Quarterback Abstract

John Maxymuk

TRIUMPH
BOOKS

Triumph Books and colophon are registered trademarks of Random House, Inc.

Library of Congress Cataloging-in-Publication Data

Maxymuk, John.
  The quarterback abstract / by John Maxymuk.
      p. cm.
  Includes bibliographical references.
  ISBN 978-1-60078-268-8
  1. Quarterbacks (Football)—Statistics. 2. Quarterbacks (Football)—
History. 3. Quarterbacking (Football) I. Title.
  GV938.M386 2009
  796.332092—dc22

                        2009017455

This book is available in quantity at special discounts for your group or organization. For further information, contact:

Triumph Books
542 South Dearborn Street
Suite 750
Chicago, Illinois 60605
(312) 939-3330
Fax (312) 663-3557
www.triumphbooks.com

Printed in U.S.A.
ISBN: 978-1-60078-268-8

Design by Patricia Frey

...ographs on pages xiii (top), 25, 33, 67, 85, 93, 99, 112, 117, 119, 125, ...41, 209, 210, 228, 299, 334, and 355 courtesy of AP Images. All ...photographs courtesy of Getty Images.

*This book is dedicated to my loving and
unbeatable family—Suzanne, Juliane,
Katie—and my faithful, furry friend, Augie.*

Contents

Preface

There have been a number of books written about quarterbacks over the years, but they have tended to focus exclusively on only the best, whether that's the 25 greatest or the 50 greatest. That approach, though, leaves out a lot of interesting field generals. Since the T formation became the basic offense in the NFL in the 1940s and elevated one man, the quarterback, to a position of greater importance than any other on the field, there have been hundreds of NFL quarterbacks. This book views the broader picture of quarterbacks at all levels of achievement and ability and attempts to answer three questions about each quarterback: Who was he? What was his playing style? How good was he?

This book contains entries for 366 men. The bulk of the group is made up of the 339 quarterbacks who have started at least 10 games in the NFL since 1950. Beginning with 1950, two-platoon football became permanent, allowing the T-formation quarterback to focus solely on offense without also having to play defensive back. The advent of the two-platoon game also made it easier to track starting quarterbacks. In addition, I have included 27 pre-1950 signal-callers, some of whom played at least part of their careers as single-wing tailbacks. These men either were likely to have started at least 10 games at quarterback or were passers of such significance that they could not be ignored.

Each entry includes basic biographical data: birth date, height, weight, college attended, draft position, teams played for, and years played. Full regular-season statistics are given, as are postseason career totals. All statistics are compiled through the 2008 season and postseason. In addition to the basic passing and rushing numbers, I have added a few statistics that I have accumulated and compiled myself.

"Relative passer rating" takes the quarterback's career passer rating and compares it to the league average for the years in which he was active. It is expressed in a percentage with 100 percent denoting the league average. Thus, a relative percentage of 90 percent means that this quarterback's passer rating was 10 percent less than that of an average passer during his career, while a relative percentage of 110 percent means that this quarterback was 10 percent better than an average passer during his career. Relativizing passer ratings allows us to better compare the efficiency of passers across time, which is impossible by simply looking at the passer rating itself, because the game continually changes so much. The relative passer rating is not figured for postseason statistics.

"Record" is self-explanatory; it represents the quarterback's won-lost record as a starter. There are certainly arguments to be made against this statistic because football is such a team game that the record reflects the efforts of 22 men on both sides of the ball plus special teams, but the quarterback is still the most important player on the field. The quarterback literally is the man with the ball in his hands, and we have come to accept a quarterback's won-lost record as having a great deal of validity as a factor in ranking quarterbacks. Won-lost records going back to the mid-1980s are easy enough to compile from the *NFL Record and Fact Book*, but to go back to 1950 required a lot of digging through old newspapers. For pre-1950 passers, I have included an estimated won-lost record based on the team's record and the games played by the player.

"Comebacks" refers to games in which the quarterback led a game-winning drive in either the fourth quarter or in overtime. From newspapers and line scores, I compiled this data all the way back to the 1920s for both the regular season and the playoffs. As the passing game became more prevalent, so too did comebacks, because it became more possible to surmount a late deficit by moving the ball quickly through the air.

Finally, each quarterback is rated along an evenly divided scale that allows me to assign each a "Quarterback Proficiency Rating" (QPR). Devising a system that accurately ranks quarterbacks is a daunting task. This is not a cut-and-dried exercise like ranking outfielders in baseball. The quarterback position is so multifaceted, and so much of it is not measured by statistics. I tried to focus on what qualities top quarterbacks share. I began by adding together Relative Passer Rating which is described above and Relative Points, which compares how many points a quarterback's team scored to the league average in the years in which he was the primary starter. Relative Rating measures a quarterback's passing efficiency. When you add these two relative numbers and subtract 200, you get the percentage a quarterback differed from an average quarterback during his time in these two areas. Because the competition was so different in the early days of the NFL, relative statistics are greatly inflated for the better passers of that time. To adjust for these anomalies, I divided the result for pre–World War II players by 10 and the result for early T quarterbacks whose careers extended into the postwar 1940s by two. For example, Cecil Isbell's RR of 188 and his RP of 146 add up to 334, but when that total is divided by 10, he ends up with an adjusted score of 33, putting him in the company of Charlie Conerly and John Hadl and not Otto Graham. Sammy Baugh's career began just one year before Isbell's but lasted until 1952, so his total of 57 is divided by two for an adjusted score of 29.

Another basic problem with an average is that it doesn't take into account the importance of maintaining a level of performance over time, so I added a weight for games started to correct for that. The 152 quarterbacks who started at least 55 games were given 55 additional points; the 98 quarterbacks who started between 25 and 54 games were given 25 additional points; and the 116 quarterbacks who started fewer than 25 games were given no extra points because they had not established a true level of performance. Thus, Cecil Isbell increased his score from 13 to 68, while Sammy Baugh gained 55 points to reach 84 points. To use two more recent quarterbacks, Philip Rivers' initial score of 47 was supplemented by 25 points for his number of starts, but Aaron Rodgers' initial score of 15 is not augmented since he has started just 16 games.

However, this number still did not address the most essential components of great field generals: leadership and clutch performance. Hall of Fame quarterbacks have long tenures as their team's starters (all except for old-timers Benny Friedman and Ace Parker served as their teams' primary starter for at least eight years) and win championships (the 28 Hall of Fame quarterbacks have won 54 championships, while the remaining 338 quarterbacks in this book have won 34). Using these two factors as de facto measures of leadership and clutch performance, I gave each quarterback two points for each year he started at least half his team's games, five points for each championship-game start, and five more points for each championship won. Continuing on with our examples, Sammy Baugh's total thus far of 84 is augmented by 30 points for 15 years as a starter, 20 points for two championships won, and 15 for three championship game losses, for a total score of 149. Isbell's 68 is augmented by 10 for five years as a starter, 10 for one championship, and five for one title game loss, to total 93. Rivers gains six for three years as a starter for a total of 78, and Rodgers gains two for one year starting for a total of 17.

Using this total score, I aligned the quarterbacks along a 10-point scale to get their QPR. Each half-point on the scale comprises roughly 18 quarterbacks. From Graham, Luckman, Starr, and Montana at the top end of the 10s to Jug Girard, Dan Darragh, and Stan Gelbaugh at the bottom of the 0.5s, all 366 quarterbacks are ranked. You can read about each one of them on the pages that follow.

10	Pinnacle Hall of Famers
9.5	Ken Anderson Division of Great Quarterbacks
9.0	Jim Plunkett Division of Very Good Quarterbacks
8.0–8.5	Drew Bledsoe Division of Good Quarterbacks
7.0–7.5	Vinny Testaverde Division of Above Average Quarterbacks
6.0–6.5	Dan Pastorini Division of Average Quarterbacks
5.0–5.5	Tommy Maddox Division of Struggling Starters
4.0–4.5	Todd Blackledge Division of Failing Starters
3.0–3.5	Frank Reich Division of Strictly Backups
2.0–2.5	The Jeff Rutledge Practice Squad
Below 2	Chris Weinke's College Boys

Statistical Note

The 1940s present a number of complications for football historians. As I stated in the preface, the permanent establishment of two-platoon football in 1950 allowed for easier tracking of quarterback won-lost records, and by then the position of T-formation quarterback was becoming firmly defined. Throughout the 1940s, teams moved to the T from the single wing, and there was a great deal of experimentation with substitution patterns. Thus, the player who started often was not the team's true leader for the game. Sid Luckman frequently entered games only after Charlie O'Rourke or Bob Snyder or Johnny Long or Gene Ronzani first played the role of scout, probing the defense for weaknesses that Luckman could later exploit. However, Luckman was clearly the Bears' starter regardless of whether he was on the field for the first snap.

For these reasons, I list the quarterback records from this time as "est." or estimates. Parenthetically, I have also included a handful of single-wing tailbacks from the time who acted as a team's signal-caller, ball-handler, and primary passer, similar to a T quarterback. Great players like Sid Luckman and Sammy Baugh were plainly their teams' leaders, and I credit them with the outcomes of all games in which they played throughout most of the '40s until viable alternatives like Johnny Lujack and Harry Gilmer began to appear for the Bears and Redskins. Furthermore, since Baugh and the underappreciated Frankie Filchock regularly alternated quarters for Washington in the early 1940s, first as tailbacks then as quarterbacks, I double-count and credit both Baugh and Filchock for those games. For other quarterbacks during the decade, I have tried to assess the primary quarterback game by game. With this effort being more of an art than science, these records are also noted as estimates.

Post-1949, I have made three exceptions to strictly listing the starting quarterback as the sole quarterback of record in games. The first is with the Rams Hall of Fame pair of Bob Waterfield and Norm Van Brocklin, who alternated quarters as equals from 1950 to 1952. Since they essentially shared the job equally, I have again double-counted those Rams games for both Waterfield and Van Brocklin. Second, from 1954 through 1958, the Giants used backup quarterback Don Heinrich to start games in a scouting function for real starter Charlie Conerly, who would enter the game sometime afterward, similar to the Bears' use of Luckman in the 1940s. I have given credit to both quarterbacks in the games in which this practice was employed. Finally, in 1962, Cowboys coach Tom Landry alternated Eddie LeBaron and Don Meredith on each down so Landry could call the plays. Again, I have credited each quarterback for each game that year. In all three exceptions, the team had a clearly established regular substitution pattern that essentially amounted to two quarterbacks sharing the starter's status, and I have decided to reflect that reality in my record-keeping because the purpose of tallying up all this starter data is to assign responsibility for the team's outcome, not to simply note who took the first snap from center. Without double-counts, I have Filchock at 26–12–3, Baugh at 78–50–4, Waterfield at 48–23–4, Van Brocklin at 61–36–4, Conerly at 68–44, LeBaron at 26–52–3, and Meredith at 48–33–4.

Lastly, I have included All-America Football Conference players and statistics in this book. For quarterbacks who appeared in both the AAFC and the NFL, like Otto Graham and Frankie Albert, their statistical totals reflect the combined figures from both leagues. Although the NFL does not officially recognize these numbers, the AAFC deserves full recognition because it was a major league, nearly comparable to the NFL, and because the two leagues ultimately merged. Not only were the Browns, 49ers, and Colts accepted into the NFL in 1950, but also the players from the teams in New York and Los Angeles were part of team merger arrangements with the Giants, Yanks, and Rams. The AAFC was more comparable to the AFL of the 1960s than the USFL of the 1980s. Hence, I have included the AAFC records.

Introduction

Ranking the Very Best

In this book, each quarterback who started at least 10 games is ranked by a QPR score, but I felt the immortals deserved a complementary approach that would further fine-tune the differences amongst the very best. It's tough enough to choose between Tom Brady or Peyton Manning as the best quarterback of the current decade, but with the vast changes in the rules of the game and the style of play over time, it seems a near-impossible task to rank the greatest of all time. But that doesn't mean it's not fun to try.

I started by narrowing the population to consider. There are 30 men in the Hall of Fame who are listed as quarterbacks. Of those, I dropped six: Paddy Driscoll and Fritz Pollard from the 1920s because they were not T-formation quarterbacks, nor did they pass the ball much. Benny Friedman was the first great passer in the NFL, but he played before statistics were officially kept and was a single-wing tailback like Arnie Herber and Ace Parker. George Blanda was a fine quarterback but was elected to the Hall of Fame more for being the league's top scorer as a kicker and for his 26-year longevity than as a quarterback.

To the 24 Hall of Fame quarterbacks who remained, I added three quarterbacks who had been finalists to the Hall (Charlie Conerly, Ken Anderson, and Ken Stabler) and three current players who will be first-ballot enshrines five years after they retire (Brett Favre, Manning, and Brady). That left me with a group of 30 to rank according to five criteria I set out as the essential elements for any great quarterback: 1) passing efficiency; 2) offensive effectiveness; 3) running ability and mobility; 4) leadership and play-calling skills; and 5) clutch performance. Each of the five criteria I tied to a statistical measure described here and then

ranked the results in quintiles of six quarterbacks each. Quarterbacks in the top quintile scored five points, while those in the bottom quintile scored one. Then, I cumulated the points for each criterion in one overall ranking, with number of championships and then number of wins serving as the tiebreakers.

For the passing efficiency criterion, I used the statistic of relative passer rating described in the preface. Relative passer rating compares a quarterback's career passer rating to the league average during his time. It's not surprising that Sid Luckman and Sammy Baugh top this category because they were so far superior to the primitive passing numbers of the 1940s. Rounding out the top six are Otto Graham, Len Dawson, Roger Staubach, and Norm Van Brocklin. Perhaps most impressive was the seventh-place finish of Steve Young, who was 27 percent better than the average passer in the highly evolved passing game of the 1990s. At the bottom of the list were bombers Joe Namath, Bobby Layne, Terry Bradshaw, and John Elway, for whom passing for touchdowns was more important than the efficiency that passer rating measures.

For offensive effectiveness, I used another relative statistic of my own devising, "relative points." The object of the offense is to score, so it would reason that the best quarterbacks would drive their teams to score more points than the league average. At the top here are Sid Luckman, Bob Waterfield, Steve Young, Otto Graham, and Norm Van Brocklin—all quarterbacks of dominant offensive teams. At the bottom are Charlie Conerly of the defensive-minded Giants, Sonny Jurgensen of some very poor teams, and the inconsistent Y.A. Tittle.

For running ability and mobility, I used the quarterbacks' average gain–per–rushing attempt. It's no shock to see Steve Young at the very top, along with scramblers Roger Staubach and Fran Tarkenton. However, few would expect that Ken Anderson, Bart Starr, and Terry Bradshaw round out the top quintile over more well-known moving passers such as John Elway, Bobby Layne, and Bob Griese. Some of the least-mobile quarterbacks by this measure were punished by 1940s statistical practices that lumped sacks in with rushing attempts, so Sid Luckman, Bob Waterfield, and Sammy Baugh are treated a bit unfairly in this category. Dan Marino and Norm Van Brocklin, though, fully belong in the bottom.

For leadership and play-calling skills I use the statistic where those subjective talents are best reflected, the quarterback's winning percentage. Although play-calling is largely done by the coach today, the better quarterbacks still read the defense at the line of scrimmage and audible out of doomed play-calls. As for leadership, leaders consistently win; it's that simple. The top five in this category all won more than 70 percent of their starts and all won multiple championships: Otto Graham, Tom Brady, Sid Luckman, Roger Staubach, and Joe Montana. At the bottom, two quarterbacks had losing records—Sonny Jurgensen and Joe Namath—while Warren Moon and Dan Fouts were just barely over .500.

The final category of clutch performance is best demonstrated by a quarterback's postseason winning percentage, and the best of all was Bart Starr, who won nine of 10 playoff games. The other five in the top quintile all won at least three-fourths of their postseason games: Sid Luckman, Tom Brady, Johnny Unitas, Bobby Layne, and Otto Graham. Again, all won multiple championships. Great quarterbacks who came up small in the playoffs include Y.A. Tittle and Warren Moon. Sonny Jurgensen is the only Hall of Fame quarterback to never start a postseason game.

Cumulating the results of these five categories results in the final ranking in this table:

Rank	Quarterback	Relative Rating	Relative Points	W/L %	Playoff %	Rush Avg.	Total	Tiebreakers Champs.	Wins
1	Graham, Otto	5	5	5	5	2	22	7	103
2	Staubach, Roger	5	3	5	4	5	22	2	85
3	Montana, Joe	4	4	5	4	4	21	4	117
4	Luckman, Sid	5	5	5	5	1	21	4	73
5	Young, Steve	4	5	4	3	5	21	1	94
6	Brady, Tom	3	4	5	5	2	19	3	86
7	Starr, Bart	4	1	3	5	5	18	5	94
8	Bradshaw, Terry	1	4	4	4	5	18	4	107
9	Unitas, Johnny	3	2	4	5	4	18	3	118
10	Dawson, Len	5	3	3	3	4	18	2	94
11	Elway, John	1	4	4	4	4	17	2	148
12	Manning, Peyton	4	5	4	2	2	17	1	105
13	Griese, Bob	3	3	3	3	4	16	2	92
14	Van Brocklin, Norm	5	5	3	1	1	15	2	75
15	Waterfield, Bob	2	5	5	2	1	15	2	59
16	Favre, Brett	2	4	3	3	3	15	1	160
17	Tarkenton, Fran	4	2	1	3	5	15	0	124
18	Layne, Bobby	1	1	2	5	4	13	2	82
19	Stabler, Ken	2	3	4	3	1	13	1	96
20	Kelly, Jim	2	3	3	2	3	13	0	101
21	Baugh, Sammy	5	2	2	2	1	12	2	92
22	Anderson, Ken	3	2	1	1	5	12	0	91
23	Aikman, Troy	1	1	2	4	3	11	3	94
24	Marino, Dan	2	4	2	2	1	11	0	147
25	Namath, Joe	1	2	1	4	2	10	1	62
26	Tittle, Y.A.	3	1	2	1	3	10	0	86
27	Fouts, Dan	2	3	1	2	2	10	0	86
28	Jurgensen, Sonny	4	1	1	1	3	10	0	69
29	Conerly, Charlie	3	1	2	1	2	9	1	84
30	Moon, Warren	1	2	1	1	3	8	0	102

In a New York City hotel in 1938, the three greatest NFL passers prior to 1950 pose: Sammy Baugh, Benny Friedman, and Sid Luckman.

Known as a pocket passer, Otto Graham could do it all, including tuck the ball under his arm and run.

Bart Starr culminates the Packers' 68-yard game-winning drive in the Ice Bowl on this quarterback sneak with just 13 seconds to play.

The annual duels between Peyton Manning (18) and Tom Brady (12) have been the most consequential series of games between future Hall of Famers since Johnny Unitas and Bart Starr in the 1960s.

Otto Graham and Roger Staubach tie at the top with 22 points, but Graham had more championships and victories to win the tiebreakers. Graham, along with Sid Luckman at No. 4, fell down only in the running category, where they were both punished by having sacks thrown in with rushing attempts. That is particularly true for Graham, who was a very good runner and scored more rushing touchdowns than any other quarterback. Staubach was just middling in team scoring, while Joe Montana was very good across the board and finished two slots ahead of the man who followed him, Steve Young. Rounding out the top 10 are Tom Brady, Bart Starr, Terry Bradshaw,

Johnny Unitas, and Len Dawson. Warren Moon finishes at the very bottom of the list, No. 30, just behind seven-time Hall of Fame finalist Charlie Conerly. The other two non-enshrined finalists, Ken Stabler and Ken Anderson, finished 19th and 22nd respectively.

I then redid the rankings using raw scores and not quintiles and came up with this table:

Rank	Quarterback	Relative Rating	Relative Points	W/L %	Playoff %	Rush Avg.	Total	Tiebreaker Champs.
1	Graham, Otto	28	27	30	27	10	122	7
2	Young, Steve	24	28	21	16	30	119	1
3	Luckman, Sid	30	30	28	29	1	118	4
4	Staubach, Roger	26	13	27	19	28	113	2
5	Montana, Joe	22	23	26	22	19	112	4
6	Brady, Tom	17	24	29	28	7	105	3
7	Dawson, Len	27	18	13	18	23	99	2
8	Bradshaw, Terry	3	21	24	24	25	97	4
9	Starr, Bart	20	6	14	30	26	96	5
10	Unitas, Johnny	16	12	20	26	21	95	3
11	Elway, John	4	19	19	21	24	87	2
12	Manning, Peyton	19	25	23	9	11	87	1
13	Griese, Bob	14	17	15	13.5	20	79.5	2
14	Favre, Brett	8	22	17	15	16	78	1
15	Waterfield, Bob	11	29	25	10.5	2	77.5	2
16	Van Brocklin, Norm	25	26	16	5.5	4	76.5	2
17	Tarkenton, Fran	21	7	6	13.5	27	74.5	0
18	Kelly, Jim	9	16	18	12	18	73	0
19	Stabler, Ken	7	15	22	17	5	66	1
20	Baugh, Sammy	29	8	11	10.5	6	64.5	2
21	Layne, Bobby	2	5	9	25	22	63	2
22	Anderson, Ken	15	9	5	4	29	62	0
23	Aikman, Troy	5	4	8	23	14	54	3
24	Marino, Dan	12	20	10	8	3	53	0
25	Tittle, Y.A.	18	3	7	2	17	47	0
26	Fouts, Dan	10	14	4	7	9	44	0
27	Conerly, Charley	13	1	12	5.5	12	43.5	1
28	Namath, Joe	1	10	2	20	8	41	1
29	Jurgensen, Sonny	23	2	1	1	13	40	0
30	Moon, Warren	6	11	3	3	15	38	0

For the most part the rankings stayed the same, with only four quarterbacks moving up or down more than two slots, but the biggest change was right at the top where Steve Young jumped three spots from No. 5 all the way to No. 2, passing his old teammate and rival Joe Montana on the way. Otto Graham remained No. 1. Len Dawson also jumped three slots from No. 10 to No. 7, while Bobby Layne fell from No. 18 to No. 21 and Joe Namath from No. 25 to No. 28. There is no change to the makeup of the top 10. Warren Moon remains locked in at No. 30. Personally, I like the quintiles better because the differences between any two quarterbacks in any one category are generally very slight, so that quintile grouping seems a bit more fair.

No matter what criteria and measures you choose to rank these greatest of all quarterbacks,

they were all brilliant once and all deserve to be honored. Ultimately, we all will judge who was the greatest according to our own subjective reasons and biases. If someone were to ask me who was the greatest quarterback of all time, I would think long and hard about Otto Graham and Joe Montana, but my response would be Bart Starr because he best answers this question for me: who would you choose as quarterback if you had one game to win? Starr won his last nine postseason games and won five championships in the process. His game-winning drive under the frigid conditions in the Ice Bowl has never been topped. Bart Starr was the greatest quarterback of all time in my mind. Of course, I'm a Packers fan, so I may be prejudiced.

The Quarterbacks

From Adams to Zorn

Tony Adams

QPR 2.0

Height: 6'0" **Weight:** 198 lbs. **Birthdate:** 3/9/1950
College: Utah State **Draft:** San Diego 1973-14th
**1974 WFL; 1975–78 Kansas City; 1979–80, 1982–84
CFL; 1987 Minnesota**
Regular Season Record: 1–9, 1 comeback
Postseason Record: NA
Relative Rating: 82%

Passing

Year	G	Comp./Att.	%	Yards	Y/Att.	TD	INT	Rating
1975	6	36/77	46.8	445	5.8	2	4	52.1
1976	14	36/71	50.7	575	8.1	3	4	68.7
1977	14	47/92	51.1	691	7.5	2	11	43.6
1978	16	44/79	55.7	415	5.3	2	3	63.0
1987	3	49/89	55.1	607	6.8	3	5	64.2
Total	53	212/408	52.0	2,753	6.6	12	27	55.5

Rushing

Year	Att.	Yards	Avg.	TD
1975	8	42	5.3	0
1976	5	46	9.2	0
1977	5	21	4.2	0
1978	9	15	1.7	0
1987	11	31	2.8	0
Total	38	155	4.1	0

The scatter-armed Tony Adams got his money's worth out of football. Throwing for more than 3,900 yards and 23 touchdowns with the Southern California Sun in 1974, Tony was named co-MVP of the World Football League with Tommy Reamon and J.J. Jennings. In keeping with the bizarre nature of that collapsing league, each was presented with a bulging bag of $3,333 in cash at halftime of the World Bowl Championship. Tony parlayed that payday into a quarterback slot with the Chiefs but over four years was unable to dislodge the mediocre Mike Livingston from the starting position. In Kansas City, Adams threw for less yardage and fewer touchdowns than he had in his one season in the WFL. In his only win, the Chiefs beat San Diego on a fourth-quarter fumble recovery for a touchdown. Adams then spent five seasons in the Canadian Football League before retiring in 1985.

However, during the 1987 players' strike, 37-year-old Tony was signed by Minnesota, whose lead scout, Paul Wiggins, had been Adams' coach with the Chiefs. The hapless Vikings replacement players lost all three of their games but still profited by receiving a bonus share of the playoff money when the real Vikings team went 8–4 and made it all the way to the NFC Championship Game.

Troy Aikman

QPR 9.5

Height: 6'4" **Weight:** 219 lbs. **Birthdate:** 11/21/1961
College: UCLA **Draft:** Dallas 1989-1st
1989–2000 Dallas Cowboys
Regular Season Record: 94–71, 15 comebacks
Postseason Record: 11–4, 1 comeback
Relative Rating: 105%

Passing

Year	G	Comp./Att.	%	Yards	Y/Att.	TD	INT	Rating
1989	11	155/293	52.9	1749	6.0	9	18	55.7
1990	15	226/399	56.6	2579	6.5	11	18	66.6
1991	12	237/363	65.3	2754	7.6	11	10	86.7
1992	16	302/473	63.8	3445	7.3	23	14	89.5
1993	14	271/392	69.1	3100	7.9	15	6	99.0
1994	14	233/361	64.5	2676	7.4	13	12	84.9
1995	16	280/432	64.8	3304	7.6	16	7	93.6
1996	15	296/465	63.7	3126	6.7	12	13	80.1
1997	16	292/518	56.4	3283	6.3	19	12	78.0
1998	11	187/315	59.4	2330	7.4	12	5	88.5
1999	14	263/442	59.5	2964	6.7	17	12	81.1
2000	11	156/262	59.5	1632	6.2	7	14	64.3
Total	165	2,898/4,715	61.5	32,492	7.0	165	141	81.6
PS:	16	320/502	63.7	3,849	7.7	23	17	88.3

Rushing

Year	Att.	Yards	Avg.	TD
1989	38	302	7.9	0
1990	40	172	4.3	1
1991	16	5	0.3	1
1992	37	105	2.8	1
1993	32	125	3.9	0
1994	30	62	2.1	1
1995	21	32	1.5	1
1996	35	42	1.2	1
1997	25	79	3.2	0
1998	22	69	3.1	2
1999	21	10	0.5	1
2000	10	13	1.3	0
Total	327	1,016	3.1	9

In the pocket Troy Aikman stood as tall and rooted as a redwood—the epitome of a classic drop-back passer—and at the outset of his career

Troy Aikman was the most successful of all Cowboy quarterbacks, leading Dallas to three championships.

took a beating without complaint. The Eagles once sacked him 11 times in one game despite his quick release. Ultimately, though, he suffered a series of concussions that shortened his career. Aikman had a strong and accurate arm and, unlike many other pocket passers, such as Craig Morton and Drew Bledsoe, rarely threw interceptions. Troy spread the ball around and made good use of his tight ends and backs as well as Michael Irvin and his other wide receivers. Schooled in Norv Turner's offense, Troy liked to throw the ball down the field and stretch the defense. Although detractors tried to denigrate him as an overrated game manager in Dallas' run-based attack, he averaged well over seven yards per pass in his best years.

On the field, he was an unquestioned leader; off the field, Aikman was a figure of sanity and stability in the atmosphere of swaggering debauchery that surrounded the 1990s Cowboys. He formed a strong bond with his first coach, Jimmy Johnson, and was appalled at the complete disintegration of discipline that enveloped the team and led to its demise after Barry Switzer took over as coach in 1994. Above all, though, he was supportive of teammates, no matter what trouble they ran into with the law or the media.

Aikman won three championships with that great team and was at his best in the postseason, raising his completion percentage, yards per attempt, and passer rating above his regular-season rates. In fact, he played in exactly one season's worth of playoff games, and if you look at his postseason statistics that way, what a "season" that was, with close to 4,000 yards and 11 wins in 15 starts against the toughest competition. Troy was elected to the Hall of Fame in his first year of eligibility, 2006.

Frankie Albert QPR  9.0

Height: 5'10" **Weight:** 166 lbs. **Birthdate:** 1/27/1920
College: Stanford **Draft:** Chicago Bears 1942-1st
1946–52 San Francisco 49ers; 1953 CFL
Regular Season Record: 51–30–3, 6 comebacks
Postseason Record: 1–1, no comebacks
Relative Rating: 122%

Passing

Year	G	Comp./Att.	%	Yards	Y/Att.	TD	INT	Rating
1946	14	104/197	52.8	1404	7.1	14	14	69.8
1947	14	128/242	52.9	1692	7.0	18	15	74.3
1948	14	154/264	58.3	1990	7.5	29	10	102.9
1949	12	129/260	49.6	1862	7.2	27	16	82.2
1950	12	155/306	50.7	1767	5.8	14	23	52.3
1951	12	90/166	54.2	1116	6.7	5	10	60.2
1952	12	71/129	55	964	7.5	8	10	67.5
Total	90	831/1,564	53.1	10,795	6.9	115	98	79.2
PS:	2	17/41	41.5	204	5.0	2	2	53.3

Rushing

Year	Att.	Yards	Avg.	TD
1946	69	-10	-0.1	4
1947	46	179	3.9	5
1948	69	349	5.1	8
1949	35	249	7.1	3
1950	53	272	5.1	3
1951	35	146	4.2	3
1952	22	87	4.0	1
Total	329	1,272	3.9	27
PS:	5	41	8.2	0

Frankie Albert was a mediocre single-wing tailback on a losing Stanford team in 1939 when Clark

Shaugnessy arrived from Chicago to install the modern T formation offense he had fine-tuned for George Halas' Chicago Bears. Shaughnessy's 1940 Stanford team went undefeated and won the Rose Bowl behind the retooled left-handed T formation quarterback Frankie Albert. Much like future 49er quarterback Jeff Garcia, Albert was small and not particularly fast and did not have a strong arm, but he was expert at ball handling and faking and was a deadly accurate passer when rolling out.

Albert's collegiate heroics were immortalized in a dreadful 1942 movie, *The Spirit of Stanford*, in which Frankie played himself. Later that year, he was selected in the first round by the Bears but went into the navy during the war. When he came out, the All-America Football Conference was starting up with a new team in San Francisco, so Frankie signed on to be the first in a line of excellent quarterbacks in the Bay Area rather than Sid Luckman's backup in his native Chicago. In the four years of the AAFC, Albert threw more touchdown passes, 88, than any other quarterback in the league and was co-MVP in 1948. The 49ers had a ferocious ground game and twice led the league in scoring while continually battling the Cleveland Browns at the top of the league. One of Cleveland's four AAFC losses was delivered by San Francisco, and Albert's 49ers went 38–14–2 over the life of the league.

TOP 10
Underrated Quarterbacks

10. Bart Starr—five-time champion considered Unitas' equal in the 1960s
9. Len Dawson—three-time AFL champion
8. Boomer Esiason—overshadowed by the class of 1983
7. Rich Gannon—late bloomer
6. Frank Ryan—two-time NFL leader in TD passes
5. Tommy Thompson—second T formation quarterback; two-time champion
4. Jim Plunkett—two-time champion
3. Bert Jones—undone by shoulder injuries
2. Charlie Conerly—seven-time Hall of Fame finalist
1. Ken Anderson—should be in the Hall of Fame

Albert also was the team's punter, played defensive back at times, and was probably the best bootleg runner of his time, scoring 27 touchdowns. By the time the 49ers joined the NFL in 1950, Frankie was reaching the downside of his career. He played only three years in the NFL and fought Y.A. Tittle for playing time in the last one. Albert retired in 1953 but was lured back to the game by a lucrative offer from Canada and spent one last season in the CFL. A natural leader, Albert returned to the 49ers as coach in 1956 but quit after three years of middling success.

Derek Anderson

QPR 5.0

Height: 6'6" **Weight:** 229 lbs. **Birthdate:** 6/15/1983
College: Oregon State **Draft:** Baltimore Ravens 2005-6th
2006–08 Cleveland Browns
Regular Season Record: 13–14, 3 comebacks
Postseason Record: NA
Relative Rating: 94%

Passing

Year	G	Comp./Att.	%	Yards	Y/Att.	TD	INT	Rating
2006	5	66/117	56.4	793	6.8	5	8	63.1
2007	16	298/527	56.5	3787	7.2	29	19	82.5
2008	10	142/283	50.2	1615	5.7	9	8	66.5
Total	**31**	**506/927**	**54.5**	**1,615**	**6.7**	**43**	**35**	**75.1**

Rushing

Year	Att.	Yards	Avg.	TD
2006	4	47	11.8	0
2007	32	70	2.2	3
2008	25	55	2.2	0
Total	**61**	**172**	**2.8**	**3**

The 6'6" Derek Anderson hails from Scappoose, Oregon, and has been called the "Moose from Scappoose," but teammates think he better resembles the Disney character Goofy. Cleveland GM Phil Savage brought Anderson with him when he came from the Ravens, and Derek made the team as an awkward-looking backup to Charlie Frye in 2006. When Frye was hopeless in the season opener against the Steelers, coach Romeo Crennell inserted Anderson, who threw a touchdown pass and showed enough promise to earn a start the next week against the Bengals. In a passing exhibition, Anderson matched up against the more celebrated

Carson Palmer and more than held his own. While Palmer threw for more than 400 yards and six touchdowns, Anderson threw for 328 yards, five touchdowns, and the win, 51–45. Anderson threw for 29 touchdowns and close to 4,000 yards over the season, all the while keeping top draft pick Brady Quinn on the bench wondering why he held out so long in training camp.

Anderson, who played with Rams runner Steven Jackson at Oregon State and who grew up with 2007 Playboy Playmate of the Year Sara Jean Underwood, was able to parlay his surprising on-field success into a lucrative contract for the 2008 season and a tentative hold on the Browns' starting quarterback position. His hot and cold tendencies sent him to the bench in midseason, but he returned when Quinn injured his finger and then went down to a season-ending injury of his own.

Ken Anderson

 QPR 9.5

Height: 6'2" **Weight:** 212 lbs. **Birthdate:** 2/15/1949
College: Augustana **Draft:** Cincinnati 1971-3rd
1971–86 Cincinnati Bengals
Regular Season Record: 91–81, 16 comebacks
Postseason Record: 2–4, 1 comeback
Relative Rating: 117%

Passing

Year	G	Comp./Att.	%	Yards	Y/Att.	TD	INT	Rating
1971	11	72/131	55	777	5.9	5	4	72.6
1972	13	171/301	56.8	1,918	6.4	7	7	74.0
1973	14	179/329	54.4	2,428	7.4	18	12	81.2
1974	13	213/328	64.9	2,667	8.1	18	10	95.7
1975	13	228/377	60.5	3,169	8.4	21	11	93.9
1976	14	179/338	53	2,367	7.0	19	14	76.9
1977	14	166/323	51.4	2,145	6.6	11	11	69.7
1978	12	173/319	54.2	2,219	7.0	10	22	58.0
1979	15	189/339	55.8	2,340	6.9	16	10	80.7
1980	13	166/275	60.4	1,778	6.5	6	13	66.9
1981	16	300/479	62.6	3,754	7.8	29	10	98.4
1982	9	218/309	70.6	2,495	8.1	12	9	95.3
1983	13	198/297	66.7	2,333	7.9	12	13	85.6
1984	11	175/275	63.6	2,107	7.7	10	12	81.0
1985	3	16/32	50	170	5.3	2	0	86.7
1986	8	11/23	47.8	171	7.4	1	2	51.2
Total	192	2,654/4,475	59.3	32,938	7.3	197	160	89.1
PS:	6	110/166	66.3	1,321	8.0	9	6	93.5

Rushing

Year	Att.	Yards	Avg.	TD
1971	22	125	5.7	1
1972	22	94	4.3	3
1973	26	97	3.7	0
1974	43	314	7.3	2
1975	49	188	3.8	2
1976	31	134	4.3	1
1977	26	128	4.9	2
1978	29	167	5.8	1
1979	28	235	8.4	2
1980	16	122	7.6	0
1981	46	320	7.0	1
1982	25	85	3.4	4
1983	22	147	6.7	1
1984	11	64	5.8	0
1985	1	0	0.0	0
Total	397	2,220	5.6	20
PS:	19	101	5.3	0

There was a lot of timing and luck involved in the surprising rise of Ken Anderson from little Augustana College to Pro Bowl quarterback of the Cincinnati Bengals, but Anderson deserves accolades for fully taking advantage of his opportunity. Because of the career-ending shoulder miseries of the strong-armed Greg Cook, Bengals offensive coach Bill Walsh was forced to retool from a down-the-field passing offense to one that emphasized short, timed patterns that backup quarterback Virgil Carter could execute well. What became known as the West Coast offense was ideal for third-rounder Anderson as well. Although Ken's arm was stronger than Carter's, he also excelled at the short–passing game and had the mobility and intelligence to thrive in that type of attack.

In training camp, Walsh spent weeks working with Anderson's footwork and mechanics without even having him throw a pass. Upon Walsh's death in 2007, Anderson said, "He took a kid from Augustana College and made him into an NFL quarterback. He was the basis for everything I know about playing quarterback." Anderson's development culminated in his being named NFL Player of the Year in 1981 when he led the Bengals to the Super Bowl, where they lost to Walsh's 49ers 26–21 despite 300 yards in passing from Ken. The following year, Anderson set an all-time record by completing 70.6 percent of his passes during the 1982 strike-shortened season.

Four times he led the NFL in passer rating, three times in completion percentage, and twice in yards. His roommate, guard Dave Lapham, once said of Anderson's accuracy, "If he made a receiver move more than six inches for a football, he thought he threw a bad pass."

Moreover, when Anderson retired, his total of 2,220 yards rushing was eighth in NFL history for quarterbacks. Of the seven above him, only Greg Landry and Bobby Douglass topped Anderson's 5.6 yards per carry. Above all, Ken had a 91–81 won-lost record as a starter...and that was with the Bengals. None of his successors in Cincinnati can touch that. Although he was twice a Canton finalist, he is the finest quarterback still not in the Hall of Fame.

David Archer

 **QPR 0.5**

Height: 6'2" **Weight:** 207 lbs. **Birthdate:** 2/15/1962
College: Iowa State **Draft:** Free Agent
1984–87 Atlanta Falcons; 1988 Washington Redskins; 1989 San Diego Chargers; 1991–92 WLAF; 1993–98 CFL
Regular Season Record: 9–13–1, 2 comebacks
Postseason Record: NA
Relative Rating: 83%

Passing

Year	G	Comp./Att.	%	Yards	Y/Att.	TD	INT	Rating
1984	2	11/18	61.1	181	10.1	1	1	90.3
1985	16	161/312	51.6	1,992	6.4	7	17	56.5
1986	11	150/294	5.01	2,007	6.8	10	9	71.6
1987	9	9/23	39.1	95	4.1	0	2	15.7
1988	1	0/2	0.0	0	0.0	0	0	39.6
1989	16	5/12	41.7	62	5.2	0	1	23.6
Total	55	336/661	50.8	4,337	6.6	18	30	61.9

Rushing

Year	Att.	Yards	Avg.	TD
1984	6	38	6.3	0
1985	70	347	5.0	2
1986	52	298	5.7	0
1987	2	8	4.0	0
1988	3	1	0.3	0
1989	2	14	7.0	0
Total	135	706	5.2	2

Four games into the 1986 season was the high point of unheralded free agent David Archer's NFL career; he had led the Falcons to a 4–0 start, averaging more than 30 points a game. Seven weeks later, the team was 5–5–1 and Archer was on the bench watching Turk Schonert take snaps. Over the next four years, Archer would be beaten out on NFL rosters by Scott Campbell, 37-year-old Ron Jaworski, 33-year-old Doug Williams, Mark Vlasic, Pat Ryan, and Chuck Long. By 1992, Archer was leading the Sacramento Surge to the championship of the World League of American Football, precursor to NFL Europe. From there it was on to the CFL where he threw for more than 6,000 yards in one season and accumulated more than 20,000 yards passing in five years before retiring and going into broadcasting.

Archer was a nifty scrambler who led all NFL quarterbacks with 347 yards rushing in 1985. However, as an NFL passer, Archer had a weak arm and tended to spray the ball inaccurately, leading to interceptions and a seat on the bench on his way to being cut from the team. The unanswered question is whether his success after the NFL was due to the lower level of competition or to maturation.

Bob Avellini

 QPR 4.0

Height: 6'2" **Weight:** 208 lbs. **Birthdate:** 8/28/1953
College: Maryland **Draft:** 1975-6th
1975–79, 1981–84 Chicago Bears
Regular Season Record: 23–27, 10 comebacks
Postseason Record: 0–1, no comebacks
Relative Rating: 77%

Passing

Year	G	Comp./Att.	%	Yards	Y/Att.	TD	INT	Rating
1975	8	67/126	53.2	942	7.5	6	11	57.0
1976	14	118/271	43.5	1,580	5.8	8	15	49.4
1977	14	154/293	52.6	2,004	6.8	11	18	61.3
1978	13	141/264	53.4	1,718	6.5	5	16	54.8
1979	7	27/51	52.9	310	6.1	2	3	60.1
1981	9	15/32	46.9	185	5.8	1	3	36.6
1982	2	8/20	40.0	84	4.2	0	0	52.9
1983	2	0/0	0.0	0	0.0	0	0	0.0
1984	4	30/53	56.6	288	5.4	0	3	48.3
Total	73	560/1,110	50.5	7,111	6.4	33	69	54.8
PS:	1	15/25	60.0	177	7.1	1	4	55.3

Rushing

Year	Att.	Yards	Avg.	TD
1975	4	-3	-0.8	1
1976	18	58	3.2	1
1977	37	109	2.9	1
1978	34	54	1.6	2
1979	3	10	3.3	0
1981	5	2	0.4	0
1984	3	-5	-1.7	0
Total	104	225	2.2	5
PS:	1	4	4.0	0

Bob Avellini had all the earmarks of post–Luckman Bear quarterbacks. He struggled to complete half his passes, averaged fewer than 6.5 yards per pass, and had an abysmal touchdown-to-interception ratio of 33–69. How does a slow-footed, inaccurate, weak-armed, inconsistent quarterback like this get to start 50 games over 10 years? Because the alternatives were no better—Bobby Douglass, Vince Evans, Gary Huff, Mike Phipps, and so on until Jim McMahon arrived in 1982. Still, Avellini took part in one record-setting performance by Bears quarterbacks in 1984 when five different ones started games.

Avellini's golden moment in Bear history occurred in Week 9 of 1977 when his 37-yard touchdown pass to Greg Latta beat Kansas City with three seconds left in the game. Somehow, that ignited Chicago on a six-game winning streak, and Avellini led the Bears to the playoffs with a 9–5 record. However, the Cowboys squashed them like slow-moving bugs 37–7 in the playoffs. Dallas safety Charlie Waters stated the obvious after Avellini's fumble and four interceptions in his only postseason appearance: "We were inviting him to throw. We laid back and tried to make it look like he had men open. We were betting on his inexperience. It worked." Two seasons later, Phipps succeeded Avellini as starter, and the Chicago quarterback carousel continued.

QPR **6.5**

Tony Banks

Height: 6'4" **Weight:** 230 lbs. **Birthdate:** 4/5/1973
College: Michigan State **Draft:** St. Louis Rams 1996-2nd
1996-98 St. Louis Rams; 1999–2000 Baltimore Ravens; 2001 Washington Redskins; 2003–05 Houston Texans
Regular Season Record: 35–43, 9 comebacks
Postseason Record: 0–0, no comebacks
Relative Rating: 92%

Passing

Year	G	Comp./Att.	%	Yards	Y/Att.	TD	INT	Rating
1996	14	192/368	52.2	2,544	6.9	15	15	71.0
1997	16	252/487	51.7	3,254	6.7	14	13	71.5
1998	14	241/408	59.1	2,535	6.2	7	14	68.6
1999	12	169/320	52.8	2,136	6.7	17	8	81.2
2000	11	150/274	54.7	1,578	5.8	8	8	69.3
2001	15	198/370	53.5	2,386	6.4	10	10	71.3
2003	7	61/102	59.8	693	6.8	5	3	84.3
2004	5	1/2	50.0	16	8.0	0	0	77.1
2005	3	14/25	56.0	173	6.9	1	2	57.6
Total	97	1,278/2,356	54.2	15,315	6.5	77	73	72.4
PS:	3	0/3	0.0	0	0.0	0	0	39.6

Rushing

Year	Att.	Yards	Avg.	TD
1996	61	212	3.5	0
1997	47	186	4.0	1
1998	40	156	3.9	3
1999	24	93	3.9	0
2000	19	57	3.0	0
2001	47	152	3.2	2
2003	6	27	4.5	0
2005	2	-2	-1.0	0
Total	246	881	3.6	6
PS:	1	-1	-1.0	0

Tony Banks was stout and sturdy with a strong arm and better than average running ability, but the only category in which he ever led the league was fumbles, with a record of 21 as a rookie. Why was he such a disappointment as a starting quarterback?

Primarily, Banks, who named his dog Felony, had a questionable attitude; he was lackadaisical and tried to get by on talent alone, doing little film study to improve his performance. In his third and final year as a Ram, he chose not to fly home with the team after a 14–0 loss to the Dolphins and missed the next day's team meetings. At the end of the season, the Rams traded him to the Ravens for two low draft picks, but again his bad habits got him into the coach's doghouse. However, Baltimore won six of its final 10 games in 1999, and Tony earned the starting job for 2000. After a decent start, the offense stopped functioning and did not score a touchdown in four straight games. Because of the stalled attack, Banks lost his job for good to journeyman Trent Dilfer, who managed a lackluster but turnover-free offense to a Super Bowl title. Tony spent the next season managing a ball-control attack under Marty Schottenheimer in Washington before finishing his career as a backup to David Carr on the Texans. Although Banks tended to spray the ball passing and fumbled 73 times in 97 games, he had the skill set to achieve much more than he did.

Steve Bartkowski

QPR **8.0**

Height: 6'4" **Weight:** 216 lbs. **Birthdate:** 11/12/1952
College: California **Draft:** Atlanta 1975-1st
1975–85 Atlanta Falcons; 1986 LA Rams
Regular Season Record: 59–68, 23 comebacks
Postseason Record: 1–3, 1 comeback
Relative Rating: 105%

Passing

Year	G	Comp./Att.	%	Yards	Y/Att.	TD	INT	Rating
1975	11	115/255	45.1	1,662	6.5	13	15	59.3
1976	5	57/120	47.5	677	5.6	2	9	39.5
1977	8	64/136	47.1	796	5.9	5	13	38.4
1978	14	187/369	50.7	2,489	6.7	10	18	61.1
1979	14	204/380	53.7	2,505	6.6	17	20	67.3
1980	16	257/463	55.5	3,544	7.7	31	16	88.2
1981	16	297/533	55.7	3,829	7.2	30	23	79.2
1982	9	166/262	63.4	1,905	7.3	8	11	77.9
1983	14	274/432	63.4	3,167	7.3	22	5	97.6
1984	11	181/269	67.3	2,158	8.0	11	10	89.7
1985	5	69/111	62.2	738	6.6	5	1	92.8
1986	6	61/126	48.4	654	5.2	2	3	59.4
Total	129	1,932/3,456	55.9	24,124	7.0	156	144	75.4
PS:	4	53/111	47.7	792	7.1	5	8	56.6

Rushing

Year	Att.	Yards	Avg.	TD
1975	14	15	1.1	2
1976	8	-10	-1.3	1
1977	18	13	0.7	0
1978	33	60	1.8	2
1979	14	36	2.6	2
1980	25	35	1.4	2
1981	11	2	0.2	0
1982	13	4	0.3	1
1983	16	38	2.4	1
1984	15	34	2.3	0
1985	5	9	1.8	0
1986	6	3	0.5	0
Total	178	239	1.3	11
PS:	2	3	1.5	0

As the first overall pick from the 1975 NFL draft, Steve Bartkowski was starting to look like a monumental bust when he lost his starting job to the undrafted June Jones at the beginning of the 1978 season. To that point, Peachtree Bart had been a superstar only after dark. He had completed fewer than 47 percent of his passes and thrown 20 touchdowns to 37 interceptions in his first three years in the NFL. Just as he saw his career begin to slip away, though, Bartkowski got serious about his work and even his religious faith. Steve won back his starting job by Week 4 and led the Falcons to the playoffs for the first time in team history that season.

Although the Falcons won only one postseason game in Steve's tenure in Atlanta, he did get them there three times. Steve also became the first NFL quarterback since Y.A. Tittle to throw at least 30 touchdown passes in consecutive seasons when he threw 31 in 1980 and 30 in 1981. His best season, though, was 1983, when he led the NFL with a 97.6 passer rating and threw 22 touchdowns to just five interceptions.

Bartkowski was a prototype pocket passer with an accurate rocket arm who loved to go deep. Paul Hackett, his college coach, claimed that Steve had thrown the ball 100 yards in the air at practice. Although Steve was a natural athlete who was an All-American first baseman at Cal, he had no mobility even when young and was a frequent target of pass rushers. He was sacked more than 350 times during his career and continually had shoulder and knee problems as a result. In fact, six operations on his right knee essentially ended his career even though his arm was still strong. Today, Bartkowski still resides in Atlanta and sits on the board of directors for the Falcons.

QPR 5.5

Charlie Batch

Height: 6'2" **Weight:** 220 lbs. **Birthdate:** 12/5/1974
College: Eastern Michigan **Draft:** Detroit 1998-2nd
1998–2001 Detroit Lions; 2003, 2005–07 Pittsburgh Steelers
Regular Season Record: 22–28, 9 comebacks
Postseason Record: NA
Relative Rating: 102%

Passing

Year	G	Comp./Att.	%	Yards	Y/Att.	TD	INT	Rating
1998	12	173/303	57.1	2,178	7.2	11	6	83.5
1999	11	151/270	55.9	1,957	7.2	13	7	84.1
2000	15	221/412	53.6	2,489	6.0	13	15	67.3
2001	10	198/341	58.1	2,392	7.0	12	12	76.8
2003	4	4/8	50.0	47	5.9	0	0	68.2
2005	4	23/36	63.9	246	6.8	1	1	81.5
2006	8	31/53	58.5	492	9.3	5	0	121.0
2007	7	17/36	47.2	232	6.4	2	3	52.1
Total	71	818/1,459	56.1	10,033	6.9	57	44	77.9

Rushing

Year	Att.	Yards	Avg.	TD
1998	41	229	5.6	1
1999	28	87	3.1	2
2000	44	199	4.5	2
2001	12	45	3.8	0
2003	1	11	11.0	0
2005	11	30	2.7	1
2006	13	15	1.2	0
2007	12	-7	-0.6	0
Total	162	609	3.8	6

Although the debate at the 1998 NFL draft was whether Peyton Manning or Ryan Leaf would go No. 1 overall, the rookie quarterback with the highest passer rating that season turned out to

TOP 10
Quarterback Fumblers

10. Paul Christman—led NFL in fumbles the first two years fumbles were counted
9. Tony Banks—first to fumble 20 times, with 21 in 1998
8. David Carr—two-time league leader
7. Jack Kemp—three-time AFL leader
6. Brett Favre—eventual all-time leader if he returns in 2009
5. Kurt Warner—once fumbled six times in one game
4. Kerry Collins—set record with 23 fumbles in 2001
3. Daunte Culpepper—98 fumbles in 97 games through 2008
2. Dave Krieg—second all time with 153 fumbles
1. Warren Moon—all-time leader with 161 fumbles in 208 games

be the Lions' second-round pick, Charlie Batch. Manning established his superstar status soon enough, and Leaf was raked out of the league in five embarrassing years, but Batch settled somewhere in the middle of those two extremes. Batch has an average but accurate arm and better than average mobility but was supplanted as a starter with the Lions by Joey Harrington. The highlight of his time in Detroit was leading the league with five fourth-quarter game-winning drives in 2000. Batch is a dependable, low-key backup who has been popular as a local favorite both in Detroit, near where he attended college, and Pittsburgh, near his roots of Homestead where he has been very active in the community. Knee and shoulder problems have sidelined him for seasons at a time, and his career may have ended with a 2008 preseason injury.

Sammy Baugh

Height: 6'2" **Weight:** 182 lbs. **Birthdate:** 3/17/1914
College: TCU **Draft:** Washington 1937-1st
1937–52 Washington Redskins
Regular Season Record: 92–57–5 est., 19 comebacks
Postseason Record: 3–3, no comebacks
Relative Rating: 152%

Passing

Year	G	Comp./Att.	%	Yards	Y/Att.	TD	INT	Rating
1937	11	81/171	47.4	1,127	6.6	8	14	50.5
1938	9	63/128	49.2	853	6.7	5	11	48.1
1939	9	53/96	55.2	518	5.4	6	9	52.3
1940	11	111/177	62.7	1,367	7.7	12	10	85.6
1941	11	106/193	54.9	1,236	6.4	10	19	52.2
1942	11	132/225	58.7	1,524	6.8	16	11	82.5
1943	10	133/239	55.6	1,754	7.3	23	19	78.0
1944	8	82/146	56.2	849	5.8	4	8	59.4
1945	8	128/182	70.3	1,669	9.2	11	4	109.9
1946	11	87/161	54.0	1,163	7.2	8	17	54.2
1947	12	210/354	59.3	2,938	8.3	25	15	92.0
1948	12	185/315	58.7	2,599	8.3	22	23	78.3
1949	12	145/255	56.9	1,903	7.5	18	14	81.2
1950	11	90/166	54.2	1,130	6.8	10	11	68.1
1951	12	67/154	43.5	1,104	7.2	7	17	43.8
1952	7	20/33	60.6	152	4.6	2	1	79.4
Total	165	1,693/2,995	56.5	21,886	7.3	187	203	72.2
PS:	6	56/102	54.9	844	8.3	7	8	72.5

Rushing

Year	Att.	Yards	Avg.	TD
1937	86	240	2.8	1
1938	21	35	1.7	0
1939	14	46	3.3	0
1940	20	16	0.8	0
1941	27	14	0.5	0
1942	20	61	3.1	1
1943	19	-43	-2.3	0
1944	19	-38	-2.0	0
1945	19	-71	-3.7	0
1946	18	-76	-4.2	1
1947	25	47	1.9	2
1948	4	4	1.0	1
1949	13	67	5.2	2
1950	7	27	3.9	1
1951	11	-5	-0.5	0
1952	1	1	1.0	0
Total	324	325	1.0	9
PS:	5	38	7.6	0

Sammy Baugh's statistical dominance of the record book made him a charter member of the Hall of Fame in 1963. Baugh led the league in pass attempts four times, completions five times, completion percentage nine times, passing yards four times, touchdowns twice, interception percentage six times, yards per attempt three times, punting average five times, and interceptions once. In 1943, he led the NFL in passing, punting, and interceptions, a sort of Triple Crown for two-way players, and his 31 lifetime interceptions are more than any other quarterback. When this four-time consensus All-Pro retired, he was the all-time leader in passes, completions, completion percentage, yards, touchdowns, interception percentage, and punting average.

Beyond that, he was a winner and led all 1940s signal-callers with 12 fourth-quarter comebacks during the decade. In his first nine years in the NFL,

Sammy Baugh's Signature Play: In his rookie year, Baugh led the Redskins to the 1937 NFL championship with three touchdown passes to beat the Bears 28–21. The last one went for 55 yards to Ed Justice.

Sammy Baugh in the Clutch: On October 19, 1941, the Redskins trailed the Eagles 17–13 in the last minutes of the game when Baugh drove Washington 56 yards on three passes, culminating in the winning touchdown to Bob Masterson from the 22. Baugh then clinched the game by intercepting a Tommy Thompson pass after the ensuing kickoff.

Sammy Baugh starred as a defensive back, too. He is still the only quarterback to lead the league in interceptions, and here picks off a Packer pass in the 1940s.

Sammy Baugh's Five Highest Honors

5. Member of the College Football Hall of Fame
4. Selected for the NFL's 75th Anniversary Team
3. Selected for six All-Star Games
2. Nine-time All-Pro and a four-time consensus All-Pro
1. Elected to the Pro Football Hall of Fame in 1963

The Five Quarterbacks Most Similar to Sammy Baugh

5. Ed Danowski
4. Chad Pennington
3. Charlie Conerly
2. Y.A. Tittle
1. Glenn Dobbs

Sammy Baugh's Five Top Touchdown Targets

5. Bob Masterson, 9 TDs
4. Joe Aguirre, 9 TDs
3. Wilbur Moore, 13 TDs
2. Dick Todd, 15 TDs
1. Hugh Taylor, 22 TDs

Sammy Baugh's Five Toughest Rivals

5. Baugh was 3–6 against the Packers.
4. Baugh was 11–2–1 against the Brooklyn Dodgers.
3. Baugh was 15–10 against the Eagles.
2. Baugh was 3–6 against the Bears in the regular season and 2–2 in the playoffs.
1. Baugh was 10–17–1 against the Giants in the regular season and 1–0 in the playoffs.

Five Random Sammy Baugh Statistics

5. Baugh played for eight head coaches.
4. Baugh's Redskins scored 5 percent more points than the league average.
3. Baugh threw for five touchdowns against the Eagles on September 28, 1947, and for six touchdowns against the Dodgers on October 31, 1943, and the Cardinals on November 23, 1947.
2. Baugh threw for more than 300 yards seven times and over 400 yards once.
1. Baugh led the league in completion percentage nine times, passing yards four times, touchdown passes twice, yards per attempts three times, and interceptions once.

his teams never had a losing record and played for the championship five times, winning it all twice. In the postwar period, Baugh continued to star, but the Redskins deteriorated. In his last seven seasons from 1946 to '52, Sammy played for only one winning team. During the most successful half of his career, Baugh was a single-wing tailback, getting pounded on every play. When the Redskins shifted to the T formation in 1944, Sammy struggled a bit to pick it up, throwing only four touchdowns and averaging just 5.8 yards per pass. By 1945, though, Baugh mastered the T, completing 70.3 percent of his passes in leading Washington to the title game one last time. That seasonal mark wasn't topped for 37 years until Ken Anderson bested it in 1982.

Baugh, who won a national championship at TCU, led the Redskins over the Bears in the 1937 championship as a rookie by throwing for three touchdowns and 358 yards. The next title match between those teams was the infamous 73–0 game from 1940. Baugh was asked after the game whether it would have been different if Charley Malone hadn't dropped Baugh's first-quarter potential touchdown pass. "Yes," he replied, "it would have been 73–6." Washington got revenge on the Bears with a 14–6 title game upset in 1942, but Sammy's last two championship appearances were marred by injury. In 1943, punt returner Sid Luckman inadvertently kicked punter Sammy Baugh in the head and left him with a concussion. In 1945, Baugh played with broken ribs in freezing Cleveland and supplied the Rams with their winning points when his end zone pass hit the goal post for a safety, the rule at the time.

Slingin' Sam got his famous nickname as a third-base prospect of the St. Louis Cardinals but was one of the greatest football players, not just quarterbacks, who ever lived.

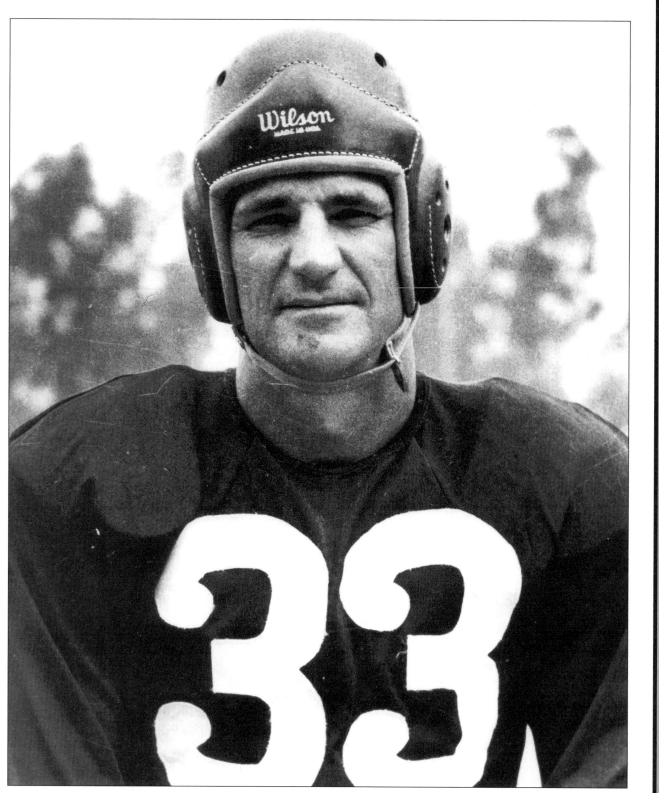

Sammy Baugh quarterbacked the Redskins for 16 years and then coached at both the college and pro levels for several years.

Pete Beathard

QPR 4.0

Height: 6'1" **Weight:** 200 lbs. **Birthdate:** 3/7/1942
College: USC **Draft:** Kansas City 1964-1st; Detroit 1964-1st
1964–67, 1973 Kansas City Chiefs; 1967–69 Houston Oilers; 1970–71 St. Louis Cardinals; 1972 L.A. Rams; 1974–75 WFL
Regular Season Record: 18–16–1, 1 comeback
Postseason Record: 0–2, no comebacks
Relative Rating: 79%

Passing

Year	G	Comp./Att.	%	Yards	Y/Att.	TD	INT	Rating
1964	14	39912	44.4	50	5.6	1	2	59.7
1965	14	36/89	40.4	632	7.1	1	6	41.0
1966	14	39/90	43.3	578	6.4	4	4	61.3
1967	11	94/231	40.7	1,114	4.8	9	14	43.8
1968	9	105/223	47.1	1,559	7.0	7	16	51.0
1969	12	180/370	48.6	2,455	6.6	10	21	55.6
1970	4	40011	41.2	114	6.7	2	1	79.0
1971	9	60/141	42.6	1,030	7.3	6	12	46.7
1972	14	19/48	39.6	255	5.3	1	7	24.6
1973	9	31/64	48.4	389	6.1	2	1	71.7
Total	110	575/1,282	44.9	8,176	6.4	43	84	49.9
PS:	3	34/86	39.5	368	4.3	2	4	41.2

Rushing

Year	Att.	Yards	Avg.	TD
1964	4	43	10.8	0
1965	25	138	5.5	4
1966	20	152	7.6	1
1967	32	133	4.2	1
1968	18	79	4.4	2
1969	19	89	4.7	2
1970	2	2	1.0	0
1971	4	29	7.3	0
1972	1	-1	-1.0	0
1973	6	16	2.7	1
Total	131	680	5.2	11
PS:	5	7	1.4	0

Pete Beathard's glory days were in college when he led USC to a national championship in 1962 that was capped by a thrilling 42–37 win over Wisconsin in the Rose Bowl. A year later, he was a high first-round pick of both the Chiefs in the AFL and the Lions in the NFL but signed on as Len Dawson's backup in Kansas City where his older brother Bobby worked as a part-time scout. At the beginning of his fourth season with the Chiefs,

Beathard had gotten only two starts but had shown enough potential that the Oilers traded defensive tackle Ernie Ladd, backup quarterback Jacky Lee, and a No. 1 draft pick for Pete. The Oilers had a swarming defense but a hole at quarterback, so it was an ideal situation for Beathard.

Pete started the last nine games of 1967 and drove Houston into the playoffs with a 9–4–1 record where they were crushed 40–7 by Oakland. Over the next couple of seasons in Houston, Beathard got his chance as a starter and showed that he was no more than a capable backup. He was a clever scrambler with a strong arm but was maddeningly erratic and injury prone. For his career, he threw almost twice as many interceptions as touchdowns and never was able to last a full season as a starter. He led the Oilers to the playoffs again in 1969 with a meager 6–6–2 record, and again the Raiders devoured them 56–7. Beathard then bounced from team to team before ending up where he started—as a backup in Kansas City. He finished his career with two seasons in the WFL where, even as a veteran throwing against inferior competition, he threw twice as many interceptions as touchdowns.

Bob Berry

QPR 6.0

Height: 5'11" **Weight:** 185 lbs. **Birthdate:** 3/10/1942
College: Oregon **Draft:** Philadelphia 1964-11th
1965–67, 1973–75 Minnesota Vikings; 1968–72 Atlanta Falcons
Regular Season Record: 20–29–3, 6 comebacks
Postseason Record: NA
Relative Rating: 117%

Passing

Year	G	Comp./Att.	%	Yards	Y/Att.	TD	INT	Rating
1965	2	0/2	0.0	0	0.0	0	0	39.6
1966	3	13/37	35.1	215	5.8	1	5	25.0
1967	2	3/7	42.9	43	6.1	0	0	63.4
1968	10	81/153	52.9	1,433	9.4	7	13	65.1
1969	7	71/124	57.3	1,087	8.8	10	2	106.5
1970	12	156/269	58.0	1,806	6.7	16	13	78.1
1971	11	136/226	60.2	2,005	8.9	11	16	75.9
1972	14	154/277	55.6	2,158	7.8	13	12	78.5
1973	6	10/24	41.7	121	5.0	1	2	37.0
1974	10	34/48	70.8	305	6.4	5	1	113.6
1975	1	3/6	50.0	24	4.0	0	0	60.4
Total	78	661/1,173	56.4	9,197	7.8	64	64	77.2

Rushing

Year	Att.	Yards	Avg.	TD
1966	3	12	4.0	0
1968	26	139	5.3	2
1969	20	68	3.4	0
1970	13	60	4.6	0
1971	19	31	1.6	0
1972	24	86	3.6	2
1973	2	5	2.5	0
1974	1	8	8.0	0
1975	1	0	0.0	0
Total	109	409	3.8	4

Like so many undersized quarterbacks, Bob Berry thrived on competition. His contemporaries often compared him to Billy Kilmer because of his leadership capabilities. Berry's physical capabilities, though, were limited. He was a scrambler with a weak arm who liked to roll out to see the field better. He relied heavily on short, accurate passes to his backs and tight ends, which tended to inflate his passer rating beyond his actual skills. He also was especially prone to being sacked. Until Rob Johnson came along, Berry had the highest sack rate of any quarterback; he was dropped on 14.1 percent of pass plays. Part of that is attributable to the lousy Falcons teams, but part is on Berry for not getting rid of the ball quickly enough.

Berry owed his career to coach Norm Van Brocklin. Van Brocklin traded for his fellow Oregon Duck in 1964 in Minnesota and then brought him to Atlanta and gave him a chance to start in 1968. In 1972, though, Van Brocklin traded Berry back to Minnesota along with a No. 1 draft pick for Bob Lee and Lonnie Warwick. In his last three years as a backup, Berry got to go to the playoffs three times and the Super Bowl twice. He ended his career the same way he began it, watching Fran Tarkenton from the sidelines.

QPR 2.0

Angelo Bertelli

Height: 6'1"   **Weight:** 190 lbs.   **Birthdate:** 6/18/1921
College: Notre Dame   **Draft:** Boston Yanks 1944-1st
1946 Los Angeles Dons; 1947–48 Chicago Rockets
Regular Season Record: 5-7-2 est., no comebacks
Relative Rating: 67%

Passing

Year	G	Comp./Att.	%	Yards	Y/Att.	TD	INT	Rating
1946	12	67/127	52.8	917	7.2	7	14	54.9
1947	1	2/7	28.6	-5	-0.7	0	2	0.0
1948	3	7/32	21.9	60	1.9	1	3	10.9
Total	16	76/166	45.8	972	5.9	8	19	41.1

Rushing

Year	Att.	Yards	Avg.	TD
1946	11	-16	-1.5	1
1947	1	2	2.0	0
1948	2	-1	-0.5	0
Total	14	-15	-1.1	1

When coach Frank Leahy decided to install the T formation as Notre Dame's offense, Angelo Bertelli became the school's very first quarterback in 1942. Although he played in only six games the following season before going into the U.S. Marines, Bertelli won the 1943 Heisman Trophy. He was the first of four Fighting Irish quarterbacks to do so. In fact, Notre Dame formed a veritable pipeline of professional quarterbacks during the early days of the T in the 1940s. Nineteen-forties quarterbacks Johnny Lujack, Boley Dancewicz, Frank Tripucka, George Ratterman, George Terlep, Steve Nemeth, Joe Gasparella, and Bob Williams all graduated to the NFL or All-America Football Conference, and five were first-round draft picks.

Bertelli was selected in 1944 by the Boston Yanks as the first overall draft pick but was fighting in the Pacific at the time. In April 1946, though, he signed a contract with the AAFC's Los Angeles Dons; a month later, the "Springfield Rifle" returned home to Massachusetts and signed with Boston of the NFL. The dispute shifted to the courtroom, and in September, Bertelli was ordered to play with Los Angeles or not at all. The rusty Bertelli was unimpressive with the Dons and was outplayed by the team's other quarterback, Charley O'Rourke. At the outset of the 1947 season, the Dons traded Bertelli in a three-way deal that saw Bertelli going to the Chicago Rockets, Chicago's Bob Hoernschemeyer going to the Brooklyn Dodgers, and Brooklyn's Glenn Dobbs coming to L.A. Bertelli spent two seasons with the Rockets but underwent multiple knee surgeries and threw just 39 passes in Chicago.

Steve Beuerlein

QPR 7.0

Height: 6'3" **Weight:** 220 lbs. **Birthdate:** 3/7/1965
College: Notre Dame **Draft:** Oakland 1987-4th
1988–89 Oakland Raiders; 1991–92 Dallas Cowboys; 1993–94 Arizona Cardinals; 1995 Jacksonville Jaguars; 1996–2000 Carolina Panthers; 2002–03 Denver Broncos
Regular Season Record: 47–55, 15 comebacks
Postseason Record: 1–1, no comebacks
Relative Rating: 104%

Passing

Year	G	Comp./Att.	%	Yards	Y/Att.	TD	INT	Rating
1988	10	105/238	44.1	1,643	6.9	8	7	66.6
1989	10	108/217	49.8	1,677	7.7	13	9	78.4
1991	8	68/137	49.6	909	6.6	5	2	77.2
1992	16	12/18	66.7	152	8.4	0	1	69.7
1993	16	258/418	61.7	3,164	7.6	18	17	82.5
1994	9	130/255	51.0	1,545	6.1	5	9	61.6
1995	7	71/142	50.0	952	6.7	4	7	60.5
1996	8	69/123	56.1	879	7.1	8	2	93.5
1997	7	89/153	58.2	1,032	6.7	6	3	83.6
1998	12	216/343	63.0	2,613	7.6	17	12	88.2
1999	16	343/571	60.1	4,436	7.8	36	15	94.6
2000	16	324/533	60.8	3,730	7.0	19	18	79.7
2002	8	68/117	58.1	925	7.9	6	5	82.7
2003	4	33/63	52.4	389	6.2	2	5	49.0
Total	147	1,894/3,328	56.9	24,046	7.2	147	112	80.3
PS:	3	16/31	51.6	271	8.7	1	1	78.8

Rushing

Year	Att.	Yards	Avg.	TD
1988	30	35	1.2	0
1989	16	39	2.4	0
1991	7	-14	-2.0	0
1992	4	-7	-1.8	0
1993	22	45	2.0	0
1994	22	39	1.8	1
1995	5	32	6.4	0
1996	12	17	1.4	0
1997	4	32	8.0	0
1998	22	26	1.2	0
1999	27	124	4.6	2
2000	44	106	2.4	1
2002	5	9	1.8	1
2003	5	13	2.6	0
Total	225	496	2.2	5
PS:	6	5	0.8	0

Although the tall pocket-passer Steve Beuerlein was never a star, he did develop into a solid NFL quarterback, able to do a decent job either as a starter or backup. His qualities are familiar ones. He could throw the long ball and was an accurate passer but was also an immobile sitting duck for pass rushers. If he had come along 20 years earlier, he may have been a No. 1 draft pick as a classic drop-back passer from Notre Dame, but the Fighting Irish brand for quarterbacks had begun to decline by the time Beuerlein graduated in 1987; he was a fourth-round selection of the Raiders.

Steve struggled in Oakland and was sent to Dallas where he relieved an injured Troy Aikman to win the last four games in 1991 and drive the Cowboys into the playoffs, where they went 1–1. After two years in Dallas as a backup with brief mop-up duty in Super Bowl XXVII, Beuerlein headed for the Arizona desert and another disappointing try as a starter. Left unprotected in the expansion draft, he was the first pick of Jacksonville and became the Jaguars' first starting quarterback. By Week 7, however, Steve yielded his starting slot to the more mobile Mark Brunell, and it was on to Carolina to back up young Kerry Collins. Two years later, the immature Collins had an emotional meltdown that drove him off the team, and Beuerlein finally got a chance to shine as a starter at the age of 33. In three years as the Panthers' starter, Steve racked up more than

10,000 yards and tossed 72 touchdowns to just 45 interceptions. By then, he was deemed too old and jettisoned in a youth movement for 29-year-old rookie Chris Weinke. Beuerlein finished his career with two seasons as a backup in Denver before moving to the broadcast booth.

Todd Blackledge

Height: 6'3" **Weight:** 225 lbs. **Birthdate:** 2/25/1961
College: Penn State **Draft:** Kansas City 1983-1st
1983-87 Kansas City Chiefs; 1988-89 Pittsburgh Steelers
Regular Season Record: 15–14, 2 comebacks
Postseason Record: 0–1, no comebacks
Relative Rating: 80%

Passing

Year	G	Comp./Att.	%	Yards	Y/Att.	TD	INT	Rating
1983	4	20/34	58.8	259	7.6	3	0	112.3
1984	11	147/294	50.0	1,707	5.8	6	11	59.2
1985	12	86/172	50.0	1,190	6.9	6	14	50.3
1986	10	96/211	45.5	1,200	5.7	10	6	67.6
1987	3	15/31	48.4	154	5.0	1	1	60.4
1988	3	38/79	48.1	494	6.3	2	3	60.8
1989	3	22/60	36.7	282	4.7	1	3	36.9
Total	46	424/881	48.1	5,286	6.0	29	38	60.2
PS:	1	12/21	57.1	80	6.7	0	2	26.0

Rushing

Year	Att.	Yards	Avg.	TD
1983	1	0	0.0	0
1984	18	102	5.7	1
1985	17	97	5.7	0
1986	23	60	2.6	0
1987	5	21	4.2	0
1988	8	25	3.1	1
1989	9	20	2.2	0
Total	81	325	4.0	2
PS:	4	33	8.3	0

The second quarterback selected in the fabled 1983 draft class of six first-round quarterbacks, Todd Blackledge was the only complete failure as a professional. He had led Penn State to a national championship and a 31–5 record over three years, but in seven years in Kansas City and Pittsburgh he was 15–14, completing less than 50 percent of his passes and tossing more interceptions than touchdowns.

After spending his rookie season on the Chiefs' bench, Blackledge got his first start in the 1984 opener against his hometown team, the Steelers. Although starting only because Bill Kenney broke his thumb, Blackledge led the Chiefs to a 37–27 upset of Pittsburgh, running for one score and throwing for another. The Chiefs won again the next week, but then reality set in. Blackledge's throwing mechanics were flawed, he was immobile and indecisive, and he got sacked too much. In Week 8, Bill Kenney came in to relieve Blackledge and regained the starting job. There would be few pro highlights for Todd; he never threw for 300 yards or threw more than three touchdowns in a game, and he played for just one playoff team. The Steelers obtained Blackledge for a fourth-round pick in 1988 and cut him two years later, hastening his broadcasting career.

Jeff Blake

Height: 6'1" **Weight:** 223 lbs. **Birthdate:** 12/4/1970
College: East Carolina **Draft:** New York Jets 1992-6th
1992 New York Jets; 1994–99 Cincinnati Bengals; 2000–01 New Orleans Saints; 2002 Baltimore Ravens; 2003 Arizona Cardinals; 2004 Philadelphia Eagles; 2005 Chicago Bears
Regular Season Record: 39–61, 17 comebacks
Postseason Record: NA
Relative Rating: 99%

Passing

Year	G	Comp./Att.	%	Yards	Y/Att.	TD	INT	Rating
1992	3	4/9	44.4	40	4.4	0	1	18.1
1994	10	156/306	51.0	2,154	7.0	14	9	76.9
1995	16	326/567	57.5	3,822	6.7	28	17	82.1
1996	16	308/549	56.1	3,624	6.6	24	14	80.3
1997	11	184/317	58.0	2,125	6.7	8	7	77.6
1998	8	51/93	54.8	739	7.9	3	3	78.2
1999	14	215/389	55.3	2,670	6.9	16	12	77.6
2000	11	184/302	60.9	2,025	6.7	13	9	82.7
2001	1	0/1	0.0	0	0.0	0	0	39.6
2002	11	165/295	55.9	2,084	7.1	13	11	77.3
2003	13	208/367	56.7	2,247	6.1	13	15	69.6
2004	3	18/37	48.6	126	3.4	1	1	54.6
2005	3	8/9	88.9	55	6.1	1	0	129.2
Total	120	1,827/3,241	56.4	21,711	6.7	134	99	78.0

Rushing

Year	Att.	Yards	Avg.	TD
1992	2	-2	-1.0	0
1994	37	204	5.5	1
1995	53	309	5.8	2
1996	72	317	4.4	2
1997	45	234	5.2	3
1998	15	103	6.9	0
1999	63	332	5.3	2
2000	57	243	4.3	1
2001	1	-1	-1.0	0
2002	39	106	2.7	1
2003	30	177	5.9	2
2004	3	6	2.0	0
2005	1	-1	-1.0	0
Total	418	2,027	4.8	14

A late-round pick of the Jets in 1992, Jeff Blake made quite a splash with the Bengals when he took over the starting job from the abysmal first-round bust David Klingler in the middle of the 1994 season. In his first full season as a starter, Jeff threw for 28 touchdowns and was named to the 1995 Pro Bowl. The following season, Blake tossed another 24 touchdowns before his career inexplicably began to unravel as he lost the confidence of coach Bruce Coslet. To unseat Blake, Coslet brought back Boomer Esiason in 1997, signed Neil O'Donnell in 1998, and drafted Akili Smith in 1999, but none was able to outplay Jeff.

In his two prime years, Blake established himself as the finest long-ball thrower in the league, maybe the best since Daryle Lamonica at the bomb. He was a good runner who rushed for more than 2,000 yards during his career and was a brash and confident leader on the field. Perhaps a bit too bold at times, he also was not afraid to challenge management, and he found himself bouncing to six teams in the last seven years of his career. Ultimately, his won-lost record is pretty ugly, but the long, arcing spirals he once threw to Carl Pickens and Darnay Scott in Cincinnati were a thing of beauty.

George Blanda

QPR 9.5

Height: 6'2" **Weight:** 215 lbs. **Birthdate:** 9/17/1927
College: Kentucky **Draft:** Chicago Bears 1949-12th
1949-58 Chicago Bears; 1950 Baltimore Colts; 1960-66 Houston Oilers; 1967-75 Oakland Raiders
Regular Season Record: 53-50-1, 14 comebacks
Postseason Record: 2-1, no comebacks
Relative Rating: 99%

Passing

Year	G	Comp./Att.	%	Yards	Y/Att.	TD	INT	Rating
1949	12	9/21	42.9	197	9.4	0	5	37.3
1950	12	0/1	0.0	0	0.0	0	0	39.6
1951	12	0/0	0.0	0	0.0	0	0	0.0
1952	12	47/131	35.9	664	5.1	8	11	38.5
1953	12	169/362	46.7	2,164	6.0	14	23	52.3
1954	8	131/281	46.6	1,929	6.9	15	17	62.1
1955	12	42/97	43.3	459	4.7	4	7	41.6
1956	12	37/69	53.6	439	6.4	7	4	82.9
1957	12	8/19	42.1	65	3.4	0	3	11.8
1958	12	2/7	28.6	19	2.7	0	0	39.6
1960	14	169/363	46.6	2,413	6.6	24	22	65.4
1961	14	187/362	51.7	3,330	9.2	36	22	91.3
1962	14	197/418	47.1	2,810	6.7	27	42	51.3
1963	14	224/423	53.0	3,003	7.1	24	25	70.1
1964	14	262/505	51.9	3,287	6.5	17	27	61.4
1965	14	186/442	42.1	2,542	5.8	20	30	47.9
1966	14	122/271	45.0	1,764	6.5	17	21	55.3
1967	14	15/38	39.5	285	7.5	3	3	59.6
1968	14	30/49	61.2	522	10.7	6	2	120.1
1969	14	6/13	46.2	73	5.6	2	1	71.5
1970	14	29/55	52.7	461	8.4	6	5	79.4
1971	14	32/58	55.2	378	6.5	4	6	58.6
1972	14	5/15	33.3	77	5.1	1	0	73.5
1973	14	0/0	0.0	0	0.0	0	0	0.0
1974	14	1/4	25.0	28	7.0	1	0	95.8
1975	14	1/3	33.3	11	3.7	0	1	5.6
Total	340	1,911/4,007	47.7	26,920	6.7	236	277	79.2
PS:	8	89/189	47.1	1,190	6.3	7	17	42.4

Rushing

Year	Att.	Yards	Avg.	TD
1949	2	9	4.5	1
1952	20	104	5.2	1
1953	24	62	2.6	0
1954	19	41	2.2	0
1955	15	54	3.6	2
1956	6	47	7.8	0
1957	5	-5	-1.0	1
1960	16	16	1.0	4
1961	7	12	1.7	0
1962	3	6	2.0	0
1963	4	1	0.3	0
1964	4	-2	-0.5	0
1965	4	-6	-1.5	0
1966	3	1	0.3	0
1969	1	0	0.0	0
1970	2	4	2.0	0
Total	135	344	2.5	9
PS:	3	0	0.0	0

George Blanda is in Canton for his kicking and for his longevity—a remarkable 26-year career under 10 coaches that lasted until he was 48 years old. As a quarterback, he was very good but with clear flaws that kept him from greatness. He was never noted as a deep passer but was very good at shorter passes. He once led the league with 36 touchdowns, but the next year he threw an all-time record 42 interceptions. In fact, he led the AFL in interceptions four times and retired with the dubious NFL record of 277 pass interceptions that Brett Favre has since exceeded. However, gruff George was an indisputable leader, in charge of the huddle and reliable in the clutch.

Blanda's professional career can be divided neatly into thirds. He played under Bear Bryant at Kentucky and was a 12th-round draft pick of the Chicago Bears in 1949. He hated Bears owner/coach George Halas right from the start for being too autocratic and for running a needlessly complex offense. Halas actually sent Blanda to Baltimore in a multiplayer deal for Dick Barwegan in 1950 but brought him back a week later in a separate cash deal. Blanda steamed, "He took away my best 10 years in pro football." For 10 seasons in Chicago, he battled unsuccessfully for playing time against a steady stream of quarterbacks, including Sid Luckman, Johnny Lujack, Bobby Williams, Steve

Romanik, Tommy O'Connell, Zeke Bratkowski, and Ed Brown. At times, Blanda even played linebacker and defensive back, but mostly he was a kicker, once hitting 156 consecutive extra points.

Blanda finally tired of being just a kicker and retired in 1959. However, when the American Football League opened for business, he found himself courted by both the Chargers and Oilers to be their initial quarterback. George signed with the Oilers and led them to three straight title games and the first two AFL championships with his passing and kicking. The Oilers had a wild passing offense that sometimes used a spread attack to get all their speedy receivers into play. They won the very first AFL Championship Game in 1960 on a spectacular 88-yard touchdown pass from Blanda to Billy Cannon in the fourth quarter. By 1966, though, the team was bad, and George was being pelted by snow cones at home.

At 40, Blanda was released by Houston, signed by Oakland in 1967, and began the third phase to his career, still kicking but now a relief passer for Daryle Lamonica in the Raiders' vertical passing offense. Blanda got to start only one game in Oakland but threw four touchdown passes in it against Denver in 1968. Two years later in 1970, Blanda captured the imagination of the American

TOP 10
Movie/TV Roles for Quarterbacks

10. Dan Pastorini in *Killer Fish*
9. Jack Concannon in *M*A*S*H* and *Brian's Song*
8. Brett Favre in *There's Something About Mary*
7. Joe Kapp as a prison guard in the original *The Longest Yard*
6. Don Meredith as a regular on the series *Police Story*
5. Roman Gabriel as Blue Boy in *The Undefeated*
4. Terry Bradshaw's nude scene in *Failure to Launch*
3. Joe Namath in *C.C. and Company* with Ann-Margret
2. Sammy Baugh as the lead in the 1941 serial *King of the Texas Rangers*
1. Carlos Brown, known as Alan Autry, playing Bubba on the series *In the Heat of the Night*

public with an amazing five-week run of clutch performances as the 43-year-old wunderkind of the Raiders. Oakland's record was 2–2–1 that year when in successive weeks Blanda threw three second-half touchdown passes to beat Pittsburgh, kicked a last-second 48-yard field goal to tie Kansas City, threw a touchdown pass and kicked a 52-yard field goal in the last four minutes to edge Cleveland, threw the fourth-quarter winning touchdown pass to nip Denver, and beat San Diego with a chip-shot 16-yard field goal on the game's final play. Blanda's fireman routine won him the Bert Bell Player of the Year Award and made him a legend even though he had thrown just 55 passes for six touchdowns during the year. By the time Blanda was finally forced out after the 1975 season, he had scored a league record 2,002 points, and he was elected to the Hall of Fame in 1981.

Drew Bledsoe   QPR 8.5

Height: 6'5" **Weight:** 238 lbs. **Birthdate:** 2/14/1972
College: Washington State **Draft:** New England 1993-1st
1993–2001 New England Patriots; 2002–04 Buffalo Bills; 2005–06 Dallas Cowboys
Regular Season Record: 98–95, 31 comebacks
Postseason: 3–3, no comebacks
Relative Rating: 102%

Passing

Year	G	Comp./Att.	%	Yards	Y/Att.	TD	INT	Rating
1993	13	214/429	49.9	2,494	5.8	15	15	65.0
1994	16	400/691	57.9	4,555	6.6	25	27	73.6
1995	15	323/636	50.8	3,507	5.5	13	16	63.7
1996	16	373/623	59.9	4,086	6.6	27	15	83.7
1997	16	314/522	60.2	3,706	7.1	28	15	87.7
1998	14	263/481	54.7	3,633	7.6	20	14	80.9
1999	16	305/539	56.6	3,985	7.4	19	21	75.6
2000	16	312/531	58.8	3,291	6.2	17	13	77.3
2001	2	40/66	60.6	400	6.1	2	2	75.3
2002	16	375/610	61.5	4,359	7.1	24	15	86.0
2003	16	274/471	58.2	2,860	6.1	11	12	73.0
2004	16	256/450	56.9	2,932	6.5	20	16	76.6
2005	16	300/499	60.1	3,639	7.3	23	17	83.7
2006	6	90/169	53.3	1,164	6.9	7	8	69.2
Total	194	3,839/6,717	57.2	44,611	6.6	251	206	77.1
PS:	7	129/252	51.2	1,335	5.3	6	12	54.9

Rushing

Year	Att.	Yards	Avg.	TD
1993	32	82	2.6	0
1994	44	40	0.9	0
1995	20	28	1.4	0
1996	24	27	1.1	0
1997	28	55	2.0	0
1998	28	44	1.6	0
1999	42	101	2.4	0
2000	47	158	3.4	2
2001	5	18	3.6	0
2002	27	67	2.5	2
2003	24	29	1.2	2
2004	22	37	1.7	0
2005	34	50	1.5	2
2006	8	28	3.5	2
Total	385	764	2.0	10
PS:	13	-1	-0.1	0

Drew Bledsoe threw a lot of passes for a ton of yards in 14 years, but after his fifth season, his career went into a long, slow decline that transformed him from a slight asset to a slight liability. He was an average NFL starting quarterback—not a bust as the No. 1 overall pick in the 1993 draft but not quite living up to that exalted billing either. He was a big-armed statue who took too many sacks, fumbled 123 times in 194 games, and threw too many key interceptions, but against weaker opponents he could put up some big numbers. He could throw hard and with touch but would get rattled after being hit and start to make poor decisions with the ball. On the plus side, Bledsoe was a classy, team guy who was a credit to any organization for whom he played.

Under Bill Parcells, Bledsoe led the 1996 Patriots to the Super Bowl in his finest season but threw four picks to the Packers in a losing effort in the big game. Bledsoe's career reached its flash point in 2001. In the off-season, he signed a 10-year, $100 million contract that seemed to cement him as a New England fixture for the rest of his playing days; however, he was traded to Buffalo less than a year later. For the ninth year in a row, Bledsoe began 2001 as the Patriots' starter but was drilled so hard by Jet linebacker Mo Lewis in the second game that internal bleeding put him on the sidelines for several weeks. In the interim, little-known backup Tom Brady asserted himself and the underrated Patriots began winning. Although Bledsoe felt that coach Bill Belichick wasn't honest with him and wasn't giving him a chance to win back his job, Drew never publicly complained or roiled the team chemistry. Bledsoe made one final appearance as a Patriot in the conference championship in Pittsburgh when Brady hurt his ankle in the second quarter. Bledsoe went in and led the team to a touchdown to close out the half and then neatly managed the game in the second half to ensure a trip to the Super Bowl. Drew completed only 10 of 21 passes for 102 yards in the game, but it was enough, and Bledsoe got his lone Super Bowl ring as Brady's backup one week later.

Bledsoe finished his career with three seasons in Buffalo and two in Dallas, giving way to younger, more mobile quarterbacks in both cities. With Dallas, he ended his career back under Bill Parcells, no longer chafing under the grumpy old coach's barbs.

Kyle Boller wowed the scouts at the NFL Combine in 2003 by dropping to his knees to throw a ball through the uprights from 50 yards away. Ravens coach Brian Billick said at the time, "The Boller kid has it all. He has all the measurables. I'm very impressed with him." Two months later, Billick drafted him and then spent the last five years of his tenure as Ravens coach trying to coax a consistent, winning performance from a very mediocre quarterback who never quite seemed to develop. Boller clearly found it much more difficult to throw accurately on his feet when he was surrounded by defensive linemen than by adoring scouts.

In 2008, Boller injured his shoulder in an exhibition game and essentially ended his time in Baltimore as coach John Harbaugh moved on with rookie Joe Flacco and second-year man Troy Smith. The streaky Boller will get a chance at redemption with the St. Louis Rams in 2009.

Kyle Boller

QPR

Height: 6'3" **Weight:** 220 lbs. **Birthdate:** 6/17/1981
College: California **Draft:** Baltimore 2003-1st
2003–08 Baltimore Ravens
Regular Season Record: 20–22, 6 comebacks
Postseason Record: NA
Relative Rating: 90%

Passing

Year	G	Comp./Att.	%	Yards	Y/Att.	TD	INT	Rating
2003	11	116/224	51.8	1,260	5.6	7	9	62.4
2004	16	258/464	55.6	2,559	5.5	13	11	70.9
2005	9	171/293	58.4	1,799	6.1	11	12	71.8
2006	5	33/55	60.0	485	8.8	5	2	104.0
2007	12	168/275	61.1	1,743	6.3	9	10	75.2
Total	53	746/1,311	56.9	7,846	6.0	45	44	71.9

Rushing

Year	Att.	Yards	Avg.	TD
2003	30	62	2.1	0
2004	53	189	3.6	1
2005	23	66	2.9	1
2006	22	34	1.5	0
2007	19	89	4.7	0
Total	147	440	3.0	2

Brooks Bollinger

QPR

Height: 6'1" **Weight:** 205 lbs. **Birthdate:** 11/15/1979
College: Wisconsin **Draft:** New York Jets 2003-6th
2004–05 New York Jets; 2006–07 Minnesota Vikings
Regular Season Record: 2–8, no comebacks
Postseason Record: NA
Relative Rating: 93%

Passing

Year	G	Comp./Att.	%	Yards	Y/Att.	TD	INT	Rating
2004	1	5/9	55.6	60	6.7	0	0	76.2
2005	11	150/266	56.4	1,558	5.9	7	6	72.9
2006	2	13/18	72.2	146	8.1	0	1	72.9
2007	5	33/50	66.0	391	7.8	1	1	88.0
2008	2	10/17	58.8	71	4.2	1	1	63.6
Total	21	211/360	58.6	2,226	6.2	9	9	74.6

Rushing

Year	Att.	Yards	Avg.	TD
2004	1	2	2.0	0
2005	35	135	3.9	0
2007	5	18	3.6	0
Total	41	155	3.8	0

Brooks Bollinger is more of a runner than a passer. At Wisconsin, he set the school rushing record for quarterbacks and led the team to three bowl victories. He does not have the tools to succeed as a starting quarterback in the NFL although he is smart enough to stick around as a backup for several years before going into coaching. In his one extended trial as a starter for the 2005 Jets, Bollinger did manage to throw for more than 300 yards in one game and was named the team's MVP for the month of December by leading them to two victories in four games. The next year, he was in Minnesota backing up Brad Johnson and Tarvaris Jackson and in 2008 moved on to Dallas as their third quarterback.

Steve Bono

QPR 5.5

Height: 6'4" **Weight:** 215 lbs. **Birthdate:** 5/11/1962
College: UCLA **Draft:** Minnesota 1985-6th
1985-86 Minnesota Vikings; 1987-88 Pittsburgh Steelers; 1989, 1991-93 San Francisco 49ers; 1994-96 Kansas City Chiefs; 1997 Green Bay Packers; 1998 St. Louis Rams; 1999 Carolina Panthers
Regular Season Record: 28-14, 5 comebacks
Postseason Record: 0-1, no comebacks
Relative Rating: 98%

Year	G	Comp./Att.	%	Yards	Y/Att.	TD	INT	Rating
1985	1	1/10	10.0	5	0.5	0	0	39.6
1986	1	1/1	100.0	3	3.0	0	0	79.2
1987	3	34/74	45.9	438	5.9	5	2	76.3
1988	2	10/35	28.6	110	3.1	1	2	25.9
1989	1	4/5	80.0	62	12.4	1	0	157.9
1991	9	141/237	59.5	1,617	6.8	11	4	88.5
1992	16	36/56	64.3	463	8.3	2	2	87.1
1993	8	39/61	63.9	416	6.8	0	1	76.9
1994	7	66/117	56.4	796	6.8	4	4	74.6
1995	16	293/520	56.3	3,121	6.0	21	10	79.5
1996	14	235/438	53.7	2,572	5.9	12	13	68.0
1997	2	5/10	50.0	29	2.9	0	0	56.2
1998	6	69/136	50.7	807	5.9	5	4	69.1
1999	2	0/1	0.0	0	0.0	0	0	39.6
Total	88	934/1,701	54.9	10,439	6.1	62	42	75.3
PS:	2	13/27	48.1	137	5.1	1	3	36.1

Rushing

Year	Att.	Yards	Avg.	TD
1987	8	27	3.4	1
1991	17	46	2.7	0
1992	15	23	1.5	0
1993	12	14	1.2	1
1994	4	-1	-0.3	0
1995	28	113	4.0	5
1996	26	27	1.0	0
1997	3	-3	-1.0	0
1998	10	13	1.3	0
1999	2	-2	-1.0	0
Total	125	257	2.1	7
PS:	0	0	0.0	0

As a third-string rookie behind Wade Wilson and Tommy Kramer on the 1985 Vikings, Steve Bono looked wryly into his future, "If I'm fortunate, in five or six years I'll be the one being booed." It did take Steve six years to become even an interim starter, and he did not become a full-time starter for another four years after that. At that point, the longtime backup's limitations became clear.

Bono lasted just two years in Minnesota and got his second chance as a replacement player for the Steelers during the 1987 strike. His 2–1 stint that year earned him another shot in 1988, but when Pittsburgh released him in 1989, he found a regular job as a stockbroker. The 49ers' offensive coach, Mike Holmgren, brought Bono to training camp that summer, though, and he won the third-string job behind Hall of Famers Joe Montana and Steve Young. Bono was able to maintain good relations with both of those feuding rivals and had a front-row seat on the bench for Super Bowl XXIV. When Montana was traded to Kansas City two years later, Young stepped in and played well but had trouble winning over the fans. After Young went down to injury, Bono won five of six games in a very methodical, efficient way and became a fan favorite. He backed up Young for two more seasons and then was traded to the Chiefs to back up Montana in Joe's final season.

In 1995, at long last, the starting job was Bono's. The Chiefs went 13–3 but lost in the first game of the playoffs. The most surprising play of his career came that year against the Cardinals when he took off on a play-action bootleg run of 76 yards, tying Greg Landry's mark for the longest run by a quarterback. That one run makes up nearly one-third of Bono's career rushing total. After a disappointing 9–7 finish in 1996, Kansas City released Bono and went with another 49er castoff at quarterback, Elvis Grbac. Bono bounced from the Packers to the Rams to the Panthers over the next three seasons, his brief life as a starter finished. Despite having a strong, accurate arm, Bono was essentially an overly mechanical system quarterback with little talent for improvisation who was unable to beat a really good team at crunch time.

Mike Boryla

QPR 1.0

Height: 6'3" **Weight:** 200 lbs. **Birthdate:** 3/6/1951
College: Stanford **Draft:** Cincinnati 1974-4th
1974–76 Philadelphia Eagles; 1978 Tampa Bay Bucs
Regular Season Record: 8–11, 1 comeback
Postseason Record: NA
Relative Rating: 90%

Passing

Year	G	Comp./Att.	%	Yards	Y/Att.	TD	INT	Rating
1974	4	60/102	58.8	580	5.7	5	3	78.9
1975	7	87/166	52.4	996	6.0	6	12	52.7
1976	11	123/246	50.0	1,247	5.1	9	14	53.4
1978	1	2/5	40.0	15	3.0	0	0	47.9
Total	23	272/519	52.4	2,838	5.5	20	29	58.1

Rushing

Year	Att.	Yards	Avg.	TD
1974	6	25	4.2	0
1975	8	33	4.1	0
1976	29	166	5.7	2
Total	43	224	5.2	2

Mike Boryla, whose father Vince was an NBA player, coach, and executive, succeeded Jim Plunkett and Don Bunce as the starting quarterback at Stanford and was the No. 1 pick of the then-unnamed New York franchise in the fledgling World Football League in 1974. Meanwhile, the Cincinnati Bengals selected him in the fourth round of the NFL draft.

TOP 10
Top 10 Quarterback Kickers

10. Doug Flutie—converted first NFL drop-kick XP in 65 years in 2006
9. Cotton Davidson—2 FGs and 31 XPs
8. Milt Plum—6 FGs and 16 XPs
7. Gary Kerkorian—10 FGs and 47 XPs
6. Benny Friedman—2 FGs and 71 XPs
5. Roy Zimmerman—18 FGs and 133 XPs
4. Johnny Lujack—4 FGs and 130 XPs
3. Bobby Layne—34 FGs and 120 XPs
2. Bob Waterfield—60 FGs and 315 XPs
1. George Blanda—335 FGs and 943 XPs

The Eagles then traded a No. 1 pick in the 1976 draft to the Bengals for the fourth-rounder before he ever played a down. Mike had some rookie success when he got to start the last three games and won them all after Eagles starter Roman Gabriel was hurt late in 1974. When Gabriel had more injury problems in 1975, Boryla closed out that year as the starter again but with less success.

Boryla was a dink-and-dunk passer who averaged just 5.5 yards per pass as a pro. For the 1974 season, Mike threw just six touchdowns to 12 interceptions, averaged only six yards per pass, and won two of five starts. It was hardly a sterling performance, but it took him to the Pro Bowl. That year Fran Tarkenton, Archie Manning, Roger Staubach, James Harris, Billy Kilmer, and Steve Bartkowski all claimed injury or prior commitments, so the NFL begged Boryla to join Jim Hart on the NFC's team. Even stranger, Hart struggled in the game and was yanked in the fourth quarter with the AFC in front 20–9, allowing Boryla to come in and throw two touchdown passes to win the game. Boryla got to start 10 games for the Eagles in 1976 but declined further in productivity and moved on to Tampa to finish his overrated career.

Terry Bradshaw

QPR 10.0

Height: 6'3" **Weight:** 215 lbs. **Birthdate:** 9/2/1948
College: Louisiana Tech **Draft:** Pittsburgh 1970-1st
1970–83 Pittsburgh Steelers
Regular Season Record: 107–51, 24 comebacks
Postseason Record: 14–5, 4 comebacks
Relative Rating: 104%

Passing

Year	G	Comp./Att.	%	Yards	Y/Att.	TD	INT	Rating
1970	13	83/218	38.1	1,410	6.5	6	24	30.4
1971	14	203/373	54.4	2,259	6.1	13	22	59.7
1972	14	147/308	47.7	1,887	6.1	12	12	64.1
1973	10	89/180	49.4	1,183	6.6	10	15	54.5
1974	8	67/148	45.3	785	5.3	7	8	55.2
1975	14	165/286	57.7	2,055	7.2	18	9	88.0
1976	10	92/192	47.9	1,177	6.1	10	9	65.4
1977	14	162/314	51.6	2,523	8.0	17	19	71.4
1978	16	207/368	56.3	2,915	7.9	28	20	84.7
1979	16	259/472	54.9	3,724	7.9	26	25	77.0
1980	15	218/424	51.4	3,339	7.9	24	22	75.0
1981	14	201/370	54.3	2,887	7.8	22	14	83.9
1982	9	127/240	52.9	1,768	7.4	17	11	81.4
1983	1	5/8	62.5	77	9.6	2	0.0	133.9
Total	**168**	**2,025/3,091**	**51.9**	**27,989**	**7.2**	**212**	**210**	**70.9**
PS:	19	261/456	57.2	3,833	8.4	30	26	83

Rushing

Year	Att.	Yards	Avg.	TD
1970	32	233	7.3	1
1971	53	247	4.7	5
1972	58	346	6.0	7
1973	34	145	4.3	3
1974	34	224	6.6	2
1975	35	210	6.0	3
1976	31	219	7.1	3
1977	31	171	5.5	3
1978	32	93	2.9	1
1979	21	83	4.0	0
1980	36	111	3.1	2
1981	38	162	4.3	2
1982	8	10	1.3	0
1983	1	3	3.0	0
Total	**44**	**2,257**	**5.1**	**32**
PS:	51	288	5.6	3

Terry Bradshaw had the worst rookie year and longest development period of any Hall of Fame quarterback. Bradshaw was the No. 1 overall pick in the 1970 draft because he could throw the ball like a javelin thrower and run with it like a halfback. As a rookie, he was as overmatched at trying to read defenses as anyone ever has been and ended up throwing just six touchdowns to 24 interceptions and completing 38 percent of his passes. He was trapped in his own end zone three times—twice for safeties and once having a punt blocked for an opposition touchdown. It wasn't until his sixth season that he threw more touchdowns than interceptions, and that was just the second season that he completed at least half of his passes. However, Bradshaw's passer rating of 78.8 for the remainder of his career was 13 percent better than the league average. After a horrible 48–81 touchdown-to-interception ratio in his first five years, Terry improved to 164–129 starting in 1975. Behind him, the Steelers scored 15 percent more points than the league average. And then there are those four Super Bowl rings and two Super Bowl MVP trophies.

Bradshaw also had an effervescent personality as big as his arm, a personality still on view on the Fox NFL pregame show. Even in his darkest days on the field, he was a leader who made his teammates believe in him. Who could question the quarterback who threw the Immaculate Reception? As he often told them, "You can lose with me, but

Terry Bradshaw's Signature Play: The Immaculate Reception. Behind 7–6 and facing fourth-and-10 from the Steelers' own 40 with 22 seconds left, Bradshaw hoisted a desperation pass to Frenchy Fuqua who collided with Jack Tatum and the ball, which ricocheted back to a trailing Franco Harris. Harris raced to the end zone to beat Oakland in the playoffs on a controversial 60-yard touchdown pass.

Terry Bradshaw was a fast and powerful runner as well as a championship passer.

Bradshaw's relationship with steely coach Chuck Noll was contentious, but lasted Terry's entire 14 seasons. The two won four Super Bowls together.

Terry Bradshaw in the Clutch: Bradshaw missed nearly the entire 1983 season after elbow surgery. He returned for the penultimate game of the season against the Jets with the Steelers' playoff hopes in jeopardy. Bradshaw played just the opening two series, yet led Pittsburgh to two scores on his final two NFL touchdown passes before hearing a pop in his elbow. Pittsburgh was in the playoffs, but his career was over.

you'll never win without me." Terry beat back competitors Terry Hanratty and Joe Gilliam and the doubts of his coach, Chuck Noll, to win the starting job for good in 1974, taking Pittsburgh to its first Super Bowl that year. His wide-open style helped make acrobatic receivers Lynn Swann and John Stallworth into Hall of Famers with his long, high tosses that they brought down for touchdowns.

Dallas linebacker Thomas Henderson famously derided Bradshaw's intelligence before Super Bowl XIII, saying, "He couldn't spell cat if you spotted him the C and the A." With the 21–17 victory for Pittsburgh's second title, though, Bradshaw quieted his "brainy" critics. With subsequent thrilling victories in Super Bowl XIII against Dallas and XIV against the Rams, he solidified his status as an all-time great. Besides his flamboyant passing, two things are often forgotten about Bradshaw. First, he called his own plays, which was a dying art by the 1980s when he retired, so there should be no doubts about his football intelligence. Second, Terry was a bull of a runner who averaged 5.2 yards per carry in gaining more than 2,200 yards rushing.

Elbow surgery kept Bradshaw on the sidelines for the first 14 weeks of the 1983 season, but with Pittsburgh needing a win over the Jets to clinch a playoff spot, Terry played his final game for Pittsburgh December 10. In two drives, Bradshaw completed five of eight passes for 77 yards and two touchdowns to start the 34–7 rout before having to leave the game with a dead arm. Bradshaw was full of life and a great champion. Thankfully, he's the only Hall of Fame quarterback with a nude scene in a Hollywood movie, the 2006 comedy *Failure to Launch*.

Terry Bradshaw's Five Highest Honors
5. Selected for three Pro Bowls
4. Six-time All-Pro and a consensus All-Pro once
3. Two-time Super Bowl MVP
2. 1978 Player of the Year
1. Elected to the Pro Football Hall of Fame in 1989

The Five Quarterbacks Most Similar to Terry Bradshaw
5. Doug Williams
4. Jim Kelly
3. John Elway
2. Bobby Layne
1. Brett Favre

Terry Bradshaw's Five Top Touchdown Targets
5. Ron Shanklin, 14 TDs
4. Bennie Cunningham, 16 TDs
3. Jim Smith, 21 TDs
2. John Stallworth, 44 TDs
1. Lynn Swann, 49 TDs

Terry Bradshaw's Five Toughest Rivals
5. Bradshaw was 2–1 against the Cowboys in the regular season and 2–0 in the Super Bowl.
4. Bradshaw was 12–9 against the Bengals.
3. Bradshaw was 15–7 against the Oilers in the regular season and 2–0 in the playoffs.
2. Bradshaw was 16–5 against the Browns.
1. Bradshaw was 2–6 against the Raiders in the regular season and 3–1 in the playoffs.

Five Random Terry Bradshaw Statistics
5. Bradshaw played for one head coach.
4. Bradshaw's Steelers outscored the league average by 15 percent.
3. Bradshaw threw for five touchdowns on November 15, 1981, against Atlanta.
2. Bradshaw threw for more than 300 yards four times.
1. Bradshaw led the league in touchdown passes twice and interceptions once.

Tom Brady

QPR **10.0**

Height: 6'4" **Weight:** 225 lbs. **Birthdate:** 8/3/1977
College: Michigan **Draft:** New England 2000-6th
2001–08 New England Patriots
Regular Season Record: 86–24, 22 comebacks
Postseason Record: 14–3, 6 comebacks
Relative Rating: 117%

Passing

Year	G	Comp./Att.	%	Yards	Y/Att.	TD	INT	Rating
2000	1	1/3	33.3	6	2.0	0	0	42.4
2001	15	264/413	63.9	2,843	6.9	18	12	86.5
2002	16	373/601	62.1	3,764	6.3	28	14	85.7
2003	16	317/527	60.2	3,620	6.9	23	12	85.9
2004	16	288/474	60.8	3,692	7.8	28	14	92.6
2005	16	334/530	63.0	4,110	7.8	26	14	92.3
2006	16	319/516	61.8	3,529	6.8	24	12	87.9
2007	16	398/578	68.9	4,806	8.3	50	8	117.2
2008	1	7/11	63.6	76	6.9	0	0	83.9
Total	113	2,301/3,653	63.0	26,446	7.2	197	86	92.9
PS:	17	372/595	62.5	3,954	6.6	26	12	88.0

Rushing

Year	Att.	Yards	Avg.	TD
2001	36	43	1.2	0
2002	42	110	2.6	1
2003	42	63	1.5	1
2004	43	28	0.7	0
2005	27	89	3.3	1
2006	49	102	2.1	0
2007	37	98	2.6	2
Total	276	533	1.9	5
PS:	40	65	1.6	1

After going through quarterbacks Tom Dimitroff, Tom Greene, Tom Yewcic, Tom Sherman, Tom Flick, Tom Owen, Tom Ramsey, Tom Hodson, and Tom Tupa, the Patriots finally found their Tom Terrific when Tom Brady took over for injured Drew Bledsoe in the second game of the 2001 season. Brady's fairy-tale rise is familiar. He struggled for playing time at Michigan against Scott Driesbach and Brian Griese as a freshman and sophomore and then against Drew Henson as a senior. He wasn't drafted until the sixth round of the 2000 draft and was the 199th player taken—a background eerily similar to Hall of Famer Bart Starr, who lost his starting job at Alabama and was the 200th player drafted in 1956. Brady reported as a spindly fourth-stringer and, through film study and work in the weight room, built himself into a viable NFL backup when he got an opportunity in his second season. Three Super Bowl championships in four years followed as Brady established himself at the top of the quarterback class with Peyton Manning.

Brady is a tribute to the effects of diligence and hard work. As a rookie, he didn't have enough heft or arm strength to throw the ball hard enough to succeed in the NFL. The weight room built his body, and the practice field honed his skills. What he had from the start was the ability to lead a team and the poise to produce his best drives in the most dire circumstances—in the snow against Oakland in 2001, last-minute Super Bowl–winning drives against the Rams and the Panthers, and even the potential game-winning touchdown pass with 2:42 to play when the 18–0 Patriots were upended by the Giants in Super Bowl XLII. Tom has led more postseason fourth-quarter game-winning drives—six—than anyone other than John Elway.

When Brady went down to injury in the 2008 opener, ending his streak of consecutive starts at 111, it was clear that the Patriots would not be returning to the Super Bowl that season. Behind Tom, the Patriots have outscored the league average by nearly 25 percent. He is the most irreplaceable player in the league because he paradoxically understands how he is part of a team and cannot win by himself. As he once said, "You never want to lose the respect of the guys you play with, because that's everything."

Tom Brady's Signature Play: In the 2007 season finale, Brady hit Randy Moss for a 65-yard touchdown pass against the Giants to give the undefeated Patriots a fourth-quarter lead, 31–28. It was Brady's record-setting 50th touchdown pass and Moss' record-setting 23rd touchdown reception of the season.

Tom Brady uncorks a bomb against the Giants in the Patriots' undefeated 2007 regular season.

Tom Brady in the Clutch: In Brady's first postseason game in 2001 against the Raiders in the snow, Tom led the Patriots to 10 fourth-quarter points to send the game to overtime. In the game-winning 15-play, 61-yard drive, Brady completed eight of eight passes for 45 yards to set up Adam Vinatieri's 23-yard winning field goal.

Tom Brady emphatically celebrates a touchdown in Super Bowl XLII. Brady is a vocal leader on the Patriots.

Tom Brady's Five Highest Honors

5. 2005 *Sports Illustrated* Sportsman of the Year
4. Selected to four Pro Bowls
3. Four-time All-Pro and consensus All-Pro once
2. Two-time Super Bowl MVP
1. 2007 Player of the Year

The Five Quarterbacks Most Similar to Tom Brady

5. Ken Anderson
4. Bart Starr
3. Troy Aikman
2. Johnny Unitas
1. Joe Montana

Tom Brady's Five Top Touchdown Targets

5. Deion Branch, 14 TDs
4. Troy Brown, 15 TDs
3. David Patten, 16 TDs
2. Daniel Graham, 17 TDs
1. Randy Moss, 23 TDs

Tom Brady's Five Toughest Rivals

5. Brady is 2–1 against the Steelers in the regular season and 2–0 in the playoffs.
4. Brady is 2–2 against the Chargers in the regular season and 2–0 in the playoffs.
3. Brady is 9–5 against the Dolphins.
2. Brady is 11–2 against the Jets in the regular season and 1–0 in the playoffs.
1. Brady is 5–2 against the Colts in the regular season and 2–1 in the playoffs.

Five Random Tom Brady Statistics

5. Brady has played for only one head coach.
4. Brady's Patriots have outscored the league average by 23 percent.
3. Brady threw for five touchdowns against the Cowboys on October 14, 2007, the Bills on November 18, 2007, and threw for six against the Dolphins on October 21, 2007.
2. Brady has thrown for over 300 yards 23 times and more than 400 on September 22, 2002, against the Chiefs.
1. Brady has led the league in completion percentage once, passing yards twice, touchdown passes twice, yards per attempt once, and passing rating once.

Zeke Bratkowski

QPR 3.0

Height: 6'2" **Weight:** 210 lbs. **Birthdate:** 10/20/1931
College: Georgia **Draft:** Chicago Bears 1953-2nd
1954, 1957–60 Chicago Bears; 1961–63 Los Angeles Rams; 1963–68, 1971 Green Bay Packers
Regular Season Record: 16–30–1, 7 comebacks
Postseason Record: 0–0, 1 comeback
Relative Rating: 80%

Passing

Year	G	Comp./Att.	%	Yards	Y/Att.	TD	INT	Rating
1954	12	67/130	51.5	1,087	8.4	8	17	60.8
1957	12	37/80	46.3	527	6.6	1	9	32.7
1958	12	41/90	45.6	571	6.3	7	6	64.6
1959	12	31/62	50.0	403	6.5	2	5	48.0
1960	11	87/175	49.7	1,051	6.0	6	21	40.4
1961	13	124/230	53.9	1,547	6.7	8	13	63.1
1962	13	110/219	50.2	1,541	7.0	9	16	56.5
1963	6	49/93	52.7	567	6.1	4	9	46.1
1964	5	19/36	52.8	277	7.7	1	1	75.8
1965	6	21/48	43.8	348	7.3	3	4	54.9
1966	8	36/64	56.3	569	8.9	4	2	93.8
1967	6	53/94	56.4	724	7.7	5	9	59.3
1968	10	68/126	54.0	835	6.6	3	7	59.5
1971	6	19/37	51.4	298	8.1	4	3	80.7
Total	**132**	**762/1,484**	**51.3**	**10,435**	**7.0**	**65**	**122**	**54.3**
PS:	2	22/40	55	248	6.2	0	2	52.9

Rushing

Year	Att.	Yards	Avg.	TD
1954	15	35	2.3	1
1957	12	83	6.9	0
1958	3	0	0.0	0
1959	7	86	12.3	0
1960	8	20	2.5	0
1961	12	36	3.0	3
1962	7	14	2.0	0
1963	4	-3	-0.8	0
1964	2	0	0.0	0
1965	4	-1	-0.3	0
1966	4	7	1.8	0
1967	5	6	1.2	0
1968	8	24	3.0	0
1971	1	1	1.0	1
Total	**92**	**308**	**3.3**	**5**
PS:	0	0	0.0	0

Zeke Bratkowski's nearly 1:2 ratio both of touchdowns to interceptions and wins to losses as a starter does not paint an attractive portrait of the 14-year NFL veteran, but it does not paint a full one either. Bratkowski was a terrible interception-prone starter with the Bears and Rams but found his niche as Bart Starr's backup for the end of the Packers' 1960s dynasty.

As a sometime starter in Green Bay, Zeke went only 4–4–1 but is remembered fondly for his clutch performances as a relief pitcher when Starr was felled by injury during key games. Most prominent was the 1965 playoff between the Colts, led by halfback Tom Matte playing quarterback, and the Packers. Starr was forced to leave the game on the first play when his ribs were bruised trying to prevent linebacker Don Shinnick from scoring on a fumble recovery. Bratkowski came in cold and directed the offense, eventually leading a game-tying drive in the final minutes and then the game-winning drive in overtime. The following season, Zeke again picked on the Colts when he came in for Starr, who was felled by back spasms in the 13th game of the year. Bratkowski directed the offense for the second half and led a game-winning, fourth-quarter touchdown drive of 80 yards to clinch the division title.

Bratkowski had a close relationship with Starr, whom he had competed against in college. The two studied film together for hours, and Zeke later served as Starr's offensive coach on the Packers. Bratkowski coached for decades in the NFL with the Bears, Colts, Jets, Browns, and Eagles, and his son Bob has been the offensive coordinator for both the Seahawks and Bengals.

TOP 10
Late-Round Draft Picks

10. Marlin Briscoe—10th round, 357th player chosen
9. Bob Lee—17th round, 441st player chosen
8. Steve DeBerg—24th round, 275th player chosen
7. Jack Kemp—17th round, 203rd player chosen
6. Brian Sipe—13th round, 330th player chosen
5. Doug Flutie—11th round, 285th player chosen
4. Trent Green—8th round, 222nd player chosen
3. Brad Johnson—9th round, 227th player chosen
2. Tom Brady—6th round, 199th player chosen
1. Bart Starr—17th round, 200th player chosen

Drew Brees

QPR 9.0

Height: 6'0" **Weight:** 209 lbs. **Weight:** 1/15/1979
College: Purdue **Draft:** San Diego 2001-2nd
2001–05 San Diego Chargers; 2006–08 New Orleans Saints
Regular Season Record: 55–51, 12 comebacks
Postseason Record: 1–2, no comebacks
Relative Rating: 112%

Passing

Year	G	Comp./Att.	%	Yards	Y/Att.	TD	INT	Rating
2001	1	15/27	55.6	221	8.2	1	0	94.8
2002	16	320/526	60.8	3,284	6.2	17	16	76.9
2003	11	205/356	57.6	2,108	5.9	11	15	67.5
2004	15	262/400	65.5	3,159	7.9	27	7	104.8
2005	16	323/500	64.6	3,576	7.2	24	15	89.2
2006	16	356/554	64.3	4,418	8.0	26	11	96.2
2007	16	440/652	67.5	4,423	6.8	28	18	89.4
2008	16	413/635	65.0	5,069	8.0	34	17	96.2
Total	107	2,334/3,650	63.9	26,258	7.2	168	99	89.4
PS:	3	78/123	63.4	916	7.4	5	2	92.7

Rushing

Year	Att.	Yards	Avg.	TD
2001	2	18	9.0	0
2002	38	130	3.4	1
2003	21	84	4.0	0
2004	53	85	1.6	2
2005	21	49	2.3	1
2006	42	32	0.8	0
2007	23	52	2.3	1
2008	22	-1	0.0	0
Total	222	449	2.0	5
PS:	9	23	2.6	0

Doug Flutie (7) even had to look up to 6' Drew Brees (9) after directing a Charger win in 2003.

Despite being one of the shortest quarterbacks in the NFL, Drew Brees is also one of the best. He's an accurate passer with great touch and timing as well as a fine leader. Ultimately, though, he may be better remembered for his magnanimous charitable work in the New Orleans community in the wake of Hurricane Katrina in 2005. His expert quarterbacking the following football season also had a buoying effect on the spirits of our most spirited city and earned him popularity and respect in the Crescent City.

Brees was the Academic All-American Player of the Year at Purdue in 2000 but was marked down in the NFL draft because of his size. The Chargers that year had the top pick but were not overly enamored with top-rated Michael Vick and thus swung a deal with Atlanta that netted San Diego LaDainian Tomlinson in the first round and Drew Brees in the second—two tough Texans to build around. Brees sat on the bench as a rookie but threw for more than 3,000 yards in 2002 before struggling in 2003. Because of Drew's decline, the Chargers drafted Eli Manning in 2004 and then traded him for the Giants' pick, Philip Rivers.

Spurred by the lack of respect, Brees returned to form and threw for more than 3,000 yards and 20 touchdowns in both 2004 and 2005. The year 2005 marked the end of his contract, but Drew badly tore up his shoulder in the final game of the season, so San Diego opted to give the starting job to Rivers. Brees negotiated with the Dolphins and Saints, but the Dolphins also were nervous about his shoulder and signed Daunte Culpepper off knee surgery instead. While Culpepper and the Dolphins headed down the dumper in 2006, Brees revived the Saints' franchise and took them to the playoffs, where they ultimately lost to the Bears. Although they are a flawed team, the Saints have continued as a quasi contender in the last couple of years on the limber arm of Brees.

Bubby Brister

QPR 6.0

Height: 6'3" **Weight:** 205 lbs. **Birthdate:** 8/15/1962
College: Louisiana-Monroe **Draft:** Pittsburgh 1986-3rd
**1986–92 Pittsburgh Steelers; 1993–94 Philadelphia
Eagles; 1995 New York Jets; 1997–99 Denver
Broncos; 2000 Minnesota Vikings**
Regular Season Record: 37–38, 10 comebacks
Postseason Record: 1–1, 1 comeback
Relative Rating: 94%

Passing

Year	G	Comp./Att.	%	Yards	Y/Att.	TD	INT	Rating
1986	2	21/60	35.0	291	4.9	0	2	37.6
1987	2	4/12	33.3	20	1.7	0	3	2.8
1988	13	175/370	47.3	2,634	7.1	11	14	65.3
1989	14	187/342	54.7	2,365	6.9	9	10	73.1
1990	16	223/387	57.6	2,725	7.0	20	14	81.6
1991	8	103/190	54.2	1,350	7.1	9	9	72.9
1992	6	63/116	54.3	719	6.2	2	5	61.0
1993	10	181/309	58.6	1,905	6.2	14	5	84.9
1994	7	51/76	67.1	507	6.7	2	1	89.1
1995	9	93/170	54.7	726	4.3	4	8	53.7
1997	1	6/9	66.7	48	5.3	0	0	79.9
1998	7	78/131	59.5	986	7.5	10	3	99.0
1999	2	12/20	60.0	87	4.4	0	3	30.6
2000	2	10/20	50.0	82	4.1	0	1	40.0
Total	99	1,207/2,212	54.6	14,445	6.5	81	78	72.3
PS:	2	62/34	54.8	356	5.7	1	0	77.1

Rushing

Year	Att.	Yards	Avg.	TD
1986	6	10	1.7	1
1988	45	209	4.6	6
1989	27	25	0.9	0
1990	25	64	2.6	0
1991	11	17	1.5	0
1992	10	16	1.6	0
1993	20	39	2.0	0
1994	1	7	7.0	0
1995	16	18	1.1	0
1997	4	2	0.5	0
1998	19	102	5.4	1
1999	2	17	8.5	0
2000	5	20	4.0	0
Total	191	546	2.9	8
PS:	3	5.0	1.7	0

Like any confident, spirited quarterback, Bubby Brister thought of himself as a starter, but in reality he was a born backup. He came to the Steelers out of a small school in Louisiana and earned the starting nod by 1988. The following season, Pittsburgh started out losing its first two games by a combined 92–10 score but then rallied behind Brister to make the playoffs and get nipped 24–23 in the divisional round by John Elway's Broncos. Despite the success, Brister was an impatient play caller and an often inaccurate passer whose starting days were numbered.

Bubby was not happy that rookie Neil O'Donnell had pushed past him as starting quarterback in December 1991 and felt that he was caught in the middle between unpopular offensive coach Joe Walton and O'Donnell. When he was told to go in and replace O'Donnell late in a 31–6 loss to the Oilers, Brister replied, "I'm no relief quarterback. I don't mop up for anyone." When asked about it later, Coach Noll said that the bristly Brister would not be fined and even gave him his starting job back for the last two games of the year.

Brister moved on to Philadelphia in 1993 and the Jets in 1995 before slipping out of the game entirely in 1996. Ironically, when O'Donnell left Pittsburgh as a free agent five years later, he replaced Brister as the Jets' quarterback. However, former Eagle teammate Bill Romanowski recommended Bubby to coach Mike Shanahan, and Brister was brought in as Elway's backup just in time for Denver's back-to-back Super Bowl titles. Brister hoped to succeed Elway in 1999 but was beaten out by Brian Griese and angrily left for Minnesota, which proved to be his final NFL stop in 2000.

Dieter Brock

QPR 5.0

Height: 6'0" **Weight:** 195 lbs. **Birthdate:** 2/12/1951
College: Jacksonville State (AL) **Draft:** Free agent
1974–84 CFL; 1985 Los Angeles Rams
Regular Season Record: 11–4, 1 comeback
Postseason: 1–1, no comebacks
Relative Rating: 112%

Passing

Year	G	Comp./Att.	%	Yards	Y/Att.	TD	INT	Rating
1985	15	218/365	59.7	2,658	7.3	16	13	82.0
PS:	2	16/53	30.2	116	2.2	0	2	24.0

Rushing

Year	Att.	Yards	Avg.	TD
1985	20	38	1.9	0
PS:	1	0	0.0	0

At the outset of his career in Canada, Dieter Brock was criticized for trying to force too many deep balls when shorter passes were more open. Ironically, in his one year in the NFL, Brock was criticized for never going for the bomb, but by that time he was 34 years old and probably had lost his fastball.

Brock began as the understudy to Heisman Trophy winner Pat Sullivan at Auburn before transferring to little Jacksonville State in his native Alabama. Because NFL scouts seemed to show little interest in him, Dieter signed with Winnipeg in the CFL before the NFL draft. In 11 seasons, Brock led the league four times in passing, was a two-time MVP, and would eventually be elected to the Canadian Football Hall of Fame. In 1985, the Rams signed Brock to a four-year, $2.1 million contract to punch up their passing game. In the previous four seasons, Los Angeles had gone through Pat Haden, Dan Pastorini, Bert Jones, Vince Ferragamo, and Jeff Kemp at quarterback and gone 27–30. Brock had the third-highest passer rating in the NFL in 1985 and led the Rams to an 11–5 record and the NFC conference championship but never played in the NFL again. However, although Brock was very efficient, he was also very conservative. The Rams were 26th in passing yards, and Brock was downright embarrassing in the playoffs. In beating Dallas, Dieter completed six of 22 passes for 50 yards and one interception. In windy Soldier Field against the Bears the next week, he was worse—completing just 10 of 31 wobbly passes for 66 yards and again one interception. Dieter remained on the Rams' roster in 1986 but was troubled by a bad back and then had knee surgery. Veteran Steve Bartkowski and rookie Jim Everett were imported to handle the quarterbacking, and Brock retired at the end of the year.

QPR 9.0

John Brodie

Heigh: 6'1" **Weight:** 198 lbs. **Birthdate:** 8/14/1935
College: Stanford **Draft:** San Francisco 1957-1st
1957–73 San Francisco 49ers
Regular Season Record: 74–77, 14 comebacks
Postseason Record: 2–3, no comebacks
Relative Rating: 108%

Passing

Year	G	Comp./Att.	%	Yards	Y/Att.	TD	INT	Rating
1957	5	11/21	52.4	160	7.6	2	3	69.6
1958	12	103/172	59.9	1,224	7.1	6	13	61.8
1959	12	30/64	46.9	354	5.5	2	7	35.0
1960	11	103/207	49.8	1,111	5.4	6	9	57.5
1961	14	155/283	54.8	2,588	9.1	14	12	84.7
1962	14	175/304	57.6	2,272	7.5	18	16	79.0
1963	3	30/61	49.2	367	6.0	3	4	57.2
1964	14	193/392	49.2	2,498	6.4	14	16	64.6
1965	13	242/391	61.9	3,112	8.0	30	16	95.3
1966	14	232/427	54.3	2,810	6.6	16	22	65.8
1967	14	168/349	48.1	2,013	5.8	11	16	57.6
1968	14	234/404	57.9	3,020	7.5	22	21	78.0
1969	13	194/347	55.9	2,405	6.9	16	15	74.9
1970	14	223/378	59.0	2,941	7.8	24	10	93.8
1971	14	208/387	53.7	2,642	6.8	18	24	65.0
1972	6	70/110	63.6	905	8.2	9	8	86.4
1973	14	98/194	50.5	1,126	5.8	3	12	47.7
Total	201	2,469/4,491	55.0	31,548	7.0	214	224	72.3
PS:	5	71/143	49.7	973	6.8	4	7	60.7

Rushing

Year	Att.	Yards	Avg.	TD
1957	2	0	0.0	0
1958	11	-12	-1.1	1
1959	5	6	1.2	0
1960	18	171	9.5	1
1961	28	90	3.2	2
1962	37	258	7.0	4
1963	7	63	9.0	0
1964	27	135	5.0	2
1965	15	60	4.0	1
1966	5	18	3.6	3
1967	20	147	7.4	1
1968	18	71	3.9	0
1969	11	62	5.6	0
1970	9	29	3.2	2
1971	14	45	3.2	3
1972	3	8	2.7	1
1973	5	16	3.2	1
Total	235	1,167	5.0	22
PS:	2	3	1.5	1

John Brodie had all the tools to be a great quarterback. At times he was, but ultimately his inconsistency undermined his best efforts. In 1965, Brodie completed 62 percent of his passes for 3,112 yards and 30 touchdowns. However, in 1966 and 1967, he completed 54 percent and 48 percent of his passes for 27 touchdowns and 38 interceptions. His career was an up-and-down cable car journey that left him with more interceptions than touchdowns and more losses than wins.

Brodie was born in San Francisco and attended nearby Stanford University before being drafted by his hometown 49ers in 1957. In the early years, fans were booing incumbent Y.A. Tittle and calling for Brodie, but when John took over he was not so popular with fans who then called for younger backups George Mira and Steve Spurrier whenever Brodie struggled. John was courted by the Houston Oilers of the AFL after the 1965 season and came to an agreement on a five-year, $750,000 contract. When the two leagues agreed to merge, Brodie insisted that his deal be honored. John worked out a million-dollar settlement with the NFL to stay a 49er. Brodie eventually turned to Scientology and became an early advocate of it as he began the most satisfying run of his career at the beginning of the 1970s. Brodie took the 49ers to the playoffs three straight years but each time lost to the Cowboys in the postseason.

Some critics said Brodie had trouble reading defenses, others thought he could be pressured into mistakes, and some questioned his dedication.

John himself told *Sports Illustrated* at the height of his success, "The whole overemphasis on the quarterback is misplaced if you really understand what football is about." Yet, when he was on his game, there was none better. After his retirement, Brodie went into broadcasting and then joined the Senior PGA Golf Tour for nearly 15 years. His son-in-law is longtime NFL quarterback Chris Chandler.

Aaron Brooks

QPR 7.0

Height: 6'4" **Weight:** 220 lbs. **Birthdate:** 3/24/1976
College: Virginia **Draft:** Green Bay 1999-4th
2000–05 New Orleans Saints; 2006 Oakland Raiders
Regular Season Record: 38–52, 18 comebacks
Postseason Record: 1–1, no comebacks
Relative Rating: 99%

Passing

Year	G	Comp./Att.	%	Yards	Y/Att.	TD	INT	Rating
2000	8	113/194	58.2	1514	7.8	9	6	85.7
2001	16	312/558	55.9	3832	6.9	26	22	76.4
2002	16	283/528	53.6	3572	6.8	27	15	80.1
2003	16	306/518	59.1	3546	6.8	24	8	88.8
2004	16	309/542	57.0	3810	7.0	21	16	79.5
2005	13	240/431	55.7	2882	6.7	13	17	70.0
2006	8	110/192	57.3	1105	5.8	3	8	61.7
Total	93	1,673/2,963	56.5	20,261	6.8	123	92	78.5
PS:	2	46/77	59.7	561	7.3	6	3	92.0

Rushing

Year	Att.	Yards	Avg.	TD
2000	41	170	4.1	2
2001	80	358	4.5	1
2002	62	253	4.1	2
2003	54	175	3.2	2
2004	58	173	3.0	4
2005	45	281	6.2	2
2006	22	124	5.6	0
Total	362	1,534	4.2	13
PS:	15	55	3.7	0

Michael Vick's cousin was a middle-round draft choice of the Packers in 1999 and spent one season backing up Brett Favre and Matt Hasselbeck before being dealt to New Orleans at the onset of the new century to back up Jeff Blake, whom the Saints

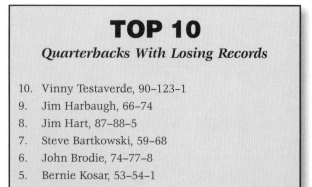

TOP 10

Quarterbacks With Losing Records

10. Vinny Testaverde, 90–123–1
9. Jim Harbaugh, 66–74
8. Jim Hart, 87–88–5
7. Steve Bartkowski, 59–68
6. John Brodie, 74–77–8
5. Bernie Kosar, 53–54–1
4. Dan Pastorini, 56–61
3. Boomer Esiason, 80–93
2. Sonny Jurgensen, 69–73–7
1. Joe Namath, 62–63–4

signed as a free agent. When Blake was hurt in the 11th game, Aaron Brooks replaced him and led the Saints into the playoffs, where they upset the mighty Rams before falling to the Vikings. Blake threw only one more pass in New Orleans before leaving after the 2001 season.

The lanky Brooks was surprisingly durable, starting 82 games in a row over the next five seasons until he was benched for poor play late in 2005. Aaron was an excellent runner who had a strong arm and was especially good in late-game rallies, directing 18 fourth-quarter game-winning drives in New Orleans. He was also impatient and given to making poor choices, throwing too many inopportune interceptions and fumbling 63 times in 93 games. Although it could be argued that he was a better Saints quarterback than the revered Archie Manning, Brooks wore out his welcome and left for Oakland as a free agent in 2006. As a Raider, his game seemed to deteriorate even further, to the point where he was unable to find a job in the NFL at 31 despite being in good health.

Dave Brown

QPR 5.5

Height: 6'5" **Weight:** 230 lbs. **Birthdate:** 2/25/1970
College: Duke **Draft:** New York Giants 1992-1st
1992–97 New York Giants; 1998–2001 Arizona Cardinals
Regular Season Record: 26–34, 5 comebacks
Postseason Record: 0–0, no comebacks
Relative Rating: 87%

Passing

Year	G	Comp./Att.	%	Yards	Y/Att.	TD	INT	Rating
1992	2	4/7	57.1	21	3	0	0	62.2
1993	1	0/0	0.0	0	0	0	0	0.0
1994	15	201/350	57.4	2536	7.2	12	16	72.5
1995	16	254/456	55.7	2814	6.2	11	10	73.1
1996	16	214/398	53.8	2412	6.1	12	20	61.3
1997	7	93/180	51.7	1023	5.7	5	3	71.1
1998	1	2/5	40.0	31	6.2	0	0	61.2
1999	8	84/169	49.7	944	5.6	2	6	55.9
2000	6	40/69	58.0	467	6.8	2	3	70.1
2001	1	0/0	0.0	0	0.0	0	0	0.0
Total	73	892/1,634	54.6	10,248	6.3	44	58	67.9
PS:	1	6/10	60.0	56	5.6	0	1	35.8

Rushing

Year	Att.	Yards	Avg.	TD
1992	2	-1	-0.5	0
1993	3	-4	-1.3	0
1994	60	196	3.3	2
1995	45	228	5.1	4
1996	50	170	3.4	0
1997	17	29	1.7	1
1998	1	2	2.0	0
1999	13	49	3.8	0
2000	1	0	0.0	0
Total	192	669	3.5	7
PS:	1	8	8.0	0

Dave Brown was a major miscalculation on the part of Giants GM George Young, who chose Brown as a first-round pick in the 1992 supplemental draft. Brown sat on the bench with fellow 6'5" rookie quarterback Kent Graham in 1992 and 1993 while Phil Simms and Jeff Hostetler played. With Hostetler gone to free agency and Simms to retirement, Brown beat out Graham for the starting job in 1994 and led the plodding Giants to a 9–7 record. Brown was not very impressive in his first year but then got worse, declining each year in completion percentage and yards per attempt. He was awkward and mechanical and displayed no feel for playing the position. His passing was inaccurate, and he was unable to deliver a big play at key moments. Jim Fassel replaced Dan Reeves as the Giants coach in 1997, but Brown showed no improvement and left for Arizona as a free agent in 1998. For the Cardinals, Brown replaced his old teammate Kent Graham while Graham returned to New York to succeed Brown. In the desert, Brown got to start just seven games in four years playing behind Jake Plummer, although he did beat the Giants in one of those starts in 1999. He was released in 2002.

Ed Brown

QPR **7.5**

Height: 6'2" **Weight:** 200 lbs. **Birthdate:** 10/26/1928
College: San Francisco **Draft:** Chicago Bears 1952-6th
1954–61 Chicago Bears; 1962–65 Pittsburgh Steelers;
1965 Baltimore Colts
Regular Season Record: 55–38–5, 13 comebacks
Postseason Record: 0–1, no comebacks
Relative Rating: 93%

Passing

Year	G	Comp./Att.	%	Yards	Y/Att.	TD	INT	Rating
1954	12	10/17	58.8	283	16.6	3	1	118.3
1955	12	85/164	51.8	1307	8.0	9	10	71.4
1956	12	96/168	57.1	1667	9.9	11	12	83.1
1957	12	84/185	45.4	1321	7.1	6	16	44.4
1958	12	102/218	46.8	1418	6.5	10	17	51.0
1959	12	125/247	50.6	1881	7.6	13	10	76.7
1960	12	59/149	39.6	1079	7.2	7	11	50.2
1961	14	46/98	46.9	742	7.6	4	11	46.8
1962	14	43/84	51.2	726	8.6	5	6	70.8
1963	14	168/362	46.4	2982	8.2	21	20	71.4
1964	14	121/272	44.5	1990	7.3	12	19	55.2
1965	14	10/23	43.5	204	8.9	1	5	50.2
Total	154	949/1,987	47.8	15,600	7.9	102	138	62.8
PS:	1	8/20	40.0	97	4.9	0	1	34.8

Rushing

Year	Att.	Yards	Avg.	TD
1954	9	36	4.0	0
1955	43	203	4.7	2
1956	40	164	4.1	1
1957	31	129	4.2	1
1958	32	94	2.9	3
1959	33	108	3.3	1
1960	19	89	4.7	2
1961	13	18	1.4	0
1962	2	-8	-4.0	0
1963	15	20	1.3	2
1964	26	110	4.2	2
1965	2	-3	-1.5	0
Total	265	960	3.6	14
PS:	5	-3	-0.6	0

Ed Brown was the quarterback on the fabled 1951 University of San Francisco team that went undefeated and sent 11 players to the NFL, but was denied a bowl invitation because the Dons featured two black starters. San Francisco dropped its football program the next year, and its quarterback went into the U.S. Marines for a two-year stint. In 1954, Brown joined the Bears where he watched Zeke Bratkowski and George Blanda for a year before winning the starting slot in 1955. The following season, Brown led the Bears to the NFL title game. Unfortunately, the Giants destroyed Chicago 47–7 on an icy field while Brown completed just eight of 20 passes for 97 yards in the first half before being relieved by Blanda in the second half.

Brown's strength was the bomb; he threw the best deep ball in the league and is second only to Arnie Herber in yards per completion at 16.4. His 7.9 yards per attempt is eighth of all time. On the other hand, his lifetime completion percentage is below 48; he threw a lot of interceptions and became as immobile as a stump as he aged. By 1962, George Halas had seen enough of Brown and sent him to Pittsburgh to back up Bobby Layne. When Layne retired, Brown became the starter in 1963.

Brown has an excellent winning percentage, but in his two biggest games he came up small. The 1956 championship game was his only postseason contest, but in 1963 the Steelers came to New York to face the Giants in the season finale in a game to determine the Eastern Conference champion. Pittsburgh broadcaster Myron Cope later claimed that, befitting the seriousness of the occasion, Brown stayed out of the local taverns all week, unlike his usual routine. Come game time, though, Brown was awful. His passes sailed all over the field, missing open targets, and he finished with 13 completions in 33 attempts and three interceptions. The Giants won 33–17, and the Steelers' season was over.

Brown played two more years in Pittsburgh before being picked up by the Colts for their season finale in 1965. Halfback Tom Matte was pressed into service as quarterback with Johnny Unitas and Gary Cuozzo both injured, and Brown got to throw his last five NFL passes against the Rams that day, including the 68-yard game-winning touchdown to John Mackey, one last bomb for Ed Brown.

Mark Brunell

QPR 8.5

Height: 6'1" **Weight:** 217 lbs. **Birthdate:** 9/17/1970
College: Washington **Draft:** Green Bay 1993-5th
1994 Green Bay Packers; 1995–2003 Jacksonville Jaguars; 2004–07 Washington Redskins; 2008 New Orleans Saints
Regular Season Record: 78–72, 25 comebacks
Postseason Record: 5–5, 1 comeback
Relative Rating: 107%

Passing

Year	G	Comp./Att.	%	Yards	Y/Att.	TD	INT	Rating
1994	2	12/27	44.4	95	3.5	0	0	53.8
1995	13	201/346	58.1	2168	6.3	15	7	82.6
1996	16	353/557	63.4	4367	7.8	19	20	84.0
1997	14	264/435	60.7	3281	7.5	18	7	91.2
1998	13	208/354	58.8	2601	7.3	20	9	89.9
1999	15	259/441	58.7	3060	6.9	14	9	82.0
2000	16	311/512	60.7	3640	7.1	20	14	84.0
2001	15	289/473	61.1	3309	7.0	19	13	84.1
2002	15	245/416	58.9	2788	6.7	17	7	85.7
2003	3	54/82	65.9	484	5.9	2	0	89.7
2004	9	118/237	49.8	1194	5.0	7	6	63.9
2005	16	262/454	57.7	3050	6.7	23	10	85.9
2006	10	162/260	62.3	1789	6.9	8	4	86.5
2008	2	0/0	0.0	0	0.0	0	0	0.0
Total	157	2,738/4,594	59.6	31,826	6.9	182	106	84.2
PS:	11	156/307	50.8	1,833	6.0	11	11	66.3

Rushing

Year	Att.	Yards	Avg.	TD
1994	6	7	1.2	1
1995	67	480	7.2	4
1996	80	396	5.0	3
1997	48	257	5.4	2
1998	49	192	3.9	0
1999	47	208	4.4	1
2000	48	236	4.9	2
2001	39	224	5.7	1
2002	43	207	4.8	0
2003	8	19	2.4	1
2004	19	62	3.3	0
2005	42	111	2.6	0
2006	13	34	2.6	0
Total	509	2,433	4.8	15
PS:	39	147	3.8	0

The mild-mannered Mark Brunell did not shy away from competition. In college, he played for a Washington Husky powerhouse that went 31–5 and won two of three consecutive Rose Bowls. However, Mark tore up his knee in his junior year and lost the starting job to Billy Joe Hobert until the NCAA suspended Hobert during the following season. Due to his injury history, Brunell was not drafted until the fifth round—the 118th pick—by Green Bay. By contrast, the fast-living Hobert was picked in the third round by Oakland, 60 slots ahead of his teammate. While Hobert floundered in Oakland, Brunell sat behind Brett Favre in Green Bay. When the Packers' assistant coach Ray Rhodes took over the Eagles in 1995, he worked out a deal for Brunell, but Philadelphia's management objected to Mark's salary demands. Instead, Brunell was traded to the expansion Jacksonville Jaguars soon after.

By midseason, the much more mobile Brunell swept aside starter Steve Beurelein and took over the 1–5 Jags. Brunell led Jacksonville to a 4–12 record in their first year and then to a playoff berth the next. In that second season, Brunell joined Johnny Unitas and Tobin Rote as the only three players in history to lead all quarterbacks in both passing and rushing yards. Brunell threw for 4,367 yards and ran for 480 in 1996 as the Cinderella Jags went all the way to the conference championship. Although he passed for more than 3,000 yards three more times and accumulated more than 2,400 rushing yards in his career, Mark would never have a better season.

In his eight years as the Jaguars' starting quarterback, Brunell drove the team to the playoffs four straight seasons before salary cap problems caused the team to disintegrate under coach Tom Coughlin. Mark was supplanted as a starter by rookie Byron Leftwich in 2003 under new coach Jack Del Rio. Because Brunell was a scrambling, left-handed quarterback who wore the No. 8, he often was compared to Steve Young. Mark was a three-time Pro Bowl quarterback, but he could not approach the precision passing of Young, although he did set the NFL mark for consecutive completions with 22 while with the Redskins. By that point, though, Brunell had lost a good deal of mobility and arm strength and was no longer the same quarterback. Even then, Brunell remained a true professional who always played the game with heart.

Scott Brunner

QPR **2.5**

Height: 6'5" **Weight:** 206 lbs. **Birthdate:** 3/24/1957
College: Delaware **Draft:** New York Giants 1980-6th
1980–83 New York Giants; 1985 St. Louis Cardinals
Regular Season Record: 12–18, 7 comebacks
Postseason Record: 1–1, no comebacks
Relative Rating: 75%

Passing

Year	G	Comp./Att.	%	Yards	Y/Att.	TD	INT	Rating
1980	16	52/112	46.4	610	5.4	4	6	53.1
1981	16	79/190	41.6	978	5.1	5	11	42.8
1982	9	161/298	54.0	2017	6.8	10	9	73.9
1983	16	190/386	49.2	2516	6.5	9	22	54.3
1985	16	30/60	50.0	336	5.6	1	6	33.1
Total	73	512/1,046	48.9	6,457	6.2	29	54	56.3
PS:	2	25/51	49.0	386	7.6	6	3	89.2

Rushing

Year	Att.	Yards	Avg.	TD
1980	10	18	1.8	0
1981	14	20	1.4	0
1982	19	27	1.4	1
1983	26	64	2.5	0
1985	3	8	2.7	0
Total	72	137	1.9	1
PS:	8	9	1.1	0

Phil Simms' misfortune was Scott Brunner's opportunity. Without the injury problems of Simms early in his career, Brunner may never have had the chance to prove he was *not* an NFL starting quarterback. He faced a similar roadblock playing behind Jeff Komlo at Delaware. In Scott's senior year, though, he led the Blue Hens to the Division II championship game where they came back from a 31-7 halftime deficit to win 51–45. Drafted by the Giants, Brunner then spent a season and a half watching Simms until Phil separated his shoulder late in 1981. Brunner quarterbacked the defense-oriented New York into the playoffs for the first time in 18 years and even beat the Eagles in the first round before succumbing to San Francisco, the eventual Super Bowl champion.

In 1982, Simms blew out his knee in an exhibition game, and Brunner continued as the Giants' mediocre starter. The following season, new coach Bill Parcells chose Brunner over the returning Simms at quarterback, but Scott struggled so much that Parcells went back to Simms—only to watch Phil break his thumb. Brunner completed fewer than half his passes that season with nine touchdowns and 22 interceptions. He was an awkward runner and threw fluttering, inaccurate passes. He had proved he was a backup at best.

With Simms back for good in 1984, the Giants traded Brunner to Denver, where he spent the season on injured reserve before concluding his career with one forgettable year with the Cardinals. Ultimately, Brunner shrewdly summed up his skills to the *New York Times* in 1982: "I play with my head a lot more than I play with my body. When I'm not playing with my head, I can be very bad. I'm not a great athlete."

Rudy Bukich

QPR **5.5**

Height: 6'1" **Weight:** 195 lbs. **Birthdate:** 3/15/1932
College: USC **Draft:** Los Angeles Rams 1953-2nd
1953, 1956 Los Angeles Rams; 1957–58 Washington Redskins; 1958–59, 1962–68 Chicago Bears; 1960–61 Pittsburgh Steelers
Regular Season Record: 21–14–3, 7 comebacks
Postseason Record: NA
Relative Rating: 100%

Passing

Year	G	Comp./Att.	%	Yards	Y/Att.	TD	INT	Rating
1953	8	14/32	43.8	169	5.3	0	3	21.5
1956	3	10/23	43.5	130	5.7	1	3	36.8
1957	7	6/28	21.4	103	3.7	0	3	2.8
1958	4	8/23	34.8	166	7.2	1	1	57.5
1959	5	0/0	0.0	0	0.0	0	0	0.0
1960	12	25/51	49.0	358	7.0	2	3	60.7
1961	11	89/156	57.1	1253	8.0	11	16	67.0
1962	5	3/13	23.1	79	6.1	1	4	38.5
1963	6	29/43	67.4	369	8.6	3	2	97.9
1964	9	99/160	61.9	1099	6.9	12	7	89.0
1965	14	176/312	56.4	2641	8.5	20	9	93.7
1966	14	147/309	47.6	1858	6.0	10	21	49.3
1967	3	18/33	54.5	185	5.6	0	2	45.6
1968	2	2/7	28.6	23	3.3	0	0	40.8
Total	103	626/1,190	52.6	8,433	7.1	61	74	66.6

Rushing

Year	Att.	Yards	Avg.	TD
1953	14	28	2.0	1
1956	1	8	8.0	0
1957	8	-2	-0.3	0
1958	2	16	8.0	0
1959	1	0	0.0	0
1960	3	-8	-2.7	0
1961	14	4	0.3	2
1963	7	1	0.1	1
1964	12	28	2.3	0
1965	28	33	1.2	3
1966	18	14	0.8	2
1967	4	-13	-3.3	0
Total	112	109	1.0	9

Rudy Bukich probably had the longest apprenticeship of any NFL passing leader, which he became in 1965, his 11th season as a pro. Bukich had been a longtime backup with several teams in the NFL and had been a reserve behind All-American Jim Sears at USC as well. When Sears got hurt in the 1953 Rose Bowl, though, Bukich came in and led the Trojans to victory over Wisconsin. The hometown Rams drafted Rudy in the second round that year to back up Norm Van Brocklin at quarterback. Bukich then went into the service for two years and quarterbacked Fort Ord to the national service championship before returning to the Rams in 1956. In the interim, he had fallen to third string behind Van Brocklin and Bill Wade.

The Rams traded Rudy to the Redskins in 1957, and Washington sent him to the Bears in 1958. George Halas already had Ed Brown, Zeke Bratkowski, and George Blanda, so he sent Bukich to Pittsburgh in 1959 for a player to be named later. With the Steelers, Bukich started eight games behind a banged-up Bobby Layne in 1960 and 1961 and played pretty well. Halas then made Bukich the "player to be named later" from the earlier lend-lease deal and brought him back to Chicago to play behind Bill Wade again. Bukich did not get a chance to start for the Bears until 1964, his third year back, but the pocket passer took over as starter in 1965, led the team to a 9–5 record, and led the league in passing at age 33. He would be the last Bear for 30 years to toss 20 touchdowns, until Erik Kramer in 1995.

TOP 10
Long Bombers

10. Arnie Herber
9. Steve Bartkowski
8. Sid Luckman
7. Ed Brown
6. Jim Plunkett
5. Jeff Blake
4. Terry Bradshaw
3. Joe Namath
2. Norm Van Brocklin
1. Daryle Lamonica

Bukich continued as the starter for one more season, but both he and the Bears struggled in 1966. Halas then traded Mike Ditka to the Eagles for Jack Concannon, and Rudy spent his last two seasons back on the bench. Bukich was an intelligent play-caller and accurate passer, and he had the strongest arm in the league, although he fumbled too much. He had to wait too long to get the chance to show that he could play.

Marc Bulger

QPR 7.5

Height: 6'3" **Weight:** 215 lbs. **Birthdate:** 4/5/1977
College: West Virginia **Draft:** New Orleans 2000-6th
2002–08 St. Louis Rams
Regular Season Record: 40–47, 14 comebacks
Postseason Record: 1–2, 1 comeback
Relative Rating: 107%

Passing

Year	G	Comp./Att.	%	Yards	Y/Att.	TD	INT	Rating
2002	7	138/214	64.5	1,826	8.5	14	6	101.5
2003	15	336/532	63.2	3,845	7.2	22	22	81.4
2004	14	321/485	66.2	3,964	8.2	21	14	93.7
2005	8	192/287	66.9	2,297	8.0	14	9	94.4
2006	16	370/588	62.9	4,301	7.3	24	8	92.9
2007	12	221/378	58.5	2,392	6.3	11	15	70.3
2008	15	251/440	57.0	2,720	6.2	11	13	71.4
Total	87	1,829/2,924	62.6	21,345	7.3	117	87	85.6
PS:	3	68/113	60.2	944	8.4	4	5	80.4

Rushing

Year	Att.	Yards	Avg.	TD
2002	12	-13	-1.1	1
2003	29	75	2.6	4
2004	19	89	4.7	3
2005	9	29	3.2	0
2006	18	44	2.4	0
2007	9	13	1.4	0
2008	14	41	2.9	0
Total	110	278	2.5	8
PS:	8	25	3.1	0

Despite a celebrated career at West Virginia, Marc Bulger wasn't drafted until the sixth round by the Saints in 2000 and then was cut during training camp. After a brief trial with Atlanta, Bulger was picked up by the Rams and made the team as a third quarterback in 2001. In 2002, backup Trent Green was traded to Kansas City and starter Kurt Warner had thumb problems that caused the team to get off to a 0–5 start. Bulger stepped in and began to run Mike Martz's offense in the way St. Louis was accustomed. The Rams won Marc's first six starts. However, he was sidelined for a few games with hand and back injuries, and the team missed the playoffs.

Bulger had the offense roaring and the team back in the playoffs in 2003, while the demoted Warner watched from the sidelines. Bulger was named to the Pro Bowl that season and again in 2006 after he threw for more than 4,000 yards, but the declining Rams have not finished above .500 since 2003. Bulger has a good arm and can be an effective quarterback throwing both short and long, but he is fairly immobile and takes a lot of sacks, especially in front of the substandard Rams lines. He has racked up some big passing numbers, but his yards per pass average has declined since the Martz years, and he has always been prone to throw interceptions in key moments.

Adrian Burk

QPR 4.5

Height: 6'2" **Weight:** 190 lbs. **Birthdate:** 12/14/1927
College: Baylor **Draft:** Baltimore Colts 1950-1st
1950 Baltimore Colts; 1951–56 Philadelphia Eagles
Regular Season Record: 15–23–3, 2 comebacks
Postseason Record: NA
Relative Rating: 92%

Passing

Year	G	Comp./Att.	%	Yards	Y/Att.	TD	INT	Rating
1950	12	43/119	36.1	798	6.7	6	12	37.4
1951	12	92/218	42.2	1,329	6.1	14	23	44.5
1952	12	37/82	45.1	561	6.8	4	5	59.0
1953	10	56/119	47.1	788	6.6	4	9	48.6
1954	12	123/231	53.2	1,740	7.5	23	17	80.4
1955	12	110/228	48.2	1,359	6.0	9	17	49.2
1956	12	39/82	47.6	426	5.2	1	6	36.9
Total	82	500/1,079	46.3	7,001	6.5	71	89	52.2

Rushing

Year	Att.	Yards	Avg.	TD
1950	11	19	1.7	1
1951	28	12	0.4	1
1952	7	28	4.0	0
1953	8	54	6.8	3
1954	15	18	1.2	0
1955	36	132	3.7	2
1956	17	61	3.6	0
Total	122	324	2.7	4

Adrian Burk was something of a Zeliglike figure in pro football, turning up with some sort of role in a number of big and strange moments in NFL history. He is most remembered as the second NFL quarterback to throw for seven touchdowns in a game in 1954, but he also has a connection to each of the three times the feat was duplicated after that. Burk was a first-round pick of the Baltimore Colts in 1950 when they were part of the merger between the NFL and All-America Football Conference. On that sorry 1–11 Colts team, Burk often relieved starter Y.A. Tittle; Tittle later threw seven touchdowns in a 1962 game for the Giants.

The Colts folded at the end of the year, and Burk, who completed only 36 percent of his passes as a rookie, was allocated to the Eagles. He started all

12 games in 1951 and improved a little, completing 42 percent of his passes, but he also led the league with 23 interceptions. The Eagles traded for Bobby Thomason in 1952, and for the next five years, Burk shared the quarterbacking burden and was the team's punter. Thomason threw for 8,850 yards, 53 touchdowns, and 70 interceptions in that time, while Burk threw for 4,874 yards, 41 touchdowns, and 54 interceptions. Burk's greatest season was 1954, when he threw 23 touchdowns and made the Pro Bowl. Not only did he throw seven touchdowns against the Redskins that October, but he threw five more the next month when Washington came to Philly—12 of 23 TDs came against one team.

Burk became an attorney and was hired by Bud Adams to help put together the Houston Oilers in 1959. He signed Heisman Trophy winner Billy Cannon under the goal posts at the conclusion of the 1960 Sugar Bowl, a signing that put both the AFL and the Oilers on the football map. In addition, Cannon caught three of Houston quarterback George Blanda's seven touchdown passes in a 1961 game.

Burk next became an NFL official and worked a number of significant games. In 1968, he was part of the officiating crew that was suspended for one week after a mistake by the man handling the down marker cost the Rams a down in a loss to the Bears. The following season, Burk was on the field for Joe Kapp's seven-touchdown performance against the Colts—the last time that has been accomplished. Then in 1971, Burk was part of the crew that worked the longest playoff game in history between Miami and Kansas City. Finally, Burk was the back judge who signaled a touchdown on Franco Harris' Immaculate Reception in the Steelers' improbable 1972 playoff win over the Raiders. In his later years, the talented Mr. Burk became a Baptist minister and served as a missionary with his wife for several years.

Jason Campbell has all the tools but has struggled to establish himself as a top-flight NFL quarterback.

Jason Campbell

QPR 5.0

Height: 6'5" **Weight:** 223 lbs. **Birthdate:** 12/31/1981
College: Auburn **Draft:** Washington 2005-1st
2006–08 Washington Redskins
Regular Season Record: 16–20, 3 comebacks
Postseason Record: NA
Relative Rating: 100%

Passing

Year	G	Comp./Att.	%	Yards	Y/Att.	TD	INT	Rating
2006	7	110/207	53.1	1,297	6.3	10	6	76.5
2007	13	250/417	60.0	2,700	6.5	12	11	77.6
2008	16	315/506	62.3	3,245	6.4	13	6	84.3
Total	36	675/1,130	59.7	7,242	6.4	35	23	80.4

Rushing

Year	Att.	Yards	Avg.	TD
2006	24	107	4.5	0
2007	36	185	5.1	1
2008	47	258	5.5	1
Total	107	550	5.1	2

Throughout his college and short pro career, the strong-armed Jason Campbell has bounced from one offensive system to another as the coaches around him keep changing. Campbell, who led the 2004 Auburn Tigers with Cadillac Williams and Ronnie Brown to an undefeated season, began to take over for starter Mark Brunell in 2006. He showed promise but struggled in the complicated seven-step-drop, down-the-field offense of Al Saunders in 2007 before injuring his knee late in the season. In 2008 under Jim Zorn's three-step-drop West Coast offense, Jason showed improvement and drove the Redskins to an 8–8 season. He's a good runner, a fairly accurate passer, and protects the ball well but doesn't make many big plays.

Scott Campbell

QPR 0.5

Height: 6'0" **Weight:** 196 lbs. **Birthdate:** 4/15/1962
College: Purdue **Draft:** Pittsburgh Steelers 1984-7th
1984–86 Pittsburgh Steelers; 1986–90 Atlanta Falcons; 1992 CFL
Regular Season Record: 2–11, 3 comebacks
Postseason Record: NA
Relative Rating: 82%

Passing

Year	G	Comp./Att.	%	Yards	Y/Att.	TD	INT	Rating
1984	5	8/15	53.3	109	7.3	1	1	71.3
1985	16	43/96	44.8	612	6.4	4	6	53.8
1986	4	1/7	14.3	7	1.0	0	0	39.6
1987	12	136/260	52.3	1,728	6.6	11	14	65
1989	1	0/0	0.0	0	0.0	0	0	0.0
1990	7	36/76	47.4	527	6.9	3	4	61.7
Total	45	224/454	49.3	2,983	6.6	19	25	61.6

Rushing

Year	Att.	Yards	Avg.	TD
1984	3	-5	-1.7	0
1985	9	28	3.1	0
1986	1	7	7.0	0
1987	21	102	4.9	2
1990	9	38	4.2	0
Total	43	170	4.0	2

Scott Campbell was a quarter inch shy of 6' but was a big star at Purdue where he was the team's MVP for his senior year. Campbell even set a school record of throwing for 516 yards against Ohio State that year, although Boilermakers Kyle Orton and Drew Brees later exceeded that. A late draft choice of the

Steelers, Scott spent two and a half unimpressive seasons in Pittsburgh as a backup who completed just 44 percent of his passes.

Campbell was released in the middle of 1986 when rookie Bubby Brister emerged as Mark Malone's new caddy. In November, Atlanta brought Campbell in to work him out for the following season. While in Atlanta, Scott attended the Falcons game against the Bears in which starting quarterback David Archer suffered a separated shoulder to end his season. At halftime, the Falcons announced over the PA that Scott Campbell should report to the locker room after the game. Atlanta signed Campbell to back up Turk Schonert, and he got to play a little the following week against the 49ers. In 1987, Campbell got his one real chance to start when he beat out Archer and rookie Chris Miller during the non-strike portion of the year. Unfortunately, Campbell threw more interceptions than touchdowns, and the Falcons went 2–7 in his nine starts. Campbell did not have the physical tools to be a starter but stuck around on the Falcons' bench for a few more years and then finished his career holding a clipboard for Ottawa in Canada in 1992.

Cody Carlson

QPR 3.0

Height: 6'3" **Weight:** 202 lbs. **Birthdate:** 11/5/1963
College: Baylor **Draft:** Houston Oilers 1987-3rd
1988–94 Houston Oilers
Regular Season Record: 11–8, 3 comebacks
Postseason Record: 0–1, no comebacks
Relative Rating: 92%

Passing

Year	G	Comp./Att.	%	Yards	Y/Att.	TD	INT	Rating
1989	6	15/31	48.4	155	5.0	0	1	49.8
1990	6	37/55	67.3	383	7.0	4	2	96.2
1991	3	7/12	58.3	114	9.5	1	0	118.1
1992	11	149/227	65.6	1,710	7.5	9	11	81.2
1993	8	51/90	56.7	605	6.7	2	4	66.2
1994	5	59/132	44.7	727	5.5	1	4	52.2
Total	45	370/659	56.1	4,469	6.8	21	28	70.0
PS:	1	16/33	48.5	165	5.0	2	1	70.9

Rushing

Year	Att.	Yards	Avg.	TD
1988	12	36	3.0	1
1989	3	-3	-1.0	0
1990	11	52	4.7	0
1991	4	-3	-0.8	0
1992	27	77	2.9	1
1993	14	41	2.9	2
1994	10	17	1.7	0
Total	81	217	2.7	4
PS:	4	22	5.5	0

Cody Carlson was Warren Moon's caddy for seven seasons in Houston and got to experience more than the usual highs and lows of being a mediocre professional quarterback. Carlson did not play at all as a rookie in the 1987 strike season and felt that coach Jerry Glanville was being vindictive to him for carrying a picket sign. The following season, Carlson got five starts when Moon was hurt but was not called on again till the last game of 1990. The Oilers needed to beat the Steelers out for the last playoff spot. Cody's three touchdown passes that game earned him AFC Offensive Player of the Week honors and the nickname "Commander Cody," like the country-rock musician. It also earned the Oilers

a wild-card match with the Bengals, but Carlson's heroics were short lived as Cincinnati crushed Houston 41–14 the next week.

Two years later, Warren Moon broke his arm in the 10th week of the season, and Cody started the last six games of the year, leading the Oilers to four wins. In the last game, Moon returned in the second quarter against the Bills, who then lost their starter, Jim Kelly, for the next week's postseason match between the Oilers and Bills. In that game, Bills backup Frank Reich led the Bills in erasing a 32-point second-half deficit to beat Moon and the Oilers in overtime 41–38. The next season, Moon was benched for ineffective play before the sixth game, but Cody suffered a groin injury in the first quarter and Moon regained his job. In 1994, Moon left Houston as a free agent, and Carlson got his chance to start in between shoulder and knee injuries. In the face of heavy booing, he was the quarterback for one of the Oilers' two victories that season. Things got so bad that owner Bud Adams told reporters that Cody was too fragile to lead the Oilers. Carlson failed the team's physical in 1995 and retired.

TOP 10

Quarterbacks Who Became Pro Football Officials

10. Tommy Hughitt, 1920s player and AAFC official
9. Paddy Driscoll, 1920s Hall of Famer
8. Leo Miles, black quarterback in college shifted to defensive back on the Giants
7. Benny Friedman, Hall of Fame passing tailback
6. Davey O'Brien, 5'7" passing tailback
5. Dean Look, threw one pass for the 1962 Titans
4. Fred Wyant, left-hander threw two passes for the 1956 Redskins
3. Gary Lane, Browns backup
2. Pete Liske, played with the Jets, Broncos, and Eagles and in the CFL
1. Adrian Burk, starter for the Colts and Eagles

QPR

David Carr

Height: 6'3" **Weight:** 215 lbs. **Birthdate:** 7/21/1979
College: Fresno State **Draft:** Houston Texans 2002-1st
2002–06 Houston Texans; 2007 Carolina Panthers;
2008 New York Giants
Regular Season Record: 23–56, 11 comebacks
Postseason Record: NA
Relative Rating: 94%

Passing

Year	G	Comp./Att.	%	Yards	Y/Att.	TD	INT	Rating
2002	16	233/444	52.5	2,592	5.8	9	15	62.8
2003	12	167/295	56.6	2,013	6.8	9	13	69.5
2004	16	285/466	61.2	3,531	7.6	16	14	83.5
2005	16	256/423	60.5	2,488	5.9	14	11	77.2
2006	16	302/442	68.3	2,767	6.3	11	12	82.1
2007	6	73/136	53.7	635	4.7	3	5	58.3
2008	3	9/12	75.0	115	9.6	2	0	144.1
Total	87	1,325/2,218	59.7	14,141	6.4	64	70	74.9

Rushing

Year	Att.	Yards	Avg.	TD
2002	59	282	4.8	3
2003	27	151	5.6	2
2004	73	299	4.1	0
2005	56	308	5.5	1
2006	53	195	3.7	2
2007	17	59	3.5	0
2008	8	10	1.3	0
Total	293	1,304	4.5	8

As the first overall pick of the 2002 draft and the first-ever draft choice of the expansion Houston Texans, David Carr has to be considered a colossal bust with his 23–56 lifetime won-lost record. Even taking into account the crappiness of the Texan teams he led for five years, there are not a lot of positives that can be said about Carr's performance. He told *Sports Illustrated* when he left Houston as a free agent, "I haven't accomplished anything I've wanted to accomplish in the NFL. I came in with very high hopes. I want to win Super Bowls." Instead, he is remembered as an inaccurate dink passer who led the NFL three times in being sacked, and for his career he was sacked on 10.6 percent of pass plays.

Too often, sacks are attributed solely to the offensive line. In fact, the quarterback plays a big role in a team's sack total. If a quarterback can't quickly decide where to go with the ball or holds onto it too long waiting for a play to open up, he's going to get sacked behind any line. In his one season in Carolina, Carr took over from an injured Jake Delhomme but played so badly that he lost his job to Vinny "Methuselah" Testaverde and then to unheralded rookie Matt Moore. The sack percentage of the other three Panther quarterbacks that year ranged from 5.0 to 5.5; Carr's percentage was 8.7, and he was barely completing half his passes for a miniscule 4.7 yards per pass. It was no surprise that Carolina released him in 2008, but Carr landed on his feet, signing with the defending champion Giants.

QPR 3.0

Quincy Carter

Height: 6'2" **Weight:** 213 lbs. **Birthdate:** 10/13/1977
College: Georgia **Draft:** Dallas Cowboys 2001-2nd
2001–03 Dallas Cowboys; 2004 New York Jets
Regular Season Record: 18–16, 7 comebacks
Postseason Record: 0–1
Relative Rating: 90%

Passing

Year	G	Comp./Att.	%	Yards	Y/Att.	TD	INT	Rating
2001	8	90/176	51.1	1,072	6.1	5	7	63.0
2002	7	125/221	56.6	1,465	6.6	7	8	72.3
2003	16	292/505	57.8	3,302	6.5	17	21	71.4
2004	7	35/58	60.3	498	8.6	3	1	98.2
Total	38	542/960	56.5	6,337	6.6	32	37	71.7
PS:	1	21/36	58.3	154	4.3	0	1	56.9

Rushing

Year	Att.	Yards	Avg.	TD
2001	45	150	3.3	1
2002	27	91	3.4	0
2003	68	257	3.8	2
2004	12	20	1.7	0
Total	152	518	3.4	3
PS:	4	25	6.3	0

Quincy Carter fought off stiffs Anthony Wright, Clint Stoerner, Ryan Leaf, and Chad Hutchinson to become Troy Aikman's replacement on the Cowboys, but the scrambling, scatter-armed, drug-tested Carter was as unlike Aikman as anyone could be. Carter originally played outfield in the Cubs' organization before a batting average in the low .200s drove him back to the gridiron. Most scouts saw Dallas grabbing the inconsistent Carter in the second round as a reach in 2001, but when Bill Parcells took over the Cowboys in 2003, Carter won the starting job and showed big play potential. He threw more interceptions than touchdowns and averaged only 6.5 yards per pass, but he did throw for more than 3,000 yards and run for 257, leading Dallas to the postseason for the first time in four years.

Things began to fall apart that off-season, though. The Cowboys signed Vinny Testaverde and Drew Henson to compete for the starting job, and

Carter overreacted. In addition, he failed a drug test. In August, Dallas released Carter, saying that he "could not be trusted with the leadership of the team." On the field, Carter was too eager to run, had trouble reading defenses, and made poor decisions. Off the field, he just made poor decisions. He was signed by the Jets to back up Chad Pennington in 2004 and helped them reach the playoffs but was in drug rehab by the postseason and was released. Since then, Carter has had trials in Canada and in Arena Football, but those, too, have been marred by disciplinary suspensions and drug arrests that have made him radioactive to the NFL.

Virgil Carter

QPR 6.0

Height: 6'1" **Weight:** 192 lbs. **Birthdate:** 11/9/1945
College: BYU **Draft:** Chicago Bears 1967-6th
1968–69, 1976 Chicago Bears; 1970–72 Cincinnati Bengals; 1974 WFL; 1975 San Diego Chargers
Regular Season Record: 16–14, 3 comebacks
Postseason Record: 0–1, no comebacks
Relative Rating: 106%

Passing

Year	G	Comp./Att.	%	Yards	Y/Att.	TD	INT	Rating
1968	7	55/122	45.1	769	6.3	4	5	59.8
1969	3	36/71	50.7	343	4.8	2	5	44.5
1970	13	143/278	51.4	1,647	5.9	9	9	66.9
1971	10	138/222	62.2	1,624	7.3	10	7	86.2
1972	10	47/82	57.3	579	7.1	3	4	71.1
1975	1	3/5	60.0	24	4.8	0	1	32.5
1976	8	3/5	60.0	77	15.4	1	0	143.7
Total	52	425/785	54.1	5,063	6.4	29	31	69.9
PS:	1	7/20	35	64	3.2	0	1	23.8

Rushing

Year	Att.	Yards	Avg.	TD
1968	48	265	5.5	4
1969	4	19	4.8	0
1970	34	246	7.2	2
1971	8	42	5.3	0
1972	12	57	4.8	2
1975	2	11	5.5	0
1976	1	0	0.0	0
Total	109	640	5.9	8
PS:	2	16	8.0	0

The modern game of football owes a great deal to Virgil Carter. The short, weak-armed Carter was next man up for Cincinnati in 1970 when the tall, long-ball throwing Greg Cook had career-ending shoulder problems. Resourceful Bengals offensive coach Bill Walsh turned lemons into lemonade by drawing up a new offense to take advantage of the skills that Virgil did possess—he was smart, mobile, and accurate. The misnamed West Coast offense of short, quick, timed passes to a whole progression of receivers was born.

The brainy Carter went to college on an academic scholarship and earned an advanced degree in mathematics. He was the forerunner of a string of star quarterbacks at BYU, where he set an NCAA record by throwing for 513 yards in a 1966 game in which he also ran for 86 yards. Carter sat on the Bears bench as a rookie in 1967, but the next year he got a chance to start and won four straight games before breaking his ankle. In 1969, though, Carter didn't get another chance to start until the 12th game and was yanked for good at the half of game 13. The mild-mannered Virgil was furious. He called coach Jim Dooley a liar, ripped sainted quarterback coach Sid Luckman, and called George Halas "chickenshit," a major epithet from the Mormon quarterback. The next year Carter found himself in Cincinnati where Paul Brown said of him, "Carter is the best quarterback I ever had at analyzing a game in progress." Carter led the Bengals to the playoffs for the first time in 1970, but over the next two years he lost his job to the younger and more talented Ken Anderson. Virgil missed 1973 with a broken collarbone and jumped to the Chicago Fire in the WFL in 1974. After a year on San Diego's bench, Virgil finished his career on the Bears sidelines in 1976, watching the execrable Bob Avellini start all 14 games.

Matt Cassel

QPR **5.5**

Height: 6'5" **Weight:** 230 lbs. **Birthdate:** 4/17/1982
College: USC **Draft:** New England 2005-7th
2005–08 New England Patriots
Regular Season Record: 10–5, 2 comebacks
Postseason Record: NA
Relative Rating: 111%

Passing

Year	G	Comp./Att.	%	Yards	Y/Att.	TD	INT	Rating
2005	2	13/24	54.2	183	7.6	2	1	89.4
2006	6	5/8	62.5	32	4.0	0	0	70.8
2007	6	4/7	57.1	38	5.4	0	1	32.7
2008	16	327/516	63.4	3,693	7.2	21	11	89.4
Total	30	349/555	62.9	3,946	7.1	23	13	88.2

Matt Cassel's statistics for his first season were remarkably similar to those of Tom Brady in 2001.

Rushing

Year	Att.	Yards	Avg.	TD
2005	6	12	2.0	0
2006	2	4	2.0	0
2007	4	12	3.0	1
2008	73	270	3.7	2
Total	85	298	3.5	3

The guys at Football Outsiders devised a quick and dirty way to assess the chances of a college quarterback playing well in the NFL. They look at two numbers: how many games the quarterback started in college and his completion percentage. There is an intuitive logic to this when you think about it. In making the jump to the faster-paced NFL, a quarterback has to be poised and accurate. The best way to gain or improve poise is through experience. Thus, a quarterback who has started for three or four years will have experienced and learned to deal with a much wider range of situations than one who has started only as a senior. Similarly, a quarterback with a higher completion percentage has proven under fire the ability to hit receivers; he will need that accuracy to connect with much more tightly covered receivers in the pros.

When four-year reserve Matt Cassel was given the ball upon Tom Brady's knee injury in Week 1 of 2008, he had not started a game at quarterback since high school. At USC, he held the clipboard for Carson Palmer and then Matt Leinart, even playing a little tight end. That the Patriots got as much as they did with Cassel at quarterback in 2008 is a tribute to the intelligence of Cassel and the quality of the New England coaching staff. Cassel showed he has a good arm, good accuracy, and the courage to stay in the pocket. What he lacked at first was the instinct that comes at least partly from playing much more at a young age. He was too slow in reading what defenses were doing and took too many sacks. He was indecisive and hesitant at key moments and was not a quarterback you would trust to win the game. However, Cassel developed by leaps throughout the season, enough to earn a big payday after being traded to the Chiefs in the off-season. Should he fail at that, he still established himself as a viable NFL backup, and that's not bad, considering his limited background.

Matt Cavanaugh

QPR 3.0

Height: 6'2" **Weight:** 212 lbs. **Birthdate:** 10/27/1956
College: Pittsburgh **Draft:** New England 1978-2ⁿᵈ
1979–82 New England Patriots; 1983–85 San Francisco 49ers; 1986–89 Philadelphia Eagles; 1990–91 New York Giants
Regular Season Record: 8–11, 3 comebacks
Postseason Record: 0–0, no comebacks
Relative Rating: 96%

Passing

Year	G	Comp./Att.	%	Yards	Y/Att.	TD	INT	Rating
1979	13	1/1	100.0	10	10.0	0	0	108.3
1980	16	63/105	60.0	885	8.4	9	5	95.9
1981	16	115/219	52.5	1,633	7.5	5	13	59.8
1982	7	27/60	45.0	490	8.2	5	5	66.7
1983	5	0/0	0.0	0	0.0	0	0	0.0
1984	8	33/61	54.1	449	7.4	4	0	99.7
1985	16	28/54	51.9	334	6.2	1	1	69.5
1986	10	28/58	48.3	397	6.8	2	4	53.6
1987	3	0/0	0.0	0	0.0	0	0	0.0
1988	5	7/16	43.8	101	6.3	1	1	59.6
1989	9	3/5	60.0	33	6.6	1	1	79.6
1990	0	0/0	0.0	0	0.0	0	0	0.0
1991	4	0/0	0.0	0	0.0	0	0	0.0
Total	112	305/579	52.7	4,332	7.5	28	30	71.7

PS: 2 1/2 50.0 3 1.5 0 0 56.3

Rushing

Year	Att.	Yards	Avg.	TD
1979	1	-2	-2.0	0
1980	19	97	5.1	0
1981	17	92	5.4	3
1982	2	3	1.5	0
1983	1	8	8.0	0
1984	4	-11	-2.8	0
1985	4	5	1.3	0
1986	9	26	2.9	0
1987	1	-2	-2.0	0
1989	2	-3	-1.5	0
Total	60	213	3.6	3

PS: 1 2 2.0 0

Matt Cavanaugh went from being the quarterback for the national championship Pittsburgh Panthers of Tony Dorsett in 1976 to being a 14-year backup in the NFL. If you look at his cumulative statistics, they equate to about one season for a full-time starter. For that 14-year "season," Cavanaugh threw

for 28 touchdowns, more than 4,000 yards, and averaged 7.5 yards per pass. Clearly, he liked to throw the ball down the field. Of course, he also threw 30 interceptions and completed just over half his passes. In his only extended trial as a starter, he went 1–7 with the 1981 Patriots. He was a backup but earned Super Bowl rings with both the 49ers and Giants. Perhaps his most famous moment in the NFL came with San Francisco in 1985 when he came on to hold for a 19-yard Ray Wersching field-goal attempt in the final minute of a game in Denver. As the ball was snapped, a snowball thrown by a Broncos fan landed in front of Cavanaugh, who bobbled the snap and then threw an incomplete pass. The 49ers lost the game by a point and were furious that the officials did not order the play replayed. Since Cavanaugh's retirement, he has worked consistently as an assistant coach for several NFL teams—winning a third Super Bowl ring with Baltimore—and for his alma mater, Pittsburgh.

Bob Celeri

QPR 4.0

Height: 5'10" **Weight:** 180 lbs. **Birthdate:** 6/1/1927
College: California **Draft:** San Francisco 1950-10ᵗʰ
1951 New York Yanks; 1952 Dallas Texans
Regular Season Record: 1–9–1, 1 comeback
Postseason Record: NA
Relative Rating: 107%

Passing

Year	G	Comp./Att.	%	Yards	Y/Att.	TD	INT	Rating
1951	11	102/238	42.9	1,797	7.6	12	15	59.8
1952	8	31/75	41.3	490	6.5	3	3	60.4
Total	19	133/313	42.5	2,287	7.3	15	18	60.2

Rushing

Year	Att.	Yards	Avg.	TD
1951	36	107	3.0	0
1952	17	135	7.9	0
Total	53	242	4.6	0

At Cal, Bob Celeri, the "Mad Engineer," led the Golden Bears to consecutive Rose Bowls and as a senior was runner-up to Eddie LeBaron for the Pop Warner Award, given to the best player on the West Coast in 1949. The debate about which graduating, undersized, ball-handling magician was better reached such proportions in California that a game between the Eddie LeBaron All-Stars and the Bob Celeri All-Stars was played in Lodi in February 1950 before more than 24,000 people and was won by LeBaron 7–6. It was the first professional game for either quarterback.

Celeri was drafted by the 49ers that year but was cut in September. The next year, though, he made the New York Yanks roster and took over as starter from struggling John Rauch in October. When the Yanks' lanky 1950 starter, George Ratterman, returned from a stint in the CFL in November, it was thought that he immediately would get his old job back. Actually, Ratterman got only one start that year and played behind Celeri. The 5'10" Celeri was a daring passer whom coach Jimmy Phelan often put in short punt formation, an early version of the shotgun, to take advantage of his passing skills. In 1952, the 1–9–2 Yanks were bought by Texas investors who moved the team to Dallas and renamed them the Texans. Celeri got hurt at midseason and lost his job to Frank Tripucka. By that time, the failing Texans had been taken over by the league and finished the year as a traveling team based in Hershey, Pennsylvania.

In 1953, Celeri was cut by the Hamilton Tiger Cats in Canada but went on to star in Canadian minor-league football for the rest of the decade. He then coached in Canada for several years before he was hired in 1968 as an assistant by new Buffalo coach Harvey Johnson, his old Yank teammate. Celeri became a scout for the Bills and a few years later died from a heart attack at the age of 47.

Chris Chandler

QPR 7.5

Height: 6'4" **Weight:** 224 lbs. **Birthdate:** 10/12/1965
College: Washington   **Draft:** Indianapolis 1988-3rd
1988–89 Indianapolis Colts; 1990–91 Tampa Bay Bucs; 1991–93 Arizona Cardinals; 1994 Los Angeles Rams; 1995–96 Houston Oilers; 1997–2001 Atlanta Falcons; 2002–03 Chicago Bears; 2004 St. Louis Rams
Regular Season Record: 67–85, 15 comebacks
Postseason Record: 2–1, 1 comeback
Relative Rating: 102%

Passing

Year	G	Comp./Att.	%	Yards	Y/Att.	TD	INT	Rating
1988	15	129/233	55.4	1,619	6.9	8	12	67.2
1989	3	39/80	48.8	537	6.7	2	3	63.4
1990	7	42/83	50.6	464	5.6	1	6	41.4
1991	9	78/154	50.6	846	5.5	5	10	50.9
1992	15	245/413	59.3	2,832	6.9	15	15	77.1
1993	4	52/103	50.5	471	4.6	3	2	64.8
1994	12	108/176	61.4	1,352	7.7	7	2	93.8
1995	13	225/356	63.2	2,460	6.9	17	10	87.8
1996	12	184/320	57.5	2,099	6.6	16	11	79.7
1997	14	202/342	59.1	2,692	7.9	20	7	95.1
1998	14	190/327	58.1	3,154	9.6	25	12	100.9
1999	12	174/307	56.7	2,339	7.6	16	11	83.5
2000	14	192/331	58.0	2,236	6.8	10	12	73.5
2001	14	223/365	61.1	2,847	7.8	16	14	84.1
2002	9	103/161	64.0	1,023	6.4	4	4	79.8
2003	8	107/192	55.7	1,050	5.5	3	7	61.3
2004	5	35/62	56.5	463	7.5	2	8	51.4
Total	180	2,328/4,005	58.1	28,484	7.1	170	146	79.1
PS:	3	59/97	60.8	728	7.5	4	4	80.6

Rushing

Year	Att.	Yards	Avg.	TD
1988	46	139	3.0	3
1989	7	57	8.1	1
1990	13	71	5.5	1
1991	26	111	4.3	0
1992	36	149	4.1	1
1993	3	2	0.7	0
1994	18	61	3.4	1
1995	28	58	2.1	2
1996	28	113	4.0	0
1997	43	158	3.7	0
1998	36	121	3.4	2
1999	16	57	3.6	1
2000	21	60	2.9	0
2001	25	84	3.4	0
2002	10	32	3.2	0
2003	14	35	2.5	0
2004	1	2	2.0	0
Total	371	1,310	3.5	12
PS:	6	45	7.5	0

The oft-injured Chris Chandler was once cruelly but accurately dubbed "Crystal Chandelier" and indeed never played a full 16-game season in his 17-year career. When he was healthy and playing in a compatible offense, though, Chandler could be a surprisingly effective quarterback. After all, he was the first quarterback to direct the lowly Atlanta franchise to the Super Bowl.

Chandler bounced around more than any other quarterback, starting for a record seven different franchises—most of them bad—and playing under 10 head coaches. As a rookie, he started most of the year for a 9–7 Colts team, but he was devastated by injuries the next year and displaced by No. 1 draft pick Jeff George. Chandler moved on to the hopeless Buccaneers for a season and a half behind Vinny Testaverde, then to the always malfunctioning Cardinals for two and a half more, and then a losing season with the Rams. In 1994, he got a chance to start again with the Houston Oilers and spent two seasons as the primary starter while the team groomed Steve McNair to take over. When McNair was ready, Chandler was traded to the Falcons for fourth- and sixth-round draft picks, and he played his best football in his early thirties. Chris was an accurate passer when given time but did not get rid of the ball quickly and took a lot of sacks.

Chandler finished his career with two seasons in the quarterback hell of Chicago and then took a return trip to the Rams, where classy St. Louis coach Mike Martz said of his play, "[Chandler] has the knowledge of the offense. He just doesn't play it in the games. There's no preparation for what we did out there. It's tragic that [Chandler] holds this team hostage." Like his father-in-law, John Brodie, Chris withstood heavy criticism over a long career spent mostly with the league's bottom-dwellers. His lifetime winning percentage is an unimpressive .441, but that is considerably better than that of his teams, which won at only a .409 clip. Chandler was not great, but he was an upstanding quarterback when he was indeed up standing.

Paul Christman

QPR 6.5

Height: 6'0" **Weight:** 210 lbs. **Birthdate:** 3/5/1918
College: Missouri **Draft:** Chicago Cardinals 1941-2nd
1945–49 Chicago Cardinals; 1950 Green Bay Packers
Regular Season Record: 22–21 est., 8 comebacks
Postseason Record: 1–0, no comebacks
Relative Rating: 102%

Passing

Year	G	Comp./Att.	%	Yards	Y/Att.	TD	INT	Rating
1945	8	89/219	40.6	1,147	5.2	5	12	42.6
1946	11	100/229	43.7	1,656	7.2	13	18	54.8
1947	12	138/301	45.8	2,191	7.3	17	22	59.0
1948	7	51/114	44.7	740	6.5	5	4	66.4
1949	12	75/151	49.7	1,015	6.7	11	13	59.9
1950	11	51/126	40.5	545	4.3	7	7	49.2
Total	61	504/1,140	44.2	7,294	6.4	58	76	54.8
PS:	1	3/14	21.4	54	3.9	0	2	3.6

Rushing

Year	Att.	Yards	Avg.	TD
1945	30	-34	-1.1	1
1946	28	-61	-2.2	3
1947	8	11	1.4	2
1948	8	6	0.8	1
1949	4	34	8.5	0
1950	7	18	2.6	1
Total	85	-26	-0.3	8
PS:	8	2	0.3	0

Pitchin' Paul Christman was one of the earliest T formation quarterbacks, first at the University of Missouri and then as part of the Chicago Cardinals' "Million Dollar Backfield" in the 1940s. An All-American, Christman led the nation in touchdown passes as a senior and had his No. 44 retired by the Tigers. As a professional, Christman quarterbacked

TOP 10

First-Year Expansion Team Quarterbacks

10. John Stofa, 1–0 for the 1966 Miami Dolphins and 2–5 for the 1968 Cincinnati Bengals
9. Tim Couch, 2–12 as starter for the 1999 Cleveland Browns
8. Randy Johnson, 3–8 for the 1966 Atlanta Falcons
7. David Carr, 4–12 for the 2002 Houston Texans
6. Jim Zorn, 2–12 for the 1976 Seattle Seahawks
5. Billy Kilmer, 0–4 for the 1967 New Orleans Saints
4. Eddie LeBaron, 0–11–1 for the 1960 Dallas Cowboys
3. Fran Tarkenton, 3–8 for the 1961 Minnesota Vikings
2. Mark Brunell, 3–7 for the 1995 Jacksonville Jaguars
1. Kerry Collins, 7–6 for the 1995 Carolina Panthers

the Cardinals to the only championship game they ever won. With Christman, the offense was not always pretty, but his teams won. He led all quarterbacks in fumbles in both 1945 and 1946 and once fumbled five times in one game, but the only other Cardinal quarterback with at least 20 starts who won more games than he lost was Charley Johnson in the 1960s.

In his one title game appearance, Christman had an awful game throwing in icy, 28-degree weather, so the Cardinals beat the Eagles on four long runs. The following year, the Cardinals and Eagles had a rematch, but Paul missed several games during the season with a broken wrist and missed the championship with a broken finger as the Cardinals lost. The 30-year-old Christman, who missed four seasons while in the service during World War II, played only two more seasons in the NFL. He was a popular broadcaster throughout the 1960s and died of cancer in 1970 at 51.

Kerry Collins

QPR 7.0

Height: 6'5"   **Weight:** 248 lbs.   **Birthdate:** 12/30/1972
College: Penn State   **Draft:** Carolina 1995-1st
1995–98 Carolina Panthers; 1998 New Orleans Saints;
1999–2003 New York Giants; 2004–05 Oakland
Raiders; 2006–08 Tennessee Titans
Regular Season Record: 79–85, 26 comebacks
Postseason Record: 3–4, no comebacks
Relative Rating: 93%

Passing

Year	G	Comp./Att.	%	Yards	Y/Att.	TD	INT	Rating
1995	15	214/433	49.4	2,717	6.3	14	19	61.9
1996	13	204/364	56.0	2,454	6.7	14	9	79.4
1997	13	200/381	52.5	2,124	5.6	11	21	55.7
1998	11	170/353	48.2	2,213	6.3	12	15	62.0
1999	10	190/331	57.4	2,318	7.0	8	11	73.3
2000	16	311/529	58.8	3,610	6.8	22	13	83.1
2001	16	327/568	57.6	3,764	6.6	19	16	77.1
2002	16	335/545	61.5	4,073	7.5	19	14	85.4
2003	13	284/500	56.8	3,110	6.2	13	16	70.7
2004	14	289/513	56.3	3,495	6.8	21	20	74.8
2005	15	302/565	53.5	3,759	6.7	20	12	77.3
2006	4	42/90	46.7	549	6.1	1	6	42.3
2007	6	50/82	61.0	531	6.5	0	0	79.9
2008	16	242/415	58.3	2,676	6.4	12	7	80.2
Total	178	3,160/5,669	55.7	37,393	6.6	186	179	73.8
PS:	7	141/241	58.5	1,556	6.5	12	11	75.3

Rushing

Year	Att.	Yards	Avg.	TD
1995	42	74	1.8	3
1996	32	38	1.2	0
1997	26	65	2.5	1
1998	30	153	5.1	1
1999	19	36	1.9	2
2000	41	65	1.6	1
2001	39	73	1.9	0
2002	44	-3	-0.1	0
2003	17	49	2.9	0
2004	16	36	2.3	0
2005	17	39	2.3	1
2007	3	-3	-1.0	0
2008	25	49	2.0	0
Total	351	671	1.9	9
PS:	19	33	1.7	0

Kerry Collins had a great deal of early success in his career. He led Penn State to a Rose Bowl win in 1995 and a claim to the national championship. He was the first-ever draft choice of the expansion Carolina Panthers and led them to the NFC Championship Game in both his and their second season. However, shortly after that, his life quickly descended in an alcohol-driven downward spiral. Reeling from the effects of some racially tinged remarks he made to teammates, he went to Carolina coach Dom Capers to request to be benched while he cleared his head. Capers saw him as a quitter, though, and cut him midseason in 1998. Signed by New Orleans, he was next seen in Carolina being arrested for a DUI when the Saints came to visit the Panthers. The Saints released the careening, carousing Collins at the end of the season. The Giants then shocked everyone by signing the unsaintly quarterback to a $16 million contract in 1999.

GM Ernie Accorsi and coach Jim Fassel had thoroughly checked out Collins, though, and were convinced he had confronted his alcoholism and had turned his life around. They were proven correct, and Fassel and quarterbacks coach Sean Payton were able to accentuate Collins' positives to produce his best work in New York. Collins was big and durable with a strong arm. He also had limitations that kept him from being a great quarterback: he was immobile, inconsistent, a record-setting fumbler, and interception prone.

The Giants got four years of more than 3,000 yards and one of more than 4,000 from Collins in addition to a trip to the Super Bowl. When New York drafted Eli Manning in 2004, though, Kerry left with some bitterness. After two more mediocre seasons as a starter in Oakland, Collins found a new home in Tennessee as Vince Young's backup. Ironically, when Young's life began to spin out of control, the now-cool Collins stepped in to lead the Titans to the top seed in the playoffs while offering experienced help to the confused Young.

Todd Collins

Height: 6'4" **Weight:** 225 lbs. **Birthdate:** 11/5/1971
College: Michigan **Draft:** Buffalo 1995-2ⁿᵈ
1995–97 Buffalo Bills; 2001–05 Kansas City Chiefs; 2006–08 Washington Redskins
Regular Season Record: 10-10, 6 comebacks
Postseason Record: 0-1, no comebacks
Relative Rating: 96%

Passing:

Year	G	Comp./Att.	%	Yards	Y/Att.	TD	INT	Rating
1995	7	14/29	48.3	112	3.9	0	1	44.0
1996	7	55/99	55.6	739	7.5	4	5	71.9
1997	14	215/391	55.0	2,367	6.1	12	13	69.5
2001	1	3/4	75.0	40	10.0	0	0	106.2
2002	3	5/6	83.3	73	12.2	1	0	156.9
2003	5	9/12	75.0	74	6.2	0	0	90.3
2004	2	1/5	20.0	42	8.4	0	0	62.1
2005	2	0/0	0.0	0	0.0	0	0	0.0
2006	1	0/0	0.0	0	0.0	0	0	0.0
2007	4	67/105	63.8	888	8.5	5	0	106.4
Total	46	369/651	56.7	4,335	6.7	22	19	76.2
PS:	2	30/54	55.6	273	5.1	2	2	66.4

Rushing

Year	Att.	Yards	Avg.	TD
1995	9	23	2.6	0
1996	21	43	2.0	0
1997	30	77	2.6	0
2001	2	6	3.0	0
2002	1	7	7.0	0
2003	8	-7	-0.9	0
2004	1	4	4.0	0
2005	2	-2	-1.0	0
2007	8	1	0.1	0
Total	82	152	1.9	0
PS:	2	2	1.0	0

Todd Collins captured the attention of the nation in 2007 when he took over a foundering Redskins team still in shock from the shooting death of safety Sean Taylor and drove them into the playoffs with four straight wins, throwing for five touchdowns and no interceptions. Collins was a longtime backup who had not started a game for 10 years when starter Jason Campbell dislocated his knee against the Bears. In relief, Collins completed 15 of 20 for 224 yards and was named NFC Offensive Player of the Week. He then led Washington over the Giants, Vikings, and Cowboys to clinch a playoff spot.

Collins had failed at his first NFL stop, trying to replace Jim Kelly in Buffalo in the late 1990s. Moving on to Kansas City, he served as the Chiefs' third quarterback for three seasons without seeing any action. When Dick Vermeil was hired as Chiefs coach in 2001, he brought in Al Saunders as his offensive coach, and Collins moved up to second string. He still saw little action, though, as Trent Green started 80 games in a row. When Saunders moved on to Washington in 2006, his number one pupil, Collins, followed him, although it was back to third string for Todd at first. Collins was so anonymous that two fans created a fictional Todd Collins blog in 2005, humorously purporting to be the diary of an NFL quarterback who gets paid to sit around and do nothing. Collins was not amused, although the blog continued into the 2008 season with Collins back on the bench.

Collins was adept at reading defenses and delivering accurate passes in rhythm. When he reached the postseason against Seattle, though, the Seahawks disrupted that rhythm and showed why Collins was a backup, not a starter. Seattle picked him off twice, his first interceptions in 10 years, and easily beat the Redskins. When Saunders moved on to the Rams, there was speculation that Collins would follow his coach again, but Todd re-signed with Washington for $9 million and three years.

Jack Concannon had more success playing a quarterback in the movies than in the NFL.

Rushing

Year	Att.	Yards	Avg.	TD
1964	16	134	8.4	1
1965	9	104	11.6	0
1966	25	195	7.8	2
1967	67	279	4.2	3
1968	28	104	3.7	2
1969	22	62	2.8	1
1970	42	136	3.2	2
1971	5	5	1.0	0
1974	3	7	2.3	1
Total	**217**	**1,026**	**4.7**	**12**

Boston columnist Bob Ryan eulogized the late Jack Concannon as being "Flutie before Flutie" because both were larger-than-life local legends known for being thrilling, scrambling quarterbacks. However, Concannon was 6'3", not 5'9", and his most famous moment at Boston College wasn't a 50-yard Hail Mary pass to beat Miami but instead the 79-yard "Serpentine Run" for a spectacular touchdown in a loss to Ernie Davis' Syracuse team in 1961. In 1963, the celebrated Concannon was even on the cover of the *NCAA Guide*.

Despite being the top pick of the hometown Patriots in 1964, the BC Eagle quarterback signed with the Philadelphia Eagles because they made a more lucrative offer. With Philadelphia, however, He fell into a three-quarterback competition with Norm Snead and King Hill and would attempt only 103 passes in three years, completing fewer than half of them for four touchdowns and eight interceptions. His first NFL start came in the final home game of his rookie year against the Cowboys. Joe Kuharich felt that the rookie's scrambling would counter the Cowboy blitzes, and Concannon gained 99 yards on eight carries with his scrambles and completed 10 passes for 134 yards and two scores in a win over Dallas. However, Concannon would not start again for Philadelphia until the end of the 1966 season when he led the Eagles to victories over the Steelers and Browns.

The following season, he was traded to the Bears for Mike Ditka and spent five mostly unsuccessful seasons in Chicago, although he did appear in both *M*A*S*H* and *Brian's Song* during that time. He finished a lackluster career with two seasons as a backup in Green Bay and Detroit. Concannon averaged close to five yards per carry during his career but was not an NFL passer. He had trouble

Jack Concannon

QPR 3.5

Height: 6'3" **Weight:** 205 lbs. **Birthdate:** 2/25/1943
College: Boston College **Draft:** Philadelphia 1964-2nd; Boston Patriots 1964-1st
1964–66 Philadelphia Eagles; 1967–71 Chicago Bears; 1974 Green Bay Packers; 1975 Detroit Lions
Regular Season Record: 20–24–1, 1 comeback
Postseason Record: NA
Relative Rating: 83%

Passing

Year	G	Comp./Att.	%	Yards	Y/Att.	TD	INT	Rating
1964	4	12/23	52.2	199	8.7	2	1	92.5
1965	3	12/29	41.4	176	6.1	1	3	33.8
1966	11	21/51	41.2	262	5.1	1	4	31.7
1967	13	92/186	49.5	1,260	6.8	6	14	50.9
1968	7	71/143	49.7	715	5.0	5	9	49.7
1969	14	87/160	54.4	783	4.9	4	8	55.3
1970	14	194/385	50.4	2,130	5.5	16	18	61.5
1971	3	42/77	54.5	334	4.3	0	3	49.4
1974	14	28/54	51.9	381	7.1	1	3	57.7
1975	7	1/2	50.0	30	15.0	0	0	95.8
Total	**90**	**560/1,110**	**50.5**	**6,270**	**5.6**	**36**	**63**	**54.8**

finding secondary receivers, threw a lot of interceptions, and averaged a puny 5.6 yards per pass. He was often said to be a halfback playing quarterback and probably would have had a better career as a running back.

Charlie Conerly

 QPR 9.5

Height: 6'1"   **Weight:** 185 lbs.   **Birthdate:** 9/19/1921
College: Mississippi   **Draft:** Washington 1945-13th
1948–61 New York Giants
Regular Season Record: 84–52–2, 20 comebacks
Postseason Record: 2–3, no comebacks
Relative Rating: 113%

Passing

Year	G	Comp./Att.	%	Yards	Y/Att.	TD	INT	Rating
1948	12	162/299	54.2	2,175	7.3	22	13	84.0
1949	12	152/305	49.8	2,138	7.0	17	20	64.1
1950	11	56/132	42.4	1,000	7.6	8	7	67.1
1951	12	93/189	49.2	1,277	6.8	10	22	49.3
1952	11	82/169	48.5	1,090	6.4	13	10	70.4
1953	12	143/303	47.2	1,711	5.6	13	25	44.9
1954	10	103/210	49.0	1,439	6.9	17	11	76.7
1955	12	98/202	48.5	1,310	6.5	13	13	64.2
1956	12	90/174	51.7	1,143	6.6	10	7	75.0
1957	12	128/232	55.2	1,712	7.4	11	11	74.9
1958	10	88/184	47.8	1,199	6.5	10	9	66.8
1959	10	113/194	58.2	1,706	8.8	14	4	102.7
1960	12	66/134	49.3	954	7.1	8	7	70.9
1961	13	44/106	41.5	634	6.0	7	8	52.2
Total	161	1,418/2,833	50.1	19,488	6.9	173	167	68.2
PS:	6	47/90	52.2	793	8.8	4	4	78.6

Rushing

Year	Att.	Yards	Avg.	TD
1948	40	160	4.0	5
1949	23	42	1.8	0
1950	23	22	1.0	1
1951	17	65	3.8	1
1952	27	115	4.3	0
1953	24	91	3.8	0
1954	24	107	4.5	1
1955	12	10	0.8	0
1956	11	11	1.0	0
1957	15	24	1.6	1
1958	12	-17	-1.4	0
1959	15	38	2.5	1
1960	14	1	0.1	0
1961	13	16	1.2	0
Total	270	685	2.5	10
PS:	4	15	3.8	1

Chuckin' Charlie Conerly was originally drafted by Washington in 1945 as a single-wing tailback, but the taciturn Mississippi signal-caller was serving his country as a marine involved in several island assaults in the Pacific at the time. After he used up his college eligibility, Conerly's rights were traded to the Giants for Howie Livingston in 1948, and in his rookie season he threw for 22 touchdowns and 2,175 yards. However, he struggled to learn the T formation while still playing in coach Steve Owen's outdated A formation over the next five years. Conerly and the Giants were plagued by a poor line, slow receivers, and an unimaginative attack, and Charlie felt the brunt of it. He was sacked repeatedly and booed unmercifully as the

TOP 10
Worst Winning Performances in a Championship Game

10. Bob Waterfield—completed nine of 24 passes with two interceptions for the Rams in 1951
9. Terry Bradshaw—completed nine of 14 passes for 96 yards for Pittsburgh in 1974
8. Trent Dilfer—completed 12 of 25 passes for 153 for the Ravens in 2000
7. Bill Wade—completed 10 of 28 passes for 138 yards for the Bears in 1963
6. Jack Kemp—completed eight of 19 passes for 155 yards for Buffalo in 1965
5. Earl Morrall—completed 6 of 17 passes with three interceptions for Baltimore in 1969
4. George Blanda—one TD and five interceptions for Houston in 1961
3. Tommy Thompson—completed two of 12 for seven yards with two interceptions in a blizzard for Philadelphia in 1948
2. Paul Christman—completed three of 14 passes and two interceptions for the Cardinals in 1947
1. Ben Roethlisberger—completed nine of 21 passes for 123 yards with two interceptions for Pittsburgh in 2005

stands were festooned with signs reading "Back to the Farm," "Charlie Must Go," and worse.

Conerly's career turned around at age 33 in 1954 when Vince Lombardi was hired to handle the offense. In that year, Charlie became the third quarterback to reach 100 career touchdown passes. For the next eight seasons under Lombardi and then Allie Sherman, Conerly enjoyed a golden period in which the team won and the fans were on his side at last. His teammates were always behind this quiet, unflappable, forceful, respected leader who was named league MVP in 1959 when he led the league in passing at age 38.

Conerly led the Giants to three NFL title games and won the championship in 1956 when he completed seven of 10 passes for 195 yards and two touchdowns. In 1958, he was already voted MVP of the championship game when Johnny Unitas brought the Colts back to win in sudden death in that watershed moment. Charlie was an accurate passer and talented reader of defenses who once said modestly of his skills, "I don't know if I was a good passer or not, but I could see the field. I thought I was average. I couldn't throw the ball too far, but then, I usually never had anybody who could go deep."

When he retired at age 40 in 1961, only Otto Graham had won more quarterback starts than Charlie's 84. Conerly also led 20 fourth-quarter game-winning comebacks and finished as the Giants' all-time leader with more than 19,000 yards passing and 173 touchdowns. Giants owner Wellington Mara often said that Charlie was the "best player not in the Pro Football Hall of Fame." His No. 42 was retired by the team.

Greg Cook

QPR 6.0

Height: 6'4"   **Weight:** 220 lbs.   **Birthdate:** 11/20/1946
College: Cincinnati   **Draft:** Cincinnati 1969-1st
1969, 1973 Cincinnati Bengals
Regular Season Record: 4–6–1, no comebacks
Postseason Record: NA
Relative Rating: 137%

Passing

Year	G	Comp./Att.	%	Yards	Y/Att.	TD	INT	Rating
1969	11	106/197	53.8	1,854	9.4	15	11	88.3
1973	1	1/3	33.3	11	3.7	0	0	45.1
Total	12	107/200	53.5	1,865	9.3	15	11	88.3

Rushing

Year	Att.	Yards	Avg.	TD
1969	25	148	5.9	1

The greatest "what if" story among all NFL quarterbacks, Greg Cook struck like lightning out of the University of Cincinnati as a rookie in 1969, tore up his shoulder, and was done. Cook led the second-year Bengals to three straight wins at the start of the season and then landed on his shoulder in the third game against Kansas City and missed the next three games—all losses. Without the modern diagnostic tools to determine that not only had Cook torn his rotator cuff but also detached his bicep, Greg returned in Week 7 shot up with cortisone. Cook played out his rookie season and led the league in completion percentage, yards per attempt, and yards per completion. His 9.4 yards per pass has been exceeded only twice in the last 40 years (Chris Chandler in 1998 and Kurt Warner in 2000), and his 17.5 yards per completion has been topped only by Craig Morton in 1970.

Cook had a quick release, big arm, and the vision to find secondary receivers. At 6'4" and 220 pounds, he was also a gifted scrambler who averaged almost six yards per carry in 1969. After repeated operations, he appeared in only one more game four years later when he completed one of three passes for 11 yards in the 1973 opener against the Broncos. With Cook's premature demise as a player, Bengals offensive coach Bill Walsh had to jettison the long-ball attack he favored for a offense of short, timed passes that came to be known as the West Coast offense. A healthy Cook would have been more spectacular to watch.

Tim Couch

QPR 6.0

Height: 6'4"   **Weight:** 220 lbs.   **Birthdate:** 7/31/1977
College: Kentucky   **Draft:** Cleveland 1999-1st
1999–2003 Cleveland Browns
Regular Season Record: 22–37, 11 comebacks
Postseason Record: NA
Relative Rating: 96%

Passing

Year	G	Comp./Att.	%	Yards	Y/Att.	TD	INT	Rating
1999	15	223/399	55.9	2,447	6.1	15	13	73.2
2000	7	137/215	63.7	1,483	6.9	7	9	77.3
2001	16	272/454	59.9	3,040	6.7	17	21	73.1
2002	14	273/443	61.6	2,842	6.4	18	18	76.8
2003	10	120/203	59.1	1,319	6.5	7	6	77.6
Total	62	1,025/1,714	59.1	11,131	6.5	64	67	75.1

Rushing

Year	Att.	Yards	Avg.	TD
1999	40	267	6.7	1
2000	12	45	3.8	0
2001	38	128	3.4	0
2002	23	77	3.3	0
2003	11	39	3.5	1
Total	124	556	4.5	2

Of the five quarterbacks taken in the first round of the 1999 NFL draft, Tim Couch was the first selected, the first pick overall, and the first pick of the reborn Cleveland Browns franchise. The Browns passed on Donovan McNabb because they didn't think he was a good enough passer. They passed on Daunte Culpepper because he had not played against a very high level of competition in college. Akili Smith was too inexperienced, and Cade McNown was not highly rated, so the choice was Couch. Tim had completed 72 percent of his passes as a senior, although almost all were short tosses. The Browns felt he was ideal for their offense. What a letdown his career was.

Couch was made the starter on the expansion Browns for their second game, and he was tossed around like a rag doll behind a raggedy offensive line. In his second season, he missed most of the year with a thumb injury but played all of the

2001 season when the Browns won seven games. In 2002, a quarterback controversy arose as Couch competed with backup Kelly Holcomb. His low point came against the Ravens, when he was knocked out of the game with a concussion that was cheered by Cleveland fans. The sensitive Couch choked back tears in the locker room after the game, but he led the Browns to the playoffs with a 9–7 record that year. Unfortunately, Tim broke his leg in the season finale and had to watch Holcomb in the postseason. The next year, the Browns went back and forth between the two quarterbacks, and Couch began to fold under the pressure.

Cleveland cut Couch in the off-season, and he tried to hook on with the Packers but had a bad shoulder and played so terribly that he was booed off Lambeau Field in the exhibition season. After Green Bay cut him, he underwent shoulder surgery and tested positive for HGH during his rehabilitation. Couch, who is married to one-time Playboy Playmate of the Year Heather Kozar, has since failed tryouts in the CFL and with the Jaguars and moved on with his life.

Daunte Culpepper

QPR 8.5

Height: 6'4"   **Weight:** 264 lbs.   **Birthdate:** 1/28/1977
College: Central Florida   **Draft:** Minnesota 1999-1st
1999–2005 Minnesota Vikings; 2006 Miami Dolphins;
2007 Oakland Raiders; 2008 Detroit Lions
Regular Season Record: 41–54, 14 comebacks
Postseason Record: 2–2, no comebacks
Relative Rating: 114%

Passing

Year	G	Comp./Att.	%	Yards	Y/Att.	TD	INT	Rating
1999	1	0/0	0.0	0	0.0	0	0	0.0
2000	16	297/474	62.7	3,937	8.3	33	16	98.0
2001	11	235/366	64.2	2,612	7.1	14	13	83.3
2002	16	333/549	60.7	3,853	7.0	18	23	75.3
2003	14	295/454	65.0	3,479	7.7	25	11	96.4
2004	16	379/548	69.2	4,717	8.6	39	11	110.9
2005	7	139/216	64.4	1,564	7.2	6	12	72.0
2006	4	81/134	60.4	929	6.9	2	3	77.0
2007	7	108/186	58.1	1,331	7.2	5	5	78.0
2008	5	60/115	52.2	786	6.8	4	6	63.9
Total	97	1,927/3,042	63.3	23,208	7.6	146	100	89.0
PS:	4	73/134	54.5	980	7.3	8	5	82.3

Rushing

Year	Att.	Yards	Avg.	TD
1999	3	6	2.0	0
2000	89	470	5.3	7
2001	71	416	5.9	5
2002	106	609	5.7	10
2003	73	422	5.8	4
2004	88	406	4.6	2
2005	24	147	6.1	1
2006	10	20	2.0	1
2007	20	40	2.0	3
2008	12	25	2.1	1
Total	**496**	**2,561**	**5.2**	**34**
PS:	17	140	8.2	1

Daunte Culpepper was the fourth of five quarterbacks taken in the first round of the 1999 NFL draft and for a short time was a superstar in the league before injuries and off-field incidents derailed his career. Culpepper spent his rookie year on the sidelines watching Jeff George and Randall Cunningham throwing bombs to Randy Moss and Cris Carter. The Vikings got rid of both veteran quarterbacks in 2000, though, and turned the team over to the massive Culpepper. Daunte quickly proved himself a powerful runner and strong-armed passer and led Minnesota to the NFC conference championship. Although the Vikings lost that game, Culpepper threw for 33 touchdowns, just 16 interceptions, and nearly 4,000 yards in his first season.

Unfortunately, the team around Culpepper declined and went just 28–36 in the next four seasons. Daunte struggled with interceptions in 2001 and 2002 but rebounded in 2003 and 2004 to throw for a combined 64 touchdowns and only 22 interceptions for more than 8,000 yards. Moss was on board to supply spectacular touchdown catches and endless off-field drama as the Vikings were viewed as perennial underachievers. Moss was cut loose in 2005, and Culpepper got off to a horrendous start, throwing just six touchdowns to 12 interceptions in the first seven games before tearing up his knee. To make matters worse, Daunte's name was implicated in the reports of the Viking players' infamous "Love Boat" cruise scandal that gave the impression that the team was out of control.

New coach Brad Childress found the recovering Culpepper more interested in money than the team in the off-season and traded him to Miami for a second-round pick. Culpepper swore he would be back by the start of the 2006 season. He did start the first four games for Miami but looked sluggish and was benched. In November, he underwent another knee surgery, and the Dolphins tired of him. Miami released him during training camp in 2007, and he signed on with Oakland. As a Raider, Culpepper shared the job with perennial backup Josh McCown and was released at the end of the year.

Since 2006, Culpepper has acted as his own agent and tried to sell himself only as a starter in 2008, blowing off the Packers and Steelers, who were interested in Daunte as a backup. When he drew no offers, Culpepper announced his retirement in September, saying, "I would rather shut the door to such 'opportunity' than continue to wait for one of my fellow quarterbacks to suffer a serious injury. Since I was not given a fair chance to come in and compete for a job, I would rather move on and win in other arenas of life." Culpepper seemed not to realize that injuries had destroyed his once prodigious skills. Although he was once an unstoppable runner who scored 33 rushing touchdowns, more than all but nine other quarterbacks, now Culpepper is an immobile, injury-prone liability not able to use his cannon arm effectively. From 2005 through 2007, Culpepper played in just 17 of 48 games and was sacked 73 times—12 percent of pass plays. Through 2008, he is the only quarterback to have more fumbles, 98, than games played, 97. The highs and lows of his life are striking: rising from being born to a mother in prison to a three-time Pro Bowl quarterback and then having all the glory fall away. In October, Culpepper announced he was ready to end his retirement for the highest bidder, which turned out to be the winless Lions, for whom he started five games.

Randall Cunningham

QPR **8.5**

Height: 6'4" **Weight:** 212 lbs. **Birthdate:** 3/27/1963
College: UNLV **Draft:** Philadelphia 1985-2nd
1985–95 Philadelphia Eagles; 1997–99 Minnesota
Vikings; 2000 Dallas Cowboys; 2001 Baltimore Ravens
Regular Season Record: 82–52–1, 23 comebacks
Postseason Record: 4–6, 2 comebacks
Relative Rating: 106%

Passing

Year	G	Comp./Att.	%	Yards	Y/Att.	TD	INT	Rating
1985	6	34/81	42.0	548	6.8	1	8	29.8
1986	15	111/209	53.1	1,391	6.7	8	7	72.9
1987	12	223/406	54.9	2,786	6.9	23	12	83.0
1988	16	301/560	53.8	3,808	6.8	24	16	77.6
1989	16	290/532	54.5	3,400	6.4	21	15	75.5
1990	16	271/465	58.3	3,466	7.5	30	13	91.6
1991	1	1/4	25.0	19	4.8	0	0	46.9
1992	15	233/384	60.7	2,775	7.2	19	11	87.3
1993	4	76/110	69.1	850	7.7	5	5	88.1
1994	14	265/490	54.1	3,229	6.6	16	13	74.4
1995	7	69/121	57.0	605	5.0	3	5	61.5
1997	6	44/88	50.0	501	5.7	6	4	71.3
1998	15	259/425	60.9	3,704	8.7	34	10	106.0
1999	6	124/200	62.0	1,475	7.4	8	9	79.1
2000	6	74/125	59.2	849	6.8	6	4	82.4
2001	6	54/89	60.7	573	6.4	3	2	81.3
Total	161	2,429/4,289	56.6	29,979	7.0	207	134	81.5
PS:	12	192/365	52.6	2,426	6.6	12	9	74.3

Rushing

Year	Att.	Yards	Avg.	TD
1985	29	205	7.1	0
1986	66	540	8.2	5
1987	76	505	6.6	3
1988	93	624	6.7	6
1989	104	621	6.0	4
1990	118	942	8.0	5
1992	87	549	6.3	5
1993	18	110	6.1	1
1994	65	288	4.4	3
1995	21	98	4.7	0
1997	19	127	6.7	0
1998	32	132	4.1	1
1999	10	58	5.8	0
2000	23	89	3.9	1
2001	14	40	2.9	1
Total	775	4,928	6.4	35
PS:	46	254	5.5	1

Randall Cunningham was a human highlight reel. There was the time against the Oilers in 1988 when Randall rolled out to the left, found no one open, and doubled back to the other side of the field. With still no passing options, he took off and juked and sprinted his way for a 33-yard touchdown run. The next week against the Giants, Randall rolled right and found linebacker Carl Banks going for his legs. Randall broke his hurdling fall with his hand, popped up and threw a touchdown pass to Jimmie Giles. In 1989, he proved his leg was as powerful as his arm when he booted a 91-yard punt against the Giants. Against the Bills in 1990, Cunningham dropped back in his own end zone, eluded the charging Bruce Smith, dashed to his left, and launched the ball 60 yards in the air where Fred Barnett leaped to snare it and race the rest of the way on a remarkable 95-yard touchdown pass play.

Coach Buddy Ryan told Randall that the offensive plan was for him to make four or five big plays to win the game. *Sports Illustrated* famously dubbed Cunningham the Ultimate Weapon at the time, but he was not a complete player and was not interested in bettering himself through film study. Instead he came up with new slogans each year: "Any questions, call my agent," "Let me be me," "I'm

TOP 10
40-Year-Old Quarterbacks

10. Vince Evans—best full-season passer rating at 40
9. Charlie Conerly—seven TD passes at 40
8. Len Dawson—66 percent completions and five TD passes at 40
7. Steve DeBerg—started last game at 44
6. Earl Morrall—averaged 11.1 yards per pass at 40
5. Vinny Testaverde—3,532 passing yards and 17 TD passes at 40
4. Doug Flutie—nine TD passes at 40
3. Sonny Jurgensen—64 percent completions and 11 TD passes at 40
2. Warren Moon—3,678 passing yards and 25 TD passes at 40
1. George Blanda—1970 MVP for late-game heroics at 43

still scrambling." It's true that he was estranged from his revered big brother Sam, a former Patriot star fullback; that he and Warren Moon were the first star black quarterbacks; and that he played in front of a bad offensive line, assisted by no true running backs and no great receivers. However, Cunningham's immaturity detracted from his play. He won almost as many MVP trophies (three) as playoff games (four), and his weakness at reading defenses led to key interceptions in big games.

He led the Eagles and all NFL quarterbacks in rushing four straight years, including 942 yards in 1990, and four times was the team's offensive MVP. Then, he suffered a knee injury in the 1991 opener. Randall worked hard and won the Comeback Player Award the next season but broke his leg in the fourth game of 1993 and was lost for another season. He came back again in 1994, but when he lost his starting job to Bubby Brister, he reacted petulantly by packing up his locker and wearing his team jacket inside out on the sidelines. Failing to function in the West Coast offense in 1995, a struggling Cunningham was benched for journeyman Rodney Peete after the team started 1–3. Randall pouted and withdrew again. When Peete got injured in the playoffs, Randall played in a fog, unprepared and confused, as the Eagles got pummeled by the Cowboys.

Cunningham abruptly retired to do masonry in Nevada. The following season, he returned to the league as a Viking, and in his second season in Minnesota he threw 34 touchdowns to the likes of Randy Moss and Cris Carter, leading the Vikings to a 15–1 record. In the NFC championship, though, the Falcons upset Minnesota, a key play being a costly interception Randall threw right before the half. He spent three more seasons in the league with the Vikings, Cowboys, and Ravens before retiring for good in 2002 as the all-time rushing leader among quarterbacks and the winner of 82 regular-season starts, but somehow less than the sum of his great parts.

Gary Cuozzo

Height: 6'0" **Weight:** 195 lbs. **Birthdate:** 4/26/1941
College: Virginia **Draft:** Free Agent
1963–66 Baltimore Colts; 1967 New Orleans Saints;
1968–71 Minnesota Vikings; 1972 St. Louis Cardinals
Regular Season Record: 21–19, 4 comebacks
Postseason Record: 0–2, comebacks
Relative Rating: 92%

Passing

Year	G	Comp./Att.	%	Yards	Y/Att.	TD	INT	Rating
1963	5	10/17	58.8	104	6.1	0	0	76.6
1964	9	15/36	41.7	163	4.5	2	3	39.5
1965	7	54/105	51.4	700	6.7	7	4	79.1
1966	7	26/50	52.0	424	8.5	4	2	90.7
1967	13	134/260	51.5	1,562	6.0	7	12	59.8
1968	4	24/33	72.7	297	9.0	1	0	110.3
1969	9	49/98	50.0	693	7.1	4	5	65.6
1970	12	128/257	49.8	1,720	6.7	7	10	64.3
1971	8	75/168	44.6	842	5.0	6	8	52.2
1972	8	69/158	43.7	897	5.7	5	11	43.7
Total	82	584/1,182	49.4	7,402	6.3	43	55	62.1
PS:	3	22/52	42.3	286	5.5	2	5	33.5

Although Gary Cuozzo was an undrafted free agent, he was traded for three No. 1 draft picks in his journeyman's career.

Rushing

Year	Att.	Yards	Avg.	TD
1963	3	26	8.7	0
1964	7	-2	-0.3	0
1965	6	8	1.3	0
1966	1	9	9.0	0
1967	19	43	2.3	1
1968	1	4	4.0	0
1969	3	-4	-1.3	0
1970	17	61	3.6	0
1971	15	24	1.6	0
1972	4	7	1.8	0
Total	76	176	2.3	1
PS:	1	11	11.0	0

Gary Cuozzo was one of the most overvalued quarterbacks in league history. After he attained a 1–2 record in four years as Johnny Unitas' backup in Baltimore, the Colts traded him for center Bill Curry and the No. 1 pick in the 1967 draft that they used for Bubba Smith. Cuozzo spent one season in the Big Easy, throwing almost twice as many interceptions as touchdowns and averaging just six yards per pass before losing his job to Billy Kilmer. Yet the Saints were able to trade Cuozzo to the Vikings in 1968 for *two* No. 1 picks. Somehow the price for mediocrity had gone up. he spent four seasons in Minnesota, the first two behind Joe Kapp, and completed fewer than half his passes as well as tossing more interceptions than touchdowns. Still, in 1972, Minnesota traded the 31-year-old journeyman to the Cardinals for speedy receiver John Gilliam and a No. 2 pick. In St. Louis, Cuozzo finished his career by throwing for five touchdowns and 11 interceptions while winning just one of six starts.

Cuozzo made his reputation by throwing for five touchdowns in relief of Unitas during one game in 1965. Writers compared his drop-back form to Unitas, and T formation guru Clark Shaughnessy thought he had the footwork, setup, and balance to be a star. Cuozzo was an intelligent, accurate touch passer but did not have the strong arm or inspirational manner of a star. He was a career backup who was traded for three No. 1 picks, a No. 2 pick, and two Pro Bowl players during his lackluster career.

Jay Cutler

QPR 6.0

Height: 6'3" **Weight:** 225 lbs. **Birthdate:** 4/29/1983
College: Vanderbilt **Draft:** Denver 2006-1st
2006–08 Denver Broncos
Regular Season Record: 17–20, 6 comebacks
Postseason Record: NA
Relative Rating: 108%

Passing

Year	G	Comp./Att.	%	Yards	Y/Att.	TD	INT	Rating
2006	5	81/137	59.1	1,001	7.3	9	5	88.5
2007	16	297/467	63.6	3,497	7.5	20	14	88.1
2008	16	384/616	62.3	4,526	7.3	25	18	86.0
Total	37	762/1,220	62.5	9,024	7.4	54	37	87.1

Rushing

Year	Att.	Yards	Avg.	TD
2006	12	18	1.5	0
2007	44	205	4.7	1
2008	57	200	3.5	2
Total	113	423	3.7	3

With Vince Young and Matt Leinart having trouble staying on the field due to both on- and off-field issues, it's becoming increasingly likely that the best quarterback to emerge from the 2006 draft will be the third selected, Jay Cutler, the pride of Santa Claus, Indiana. Cutler came into the pros well tested, having started 45 games in four years for the 12–34 Vanderbilt Commodores. He boasts good size, nimble feet, and a Favreian arm along with a tendency to play a bit frantically.

During Cutler's rookie year, he was given the starting position on the 7–4 Broncos with coach Mike Shanahan saying, "I think he gives us the best chance to win now." Actually, Jake Plummer gave Denver the best chance to win in 2006, but Shanahan was tired of Plummer's shortcomings and wanted to see what Cutler could do. The Broncos went 2–3 down the stretch and missed the playoffs, but Shanahan saw enough of Cutler's potential that he traded Plummer to Tampa after the season. In 2007, the job was Cutler's, and he played well for a second-year quarterback. However, he started to lose weight and run short on energy as the season progressed. In May 2008, Jay was diagnosed with Type 1 diabetes and equipped with an insulin pump. Cutler began the 2008 on season on fire, fully able to cope with his ongoing condition and poised for a bright future in the NFL. As usual, the Broncos faded in the second half of the season, but Cutler had an outstanding year. In the off-season, though, a surprisingly intransigent conflict with new coach Josh McDaniel erupted, and got Cutler traded to the Bears.

Gary Danielson

QPR 7.0

Height: 6'2" **Weight:** 195 lbs. **Birthdate:** 9/10/1951
College: Purdue **Draft:** Free Agent
1974–75 WFL; 1976–78, 1980–84 Detroit Lions; 1985, 1987–88 Cleveland Browns
Regular Season Record: 28–31–1, 8 comebacks
Postseason Record: 0–1, no comebacks
Relative Rating: 106%

Passing

Year	G	Comp./Att.	%	Yards	Y/Att.	TD	INT	Rating
1976	1	0/0	0.0	0	0.0	0	0	0.0
1977	13	42/100	42.0	445	4.5	1	5	38.1
1978	16	199/351	56.7	2,294	6.5	18	17	73.5
1980	16	244/417	58.5	3,223	7.7	13	11	82.4
1981	6	56/96	58.3	784	8.2	3	5	73.4
1982	8	100/197	50.8	1,343	6.8	10	14	60.1
1983	10	59/113	52.2	720	6.4	7	4	78.0
1984	15	252/410	61.5	3,076	7.5	17	15	83.1
1985	8	97/163	59.5	1,274	7.8	8	6	85.3
1987	6	25/33	75.8	281	8.5	4	0	140.3
1988	2	31/52	59.6	324	6.2	0	1	69.7
Total	101	1,105/1,932	57.2	13,764	7.1	81	78	76.6
PS:	1	24/38	63.2	236	6.2	0	5	41.0

Rushing

Year	Att.	Yards	Avg.	TD
1977	7	62	8.9	0
1978	22	93	4.2	0
1980	48	232	4.8	2
1981	9	23	2.6	2
1982	23	92	4.0	0
1983	6	8	1.3	0
1984	41	218	5.3	3
1985	25	126	5.0	0
1987	1	0	0.0	0
1988	4	3	0.8	0
Total	186	857	4.6	7
PS:	4	17	4.3	0

Gary Danielson was born in Detroit, grew up in nearby Dearborn, and even quarterbacked a high school championship game in Tiger Stadium in 1967. When he was a small boy, he wore a Bobby Layne jersey and then got to follow Layne's legacy as the Lions' leader in the late 1970s and early 1980s. Danielson did not experience the triumph of Layne as a Lion, though. Of course, no one has on this dysfunctional franchise.

Danielson followed All-Americans Bob Griese and Mike Phipps as Purdue's quarterback and was a three-year starter for the mediocre Boilermakers. Undrafted, Gary signed with the WFL and served as a backup for three teams in two seasons, throwing just 75 passes from 1974 to 1975. He signed with the Lions as a free agent in 1976 and finally beat out Greg Landry as the starter in 1978. Gary played well but then suffered a knee injury in the fourth quarter of the final exhibition game of the 1979 preseason and was out for the year. When he returned in 1980, Gary threw for more than 3,000 yards for the first time but then hurt his wrist in 1981 and was replaced by Eric Hipple. Danielson and Hipple would battle for the starting job over the next four years. After a second season of more than 3,000 yards passing in 1984, Danielson was traded to the Browns to groom rookie Bernie Kosar. By Week 6 of 1985, Kosar was the starter and Danielson was his able backup for the next four years. Danielson was never a great quarterback but was smart, mobile, and fairly accurate, the very essence of an average quarterback. He has since had a long career as a very capable college football broadcaster.

TOP 10
Quarterback Imports from Rival Leagues

10. Gary Danielson from the WFL
9. Pat Haden from the WFL
8. Bobby Hebert from the USFL
7. Danny White from the WFL
6. Doug Flutie from the USFL
5. Frankie Albert from the AAFC
4. Y.A. Tittle from the AAFC
3. Jim Kelly from the USFL
2. Steve Young from the USFL
1. Otto Graham from the AAFC

Ed Danowski

QPR 9.0

Height: 6'1" **Weight:** 198 lbs. **Birthdate:** 9/30/1911
College: Fordham **Draft:** Free agent
1934–39, 1941 New York Giants
Regular Season Record: 35–17–5 est., 6 comebacks
Postseason Record: 2–2, 1 comeback
Relative Rating: 174%

Passing

Year	G	Comp./Att.	%	Yards	Y/Att.	TD	INT	Rating
1934	8	15/32	46.9	230	7.2	2	3	52.9
1935	12	57/113	50.4	794	7.0	10	9	69.7
1936	12	47/104	45.2	515	5.0	5	10	36.8
1937	11	66/134	49.3	814	6.1	8	5	72.8
1938	11	70/129	54.3	848	6.6	7	8	66.9
1939	11	42/101	41.6	437	4.3	3	6	39.9
1941	6	12/24	50.0	179	7.5	2	3	63.0
Total	71	309/637	48.5	3,817	6.0	37	44	58.1
PS:	4	22/43	51.2	325	7.6	4	6	67.6

Rushing

Year	Att.	Yards	Avg.	TD
1934	75	248	3.3	0
1935	130	335	2.6	2
1936	91	259	2.8	0
1937	66	95	1.4	1
1938	48	215	4.5	1
1939	25	21	0.8	0
1941	0	0	0.0	0
Total	435	1,173	2.7	4
PS:	1	4	4.0	1

Single-wing tailback Ed Danowski was one of the finest passers of his era. He did not have a particularly strong arm, but he had great touch and accuracy. He was a clever play caller and able runner, and he was a skilled punter and defensive back as well. Above all, he was a winner who continually had the Giants at the top of the league.

Danowski was the signal-caller for the Fordham Ram team that featured the original Seven Blocks of Granite line. The Giants signed him off the nearby Fordham campus where Wellington Mara was a sophomore in 1934. When starting passer Harry Newman went down with a season-ending injury that year, rookie Ed Danowski led the Giants

to the NFL title in the famous "Sneakers Game." The following season, Danowski held on to the starting job and led the NFL in passing as New York returned to the title game, where they lost to the Lions. Ed again led the league in passing in 1938 and topped that season by connecting with Hank Soar for the 23-yard touchdown pass that beat Green Bay for the championship. Ed led the Giants back to the title game in 1939 and then retired to play semi-pro ball in 1940. The three-time All-Pro returned to the Giants for the second half of 1941 but then went into the navy for the bulk of World War II. Danowski was named varsity football coach at Fordham in 1946 and continued there until the Rams gave up the sport in 1955. He spent the remainder of his career as a local high school gym teacher and coach. His son, John, has had a long, successful career as a collegiate lacrosse coach.

Dan Darragh

QPR 0.5

Height: 6'3" **Weight:** 196 lbs. **Birthdate:** 11/28/1946
College: William & Mary **Draft:** Buffalo 1968-13th
1968–70 Buffalo Bills
Regular Season Record: 1–10, no comebacks
Postseason Record: NA
Relative Rating: 44%

Passing

Year	G	Comp./Att.	%	Yards	Y/Att.	TD	INT	Rating
1968	11	92/215	42.8	917	4.3	3	14	33.0
1969	3	24/52	46.2	365	7.0	1	6	36.6
1970	3	11/29	37.9	71	2.4	0	2	17.5
Total	17	127/296	42.9	1,353	4.6	4	22	30.4

Rushing

Year	Att.	Yards	Avg.	TD
1968	13	11	0.8	0
1969	6	14	2.3	0
1970	1	26	26.0	0
Total	20	51	2.6	0

Dan Darragh is quite possibly the worst quarterback to ever start 10 games in the NFL. That he lasted three seasons in Buffalo is simply unfathomable. As Darragh himself once said, "When I was there, we were abominable. We won eight games in three years." The man threw four touchdowns and 22 interceptions. He averaged 4.6 yards per pass. He completed 43 percent of his passes. His passer rating of 30.4 is just 44 percent of the league average during that time, the lowest relative rating of anyone. His passer rating would have been below the league average in 1937.

Darragh was a three-year starter for coach Marv Levy at William & Mary and went from being a 13th-round draft pick to starting the season opener in his rookie year. In 1968, the Bills had one of the most extraordinary quarterbacking disasters in history. Starter Jack Kemp was injured in August when coach Joel Collier ordered a "get tough" scrimmage after he was dissatisfied with his team's effort—Collier was fired two games into the season. Backup Tom Flores was suffering from a sore arm and would ultimately appear in just one game during the season. That left Darragh as the next man up, and Dan started six of the first seven games. The only victory of his three-year career came when the Bills beat the Super Bowl–bound Jets on three interceptions returned for touchdowns against Joe Namath. After Tom Flores tried to start in Week 6, Darragh was back in Week 7 but sprained his ankle and hurt his arm. Kay Stephenson started the next three games and then broke his collarbone, leading to Dan's return in Week 11, when he suffered cracked ribs and was done for the year, leaving the quarterbacking to emergency QB Ed Rutkowski. In four of Darragh's seven starts he threw for fewer than 100 yards and never exceeded 160 yards passing.

The Bills brought Dan back for three starts in 1969 before he separated his shoulder. In his final season, Darragh started the first two games of the year before yielding to rookie Dennis Shaw and getting on with his life as an attorney.

Cotton Davidson **QPR** 5.0

Height: 6'1" **Weight:** 182 lbs. **Birthdate:** 11/30/1931
College: Baylor **Draft:** Baltimore Colts 1954-1st
1954, 1957 Baltimore Colts; 1958–59 CFL; 1960–62 Dallas Texans; 1962–66, 1968 Oakland Raiders
Regular Season Record: 20–33–1, 3 comebacks
Postseason Record: NA
Relative Rating: 90%

Passing

Year	G	Comp./Att.	%	Yards	Y/Att.	TD	INT	Rating
1954	12	28/64	43.8	309	4.8	0	5	26.1
1957	12	0/2	0.0	0	0.0	0	1	0.0
1960	14	179/379	47.2	2,474	6.5	15	16	64.2
1961	14	151/330	45.8	2,445	7.4	17	23	59.2
1962	14	119/321	37.1	1,977	6.2	7	23	36.1
1963	14	77/194	39.7	1,276	6.6	11	10	60.0
1964	14	155/320	48.4	2,497	7.8	21	19	72.1
1965	2	1/1	100.0	8	8.0	0	0	100
1966	14	59/139	42.4	770	5.5	2	11	32.4
1968	1	1/2	50.0	4	2.0	0	0	56.2
Total	**111**	**770/1,752**	**43.9**	**11,760**	**6.7**	**73**	**108**	**54.9**

Rushing

Year	Att.	Yards	Avg.	TD
1954	11	31	2.8	0
1960	14	36	2.6	1
1961	21	123	5.9	1
1962	25	54	2.2	3
1963	23	133	5.8	4
1964	29	167	5.8	2
1966	6	-11	-1.8	0
Total	**129**	**533**	**4.1**	**11**

Cotton Davidson was the No. 1 draft pick of the Baltimore Colts in 1954 but threw only 64 passes for the Colts before going into the service for two years. By the time he came out in 1957, the Colts had drafted George Shaw with the first pick of 1955, and Shaw had lost his job to a young unknown, Johnny Unitas. Davidson stuck with Baltimore in 1957 as the punter but tried his lot with Calgary in the CFL the following season.

When the American Football League began in 1960, Cotton was signed by Hank Stram to direct the Dallas Texans offense. Davidson was skinny and elusive; he was a good scrambler who threw a hard pass and a good deep ball. His 15.3 yards per completion average is sixth of all time among quarterbacks who threw at least 1,000 passes. Inaccuracy and inconsistency were his big flaws. Cotton started for the Texans for two years and even was the MVP of the 1961 AFL All-Star Game. His most memorable moment was the "12th Man" incident in a game in Boston in 1961. Trailing 28–21, Davidson drove the Texans to the Patriot 11 with just seconds left and fans pouring onto the field. Chased by Larry Eisenhauer, Davidson tried to hit Chris Burford in the middle of the end zone, but the ball bounced away incomplete. When Stram reviewed the game film, he noticed that a fan in a raincoat had wandered into the end zone on that last play and knocked the ball away before disappearing into the crowd undetected by the referees.

When Len Dawson joined Dallas in 1962, Cotton was traded to Oakland for a No. 1 pick that turned out to be Buck Buchanan. Cotton completed barely more than a third of his passes for the 1–13 Raiders in 1962 but had better fortune when Al Davis took over as coach in 1963. In the 1963 and 1964 seasons, Davidson shared the quarterbacking with Tom Flores and was used to his best advantage. In those two years, Cotton threw for more than 3,700 yards and 32 touchdowns. He missed 1965 with a shoulder problem, returned as a backup in 1966, and was joined on the bench by George Blanda in 1967. In 1968, Oakland owner Wayne Valley said of his backups, "We're the only club in pro football with two quarterbacks old enough to run for President." Cotton retired at the end of 1968 and later coached at his alma mater, Baylor.

Bob Davis

QPR 0.5

Height: 6'2" **Weight:** 205 lbs. **Birthdate:** 9/15/1945
College: Virginia **Draft:** Houston Oilers 1967-2nd
1967–69 Houston Oilers; 1970–72 New York Jets; 1973 New Orleans Saints
Regular Season Record: 6-7-1, 1 comeback
Postseason Record: NA
Relative Rating: 64%

Passing

Year	G	Comp./Att.	%	Yards	Y/Att.	TD	INT	Rating
1967	2	9/19	47.4	71	3.7	0	2	17.5
1968	6	33/86	38.4	441	5.1	0	6	26.4
1969	2	25/42	59.5	223	5.3	2	4	50.1
1970	1	6.17	35.3	66	3.9	0	0	47.7
1971	13	49/121	40.5	624	5.2	10	8	57.3
1972	14	10/22	45.5	114	5.2	2	1	72.9
1973	2	5/17	29.4	14	0.8	0	2	0.0
Total	40	137/324	42.3	1,553	4.8	14	23	42.1

Rushing

Year	Att.	Yards	Avg.	TD
1967	5	32	6.4	0
1968	15	91	6.1	1
1969	3	2	0.7	0
1970	2	11	5.5	0
1971	18	154	8.6	1
1972	6	32	5.3	0
1973	3	10	3.3	0
Total	52	332	6.4	2

Bob Davis was heavily recruited out of high school as a quarterback; he was from Neptune, New Jersey, and ultimately chose to go to Virginia. On the final play of the last game of his senior year, Davis tore his MCL but still was the fourth quarterback selected after first-rounders Steve Spurrier, Bob Griese, and Don Horn. Davis spent three seasons in Houston as Pete Beathard's backup, but the Oilers cut their ties to both quarterbacks in 1970. Bob got a tryout with the Jets, but because the Mets were playing at Shea that day, the audition was held at Rikers Island Prison in front of 7,000 prisoners. Davis impressed the inmates and coach Weeb Ewbank and was signed.

Davis stayed with the Jets for three years and got a chance to start seven games in 1971 when both Joe Namath and Al Woodall went down to injuries. The Jets won three of the seven. Davis did manage to throw more touchdowns than interceptions, but he was a game manager at best, averaging fewer than 5 yards per pass for his career. After one final season backing up Archie Manning in New Orleans, Bob signed on with the WFL and surprisingly accumulated the most passing yards in that league's one and a half seasons before it folded, 4,193 yards with 28 touchdowns and 35 interceptions.

Len Dawson

QPR 10.0

Height: 6'0" **Weight:** 190 lbs. **Birthdate:** 6/20/1935
College: Purdue **Draft:** Pittsburgh 1957-1st
1957–59 Pittsburgh Steelers; 1960–61 Cleveland Browns; 1962–75 Dallas Texans/Kansas City Chiefs
Regular Season Record: 94–57–8, 17 comebacks
Postseason Record: 5–3, 2 comebacks
Relative Rating: 129%

Passing

Year	G	Comp./Att.	%	Yards	Y/Att.	TD	INT	Rating
1957	3	2/4	50.0	25	6.3	0	0	69.8
1958	4	1/6	16.7	11	1.8	0	2	0.0
1959	12	3/7	42.9	60	8.6	1	0	113.1
1960	2	8/13	61.5	23	1.8	0	0	65.9
1961	7	7/15	46.7	85	5.7	1	3	47.2
1962	14	189/310	61.0	2,759	8.9	29	17	98.3
1963	14	190/352	54.0	2,389	6.8	26	19	77.5
1964	14	199/354	56.2	2,879	8.1	30	18	89.9
1965	14	163/305	53.4	2,262	7.4	21	14	81.3
1966	14	159/284	56.0	2,527	8.9	26	10	101.7
1967	14	206/357	57.7	2,651	7.4	24	17	83.7
1968	14	131/224	58.5	2,109	9.4	17	9	98.6
1969	9	98/166	59.0	1,323	8.0	9	13	69.9
1970	14	141/262	53.8	1,876	7.2	13	14	71.0
1971	14	167/301	55.5	2,504	8.3	15	13	81.6
1972	14	175/305	57.4	1,835	6.0	13	12	72.8
1973	8	66/101	65.3	725	7.2	2	5	72.4
1974	14	138/235	58.7	1,573	6.7	7	13	65.8
1975	12	93/140	66.4	1,095	7.8	5	4	90.0
Total	211	2,136/3,741	57.1	28,711	7.7	239	183	82.6
PS:	8	107/188	56.9	1,497	8.0	7	8	77.4

Rushing

Year	Att.	Yards	Avg.	TD
1957	3	31	10.3	0
1958	2	-1	-0.5	0
1959	4	20	5.0	0
1960	1	0	0.0	0
1961	1	-10	-10.0	0
1962	38	252	6.6	3
1963	37	272	7.4	2
1964	40	89	2.2	2
1965	43	142	3.3	2
1966	24	167	7.0	0
1967	20	68	3.4	0
1968	20	40	2.0	0
1969	1	3	3.0	0
1970	11	46	4.2	0
1971	12	24	2.0	0
1972	15	75	5.0	0
1973	6	40	6.7	0
1974	11	28	2.5	0
1975	5	7	1.4	0
Total	294	1,293	4.4	9
PS:	21	103	4.9	0

Len Dawson illustrates the role of fortune in the lives of football players. Cleveland's Paul Brown hoped to draft the Purdue star in the first round in 1957 but was beaten to it by the Steelers. A disappointed Brown then had to settle for fullback Jim Brown. Dawson instead signed with the Steelers and spent three seasons watching first Earl Morrall then Bobby Layne play quarterback. Cleveland packaged Preston Carpenter and Junior Wren to finally obtain Dawson in 1960, but the rusty Dawson spent two more seasons on the bench watching Milt Plum play quarterback. In 1962, Dawson asked Paul Brown for his release and signed with the Dallas Texans of the AFL, who were coached

Len Dawson in the Clutch: In the third quarter of the final AFL Championship Game in 1969, the Raiders had the Chiefs pinned at the 2 and facing a second and 14 in a 7–7 game. Dawson dropped back to pass and threaded a sideline pass to Otis Taylor between defenders Willie Brown and George Atkinson at the Kansas City 37 for a big first down. Dawson then led the Chiefs on a back-breaking 94-yard touchdown drive that helped propel Kansas City to the Super Bowl.

The surprisingly elusive Len Dawson scampers away from the Raiders pass rush in 1966.

Len Dawson's Signature Play: In Super Bowl IV, Dawson hit Otis Taylor for a 5-yard sideline pattern on the first drive of the second half. Taylor stiff-armed Earsel Mackbee and raced for a 46-yard touchdown that put the Chiefs up 23–7.

Len Dawson's Five Highest Honors

5. 1973 NFL Man of the Year (now called the Walter Payton Award)
4. Selected to seven All-Star Games
3. Six-time All-Pro and consensus All-Pro twice
2. Super Bowl IV MVP
1. Elected to the Pro Football Hall of Fame in 1987

The Five Quarterbacks Most Similar to Len Dawson

5. Neil O'Donnell
4. Ken O'Brien
3. Rich Gannon
2. Bob Griese
1. Bart Starr

Len Dawson's Five Top Touchdown Targets

5. Abner Haynes, 11 TDs
4. Frank Jackson, 18 TDs
3. Fred Arbanas, 33 TDs
2. Chris Burford, 43 TDs
1. Otis Taylor, 46 TDs

Len Dawson's Five Toughest Rivals

5. Dawson was 11–3 against the Oilers in the regular season and 1–0 in the playoffs.
4. Dawson was 4–8–1 against the Bills in the regular season and 1–0 in the playoffs.
3. Dawson was 20–2 against the Broncos.
2. Dawson was 12–11–1 against the Chargers.
1. Dawson was 10–13–2 against the Raiders in the regular season and 1–1 in the playoffs.

Five Random Len Dawson Statistics

5. Dawson played for four head coaches.
4. Dawson's Chiefs outscored the league average by 11 percent.
3. Dawson threw for five touchdowns against the Patriots on September 25, 1966, and against Miami on October 8, 1967, while throwing for six against Denver on November 1, 1964.
2. Dawson threw for more than 300 yards nine times and more than 400 on November 1, 1964, against Denver.
1. Dawson led the league in completion percentage six times, touchdown passes four times, yards per attempts three times, and passer rating six times.

by Hank Stram, Len's backfield coach from college.

In five years, Dawson had thrown just 45 passes and started just two games. When Len reported to Dallas, Stram was shocked at how far his skills had deteriorated and worked intensively with him throughout training camp. By the start of the season, Lenny the Cool was back. Dawson stormed through the AFL in 1962, leading the league in completion percentage, yards per pass, and touchdown passes as the Texans won the league title. The next year the Texans moved to Kansas City and became the Chiefs but slipped in the standings. By 1966, the Chiefs were back on top, as Dawson led them to a second AFL title and the very first Super Bowl against the Green Bay Packers. The match with the Packers was appropriate because Dawson and Bart Starr were very similar types of quarterbacks. Both were smart, quiet, poised, competitive leaders who excelled at reading defenses and clever play calling. Both were surprisingly mobile and the most accurate passers in their leagues. Both had slight builds and were given to missing a game or two to injury each year. And both finished with 94 wins in their careers—Dawson with a .616 winning percentage and Starr with .618.

The Packers were a superior team and won Super Bowl I handily, but three years later the Chiefs had improved considerably as Dawson led them to the final AFL championship and a trip to Super Bowl IV to meet the favored Vikings. During the week leading up to the game, Lenny had to deal with erroneous reports that linked him to a

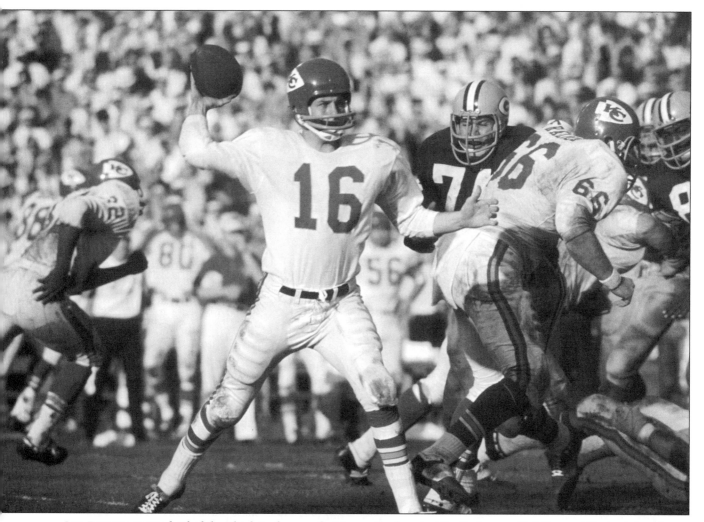

Len Dawson quarterbacked the Chiefs in the very first Super Bowl against the Packers and led Kansas City to victory three years later in the last Super Bowl before the NFL/AFL merger.

known gambler also named Dawson. In the game he directed a masterful attack from the Chiefs' moving pocket to pick apart the vaunted Vikings. This Super Bowl victory proved that the Jets' upset of the Colts the previous year was no fluke, and the two leagues merged as equals.

Dawson played another six seasons and solidified his case for the Hall of Fame. Three times he led the league in yards per pass, four times in touchdown passes, and six times in completion percentage and passer rating. Three times he led all AFL quarterbacks in yards rushing, and his 12 fourth-quarter comebacks in the 1960s were the best in the American Football League. If he had walked away in 1962 or if Stram hadn't been around to resuscitate his career, Dawson would be remembered today as just another first-round bust. Both Dawson and pro football are fortunate that Lenny finally got the chance to show what a great quarterback he was.

Steve DeBerg

QPR 7.0

Height: 6'3" **Weight:** 210 lbs. **Birthdate:** 1/19/1954
College: San Jose State **Draft:** Dallas 1977-10th
1978–80 San Francisco 49ers; 1981–83 Denver Broncos; 1984–87, 1992–93 Tampa Bay Bucs; 1988–91 Kansas City Chiefs; 1993 Miami Dolphins; 1998 Atlanta Falcons
Regular Season Record: 53–86–1, 22 comebacks
Postseason Record: 1–3, no comebacks
Relative Rating: 99%

Passing

Year	G	Comp./Att.	%	Yards	Y/Att.	TD	INT	Rating
1978	12	137/302	45.4	1,570	5.2	8	22	40
1979	16	347/578	60.0	3,652	6.3	17	21	73.1
1980	11	186/321	57.9	1,998	6.2	12	17	66.7
1981	14	64/108	59.3	797	7.4	6	6	77.6
1982	9	131/223	58.7	1,405	6.3	7	11	67.2
1983	10	119/215	55.3	1,617	7.5	9	7	79.9
1984	16	308/509	60.5	3,554	7.0	19	18	79.3
1985	11	197/370	53.2	2,488	6.7	19	18	71.3
1986	16	50/96	52.1	610	6.4	5	12	49.7
1987	12	159/275	57.8	1,891	6.9	14	7	85.3
1988	13	224/414	54.1	2,935	7.1	16	16	73.5
1989	12	196/324	60.5	2,529	7.8	11	16	75.8
1990	16	258/444	58.1	3,444	7.8	23	4	96.3
1991	16	256/434	59.0	2,965	6.8	17	14	79.3
1992	6	76/125	60.8	710	5.7	3	4	71.1
1993	8	136/227	59.9	1,707	7.5	7	10	75.3
1998	8	30/59	50.8	369	6.3	3	1	80.4
Total	206	2,874/5,024	57.2	34,241	6.8	196	204	74.2
PS:	4	45/72	62.5	511	7.1	3	3	80.3

Rushing

Years	Att.	Yards	Avg.	TD
1978	15	20	1.3	1
1979	17	10	0.6	0
1980	6	4	0.7	0
1981	9	40	4.4	0
1982	8	27	3.4	1
1983	13	28	2.2	1
1984	28	59	2.1	2
1985	9	28	3.1	0
1986	2	1	0.5	1
1987	8	-8	-1.0	0
1988	18	30	1.7	1
1989	14	-8	-0.6	0
1990	21	-5	-0.2	0
1991	21	-15	-0.7	0
1992	3	3	1.0	0
1993	4	-4	-1.0	0
1998	8	-10	-1.3	0
Total	204	206	1.0	7
PS:	3	-5	-1.7	0

In the early days of Steve DeBerg's long, strange, and mediocre career, coach Bill Walsh said of the journeyman quarterback, "Steve is one of the best young quarterbacks in the league. He is very accurate on short passes and has an outstanding grasp of the pro game." Within a couple of years, though, Walsh was complaining that DeBerg was "just good enough to get you beat." That would be the mantra of Steve's lengthy career under 10 head coaches.

DeBerg was drafted in the 10th round by Dallas in 1977 but was cut. The following season, he was the primary starter on the 2–14 San Francisco 49ers and repeated that trick in Walsh's first season of 1979. By 1980, Steve had lost his job for the first time to a young future Hall of Famer, Joe Montana. The 49ers then sent DeBerg to the Broncos for a fourth-round pick in 1981. For two years, Steve battled the ancient Craig Morton for the starting job, and then Denver traded for the rights to rookie John Elway in 1983. Once again, it was only a matter of time, and Bronco fans booed Steve when he played during the preseason because he was not Elway. In 1985, Denver sent DeBerg to Tampa for two draft picks so he could compete with rookie Steve Young, and he even managed to hold the raw Young at bay until 1987. That year, Young was sent to San Francisco, and Tampa drafted Heisman

TOP 10

Quarterback/Coach Pairs

10. Otto Graham/Paul Brown, 10 years, 124 starts
9. Donovan McNabb/Andy Reid, 10 years, 128 starts
8. Roger Staubach/Tom Landry, 11 years, 114 starts
7. Bob Griese/Don Shula, 11 years, 119 starts
6. Steve McNair/Jeff Fisher, 11 years, 131 starts
5. Jim Kelly/Marv Levy, 11 years, 153 starts
4. Bobby Layne/Buddy Parker, 12 years, 127 starts
3. Len Dawson/Hank Stram, 13 years, 157 starts
2. Dan Marino/Don Shula, 13 years, 184 starts
1. Terry Bradshaw/Chuck Noll, 14 years, 158 starts

Although Steve DeBerg played for six different teams in his 17-year career, he spent the longest time in Tampa Bay, where he played for six seasons.

DeBerg categorized himself to *Sports Illustrated*, "I have average talent, but I've made myself better than 10,000 quarterbacks who had more talent because they weren't as committed as I was." It's a wonder how the weight room and film room can extend a career in the NFL.

Al Dekdebrun

QPR 3.0

Height: 5'11"   **Weight:** 185 lbs.   **Birthdate:** 5/11/1921
College: Cornell   **Draft:** Boston Yanks 1946-9th
1946 Buffalo Bisons; 1947 Chicago Rockets; 1948 New York Yankees; 1948 Boston Yanks; 1949–53 CFL
Regular Season Record: 4–9 est., 1 comeback
Postseason Record: NA
Relative Rating: 102%

Passing

Year	G	Comp./Att.	%	Yards	Y/Att.	TD	INT	Rating
1946	14	28/66	42.4	517	7.8	8	8	70.1
1947	12	45/75	60.0	556	7.4	5	7	66.3
1948	6	11/23	47.8	151	6.6	0	3	29.7
Total	36	84/164	51.2	1,224	7.5	13	18	62.7

Rushing

Year	Att.	Yards	Avg.	TD
1946	25	-55	-2.2	0
1947	20	71	3.6	0
1948	9	38	4.2	0
Total	54	54	1.0	1

Trophy winner Vinny Testaverde. A year later, the job was Vinny's, and Steve was sent to Kansas City for safety Mark Robinson and a draft pick. There he competed with fellow journeyman Bill Kenney.

When Marty Schottenheimer arrived in 1989, though, he found the master ball handler DeBerg to be perfect for the play-action Marty Ball offense, and Steve had his best years as a Chief. In 1990, he threw for 23 touchdowns and just four interceptions, both personal bests. However, he could not take the Chiefs to the Super Bowl. Steve was released in 1992 to make way for Dave Krieg and returned to the Bucs. After a year and a half in Tampa and a few games in Miami replacing an injured Dan Marino, DeBerg called it quits in 1993 at age 39. As a fitting coda to his career, he returned in 1998 when Chris Chandler was hurt during the Falcons' Super Bowl season to become the oldest quarterback to start a game at 44 and the oldest player to appear on a Super Bowl roster at 45.

Cornell's captain, Al Dekdebrun, led the nation in passing yards in 1945 but was declared ineligible for his senior season because he had played four minutes in a game for Columbia in 1942 although never enrolled there as a student. As a senior, Dekdebrun starred in the 1945 East-West Shrine Game, scoring the tying touchdown on a 42-yard run, and was named player of the game. In 1946, Buffalo coach Red Dawson signed Al as the Bisons' first player for their inaugural season in the All-America Football Conference. Dekdebrun played for three losing teams in three years in the AAFC before throwing three passes in 1948 for the NFL's Boston Yanks, which originally had drafted him two years before.

The slightly built Dekdebrun continued his career in Canada for Hamilton, Toronto, and

Montreal. In 1950, Al helped lead Toronto to the Grey Cup championship on a muddy field that turned the game into a sloppy mess. Using his Ivy League intelligence, he taped thumbtacks to his fingers to improve his grip on the slippery ball and scored the only touchdown in the game. Dekdebrun later served two terms as mayor in Amherst, New York.

Jake Delhomme  QPR 8.0

Height: 6'2" **Weight:** 215 lbs. **Birthdate:** 1/10/1975
College: Louisiana-Lafayette **Draft:** Free Agent
1999, 2002 New Orleans Saints; 2003–08 Carolina Panthers
Regular Season Record: 50–31, 19 comebacks
Postseason Record: 4–3, 1 comeback
Relative Rating: 106%

Passing

Year	G	Comp./Att.	%	Yards	Y/Att.	TD	INT	Rating
1999	2	42/76	55.3	521	6.9	3	5	62.4
2002	4	8/10	80.0	113	11.3	0	0	113.7
2003	16	266/449	59.2	3,219	7.2	19	16	80.6
2004	16	310/533	58.2	3,886	7.3	29	15	87.3
2005	16	262/435	60.2	3,421	7.9	24	16	88.1
2006	13	263/431	61.0	2,805	6.5	17	11	82.6
2007	3	55/86	64.0	624	7.3	8	1	111.8
2008	16	246/414	59.4	3,288	7.9	15	12	84.7
Total	**86**	**1,452/2,434**	**59.7**	**17,877**	**7.3**	**115**	**76**	**85.1**
PS:	8	130/226	57.5	1,847	8.2	12	10	83.3

Rushing

Year	Att.	Yards	Avg.	TD
1999	11	72	6.5	2
2002	4	-2	-0.5	0
2003	42	39	0.9	1
2004	25	71	2.8	1
2005	24	31	1.3	1
2006	18	12	0.7	0
2007	6	26	4.3	0
2008	20	21	1.1	2
Total	**150**	**270**	**1.8**	**7**
PS:	0	0	0.0	0

Jake Delhomme has been a surprisingly effective quarterback in the NFL, particularly in the closing minutes of games. More than a third of his wins were engineered by fourth-quarter comebacks. In fact, Jake set a league record with eight fourth-quarter game-winning drives in 2003 if you include his one postseason comeback that year. He is creative on the run and has a quick release. His spirals aren't always perfect, but as his lead receiver Steve Smith once said, "They get there."

Delhomme's career took the same wobbly route as his passes. As a high school senior, he was a skinny passing star in Lafayette, Louisiana, who was overshadowed in the state by high school juniors Peyton Manning and Josh Booty. Jake stayed home at Southwestern Louisiana for college and threw for more than 9,000 yards as a four-year starter. However, he was neither invited to the NFL Combine nor drafted. The Saints signed the local prospect as a free agent, and Jake spent two seasons on the practice squad and two off-seasons playing in NFL's development league in Europe. In Europe, he spent one season backing up Kurt Warner and a second sharing the quarterbacking with Cal's Pat Barnes. By 1999, Delhomme worked his way up to third string but got into just six games in four years, going 1–1 as a starter. Frustrated behind the inconsistent Aaron Brooks, Delhomme left New Orleans in 2003 as free agent. Although courted by the Cowboys, Jake signed a more lucrative deal with Carolina, which then went with veteran journeyman Rodney Peete in their opening game. However, Delhomme relieved Peete and won that game on a touchdown pass to Ricky Proehl with 16 seconds left. He has been the Panthers' starter ever since, with the high point coming in Super Bowl XXXVIII when he led three fourth-quarter scoring drives to overcome an 11-point deficit. Unfortunately, Tom Brady and the Patriots had the last word in that game, but Delhomme proved himself a fearless leader and a hero to his fellow Cajuns back home in Louisiana.

Even after his Super Bowl heroics, Delhomme remained a humble guy, all too aware of who he is and how hard he has had to work to succeed. As he told *Sports Illustrated* the next season, "I know the kind of player I am. I'm not the biggest guy or the fastest. I don't have the best arm. I'm lucky to be on this team." Jake underwent Tommy John surgery with a ligament from his hamstring used to repair his right elbow in 2007. Delhomme came back in

2008 to lead the Panthers to the second seed in the playoffs before throwing five interceptions in a divisional-round loss to the Cardinals on his 34th birthday. He will have to prove himself all over again in 2009.

Ty Detmer

 QPR 5.5

Height: 6'0" **Weight:** 190 lbs. **Birthdate:** 10/30/1967
College: BYU   **Draft:** Green Bay 1992-9th
1993, 1995 Green Bay Packers; 1996–97 Philadelphia Eagles; 1998 San Francisco 49ers; 1999 Cleveland Browns; 2001, 2003 Detroit Lions
Regular Season Record: 11–14, 5 comebacks
Postseason Record: 0–1, no comebacks
Relative Rating: 96%

Passing:

Year	G	Comp./Att.	%	Yards	Y/Att.	TD	INT	Rating
1993	3	3/5	60.0	26	5.2	0	0	73.7
1995	4	8/16	50.0	81	5.1	1	1	59.6
1996	13	238/401	59.4	2,911	7.3	15	13	80.8
1997	8	134/244	54.9	1,567	6.4	7	6	73.9
1998	16	24/38	63.2	312	8.2	4	3	91.1
1999	5	47/91	51.6	548	6.0	4	2	75.7
2001	4	92/151	60.9	906	6.0	3	10	56.9
2003	1	0/0	0.0	0	0.0	0	0	0.0
Total	54	546/946	57.7	6,531	36.7	34	35	74.7
PS:	1	14/21	66.7	148	7.0	0	2	47.4

Rushing

Year	Att.	Yards	Avg.	TD
1993	1	-2	-2.0	0
1995	3	3	1.0	0
1996	31	59	1.9	1
1997	14	46	3.3	1
1998	8	7	0.9	0
1999	6	38	6.3	1
2001	9	26	2.9	0
Total	72	177	2.5	3
PS:	0	0	0.0	0

Ty Detmer was Texas Player of the Year for his senior year of high school in San Antonio, where his father Sonny was his coach, but he was so frail looking that there was no major push to recruit him. Brigham Young coach La Vell Edwards often told the story that when Detmer visited Provo that Edwards expected to see John Elway, when "in walks Pee-wee Herman." At BYU, though, Ty racked up an NCAA record 15,031 yards passing with 121 TD passes in three and a half years. He threw at least one touchdown pass in 35 consecutive games at BYU and won the Heisman Trophy as a junior and the Davey O'Brien Award for the nation's top college quarterback as both a junior and senior.

What NFL scouts saw was a small, fragile player who was suspect as both a Heisman winner and a BYU quarterback. Detmer was not drafted until the ninth round by Green Bay. In four years backing up Brett Favre in Green Bay, Ty got into only eight games, but the Eagles signed him in 1996 as someone who was familiar with coordinator Jon Gruden's offense. Early in the 1996 season, Eagles starter Rodney Peete hurt his knee, and Detmer finally got his chance. The Eagles won Ty's first four starts, but in the second half of the year both Detmer and the Eagles were exposed a bit. The team made the playoffs but played poorly, being shut out by San Francisco in a first-round game. The next year, Detmer just barely won the starting job in training camp and was shuffled in and out of the lineup all season.

At the end of the season, Detmer left Philadelphia to back up Steve Young in San Francisco. After just one year, it was on to the expansion Cleveland Browns where he prepped vaunted rookie Tim Couch for a year. Ty next spent three years in Detroit where he threw seven interceptions in his first start and mentored another vaunted rookie, Joey Harrington, before finishing his career as a third stringer in Atlanta. Despite being too short to see, too slight to endure, and too weak-armed to throw, his pro career lasted more than 10 years. Detmer was smart, competitive, and mobile. He could manage a game plan and was a nice touch passer. He was an ideal NFL backup.

Lynn Dickey

QPR 7.0

Height: 6'3" **Weight:** 214 lbs. **Birthdate:** 10/19/1949
College: Kansas State **Draft:** Houston Oilers 1971-3rd
**1971, 1973–75 Houston Oilers; 1976–77, 1979–85
Green Bay Packers**
Regular Season Record: 45–63–3, 19 comebacks
Postseason Record: 1–1, no comebacks
Relative Rating: 102%

Passing

Year	G	Comp./Att.	%	Yards	Y/Att.	TD	INT	Rating
1971	7	19/57	33.3	315	5.5	0	9	13.3
1973	12	71/120	59.2	888	7.4	6	10	64.2
1974	14	63/113	55.8	704	6.2	2	8	50.9
1975	14	2/4	50.0	46	11.5	0	1	52.1
1976	10	115/243	47.3	1,465	6.0	7	14	52.2
1977	9	113/220	51.4	1,346	6.1	5	14	51.4
1979	5	60/119	50.4	787	6.6	5	4	71.7
1980	16	278/478	58.2	3,529	7.4	15	25	70.0
1981	13	204/354	57.6	2,593	7.3	17	15	79.0
1982	9	124/218	56.9	1,790	8.2	12	14	75.3
1983	16	289/484	59.7	4,458	9.2	32	29	87.3
1984	15	237/401	59.1	3,195	8.0	25	19	85.6
1985	12	172/314	54.8	2,206	7.0	15	17	70.4
Total	**152**	**1,747/3,125**	**55.9**	**23,322**	**7.5**	**141**	**179**	**70.9**
PS:	2	36/59	61.0	592	10.0	5	3	101.8

Rushing

Year	Att.	Yards	Avg.	TD
1971	1	4	4.0	0
1973	6	9	1.5	0
1974	3	7	2.3	0
1975	1	3	3.0	0
1976	11	19	1.7	1
1977	5	24	4.8	0
1979	5	13	2.6	0
1980	19	11	0.6	1
1981	19	6	0.3	0
1982	13	19	1.5	0
1983	21	12	0.6	3
1984	18	6	0.3	3
1985	18	-12	-0.7	1
Total	**140**	**121**	**0.9**	**9**
PS:	2	0	0.0	0

Lynn Dickey had to overcome bad luck of biblical proportions and devastating injuries to establish himself as an NFL quarterback. In the sterling 1971 NFL draft, Jim Plunkett, Archie Manning, and Dan Pastorini were all picked in the first round; Dickey and Ken Anderson went in the third; and Joe Theismann went in round four. Dickey and Pastorini were both drafted by the Oilers, though. Dan won the starting job as a rookie, but there was an open competition the next year when Lynn both dislocated and broke his left hip in an exhibition game. After a year of rehabilitation, he served as a spot starter in 1973 and 1974 but could not win the top job. Finally in 1976, Green Bay traded for Dickey to be their starter, but Lynn went down with a shoulder separation in the 10th game. The next year, Lynn had his leg so badly broken on the last play of the ninth game that he did not return until late in the 1979 season, missing all of 1978.

By the start of the 1980 season, Dickey had endured the football trials of Job. He had missed 30 of 60 games due to injury in his four years in Green Bay and 53 games altogether in his nine-year career. In that choppy span, he had thrown 25 touchdowns and 60 interceptions. By contrast, Lynn would throw for 116 touchdowns and 119 interceptions in the remaining six years of his career. He was a pure passer who was very accurate throwing both short and long, although he could not run at all and was prone to interceptions. His best year was 1983, with 4,458 passing yards and a league-leading 32 touchdown passes.

The most memorable game of his career was on Monday night, October 17, 1983, against the defending champion Washington Redskins. That night, the two teams scored 95 points and ran up 1,025 yards of offense—552 for Washington, who had the ball for 39 minutes, and 473 for Green Bay, who held the ball for only 21 minutes. Redskin quarterback Joe Theismann threw for 398 yards and two scores, while Dickey completed 22 of 30 for 387 yards and three touchdowns. When the Redskins' reliable Mark Moseley lined up for a 39-yard field goal on the last play of the game with the Skins trailing 48–47, Dickey said to Packers kicker Jan Stenerud, "Can you believe we're going to lose this game?" But Moseley missed, and the Packers won.

Dickey's final game was the Snow Bowl against Tampa in 1985 before only 19,000 fans at Lambeau. Playing in a blizzard that dumped more than a foot of snow in Green Bay that day, Dickey completed 22 of 36 passes for 299 yards in a 21–0 win over the Bucs. The next week, Lynn hurt himself on a weight-training machine and never played again. Lynn Dickey was the epitome of toughness, coming back time after time from serious injury and playing stoically through chronic pain.

Trent Dilfer

QPR **6.5**

Height: 6'4" **Weight:** 225 lbs. **Birthdate:** 3/13/1972
College: Fresno State **Draft:** Tampa 1994-1st
1994–99 Tampa Bay Bucs; 2000 Baltimore Ravens;
2001–04 Seattle Seahawks; 2005 Cleveland Browns;
2007 San Francisco 49ers
Regular Season Record: 58–55, 14 comeback
Postseason Record: 5–1, no comebacks
Relative Rating: 89%

Passing

Year	G	Comp./Att.	%	Yards	Y/Att.	TD	INT	Rating
1994	5	38/82	46.3	433	5.3	1	6	36.3
1995	16	224/415	54.0	2,774	6.7	4	18	60.1
1996	16	267/482	55.4	2,859	5.9	12	19	64.8
1997	16	217/386	56.2	2,555	6.6	21	11	82.8
1998	16	225/429	52.4	2,729	6.4	21	15	74.0
1999	10	146/244	59.8	1,619	6.6	11	11	75.8
2000	11	134/226	59.3	1,502	6.6	12	11	76.6
2001	6	73/122	59.8	1,014	8.3	7	4	92.0
2002	6	94/168	56.0	1,182	7.0	4	6	71.1
2003	5	4/8	50.0	31	3.9	1	1	59.9
2004	5	25/58	43.1	333	5.7	1	3	46.1
2005	11	199/333	59.8	2,321	7.0	11	12	76.9
2007	7	113/219	51.6	1,166	5.3	7	12	55.1
Total	130	1,759/3,172	55.5	20,158	6.5	113	1129	70.2
PS:	6	59/135	43.7	971	7.2	4	4	66.0

TOP 10
Undrafted Free-Agent Quarterbacks

10. Gary Danielson
9. Jim Zorn
8. Bobby Hebert
7. Jake Delhomme
6. Jim Hart
5. Tommy Thompson
4. Jeff Garcia
3. Dave Krieg
2. Kurt Warner
1. Warren Moon

Rushing

Year	Att.	Yards	Avg.	TD
1994	2	27	13.5	0
1995	23	115	5.0	2
1996	32	124	3.9	0
1997	33	99	3.0	1
1998	40	141	3.5	2
1999	35	144	4.1	0
2000	20	75	3.8	0
2001	11	17	1.5	0
2002	10	27	2.7	0
2003	2	-1	-0.5	0
2004	10	14	1.4	0
2005	20	46	2.3	0
2007	10	25	2.5	0
Total	248	853	3.4	5
PS:	15	7	0.5	0

Although Trent Dilfer set an NCAA record by throwing 271 passes without an interception at Fresno State, he never displayed that cautiousness as a pro. In his first full season as a starter, he threw for just four touchdowns and 18 interceptions for Tampa in 1995. Two years after that, though, Dilfer threw for 21 touchdowns in his finest season passing. He made the Pro Bowl, and the Bucs made the playoffs. Two years later, he lost his job to rookie Shaun King and became a free agent.

By then it was clear that Dilfer had a strong arm but not a very accurate one, and he often made bad decisions by forcing passes, trying to make a big play. He signed with the Ravens as Tony Banks' backup in 2000 and at midseason took over a Baltimore offense that had not scored a touchdown in four games. The offense did not score again that first week and the team lost, but they would not lose another game the rest of the season. Under Dilfer's leadership, the Ravens scored enough points to support their defense and win the last seven games of the year. As a wild-card team, the Ravens went 4–0 in the postseason to win the Super Bowl. The key plays in the playoff run were Dilfer's 96-yard touchdown pass to Shannon Sharpe to beat Oakland in the conference championship and his 38-yard strike to Brandon Stokley in the Super Bowl win over New York.

Yet Dilfer became the first Super Bowl–winning quarterback to be released the following season as the Ravens chased after prettier passer Elvis Grbac.

Ravens defensive end Rob Burnett said at the time, "Did most of us want Trent back? Absolutely. In addition to being a winning quarterback, he's a first-class person who touched a lot of people in that locker room." Grbac turned out to be a one-year washout in Baltimore, while Dilfer signed on with Seattle to begin the second phase of his career as a mentor. With the Seahawks he battled with Matt Hasselbeck for the starting job while also helping Matt to develop as a quarterback. After that, he worked with Charlie Frye in Cleveland and Alex Smith in San Francisco.

What mattered to Dilfer was winning, and his 2000 season was the ultimate triumph of the game manager quarterback—don't turn the ball over, rely on the running game, and support the defense. For his efforts, he got something that Dan Marino, Dan Fouts, and Sonny Jurgensen all lack—a Super Bowl ring.

Steve Dils

QPR 4.0

Height: 6'1" **Weight:** 190 lbs. **Birthdate:** 12/8/1955
College; Stanford **Draft:** Minnesota 1979-4th
1979–84 Minnesota Vikings; 1984–87 Los Angeles Rams; 1988 Atlanta Falcons
Regular Season Record: 10–17, 4 comebacks
Postseason Record: NA
Relative Rating: 88%

Passing

Year	G	Comp./Att.	%	Yards	Y/Att.	TD	INT	Rating
1979	1	0/0	0	0	0.0	0	0	0.0
1980	16	32/51	62.7	352	6.9	3	0	102.7
1981	2	54/102	52.9	607	6.0	1	2	66.1
1982	9	11/26	42.3	68	2.6	0	0	49.8
1983	16	239/444	53.8	2,840	6.4	11	16	66.8
1984	10	4/7	57.1	44	6.3	1	1	75.9
1985	15	0/0	0	0	0.0	0	0	0.0
1986	15	59/129	45.7	693	5.4	4	4	60
1987	15	56/114	49.1	646	5.7	5	4	66.6
1988	7	49/99	49.5	566	5.7	2	5	52.8
Total	106	504/972	51.9	5,816	6.0	27	32	65.8

Rushing

Year	Att.	Yards	Avg.	TD
1980	3	26	8.7	0
1981	4	14	3.5	0
1982	1	5	5.0	0
1983	16	28	1.8	0
1985	2	-4	-2.0	0
1986	10	5	0.5	0
1987	7	-4	-0.6	0
1988	2	1	0.5	1
Total	45	171	1.6	1

Under Bill Walsh at Stanford, Steve Dils won an NCAA passing title and the Sammy Baugh Trophy as the best passer in college football. Upon Walsh's death in 2007, the modestly talented Dils remarked, "Before Bill arrived at Stanford, the odds of me playing pro football were slim. Because of him, I played 10 years. He changed the trajectory of my life."

Dils was primarily a backup quarterback in the NFL. His only extended series of starts came with Minnesota in 1983 when Tommy Kramer was lost for the year in the third game. Steve went 5–7 as a starter that year, but by the end of the year, he was being pushed by the young Wade Wilson. Steve was dealt to Los Angeles the following season for a low draft pick. The weak-armed Dils was not especially mobile and not especially accurate. He finished a lackluster career as a backup with the Rams and then the Falcons.

Glenn Dobbs

QPR 5.5

Height: 6'4" **Weight:** 210 lbs. **Birthdate:** 7/12/1920
College: Tulsa **Draft:** Chicago Cardinals 1943-1st
1946–47 Brooklyn Dodgers; 1947–49 Los Angeles Dons; 1951–54 CFL
Regular Season Record: 20–32–1 est., 4 comebacks
Postseason Record: NA
Relative Rating: 100%

Passing

Year	G	Comp./Att.	%	Yards	Y/Att.	TD	INT	Rating
1946	12	135/269	50.2	1,886	7.0	13	15	66.0
1947	11	61/143	42.7	762	5.3	7	8	52.8
1948	14	185/369	50.1	2,403	6.5	21	20	67.4
1949	12	65/153	42.5	825	5.4	4	9	44.2
Total	49	446/934	47.8	5,876	6.3	45	52	61.0

Rushing

Year	Att.	Yards	Avg.	TD
1946	95	208	2.2	4
1947	42	131	3.1	1
1948	91	539	5.9	4
1949	34	161	4.7	3
Total	262	1,039	4.0	12

Glenn Dobbs played very little quarterback in his career but was one of the best passers of his time, primarily as a single-wing tailback. The All-American led Tulsa to a 10–1 record as a senior and was the first pick of the Cardinals for 1943 but went into the air force instead. After the war, Dobbs signed with Brooklyn of the fledgling All-America Football Conference and was the MVP of the league in 1946. Because he was tall and thin and the league's top punter as well as a star passer, he was known as the AAFC's Sammy Baugh, although Glenn's 46.4 lifetime punting average bested Sammy's 44.9 by a yard and a half.

Brooklyn had financial problems, though, and made a three-way deal in 1947 that sent Dobbs to the Los Angeles Dons for $60,000 cash and the Chicago Rockets' Bob Hoernschemeyer, while the Rockets received Angelo Bertelli from the Dons. Unlike Brooklyn, the Dons were running the T formation, and Dobbs struggled to pick it up as all his passing numbers declined. Under new coach Jimmy Phelan in 1948, though, Dobbs was put back in the single-wing with a new wrinkle called the Phelan Spread, in which the other three backs were all spread on the wing to one side with only Dobbs in the backfield. He thrived in the new system, which also called on him to show his talent for running. In the four years of the AAFC, Dobbs gained more than 1,000 yards on the ground as well as nearly 6,000 through the air. He also returned kicks and punts, twice led the league in punting, and played defensive back.

Dobbs retired when the leagues merged but returned a year later to play in Canada. In his first season up north, he threw 28 touchdown passes for Saskatchewan and then was named player/coach. He returned home in 1955 as athletic director at Tulsa and served as football coach there from 1961 to 1968. As coach, Dobbs ran the most pass-oriented offense in the nation, relying on short, quick, timed patterns similar to what later became known as the West Coast offense. "We throw first, run second," Dobbs said. He added, "Defense is simply something you play when the offensive players need a rest."

Marty Domres

Height: 6'4" **Weight:** 220 lbs. **Birthdate:** 4/17/1947
College: Columbia **Draft:** San Diego 1969-1st
1969–71 San Diego Chargers; 1972–75 Baltimore Colts; 1976 San Francisco 49ers; 1977 New York Jets
Regular Season Record: 12–20, 1 comeback
Postseason Record: 0–0, no comebacks
Relative Rating: 83%

Passing

Year	G	Comp./Att.	%	Yards	Y/Att.	TD	INT	Rating
1969	10	47/112	42.0	631	5.6	2	10	29.3
1970	8	28/55	50.9	491	8.9	2	4	63.5
1971	4	7/12	58.3	97	8.1	1	3	72.6
1972	12	115/222	51.8	1,392	6.3	11	6	76.6
1973	11	93/191	48.7	1,153	6.0	9	13	55.2
1974	14	77/153	50.3	803	5.2	0	12	33.2
1975	14	8/10	80.0	123	12.3	1	0	151.2
1976	5	7/14	50.0	101	7.2	0	1	44.0
1977	12	17/40	42.5	113	2.8	1	1	47.9
Total	90	399/809	43.9	4,904	6.1	27	50	53.8
PS:	1	2/11	18.2	9	0.8	1	2	30.3

Rushing

Year	Att.	Yards	Avg.	TD
1969	19	145	7.6	4
1970	14	39	2.8	0
1971	1	0	0.0	0
1972	30	137	4.6	1
1973	32	126	3.9	2
1974	22	145	6.6	2
1975	4	46	11.5	1
1976	4	18	4.5	0
1977	4	23	5.8	0
Total	130	679	5.2	10
PS:	4	17	4.3	0

The mediocre skills of Marty Domres were responsible for getting two coaches fired, one for not playing him and a second for not benching him. Domres broke the passing records of Sid Luckman and Paul memoir, *Bump and Run: Days and Nights of a Rookie Quarterback.*

TOP 10
Quarterback Punters

10. Tom Tupa, 873 punts, 43.4 ave.
9. King Hill, 368 punts, 41.3 ave.
8. Danny White, 610 punts, 40.2 ave. (the last to hold both jobs at once in the NFL)
7. Ed Brown, 493 punts, 40.6 ave.
6. Adrian Burk, 474 punts, 40.9 ave.
5. Bob Waterfield, 315 punts, 42.5 ave.
4. Frankie Albert, 299 punts, 43 ave.
3. Norm Van Brocklin, 523 punts, 42.9 ave.
2. Glenn Dobbs, 231 punts, 46.4 ave.
1. Sammy Baugh, 338 punts, 44.9 ave., five-time NFL leader

Al Dorow

QPR

Height: 6'0" **Weight:** 193 lbs. **Birthdate:** 11/15/1929
College: Michigan State **Draft:** Washington 1952-3rd
1954–56 Washington Redskins; 1957 Philadelphia Eagles; 1958–59 CFL; 1960–61 New York Titans; 1962 Buffalo Bills
Regular Season Record: 19–25, 5 comebacks
Postseason Record: NA
Relative Rating: 95%

Passing

Year	G	Comp./Att.	%	Yards	Y/Att.	TD	INT	Rating
1954	11	70/138	50.7	997	7.2	8	17	54.2
1955	8	2/12	16.7	37	3.1	0	1	5.2
1956	12	55/112	49.1	730	6.5	8	8	64.2
1957	6	17/36	47.2	212	5.9	1	4	35.6
1960	14	201/396	50.8	2,748	6.9	26	26	67.8
1961	14	197/438	45.0	2,651	6.1	19	30	50.7
1962	4	30/75	40.0	333	4.4	2	7	23.9
Total	69	572/1,207	47.4	7,708	6.4	64	93	53.8

Rushing

Year	Att.	Yards	Avg.	TD
1954	34	117	3.4	3
1955	8	49	6.1	0
1956	30	105	3.5	0
1957	17	52	3.1	2
1960	90	453	5.0	7
1961	54	317	5.9	4
1962	15	57	3.8	0
Total	248	1,150	4.6	16

Governali at Columbia, and he became the last Ivy League quarterback to be drafted in the first round when the Chargers picked him in 1969. Marty spent three seasons learning from Sid Gillman and watching John Hadl play before San Diego traded him to the Colts in 1972 for a No. 1 pick.

Controversial general manager Joe Thomas brought Domres to Baltimore to replace Johnny Unitas, but Unitas wasn't ready to leave. With the Colts sitting at 1–4 in October, Thomas ordered coach Don McCafferty to play Domres. When McCafferty remained loyal to Unitas, Thomas replaced him with John Sandusky, who announced that Unitas would not play again unless Domres got hurt. By 1973, both Sandusky and Unitas were gone; the Colts hired Howard Schnellenberger as their new coach and drafted quarterback Bert Jones with their No. 1 draft pick. When Schnellenberger was still starting Domres in 1974, owner Robert Irsay ordered him to start Jones instead. Schnellenberger refused and was replaced by Joe Thomas, who sat down Domres for Jones. Marty stuck around Baltimore for one more year and then spent one season with the 49ers and another with the Jets as a backup. Domres was smart, big, and strong but threw interceptions and was not much of a leader. Part of his problem may have been that he tended not to spend his nights on film study as he indicated in a now-forgotten

Al Dorow was recruited to Michigan State as a halfback and converted to quarterback as a sophomore. By his senior year in 1953, the Spartans were 9–0 and second in the nation, and Dorow was backed up by Tom Yewcic, who would later play for the Patriots, and Willie Thrower, who would become the first black quarterback in the NFL with the Bears. As a former halfback, Dorow loved to run and was a scrambling quarterback who twice led the AFL quarterbacks in rushing. He didn't have the strongest or most accurate arm but was an inspirational leader.

Dorow was drafted by Washington but first served a two-year hitch in the air force. When he joined the Redskins in 1954, Eddie LeBaron had just left to play in Canada, so Dorow shared the job with second-year man Jack Scarbath and showed some potential. LeBaron returned the following year and led the Skins to a winning season but then injured his knee in 1956, giving Dorow another chance. Al played well enough to be selected to the Pro Bowl, but after a salary dispute with owner George Preston Marshall in the off-season, he was shipped off to Philadelphia for a third-round pick. Dorow played little with the Eagles and headed to Canada for two seasons before the American Football League began in 1960.

For the New York Titans in the AFL, Dorow spent two years throwing bombs to Don Maynard and Art Powell in coach Sammy Baugh's wide-open passing attack. Al threw 45 touchdowns and 56 interceptions for two 7–7 teams. With a sore shoulder in 1962, Al was traded to Buffalo, still owed money by the Titans owner, Harry Wismer. After four games with the Bills, Dorow's shoulder froze up, and he never played again, although he did do some coaching in college and in the CFL.

Rushing

Year	Att.	Yards	Avg.	TD
2004	5	7	1.4	0
2005	4	11	2.8	0
2008	2	0	0.0	0
Total	11	18	1.6	0

Ken Dorsey led the Miami Hurricanes to the 2001 national championship and just barely lost the 2002 BCS National Championship Game to Ohio State in double overtime. As a starter, Dorsey was 38–2 in college but just 2–11 in five years in the pros. In college, Dorsey was a poised leader who used all the weapons that the Hurricanes made available to him. With the 49ers and Browns, though, he was not surrounded by such superior talent that could mask his deficiencies, and he struggled. Dorsey did not have a quick release, and his arm was not of NFL caliber. His passes tended to float to the receiver, and he had trouble throwing deep at all. In his three 2008 starts, Dorsey averaged 125 yards per game, threw no touchdowns and seven interceptions, and the Browns did not score an offensive touchdown.

Ken Dorsey

QPR 0.5

Height: 6'4"   **Weight:** 218 lbs.   **Birthdate:** 4/22/1981
College: Miami   **Draft:** San Francisco 2003-7th
2004–05 San Francisco 49ers; 2006–08 Cleveland Browns
Regular Season Record: 2–11, 1 comeback
Postseason Record: NA
Relative Rating: 69%

Passing

Year	G	Comp./Att.	%	Yards	Y/Att.	TD	INT	Rating
2004	9	123/226	54.4	1,231	5.4	6	9	62.4
2005	3	48/90	53.3	481	5.3	2	2	66.9
2006	1	0/1	0	0	0.0	0	0	39.6
2007	1	0/0	0	0	0.0	0	0	0.0
2008	4	43/91	47.3	370	4.1	0	7	26.4
Total	18	214/408	52.5	2,086	5.1	8	18	55.2

Bobby Douglass

QPR 2.0

Height: 6'4"   **Weight:** 225 lbs.   **Birthdate:** 6/22/1947
College: Kansas   **Draft:** Chicago Bears 1969-2nd
1969–75 Chicago Bears; 1975 San Diego Chargers; 1976–77 New Orleans Saints; 1978 Green Bay Packers
Regular Season Record: 16–36–1, 4 comebacks
Postseason Record: NA
Relative Rating: 65%

Passing

Year	G	Comp./Att.	%	Yards	Y/Att.	TD	INT	Rating
1969	11	68/148	45.9	773	5.2	5	8	50.9
1970	3	12/30	40.0	218	7.3	4	3	65.7
1971	12	91/225	40.4	1,164	5.2	5	15	37.0
1972	14	75/198	37.9	1,246	6.3	9	12	49.8
1973	13	81/174	46.6	1,057	6.1	5	7	59.0
1974	7	41/100	41.0	387	3.9	2	4	42.4
1975	4	15/47	31.9	140	3.0	0	3	14.6
1976	11	103/213	48.4	1,288	6.0	4	8	58.2
1977	4	16/31	51.6	130	4.2	1	3	33.7
1978	12	5/12	41.7	90	7.5	1	1	61.1
Total	91	507/1,178	43.0	6,493	5.5	36	64	48.5

Rushing

Year	Att.	Yards	Avg.	TD
1969	51	408	8.0	2
1970	7	22	3.1	0
1971	39	284	7.3	3
1972	141	968	6.9	8
1973	94	525	5.6	5
1974	36	229	6.4	1
1975	15	76	5.1	1
1976	21	92	4.4	2
1977	2	23	11.5	0
1978	4	27	6.8	0
Total	**410**	**2,654**	**65.0**	**22**

It's not accurate to say that Bobby Douglass couldn't throw the ball, but inaccuracy indeed was his downfall. It was said that the husky blond left-hander could throw a football through a brick wall...if only the 43 percent passer could hit the wall. On the plus side, Douglass was a fearsome runner with the build of a fullback and the speed of a halfback. Three times he led all NFL quarterbacks in rushing and in 1972 set the seasonal rushing mark for quarterbacks with 968 yards in 14 games. That record stood for 34 years till Michael Vick topped 1,000 yards in 16 games in 2006.

Douglass averaged a robust 6.5 yards per carry running. Unfortunately, that was a full yard more than he averaged with his pathetic passes. Douglass was miscast as a quarterback and started as many games as he did only because the Bears and Saints teams for which he played were so toothless. In 1971, head coach Jim Dooley was so intent on mentoring Bobby as a quarterback that he moved into Douglass' bachelor apartment the week before the Lions game. The Bears won that week, but by the end of the season Dooley was fired and Douglass was still a mess.

Although Bobby married a Playboy Playmate of the Month when that magazine was still based in Chicago, his popularity at home dwindled. Soldier Field fans even cheered when he hurt his knee in 1973. Douglass' response to his critics was, "I don't think anyone's been silly enough to say I'm not a good football player. The difference between me and them is that I'm sure I'm a good quarterback." He never could read defenses and always looked awkward in his dropbacks. At the first sign of trouble, he would take off, which is understandable, considering it was much more likely that he would be able to run for a first down than pass for one. Still, Bobby was sacked on 13.3 percent of pass plays, the third highest of all time. Ultimately, the only NFL quarterbacks to start at least 50 games and have a lower winning percentage than Douglass were Archie Manning and David Carr.

Tony Eason

Height: 6'4"   **Weight:** 212 lbs.   **Birthdate:** 10/8/1959
College: Illinois   **Draft:** New England 1983-1st
1983–89 New England Patriots; 1989–90 New York Jets
Regular Season Record: 28–23, 8 comebacks
Postseason Record: 3–2, no comebacks
Relative Rating: 106%

Passing

Year	G	Comp./Att.	%	Yards	Y/Att.	TD	INT	Rating
1983	16	46/95	48.4	557	5.9	1	5	48.4
1984	16	259/431	60.1	3,228	7.5	23	8	93.4
1985	16	168/299	56.2	2,156	7.2	11	17	67.5
1986	15	276/448	61.6	3,328	7.4	19	10	89.2
1987	4	42/79	53.2	453	5.7	3	2	72.4
1988	2	28/43	65.1	249	5.8	0	2	61.1
1989	5	79/141	56	1,016	7.2	4	6	70.5
1990	16	13/28	46.4	155	5.5	0	1	49.0
Total	**90**	**911/1,564**	**58.2**	**11,142**	**7.1**	**61**	**51**	**79.7**
PS:	5	42/72	58.3	561	7.8	7	0	115.6

Rushing

Year	Att.	Yards	Avg.	TD
1983	19	39	2.1	0
1984	40	154	3.9	5
1985	22	70	3.2	1
1986	35	170	4.9	0
1987	3	25	8.3	0
1988	5	18	3.6	0
1989	3	-2	-0.7	0
1990	7	29	4.1	0
Total	**134**	**503**	**3.8**	**6**
PS:	14	26	1.9	0

Tony Eason was the fourth of six quarterbacks selected in the first round of the 1983 draft. Although he didn't measure up to the three Hall of Famers in the group, he was not the total bust that Todd Blackledge was either. Due largely to persistent shoulder problems, Eason was the Patriots' primary starter only from 1984 to 1986, but in two of those years he threw for more than 3,000 yards and in the other he led New England to its first Super Bowl.

That disastrous Super Bowl against the 1985 Bears, in which Eason became the only Super Bowl starter to not complete a pass, is the most lasting image that remains of Tony, but there were mitigating factors. Eason indeed went 0–6 passing and was sacked twice and fumbled once, but the entire offense was overwhelmed and overrun by the ravenous Bear defense, perhaps the greatest defense of all time. In Eason's six offensive series, Stanley Morgan dropped two of his passes, Craig James fumbled, and only one running play gained positive yards. In fact, the Patriots gained just seven yards rushing for the entire game. Eason himself was recovering from a virus, which probably contributed to his looking shell-shocked on the field. So with 5:08 left in the second quarter and trailing 20–3, Steve Grogan replaced Eason. Although Grogan threw for 177 yards, he produced just seven points in the 46–10 shellacking.

Eason was a touch passer who threw few interceptions and was fairly mobile, although he was prone to getting sacked and injured. Tony led New England back to the playoffs in 1986, but they fell victim to one of John Elway's typical fourth-quarter comebacks. Over the next three seasons, Eason started just 13 games for the Patriots and then was traded to the Jets, where he finished his career as the backup to another quarterback from the class of 1983, Ken O'Brien.

In recent years, Eason has been the subject of an off-Broadway play called *Runt of the Litter*. It's a one-man show about sibling rivalry written by and starring Eason's brother Bo, who was an NFL defensive back.

Trent Edwards

Height: 6'4" **Weight:** 231 lbs. **Birthdate:** 10/30/1983
College: Stanford **Draft:** Buffalo 2007-3rd
2007–08 Buffalo Bills
Regular Season Record: 12–11, 4 comebacks
Postseason Record: NA
Relative Rating: 97%

Passing

Year	G	Comp./Att.	%	Yards	Y/Att.	TD	INT	Rating
2007	10	151/269	56.1	1,630	6.1	7	8	70.4
2008	14	245/374	65.5	2,699	7.2	11	10	85.4
Total	24	396/643	61.6	4,329	6.7	18	18	79.1

Rushing

Year	Att.	Yards	Avg.	TD
2007	14	49	3.5	0
2008	36	117	3.3	3
Total	50	166	3.3	3

Bill Walsh talked to his old friend Marv Levy on behalf of Stanford quarterback Trent Edwards in 2007, and Levy selected Edwards late in the third round of that year's draft. When starter J.P. Losman got hurt early in 2007, Edwards stepped in and did a credible job until hurting his wrist. Losman returned but struggled and gave the starting job back to Edwards in December. Edwards and the Bills got off to a fast start in 2008, but both displayed their limitations in the second half of the season. Edwards is very accurate on short passes but does not have the big arm that a quarterback his size should have. Trent is intelligent but can be flustered into mistakes by a pass rush. Although Edwards benefits by the comparison with Losman, a draft bust, he is essentially a game manager whose niche in the NFL is likely to be as a backup.

John Elway

QPR **10.0**

Height: 6'3" **Weight:** 215 lbs. **Birthdate:** 6/28/1960
College: Stanford **Draft:** Baltimore Colts 1983-1st
1983–98 Denver Broncos
Regular Season Record: 148–82–1, 42 comebacks
Postseason Record: 14–7, 6 comebacks
Relative Rating: 105%

Passing

Year	G	Comp./Att.	%	Yards	Y/Att.	TD	INT	Rating
1983	11	123/259	47.5	1,663	6.4	7	14	54.9
1984	15	214/380	56.3	2,598	6.8	18	15	76.8
1985	16	327/605	54.0	3,891	6.4	22	23	70.2
1986	16	280/504	55.6	3,485	6.9	19	13	79.0
1987	12	224/410	54.6	3,198	7.8	19	12	83.4
1988	15	274/496	55.2	3,309	6.7	17	19	71.4
1989	15	223/416	53.6	3,051	7.3	18	18	73.7
1990	16	294/502	58.6	3,526	7.0	15	14	78.5
1991	16	242/451	53.7	3,253	7.2	13	12	75.4
1992	12	174/316	55.1	2,242	7.1	10	17	65.7
1993	16	348/551	63.2	4,030	7.3	25	10	92.8
1994	14	307/494	62.1	3,490	7.1	16	10	85.7
1995	16	316/542	58.3	3,970	7.3	26	14	86.4
1996	15	287/466	61.6	3,328	7.1	26	14	89.2
1997	16	280/502	55.8	3,635	7.2	27	11	87.5
1998	13	210/356	59.0	2,806	7.9	22	10	93.0
Total	234	4,123/7,250	56.9	51,475	7.1	300	226	79.9
PS:	22	355/651	54.5	4,964	7.6	27	21	79.7

Rushing

Year	Att.	Yards	Avg.	TD
1983	28	146	5.2	1
1984	56	237	4.2	1
1985	51	253	5.0	0
1986	52	257	4.9	1
1987	66	304	4.6	4
1988	54	234	4.3	1
1989	48	244	5.1	3
1990	50	258	5.2	3
1991	55	255	4.6	6
1992	34	94	2.8	2
1993	44	153	3.5	0
1994	58	235	4.1	4
1995	41	176	4.3	1
1996	50	249	5.0	4
1997	50	218	4.4	1
1998	37	94	2.5	1
Total	774	3,407	4.4	33
PS:	94	461	4.9	6

John Elway is arguably the greatest quarterback of all time, although his passer rating and completion percentage don't indicate that. His 148 career wins have been topped only by Brett Favre, and his 48 fourth-quarter comebacks include some of the most unforgettable games in NFL history. Winning the Super Bowl in his last two seasons also silenced critics who claimed he couldn't win the big one and shed light on what a great achievement it was for him to drag those first three mediocre Denver teams to the Super Bowl.

Elway always had a knack for being in the center of things. His last game at Stanford featured the unforgettable five-lateral kickoff return through the marching band to beat Cal at the buzzer. Drafted No. 1 overall in the class of 1983, Elway made it clear he would not play for the Baltimore Colts and their autocratic coach, Frank Kush. To the shock of Colts GM Ernie Accorsi, Colts owner Robert Irsay

John Elway's Signature Play: With just six seconds to play in a tie game against Washington on September 18, 1995, Elway fired a fourth-down touchdown pass of 43 yards to rookie Rod Smith for the win on the game's final play.

John Elway in the Clutch: "The Drive." 98 yards in the last five minutes to tie the 1986 AFC Championship Game with the Browns. Elway then led the game-winning drive in overtime.

No lead was safe with John Elway roaming freely with the ball in the fourth quarter.

John Elway's Five Highest Honors

5. Selected to nine Pro Bowls
4. Nine-time All-Pro
3. Super Bowl XXXIII MVP
2. AFC Player of the Year in 1987 and 1993
1. Elected to the Pro Football Hall of Fame 2004

The Five Quarterbacks Most Similar to John Elway

5. Jay Cutler
4. Donovan McNabb
3. Ben Roethlisberger
2. Brett Favre
1. Bert Jones

John Elway's Five Top Touchdown Targets

5. Anthony Miller, 21 TDs
4. Mark Jackson, 22 TDs
3. Ed McCaffrey, 23 TDs
2. Vance Johnson, 35 TDs
1. Shannon Sharpe, 41 TDs

John Elway's Five Toughest Rivals

5. Elway was 20–10 against the Chargers.
4. Elway was 20–9 against the Seahawks.
3. Elway was 17–12 against the Chiefs in the regular season and 1–0 in the playoffs.
2. Elway was 13–15 against the Raiders in the regular season and 0–1 in the playoffs.
1. Elway was 7–2 against the Browns in the regular season and 3–0 in the playoffs.

Five Random John Elway Statistics

5. Elway played for three head coaches.
4. Elway's Broncos outscored the league average by 12 percent.
3. Elway threw for five touchdowns against the Vikings on November 18, 1984.
2. Elway threw for more than 300 yards 36 times and over 400 yards twice.
1. Elway led the league in passing yards once.

rashly traded Elway to Denver for quarterback Mark Herrmann, tackle Chris Hinton, and a first-round pick. Elway was actually drafted by four different teams but never played for any of them: the Colts, the Oakland Invaders of the USFL, and the Royals and Yankees in baseball.

Although Elway had many great athletic moments in his first decade leading the Broncos, he chafed under coach Dan Reeves. Elway seemed to get by on his immense athletic talent for those first 10 years, producing such memorable moments as The Drive when he led Denver 98 yards in the last five minutes of the AFC conference championship to tie the Browns and force overtime. However, his greatest years as a quarterback coincided with Reeves' departure and the chance to work with coordinator Jim Fassell and head coach Mike Shanahan. Elway's best passer rating in his first 10 years was 83.4; his worst in his last six years was 85.7. John was given more weapons and a more diversified attack, and he seemed to get better with age. The culmination was throwing for 336 yards in his last game, a Super Bowl triumph over Dan Reeves' Atlanta Falcons.

Elway had the strongest arm of his generation and could be deadly accurate with both short and long passes. He was mobile, fearlessly gaining 3,407 yards rushing in his career, and scored 33 touchdowns on the ground. Above all, he was a fiery, confident leader who was at his best when the game was on the line. He belongs at the top of the list of quarterbacks with Montana, Unitas, and Graham.

No one has ever lofted the Vince Lombardi Trophy with more joy than 37-year-old three-time loser John Elway in January 1998.

Fred Enke

QPR 3.0

Height: 6'1"   **Weight:** 208 lbs.   **Birthdate:** 12/15/1924
College: Arizona   **Draft:** Detroit 1948-7th
1948–51 Detroit Lions; 1952 Philadelphia Eagles;
1953–54 Baltimore Colts
Regular Season Record: 6–20, 2 comebacks
Postseason Record: NA
Relative Rating: 82%

Passing

Year	G	Comp./Att.	%	Yards	Y/Att.	TD	INT	Rating
1948	12	100/221	45.2	1,328	6.0	11	17	49.4
1949	12	63/142	44.4	793	5.6	6	5	61.7
1950	12	22/53	41.5	424	8.0	5	7	61.9
1951	12	2/9	22.2	22	2.4	0	1	0.0
1952	9	22/67	32.8	377	5.6	1	5	26.8
1953	8	71/169	42.0	1,054	6.2	8	15	41.9
1954	3	17/28	60.7	171	6.1	0	3	38.5
Total	68	297/698	43.1	4,169	6.1	31	53	46.2

Rushing

Year	Att.	Yards	Avg.	TD
1948	74	365	4.9	0
1949	36	134	3.7	1
1950	9	16	1.8	0
1951	4	6	1.5	0
1952	14	25	1.8	0
1953	28	91	3.3	0
1954	5	3	0.6	0
Total	170	640	3.8	1

During "Firing" Fred Enke's rookie year, Commissioner Bert Bell said, "That lad will become one of the league's best." It was talent evaluation like that that enabled Bell to achieve an NFL coaching record of 10–46–2. Enke led the nation in total offense in 1947 as a single-wing tailback but never really transferred that success to the pros. He was a better runner than passer who led all quarterbacks in rushing as a rookie but was an ordinary quarterback at best.

Enke's father, Fred Sr., was the basketball coach at Arizona, where Fred Jr. was the star guard on that squad as well as being the captain of the baseball team. Junior served in the navy during the war and left Arizona for the NFL with two years of eligibility remaining. His agent was a teammate from the basketball team, future Congressman Mo Udall, and Enke signed a no-cut contract with the

Lions in 1948. He held down the starting slot for two losing years until Bobby Layne arrived in 1950 and then sat on the bench for two more. In 1952 the Lions obtained Jim Hardy as Layne's backup and traded Enke to Philadelphia where he backed up Bobby Thomason and Adrian Burk for one year. He finished his career as the first quarterback for the new Baltimore Colts franchise in 1953 and then was pushed aside by Gary Kerkorian in 1954.

Craig Erickson

QPR 4.0

Height: 6'2"   **Height:** 209 lbs.   **Birthdate:** 5/17/1969
College: Miami   **Draft:** Philadelphia 1991-5th; Tampa 1992-4th
1992–94 Tampa Bay Bucs; 1995 Indianapolis Colts;
1996–97 Miami Dolphins
Regular Season Record: 14–21, 3 comebacks
Postseason Record: NA
Relative Rating: 96%

Passing

Year	G	Comp./Att.	%	Yards	Y/Att.	TD	INT	Rating
1992	6	15/26	57.7	121	4.7	0	0	69.6
1993	16	233/457	51.0	3,054	6.7	18	21	66.4
1994	15	225/399	56.4	2,919	7.3	16	10	82.5
1995	6	50/83	60.2	586	7.1	3	4	73.7
1996	7	55/99	55.6	780	7.9	4	2	86.3
1997	2	13/28	46.4	165	5.9	0	1	50.4
Total	52	591/1,092	54.1	7,625	7.0	41	38	74.3

Rushing

Year	Att.	Yards	Avg.	TD
1992	1	-1	-1.0	0
1993	26	96	3.7	0
1994	26	68	2.6	1
1995	9	14	1.6	0
1996	11	16	1.5	0
1997	4	8	2.0	0
Total	77	201	2.6	1

Craig Erickson led Miami to its third national championship in 1989 and then won the Johnny Unitas Award as a senior in 1990 as the best college quarterback in the country. NFL scouts had doubts about his arm to begin with, and then Craig tore up his knee at practice before the Hula Bowl and his stock dropped further. Erickson was selected by Philadelphia in the fifth round of the 1991 draft, but they could not come to agreement on a contract.

Here Craig Erickson enjoys the life of a Bucs quarterback before the arrival of coach Tony Dungy.

He spent the year rehabilitating his knee. When he was still unsigned for the 1992 draft, the Bucs took him in the fourth round.

With the Bucs, Erickson was the starter between the failed tenures of Vinny Testaverde and Trent Dilfer. Craig didn't do too badly; he was a respected leader on the field and threw for more than 2,900 yards in back-to-back seasons, but the team did not win. Of course, Erickson did have better receivers in college, with Michael Irvin, Brian Blades, and Brett Perriman, than he did at any of his pro stops. The Bucs got a No. 1 pick from the Colts for Craig, and he spent one year behind Jim Harbaugh before moving on to back up Dan Marino back in Miami for two years. When he retired, Erickson got to live every boy's dream and became a yacht broker. That's right, a yacht broker.

Boomer Esiason

QPR 9.0

Height: 6'5" **Weight:** 224 lbs. **Birthdate:** 4/17/1961
College: Maryland **Draft:** Cincinnati 1984-2nd
1984–92, 1997 Cincinnati Bengals; 1993–95 New York Jets; 1996 Arizona Cardinals
Regular Season Record: 80–93, 24 comebacks
Postseason Record: 3–2, no comebacks
Relative Rating: 106%

Passing

Year	G	Comp./Att.	%	Yards	Y/Att.	TD	INT	Rating
1984	10	51/102	50.0	530	5.2	3	3	62.9
1985	15	251/431	58.2	3,443	8.0	27	12	93.2
1986	16	273/469	58.2	3,959	8.4	24	17	87.7
1987	12	240/440	54.5	3,321	7.5	16	19	73.1
1988	16	223/388	57.5	3,572	9.2	28	14	97.4
1989	16	258/455	56.7	3,525	7.7	28	11	92.1
1990	16	224/402	55.7	3,031	7.5	24	22	77.0
1991	14	233/413	56.4	2,883	7.0	13	16	72.5
1992	12	144/278	51.8	1,407	5.1	11	15	57.0
1993	16	288/473	60.9	3,421	7.2	16	11	84.5
1994	15	255/440	58.0	2,782	6.3	17	13	77.3
1995	12	221/389	56.8	2,275	5.8	16	15	71.4
1996	10	190/339	56.0	2,293	6.8	11	14	70.6
1997	7	118/186	63.4	1,478	7.9	13	2	106.9
Total	187	2,969/5,205	57.0	37,920	7.3	247	184	81.1
PS:	5	51/99	51.5	600	6.1	4	3	71.1

Rushing

Year	Att.	Yards	Avg.	TD
1984	19	63	3.3	2
1985	33	79	2.4	1
1986	44	146	3.3	1
1987	52	241	4.6	0
1988	43	248	5.8	1
1989	47	278	5.9	0
1990	49	157	3.2	0
1991	24	66	2.8	0
1992	21	66	3.1	0
1993	45	118	2.6	1
1994	28	59	2.1	0
1995	19	14	0.7	0
1996	15	52	3.5	1
1997	8	11	1.4	0
Total	447	1,598	3.6	7
PS:	19	105	5.5	0

If he had not been redshirted for a year at Maryland, Boomer Esiason could have been part of the fabled quarterback class of 1983. Instead, the left-hander was the first quarterback taken in 1984, but that wasn't until the second round. Between that and the fact that he spent most of his career with lousy teams in Cincinnati, New York, and Arizona, it's easy to forget how good a player Esiason was.

Boomer was a big, confident leader who was very mobile in the pocket and a strong and accurate passer. He was a skilled ball handler who excelled at play-action passes and pioneered the use of the no-huddle offense in Cincinnati. Fighting off a sore shoulder, Boomer came within a legendary Joe Montana comeback drive of leading the Bengals to a world championship in Super Bowl XXIII. He can be heard from the sidelines on the NFL Films highlight film, worrying about having left too much time for Montana in that game. It was the pinnacle of his career.

Esiason had succeeded Kenny Anderson in 1985, guaranteeing Cincinnati 20 consecutive seasons of quality quarterbacking. Seven times he exceeded 3,000 yards passing, five times he threw at least 24 touchdowns, and four times he had a passer rating of more than 90. In a stunning miscalculation, the Bengals traded Boomer to the Jets in 1993 to make room for top pick David Klingler. For the Long Island native, the trade was like going home, but with the quality of the Jets' team, Esiason soon found you can't go home again. After three years with the stumbling Jets, Boomer signed with the Cardinals and had his greatest passing day in November 1996 when he threw for 522 yards and three touchdowns to beat the Redskins in overtime. Esiason returned to Cincinnati in 1997 and achieved personal bests in both completion percentage and passer rating in his final season.

He continues to be a very visible and vocal presence as a sports broadcaster in various settings. However, because his son Gunnar suffers from cystic fibrosis, Esiason has become as well known as an advocate for research into that disease as he is for football.

Sam Etcheverry

QPR **2.5**

Height: 5'11" **Weight:** 190 lbs. **Birthdate:** 5/20/1930
College: Denver **Draft:** Free Agent
1952–60 CFL, 1961–62 St. Louis Cardinals
Regular Season Record: 5–8, 3 comebacks
Postseason Record: NA
Relative Rating: 87%

Passing

Year	G	Comp./Att.	%	Yards	Y/Att.	TD	INT	Rating
1961	14	96/196	49.0	1,275	6.5	14	11	70.4
1962	14	58/106	54.7	707	6.7	2	10	42.5
Total	28	154/302	51.0	1,982	6.6	16	21	61.6

Rushing

Year	Att.	Yards	Avg.	TD
1961	33	73	2.2	0
1962	8	5	0.6	0
Total	41	78	1.9	0

Sam "the Rifle" Etcheverry joined the Montreal Alouettes out of the University of Denver in 1952 and proved himself the finest passer in Canada over the next nine seasons. He led the CFL in passing yards and completions for six years in a row and seven times threw for more than 3,000 yards in a season. His high was 4,723 yards in 1956, and his mark of 586 yards passing in one game lasted for 39 years. When he came to the NFL in 1961, though, he led the league only in fumbles.

The Giants sent Al DeRogatis to scout Etcheverry in 1954 as a possible successor to Charlie Conerly, but DeRogatis came back raving about runner Alex Webster instead. Two years later, the Cardinals took Sam to court to try to force him to play for them, but he returned to Montreal. Finally, Montreal traded Etcheverry to the Hamilton Tiger Cats in 1960, sparking an outcry among Montreal fans. Alouette coach Perry Moss defended the move by saying, "We traded two great individual stars for a better team man in [quarterback Bernie] Faloney. In Faloney we have a quarterback who can play both ways and who can run as well as pass."

In light of the trade, Etcheverry considered himself a free agent and signed with the Giants to replace George Shaw, but Commissioner Pete Rozelle invalidated the contract because Etcheverry's

NFL rights were owned by the Cardinals, who promptly signed Sam to a two-year deal. CFL commissioner Sydney Halter protested to Rozelle about the two leagues honoring each other's contracts, but Etcheverry became a 31-year-old rookie for St. Louis in 1961.

Unfortunately, Etcheverry reported to the Cardinals with a sore throwing shoulder that kept him from being able to throw the ball very well in his two seasons in St. Louis. It wasn't a total loss, though; he did help groom his talented young roommate, Charley Johnson, to take over the quarterbacking for the Cardinals. Etcheverry tried to catch on with the 49ers in 1963 but lost out to Lamar McHan. He reemerged at the end of the decade as the GM and coach in Montreal and led the Alouettes to the Grey Cup in 1970. Etcheverry is a member of the Canadian Football Hall of Fame.

Vince Evans

QPR 3.5

Height: 6'2" **Weight:** 215 lbs. **Birthdate:** 6/14/1955
College: USC **Draft:** Chicago Bears 1977-6th
1977–83 Chicago Bears; 1984–85 USFL; 1987–95 Los Angeles/Oakland Raiders
Regular Season Record: 14–25, 4 comebacks
Postseason Record: 0–0, no comebacks
Relative Rating: 85%

Passing

Year	G	Comp./Att.	%	Yards	Y/Att.	TD	INT	Rating
1977	7	0/0	0.0	0	0.0	0	0	0.0
1978	3	1/3	33.3	38	12.7	0	1	42.4
1979	4	32/63	50.8	508	8.1	4	5	66.1
1980	13	148/278	53.2	2,039	7.3	11	16	66.2
1981	16	195/436	44.7	2,354	5.4	11	20	51.1
1982	4	12/28	42.9	125	4.5	0	4	16.8
1983	9	76/145	52.4	1,108	7.6	5	7	69.0
1987	3	39/83	47.0	630	7.6	5	4	72.9
1989	1	2/2	100.0	50	25.0	0	0	118.7
1990	5	1/1	100.0	36	36.0	0	0	118.7
1991	4	6/14	42.9	127	9.1	1	2	59.8
1992	5	29/53	54.7	372	7.0	4	3	78.5
1993	8	45/76	59.2	640	8.4	3	4	77.7
1994	9	18/33	54.5	222	6.7	2	0	95.8
1995	9	100/175	57.1	1,236	7.1	6	8	71.5
Total	**100**	**704/1,490**	**50.6**	**9,485**	**6.8**	**52**	**74**	**63.0**
PS:	1	2/8	25.0	26	3.3	0	1	1

Rushing

Year	Att.	Yards	Avg.	TD
1977	1	0	0.0	0
1978	6	23	3.8	0
1979	12	72	6.0	1
1980	60	306	5.1	8
1981	43	218	5.1	3
1982	2	0	0.0	0
1983	22	142	6.5	1
1987	11	144	13.1	1
1989	1	16	16.0	0
1990	1	-2	-2.0	0
1991	8	20	2.5	0
1992	11	79	7.2	0
1993	14	51	3.6	0
1994	6	24	4.0	0
1995	14	36	2.6	0
Total	**212**	**1,129**	**5.3**	**14**
PS:	4	33	9.3	0

Vince Evans had the career that wouldn't die. Despite being the 1977 Rose Bowl MVP for USC, he was lightly regarded by NFL scouts and was not selected until the sixth round of the draft by the Bears, who then used him as a kick returner as a rookie. Evans won just 12 of his 32 starts in Chicago and completed fewer than half his passes in his seven years there. He was a skittish quarterback with a rag arm and happy feet who would never stay in the pocket. Aside from one perfect-passer-rating game in December 1980 when he went 18–22 for 306 yards and three touchdowns in beating the Packers 61–7, he took poor risks, threw a lot of interceptions, and wore out his welcome with the Bears.

TOP 10
Running Quarterbacks

10. Tobin Rote
9. Greg Landry
8. Archie Manning
7. Steve McNair
6. Donovan McNabb
5. Fran Tarkenton
4. Bobby Douglass
3. Steve Young
2. Randall Cunningham
1. Michael Vick

TOP 10
Quarterbacks Not as Good as Their Nicknames

10. Don "Majik Man" Majkowski
9. Commander Cody Carlson
8. Jefferson Street Joe Gilliam
7. Ryan Leaf, the Boy Blunder
6. Jared Lorenzen, the Hefty Lefty and the Pillsbury Throwboy
5. Jim "Chris" Everett
4. Jack Thompson, the Throwin' Samoan
3. Chris Chandler, also known as Crystal Chandelier
2. David Woodley and Don Strock, also known as Woodstrock
1. Parkway Joe Pisarcik

When Evans signed with the Chicago Blitz of the USFL in 1984, there was no public outcry from Bears fans. In two years in the USFL, Vince's numbers mirrored those of his 15 in the NFL. In roughly half as many pass attempts, Evans threw for 26 touchdowns and 38 interceptions in the USFL, compared to 52 touchdowns and 74 interceptions in the NFL. Vince was just as ineffective in the USFL as in the NFL, and when the newer league died in 1986, it seemed his career would too. For the next year and a half, Evans clamored to get back in the NFL but drew no interest until the 1987 players' strike when Vince hooked on with the Raiders as a replacement player. Against that competition, he performed credibly enough that he hung on with the team for the next nine years and even drew a few starts in his final year of 1995 when he was 40 years old.

Evans should be commended for his dedication and his work ethic, but he was a poor quarterback who had no business spending 15 seasons in the NFL. Oddly enough, when the Raiders website asked him in 2006 about his favorite games, two of the three he mentioned were preseason games, which was probably when he was at his best.

Jim Everett
QPR 8.0

Height: 6'5" **Weight:** 212 lbs. **Birthdate:** 1/3/1963
College: Purdue **Draft:** Houston Oilers 1986-1st
1986–93 Los Angeles Rams; 1994–96 New Orleans Saints; 1997 San Diego Chargers
Regular Season Record: 64–89, 14 comebacks
Postseason Record: 2–3, 1 comeback
Relative Rating: 103%

Passing

Year	G	Comp./Att.	%	Yards	Y/Att.	TD	INT	Rating
1986	6	73/147	49.7	1,018	6.9	8	8	67.8
1987	11	162/302	53.6	2,064	6.8	10	13	68.4
1988	16	308/517	59.6	3,964	7.7	31	18	89.2
1989	16	304/518	58.7	4,310	8.3	29	17	90.6
1990	16	307/554	55.4	3,989	7.2	23	17	79.3
1991	16	277/490	56.5	3,438	7.0	11	20	68.9
1992	16	281/475	59.2	3,323	7.0	22	18	80.2
1993	10	135/274	49.3	1,652	6.0	8	12	59.7
1994	16	346/540	64.1	3,855	7.1	22	18	84.9
1995	16	345/567	60.8	3,970	7.0	26	14	87.0
1996	15	267/464	57.5	2,797	6.0	12	16	69.4
1997	4	36/75	48.0	457	6.1	1	4	49.7
Total	158	2,841/4,923	57.7	34,837	7.1	203	175	78.6
PS:	5	87/176	49.4	1,120	6.4	7	11	57.0

Rushing

Year	Att.	Yards	Avg.	TD
1986	16	46	2.9	1
1987	18	83	4.6	1
1988	34	104	3.1	0
1989	25	31	1.2	1
1990	20	31	1.6	1
1991	27	44	1.6	0
1992	32	133	4.2	0
1993	19	38	2.0	0
1994	15	35	2.3	0
1995	24	42	1.8	0
1996	22	3	0.1	0
1997	5	6	1.2	0
Total	257	596	2.3	4
PS:	12	43	3.6	0

Jim Everett will always be remembered for two related incidents that highlight his softness as a player: the Phantom Sack and "Chris" Everett's fight with broadcaster Jim Rome. After them, Everett was never quite the same quarterback.

Everett was the third overall pick in the 1986 draft by Houston, but the Oilers were unable to sign Jim and traded him to the Rams, who outbid the 49ers. Coach John Robinson brought in Ernie Zampese to tutor Everett in his version of the Air Coryell offense of timing patterns and shorter dropbacks. By 1988, Everett seemed to have arrived. He threw for 31 touchdowns that year and 29 the next, with passer ratings around 90 both years. After the Rams beat the Eagles and Giants in the 1989 playoffs—the latter in overtime on a 30-yard Everett touchdown strike to Flipper Anderson—they met the 49ers for the NFC title. In a game the Rams would lose 30–3, Everett dropped back on a third-and-10 in the second quarter. With San Francisco rushing just three linemen, Everett panicked and crumpled to the ground without being touched. Announcer John Madden commented that Jim "felt the bullet when there was no bullet." It would be nearly 10 years before Everett would admit to the *Los Angeles Times*, "I took a dive." His reputation did as well.

Loudmouth talk show host Jim Rome had a great deal of fun regularly referring to Everett as "Chris Everett," as in women's tennis pro Chris Evert. By 1994, Everett had had enough. He went on Rome's show and warned Rome not to call him that. When Rome persisted, Everett flipped over a table and lunged at Rome. Although some suspected that the whole thing was a setup, it gave the impression of pathetic self-parody. By that point Everett had washed out of Los Angeles and had hooked up with the Saints.

Everett threw for more than 3,000 yards five more times after the Phantom Sack but never played for another winning team. He came to be known as Jittery Jim, who threw off his back foot and made key mistakes whenever he played against a good defense. He had a long career and accumulated some very good career passing numbers but lacked the mental toughness to be as good as his talent.

Big-armed Jim Everett could throw the ball but wilted under pressure. His stats rank him higher than he should be rated.

Brett Favre

Height: 6'2" **Weight:** 225 lbs. **Birthdate:** 10/10/1969
College: Southern Mississippi **Draft:** Atlanta 1991-2nd
**1991 Atlanta Falcons; 1992–2007 Green Bay Packers;
2008 New York Jets**
Regular Season Record: 169–10, 39 comebacks
Postseason Record: 12–10, 2 comebacks
Relative Rating: 109%

Passing

Year	G	Comp./Att.	%	Yards	Y/Att.	TD	INT	Rating
1991	2	0/4	0.0	0	0.0	0	2	0.0
1992	15	302/471	64.1	3,227	6.9	18	13	85.3
1993	16	318/522	60.9	3,303	6.3	19	24	72.2
1994	16	363/582	62.4	3,882	6.7	33	14	90.7
1995	16	359/570	63.0	4,413	7.7	38	13	99.5
1996	16	325/543	59.9	3,899	7.2	39	13	95.8
1997	16	304/513	59.3	3,867	7.5	35	16	92.6
1998	16	347/551	63.0	4,212	7.6	31	23	87.8
1999	16	341/595	57.3	4,091	6.9	22	23	74.7
2000	16	338/580	58.3	3,812	6.6	20	16	78.0
2001	16	314/510	61.6	3,921	7.7	32	15	94.1
2002	16	341/551	61.9	3,658	6.6	27	16	85.6
2003	16	308/471	65.4	3,361	7.1	32	21	90.4
2004	16	346/540	64.1	4,088	7.6	30	17	92.4
2005	16	372/607	61.3	3,881	6.4	20	29	70.9
2006	16	343/613	56.0	3,885	6.3	18	18	72.7
2007	16	356/535	66.5	4,155	7.8	28	15	95.7
2008	16	343/522	65.7	3,472	6.7	22	22	81.0
Total	273	5,720/9,280	61.6	65,127	7.0	464	310	85.4
PS:	22	438/721	60.7	5,311	7.4	39	28	85.2

Rushing

Year	Att.	Yards	Avg.	TD
1992	47	198	4.2	1
1993	58	216	3.7	1
1994	42	202	4.8	2
1995	39	181	4.6	3
1996	49	136	2.8	2
1997	58	187	3.2	1
1998	40	133	3.3	1
1999	28	142	5.1	0
2000	27	108	4.0	0
2001	38	56	1.5	1
2002	25	73	2.9	0
2003	18	15	0.8	0
2004	16	36	2.3	0
2005	18	62	3.4	0
2006	23	29	1.3	1
2007	29	12	0.4	0
2008	21	43	2.0	1
Total	576	1,829	3.2	14
PS:	51	72	1.4	1

Art Schlichter had a severe gambling problem and was dumped by the Colts after four years. Ryan Leaf battled with teammates, management, and the media and was shipped out of San Diego after three years. Todd Marinovich and Cade McNown were relentless party animals who were jettisoned by the Raiders and Bears respectively after two years. Brett Favre topped all of those first-round flops by getting bounced out of Atlanta after just one year. Favre's immense potential did not fall

Brett Favre in the Clutch: In his first extended appearance with the Packers, Favre relieved an injured Don Majkowski against the Bengals on September 20, 1992. Trailing by six with no timeouts and 1:07 to play, Favre drove the Packers 92 yards for a touchdown, scoring on a 35-yard bomb to Kittrick Taylor with 13 seconds left. Favre started for the first time the next week and never missed a start for the rest of his career.

Brett Favre's Signature Play: In Favre's first playoff game against the Lions in 1994, Green Bay trailed by three points in the last minute. From the Detroit 40, Favre scrambled to his left, turned, and whipped a strike all the way across the field to Sterling Sharpe, who streaked into the end zone for the winning score.

Expressing the excitement of a Pop Warner football player, Brett Favre celebrates his 54-yard touchdown strike to Andre Rison on his first throw in Super Bowl XXXI in January 1997.

Brett Favre's Five Highest Honors

5. 2007 *Sports Illustrated* Sportsman of the Year
4. Selected to nine Pro Bowls
3. Eight-time All-Pro and three-time consensus All-Pro
2. 1997 Co–Player of the Year with Barry Sanders
1. 1995 and 1996 Player of the Year

The Five Quarterbacks Most Similar to Brett Favre

5. Jake Delhomme
4. Ken Stabler
3. Don Meredith
2. Bobby Layne
1. Terry Bradshaw

Brett Favre's Five Top Touchdown Targets

5. Bubba Franks, 29 TDs
4. Robert Brooks, 32 TDs
3. Donald Driver, 36 TDs
2. Sterling Sharpe, 41 TDs
1. Antonio Freeman, 57 TDs

Brett Favre's Five Toughest Rivals

5. Favre was 23–9 against the Lions in the regular season and 2–0 in the playoffs.
4. Favre was 17–14 against the Vikings in the regular season and 0–1 in the playoffs.
3. Favre was 22–10 against the Bears.
2. Favre was 7–0 against the 49ers in the regular season and 4–1 in the playoffs.
1. Favre was 2–10 against the Cowboys in the regular season and 0–3 in the playoffs.

Five Random Brett Favre Statistics

5. Favre played for six head coaches.
4. Favre's Packers and Jets outscored the league average by 12 percent.
3. Favre threw for five touchdowns against the Bears on November 12, 1995, the Vikings on September 21, 1997, and the Panthers on September 27, 1998.
2. Favre threw for over 300 yards 55 times and more than 400 on December 5, 1993, against the Bears.
1. Favre led the league in completion percentage once, passing yards twice, touchdown passes four times, and interceptions three times.

victim to immaturity, though, because Brett found a coach in his second stop who turned his career around. Mike Holmgren made sure that the Hall of Fame talent of Favre was harnessed, and the Packers rode that controlled fury to a Super Bowl championship.

Favre had all the skills. He was mobile with a quick release and adept at avoiding a rush. He had the strongest arm in the league but was also an accurate passer. He was durable and nearly impossible to drive off the field, starting 269 straight games. Finally, Brett was a leader who could create great plays out of the worst circumstances. However, if the Jets were paying attention when they acquired the un-retired Favre in 2008, they were also getting a quarterback who was a headstrong gunslinger who made some unbelievably poor decisions on the field. His December 2008 collapse of throwing one touchdown and nine interceptions made the 39-year-old Jet seem as old as 38-year-old Y.A. Tittle, who retired after a horrendous 1964 season, saying, "I don't want to be a mediocre football player again."

When Favre ran onto the field for his second Super Bowl against the Broncos in 1998, he was at the pinnacle. His playoff record was nine wins against just three losses. After that, Favre went 3–7 in playoff games, and some of the losses were particularly ugly. He tossed four interceptions against the Vikings in 2005 and six interceptions against the Rams in 2002. His last pass of the 2004 postseason was a pop fly fling that went right to Brian Dawkins of the Eagles. Similarly, the 2008 postseason ended

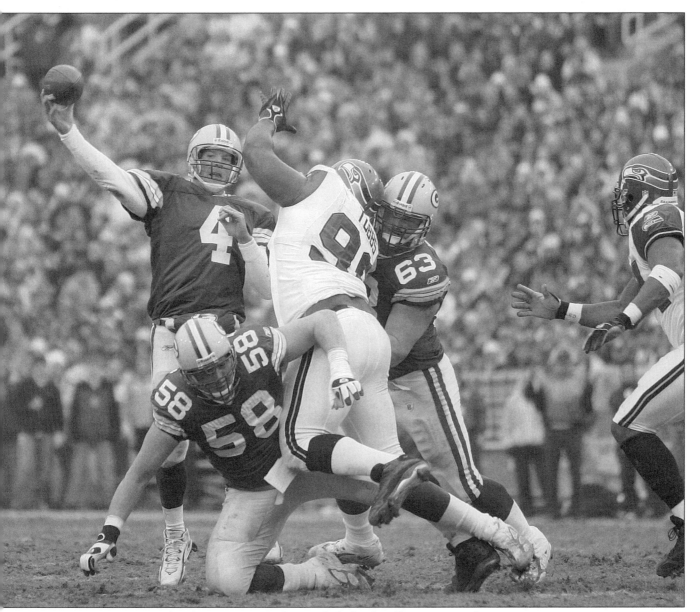

No one was tougher than Brett Favre. If you include the playoffs, Favre started 293 consecutive games over 17 seasons in the NFL.

with Corey Webster of the Giants intercepting an ill-advised, misdirected Favre pass.

At times, Favre was so impatient on the field that it seemed he had attention deficit disorder. He threw deep passes into double coverage even when the offense was moving the chains and driving down the field. It was no wonder that in addition to all of the positive passing records of Dan Marino's that Favre broke, he also took George Blanda's career interception mantle. Favre is a first-ballot Hall of Famer and one of the all-time great quarterbacks. The sad thing is that he had the talent to be the best ever if he would have had a little more self-control.

A.J. Feeley

QPR **1.5**

Height: 6'3"   **Weight:** 225 lbs.   **Birthdate:** 5/16/1977
College: Oregon   **Draft:** Philadelphia 2001-5th
2001–02, 2006–07 Philadelphia Eagles;
2004 Miami Dolphins
Regular Season Record: 7–8, 5 comebacks
Postseason Record: NA
Relative Rating: 87%

Passing

Year	G	Comp./Att.	%	Yards	Y/Att.	TD	INT	Rating
2001	1	10/14	71.4	143	10.2	2	1	114.0
2002	6	86/154	55.8	1,011	6.6	6	5	75.4
2004	11	191/356	53.7	1,893	5.3	11	15	61.7
2006	2	26/38	68.4	342	9.0	3	0	122.9
2007	3	59/103	57.3	681	6.6	5	8	61.2
Total	23	372/665	55.9	4,070	6.1	27	29	69.6

Rushing

Years	Att.	Yards	Avg.	TD
2002	12	6	0.5	0
2004	14	13	0.9	1
2006	1	3	3.0	0
2007	7	23	3.3	0
Total	34	45	1.3	1

The one thing that A.J. Feeley proved was that you don't have to be a *starting* quarterback to date well; he carried on a very public romance with attractive soccer star Heather Mitts for five years while he merely carried a clipboard on the field. Feeley is truly a lifelong backup. At Oregon, he sat behind Akili Smith as a sophomore, until he briefly won the starting job as a junior. Then he was overtaken by Joey Harrington and spent his senior year on the bench.

With the Eagles, Feeley attracted some attention when he won four of the last five games for the injured Donovan McNabb in 2002, but he was really more of a game manager who tried not to lose the game for the defense. Still, Miami gave Philadelphia a second-round pick for Feeley in 2004, and A.J. got an extended trial as starter with the Dolphins and threw more interceptions than touchdowns. The next season, he was traded to San Diego, but when the Chargers cut him in 2006, he returned to Philadelphia.

In 2007 against the undefeated Patriots in a Sunday night game, Feeley provided more evidence of why he is a backup. That night, Feeley threw for three touchdowns in keeping the game close, but he also threw three interceptions, letting it slip away at the end. The following week against the Seahawks, he threw four more interceptions. Feeley essentially is just good enough to get you beat. He doesn't have a major-league arm and ultimately tries to force the ball to make a play he is unable to make at key moments.

Joe Ferguson

QPR **7.0**

Height: 6'0"   **Weight:** 190 lbs.   **Birthdate:** 4/23/1950
College: Arkansas   **Draft:** Buffalo 1973-3rd
1973–84 Buffalo Bills; 1985–86 Detroit Lions;
1988–89 Tampa Bay Bucs; 1990 Indianapolis Colts
Regular Season Record: 79–92, 24 comebacks
Postseason Record: 1–3, no comebacks
Relative Rating: 95%

Passing

Year	G	Comp./Att.	%	Yards	Y/Att.	TD	INT	Rating
1973	14	73/164	44.5	939	5.7	4	10	45.8
1974	14	119/232	51.3	1,588	6.8	12	12	69.0
1975	14	169/321	52.6	2,426	7.6	25	17	81.3
1976	7	74/151	49.0	1,086	7.2	9	1	90.0
1977	14	221/457	48.4	2,803	6.1	12	24	54.8
1978	16	175/330	53.0	2,136	6.5	16	15	70.5
1979	16	238/458	52.0	3,572	7.8	14	15	74.4
1980	16	251/439	57.2	2,805	6.4	20	18	74.5
1981	16	252/498	50.6	3,652	7.3	24	20	74.1
1982	9	144/264	54.5	1,597	6.0	7	16	56.3
1983	16	281/508	55.3	2,995	5.9	26	25	69.3
1984	12	191/344	55.5	1,991	5.8	12	17	63.5
1985	8	31/54	57.4	364	6.7	2	3	67.2
1986	6	73/155	47.1	941	6.1	7	7	62.9
1988	2	31/46	67.4	368	8.0	3	1	104.3
1989	5	44/90	48.9	533	5.9	3	6	50.8
1990	1	2/8	25.0	21	2.6	0	2	0.0
Total	186	2,369/4,519	52.4	29,817	6.6	196	209	68.4
PS:	4	58/128	48.3	814	6.8	6	9	56

Rushing

Year	Att.	Yards	Avg.	TD
1973	48	147	3.1	2
1974	54	111	2.1	2
1975	23	82	3.6	1
1976	18	81	4.5	0
1977	41	279	6.8	2
1978	27	76	2.8	0
1979	22	68	3.1	1
1980	31	65	2.1	0
1981	20	29	1.5	1
1982	16	46	2.9	1
1983	20	88	4.4	0
1984	19	102	5.4	0
1985	4	12	3.0	1
1986	5	25	5.0	0
1988	1	0	0.0	0
1989	4	6	1.5	0
Total	353	1,217	3.4	11
PS:	3	-1	-0.3	0

Joe Ferguson started out with Buffalo as an unheralded rookie whose simple job was to hand the ball off to O.J. Simpson when he ran for a record 2,003 yards in 1973. Ferguson was given the job because he was more careful with the ball than the previous year's starter, Dennis Shaw. The Bills went 9–5 both that year and the next with Ferguson steadily improving as a field general. Joe never became a great quarterback, but he did become a pretty good one who lasted 17 years in the league, mostly as a starter.

Ferguson had a fairly good arm and was fairly mobile, running for 1,200 yards in his career. He was a smart quarterback who was very good at reading defenses. He was also durable for a slightly built guy. In fact, he and Ron Jaworski both started consecutive starts streaks in 1977 that continued for seven years. By 1984, the two shared the NFL record for consecutive quarterback starts. Joe's streak ended at 107 that year, while Jaworski continued on for another nine games. Ferguson's tenure in Buffalo also ended that year with him holding most of the team's passing records. Joe was traded to Detroit for a seventh-round draft choice and finished his career bouncing from Detroit to Tampa to Indianapolis as an aging veteran backup quarterback.

QPR 6.0

Vince Ferragamo

Height: 6'3" **Weight:** 212 lbs. **Birthdate:** 4/24/1954
College: Nebraska **Draft:** Los Angeles Rams 1977-4th
1977–80, 1982–84 Los Angeles Rams; 1981 CFL;
1985 Buffalo Bills; 1986 Green Bay Packers
Regular Season Record: 27–26, 7 comebacks
Postseason Record: 3–3, 1 comeback
Relative Rating: 97%

Passing

Year	G	Comp./Att.	%	Yards	Y/Att.	TD	INT	Rating
1977	3	9/15	60.0	83	5.5	2	0	114.7
1978	9	7/20	35.0	114	5.7	0	2	15.4
1979	8	53/110	48.2	778	7.1	5	10	49.0
1980	16	240/404	59.4	3,199	7.9	30	19	89.7
1982	7	118/209	56.5	1,609	7.7	9	9	77.6
1983	16	274/464	59.1	3,276	7.1	22	23	75.9
1984	3	29/66	43.9	317	4.8	2	8	29.2
1985	10	149/287	51.9	1,677	5.8	5	17	50.8
1986	3	23/40	57.5	283	7.1	1	3	56.6
Total	75	902/1,615	55.9	1,336	7.0	76	91	70.1
PS:	7	92/188	48.9	1,228	6.5	8	11	59.9

Rushing

Years	Att.	Yards	Avg.	TD
1977	1	0	0.0	0
1978	2	10	5.0	0
1979	3	-2	-0.7	0
1980	15	34	2.3	1
1982	4	3	0.8	1
1983	22	17	0.8	0
1984	4	0	0.0	0
1985	8	15	1.9	1
1986	1	0	0.0	0
Total	60	77	1.3	1
PS:	7	-5	-0.7	0

Years after he retired, Vince Ferragamo told *Sports Illustrated*, "My whole career was in spurts. When I got the chance I'd always play well. But I was given only short periods to do it." There is a lot of truth to that, but it also is a rose-colored view of his career. Ferragamo was a very strong-armed quarterback who could throw the deep ball with the best of them, but he could also be fooled by coverages and throw some really bad interceptions.

The Rams have a long history of quarterback controversies, and Ferragamo was caught in the middle of that throughout his career. He backed up the popular Pat Haden for two years until Haden broke his thumb late in 1979. Ferragamo rallied the Rams to four wins in their last five games and then two playoff wins to get to the Super Bowl. Against the Steelers in Super Bowl XIV, Ferragamo played a good game, but a fourth-quarter interception ended the Rams' upset dreams.

The next year, Ferragamo threw for 30 touchdowns and fancied himself a superstar. He got into a nasty salary dispute that ended with him signing with Montreal of the CFL. In Canada, Vince was awful, throwing just seven touchdowns to 25 interceptions, and he returned to Los Angeles in 1982. Over the next few seasons, Ferragamo had his moments, such as throwing for 509 yards against the Bears in 1982 and for five touchdowns against the 49ers in 1983, but he was an up-and-down player who eventually ended his career with ugly stints in Buffalo and Green Bay.

Jay Fiedler

QPR 6.5

Height: 6'2" **Weight:** 225 lbs. **Birthdate:** 12/29/1971
College: Dartmouth **Draft:** Free Agent
1995 Philadelphia Eagles; 1998 Minnesota Vikings; 1999 Jacksonville Jaguars; 2000–04 Miami Dolphins; 2005 New York Jets
Regular Season Record: 37–23, 10 comebacks
Postseason Record: 1–2, 1 comeback
Relative Rating: 98%

Passing

Year	G	Comp./Att.	%	Yards	Y/Att.	TD	INT	Rating
1995	0	0/0	0.0	0	0.0	0	0	0.0
1998	5	3/7	42.9	41	5.9	0	1	22.6
1999	8	61/94	64.9	656	7.0	2	2	83.5
2000	15	204/357	57.1	2,402	6.7	14	14	74.5
2001	16	273/450	60.7	3,290	7.3	20	19	80.3
2002	11	179/292	61.3	2,024	6.9	14	9	85.2
2003	12	179/314	57.0	2,138	6.8	11	13	72.4
2004	8	101/190	53.2	1,186	6.2	7	8	67.1
2005	2	8/13	61.5	107	8.2	1	0	113.3
Total	77	1,008/1,717	58.7	11,844	6.9	69	66	77.1
PS:	4	59/110	53.6	655	6.0	3	8	50.4

Rushing

Year	Att.	Yards	Avg.	TD
1998	4	-6	-1.5	0
1999	13	26	2.0	0
2000	54	267	4.9	1
2001	73	321	4.4	4
2002	28	99	3.5	3
2003	34	88	2.6	3
2004	12	59	4.9	0
2005	1	0	0.0	0
Total	219	854	3.9	11
PS:	13	71	5.5	0

Following in the footsteps of Jeff Kemp, Jay Fiedler was the second NFL quarterback to come out of Dartmouth. Fiedler, who is related to former Boston Pops conductor Arthur Fiedler, signed as a free agent with Philadelphia in 1995 and spent two years under contract with the Eagles but never appeared in a game. Jay persisted for a real shot in the NFL and caught on with the Vikings in 1998 when they had injuries to Randall Cunningham and Brad Johnson. The next year, Fiedler made the Jacksonville roster as Mark Brunell's backup and got his first NFL start in the season finale against the Bengals. Jay threw for more than 300 yards in that game and then got into his first playoff game in the Jags' 62–7 destruction of Miami in Dan Marino's last game.

Fiedler signed with the Dolphins in the off-season and beat out Damon Huard to succeed Marino in Miami for the new millennium. Jay started for the Dolphins for most of five years and won 36 of 59 starts in the regular season. Against the tougher postseason competition, though, he threw just one touchdown to seven interceptions in three playoff games. Fiedler was a fierce competitor who was well liked by his teammates and could usually scramble out of trouble. However, his accuracy was inconsistent, and he tended to spray the ball. Moving on from Miami, Fiedler spent one year behind Chad Pennington in New York before shoulder problems drove him out of the game.

Frank Filchock

QPR **8.0**

Height: 5'10" **Weight:** 193 lbs. **Birthdate:** 10/18/1916
College: Indiana **Draft:** Pittsburgh 1938-2nd
1938 Pittsburgh Steelers; 1938–41, 1944–45
Washington Redskins; 1946 New York Giants;
1947–53 CFL; 1950 Baltimore Colts
Regular Season Record: 44–16–3 est., 5 comebacks
Postseason Record: 0–1, no comebacks
Relative Rating: 137%

Passing

Year	G	Comp./Att.	%	Yards	Y/Att.	TD	INT	Rating
1938	12	41/101	40.6	469	4.6	3	11	25.6
1939	11	55/89	61.8	1,094	12.3	11	7	111.6
1940	10	28/54	51.9	460	8.5	6	9	78.2
1941	11	28/68	41.2	327	4.8	1	11	21.8
1944	10	84/147	57.1	1,139	7.7	13	9	86.0
1945	10	18/46	39.1	169	3.7	1	7	63.4
1946	11	87/169	51.5	1,262	7.5	12	25	60.2
1950	1	1/3	33.3	1	0.3	0	0	42.4
Total	76	342/677	50.5	4,921	7.3	47	79	58.0
PS:	3	25/63	39.7	401	6.4	4	12	43.3

Rushing

Years	Att.	Yards	Avg.	TD
1938	69	198	2.9	1
1939	103	413	4.0	1
1940	50	126	2.5	2
1941	115	383	3.3	1
1944	33	-34	-1.0	0
1945	9	21	2.3	0
1946	98	371	3.8	2
1950	0	0	0.0	0
Total	477	1,478	3.1	7
PS:	15	7	0.5	0

If Frank Filchock is remembered at all today it is for being part of a gambling scandal surrounding the 1946 NFL title game. What has been lost in his notoriety is what a tremendous football player he was.

Filchock was the second draft pick of Pittsburgh in 1938, but Art Rooney was having money problems by midseason and sold the rookie tailback to the Redskins. He began to show his skills as Sammy Baugh's relief in 1939. That year, Frank led the league in touchdown passes, averaged 12.3 yards per pass, and threw the NFL's first 99-yard touchdown pass—

it was actually a 2-yard swing pass to Andy Farkas, who then ran 97 yards for the score. In addition to playing tailback in the Redskins' single-wing attack, Filchock played defensive back and returned punts and kickoffs, while also playing minor league baseball. He was so effective that Washington coach Ray Flaherty had Frank and Sammy Baugh alternate quarters.

Filchock went into the navy in 1942, and when he returned to the Redskins in 1944, they were switching to the T formation. Frank actually had a smoother transition to the T than Baugh and led the league in touchdown passes, completions, completion percentage, and yards per pass that season. However, after Baugh made the adjustment to the T in 1945, Washington sent Filchock to the Giants for young quarterback Tommy Mont and tackle Paul Stenn. Giants coach Steve Owen brought Filchock in to run New York's A formation, a single-wing variant. Filchock led the Giants in both passing and rushing in 1946 and took them to the NFL title game. The night before the game, though, everything changed for Filchock.

Commissioner Bert Bell heard that Filchock and halfback Merle Hapes were offered bribes to

In a badly staged photo, NFL Commissioner Bert Bell hands Frank Filchock his indefinite suspension for not reporting a bribe offer from a gambler before the 1946 title game between Filchock's Giants and the Bears.

play against the point spread instead of the Bears. Hapes admitted not reporting the attempt and was suspended, but Filchock denied even being approached and was allowed to play. In the game, Frank played valiantly through a broken nose but threw six interceptions, and the Bears beat the Giants by 10 points, exactly the point spread. In the speedy trial the next month, it came out that Filchock had indeed been approached as well as Mapes, and both were suspended indefinitely by Bell immediately after the trial.

Locked out of the NFL, Filchock was courted by two Canadian teams and signed with the Hamilton Tigers for 1947. The league initially disallowed the contract because of his NFL suspension but then switched its rationale to the fact that he was a professional; Canadian football at the time was pretending to be an amateur league. Hamilton forfeited several games at the beginning of the year for using the "professional" Filchock before his contract was finally approved in October, by which time Frank was the player/coach and had instituted a single-wing offense. The Tigers dropped out of the league in 1948 and played in a minor league. By 1949, Filchock was back in the main Canadian league, playing for Montreal. In 1950, Bell reinstated Filchock, and Frank returned to play in one game for the Baltimore Colts after the Montreal season ended.

Filchock finished his career as a player/coach with Edmonton and then Saskatchewan from 1951 to 1953 and then coached Saskatchewan through 1957. He brought his old Saskatchewan quarterback, Frank Tripucka, with him when he was hired as the initial coach of the Denver Broncos of the American Football League in 1960. Filchock did not have much success with the Broncos, though, finishing 7–20–1 in two years. Frankie played quarterback only for a short time but was a star passer and runner in two countries in the early days of the pro game.

Jim Finks

QPR 5.0

Height: 5'11" **Weight:** 180 lbs. **Birthdate:** 8/31/1927
College: Tulsa **Draft:** Pittsburgh 1949-12th
1949–55 Pittsburgh Steelers; 1957 CFL
Regular Season Record: 18–27, 9 comebacks
Postseason Record: NA
Relative Rating: 98%

Passing

Year	G	Comp./Att.	%	Yards	Y/Att.	TD	INT	Rating
1949	11	24/71	33.8	322	4.5	2	8	19.0
1950	9	5/9	55.6	35	3.9	0	1	25.0
1951	12	14/24	58.3	201	8.4	1	1	82.1
1952	12	158/336	47.0	2,307	6.9	20	19	66.2
1953	11	131/292	44.9	1,484	5.1	8	14	49.8
1954	12	164/306	53.6	2,003	6.5	14	19	63.4
1955	12	165/344	48.0	2,270	6.6	10	26	47.7
Total	79	661/1,382	47.8	8,622	6.2	55	88	54.7

Rushing

Year	Att.	Yards	Avg.	TD
1949	35	135	3.9	1
1950	1	2	2.0	0
1951	3	27	9.0	0
1952	23	37	1.6	5
1953	12	0	0.0	2
1954	9	17	1.9	0
1955	35	76	2.2	4
Total	118	294	2.5	12

Jim Finks is in the Pro Football Hall of Fame as an administrator for transforming three struggling franchises—the Vikings, Bears, and Saints—into playoff teams, but he began as a player with some talent himself. Finks was a T formation quarterback for Tulsa but was drafted by the Steelers, who were the last team to convert from the single-wing. For his first three years in Pittsburgh, Finks was primarily a defensive back. When the Steelers finally made the shift to the T in 1952, Jim was in place and became their first quarterback.

In that first year, Finks led the league with 20 touchdown passes, but Pittsburgh was a mediocre team that was known more for toughness than winning. In 1954, the immobile Finks had his jaw fractured by a wild forearm from Eagle defensive end Norm "Wild Man" Willey but played the following week with a makeshift catcher's mask attached to his helmet that made him look like "a man from Mars" according to the AP. Despite the broken jaw, Finks threw for 257 yards and four touchdowns in helping Pittsburgh to beat the Browns for the very first time 55–27 on October 17, 1954, at Forbes Field. It was the worst defeat the Browns had ever suffered up to that point.

Although Finks led the NFL in passing yards with 2,270 in 1955, the 28-year-old quarterback retired to take an assistant coaching position at Notre Dame. He returned briefly as a player with Calgary in 1957, and that gave him the chance to work his way up in the Stampeder front office. After eight successful years in Calgary, the Vikings hired Jim as their GM in 1964, and he began the Hall of Fame portion of his life.

Ryan Fitzpatrick

QPR 0.5

Height: 6'2" **Weight:** 221 lbs. **Birthdate:** 11/24/1982
College: Harvard **Draft:** St. Louis Rams 2005-7th
2005-06 St. Louis Rams; 2007-08 Cincinnati Bengals
Regular Season Record: 4–10, no comebacks
Postseason Record: NA
Relative Rating: 84%

Passing

Year	G	Comp./Att.	%	Yards	Y/Att.	TD	INT	Rating
2005	4	76/135	56.3	777	5.8	4	8	58.2
2006	1	0/0	0.0	0	0.0	0	0	0.0
2007	1	0/0	0.0	0	0.0	0	0	0.0
2008	13	221/372	59.4	1,905	5.1	8	9	70.0
Total	18	297/507	58.6	2,682	5.3	12	17	66.9

Rushing

Year	Att.	Yards	Avg.	TD
2005	14	64	4.6	2
2006	3	0	0.0	0
2008	60	304	5.1	2
Total	77	368	4.8	4

Having led Harvard to two Ivy League titles, Ryan Fitzpatrick became just the third Harvard quarterback to be drafted after he aced the Wonderlic test, finishing it in just nine minutes rather than the allotted 12. When Fitzpatrick relieved injured Rams backup Jaime Martin against the Texans in November 2005, he became the first

Crimson quarterback to actually play in the NFL. Fitzpatrick threw for more than 300 yards in his debut and won the game with a 56-yard touchdown toss in overtime. That earned him starts in the next three games, but he lost each one. He joined the Bengals in 2007 and a year later became the starter when Carson Palmer went down with elbow problems in the third game. Although Fitzpatrick was one of the leading rushers among quarterbacks in 2008, he firmly established that he is a third quarterback at best. Although he is fairly accurate on short passes, Fitzpatrick can't throw a deep pass at all, takes too many sacks, and is a fumbler.

Joe Flacco

QPR 4.5

Height: 6'6" **Weight:** 236 lbs. **Birthdate:** 1/16/1985
College: Delaware **Draft:** Baltimore Ravens 2008-1st
2008 Baltimore Ravens
Regular Season Record: 11–5, 1 comeback
Postseason Record: 2–1, 1 comeback
Relative Rating: 99%

Passing

Year	G	Comp./Att.	%	Yards	Y/Att.	TD	INT	Rating
2008	16	257/428	60.0	2,971	6.9	14	12	80.3
PS:	3	33/75	44.0	437	5.8	1	3	50.8

Rushing

Year	Att.	Yards	Avg.	TD
2008	52	180	3.5	2
PS:	12	5	0.4	1

Joe Flacco resembles Vinny Testaverde facially but on the field is the second coming of Ben Roethlisberger. Like Big Ben, Flacco is huge with a big arm, is a powerful and elusive runner, and plays with unaffected poise. Coming out of Delaware, Flacco was marked down by scouts as not having faced top competition in college, and the Ravens surprised some by taking him in the first round. Then when Kyle Boller and Troy Smith were hurt in training camp, Flacco got his chance to play and won the starting job. Although the Ravens rely mostly on their defense, Flacco has improved steadily in the simplified offense he has been asked to run. Joe does not have picture-perfect quarterback mechanics, but he throws the ball with touch and has the arm to put it anywhere on the field. He has a tough, no-nonsense personality that allows him to deal calmly with teammate Terrell Suggs, asserting that Troy Smith should be starting. Flacco has the promise to be more like Rich Gannon than Scott Brunner or Jeff Komlo, among former Blue Hen quarterbacks who played in the NFL. What he showed in becoming the first rookie quarterback to win two postseason starts was a big arm and the poise to not make crucial mistakes.

Tom Flores

QPR 5.5

Height: 6'1" **Weight:** 202 lbs. **Birthdate:** 3/21/1937
College: Pacific **Draft:** Free Agent
1959 CFL; 1960–61, 1963–66 Oakland Raiders;
1967–69 Buffalo Bills; 1969 Kansas City Chiefs
Regular Season Record: 31–32–4, 8 comebacks
Postseason Record: NA
Relative Rating: 110%

Passing

Year	G	Comp./Att.	%	Yards	Y/Att.	TD	INT	Rating
1960	14	136/252	54.0	1,738	6.9	12	12	71.8
1961	14	190/366	51.9	2,176	5.9	15	19	62.1
1963	14	113/247	45.7	2,101	8.5	20	13	80.7
1964	14	98/200	49.0	1,389	6.9	7	14	54.4
1965	14	122/269	45.4	1,593	5.9	14	11	64.9
1966	14	151/306	49.3	2,638	8.6	24	14	86.2
1967	14	22/64	34.4	260	4.1	0	8	8.1
1968	1	3/5	60.0	15	3	0	1	25.0
1969	7	3/6	50.0	49	8.2	1	0	117.4
Total	106	838/1,715	48.9	11,959	7.0	93	92	67.6

Rushing

Year	Att.	Yards	Avg.	TD
1960	19	123	6.5	3
1961	23	36	1.6	1
1963	12	2	0.2	0
1964	11	64	5.8	0
1965	11	32	2.9	0
1966	5	50	10.0	1
1969	1	0	0.0	0
Total	82	307	3.7	5

Tom Flores, who was the first Mexican American starting quarterback and head coach in the NFL, was also the first person to win a Super Bowl as both a player and a coach. Flores grew up picking fruit and cotton in California and worked his way to the College of the Pacific, where he received All-American honorable mention in 1957 as a senior. When he drew no interest from the NFL, Tom tried out with Calgary in Canada but could not overcome shoulder problems. Those shoulder problems persisted in the Redskins' 1959 training camp, and he was cut again. After shoulder surgery, Flores was ready when the American Football League began in 1960, and he beat out veteran Babe Parilli for the starting slot in Oakland.

Flores led the AFL in completion percentage in 1960 and started all 14 games for the 2–12 1961 Raiders before contracting tuberculosis and missing the dreadful 1–13 1962 season. When Flores returned in 1963, Al Davis was in charge in Oakland, and the fortunes of the team turned around immediately. Davis installed his vertical passing offense that emphasized the long pass, and Tom was fairly effective running it, although he didn't have an exceptionally strong arm. However, he was fearless in the pocket and averaged 8.5 yards per pass in 1963 and 8.6 in 1966. When Davis was able to trade Flores and Art Powell for the big-armed Daryle Lamonica, he jumped at the chance. Flores was devastated, but Davis told him he would be back.

Flores had arm problems in Buffalo and threw no touchdowns and nine interceptions in parts of three years as a Bill. During the 1969 season, the Bills released Flores, and the Chiefs picked him up to back up Len Dawson. Tom threw only one pass for Kansas City but did win a Super Bowl ring in his final season as a player, retiring as one of a handful of 10-year AFL players. Flores then rejoined the Raiders as first an assistant and then head coach, wining three more Super Bowl rings. He finished his pro football career as GM and head coach of the Seahawks but was unable to repeat his Raiders coaching success in Seattle. Once again Tom returned to Oakland, but as a broadcaster.

Doug Flutie

Height: 5'9" **Weight:** 180 lbs. **Birthdate:** 10/23/1962
College: Boston College **Draft:** Los Angeles Rams 1985-11th
1985 USFL; 1986 Chicago Bears; 1987–89, 2005 New England Patriots; 1990–97 CFL; 1998–2000 Buffalo Bills; 2001–04 San Diego Chargers
Regular Season Record: 38–28, 10 comebacks
Postseason Record: 0–2, no comebacks
Relative Rating: 98%

Passing

Year	G	Comp./Att.	%	Yards	Y/Att.	TD	INT	Rating
1986	4	23/46	50.0	361	7.8	3	2	80.1
1987	2	15/25	60.0	199	8	1	0	98.6
1988	11	92/179	51.4	1,150	6.4	8	10	63.3
1989	5	36/91	39.6	493	5.4	2	4	46.6
1998	13	202/354	57.1	2,711	7.7	20	11	87.4
1999	15	264/478	55.2	3,171	6.6	19	16	75.1
2000	11	132/231	57.1	1,700	7.4	8	3	86.5
2001	16	294/521	56.4	3,464	6.6	15	18	72.0
2002	1	3/11	27.3	64	5.8	0	0	51.3
2003	7	91/167	54.5	1,097	6.6	9	4	82.8
2004	2	20/38	52.6	276	7.3	1	0	85.0
2005	5	5/10	50.0	29	2.9	0	0	56.2
Total	92	1,177/2,151	54.7	14,175	6.8	86	68	76.3
PS:	2	32/67	47.8	494	7.4	2	3	63.9

Rushing

Year	Att.	Yards	Avg.	TD
1986	9	36	4.0	1
1987	6	43	7.2	0
1988	38	179	4.7	1
1989	16	87	5.4	0
1998	48	248	5.2	1
1999	88	476	5.4	1
2000	36	161	4.5	1
2001	53	192	3.6	1
2002	1	6	6.0	0
2003	33	168	5.1	2
2004	5	39	7.8	2
2005	5	-1	-0.2	0
Total	338	1,634	4.8	10
PS:	6	41	6.8	0

Doug Flutie had a 21-year career in professional football for eight teams in three different leagues—not bad for an 11th round draft pick deemed too small to play. Altogether, he threw for 369 touchdowns,

237 interceptions, and more than 58,000 yards while running for more than 6,700 yards in his madcap scrambles.

Flutie has always been an underdog because of his 5'9" stature. Even at Boston College, where he won the Heisman Trophy and culminated his senior season with the famous 50-yard Hail Mary pass to beat Bernie Kosar and Miami 47–45, he was suspect in the eyes of some. Flutie signed with Donald Trump's New Jersey Generals out of college and played well in the USFL's final year. The Bears traded a draft pick for his rights and brought him in as a backup in 1986. Starter Jim McMahon resented Flutie and maliciously referred to him as Bambi or America's Midget. With McMahon hurt, Flutie got to start the season finale and a playoff loss to the Redskins. The next year, New England traded an eighth-round pick for him, and Flutie started the last replacement players' game in October. He struggled in his three years as a Patriot, and coach Ray Berry even advised Flutie to go into coaching before he cut him.

Instead, Flutie moved to Canada where he thrived, winning three Grey Cups and six MVP awards in eight years. In the wide-open Canadian game, Flutie said, "I feel like I've been given a chance

Doug Flutie stands with Eddie LeBaron and Davey O'Brien as the greatest short quarterbacks in NFL history.

to use all my abilities. In the NFL, I feel like a robot." Still, the ultracompetitive Flutie had a burning desire to prove the critics wrong and succeed in the NFL. Buffalo brought the 36-year-old quarterback back in 1998, and he beat out newly acquired Rob Johnson and played well enough to make the Pro Bowl. The competition with Johnson proved to be particularly nasty and divided the team. Johnson called Flutie a "self-promoter" but was consistently outperformed by the dynamic Flutie. When coach Wade Phillips named the struggling Johnson as the starter for the 2000 postseason, the team's fan base was outraged. The Bills lost to Tennessee that week in the Music City Miracle game, and some have contended that that was the beginning of the "Flutie Curse" on both Buffalo and Phillips; neither has won a playoff game since.

Flutie moved on to San Diego for four years where he was eventually beaten out by Drew Brees and then returned home to finish his career as a Patriot. Flutie did not get to play much as Tom Brady's backup, but Bill Belichik did give Flutie the opportunity to drop-kick an extra point for the first time in the NFL since 1941. Flutie was one of the most exciting players in pro football history. He was quick of foot and of mind, had a limber arm and good speed, and was a fine leader. His height did limit him against better teams, but he established himself as a legitimate starting NFL quarterback even if he never got close to winning an NFL championship.

TOP 10
Toughest Quarterbacks

10. Roman Gabriel
9. Terry Bradshaw
8. Steve McNair
7. Joe Namath
6. Doug Williams
5. Bobby Layne
4. Ron Jaworski
3. Otto Graham
2. Johnny Unitas
1. Brett Favre

John Fourcade

QPR 3.0

Height: 6'1"   **Weight:** 208 lbs.   **Birthdate:** 10/11/1960
College: Mississippi   **Draft:** Free agent
1987–90 New Orleans Saints
Regular Season Record: 7–4, 3 comebacks
Postseason Record: 0–0, no comebacks
Relative Rating: 93%

Passing

Year	G	Comp./Att.	%	Yards	Y/Att.	TD	INT	Rating
1987	3	48/89	53.9	597	6.7	4	3	75.9
1988	1	0/1	0.0	0	0.0	0	0	39.6
1989	13	61/107	57.0	930	8.7	7	4	92.0
1990	7	50/116	43.1	785	6.8	3	8	46.1
Total	24	159/313	50.8	2,312	7.4	14	15	70.1
PS:	1	5/18	27.8	79	4.4	0	2	5.8

Rushing

Year	Att.	Yards	Avg.	TD
1987	19	134	7.1	0
1989	14	91	6.5	1
1990	15	77	5.1	1
Total	48	302	6.3	2
PS:	2	13	6.5	0

John Fourcade broke the career passing marks at Ole Miss of a more famous and accomplished Saints quarterback, Archie Manning. Fourcade was a scrambling quarterback who got his chance as a replacement quarterback for the Saints in 1987 and led New Orleans to a 2–1 record in those games, winning a spot on the team for the next three years. With Bobby Hebert holding out in 1990, he even opened the season as the Saints' starter but lost that job by Week 6 due to inept play. New Orleans cut him in 1991, but his career continued for another 10 years as a player and longer still as a coach in several fly-by-night indoor leagues.

Fourcade played in the Canadian Football League in 1982 and 1983, and the USFL in 1985. After his NFL excursion, Fourcade played in the Arena Football League and the National Indoor Football League. He coached in the Arena Football League, the Indoor Professional Football League, the National Indoor Football League, the Arena Football League 2, and the Intense Football League. He served as GM/coach and quarterback for the

Mississippi Fire Dogs of the NIFL in 2001 at the age of 40 and was still coaching in football in 2008.

Dan Fouts

Height: 6'3" **Weight:** 204 lbs. **Birthdate:** 6/10/1951
College: Oregon **Draft:** San Diego 1973-3rd
1973-87 San Diego Chargers
Regular Season Record: 86-84-1, 23 comebacks
Postseason Record: 3-4, 3 comebacks
Relative Rating: 112%

Passing

Year	G	Comp./Att.	%	Yards	Y/Att.	TD	INT	Rating
1973	10	87/194	44.8	1,126	5.8	6	13	46.0
1974	11	115/237	48.5	1,732	7.3	8	13	61.4
1975	10	106/195	54.4	1,396	7.2	2	10	59.3
1976	14	208/359	57.9	2,535	7.1	14	15	75.4
1977	4	69/109	63.3	869	8.0	4	6	77.4
1978	15	224/381	58.8	2,999	7.9	24	20	83.0
1979	16	332/530	62.6	4,082	7.7	24	24	82.6
1980	16	348/589	59.1	4,715	8.0	30	24	84.7
1981	16	360/609	59.1	4,802	7.9	33	17	90.6
1982	9	204/330	61.8	2,883	8.7	17	11	93.3
1983	10	215/340	63.2	2,975	8.8	20	15	92.5
1984	13	317/507	62.5	3,740	7.4	19	17	83.4
1985	14	254/430	59.1	3,638	8.5	27	20	88.1
1986	12	252/430	58.6	3,031	7.0	16	22	71.4
1987	11	206/364	56.6	2,517	6.9	10	15	70.0
Total	181	3,297/5,604	58.8	43,040	7.7	254	242	80.2
PS:	7	159/286	55.6	2,125	7.4	12	16	70.0

Rushing

Year	Att.	Yards	Avg.	TD
1973	7	32	4.6	0
1974	19	63	3.3	1
1975	23	170	7.4	2
1976	18	65	3.6	0
1977	6	13	2.2	0
1978	20	43	2.2	2
1979	26	49	1.9	2
1980	23	15	0.7	2
1981	22	56	2.5	0
1982	9	8	0.9	1
1983	12	-5	-0.4	1
1984	12	-29	-2.4	0
1985	11	-1	-0.1	0
1986	4	-3	-0.8	0
1987	12	0	0.0	2
Total	224	476	2.1	13
PS:	8	15	1.9	0

With Dan Fouts operating the Air Coryell offense for San Diego, the Chargers led the NFL in passing yards seven of eight seasons from 1978 through 1985. However, over the past 60 years, only four teams that led the league in passing also won the championship that year—the Rams in 1951 and 1999 and the Colts in 1959 and 2006. Although passing scores points and sets up the running game, a team without some balance to its attack loses the time of possession battle and wears out its defense. Fouts' Chargers reached the AFC conference championship twice but got no further.

Fouts' passing pedigree was impeccable. As a rookie, he played with Johnny Unitas in the icon's final season. After three years of struggling, Fouts began to develop as a quarterback when Bill Walsh was brought in as offensive coordinator under Tommy Prothro in 1976. Walsh left the following year and Fouts missed the first 10 games of the season while he sued to get the NFL collective bargaining agreement overturned, but he still completed 19 of 24 passes for 279 yards in his first game back. When the Chargers started 1978 1–3, Prothro was fired and replaced with Don Coryell, and Fouts' career took flight for good. Air Coryell was a one-running-back, two-tight-end offense that used motion and timing patterns in a pass-heavy attack. Coryell brought in Joe Gibbs as his offensive coordinator, and Fouts threw for more than 4,000 yards from 1979 to 1981. In the strike season of 1982, Fouts set an NFL record by averaging 320 yards per game through the air. At his retirement, Fouts was the NFL's all-time leader in 300-yard games with 51, although Dan Marino would top him in time.

In the playoffs, Fouts was up and down. He threw five interceptions in a 1979 loss to the Oilers but threw a 50-yard touchdown pass with 2:00 left a year later to beat the Bills. His most memorable postseason games came in 1981. The Chargers overcame the resilient Dolphins 41–38 in hot, humid Miami, with Fouts throwing for 433 yards and three touchdowns in a game that was decided in overtime. A week later in minus-59-degree windchill, Fouts could manage just 185 yards in a 27–7 loss to Cincinnati in the Freezer Bowl.

Fouts was sturdily built and tough against a pass rush. He took a five-step drop, read the coverage, and delivered the ball quickly and accurately to his talented receivers. He had no mobility but got rid of the ball so quickly that he did not take an inordinate amount of sacks. He was a fine leader who was always in attack mode but would throw interceptions as well as touchdowns. Like Y.A. Tittle, Sonny Jurgensen, and Dan Marino, that style won him a Hall of Fame ring but not a championship.

Jesse Freitas

QPR 1.5

Height: 5'10"   **Weight:** 170 lbs.   **Birthdate:** 2/7/1921
College: Santa Clara   **Draft:** Pittsburgh 1944-7th
1946–47 San Francisco 49ers; 1948 Chicago Rockets; 1949 Buffalo Bills
Regular Season Record: 0–9 est., no comebacks
Postseason Record: NA
Relative Rating: 101%

Passing

Year	G	Comp./Att.	%	Yards	Y/Att.	TD	INT	Rating
1946	10	22/44	50.0	234	5.3	3	7	49.1
1947	10	13/33	39.4	215	6.5	4	2	76.4
1948	10	84/167	50.3	1,425	8.5	14	16	67.9
1949	1	4/9	44.4	10	1.1	0	2	12.0
Total	31	123/253	48.6	1,884	7.4	21	27	61.7

Rushing

Year	Att.	Yards	Avg.	TD
1946	6	-21	-3.5	0
1947	6	-9	-1.5	0
1948	24	25	1.0	0
1949	3	13	4.3	0
Total	39	8	0.2	0

Under coach Buck Shaw, Jesse Freitas Sr. starred for Santa Clara College, throwing touchdown passes to Alyn Beals before the war. When Shaw was hired as the 49ers' first coach in 1946, he signed Freitas and Beals, but Jesse did not get to play much, backing up Frankie Albert. However, all seven of Freitas' touchdown passes as a 49er went to Beals, who became a star in the All-America Football Conference. After two years, the Chicago Rockets obtained Freitas, and he split the quarterbacking with Sam Vacanti for the 1–13 Rockets in 1948. Freitas finished his career as George Ratterman's

backup in Buffalo in the final year of the AAFC and then went into high school coaching where he had a great deal of success. Two of his schoolboy quarterbacks over the years were his sons Jesse Jr., who went on to play with San Diego State and the Chargers, and Jim, who played at Long Beach State in the 1970s.

Gus Frerotte

QPR 7.0

Height: 6'3"   **Weight:** 237 lbs.   **Birthdate:** 7/31/1971
College: Tulsa   **Draft:** Washington 1994-7th
1994–98 Washington Redskins; 1999 Detroit Lions; 2000–01 Denver Broncos; 2002 Cincinnati Bengals; 2003–04, 2008 Minnesota Vikings; 2005 Miami Dolphins; 2006–07 St. Louis Rams
Regular Season Record: 45–47–1, 10 comebacks
Postseason Record: 0–2, no comebacks
Relative Rating: 94%

Passing

Year	G	Comp./Att.	%	Yards	Y/Att.	TD	INT	Rating
1994	4	46/100	46.0	600	6.0	5	5	61.2
1995	16	199/396	50.3	2,751	6.9	13	13	70.2
1996	16	270/470	57.4	3,453	7.3	12	11	79.3
1997	13	204/402	50.7	2,682	6.7	17	12	73.8
1998	3	25/54	46.3	283	5.2	1	3	45.5
1999	9	175/288	60.8	2,117	7.4	9	7	83.6
2000	10	138/232	59.5	1,776	7.7	9	8	82.1
2001	4	30/48	62.5	308	6.4	3	0	101.7
2002	4	44/85	51.8	437	5.1	1	5	46.1
2003	16	38/65	58.5	690	10.6	7	2	118.1
2004	16	0/1	0.0	0	0.0	0	0	39.6
2005	16	257/494	52.0	2,996	6.1	18	13	71.9
2006	1	1/3	33.3	27	9.0	0	0	67.4
2007	8	94/167	56.3	1,014	6.1	7	12	58.3
2008	11	178/301	59.1	2,157	7.2	12	15	73.7
Total	147	1,699/3,106	54.7	21,291	6.9	114	106	74.2
PS:	2	34/75	45.3	375	5.0	1	3	48.5

Rushing

Year	Att.	Yards	Avg.	TD
1994	4	1	0.3	0
1995	22	16	0.7	1
1996	28	16	0.6	0
1997	24	65	2.7	2
1998	3	20	6.7	0
1999	15	33	2.2	0
2000	22	64	2.9	1
2001	10	9	0.9	1
2002	4	22	5.5	0
2003	12	-2	-0.2	0
2005	27	61	2.3	0
2007	6	3	0.5	0
2008	19	7	0.4	1
Total	196	315	1.6	6
PS:	3	15	5.0	0

In 2007, Gus Frerrote tied Chris Chandler for the journeyman quarterback's record of having started for seven different NFL franchises. When the seventh-round pick came to the Redskins' camp in 1994, though, he was a long shot to start for even one. Washington selected Frerotte in the same draft that they chose All-American Heath Shuler with their top pick. However, Shuler looked so lost in the NFL that the brash Frerotte blew right by him, winning the starting job outright in 1996. Gus even went to the Pro Bowl for the first and only time that year.

Frerotte had been inconsistent in college. He told *Sports Illustrated*, "[Scouts] looked at me coming out of college and they didn't see the greatest athlete. Well, my feet are quick, I can move a little, and I can throw the rock. Plus, I pride myself on being a tough guy." In 1997, Frerotte proved not only could he throw the "rock" but also that he had rocks in his head in a game against the Giants in November. With the ball at the New York 1, Frerotte dropped back, scrambled around, and at last squirted into the end zone to give the Redskins the lead. Gus was so pumped up by his dazzling run that he headed for the stands and head-butted the wall, spraining his neck. He missed the second half of that game but returned to play the next week.

The following season, Frerotte was overtaken by Trent Green as starter, and both Gus and Trent left as free agents in 1999 with Brad Johnson coming to Washington. Frerotte spent a season

in Detroit, two in Denver, one in Cincinnati, and two in Minnesota before landing in Miami under Nick Saban. After eight years, he was a starter again and did a credible job. However, Saban lusted after Daunte Culpepper and Joey Harrington, and Frerotte moved on to St. Louis and then back to Minnesota, where Brad Childress gave up on young Tarvaris Jackson and decided that 38-year-old Gus Frerotte, who had never thrown for more than 18 touchdowns in a season, was just the guy to lead the Vikings to the Super Bowl. Although he is a fiery competitor, he is also immobile, inconsistent, and not a championship quarterback. When Frerotte was injured late in the year, Childress went back to Jackson to lead Minnesota in the postseason.

Benny Friedman

QPR 8.0

Height: 5'10" **Weight:** 183 lbs. **Birthdate:** 3/18/1905
College: Michigan **Draft:** Free agent
1927 Cleveland Bulldogs; 1928 Detroit Panthers;
1929–31 New York Giants; 1932–34 Brooklyn Dodgers
Regular Season Record: 51–25–5 est., 8 comebacks
Postseason Record: NA
Relative Rating: NA

Passing

Year	G	Comp./Att.	%	Yards	Y/Att.	TD	INT	Rating
1927*	13	96/205	NA	1,721	NA	12	11	NA
1928*	10	77/155	NA	1,348	NA	10	15	NA
1929*	15	84/156	NA	1,677	NA	20	10	NA
1930*	15	71/124	NA	1,246	NA	13	9	NA
1931*	9	42/68	NA	729	NA	3	4	NA
1932	11	23/74	31.1	319	4.3	5	10	28.9
1933	7	42/80	52.5	594	7.4	5	7	61.1
1934	1	5/13	38.5	16	1.2	0	2	7.1
Total	81	440/875	—	7,650	68	68	—	—

Rushing

Year	Att.	Yards	Avg.	TD
1927*	22	157	7.1	2
1928*	72	575	8.0	6
1929*	72	407	5.7	2
1930*	90	386	4.3	6
1931*	66	323	4.9	2
1932	88	250	2.8	0
1933	55	177	3.2	0
1934	9	31	3.4	0
Total	474	2,306	4.9	18

* incomplete and unofficial statistics

Benny Friedman was the greatest passer of his time by far and a revolutionary figure in the history of the game. However, the statistics from the time are incomplete and unofficial, so he is not much remembered today. Benny was a 5'10" single-wing tailback who led his team in rushing as well as passing in his first five years in the league. He threw for 20 touchdowns in 1929, and the next player to do that was Cecil Isbell in 1942. Friedman was the first passer who made a habit of passing on any down. His feeling was, "Why wait until third down when the defense is looking for it?" Defenses were forced to adjust to a more wide-open game when playing against Benny by having the center on the defensive line drop into a linebacking position to deal with the pass. Friedman's teams led the NFL in scoring for four consecutive seasons from 1927 to 1930, and his teams would exceed the league average in points by an astronomical 68 percent during his career. He also directed more fourth-quarter comebacks than any other signal-caller in the 1920s and 1930s.

Friedman was an All-American at Michigan under Fielding Yost before turning pro in 1927 with Cleveland, where he led the NFL in touchdown passes. The following year in Detroit, he led the league in touchdown passes again. Tim Mara wanted Benny so much as both a passer and drawing card that he bought the whole Detroit team in 1929 to get Friedman, and Benny led the league in touchdowns with 20 and spurred the team to 13 wins. He repeated that trick in 1930, although with just 13 touchdown passes this time. The team slipped a bit in 1931, but Friedman still led the league in passing yards according to the data we have. That year, he also wrote one of the first football primers, *The Passing Game*. He wanted to buy into the ownership of the Giants at this point but was rebuffed and left for the Brooklyn Dodgers, where he finished his career as a part-time player.

Friedman was supremely confident of his abilities. He coached football at CCNY and Brandeis for the next few decades but still followed the pro game with a critical eye. In 1953, he wrote an article for *Sport Magazine* titled "I Could Play Pro Football—And I'm 48." He may have been serious.

John Friesz

QPR 4.5

Height: 6'4" **Weight:** 214 lbs. **Birthdate:** 5/19/1967
College: Idaho **Draft:** San Diego 1990-6th
1990–91, 1993 San Diego Chargers; 1994 Washington Redskins; 1995–98 Seattle Seahawks; 1999–2000 New England Patriots
Regular Season Record: 13–25, 8 comebacks
Postseason Record: NA
Relative Rating: 93%

Passing

Year	G	Comp./Att.	%	Yards	Y/Att.	TD	INT	Rating
1990	1	11/22	50.0	98	4.5	1	1	58.5
1991	16	262/487	53.8	2,896	5.9	12	15	67.1
1993	12	128/238	53.8	1,402	5.9	6	4	72.8
1994	16	105/180	58.3	1,266	7.0	10	9	77.7
1995	6	64/120	53.3	795	6.6	6	3	80.4
1996	8	120/211	56.9	1,629	7.7	8	4	86.4
1997	2	15/36	41.7	138	3.8	0	3	18.1
1998	6	29/49	59.2	409	8.3	2	2	82.8
1999	1	0/0	0.0	0	0.0	0	0	0.0
2000	1	11/21	52.4	66	3.1	0	1	39.0
Total	69	745/1,364	54.6	8,699	6.4	45	42	72.3

Rushing

Year	Att.	Yards	Avg.	TD
1990	1	3	3.0	0
1991	10	18	1.8	0
1993	10	3	0.3	0
1994	1	1	1.0	0
1995	11	0	0.0	0
1996	12	1	0.1	0
1997	1	0	0.0	0
1998	5	5	1.0	0
1999	2	-2	-1.0	0
Total	53	29	0.5	0

John Friesz began his college career as the backup to future Rams coach Scott Linehan but led the Idaho Vandals to three consecutive conference championships in his three years as a starter. He also won the Walter Payton Award as the top Division I-AA player in the nation as a senior. In fact, the Idaho MVP Award is now named the John Friesz Award in his honor. It's a big leap to the NFL, though.

Friesz won the starting job in San Diego in his second year, but then he got hurt in 1993 and Stan Humphries moved past him. Friesz signed with the Redskins as a free agent in 1994 and served as a placeholder for starting quarterback for Heath Shuler for half a season. Then it was on to Seattle to back up Rick Mirer, Warren Moon, and Jon Kitna and finally New England to back up Drew Bledsoe until Tom Brady thrust Friesz aside. Friesz's career was sidetracked by injuries a number of times, but at best he was a game manager who said in 1996, "I'm just doing what I do best, which is to come in and not screw up the game."

Charlie Frye

Height: 6'4"   **Weight:** 225 lbs.   **Birthdate:** 8/28/1981
College: Akron   **Draft:** Cleveland 2005-3rd
2005–07 Cleveland Browns; 2007–08 Seattle Seahawks
Regular Season Record: 6–14, 1 comeback
Postseason Record: NA
Relative Rating: 90%

Passing

Year	G	Comp./Att.	%	Yards	Y/Att.	TD	INT	Rating
2005	7	98/164	59.8	1,002	6.1	4	5	72.8
2006	13	252/392	64.3	2,454	6.3	10	17	72.2
2007	1	4/10	40.0	34	3.4	0	1	10.0
2008	2	12/23	52.2	83	3.6	2	2	53.4
Total	**22**	366/589	62.1	3,573	6.1	16	25	70.5

Rushing

Year	Att.	Yards	Avg.	TD
2005	18	60	3.3	1
2006	47	215	4.6	3
2007	1	1	1.0	0
2008	2	30	15.0	0
Total	**68**	**306**	**4.5**	**4**

In his third preseason with the Browns, Charlie Frye held off backup Derek Anderson and rookie Brady Quinn to win the starting quarterback slot. That lasted for less than a week. In the first half of the 2007 opener against Pittsburgh, Frye was sacked five times in throwing for just 34 yards before he was pulled for Anderson. Cleveland was so disillusioned by Frye's lack of progress as an NFL quarterback that they traded him to the Seahawks for a sixth-round pick two days later. It was the first time an opening-day starting quarterback was

traded that quickly since the 1970 merger. Frye did not play again till the following season, when he was ineffective in a start against the Packers while Matt Hasselbeck was hurt. The pro game moves too quickly for the former Mid-American Conference star. Frye is indecisive under pressure, holds the ball too long, or throws it to the wrong team. His arm is adequate for short passes but not for long ones.

Steve Fuller

Height: 6'4"   **Weight:** 198 lbs.   **Birthdate:** 1/5/1957
College: Clemson   **Draft:** Kansas City 1979-1st
1979–82 Kansas City Chiefs; 1984–86 Chicago Bears
Regular Season Record: 19–23, 7 comebacks
Postseason Record: 1–1, no comebacks
Relative Rating: 94%

Passing

Year	G	Comp./Att.	%	Yards	Y/Att.	TD	INT	Rating
1979	16	146/270	54.1	1,484	5.5	6	14	55.8
1980	14	193/320	60.3	2,250	7.0	10	12	76.4
1981	13	77/134	57.5	934	7.0	3	4	74.0
1982	9	49/93	52.7	665	7.2	3	2	77.6
1984	6	53/78	67.9	595	7.6	3	0	103.3
1985	16	53/107	49.5	777	7.3	1	5	57.3
1986	16	34/64	53.1	451	7.0	2	4	60.1
Total	**90**	605/1,066	56.8	7,156	6.7	28	41	70.1
PS:	3	22/41	53.7	298	7.3	2	1	83.2

Rushing

Year	Att.	Yards	Avg.	TD
1979	50	264	5.3	1
1980	60	274	4.6	4
1981	19	118	6.2	0
1982	10	56	5.6	0
1984	15	89	5.9	1
1985	24	77	3.2	5
1986	8	30	3.8	0
Total	**186**	**908**	**4.9**	**11**
PS:	9	45	5.0	0

Steve Fuller was the third quarterback taken in the first round in 1979, behind Jack Thompson and Phil Simms and ahead of third-rounder Joe Montana. Fuller was a brainy pre-law student at Clemson who said of his future at the time of the draft, "You either have to finesse 12 people who weren't smart enough to get out of jury duty or 11 who weren't smart enough to play offense."

Fuller did not have a big-league arm, but Chiefs coach Marv Levy tried to take advantage of Steve's legs by instituting a wing-T offense in 1979 that relied more on the quarterback's ball-handling skills and ability to run with the ball than on passing. When that failed, Levy tried more of a rollout passing attack in 1980. By his third year, Fuller was on the bench and finished his career as Jim McMahon's backup in Chicago. Although he was a fine runner, Fuller was a deliberate passer who was sacked on 12.5 percent of pass plays, the third highest rate in history. His career was epitomized in the 1984 playoffs when McMahon was hurt. Steve's cautious approach was moderately effective in a win over the Redskins, but the next week he was exposed against a fierce 49er defense that sacked him nine times and allowed the Bears only 37 passing yards.

Roman Gabriel

QPR 8.5

Height: 6'5"   **Weight:** 220 lbs.   **Birthdate:** 8/5/1940
College: North Carolina State   **Draft:** Oakland Raiders 1962-1st; Los Angeles Rams 1962-1st
1962–72 Los Angeles Rams; 1973–77 Philadelphia Eagles
Regular Season Record: 86–64–7, 16 comebacks
Postseason Record: 0–2, no comebacks
Relative Rating: 112%

Passing

Year	G	Comp./Att.	%	Yards	Y/Att.	TD	INT	Rating
1962	6	57/101	56.4	670	6.6	3	2	78.4
1963	12	130/281	46.3	1,947	6.9	8	11	62.7
1964	7	65/143	45.5	1,236	8.6	9	5	82.4
1965	7	83/173	48.0	1,321	7.6	11	5	83.0
1966	14	217/397	54.7	2,540	6.4	10	16	65.9
1967	14	196/371	52.8	2,779	7.5	25	13	85.2
1968	14	184/366	50.3	2,364	6.5	19	16	70.0
1969	14	217/399	54.4	2,549	6.4	24	7	86.8
1970	14	211/407	51.8	2,552	6.3	16	12	72.2
1971	14	180/352	51.1	2,238	6.4	17	10	75.4
1972	14	165/323	51.1	2,027	6.3	12	15	63.8
1973	14	270/460	58.7	3,219	7	23	12	86.0
1974	11	193/338	57.1	1,867	5.5	9	12	66.8
1975	11	151/292	51.7	1,644	5.6	13	11	67.8
1976	4	46/92	50.0	476	5.2	2	2	63.5
1977	13	1/3	33.3	15	5	0	0	50.7
Total	**183**	**2,366/4,498**	**52.6**	**29,444**	**6.5**	**201**	**149**	**74.3**
PS:	2	63/33	52.4	336	5.3	3	2	70.6

Rushing

Year	Att.	Yards	Avg.	TD
1962	18	93	5.2	0
1963	39	132	3.4	3
1964	11	5	0.5	1
1965	23	79	3.4	2
1966	52	176	3.4	3
1967	43	198	4.6	6
1968	34	139	4.1	4
1969	35	156	4.5	5
1970	28	104	3.7	1
1971	18	48	2.7	2
1972	14	16	1.1	1
1973	12	10	0.8	1
1974	14	76	5.4	0
1975	13	70	5.4	1
1976	4	2	0.5	0
Total	**358**	**1,304**	**3.6**	**30**
PS:	7	32	4.6	0

Roman Gabriel was a No. 1 draft choice of both the Rams and the Raiders but chose to sign with the more established league in 1962. With Los Angeles, Gabriel had to battle Zeke Bratkowski, Terry Baker, and Bill Munson for playing time in a typical Rams quarterback controversy before George Allen arrived in 1966 and named Gabriel the starter. Bratkowski and Baker were already gone at that point, and Munson was soon traded. Under Allen, Los Angeles began to win when Gabriel established himself as a leader and finally mastered the art of reading defenses. From 1967 through 1969, the Rams lost only seven games in the regular season but lost both of their playoff games.

Gabriel was a very big quarterback for his time and stood like an oak in the pocket, very difficult for pass rushers to bring down. He was a hard thrower but very accurate and threw few interceptions. When he did run with the ball, he ran like a powerful fullback and gained more than 1,300 yards on the ground in his career. From 1965 to 1971, Gabriel started 89 straight games, the third-longest streak of his time. When the team began to slip after Allen was fired, Los Angeles traded for John Hadl and shipped Gabriel to Philadelphia in 1973 for Harold Jackson, Tony Baker, two first-round picks, and a third-rounder. In Philadelphia, Roman led the NFL in touchdown passes and yards while throwing to the "Fire High Gang" of tall receivers that year and won the Comeback Player of the Year Award. However, knee, elbow, and shoulder problems would haunt the final four years of his career on those dismal Eagle teams.

Although the four-time Pro Bowler was known as the "Big Indian," Gabriel was actually half Irish and half Filipino and as such was the first Asian NFL quarterback. He was a proud man who told the *Los Angeles Times* that stubbornness was a key to his success. "That's a quality that I had that carried me through 16 years of being a professional football player—denying the fact that you're hurt and daring somebody to take you down."

Bob Gagliano

QPR 2.5

Height: 6'3" **Weight:** 200 lbs. **Birthdate:** 9/5/1958
College: Utah State **Draft:** Kansas City 1981-12th
1982–83 Kansas City Chiefs; 1984–85 USFL; 1987 Arena Football; 1987 San Francisco 49ers; 1989–90 Detroit Lions; 1991–92 San Diego Chargers
Regular Season Record: 7–6, 1 comeback
Postseason Record: NA
Relative Rating: 83%

Passing

Year	G	Comp./Att.	%	Yards	Y/Att.	TD	INT	Rating
1982	1	1/1	100.0	7	7.0	0	0	95.8
1983	1	0/0	0.0	0	0.0	0	0	0.0
1987	3	16/29	55.2	229	7.9	1	1	78.1
1989	11	117/232	50.4	1,671	7.2	6	12	61.2
1990	9	87/159	54.7	1,190	7.5	10	10	73.6
1991	2	9/23	39.1	76	3.3	0	1	30.3
1992	5	19/42	45.2	258	6.1	0	3	35.6
Total	32	249/486	51.2	3,431	7.1	17	27	62.7

Rushing

Year	Att.	Yards	Avg.	TD
1989	41	192	4.7	4
1990	46	145	3.2	0
1991	3	19	6.3	0
1992	3	-4	-1.3	0
Total	95	352	3.8	4

Bob Gagliano was the epitome of a journeyman quarterback. After playing for three colleges, Gagliano was drafted in the 12th round by Kansas City in 1981 and passed through seven NFL franchises over the next 13 years. However, he threw for nearly as many yards and touchdowns in his two seasons with the Denver Gold of the USFL as he did in the NFL. In Denver, Gagliano played under Mouse Davis in the run-and-shoot offense that featured four wideouts and no tight end with the quarterback sprinting out to throw the ball often. After the USFL folded, Gagliano fell into arena football before landing with San Francisco for two years, including one start in a replacement players' game during the 1987 strike. When Davis was hired as the Lions' offensive coordinator in

1989, he brought in Gagliano to help run it. He got 11 of his 13 career starts in the next two years in Detroit before finishing his career in San Diego. Befitting his own background, Gagliano's greatest claim to fame came long after his playing days in 2000 when he tutored wifty actor Keanu Reeves in how to throw a football for his role as quarterback Shane Falco in the movie *The Replacements*.

Rich Gannon

QPR 9.0

Height: 6'3"   **Weight:** 210 lbs.   **Birthdate:** 12/20/1965
College: Delaware   **Draft:** New England 1987-4th
1987–92 Minnesota Vikings; 1993 Washington Redskins; 1995–98 Kansas City Chiefs; 1999–04 Oakland Raiders
Regular Season Record: 76–56, 18 comebacks
Postseason Record: 4–3, no comebacks
Relative Rating: 109%

Passing

Year	G	Comp./Att.	%	Yards	Y/Att.	TD	INT	Rating
1987	4	2/6	33.3	18	3.0	0	1	2.8
1988	3	7/15	46.7	90	6.0	0	0	66
1989	0	0/0	0.0	0	0.0	0	0	0.0
1990	14	182/349	52.1	2,278	6.5	16	16	68.9
1991	15	211/354	59.6	2,166	6.1	12	6	81.5
1992	12	159/279	57.0	1,905	6.8	12	13	72.9
1993	8	74/125	59.2	704	5.6	3	7	59.5
1995	2	7/11	63.6	57	5.2	0	0	76.7
1996	4	54/90	60.0	491	5.5	6	1	92.4
1997	9	98/175	56.0	1,144	6.5	7	4	79.8
1998	12	206/354	58.2	2,305	6.5	10	6	80.1
1999	16	304/515	59.0	3,840	7.5	24	14	86.5
2000	16	284/473	60.0	3,430	7.3	28	11	92.4
2001	16	361/549	65.8	3,828	7.0	27	9	95.5
2002	16	418/618	67.6	4,689	7.6	26	10	97.3
2003	7	125/225	55.6	1,274	5.7	6	4	73.5
2004	3	41/68	60.3	524	7.7	3	2	86.9
Total	157	2,533/4,206	60.2	28,743	6.8	180	104	84.7
PS:	9	154/240	64.2	1691	7.0	11	9	84.6

Rushing

Year	Att.	Yards	Avg.	TD
1988	4	29	7.3	0
1990	52	268	5.2	1
1991	43	236	5.5	2
1992	45	187	4.2	0
1993	21	88	4.2	1
1995	8	25	3.1	1
1996	12	81	6.8	0
1997	33	109	3.3	2
1998	44	168	3.8	3
1999	46	298	6.5	2
2000	89	529	5.9	4
2001	63	231	3.7	2
2002	50	156	3.1	3
2003	6	18	3.0	0
2004	5	26	5.2	0
Total	521	2,449	4.7	21
PS:	19	111	3.8	1

Rich Gannon persisted through a great deal of adversity to become a top-flight NFL quarterback finally in his thirties. New England drafted Gannon

After throwing an interception against the Rams in 2002, Rich Gannon makes a face worthy of his expressive ex-coach John "Chucky" Gruden.

and wanted to convert the speedy Delaware wing-T quarterback to a running back. When Rich balked at that, the Patriots traded him to Minnesota for a fourth-round pick. After four years, Gannon became the Vikings' primary starter, but new coach Denny Green did not appreciate Gannon's middling success and let him leave as a free agent. Rich spent a year backing up Mark Rypien in Washington and then was out of football for a year with a rotator cuff problem. He tried out with Kansas City and made the team, but coach Marty Schottenheimer couldn't see that Gannon was a better quarterback than either the cautious Steve Bono or the nervous Elvis Grbac and used Rich solely as a second quarterback. When Al Davis signed Gannon to a $16 million deal in 1999, most people couldn't see how Gannon would fit into Oakland's vaunted vertical offense.

However, the fiery, emotional Gannon was a perfect fit for coach Jon Gruden's attack. Gannon was precision passer who could throw the ball both with touch and with zip. He was creative and could extend plays with his legs when the protection broke down. In his first four years in Oakland, Gannon threw for more than 3,000 yards and went to the Pro Bowl each year, averaged 26 touchdowns and 11 interceptions per year, and led the Raiders to the playoffs three times. In 2002, he was the NFL MVP and threw for more than 4,600 yards in leading Oakland to the Super Bowl. Unfortunately, there they met the Bucs, coached by Jon Gruden, who trained his defense to recognize every play that Gannon called. He threw an uncharacteristic five interceptions in the Super Bowl, and that would prove to be the coda on his career because shoulder and neck injuries over the next two years forced him to retire. With such a long prologue and such a disappointing end to his career, Gannon remains an underrated quarterback.

TOP 10
Oddest Quarterback Trades

10. The Chargers traded the rights to top overall pick Eli Manning for the rights to Philip Rivers plus first-, third-, and fifth-round picks in 2004.

9. Harry Agganis was one of 10 Browns traded to Baltimore for five Colts in the largest NFL trade not involving draft choices. Agganis chose to play baseball instead.

8. Greg Barton was traded by the Lions to the Eagles in 1971 for three draft picks despite having thrown just one pass in his career. Barton instead signed in Canada, but Philadelphia still lost all three draft picks.

7. The Giants bought the entire Detroit Wolverines franchise in 1929 in order to obtain passer Benny Friedman.

6. The Eagles waived their 1949 first-round draft pick, Frank Tripucka, in midseason, and he was picked up by the Lions.

5. George Blanda was one of five Bears traded to the Colts in 1950 for All-Pro guard Dick Barwegan. One week later, George Halas bought Blanda back from Baltimore.

4. Cleveland's Bobby Garrett was traded to Green Bay in a deal for Babe Parilli and three others in 1954. Three years later, Garrett and Parilli were returned to their original teams in another multiplayer deal.

3. Bobby Thomason was traded by the Rams to the Packers in 1951 for first- and second-round draft picks, but only if the Packers decided to keep Thomason past December 31st of that year. Green Bay returned Thomason to the Rams in December to void the deal.

2. Jacky Lee was leased to the Broncos by the Oilers for Bud McFaddin in 1964. When Denver returned Lee to Houston in 1966, McFaddin was retired.

1. Rudy Bukich was traded by the Bears to Pittsburgh in 1960 for future considerations, which turned out to be the return of Bukich to Chicago in 1962.

Jeff Garcia

QPR 8.5

Height: 6'0" **Weight:** 195 lbs. **Birthdate:** 2/24/1970
College: San Jose State **Draft:** Free agent
1999–2003 San Francisco 49ers; 2004 Cleveland Browns; 2005 Detroit Lions; 2006 Philadelphia Eagles; 2007–08 Tampa Bay Bucs
Regular Season Record: 58–58, 17 comebacks
Postseason Record: 2–4, 2 comebacks
Relative Rating: 110%

Passing

Year	G	Comp./Att.	%	Yards	Y/Att.	TD	INT	Rating
1999	13	225/375	60.0	2,544	6.8	11	11	77.9
2000	16	355/561	63.3	4,278	7.6	31	10	97.6
2001	16	316/504	62.7	3,538	7.0	32	12	94.8
2002	16	328/528	62.1	3,344	6.3	21	10	85.6
2003	13	225/392	57.4	2,704	6.9	18	13	80.1
2004	11	144/252	57.1	1,731	6.9	10	9	76.7
2005	6	102/173	59.0	937	5.4	3	6	65.1
2006	8	116/188	61.7	1,309	7.0	10	2	95.8
2007	13	209/327	63.9	2,440	7.5	13	4	94.6
2008	12	244/376	64.9	2,712	7.2	12	6	90.2
Total	**124**	**2,264/3,676**	**61.6**	**25,537**	**6.9**	**161**	**83**	**87.5**
PS:	6	126/217	58.1	1,356	6.2	7	7	73.8

Rushing

Year	Att.	Yards	Avg.	TD
1999	45	231	5.1	2
2000	72	414	5.8	4
2001	72	254	3.5	5
2002	73	353	4.8	3
2003	56	319	5.7	7
2004	35	169	4.8	2
2005	17	51	3.0	1
2006	25	87	3.5	0
2007	35	116	3.3	1
2008	35	148	4.2	1
Total	**465**	**2,142**	**4.6**	**26**
PS:	18	88	4.9	1

Ignored by the NFL out of college, Jeff Garcia signed with Calgary in Canada to be Doug Flutie's backup. When Flutie left as a free agent two years later, Jeff became the Stampeder starter and eventually culminated an outstanding CFL career by leading Calgary to the Grey Cup in 1998. Garcia attracted the attention of Bill Walsh, who recommended that

TOP 10
Quarterback Playboys

10. Troy Aikman dated country star Lorrie Morgan.
9. Tony Romo bested Aikman by dating country singers Carrie Underwood and Jessica Simpson.
8. Bobby Douglass married Playboy Playmate Carol O'Neal.
7. Dan Pastorini married Playboy Playmate June Wilkinson.
6. Tim Couch married Playboy Playmate of the Year 1999 Heather Kozar.
5. Jeff Garcia married Playboy Playmate of the Year 2004 Carmella DeCesare.
4. Rodney Peete married actress Holly Robinson.
3. Tom Brady threw over actress Bridget Moynihan for supermodel Giselle Bundchen.
2. Joe Namath dated actresses Raquel Welch, Mamie Van Doren, and many others.
1. Bob Waterfield married his high school girlfriend, movie star Jane Russell.

the 49ers sign the Bay Area native in 1999. Garcia got his chance to play that year when Steve Young suffered a career-ending concussion, and Jeff took over as the regular starter in 2000. Garcia was an instant hit, making the Pro Bowl three straight years and throwing for more than 30 touchdowns back to back.

Much like the first 49ers quarterback, Frankie Albert, Garcia was short and did not have great arm strength but was an accurate sprint-out passer with a quick release. He was a competitive leader on the field who knew how to move the chains and proved ideal for the West Coast offense. His greatest moment in San Francisco came when he led the 49ers back from a 24-point second-half deficit to beat the Giants in the 2002 postseason. As the team declined due to ownership mismanagement, though, Garcia came under increasing fire from fans and diva receiver Terrell Owens. Jeff left as a free agent in 2004, bouncing from Cleveland to Detroit to Philadelphia in three years. Owens, meanwhile, went so far as to imply that Garcia was gay despite the fact that Jeff married a former Playboy Playmate of the Year and has two children.

In Philadelphia, Garcia backed up Donovan McNabb, another quarterback savaged by T.O.

When McNabb got hurt in the 10th game that year, Garcia came on to win five of six starts and lead the Eagles to the playoffs. His success with the Eagles restarted his career, and Jeff landed in Tampa under the intense Jon Gruden in 2007. Garcia took the Bucs to the playoffs that year, but Gruden still brought back the inconsistent Brian Griese to start in 2008 before Garcia reclaimed the starting job later in the year.

David Garrard

QPR 6.0

Height: 6'1" **Weight:** 244 lbs. **Birthdate:** 2/14/1978
College: East Carolina **Draft:** Jacksonville 2002-4th
2002-08 Jacksonville Jaguars
Regular Season Record: 24-22, 5 comebacks
Postseason Record: 1-1, 1 comeback
Relative Rating: 107%

Passing

Year	G	Comp./Att.	%	Yards	Y/Att.	TD	INT	Rating
2002	4	23/46	50.0	231	5.0	1	2	53.8
2003	2	9/12	75.0	86	7.2	1	0	122.2
2004	4	38/72	52.8	374	5.2	2	1	71.2
2005	7	98/168	58.3	1,117	6.6	4	1	83.9
2006	11	145/241	60.2	1,735	7.2	10	9	80.5
2007	12	208/325	64.0	2,509	7.7	18	3	102.2
2008	16	335/535	62.6	3,620	6.8	15	13	81.7
Total	56	856/1,399	61.2	9,672		51	29	85.4
PS:	3	34/62	54.8	486	7.8	3	3	76.4

Rushing

Year	Att.	Yards	Avg.	TD
2002	25	139	5.6	2
2004	12	76	6.3	1
2005	31	172	5.5	3
2006	47	250	5.3	0
2007	49	185	3.8	1
2008	73	322	4.4	2
Total	237	1,144	4.8	9
PS:	10	86	8.6	0

In the final game of David Garrard's college career, he was matched up against Byron Leftwich of Marshall in the 2001 GMAC Bowl. Although Garrard's East Carolina Pirates led at one time by 30 points, Leftwich led Marshall back to a 64–61 double-overtime win. It was the highest-scoring bowl game in history, but Garrard would eventually have the last laugh in Jacksonville.

Tom Coughlin drafted Garrard in the fourth round for Jacksonville as Mark Brunell's backup. The next year, new coach Jack Del Rio selected Leftwich in the first round and slotted Garrard as the third quarterback. Brunell moved on, and Garrard moved up to No. 2 again. As the backup to the frequently injured Leftwich, though, Garrad got ample opportunity to play, and he became a fan favorite. He is built like a bull and throws his body around recklessly whenever he takes off on a scramble. Del Rio tried to avoid a quarterback controversy in February 2007 by naming Leftwich the starter, but after watching the more consistent Garrard lead the team in the preseason, Del Rio changed his mind August 31. In an audacious move, the coach named Garrard the starter, and Leftwich was cut the next day. Del Rio said, "[Garrard] shows an urgency directing the offense that I like."

Garrard showed that urgency and leadership in the playoffs against Pittsburgh when his fourth-down 32-yard quarterback draw led to the winning field goal in the Jags' upset win. Although Jacksonville lost the next week to unbeaten New England, Garrard proved he could be a smart, steady, mobile quarterback, especially effective in Jacksonville's run-heavy attack. He has an accurate arm, a deft touch on his passes, and rarely turns the ball over. However, when the running game disappeared in 2008, Garrard floundered, despite his new $60 million contract extension, and started throwing interceptions.

Stan Gelbaugh

QPR 0.5

Height: 6'3" **Weight:** 207 lbs. **Birthdate:** 12/4/1962
College: Maryland **Draft:** Dallas 1986-6th
1989 Buffalo Bills; 1991 WLAF; 1991 Arizona
Cardinals; 1992–94, 1996 Seattle Seahawks
Regular Season Record: 1–11, 1 comeback
Postseason Record: NA
Relative Rating: 65%

Passing

Year	G	Comp./Att.	%	Yards	Y/Att.	TD	INT	Rating
1989	1	0/0	0.0	0	0.0	0	0	0.0
1991	6	61/118	51.7	674	5.7	3	10	42.1
1992	10	121/255	47.5	1,307	5.1	6	11	52.9
1993	1	3/5	60	39	7.8	0	1	45.0
1994	2	7/11	63.6	80	7.3	1	0	115.7
1996	1	0/2	0.0	0	0.0	0	0	39.6
Total	21	192/391	49.1	2,100	5.4	10	22	50.1

Rushing

Year	Att.	Yards	Avg.	TD
1989	1	-3	-3.0	0
1991	9	23	2.6	0
1992	16	79	4.9	0
1993	1	-1	-1.0	0
1994	1	10	10.0	0
Total	28	108	3.9	0

Trailing the Miami Hurricanes 31–0 in 1984, Maryland lifted starter Stan Gelbaugh for backup Frank Reich, who then led the Terrapins to the greatest comeback in college football history. Such was the football career of the sidearm-throwing Gelbaugh. He was drafted and cut by Dallas in 1986 and spent the season as a punter in Canada before signing with Buffalo as the third quarterback behind Jim Kelly and Frank "Never Say Die" Reich.

Gelbaugh never threw a pass in Buffalo but signed on with the London Monarchs of the World League of American Football in 1991. He was named MVP in that development league's first year, which got the rag-armed signal-caller back in the NFL, first with Arizona and then Seattle. Unworthy even to be a backup, Gelbaugh lost his first 11 NFL starts. Seattle gave Stan one last shot in the 1996 season finale with Rick Mirer and John Friesz both hurt, and Gelbaugh lasted for seven plays before he was forced to leave with a groin pull. Ironically,

in came Gino Torretta, who managed to beat the Raiders, aided by seven Oakland turnovers, and Stan Gelbaugh had his only career victory after 11 years of bouncing around the league as one of the worst quarterbacks of all time.

Jeff George

QPR 7.0

Height: 6'4" **Weight:** 218 lbs. **Birthdate:** 12/8/1967
College: Illinois **Draft:** Indianapolis 1990-1st
1990–93 Indianapolis Colts; 1994–96 Atlanta Falcons;
1997–98 Oakland Raiders; 1999 Minnesota Vikings;
2000–01 Washington Redskins
Regular Season Record: 46–78, 18 comebacks
Postseason Record: 1–2, no comebacks
Relative Rating: 103%

Passing

Year	G	Comp./Att.	%	Yards	Y/Att.	TD	INT	Rating
1990	13	181/334	54.2	2,152	6.4	16	13	73.8
1991	16	292/485	60.2	2,910	6.0	10	12	73.8
1992	10	167/306	54.6	1,963	6.4	7	15	61.5
1993	13	234/407	57.5	2,526	6.2	8	6	76.3
1994	16	322/524	61.5	3,734	7.1	23	18	83.3
1995	16	336/557	60.3	4,143	7.4	24	11	89.5
1996	3	56/99	56.6	698	7.1	3	3	76.1
1997	16	290/521	55.7	3,917	7.5	29	9	91.2
1998	8	93/169	55.0	1,186	7.0	4	5	72.7
1999	12	191/329	58.1	2,816	8.6	23	12	94.2
2000	6	113/194	58.2	1,389	7.2	7	6	79.6
2001	2	23/42	54.8	168	4.0	0	3	34.6
Total	131	2,298/3,967	57.9	27,602	7.0	154	110	80.4
PS:	3	71/129	55.0	1,001	7.8	9	3	93.8

Rushing

Year	Att.	Yards	Avg.	TD
1990	11	2	0.2	1
1991	16	36	2.3	0
1992	14	26	1.9	1
1993	13	39	3.0	0
1994	30	66	2.2	0
1995	27	17	0.6	0
1996	5	10	2.0	0
1997	17	44	2.6	0
1998	8	2	0.3	0
1999	16	41	2.6	0
2000	7	24	3.4	0
2001	4	0	0.0	0
Total	168	307	1.8	2
PS:	4	7.0	1.8	0

Falcons coach June Jones tells immature quarterback Jeff George to go stand in a corner for the rest of the season during a nationally televised Sunday night game against the Eagles in 1996.

Jeff George had all the tools to be a great quarterback in the NFL but was too self-absorbed and immature to succeed. He was an aloof, arrogant, chronic complainer who couldn't get along with his teammates, let alone lead them. At each new stop, a new, "more mature" Jeff George would claim to have changed. "I've been through a lot of turmoil, but it's made me a better person," he said when he arrived in Oakland, but that change never lasted long. Even in college, the Indiana native transferred from Purdue to Illinois. Drafted by his hometown Colts, George's first tour was punctuated by arguments with coach Ted Marchibroda and hostility toward the fans. He lasted four years there, then three in Atlanta, two in Oakland, and one in Minnesota—a

pattern of diminishing tolerance for his antics clearly emerged.

Despite leading the Falcons to the playoffs in 1995, his tenure there ended after the third game of the 1996 season when he directed a screaming sideline fit toward coach June Jones after being yanked from a Sunday night nationally televised contest against the Eagles. Jones suspended George for the rest of the year and then traded him to Oakland. For the Raiders, George had a fine year for a losing team in his first season, but then resisted new coach Jon Gruden's West Coast approach in his second year. In Minnesota, George led the Vikings to the playoffs in 1999 but was let go at the end of the year to make way for Daunte Culpepper. George's final stop was Washington, where owner Dan Snyder signed him over the objections of the Redskins' Norv Turner. George played little under either Turner that year or Marty Schottenheimer the next, and his NFL career was over. He had tryouts with the Seahawks, Bears, and Raiders in the ensuing years but never appeared in another game. Even in 2008 at age 40 and out of the league for seven years, George made inquiries into getting back into football, but there were no takers for this obstreperous quarterback.

Harry Gilmer

QPR 2.5

Height: 6'0" **Weight:** 169 lbs. **Birthdate:** 4/14/1926
College: Alabama **Draft:** Washington 1948-1st
1948–52, 1954 Washington Redskins; 1955–56 Detroit Lions
Regular Season Record: 2–12, no comebacks
Postseason Record: NA
Relative Rating: 85%

Passing

Year	G	Comp./Att.	%	Yards	Y/Att.	TD	INT	Rating
1948	1	2/5	40.0	69	13.8	0	0	87.5
1949	12	49/132	37.1	869	6.6	4	15	31.0
1950	10	63/141	44.7	948	6.7	8	12	50.8
1951	10	31/68	45.6	391	5.8	1	6	32.2
1952	12	31/58	53.4	555	9.6	4	4	80.7
1954	12	2/7	28.6	18	2.6	0	1	0.0
1955	8	58/122	47.5	633	5.2	2	4	55.1
1956	11	27/46	58.7	303	6.6	4	3	80.3
Total	76	263/579	45.4	3,786	6.5	23	45	48.0

Rushing

Year	Att.	Yards	Avg.	TD
1949	31	167	5.4	0
1950	22	145	6.6	1
1951	19	141	7.4	0
1952	100	365	3.7	0
1954	6	19	3.2	0
1955	15	67	4.5	0
1956	8	19	2.4	0
Total	201	923	4.6	1

Redskins owner George Preston Marshall thought so highly of Alabama tailback Harry Gilmer that he traded the rights to Charlie Conerly to the Giants after he drafted Gilmer with the overall top pick in 1948. Gilmer was an exciting triple-threat back for the Crimson Tide but was never more than a backup quarterback in the NFL. Marshall envisioned the slightly built Gilmer as the successor to lanky Sammy Baugh as the Washington quarterback. Ironically, it was the even smaller Eddie LeBaron who would actually take over for Baugh in 1952. By then, Gilmer had shifted to halfback and defensive back and even went to the Pro Bowl that year.

Gilmer was traded to the Lions in 1955 and served as Bobby Layne's backup for two years before retiring. His last start came in the 1955 season finale against the Giants, and Harry tossed 49 passes that day in a losing cause. The amiable, talkative Gilmer served as an assistant coach in the NFL for the next decade before being hired by the Lions as head coach in 1965. After two losing seasons in the Motor City, he was fired and went into scouting.

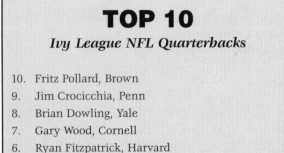

TOP 10
Ivy League NFL Quarterbacks

10. Fritz Pollard, Brown
9. Jim Crocicchia, Penn
8. Brian Dowling, Yale
7. Gary Wood, Cornell
6. Ryan Fitzpatrick, Harvard
5. Marty Domres, Columbia
4. Jason Garrett, Princeton
3. Jeff Kemp, Dartmouth
2. Jay Fiedler, Dartmouth
1. Sid Luckman, Columbia

QPR 0.5

Jug Girard

Height: 5'11" **Weight:** 176 lbs. **Birthdate:** 1/25/1927
College: Wisconsin **Draft:** Green Bay 1948-1st
1948–51 Green Bay Packers; 1952–53, 1955–56
Detroit Lions; 1957 Pittsburgh Steelers
Regular Season Record: 2–8, no comebacks
Postseason Record: NA
Relative Rating: 58%

Passing

Year	G	Comp./Att.	%	Yards	Y/Att.	TD	INT	Rating
1948	10	4/14	28.6	117	8.4	1	1	56.0
1949	12	62/175	35.4	881	5.0	4	12	31.6
1952	11	0/4	0.0	0	0.0	0	0	39.6
1953	11	0/1	0.0	0	0.0	0	0	39.6
1955	12	0/1	0.0	0	0.0	0	0	39.6
1956	10	1/1	100.0	19	19.0	0	0	118.7
1957	12	0/1	0.0	0	0.0	0	0	39.6
Total	119	67/197	34.0	1,017	5.2	5	13	32.9

Rushing

Year	Att.	Yards	Avg.	TD
1948	13	26	2.0	0
1949	45	198	4.4	1
1950	14	39	2.8	0
1951	4	20	5.0	0
1952	61	222	3.6	2
1953	19	73	3.8	0
1954	9	36	4.0	0
1955	10	27	2.7	0
1956	17	67	3.9	0
1957	2	-5	-2.5	0
Total	194	703	3.6	3

Earl "Jug" Girard was a local hero when he was drafted by the Packers in the first round of the 1948 draft. Jug was an All-American triple-threat quarterback as a 17-year-old freshman at Wisconsin who once returned two punts for scores in the same game. He did not play much as a rookie but was Green Bay's primary quarterback in 1949 and was overmatched playing on an awful team. He did lead all NFL quarterbacks with 198 yards rushing that year, but he was small and could not throw the ball very well, completing only one-third of his passes. In one game, Jug lined up behind his guard to call signals, and the center snapped the ball into the air before Girard realized his mistake. By 1950,

Jug was simply the team's punter and never played quarterback again.

The Lions picked him up in 1952, and Jug became one of coach Buddy Parker's favorites. Although he was not an NFL quarterback, he was a versatile football player who could play halfback, receiver, and defensive back as well as punt and return kicks. Girard was Parker's "Jug" of all trades in Detroit for four years where he was part of two championship teams and then for one last year in Pittsburgh. He also spent time in the farm system of the Cleveland Indians.

Paul Governali

Height: 5'11" **Weight:** 193 lbs. **Birthdate:** 1/5/1921
College: Columbia **Draft:** Boston Yanks 1943-1st
1946–47 Boston Yanks; 1947–48 New York Giants
Regular Season Record: 6–16–3 est., no comebacks
Postseason Record: NA
Relative Rating: 107%

Passing
Year	G	Comp./Att.	%	Yards	Y/Att.	TD	INT	Rating
1946	11	83/192	43.2	1,293	6.7	13	10	67.0
1947	12	108/252	42.9	1,775	7.0	17	22	53.3
1948	9	27/56	48.2	280	5.0	1	1	61.6
Total	32	218/500	43.6	3,348	6.7	31	33	59.5

Rushing
Year	Att.	Yards	Avg.	TD
1946	33	-186	-5.6	2
1947	40	151	3.8	2
1948	6	-48	-8.0	0
Total	79	-83	-1.1	4

Paul "Grover" Governali succeeded Sid Luckman as a single-wing tailback at Columbia and won the Maxwell Award as a senior in 1942 while finishing second for the Heisman Trophy. Luckman himself had finished third in the Heisman voting. As a senior, Paul led the nation with 1,442 passing yards and 19 touchdown passes. Although drafted that year by the NFL's Brooklyn Dodgers, he enlisted in the marines for the duration of the war.

When Governali came out of the service in 1946, the Dodgers were extinct, and his rights were transferred to the Boston Yanks. Paul had

1942 Heisman runner-up Paul Governali (right) watches as Joseph Taylor presents Frank Sinkwich with the Trophy.

the lowest interception percentage in the league as a rookie and threw for 13 touchdowns, but the Yanks were terrible and won only two games. Early the next season, the 1–2–1 Yanks traded Paul back home to the 0–3–1 Giants; the Yanks' win and tie both had come against the Giants. New York coach Steve Owen called Governali "the best single-wing passer in the league" when he acquired him. Governali was likewise thrilled. "I prefer to pass from the single-wing rather than the T, which is what the Yanks use." At any rate, both teams stank, whether Governali or someone else called signals.

Governali's days were numbered the next season when the Giants obtained the rights to Charlie Conerly, who took over the quarterbacking of the team. Governali retired and returned to Columbia to obtain his doctorate, which he earned with a dissertation titled, "The Professional Football Player: His Vocational Status" based on a survey Paul had conducted of his gridiron peers. In retirement, Governali worked as an assistant coach at Columbia before taking the head coaching position at San Diego State. He was succeeded there by Don Coryell and spent the rest of his life as a physical education teacher at the college.

Bruce Gradkowski

QPR **0.5**

Height: 6'1" **Weight:** 220 lbs. **Birthdate:** 1/27/1983
College: Toledo **Draft:** Tampa 2006-6th
2006–07 Tampa Bay Bucs; 2008 Cleveland Browns
Regular Season Record: 3–9, 3 comebacks
Postseason Record: NA
Relative Rating: 75%

Passing

Year	G	Comp./Att.	%	Yards	Y/Att.	TD	INT	Rating
2006	13	177/328	54.0	1,661	5.1	9	9	65.9
2007	4	13/24	54.2	130	5.4	0	1	52.4
2008	2	7/21	33.3	26	1.2	0	3	2.8
Total	19	197/373	52.8	1,817	4.9	9	13	59.9

Rushing

Year	Att.	Yards	Avg.	TD
2006	41	161	3.9	0
2007	7	20	2.9	0
2008	1	2	2.0	0
Total	49	183	3.7	0

Bruce Gradkowski went to the same Pittsburgh high school that produced Buffalo's Dan Darragh 40 years before and offered little improvement over that disastrous Bills quarterback from the late 1960s. Gradkowski set the record for highest completion percentage in Division I-A at Toledo with 68.2 percent and beat out Tim Rattay as Tampa's backup in 2006. Thrust into the starting role when Chris Simms ruptured his spleen in the fourth game, Grakowski initially performed well. However, his performance markedly declined as teams got film on him and realized that Gradkowski did not have an arm strong enough to hurt them. He barely averaged 5 yards per pass as he spent another year on Tampa's bench before being cut by both the Bucs and Rams in 2008. After three Browns quarterbacks were lost to injury, Bruce got to start Cleveland's finale against Pittsburgh and mustered a popgun attack that scored zero points.

In Denver, No. 7 is famous for John Elway and Craig Morton. In Cleveland, 7 was the number of Bruce Gradkowski (above) and Brad Goebel.

Kent Graham

QPR
4.5

Height: 6'5" **Weight:** 231 lbs. **Birthdate:** 11/1/1968
College: Ohio State **Draft:** New York Giants 1992-8th
**1992-94, 1998-99 New York Giants; 1996-97 Arizona
Cardinals; 2000 Pittsburgh Steelers; 2001 Washington
Redskins**
Regular Season Record: 17-21, 8 comebacks
Postseason Record: NA
Relative Rating: 89%

Passing

Year	G	Comp./Att.	%	Yards	Y/Att.	TD	INT	Rating
1992	6	42/97	43.3	470	4.8	1	4	44.6
1993	9	8/22	36.4	79	3.6	0	0	47.3
1994	13	24/53	45.3	295	5.6	3	2	66.2
1996	10	146/274	53.3	1,624	5.9	12	7	75.1
1997	8	130/250	52.0	1,408	5.6	4	5	65.9
1998	11	105/205	51.2	1,219	5.9	7	5	70.8
1999	9	160/271	59.0	1,697	6.3	9	9	74.6
2000	14	66/148	44.6	878	5.9	1	1	63.4
2001	3	13/19	68.4	131	6.9	2	0	122.9
Total	**83**	**694/1,339**	**51.8**	**7,801**	**5.8**	**39**	**33**	**69.0**

Rushing

Year	Att.	Yards	Avg.	TD
1992	6	36	6.0	0
1993	2	-3	-1.5	0
1994	2	11	5.5	0
1996	21	87	4.1	0
1997	13	23	1.8	2
1998	27	138	5.1	2
1999	35	132	3.8	1
2000	8	7	0.9	0
2001	7	-7	-1.0	0
Total	**121**	**424**	**3.5**	**5**

In the same year that Kent Graham was taken in the eighth round, the Giants also selected Dave Brown in the first round of the supplemental draft. The two competed for playing time for three years before Graham signed with Detroit as a free agent in 1995. Kent never played for the Lions and moved on to the Cardinals the next year. After two years as a sometime starter in Arizona, Graham returned to the Giants in 1998, the same year that Dave Brown signed with the Cardinals.

Graham took over the Giants' starting job that year and engineered an upset victory over the 13–0 Broncos, who went on to win the Super Bowl. That would prove to be the single shining moment in his otherwise drab career. Graham finished the year 5–1 as a starter, but the Giants signed the troubled Kerry Collins in the off-season to a salary four times that of Kent's. By the end of 1999, Collins was starting, and Graham was on his way out again. Kent played a year in Pittsburgh and another in Washington, always the backup. Graham had a strong arm but was wildly inconsistent and inaccurate. He was not terribly mobile and averaged fewer than 6 yards per pass throughout his career, despite his cannon arm.

Otto Graham

QPR 10.0

Height: 6'1"   **Weight:** 196 lbs.   **Birthdate:** 12/6/1921
College: Northwestern   **Draft:** Detroit 1944-1st
1946–55 Cleveland Browns
Regular Season Record: 103–17–4, 11 comebacks
Postseason Record: 9–3, 3 comebacks
Relative Rating: 150%

Passing

Year	G	Comp./Att.	%	Yards	Y/Att.	TD	INT	Rating
1946	14	95/174	54.6	1,834	10.5	17	5	112.1
1947	14	163/269	60.6	2,753	10.2	25	11	109.2
1948	14	173/333	52.0	2,713	8.1	25	15	85.6
1949	12	161/285	56.5	2,785	9.8	19	10	97.5
1950	12	137/253	54.2	1,943	7.7	14	20	64.7
1951	12	147/265	55.5	2,205	8.3	17	16	79.2
1952	12	181/364	49.7	2,816	7.7	20	24	66.6
1953	12	167/258	64.7	2,722	10.6	11	9	99.7
1954	12	142/240	59.2	2,092	8.7	11	17	73.5
1955	12	98/185	53.0	1,721	9.3	15	8	94.0
Total	**126**	**1,464/2,626**	**55.8**	**23,584**	**9.0**	**174**	**135**	**86.6**
PS:	12	159/300	53.0	2,101	7.0	14	17	67.4

Rushing

Year	Att.	Yards	Avg.	TD
1946	30	-125	-4.2	1
1947	19	72	3.8	1
1948	23	146	6.3	6
1949	27	107	4.0	3
1950	55	145	2.6	6
1951	35	29	0.8	3
1952	42	130	3.1	4
1953	43	143	3.3	6
1954	63	114	1.8	8
1955	68	121	1.8	6
Total	**405**	**882**	**2.2**	**44**
PS:	73	362	5.0	6

Automatic Otto Graham was known for the accuracy of his passing and relied heavily on timing patterns and a mix of short and long passes. He was a consistent, relentless, durable leader who was always under control. In 10 seasons as a professional quarterback, Otto led the Browns to 10 title games and won seven of them; he was 4-for-4 in the All-America Football Conference and 3-for-6 in the NFL. Three times he was the MVP in the AAFC and twice in the NFL. He led the AAFC in passer rating three times, touchdown passes twice, and passing yards three times, while he led the NFL in passer rating twice, TD passes once, and passing yards twice. Most remarkable of all, he averaged nine yards per pass, the highest mark of all time.

Graham was the first quarterback to win 100 starts and is still in the top 10 for wins today. His winning percentage is an unassailable .847 over his 10 seasons in professional football. Even limited to his time in the NFL, his won-lost record of 57–13–1 would still represent the all-time top winning percentage of .810. Cleveland coach Paul Brown claimed, "The test of a quarterback is where his team finishes. By that standard, Otto was the best of them all." Brown first saw Graham play against him as a single-wing tailback at Northwestern while Brown was coaching Ohio State. When Brown was forming the Browns, he agreed to pay Otto a stipend for the extent of his war service, and Graham chose to sign with Cleveland rather than with the NFL's Lions, who had drafted him. When Otto first got out of the navy, though, he played guard for the Rochester Royals of the National Basketball League and, of course, won the championship.

Otto Graham in the Clutch: Late in the Browns' first NFL Championship Game in 1950, they trailed the Rams 28–27. Starting from his own 32 with 1:48 to play, Graham led Cleveland to the Rams' 9 in five plays to set up Lou Groza's winning 16-yard field goal with 20 seconds to play.

Otto Graham's Signature Play: In the third quarter of a game against the Bills in the All-America Football Conference on November 2, 1947, the Browns took over on their own 1 after a goal-line stand. On the next play, Graham retreated into his end zone and hit Mac Speedie on a short sideline pattern, and Speedie raced for a 99-yard touchdown that broke open the game.

Otto Graham spurred the Browns to the championship game in each of his 10 seasons in Cleveland and won a combined seven titles in two leagues.

Otto Graham's Five Highest Honors

5. Member of the NFL's 75ᵗʰ anniversary team
4. Selected for six Pro Bowls
3. Ten-time All-Pro and nine-time consensus All-Pro
2. 1947 and 1948 AAFC MVP; 1953 and 1955 NFL Player of the Year
1. Elected to the Pro Football Hall of Fame in 1965

The Five Quarterbacks Most Similar to Otto Graham

5. Greg Cook
4. Bert Jones
3. Steve Young
2. Bob Waterfield
1. Joe Montana

Otto Graham's Five Top Touchdown Targets

5. Edgar Jones, 9 TDs
4. Ray Renfro, 11 TDs
3. Dub Jones, 18 TDs
2. Mac Speedie, 30 TDs
1. Dante Lavelli, 57 TDs

Otto Graham's Five Toughest Rivals

5. Graham was 7–0–1 against the Yankees in the regular season and 2–0 in the playoffs.
4. Graham was 9–3 against the 49ers in the regular season and 1–0 in the playoffs.
3. Graham was 8–4 against the Eagles.
2. Graham was 6–4–1 against the Giants in the regular season and 1–0 in the playoffs.
1. Graham was 0–2 against the Lions in the regular season and 1–2 in the playoffs.

Five Random Otto Graham Statistics

5. Graham played for only one head coach.
4. Graham's Browns outscored the league average by 30 percent.
3. Graham threw for six touchdowns against the L.A. Dons on October 14, 1949.
2. Graham threw for more than 300 yards 12 times and more than 400 on October 4, 1952, against the Steelers.
1. Graham led the league in completion percentage four times, passing yards five times, touchdowns three times, yards per attempt four times, passer rating four times, and interceptions once.

Although Bobby Layne's Lions had Graham's number for a time and beat him twice in the NFL title game, Otto generally came up big in big games. In the Browns' very first game in the NFL in 1950, they played the NFL champion Eagles in Philadelphia in a game that generated massive interest in pro football. Cleveland dismantled the Birds 35–10 that night as Graham picked Philadelphia's secondary apart in a much-anticipated mismatch that could be called the first Super Bowl. Three months later, in the 1950 title game against the Rams, Graham drove the Browns 68 yards in the last 1:48 to set up Lou Groza's 16-yard game-winning field goal. In that game, Otto completed 22 of 33 passes for 298 yards and four touchdowns and ran the ball 12 times for 99 more yards.

Graham threw a very catchable ball and was very mobile in the pocket. In fact, Paul Brown developed the concept of the "pocket" to protect his passer, but Graham was exceptionally tough and started 99 games in a row across two leagues. When Otto did run, he was dangerous and scored more touchdowns rushing, 44, than any other quarterback in history. Although he wasn't the greatest ball handler, the only thing he didn't do in his career was call the plays; Paul Brown did that. However, Otto proved each week that he would do whatever it took to win.

In keeping with the championship game showdown atmosphere of the 1950 NFL opening game between the defending NFL champion Eagles and the defending AAFC champion Browns, Otto Graham received the Robert French Memorial Trophy as the game's MVP. Graham, here with coach Paul Brown, led Cleveland over Philadelphia 35–10 that night.

Elvis Grbac

QPR 7.5

Height: 6'5" **Weight:** 232 lbs. **Birthdate:** 8/13/1970
College: Michigan **Draft:** San Francisco 1993-8th
1993–96 San Francisco 49ers; 1997–00 Kansas City Chiefs; 2001 Baltimore Ravens
Regular Season Record: 40–30, 11 comebacks
Postseason Record: 1–2, no comebacks
Relative Rating: 102%

Passing

Year	G	Comp./Att.	%	Yards	Y/Att.	TD	INT	Rating
1994	12	35/50	70.0	393	7.9	2	1	98.2
1995	16	127/183	69.4	1,469	8	8	5	96.6
1996	15	122/197	61.9	1,236	6.3	8	10	72.2
1997	10	179/314	57.0	1,943	6.2	11	6	79.1
1998	8	98/188	52.1	1,142	6.1	5	12	53.1
1999	16	294/499	58.9	3,389	6.8	22	15	81.7
2000	15	326/547	59.6	4,169	7.6	28	14	89.9
2001	14	265/467	56.7	3,033	6.5	15	18	71.1
Total	106	1,446/2,445	59.1	16,774	6.9	99	81	7.96
PS:	6	75/133	56.4	718	5.4	3	6	60.3

Rushing

Year	Att.	Yards	Avg.	TD
1994	13	1	0.1	0
1995	20	33	1.7	2
1996	23	21	0.9	2
1997	30	168	5.6	1
1998	7	27	3.9	0
1999	19	10	0.5	0
2000	30	110	3.7	1
2001	21	18	0.9	1
Total	163	388	2.4	7
PS:	15	52	3.5	0

Elvis Grbac played behind Steve Young for four years in San Francisco and was fairly effective despite being called a "bonehead" and an "embarrassment to humankind" by San Francisco mayor Willie Brown after a 1996 49ers loss to the Cowboys. Grbac signed as a free agent with the Chiefs and beat back the challenge of Rich Gannon to serve as the Chiefs' starter for four years. In his final year in Kansas City, Grbac went to the Pro Bowl on the strength of 28 touchdown passes and 4,169 passing yards. Grbac then signed with the world champion Baltimore Ravens, who jettisoned Super Bowl winner Trent Dilfer to go with the more accurate Grbac.

Grbac dropped to 15 touchdown passes against 18 interceptions with the Ravens and received harsh criticism from the fans and media. Grbac managed to lead Baltimore to one playoff win over Miami with just 133 passing yards but came apart the next week against the Steelers. In what would prove to be Elvis' final NFL game, he completed 18 of 37 passes for just 153 yards for no touchdowns and three interceptions. The Ravens cut him in the off-season, and Grbac retired from football at the age of 31. Elvis was a system quarterback who was lost outside the West Coast offense. He had a decent arm but was not very mobile and got rattled when he was hit. Of more importance, Grbac was a loner and not much of a team leader—reportedly the Chiefs defensive players couldn't stand him. Although Ravens coach Brian Billick saw his accuracy as a major upgrade over Dilfer, his lack of leadership was a major downgrade.

Johnny Green

QPR 2.0

Height: 6'3" **Weight:** 198 lbs. **Birthdate:** 10/12/1937
College: Tennessee-Chattanooga **Draft:** Pittsburgh 1959-21st
1960–61 Buffalo Bills; 1962–63 New York Titans/Jets
Regular Season Record: 8-11, 5 comebacks
Postseason Record: NA
Relative Rating: 94%

Passing

Year	G	Comp./Att.	%	Yards	Y/Att.	TD	INT	Rating
1960	10	89/228	39.0	1,267	5.6	10	10	54.1
1961	8	56/126	44.4	903	7.2	6	5	68.3
1962	11	128/258	49.6	1,741	6.7	10	18	55.4
1963	1	2/6	33.3	10	1.7	0	1	2.8
Total	30	275/618	44.5	3,921	6.3	26	34	56.7

Rushing

Year	Att.	Yards	Avg.	TD
1960	21	29	1.4	2
1961	14	15	1.1	1
1962	17	35	2.1	3
Total	52	79	1.5	6

Johnny Green was a late-round draft pick of Pittsburgh, whose coach, Buddy Parker, liked his arm strength. However, the Steelers waived Green in 1960 because they already had Bobby Layne and Rudy Bukich. Buffalo's coach, Buster Ramsey, had previously coached under Parker when he was in Detroit, so he called Buddy and asked about Green. Parker gave a good report to Ramsey and told Green he could stay with the Steelers on the taxi squad or sign with Buffalo in the American Football League and play. Within a week, Green was starting for the Bills.

Green had a bazooka arm but was neither accurate nor consistent. He separated his shoulder in his second season in Buffalo and the next year was traded to the Titans for the sore-armed Al Dorow. The immobile Green was the primary starter in the last confusing year of the failing Titans but was pushed aside when the Titans became the Jets under new coach Weeb Ewbank in 1963.

Trent Green

QPR 9.0

Height: 6'3" **Weight:** 217 lbs. **Birthdate:** 7/9/1970
College: Indiana **Draft:** San Diego 1993-8th
1997–98 Washington Redskins; 2000, 2008 St. Louis Rams; 2001–06 Kansas City Chiefs; 2007 Miami Dolphins
Regular Season Record: 56–57, 19 comebacks
Postseason Record: 0–2, no comebacks
Relative Rating: 109%

Passing

Year	G	Comp./Att.	%	Yards	Y/Att.	TD	INT	Rating
1997	1	0/1	0.0	0	0.0	0	0	39.6
1998	15	278/509	54.6	3,441	6.8	23	11	81.8
2000	8	145/240	60.4	2,063	8.6	16	5	101.8
2001	16	296/523	56.6	3,783	7.2	17	24	71.1
2002	16	287/470	61.1	3,690	7.9	26	13	92.6
2003	16	330/523	63.1	4,039	7.7	24	12	92.6
2004	16	369/556	66.4	4,591	8.3	27	17	95.2
2005	16	317/507	62.5	4,014	7.9	17	10	90.1
2006	8	121/198	61.1	1,342	6.8	7	9	74.1
2007	5	85/141	60.3	987	7	5	7	72.6
2008	3	38/72	52.8	525	7.3	0	6	41.7
Total	121	2,266/3,740	60.6	28,475	7.6	162	114	86.0
PS:	2	32/54	59.3	319	5.9	2	2	73

Rushing

Year	Att.	Yards	Avg.	TD
1998	42	117	2.8	2
2000	20	69	3.5	1
2001	35	158	4.5	0
2002	31	225	7.3	1
2003	26	83	3.2	2
2004	25	85	3.4	0
2005	35	82	2.3	0
2006	19	59	3.1	0
2007	7	32	4.6	0
2008	3	4	1.3	0
Total	243	914	3.8	6
PS:	4	15	3.8	0

It took Trent Green six years to work his way from the practice squad to a starting shot in the NFL, and he made the most of that chance in 1998 when he threw for 23 touchdowns and more than 3,000 yards for the Redskins. Before that, he had never been more than a third quarterback and had been on the field for just one snap in all those years. When Washington pursued hot free agent Brad Johnson in 1999, though, Green signed with the St. Louis Rams, where Mike Martz, his old position coach with the Redskins, coached under Dick Vermeil.

In the 1999 preseason, Green was outstanding in the new, wide-open Ram attack but then was felled by a Rodney Harrison blow to his knee and was lost for the year, opening the door to long shot Kurt Warner. When Green returned in 2000, the Rams were world champions, Martz was now head coach, and Trent was a backup again. After a season as a relief pitcher, Green was traded to the Chiefs, where Vermeil had taken over. Green didn't miss a start for five years in Kansas City, starting 81 straight games until a ferocious open-field tackle by the Bengals' Robert Geathers gave Green such a severe concussion that he missed eight games and wasn't the same when he did return in the second half of the year. He suffered another concussion with the Dolphins in 2007 after playing just five games. In 2008, Green returned to the Rams as a 38-year-old backup.

Green's teams outscored the league average by 20 percent over the course of his career. He was a strong and accurate passer, a clever ball handler, and a fine leader. He threw for more than 4,000 yards three years in a row and was named to two Pro Bowls.

Bob Griese

Height: 6'1" **Weight:** 190 lbs. **Birthdate:** 2/3/1945
College: Purdue **Draft:** Miami 1967-1st
1967–80 Miami Dolphins
Regular Season Record: 92–56–3, 18 comebacks
Postseason Record: 6–5, 1 comeback
Relative Rating: 115%

Passing

Year	G	Comp./Att.	%	Yards	Y/Att.	TD	INT	Rating
1967	12	166/331	50.2	2,005	6.1	15	18	61.6
1968	13	186/355	52.4	2,473	7	21	16	75.7
1969	9	121/252	48	1,695	6.7	10	16	56.9
1970	14	142/245	58	2,019	8.2	12	17	72.1
1971	14	145/263	55.1	2,089	7.9	19	9	90.9
1972	6	53/97	54.6	638	6.6	4	4	71.6
1973	13	116/218	53.2	1,422	6.5	17	8	84.3
1974	13	152/253	60.1	1,968	7.8	16	15	80.9
1975	10	118/191	61.8	1,693	8.9	14	13	86.6
1976	13	162/272	59.6	2,097	7.7	11	12	78.9
1977	14	180/307	58.6	2,252	7.3	22	13	87.8
1978	11	148/235	63	1,791	7.6	11	11	82.4
1979	14	176/310	56.8	2,160	7	14	16	72
1980	5	61/100	61	790	7.9	6	4	89.2
Total	161	1,926/3,429	56.2	25,092	7.3	192	172	77.1
PS:	12	112/208	53.8	1,467	7.1	10	12	68.3

Rushing

Year	Att.	Yards	Avg.	TD
1967	37	157	4.2	1
1968	42	230	5.5	1
1969	21	102	4.9	0
1970	26	89	3.4	2
1971	26	82	3.2	0
1972	3	11	3.7	1
1973	13	20	1.5	0
1974	16	66	4.1	1
1975	17	59	3.5	1
1976	23	108	4.7	0
1977	16	30	1.9	0
1978	9	10	1.1	0
1979	11	30	2.7	0
1980	1	0	0	0
Total	261	994	3.8	7
PS:	13	84	6.5	0

Bob Griese was something of a game manager in style, averaging just over 20 passes per game for his Hall of Fame career, but he was a talented football player who could win a game by himself when he needed to as well. At Purdue, Griese punted, kicked off, place-kicked, ran, and passed the ball to lead the Boilermakers to the school's first Rose Bowl victory in 1967. Although Florida's Steve Spurrier was the local favorite of Dolphin fans, the more mature and focused Griese was drafted by Miami and thrust into the starting role as a rookie when John Stofa broke his leg.

The Dolphins were a stumbling expansion team until Don Shula showed up in 1970. With Griese at the controls, Miami finished 10–4 that season and went to the playoffs for the first time. The next year, they were overwhelmed by Dallas in the Super Bowl, and Griese himself set a dubious

Bob Griese in the Clutch: Griese broke his leg midway through the Dolphins' undefeated 1972 season, but was ready to relieve a struggling Earl Morrall in the AFC championship against the Steelers. Down 10–7 to Pittsburgh in the third-quarter, Griese came in for the first time in two months and led two second-half touchdown drives, each requiring a fourth-down conversion. He went 3-for-5 for 70 yards passing in the drives that defeated the Steelers.

Bob Griese's Signature Play: Griese wasn't known to have a big arm, but against the defending champion Colts in the 1971 AFC title game, he hit Paul Warfield for a 75-yard touchdown on a play-action pass halfway through the first quarter. The Dolphins never trailed and dethroned the Colts 21–0.

Bob Griese was a master at mixing up his plays and took full advantage of Miami's punishing ground attack to set up his passes.

Bob Griese's Five Highest Honors

5. Member of the College Football Hall of Fame
4. Selected to eight Pro Bowls
3. Seven-time All-Pro and two-time consensus All-Pro
2. 1971 and 1977 Player of the Year
1. Elected to the Pro Football Hall of Fame in 1990

The Five Quarterbacks Most Similar to Bob Griese

5. Brian Griese
4. Rich Gannon
3. Ken Anderson
2. Roger Staubach
1. Bart Starr

Bob Griese's Five Top Touchdown Targets

5. Karl Noonan, 16 TDs
4. Howard Twilley, 17 TDs
3. Jim Mandich, 21 TDs
2. Paul Warfield, 29 TDs
1. Nat Moore, 33 TDs

Bob Griese's Five Toughest Rivals

5. Griese was 17–3–1 against the Bills.
4. Griese was 13–7 against the Jets.
3. Griese was 12–7 against the Patriots.
2. Griese was 8–7 against the Colts in the regular season and 1–0 in the playoffs.
1. Griese was 2–6–1 against the Raiders in the regular season and 1–2 in the playoffs.

Five Random Bob Griese Statistics

5. Griese played for two head coaches.
4. Griese's Dolphins outscored the league average by 11 percent.
3. Griese threw six touchdown passes against the Cardinals on November 24, 1977.
2. Griese threw for more than 300 yards three times.
1. Griese led the league in completion percentage once, touchdown passes once, and passer rating once.

record in that game by being trapped for a 29-yard loss by Bob Lilly on a misguided backward scramble. The year 1972 was the Dolphins' historic undefeated season, but Griese missed most of it after he broke his leg in October. He returned for the playoffs that year, and in Super Bowls VII and VIII combined, Bob completed 14 of 18 passes for 161 yards in leading Miami to back-to-back world championships.

With a fleet of runners such as Larry Csonka, Mercury Morris, and Jim Kiick, Griese did not pass much but was known for his accuracy. He was short and slight with questionable eyesight but was smart, disciplined, and had a quick release. Although he began his career as a scrambler, he settled down as he matured and commanded the Dolphins' punishing ground attack. He did not have a tremendous arm but could hit receivers like Paul Warfield down the field whenever he needed to.

The aging Griese became the first quarterback to wear eyeglasses under his helmet in 1977 when he led the NFL in touchdown passes with 22. He got hurt more frequently as he began to take more hits and his career wound down. After he retired in 1980, he began a long broadcasting career that was highlighted by working his son Brian's Rose Bowl win with Michigan in 1998.

Bob Griese became the first quarterback to wear eyeglasses on the field in 1977 with these oversized 1970s-styled specs.

Brian Griese

QPR 7.5

Height: 6'3" **Weight:** 215 lbs. **Birthdate:** 3/18/1975
College: Michigan **Draft:** Denver 1998-3rd
1998-02 Denver Broncos; 2003 Miami Dolphins; 2004-05, 2008 Tampa Bay Bucs; 2006-07 Chicago Bears
Regular Season Record: 45-39, 13 comebacks
Postseason Record: NA
Relative Rating: 104%

Passing

Year	G	Comp./Att.	%	Yards	Y/Att.	TD	INT	Rating
1998	1	1/3	33.3	2	0.7	0	1	2.8
1999	14	261/452	57.7	3,032	6.7	14	14	75.6
2000	10	216/336	64.3	2,688	8.0	19	4	102.9
2001	15	275/451	61.0	2,827	6.3	23	19	78.5
2002	13	291/436	66.7	3,214	7.4	15	15	85.6
2003	5	74/130	56.9	813	6.3	5	6	69.2
2004	11	233/336	69.3	2,632	7.8	20	12	97.5
2005	6	112/174	64.4	1,136	6.5	7	7	79.6
2006	6	18/32	56.3	220	6.9	1	2	62.0
2007	7	161/262	61.5	1,803	6.9	10	12	75.6
2008	5	110/184	59.8	1,073	5.8	5	7	69.4
Total	93	1,752/2,796	62.7	19,440	7.0	119	99	82.7

Rushing

Year	Att.	Yards	Avg.	TD
1998	4	-4	-1.0	0
1999	46	138	3.0	2
2000	29	102	3.5	1
2001	50	173	3.5	1
2002	37	107	2.9	1
2003	5	15	3.0	0
2004	30	17	0.6	0
2005	13	12	0.9	0
2006	6	-5	-0.8	0
2007	13	28	2.2	0
2008	5	-1	-0.2	0
Total	238	582	2.4	5

Brian Griese told *Sports Illustrated* in 2001 that the challenge of following the great John Elway in Denver was manageable because "I've been following a Hall of Famer my entire life." Brian was referring, of course, to his father, Bob, whose style he tended to emulate. Griese began as a walk-on at the University of Michigan but won 17 of 22 starts there, including a Rose Bowl win over Washington State in 1998 with his father Bob in the announcing booth.

Selected in the third round of the 1998 draft by Denver, Griese was perfectly placed to replace Elway when he retired as a champion at the end of that season. In Brian's first few years, he was hampered by shoulder and other injuries. Even so, he completed 64.3 percent of his passes for 19 touchdowns and just four interceptions in 2000. As his career progressed, though, Brian showed himself to be an accurate passer with a so-so arm who too often displayed bad judgment in throwing ill-advised passes that were intercepted. Because of his inconsistency and because he tended to be more of a loner than a leader, Griese bounced from Denver to Miami to Tampa to Chicago and then back to Tampa in the course of six seasons. In his second tour in Tampa, he won the starting job for the second time at the beginning of 2008 only to lose it again due to his variable play. Ultimately, Griese was no more successful following Jeff Garcia than he was in following John Elway and his father Bob.

Steve Grogan

QPR 8.0

Height: 6'4" **Weight:** 210 lbs. **Birthdate:** 7/24/1953
College: Kansas State **Draft:** New England 1975-5th
1975-90 New England Patriots
Regular Season Record: 75-60, 19 comebacks
Postseason Record: 0-3, no comebacks
Relative Rating: 96%

Passing

Year	G	Comp./Att.	%	Yards	Y/Att.	TD	INT	Rating
1975	13	139/274	50.7	1,976	7.2	11	18	60.4
1976	14	145/302	48.0	1,903	6.3	18	20	60.6
1977	14	160/305	52.5	2,162	7.1	17	21	65.2
1978	16	181/362	50.0	2,824	7.8	15	23	63.6
1979	16	206/423	48.7	3,286	7.8	28	20	77.4
1980	12	175/306	57.2	2,475	8.1	18	22	73.1
1981	8	117/216	54.2	1,859	8.6	7	16	63.0
1982	6	66/122	54.1	930	7.6	7	4	84.4
1983	12	168/303	55.4	2,411	8.0	15	12	81.4
1984	3	32/68	47.1	444	6.5	3	6	46.4
1985	7	85/156	54.5	1,311	8.4	7	5	84.1
1986	4	62/102	60.8	976	9.6	9	2	113.8
1987	7	93/161	57.8	1,183	7.3	10	9	78.2
1988	6	67/140	47.9	834	6	6	13	37.6
1989	7	133/261	51.0	1,697	6.5	9	14	60.8
1990	4	50/92	54.3	615	6.7	4	3	76.1
Total	149	1,879/3,593	52.3	26,886	7.5	182	208	69.6
PS:	4	48/95	50.5	571	6.0	3	7	49.1

Rushing

Year	Att.	Yards	Avg.	TD
1975	30	110	3.7	3
1976	60	397	6.6	12
1977	61	324	5.3	1
1978	81	539	6.7	5
1979	64	368	5.8	2
1980	30	112	3.7	1
1981	12	49	4.1	2
1982	9	42	4.7	1
1983	23	108	4.7	2
1984	7	12	1.7	0
1985	20	29	1.5	2
1986	9	23	2.6	1
1987	20	37	1.9	2
1988	6	12	2.0	1
1989	9	19	2.1	0
1990	4	-5	-1.3	0
Total	445	2,176	4.9	35
PS:	9	54	6.0	0

Steve Grogan was an option quarterback at Kansas State who had an awful lot to learn about playing quarterback in the NFL. As a rookie in 1975, he struggled when he was named starter over a faltering Jim Plunkett halfway through the season. Steve went 1–6 as a starter and threw 18 interceptions to just 11 touchdowns. However, coach Chuck Fairbanks had faith in Grogan and traded Plunkett to San Francisco in the off-season for a flock of high draft picks. The Patriots went 11–3 the next year with Grogan at the controls, and he set a quarterback record by scoring 12 touchdowns on the ground.

Grogan was a fiery sort who was known to throw his helmet in anger, which didn't make him the most popular teammate in New England at times. Fairbanks said in 1975, "We've got a young quarterback who can be great if he can ever learn to control his temper." Similarly, fans got frustrated with his interceptions and inconsistency and booed him unmercifully in the early years. As Grogan settled down and became a steadier quarterback, he became much more popular both with his teammates and the fans, who came to love his gritty style.

Grogan was an excellent runner as a young player, gaining 539 yards rushing in 1978 and leading all quarterbacks in rushing four times, until multiple knee problems forced him to become more

of a pocket passer and a better long-ball thrower. Hall of Fame guard John Hannah told *Sports Illustrated* in 1985, "There's only a few quarterbacks who'll do what Steve does now—he holds that ball. He'll sit there, hold it, know he'll get that lick, then throw. It makes you want to give up a little bit of your life for him." Grogan was one of the last quarterbacks to call his own plays, and more than that, also called them for Tony Eason during the Patriots' 1985 Super Bowl run. Although Grogan was never a great quarterback, he is a local legend in Boston where he spent his entire 16-year career.

Rex Grossman

Height: 6'1" **Weight:** 222 lbs. **Birthdate:** 8/23/1980
College: Florida **Draft:** Chicago Bears 2003-1st
2003–08 Chicago Bears
Regular Season Record: 19–12, 4 comebacks
Postseason Record: 2–2, 1 comeback
Relative Rating: 88%

Passing

Year	G	Comp./Att.	%	Yards	Y/Att.	TD	INT	Rating
2003	3	38/72	52.8	437	6.1	2	1	74.8
2004	3	47/84	56.0	607	7.2	1	3	67.9
2005	2	20/39	51.3	259	6.6	1	2	59.7
2006	16	262/480	54.6	3,193	6.7	23	20	73.9
2007	8	122/225	54.2	1,411	6.3	4	7	66.4
2008	4	32/62	51.6	257	4.1	2	2	59.7
Total	35	521/962	54.2	6,164	6.4	33	35	70.2
PS:	4	69/133	51.9	783	5.9	4	4	67.3

Rushing

Year	Att.	Yards	Avg.	TD
2003	3	-1	-0.3	0
2004	11	48	4.4	1
2006	24	2	0.1	0
2007	14	27	1.9	0
2008	3	4	1.3	2
Total	55	80	1.5	3
PS:	5	2	0.4	0

Steve Spurrier, his coach at Florida, called Rex Grossman "Sexy Rexy," and Rex's NFL career has been like the proverbial girl with a curl: when he's good, he's very, very good, but when he's bad, he's horrid. Bears fans never knew whether to expect Good Rex or Bad Rex in any particular game.

Grossman's grandfather, also named Rex, played for Baltimore in the All-America Football Conference in the 1940s as a contemporary of the Bears' only great quarterback, Sid Luckman. When Chicago drafted Rex No. 1 in 2003, it was desperately looking for a star. Rex had injury problems that held him to just eight games in his first three years, but he started off 2006 playing like an All-Pro for the first five weeks. Against the Cardinals in Week 6, though, Grossman threw four interceptions in a win that led to a famous tirade by Arizona coach Denny Green ("They are who we thought they were!"), and Rex's effectiveness varied wildly from week to week after that. He still managed to lead the Bears to the Super Bowl but looked astoundingly inept in that game, fumbling twice, muffing a snap, tripping over his own feet to sack himself, and throwing two late interceptions to seal the win for the Colts.

The stumbling and bumbling continued in 2007, and Rex played himself in and out of the lineup. By 2008, he lost the starting job to a maturing Kyle Orton, whose consistency was preferred by most Bear players. Grossman has a strong but erratic arm and makes too many risky decisions that result in turnovers, especially when under a pass rush. He patterned his gunslinger's game after Brett Favre but doesn't have that kind of talent.

Ralph Guglielmi

QPR 1.5

Height: 6'1" **Weight:** 196 lbs. **Birthdate:** 6/26/1933
College: Notre Dame **Draft:** Washington 1955-1st
1955, 1958–60 Washington Redskins; 1961 St. Louis Cardinals; 1962–63 New York Giants; 1963 Philadelphia Eagles
Regular Season Record: 7–16–3
Postseason Record: NA
Relative Rating: 70%

Passing

Year	G	Comp./Att.	%	Yards	Y/Att.	TD	INT	Rating
1955	9	20/62	32.3	242	3.9	2	4	29.1
1958	8	34/81	42.0	458	5.7	2	6	38.0
1959	9	36/89	40.4	617	6.9	4	11	40.1
1960	11	125/223	56.1	1,547	6.9	9	19	55.7
1961	9	56/116	48.3	927	8	5	8	61.2
1962	14	14/31	45.2	210	6.8	2	1	76.0
1963	6	7/24	29.2	118	4.9	0	3	8.0
Total	**66**	**292/626**	**46.6**	**4,119**	**6.6**	**24**	**52**	**46.5**

Rushing

Year	Att.	Yards	Avg.	TD
1955	18	51	2.8	1
1958	17	74	4.4	0
1959	26	97	3.7	0
1960	79	247	3.1	0
1961	22	101	4.6	1
1962	11	40	3.6	0
1963	4	23	5.8	0
Total	**177**	**633**	**3.6**	**2**

Coach Frank Leahy said that Ralph Guglielmi was Notre Dame's finest passer, and Ralph did go 25–3–2 as a three-year starter for the Fighting Irish. Things turned out differently in the pros where, Guglielmi once observed, "The real drawback of this business is that every year you have to make the team all over again."

Guglielmi was the top pick of Washington in 1955 and spent one season with the Redskins before entering the air force for two years. He returned to Washington in 1958 and won the starting job in 1960 for a team that went 1–9–2. Ralph did lead all quarterbacks in rushing yards that year, but the Redskins responded by drafting Norm Snead with the second overall pick in the draft and trading Guglielmi to the Cardinals for another former No. 1 pick from Notre Dame, George Izo. Guglielmi spent a year in St. Louis before the Giants traded for him to replace the retiring Charlie Conerly as Y.A. Tittle's backup.

Guglielmi seldom played in 1962 and returned as Tittle's caddy in 1963. However, he played poorly in the preseason and seemed to lose the confidence of his teammates. When Ralph was called upon to start the second game of the season against Pittsburgh because of an injury to Tittle, it was a disaster. The Steelers won 31–0, and Guglielmi completed just five of 15 passes and threw two interceptions in the loss. The Giants traded him that week to San Francisco, but Ralph refused to leave the East Coast due to his business interests. He was waived to Philadelphia a month later and ended his career there. For his career, Guglielmi threw more than twice as many interceptions as touchdowns and completed fewer than half of his passes as one of the greatest Notre Dame quarterback busts.

Pat Haden

QPR 8.0

Height: 5'11" **Weight:** 182 lbs. **Birthdate:** 1/23/1953
College: USC **Draft:** Los Angeles Rams 1975-7th
1975 WFL; 1976–81 Los Angeles Rams
Regular Season Record: 35–19–1, 6 comebacks
Postseason Record: 2–3, 1 comeback
Relative Rating: 100%

Passing

Year	G	Comp./Att.	%	Yards	Y/Att.	TD	INT	Rating
1976	10	60/105	57.1	896	8.5	8	4	94.8
1977	12	122/216	56.5	1,551	7.2	11	6	84.5
1978	16	229/444	51.6	2,995	6.7	13	19	65.1
1979	10	163/290	56.2	1,854	6.4	11	14	68.1
1980	4	19/41	46.3	185	4.5	0	4	19.9
1981	13	138/267	51.7	1,815	6.8	9	13	64.4
Total	65	731/1,363	53.6	9,296	6.8	52	60	69.6
PS:	5	55/123	44.7	728	5.9	4	12	35.3

Rushing

Year	Att.	Yards	Avg.	TD
1976	25	84	3.4	4
1977	29	106	3.7	2
1978	33	206	6.2	0
1979	16	97	6.1	0
1980	3	12	4.0	0
1981	18	104	5.8	0
Total	124	609	4.9	6
PS:	18	81	4.5	1

At USC, Pat Haden was an Academic All-American who played in three straight Rose Bowls and for two national championship teams. When he graduated, he was accepted as a Rhodes Scholar and managed to fit in a season with the Southern California Sun of the World Football League as well. With the Sun,

Haden completed 60 percent of his passes, and he signed the next year with the Rams, who had drafted the 5'11" passer in the seventh round in 1975.

In Los Angeles, the Rams were known for their annual quarterback controversies that had been going on for decades. During Haden's six seasons with Los Angeles, he found himself competing against Ron Jaworski, James Harris, Joe Namath, Vince Ferragamo, Dan Pastorini, Jeff Rutledge, and Jeff Kemp. The Rams in that time had a strong defense and running game, but the passing game was never quite right. Five of those years, the team made the playoffs, but they always ran into a more complete team eventually and lost. Because Haden was undersized and had a weak arm, he survived by using his intelligence and by minimizing mistakes. However, nagging injuries kept him off the field too often, and fans took out their frustrations with the team on Haden. They even cheered one time when it was announced that he had broken his hand. "There's tremendous pressure on me, sure. I think the thing that drives all athletes is the fear of failure. It can get scary," Haden told *Sports Illustrated*. Tired of the beatings and booings, Haden retired in 1982 to practice law while the Rams brought back Ferragamo from Canada and brought in Bert Jones from Baltimore. They did not make the playoffs.

TOP 11
Quarterback Families

11. Father Emery and son Kent Nix.
10. Jessie Freitas senior and junior.
9. Brothers Josh and Luke McCown.
8. Brothers Damon and Brock Huard.
7. Brothers Ty and Koy Detmer.
6. Brothers Carson and Jordan Palmer.
5. Brothers Matt and Tim Hasselbeck.
4. Father Phil and son Chris Simms.
3. Father Jack and son Jeff Kemp.
2. Father Bob and son Brian Griese.
1. Father Archie and sons Peyton and Eli Manning.

John Hadl

QPR 9.0

Height: 6'1" **Weight:** 214 lbs. **Birthdate:** 2/15/1940
College: Kansas **Draft:** Detroit 1962-1st; San Diego 1962-3rd
1962–72 San Diego Chargers; 1973–74 Los Angeles Rams; 1974–75 Green Bay Packers; 1976–77 Houston Oilers
Regular Season Record: 82–76–9, 17 comebacks
Postseason Record: 0–2, no comebacks
Relative Rating: 106%

Passing

Year	G	Comp./Att.	%	Yards	Y/Att.	TD	INT	Rating
1962	14	107/260	41.2	1,632	6.3	15	24	43.3
1963	14	28/64	43.8	502	7.8	6	6	63.4
1964	14	147/274	53.6	2,157	7.9	18	15	78.7
1965	14	174/348	50.0	2,798	8.0	20	21	71.3
1966	14	200/375	53.3	2,846	7.6	23	14	83.0
1967	14	217/427	50.8	3,365	7.9	24	22	74.5
1968	14	208/440	47.3	3,473	7.9	27	32	64.5
1969	14	158/324	48.8	2,253	7.0	10	11	67.8
1970	14	162/327	49.5	2,388	7.3	22	15	77.1
1971	14	233/431	54.1	3,075	7.1	21	25	68.9
1972	14	190/370	51.4	2,449	6.6	15	26	56.7
1973	14	135/258	52.3	2,008	7.8	22	11	88.8
1974	14	142/299	47.5	1,752	5.9	8	14	55.5
1975	14	191/353	54.1	2,095	5.9	6	21	52.8
1976	14	60/113	53.1	634	5.6	7	8	60.9
1977	14	11/24	45.8	76	3.2	0	3	13.9
Total	224	2,363/4,687	50.4	33,503	7.1	244	268	67.4
PS:	4	27/66	40.9	416	6.3	1	4	42.2

Rushing

Year	Att.	Yards	Avg.	TD
1962	40	139	3.5	1
1963	8	26	3.3	0
1964	20	70	3.5	1
1965	28	91	3.3	1
1966	38	95	2.5	2
1967	37	107	2.9	3
1968	23	14	0.6	2
1969	26	109	4.2	2
1970	28	188	6.7	1
1971	18	75	4.2	1
1972	22	99	4.5	1
1973	14	5	0.4	0
1974	19	25	1.3	0
1975	20	47	2.4	0
1976	7	11	1.6	0
1977	3	11	3.7	1
Total	351	1,112	3.2	16
PS:	12	48	4.0	1

John Hadl was a triple-threat running quarterback who also played defensive back at Kansas while earning All-American recognition twice. Detroit envisioned Hadl as their answer to the Packers' Paul Hornung—a former quarterback transformed into a halfback adept at the option pass—when they drafted John in the first round in 1962. Instead, Hadl signed with San Diego because coach Sid Gillman saw him as a quarterback.

Hadl had to improve his footwork, setup speed, and throwing mechanics, but no one knew how to teach quarterback fundamentals better than Gillman. When starter Jack Kemp was injured and later lost to Buffalo, Hadl was forced to start 10 games as a very green rookie. Gillman brought in veteran Tobin Rote in 1963, and Hadl learned from the bench as Rote led the Chargers to the AFL title that year. Hadl began to take over from the aging Rote in 1964 and was the full-fledged starter in 1965. Both seasons ended with Jack Kemp's Bills beating San Diego in the AFL title game.

Hadl was big and durable with a quick release and a strong arm. With San Diego, he excelled in throwing the long ball to speedy receivers Lance Alworth and Gary Garrison in the Chargers' explosive offense. John threw pretty rainbow bombs that dropped softly into the receivers' hands. Hadl's weakness was reading defenses and throwing into coverage, which led to a lot of interceptions—32 in 1968 and 26 in 1972, for instance. With Gillman gone, San Diego traded Hadl to the Rams in 1973, and he had a remarkable year, throwing 22 touchdowns to only 11 interceptions in leading the Rams to a 12–2 record.

Hadl's production declined drastically the next season, and Los Angeles sent him to Green Bay at midseason in what Packer fans call the Lawrence Welk trade, "a one and a two and a three." Actually, Green Bay gave up two No. 1s, two No. 2s, and a third-round pick for the fading Hadl. John stuck around another year in Green Bay before being sent to the Oilers for Lynn Dickey. Hadl finished his career backing up Dan Pastorini for two years in Houston. He was an exciting player who threw for a lot of touchdowns but also too many interceptions. He was Steve Young's first coach in the USFL.

Parker Hall

QPR 5.0

Height: 6'0" **Weight:** 198 lbs. **Birthdate:** 12/10/1916
College: Mississippi **Draft:** Cleveland Rams 1939-1st
1939–42 Cleveland Rams; 1946 San Francisco 49ers
Regular Season Record: 16-24-2 est., 1 comeback
Postseason Record: NA
Relative Rating: 98%

Passing

Year	G	Comp./Att.	%	Yards	Y/Att.	TD	INT	Rating
1939	11	106/208	51.0	1,227	5.9	9	13	57.5
1940	11	77/183	42.1	1,108	6.1	7	16	38.7
1941	10	84/190	44.2	863	4.5	7	19	30.5
1942	10	62/140	44.3	815	5.8	7	19	40.3
1946	11	2/8	25.0	15	1.9	0	0	39.6
Total	53	331/729	45.4	4,028	5.5	30	67	38.5

Rushing

Year	Att.	Yards	Avg.	TD
1939	120	458	3.8	2
1940	94	365	3.9	1
1941	57	232	4.1	2
1942	41	-3	-0.1	1
1946	17	31	1.8	0
Total	329	1,083	3.3	6

Single-wing tailback Parker Hall came out of Mississippi in 1939 to win the NFL MVP Award as a rookie for the Cleveland Rams. That season Hall led the league in attempts, completions, and completion percentage as the Rams improved to 5–5–1. Parker threw more passes, 208, in that first year than anyone ever had in a season before and also finished second in passing yards and fifth in rushing yards. However, Hall steadily declined during each of the next three years before he entered the military during the war. The 1939 season was the only one in which Hall's passer rating was above the league average.

From 1943 to 1945, Hall played service ball for St. Mary's Preflight and then signed with the fledgling San Francisco 49ers of the All-America Football Conference. Parker spent one season as Frankie Albert's backup, and it was the only time he ever played as a T-formation quarterback. He threw only eight passes in 1946 and then retired to Memphis to go into the lumber business.

Terry Hanratty

QPR 1.5

Height: 6'1" **Weight:** 210 lbs. **Birthdate:** 1/19/1948
College: Notre Dame **Draft:** Pittsburgh 1969-2nd
1969–75 Pittsburgh Steelers; 1976 Tampa Bay Bucs
Regular Season Record: 6-12, 3 comebacks
Postseason Record: 0-0, no comebacks
Relative Rating: 66%

Passing

Year	G	Comp./Att.	%	Yards	Y/Att.	TD	INT	Rating
1969	8	52/126	41.3	716	5.7	8	13	41.7
1970	13	64/163	39.3	842	5.2	5	8	46.1
1971	6	7/29	24.1	159	5.5	2	3	33.3
1972	7	2/4	50.0	23	5.8	0	0	67.7
1973	9	31/69	44.9	643	9.3	8	5	86.8
1974	3	3/26	11.5	95	3.7	1	5	15.5
1975	1	0/0	0.0	0	0.0	0	0	0.0
1976	3	6/14	42.9	32	2.3	0	1	20.5
Total	50	165/431	38.3	2,510	5.8	24	35	43.0
PS:	1	5/10	50.0	57	5.7	0	0	67.5

Rushing

Year	Att.	Yards	Avg.	TD
1969	10	106	10.6	0
1970	4	-5	-1.3	0
1971	1	3	3.0	1
1973	3	0	0.0	0
1974	1	-6	-6.0	0
1975	1	0	0.0	0
1976	1	1	1.0	0
Total	21	99	4.7	1
PS:	0	0	0.0	0

Teaming with wide receiver Jim Seymour, Terry Hanratty had an immediate impact on college football when the two sophomores exploded onto the scene with Notre Dame in 1966. In their first game against Purdue, they connected 13 times for 276 yards and three scores. The long-ball touchdown combination led the Fighting Irish to a national championship that year and sparked glowing assessments from pro scouts. Dallas' Gil Brandt said that both would be first-round picks in three years. The Colts' Upton Bell compared the sophomore Hanratty's arm to that of Johnny Unitas.

By the 1969 draft, though, the All-American Hanratty dropped into the second round, where

Pittsburgh grabbed the local hero. Chuck Noll gave Hanratty 11 starts in his first two seasons, but Terry won only two games and was beaten out by another Terry, Bradshaw, for good in 1971. Hanratty did have a good seat on the bench to watch the first two Steeler Super Bowl triumphs and then was let go in the 1976 expansion draft. With Tampa, Hanratty got one final start when the 0–12 Bucs traveled to Pittsburgh to get crushed 42–0 by the Steelers. Essentially, Hanratty was a bomb thrower but was too inconsistent and inaccurate to be effective. His 15.2 yards per completion compared favorably to Norm Van Brocklin, but because he completed only 38 percent of his passes, his yards per pass was an anemic 5.8. The young Terry Bradshaw was the same way initially but developed into an NFL quarterback; Hanratty never did.

Jim Harbaugh

QPR 7.5

Height: 6'3" **Weight:** 215 lbs. **Birthdate:** 12/23/1963
College: Michigan **Draft:** Chicago Bears 1987-1st
**1987–93 Chicago Bears; 1994–97 Indianapolis Colts;
1998 Baltimore Ravens; 1999–2000 San Diego
Chargers**
Regular Season Record: 66–74, 20 comebacks
Postseason Record: 2–3, no comebacks
Relative Rating: 101%

Passing

Year	G	Comp./Att.	%	Yards	Y/Att.	TD	INT	Rating
1987	6	8/11	72.7	62	5.6	0	0	86.2
1988	10	47/97	48.5	514	5.3	0	2	55.9
1989	12	111/178	62.4	1,204	6.8	5	9	70.5
1990	14	180/312	57.7	2,178	7.0	10	6	81.9
1991	16	275/478	57.5	3,121	6.5	15	16	73.7
1992	16	202/358	56.4	2,486	6.9	13	12	76.2
1993	15	200/325	61.5	2,002	6.2	7	11	72.1
1994	12	125/202	61.9	1,440	7.1	9	6	85.8
1995	15	200/314	63.7	2,575	8.2	17	5	100.7
1996	14	232/405	57.3	2,630	6.5	13	11	76.3
1997	12	189/309	61.2	2,060	6.7	10	4	86.2
1998	14	164/293	56.0	1,839	6.3	12	11	72.9
1999	14	249/434	57.4	2,761	6.4	10	14	70.6
2000	7	123/202	60.9	1,416	7.0	8	10	74.6
Total	177	2,305/3,918	58.8	26,288	6.7	129	117	77.6
PS:	5	83/163	50.9	906	5.6	6	5	67.2

Rushing

Year	Att.	Yards	Avg.	TD
1987	4	15	3.8	0
1988	19	110	5.8	1
1989	45	276	6.1	3
1990	51	321	6.3	4
1991	70	338	4.8	2
1992	47	272	5.8	1
1993	60	277	4.6	4
1994	39	223	5.7	0
1995	52	235	4.5	2
1996	48	192	4.0	1
1997	36	206	5.7	0
1998	40	172	4.3	0
1999	34	126	3.7	0
2000	16	24	1.5	0
Total	561	2,787	5.0	18
PS:	30	119	4.0	0

Jim Harbaugh was a late first-round pick of the Bears where he eventually took over the starting job after Jim McMahon was shipped out of town. Harbaugh was a good runner who had some success in Chicago, leading the Bears to back-to-back 11–5 seasons in 1990–91 but was inconsistent and inefficient in the offense and was heavily booed in Soldier Field. His time in the Windy City is best remembered for the time he was verbally undressed on the sidelines by coach Mike Ditka after throwing an interception in a loss to the Vikings.

Harbaugh left for Indianapolis as a free agent in 1994 and his career blossomed. His completion percentage improved as well as his yards per pass average. Jim was named Comeback Player of the Year in 1995 when he took the Colts to the AFC Conference championship and nearly beat Pittsburgh on a last-second Hail Mary pass. By then, Harbaugh was being called Captain Comeback for his late-game heroics. Jim and the Colts returned to the playoffs the next year, but the team slipped in 1997, and rookie Peyton Manning would replace Harbaugh in 1998.

He finished his career with stints in Baltimore, San Diego, and Carolina before getting into his father's business, coaching. As coach at San Diego State, Harbaugh led the Aztecs to a 29–6 record in three years and in 2007 was named head coach at Stanford, where his father had once served as defensive coordinator. His brother John was named the head coach of the Baltimore Ravens in 2008.

Jim Hardy

QPR 5.5

Height: 6'0" **Weight:** 180 lbs. **Birthdate:** 4/24/1923
College: USC **Draft:** Washington 1945-1st
1946–48 Los Angeles Rams; 1949–51 Chicago Cardinals; 1952 Detroit Lions
Regular Season Record: 9-13-1, no comebacks
Postseason Record: NA
Relative Rating: 96%

Passing

Year	G	Comp./Att.	%	Yards	Y/Att.	TD	INT	Rating
1946	9	24/64	37.5	285	4.5	2	7	22.7
1947	9	23/57	40.4	388	6.8	5	7	53.7
1948	12	112/211	53.1	1,390	6.6	14	7	82.1
1949	12	63/150	42.0	748	5.0	10	13	44.0
1950	11	117/257	45.5	1,636	6.4	17	24	49.7
1951	7	56/114	49.1	809	7.1	3	10	44.8
1952	9	28/59	47.5	434	7.4	3	5	53.9
Total	69	423/912	46.4	5,690	6.2	54	73	53.1

Rushing

Year	Att.	Yards	Avg.	TD
1946	10	-10	-1.0	0
1947	3	-6	-2.0	0
1948	5	14	2.8	0
1949	7	6	0.9	1
1950	10	14	1.4	1
1951	12	38	3.2	0
1952	5	16	3.2	0
Total	52	72	1.4	2

Jim Hardy was a Los Angeles native who grew up to lead USC to consecutive Rose Bowl triumphs in the 1940s, play pro football for the Rams and two other teams, and then serve as general manager of the Los Angeles Coliseum. In fact, the only Rose Bowl game that Hardy did not attend from 1930 through 2006 was the year he was in the military during the war.

Hardy was a happy-go-lucky sort who had one of the wildest two-week swings any quarterback ever had in 1950. After spending his first three years as a pro backing up Bob Waterfield on the Rams, the popular local hero was traded to the Cardinals for a first-round draft pick in 1949. Hardy

split the quarterbacking with Paul Christman that year and took over on opening day in 1950. Facing the defending champion Eagles, Hardy had a dreadful day in which nothing went right. That day, Jim threw an NFL-record eight interceptions and fumbled twice in a 45–7 loss. Frank Tripucka came in to relieve the struggling Hardy in the second half but was injured on his third play, forcing Hardy to return for still more punishment. One week later against the lowly Colts, though, Jim tossed six touchdown passes, five of them to end Bob Shaw, in a 55–13 win. The Cardinals finished 5–7 that up-and-down year. Two years later, Hardy was traded to Detroit and spent his final season as Bobby Layne's backup for the 1952 world champion Lions.

Joey Harrington

QPR 6.0

Height: 6'4" **Weight:** 220 lbs. **Birthdate:** 10/21/1978
College: Oregon **Draft:** Detroit 2002-1st
2002–05 Detroit Lions; 2006 Miami Dolphins; 2007 Atlanta Falcons; 2008 New Orleans Saints
Regular Season Record: 26–50, 8 comebacks
Postseason record: NA
Relative Rating: 87%

Passing

Year	G	Comp./Att.	%	Yards	Y/Att.	TD	INT	Rating
2002	14	215/429	50.1	2,294	5.3	12	16	59.9
2003	16	309/554	55.8	2,880	5.2	17	22	63.9
2004	16	274/489	56.0	3,047	6.2	19	12	77.5
2005	12	188/330	57.0	2,021	6.1	12	12	72.0
2006	11	223/388	57.5	2,236	5.8	12	15	68.2
2007	12	215/348	61.8	2,215	6.4	7	8	77.2
Total	81	1,424/2,538	56.1	14,693	5.8	79	85	69.4

Rushing

Year	Att.	Yards	Avg.	TD
2002	7	4	0.6	0
2003	30	86	2.9	0
2004	48	175	3.6	0
2005	24	80	3.3	0
2006	19	24	1.3	0
2007	14	33	2.4	0
Total	142	402	2.8	0

Detroit drafted Joey Harrington No. 1 in 2002 and then drafted wide receivers with their top pick for

TOP 10
Most Disappointing NFL Quarterbacks from Notre Dame

10. Tom Clements, graduated 1974
9. Boley Dancewicz, graduated 1945
8. Frank Tripucka, graduated 1948
7. George Izo, graduated 1959
6. Bob Williams, graduated 1950
5. Ralph Guglielmi, graduated 1954
4. Rick Mirer, graduated 1992
3. Angelo Bertelli, graduated 1943
2. Terry Hanratty, graduated 1968
1. John Huarte, graduated 1964

the next three years to give him passing weapons. Because Harrington has achieved the second-worst winning percentage of all quarterbacks with at least 75 starts, Matt Millen's plan clearly didn't work. Harrington certainly deserves a big part of the blame. He can be flustered easily, throws too many interceptions, and his yards per pass average is pathetic, but it should also be pointed out that the Lions have been a mostly dysfunctional franchise for decades. Two of those three first-round receivers were complete busts, and the third never became anything exceptional. Meanwhile, the team as a whole was terrible.

After four years of boos and tasteless jokes from fans and the media, Harrington was traded to Miami, another crumbling, mismanaged franchise. Harrington became the starter when the Dolphins' doomed acquisition of Daunte Culpepper didn't pan out. Joey played passably well at times and then was cut at the end of the year. Harrington moved on to the Falcons, not realizing it was a franchise on the verge of self-immolation. Of coach Bobby Petrino's offense, Joey raved, "It's the complete opposite of the West Coast offense so I feel great about this team." Chastened a bit in 2008, Harrington signed as the Saints' third quarterback. "I've obviously had a few bumps along the way," he said. "Some mistakes I made, and some I couldn't control. They've all been learning situations. I think here it gives me the chance to learn from somebody who's done it well in Drew [Brees]."

Perhaps the bland understatement provides a clue as to the fire lacking in Harrington's makeup.

James Harris

Height: 6'4" **Weight:** 210 lbs. **Birthdate:** 7/20/1947
College: Grambling **Draft:** Buffalo 1969-8th
1969–71 Buffalo Bills; 1973–76 Los Angeles Rams;
1977–79 San Diego Chargers
Regular Season Record: 25–16, 8 comebacks
Postseason Record: 1–1, 1 comeback
Relative Rating: 105%

Passing

Year	G	Comp./Att.	%	Yards	Y/Att.	TD	INT	Rating
1969	4	15/36	41.7	270	7.5	1	1	65.7
1970	7	24/50	48.0	338	6.8	3	4	56.9
1971	7	51/103	49.5	512	5.0	1	6	43.0
1973	8	7/11	63.6	68	6.2	0	0	80.9
1974	11	106/198	53.5	1,544	7.8	11	6	85.1
1975	13	157/285	55.1	2,148	7.5	14	15	73.8
1976	7	91/158	57.6	1,460	9.2	8	6	89.6
1977	9	109/211	51.7	1,240	5.9	5	11	55.8
1978	9	42/88	47.7	518	5.9	2	9	34.4
1979	8	5/9	55.6	38	4.2	0	1	26.4
Total	83	607/1,149	52.8	8,136	7.1	45	59	67.3
PS:	3	21/49	42.9	343	7.0	2	5	41

Rushing

Year	Att.	Yards	Avg.	TD
1969	10	25	2.5	0
1970	3	-8	-2.7	0
1971	6	42	7.0	0
1973	4	29	7.3	0
1974	42	112	2.7	5
1975	18	45	2.5	1
1976	12	76	6.3	2
1977	10	13	1.3	2
1978	10	7	0.7	0
1979	6	26	4.3	0
Total	121	367	3.0	10
PS:	9	34	3.8	0

James "Shack" Harris is another great "what if" quarterback, like Johnny Lujack and Greg Cook. However, injuries were not his primary problem; skin color was. Tall and strong, Harris came out of Grambling in 1969 with all the physical tools but in need of some support and polish to make the leap to the NFL.

James Harris, at the Rams training camp in 1976, was the first African American quarterback to lead his team to the NFL postseason.

He did not get much support in Buffalo. He started for the Bills on opening day of his rookie year but then lost the job to veteran Jack Kemp. Harris later suffered a knee injury and was displaced by rookie Dennis Shaw in 1970. In three years, Harris started just three games in Buffalo. As the only black starting quarterback in the NFL at the time, Harris was a pioneer. White teammates were not used to having a black man in charge of the huddle, and that made Shack's development as a leader more challenging.

Acquired by Los Angeles in 1973, Harris earned the starting job when John Hadl was traded the following season and became the first black to lead a team to the playoffs and the first to win a playoff game by beating the Redskins. Shack took the Rams to the conference championship game that year where they lost to the Vikings. Harris again led the Rams to the playoffs in 1975 but was hurt at the end of the year, so rookie Ron Jaworski took over in the postseason. Shack had the highest passer rating in the NFC in 1976 but still lost his starting job to rookie Pat Haden at midseason. The Rams lost in the conference championship game both of those years as well, so they traded for a

broken-down Joe Namath in 1977 and sent Harris to San Diego.

Harris got to start for most of 1977 with starter Dan Fouts holding out, but when Fouts returned, Shack's starting days were over. He finished his career by backing up Fouts for two more years before beginning a long, hard climb to become an NFL executive. In a life of hard-won firsts, Harris became one of the first black general managers in the NFL when he was hired by Jacksonville in 2003, having worked his way up through the Bucs, Jets, and Ravens organizations. He resigned in 2008.

Jim Hart

QPR

Height: 6'1" **Weight:** 215 lbs. **Birthdate:** 4/29/1944
College: Southern Illinois **Draft:** Free agent
1966–83 St. Louis Cardinals; 1984 Washington Redskins
Regular Season Record: 87–88–5, 21 comebacks
Postseason Record: 0–2, no comebacks
Relative Rating: 96%

Passing

Year	G	Comp./Att.	%	Yards	Y/Att.	TD	INT	Rating
1966	1	4/11	36.4	29	2.6	0	0	44.9
1967	14	192/397	48.4	3,008	7.6	19	30	58.4
1968	13	140/316	44.3	2,059	6.5	15	18	58.2
1969	9	84/169	49.7	1,086	6.4	6	12	52.5
1970	14	171/373	45.8	2,575	6.9	14	18	61.5
1971	11	110/243	45.3	1,626	6.7	8	14	54.7
1972	6	60/119	50.4	857	7.2	5	5	70.6
1973	12	178/320	55.6	2,223	6.9	15	10	80.0
1974	14	200/388	51.5	2,411	6.2	20	8	79.5
1975	14	182/345	52.8	2,507	7.3	19	19	71.7
1976	14	218/388	56.2	2,946	7.6	18	13	82.0
1977	14	186/355	52.4	2,542	7.2	13	20	64.3
1978	15	240/477	50.3	3,121	6.5	16	18	66.7
1979	14	194/378	51.3	2,218	5.9	9	20	55.2
1980	15	228/425	53.6	2,946	6.9	16	20	68.6
1981	10	134/241	55.6	1,694	7.0	11	14	68.7
1982	4	19/33	57.6	199	6.0	1	0	85.3
1983	5	50/91	54.9	592	6.5	4	8	53.0
1984	2	3/7	42.9	26	3.7	0	0	53.3
Total	201	2,593/5,076	51.1	34,665	6.8	209	247	66.6
PS:	2	40/81	49.4	491	6.1	2	4	56.1

Rushing

Year	Att.	Yards	Avg.	TD
1967	13	36	2.8	3
1968	19	20	1.1	6
1969	7	16	2.3	2
1970	18	18	1.0	0
1971	13	9	0.7	0
1972	9	17	1.9	0
1973	3	-3	-1.0	0
1974	10	21	2.1	2
1975	11	7	0.6	1
1976	8	7	0.9	0
1977	11	18	1.6	0
1978	11	11	1.0	2
1979	6	11	1.8	0
1980	9	11	1.2	0
1981	3	2	0.7	0
1983	5	12	2.4	0
1984	3	-6	-2.0	0
Total	159	207	1.3	16
PS:	1	10	10.0	0

Jim Hart was a baby-faced gunslinger at quarterback. He wasn't brash like Bobby Layne, cocky like Dan Fouts, or emotional like Brett Favre, but Hart lived and died by the long ball, flourished and perished by forcing the ball into tight coverage. Although not as talented or successful as those three Hall of Famers, Hart was a very good quarterback over a long career and guided the woeful Cardinals to their only period of success in the past 60 years, three straight 10-plus win seasons, and consecutive division championships under coach Don Coryell in the mid-1970s.

Hart was signed as an undrafted free agent in 1966 and was handed the starting job in 1967 when Charley Johnson was in the military. Jim threw 30 interceptions in his first full year but also threw for more than 3,000 yards. When the more polished Johnson returned in 1969, he reassumed the starting position but then was traded to Houston in 1970. Pete Beathard was brought in to compete with Hart for two years, and then Jim lost the starting job to journeyman Gary Cuozzo in 1972. Finally, Coryell arrived in 1973 and gave Hart the keys to a flashy new passing offense that took him to four straight Pro Bowls. Him was immobile in the pocket but got rid of the ball quickly and avoided injuries, starting 63 consecutive games at one point. At 37, Hart was succeeded by Neil Lomax but hung around

for a few more years as a backup in St. Louis and Washington before retiring to become the athletic director at his alma mater, Southern Illinois.

QPR 8.5

Matt Hasselbeck

Height: 6'4" **Weight:** 224 lbs. **Birthdate:** 9/25/1975
College: Boston College **Draft:** Green Bay 1998-6th
1999–2000 Green Bay Packers; 2001–08 Seattle Seahawks
Regular Season Record: 58-45, 21 comebacks
Postseason Record: 4-5, no comebacks
Relative Rating: 106%

Passing

Year	G	Comp./Att.	%	Yards	Y/Att.	TD	INT	Rating
1999	16	3/10	30.0	41	4.1	1	0	77.5
2000	16	10/19	52.6	104	5.5	1	0	86.3
2001	13	176/321	54.8	2,023	6.3	7	8	70.9
2002	16	267/419	63.7	3,075	7.3	15	10	87.8
2003	16	313/513	61.0	3,841	7.5	26	15	88.8
2004	14	279/474	58.9	3,382	7.1	22	15	83.1
2005	16	294/449	65.5	3,459	7.7	24	9	98.2
2006	12	210/371	56.6	2,442	6.6	18	15	76.0
2007	16	352/562	62.6	3,966	7.1	28	12	91.4
2008	7	109/209	52.2	1,216	5.8	5	10	57.8
Total	142	2,013/3,347	60.1	23,549	7.0	147	94	84.5
PS:	9	189/325	58.2	2,211	6.8	11	8	79.9

Rushing

Year	Att.	Yards	Avg.	TD
1999	6	15	2.5	0
2000	4	-5	-1.3	0
2001	40	141	3.5	0
2002	40	202	5.1	1
2003	36	125	3.5	2
2004	27	90	3.3	1
2005	36	124	3.4	1
2006	18	110	6.1	0
2007	39	89	2.3	0
2008	11	69	6.3	0
Total	257	960	3.7	5
PS:	47	107	2.3	1

In the stadium where he began his pro career, Matt Hasselbeck leaned into the referee when Seattle won the overtime coin toss in their 2004 wildcard game against the Packers in Lambeau and said, "We want the ball, and we're going to score."

One thing Hasselbeck didn't realize was that the referee's mike was live and his bold prediction was heard throughout the stadium and on television. The other thing he didn't realize was that the game would indeed end on one of his passes but on an Al Harris interception return for the winning touchdown minutes later.

Matt is the son of former NFL tight end Don Hasselbeck and the brother of former backup quarterback Tim Hasselbeck. As a late-round pick of Green Bay, Matt played well in exhibition games each preseason to attract attention behind ironman Brett Favre. Former Packer coach Mike Holmgren made a draft-day deal for Hasselbeck in 2001, and Matt has been the Seahawk starter ever since. There was some rough going in his first two years, but between the coaching of Holmgren and the mentoring of backup Trent Dilfer, Hasselbeck began to settle down in 2003. He proved himself an accurate touch passer with fine timing. He averaged almost 24 touchdowns per year over the next five seasons, and Seattle won four straight division crowns and made it to one Super Bowl.

Hasselbeck is a good scrambler and a creative playmaker. Like his friend Favre, he will throw into coverage sometimes, but he once told *Sports Illustrated*, "A quarterback can't play scared, and I never will." Although knee and back problems seem to be curtailing his career, he is creeping up steadily on Dave Krieg's team passing marks.

Bobby Hebert

QPR **8.0**

Height: 6'4"   **Weight:** 215 lbs.   **Birthdate:** 8/19/1960
College: Northwest State   **Draft:** Free agent
1983–85 USFL; 1985–89, 1991–92 New Orleans Saints; 1993–96 Atlanta Falcons
Regular Season Record: 56–44, 16 comebacks
Postseason Record: 0–3, no comebacks
Relative Rating: 102%

Passing

Year	G	Comp./Att.	%	Yards	Y/Att.	TD	INT	Rating
1985	6	97/181	53.6	1,208	6.7	5	4	74.6
1986	5	41/79	51.9	498	6.3	2	8	40.5
1987	12	164/294	55.8	2,119	7.2	15	9	82.9
1988	16	280/478	58.6	3,156	6.6	20	15	79.3
1989	14	222/353	62.9	2,686	7.6	15	15	82.7
1991	9	149/248	60.1	1,676	6.8	9	8	79.0
1992	16	249/422	59.0	3,287	7.8	19	16	82.9
1993	14	263/430	61.2	2,978	6.9	24	17	84.0
1994	10	52/103	50.5	610	5.9	2	6	51.0
1995	4	28/45	62.2	313	7.0	2	1	88.5
1996	14	294/488	60.2	3,152	6.5	22	25	72.9
Total	120	1,189/3,121	58.9	21,683	6.9	135	124	78.0
PS:	3	58/102	56.9	648	6.4	3	7	57.1

Rushing

Year	Att.	Yards	Avg.	TD
1985	12	26	2.2	0
1986	5	14	2.8	0
1987	13	95	7.3	0
1988	37	79	2.1	0
1989	25	87	3.5	0
1991	18	56	3.1	0
1992	32	95	3.0	0
1993	24	49	2.0	0
1994	9	43	4.8	0
1995	5	-1	-0.2	0
1996	15	59	3.9	1
Total	195	602	3.1	1
PS:	6	29	4.8	0

TOP 10
Quarterbacks to Wear the Same Number the Longest for One Team

10. Dan Fouts wore No. 14 for 15 years in San Diego.
9. Ken Anderson wore No. 14 for 16 years in Cincinnati.
8. Brett Favre wore No. 4 for 16 years in Green Bay.
7. Bart Starr wore No. 15 for 16 years in Green Bay.
6. Sammy Baugh wore No. 33 for 16 years in Washington.
5. John Elway wore No. 7 for 16 years in Denver.
4. John Brodie wore No. 12 for 17 years in San Francisco.
3. Dan Marino wore No. 13 for 17 years in Miami.
2. Johnny Unitas wore No. 19 for 17 years in Baltimore.
1. Jim Hart wore No. 17 for 18 years in St. Louis.

Bobby Hebert signed with the Michigan Panthers before the NFL draft in 1983 and thus went undrafted by the NFL. In the USFL, Hebert threw for more passing yards than any other quarterback and led his teams to two championship games, winning one. Three years later when the USFL folded, a number of teams courted the free agent Cajun Cannon, but the local Saints won out for the Louisiana native, who was tall with a big arm.

In New Orleans, Hebert competed for playing time with the woeful Dave Wilson in 1985 and then broke his foot in 1986. Finally, in 1987, Hebert won the starting job and led the Saints to their first winning season and playoff berth in franchise history. The team continued to be successful for the next few years with Hebert, but an acrimonious contract dispute in 1990 caused him to hold out for the entire season. That year, the Saints backed into the playoffs behind game manager Steve Walsh.

When Hebert signed for 1991, he won back his starting job and led New Orleans to the team's first divisional crown. The Saints returned to the playoffs in 1992 but lost in the first round both years. Neither Hebert nor his coach, Jim Mora, ever won a postseason game. Bobby signed with Atlanta as a free agent in 1993, with Falcon quarterback Wade Wilson signing with the Saints. Neither team made the playoffs, but Hebert was named to the Pro Bowl with 24 touchdown passes. Hebert played for three more years in Atlanta but without much success. Although he won only seven of 25 starts in Atlanta, he went 49–26 in New Orleans and was the most successful Saints quarterback ever.

Don Heinrich

QPR 5.0

Height: 6'0" **Weight:** 190 lbs. **Birthdate:** 9/19/1930
College: Washington **Draft:** New York Giants 1952-3rd
1954–59 New York Giants; 1960 Dallas Cowboys; 1962 Oakland Raiders
Regular Season Record: 20–12–2, no comebacks
Postseason Record: 2–1, no comebacks
Relative Rating: 80%

Passing

Year	G	Comp./Att.	%	Yards	Y/Att.	TD	INT	Rating
1954	2	4/9	44.4	56	6.2	0	2	25.5
1955	10	31/67	46.3	413	6.2	2	2	63.8
1956	12	37/88	42.0	369	4.2	5	5	49.9
1957	4	11/26	42.3	224	8.6	1	1	70.0
1958	7	26/68	38.2	369	5.4	4	2	63.9
1959	8	22/58	37.9	329	5.7	1	6	23.5
1960	12	23/61	37.7	371	6.1	3	3	54.7
1962	1	10/29	34.5	156	5.4	1	2	36.0
Total	56	164/406	40.0	2,287	5.6	17	23	49.6
PS:	3	6/17	35.3	65	3.8	0	2	7.8

Rushing

Year	Att.	Yards	Avg.	TD
1954	1	0	0.0	0
1955	7	4	0.6	2
1956	5	-4	-0.8	0
1957	4	10	2.5	2
1958	5	4	0.8	1
1959	2	3	1.5	0
1960	2	3	1.5	0
1962	1	4	4.0	0
Total	27	24	0.9	5
PS:	0	0	0.0	0

Don Heinrich played most of his career with the New York Giants as a backup quarterback who started. In 1955, Giants offensive coach Vince Lombardi instituted the unusual practice of starting Heinrich while real starter Charlie Conerly stood on the sidelines and watched Don probe the defense for a few series or for a whole quarter. At some undetermined point, Lombardi would wave in Conerly to try to exploit what Heinrich had found. It was an odd practice that neither player liked. Years later, Conerly said, "I never really knew why I didn't start the game." Heinrich added, "I honestly don't think a two-quarterback system is good. A team has to get used to one quarterback, and it's best to stay with him."

The one benefit to the system was that it may have extended the aging Conerly's career and kept him fresher for the end of games. The drawback was that Heinrich was not a very good passer. He was smart and had a strong arm, but he threw off his back foot and was very inaccurate; he completed only 40 percent of his passes in his career. After retiring, Heinrich was an assistant coach for six teams in 15 years before going into broadcasting.

Arnie Herber

QPR **9.5**

Height: 5'11" **Weight:** 203 lbs. **Birthdate:** 4/2/1910
College: Regis **Draft:** Free agent
1930–40 Green Bay Packers; 1944–45 New York Giants
Regular Season Record: 75–35–6 est., 8 comebacks
Postseason Record: 2–2, no comebacks
Relative Rating: 146%

Passing

Year	G	Comp./Att.	%	Yards	Y/Att.	TD	INT	Rating
1930	10	10/30	33.3	205	6.8	3	3	52.1
1931	3	5/11	45.5	78	7.1	0	0	69.5
1932	14	37/101	36.6	639	6.3	9	9	51.5
1933	11	50/124	40.3	656	5.3	3	12	26.2
1934	11	42/115	36.5	799	6.9	8	12	45.1
1935	11	40/109	36.7	729	6.7	8	14	45.4
1936	12	77/173	44.5	1,239	7.2	11	13	58.9
1937	9	47/104	45.2	684	6.6	7	10	50.0
1938	8	22/55	40.0	336	6.1	3	4	48.8
1939	10	57/139	41.0	1,107	8.0	8	9	61.6
1940	10	38/89	42.7	560	6.3	6	7	53.6
1944	10	36/86	41.9	651	7.6	6	8	53.0
1945	10	35/80	43.8	641	8.0	9	8	69.8
Total	129	496/1,216	40.8	8,324	6.9	81	109	49.5
PS:	4	24/58	41.4	431	7.4	4	8	50.9

Rushing

Year	Att.	Yards	Avg.	TD
1930	32	135	4.2	0
1931	9	11	1.2	1
1932	64	149	2.3	1
1933	62	77	1.2	0
1934	37	33	0.9	0
1935	19	0	0.0	0
1936	20	-32	-1.6	0
1937	5	9	1.8	0
1938	6	-1	-0.2	0
1939	18	-11	-0.6	1
1940	6	-23	-3.8	0
1944	7	-58	-8.3	0
1945	6	-27	-4.5	0
Total	291	262	0.9	3
PS:	5	25	5.0	0

Although Benny Friedman was the first great passer in the NFL, Arnie Herber was the first great passer after the league began officially gathering statistics in 1932. In particular, Herber threw a great deep ball; his yards per completion average of 16.7 is the highest figure of any NFL passer who threw at least 1,000 passes. His statistics seem dreadful today—40 percent completions and a passer rating of 49.5—but his passer rating was 46 percent better than the league average in his time.

Herber was from Green Bay and sold programs at Packer games in his teens. Because of the Depression, he had to drop out of college after only one year and found work as a handyman around the Packer locker room. Curly Lambeau gave the former local hero a tryout and added him to the roster in 1930. Green Bay was a single-wing team, and Arnie played tailback without a helmet. He was short, pudgy, and not much of a runner but could fling the ball deeper than any passer in that era. Herber led the league three times in passing yards and touchdown passes in the 1930s. He had very small hands but compensated by not gripping the football at all. Instead, he simply rested it on his palm with his thumb across the laces. Cradling the ball in this way allowed him to toss rainbow spirals accurately up to 70 to 80 yards through the air. Teammate Clarke Hinkle said that Herber "was more accurate at 50 yards than he was at 10," and the Packers had the best passing game in the league. Green Bay won four titles during Arnie's tenure, and it was a shock when he was released in 1941 because of a weight problem.

Herber was rejected for the military during World War II and resurfaced with the New York Giants in 1944. Older, heavier, and slower, he played against the Packers in the title game that year. His passing consistently moved the Giants down the field, but his four interceptions cinched the game for Green Bay. Herber was elected to the Pro Football Hall of Fame in 1966, just three years before his death at the age of 59.

Mark Herrmann

Height: 6'4" **Weight:** 200 lbs. **Birthdate:** 1/8/1959
College: Purdue **Draft:** Denver 1981-4th
1982 Denver Broncos; 1983–84, 1990–92 Baltimore/Indianapolis Colts; 1985–87 San Diego Chargers; 1988–89 Los Angeles Rams
Regular Season Record: 3–9, 1 comeback
Postseason Record: NA
Relative Rating: 86%

Passing

Year	G	Comp./Att.	%	Yards	Y/Att.	TD	INT	Rating
1982	2	32/60	53.3	421	7.0	1	4	53.5
1983	2	18/36	50.0	256	7.1	0	3	38.7
1984	3	29/56	51.8	352	6.3	1	6	37.8
1985	9	132/201	65.7	1,537	7.6	10	10	84.5
1986	6	51/97	52.6	627	6.5	2	3	66.8
1987	3	37/57	64.9	405	7.1	1	5	55.1
1988	6	4/5	80.0	38	7.6	0	0	98.3
1989	3	4/5	80.0	59	11.8	0	1	76.2
1990	3	1/1	100.0	6	6.0	0	0	91.7
1991	2	11/19	57.9	137	7.2	0	3	40.8
1992	1	15/24	62.5	177	7.4	1	1	81.4
Total	40	334/561	59.5	4,015	7.2	16	36	64.3

Rushing

Year	Att.	Yards	Avg.	TD
1982	3	7	2.3	1
1983	1	0	0.0	0
1985	18	-8	-0.4	0
1986	2	6	3.0	0
1987	4	-1	-0.3	0
1988	1	-1	-1.0	0
1989	2	-1	-0.5	0
1991	1	-1	-1.0	0
1992	3	-2	-0.7	0
Total	35	-1	0.0	1

When Mark Herrmann graduated from Purdue, he was the most prolific passer in NCAA history with nearly 10,000 passing yards in four years. In 11 years as a NFL backup, Herrmann accumulated less than half of that yardage. Despite his college success, Mark was never anything but a reserve in the pros. Herrmann was tall but neither a powerful passer nor a mobile runner. The one reason he is still remembered at all outside of Indiana is because he was the quarterback throw-in in the John Elway trade. Elway, the overall top draft pick in the fabled 1983 quarterback class, maintained

all along he would not play in Baltimore because he did not like the autocratic coach, Frank Kush. Over the objections of GM Ernie Accorsi, Colts owner Robert Irsay then traded Elway to the Broncos for their top pick, Chris Hinton, another No. 1 pick, and backup quarterback Mark Herrmann. Elway went to the Hall of Fame and took Denver to five Super Bowls; Herrmann is the answer to a trivia question, and Indianapolis had just five winning seasons during Elway's 16-year career.

Rusty Hilger

Height: 6'4" **Weight:** 205 lbs. **Birthdate:** 5/9/1962
College: Oklahoma State **Draft:** Los Angeles Raiders 1985-6th
1985–87 Los Angeles Raiders; 1988 Detroit Lions; 1991 Indianapolis Colts
Regular Season Record: 5–9, no comebacks
Postseason Record: NA
Relative Rating: 71%

Passing

Year	G	Comp./Att.	%	Yards	Y/Att.	TD	INT	Rating
1985	4	4/13	30.8	54	4.2	1	0	70.7
1986	2	19/38	50.0	266	7.0	1	1	70.7
1987	5	55/106	51.9	706	6.7	2	6	55.8
1988	11	126/306	41.2	1,558	5.1	7	12	48.9
1991	1	0/1	0.0	0	0.0	0	0	39.6
Total	23	204/464	44.0	2,584	5.6	11	19	52.8

Rushing

Year	Att.	Yards	Avg.	TD
1985	3	8	2.7	0
1986	6	48	8.0	0
1987	8	8	1.0	0
1988	18	27	1.5	0
Total	35	91	2.6	0

Rusty Hilger was a late-round draft pick who briefly surfaced as the Raiders' quarterback when Jim Plunkett got too old and Marc Wilson became too frustrating. Hilger went 2–3 in the strike season of 1987 and was cut. He was a little bitter about it, saying, "One year I'm the future of the Raiders. The next year, I couldn't take a snap in training camp." Hilger signed with Detroit in 1988 and assumed the starting role when Chuck Long and Eric Hipple both went down to injury. Unfortunately, he was not up to it, completing just 41 percent of his passes with nearly twice as many interceptions as touchdowns in the most extended trial of his career. He appeared in only one more game with the Colts in 1991 before his playing career ended.

King Hill

Height: 6'3" **Weight:** 212 lbs. **Birthdate:** 11/8/1936
College: Rice **Draft:** Chicago Cardinals 1958-1st
1958–60, 1969 Chicago/St. Louis Cardinals; 1961–68 Philadelphia Eagles; 1968 Minnesota Vikings
Regular Season Record: 7–22–1, 3 comebacks
Postseason Record: NA
Relative Rating: 71%

Passing
Year	G	Comp./Att.	%	Yards	Y/Att.	TD	INT	Rating
1958	7	1/9	11.1	18	2.0	0	2	0.0
1959	11	82/181	45.3	1,015	5.6	7	13	46.2
1960	12	20/55	36.4	205	3.7	1	5	16.1
1961	14	6/12	50.0	101	8.4	2	2	78.8
1962	14	31/61	50.8	361	5.9	0	5	34.9
1963	14	91/186	48.9	1,213	6.5	10	17	49.9
1964	8	49/88	55.7	641	7.3	3	4	71.3
1965	7	60/113	53.1	857	7.6	5	10	55.8
1966	10	53/97	54.6	571	5.9	5	7	59.3
1967	1	2/7	28.6	33	4.7	1	0	86.3
1968	11	33/71	46.5	531	7.5	3	6	50.9
1969	14	1/1	100.0	7	7.0	0	0	95.8
Total	123	429/881	48.7	5,553	6.3	37	71	49.3

Rushing
Year	Att.	Yards	Avg.	TD
1958	1	0	0.0	0
1959	39	167	4.3	5
1960	16	47	2.9	1
1961	2	9	4.5	0
1962	4	40	10.0	1
1963	3	-1	-0.3	0
1964	8	27	3.4	0
1965	7	20	2.9	2
1966	7	-2	-0.3	0
1968	1	1	1.0	0
Total	88	308	3.5	8

Stuart "King" Hill was the overall top pick of the 1958 draft but was outplayed in the NFL by his former backup at Rice University, Frank Ryan, who was a fifth-round pick the same year. Hill was a pretty

good punter but was an awful pro quarterback who completed fewer than half his passes, threw nearly twice as many interceptions as touchdowns, and won only one-quarter of his starts.

Hill was acquired by the Eagles in 1961 to back up Sonny Jurgensen, and the two made headlines in 1963 when they walked out of training camp together in a salary dispute. The next day the two got what they wanted—Jurgensen got a raise and Hill got the same salary as the previous year—but Philadelphia GM Vince McNally reportedly tore the arm off the chair in which he was sitting and threw it across the room during the negotiations.

When Joe Kuharich took over the Eagles in 1964, Jurgensen was traded for Norm Snead, and Jack Concannon signed out of the draft. Kuharich used all three quarterbacks in a whimsical rotation, with no one sure each week who the starting quarterback would be. During the 1968 season, Hill was traded to Minnesota for a draft pick and then finished his career as the Cardinals' punter in 1969.

Shaun Hill

Height: 6'5" **Weight:** 210 lbs. **Birthdate:** 1/9/1980
College: Maryland **Draft:** Free agent
2003 NFL Europe; 2005 Minnesota Vikings; 2007–08 San Francisco 49ers
Regular Season Record: 7–3, 3 comebacks
Postseason Record: NA
Relative Rating: 111%

Passing
Year	G	Comp./Att.	%	Yards	Y/Att.	TD	INT	Rating
2005	1	0/0	0.0	0	0.0	0	0	0.0
2007	3	54/79	68.4	501	6.3	5	1	101.3
2008	9	181/288	62.8	2,046	7.1	13	8	87.5
Total	13	235/367	64.0	2,547	6.9	18	9	90.5

Rushing
Year	Att.	Yards	Avg.	TD
2005	2	-2	-1.0	0
2007	12	14	1.2	1
2008	24	115	4.8	2
Total	38	127	3.3	3

Undrafted out of Maryland, Shaun Hill signed with Minnesota in 2002 and spent the next four years as the Vikings' third quarterback. In 2003, he was allocated to NFL Europe and threw 13 touchdowns to just five interceptions with the Amsterdam Admirals. Hill's only playing time in Minnesota came in his final game in a purple uniform when Shaun was sent in for two kneel-downs to conclude the season finale against the Bears. Hill left Minnesota and signed on as the 49ers' third quarterback in 2006. After Alex Smith and Trent Dilfer were hurt in 2007, Hill finally got a chance to play. He completed 22 of 27 passes in his first game and 21 of 28 in his first start. Hill started two games before he injured his back and missed the last game of the year. The coaches intimated that Shaun had a tired arm during training camp in 2008, but when Alex Smith went on injured reserve and J.T. O'Sullivan proved to be a turnover machine with 11 interceptions and 11 fumbles in the first eight games, new coach Mike Singletary turned to Hill. Shaun is a scrappy, roll-out quarterback—a tall version of former 49er quarterback Jeff Garcia. He has an unusual passing motion and relies heavily on check-down passes but moves the team down the field. His biggest problems come in trying to get the ball in the end zone.

Eric Hipple is one of a long line of mediocre Lions quarterbacks over the last 30 years.

Eric Hipple

QPR 6.5

Height: 6'2" **Weight:** 196 lbs. **Birthdate:** 9/16/1957
College: Utah State **Draft:** Detroit 1980-4th
1980–86, 1988–89 Detroit Lions
Regular Season Record: 28–29, 4 comebacks
Postseason Record: 0–1, no comebacks
Relative Rating: 92%

Passing

Year	G	Comp./Att.	%	Yards	Y/Att.	TD	INT	Rating
1980	15	0/0	0.0	0	0.0	0	0	0.0
1981	16	140/279	50.2	2,358	8.5	14	15	73.4
1982	9	36/86	41.9	411	4.8	2	4	45.3
1983	16	204/387	52.7	2,577	6.7	12	18	64.7
1984	8	16/38	42.1	246	6.5	1	1	62.0
1985	16	223/406	54.9	2,952	7.3	17	18	73.6
1986	16	192/305	63.0	1,919	6.3	9	11	75.6
1988	5	12/27	44.4	158	5.9	0	0	63.5
1989	1	7/18	38.9	90	5.0	0	3	15.7
Total	102	830/1,546	53.7	10,711	6.9	55	70	68.7
PS:	1	22/38	57.9	298	7.8	1	2	69.8

Rushing

Year	Att.	Yards	Avg.	TD
1981	41	168	4.1	7
1982	10	57	5.7	0
1983	41	171	4.2	3
1984	2	3	1.5	0
1985	32	89	2.8	2
1986	16	46	2.9	0
1988	1	5	5.0	0
1989	2	11	5.5	1
Total	145	550	3.8	13
PS:	6	47	7.8	0

With starter Gary Danielson lost for the season and backup Jeff Komlo ineffective, third-stringer Eric Hipple was given his first start Monday, October 19, 1981, against the Bears. Hipple astounded a national TV audience by throwing for 336 yards and four touchdowns as well as running for two more scores in a 48–17 win. It's not surprising that

Hipple would never live up to that great debut but instead was a thoroughly average NFL quarterback as a sometime starter throughout the next decade in Detroit. He was a fairly good runner and an inspirational leader but not much of a passer.

Hipple has turned up in the news twice in recent years. In 2005, he disarmed a knife-wielding assailant at a party by tackling him and holding him down till authorities arrived. Eric also has written a book called *Real Men Do Cry* about male depression in response to his 15-year-old son's suicide. Hipple travels the country raising awareness on the topic.

Billy Joe Hobert

Height: 6'0" **Weight:** 190 lbs. **Birthdate:** 1/8/1971
College: Washington **Draft:** Oakland 1993-3rd
1995–96 Oakland Raiders; 1997 Buffalo Bills;
1997–99 New Orleans Saints
Regular Season Record: 4–13, 2 comebacks
Postseason Record: NA
Relative Rating: 86%

Passing

Year	G	Comp./Att.	%	Yards	Y/Att.	TD	INT	Rating
1995	4	44/80	55.0	540	6.8	6	4	80.2
1996	8	57/104	54.8	667	6.4	4	5	67.3
1997	7	78/161	48.4	1,024	6.4	6	10	55.5
1998	1	11/23	47.8	170	7.4	1	0	87.2
1999	9	85/159	53.5	970	6.1	6	6	68.9
Total	29	275/527	52.2	3,371	6.4	23	25	67.0

Rushing

Year	Att.	Yards	Avg.	TD
1995	3	5	1.7	0
1996	2	13	6.5	0
1997	14	43	3.1	0
1998	2	13	6.5	0
1999	12	47	3.9	1
Total	33	121	3.7	1

Billy Joe Hobert led the University of Washington to a national championship, but the next year he was suspended from the team after it became known that he accepted $50,000 in loans from a Huskies backer. Hobert used the money to buy cars and guns and to pay off an ex-girlfriend. The Raiders saw this, figured that Hobert would fit right in, and drafted Billy Joe rather than his sane teammate Mark Brunell.

Hobert lost all five of his starts in three years in Oakland and was traded to Buffalo for a third-round pick in 1997. Hobert was called on by the Bills on October 12 to relieve injured starter Todd Collins against the Patriots and played terribly in the 33–6 loss, throwing two interceptions. What made it worse was that the likeable but lackadaisical Hobert admitted after the game that he hadn't bothered studying the playbook because he didn't expect to play. Marv Levy waived Billy Joe a few days later, and the desperate Saints claimed him. Hobert was no more reliable in New Orleans than he had been elsewhere, and his career petered out after three more years.

TOP 10
Quarterback Shuttles

10. Frankie Albert and Y.A. Tittle shared the quarterbacking in each game in 1950.

9. Backup Don Heinrich regularly started for the Giants to probe the defense for starter Charlie Conerly, who would enter the game anywhere from the first quarter to the fourth in the mid-1950s.

8. Randall Cunningham replaced Ron Jaworski for third-down plays in 1986.

7. In the 1954 preseason, Rams coach Hampton Pool sent backup quarterback Billy Wade to the huddle to relay the play to Norm Van Brocklin before racing right back.

6. Rookies Tommy Maddox and Shawn Moore alternated plays for Denver in one game in 1992.

5. Craig Morton and Roger Staubach alternated plays for Dallas in one game in 1971.

4. Ram quarterbacks Zeke Bratkowski, Roman Gabriel, and Terry Baker alternated plays in the 1963 preseason.

3. Don Meredith and Eddie LeBaron alternated plays for Dallas throughout the 1962 season.

2. Milt Plum and Jim Ninowski alternated plays for Cleveland in a game in 1958.

1. Norm Van Brocklin and Rudy Bukich alternated plays for the Rams in one game in 1953.

Tommy Hodson

QPR 2.5

Height: 6'3" **Weight:** 195 lbs. **Birthdate:** 1/28/1967
College: LSU **Draft:** New England 1990-3rd
1990–92 New England Patriots; 1995 New Orleans Saints
Regular Season Record: 1–11, no comebacks
Postseason Record: NA
Relative Rating: 84%

Passing

Year	G	Comp./Att.	%	Yards	Y/Att.	TD	INT	Rating
1990	7	85/156	54.5	968	6.2	4	5	68.5
1991	16	36/68	52.9	345	5.1	1	4	47.7
1992	9	50/91	54.9	496	5.5	2	2	68.8
1995	4	3/5	60.0	14	2.8	0	0	64.6
Total	36	174/320	54.4	1,823	5.7	7	11	64.1

Rushing

Year	Att.	Yards	Avg.	TD
1990	12	79	6.6	0
1991	4	0	0.0	0
1992	5	11	2.2	0
Total	21	90	4.3	0

Tommy Hodson got to start as a rookie when the 1–9 Patriots handed him the reins over the retiring Steve Grogan and Marc Wilson to finish the 1990 season. New England lost all six of Tommy's starts, but he was named the starter for 1991 anyway. Hodson actually led the team to a 16–7 win over the Colts on opening day, but when New England lost

the next two games, Hugh Millen was named the starter. The following season, Millen was lost to an injury with the team 0–6, and Hodson was brought back to lose three more starts before breaking his thumb and giving way to rookie Scott Zolak. Hodson was picked up briefly by Miami in 1993 and Dallas in 1994 but did not play. His final NFL action was as a member of the Saints, for whom he threw five passes in 1995. His 1–11 record ties him with Stan Gelbaugh as the worst winning percentage of any quarterback with 10 NFL starts.

TOP 11

Worst Quarterback Winning Percentages (minimum 10 games)

11. Craig Whelihan and Harry Gilmer, 2–12, .143
10. Bob Celeri, 1–9–1, .136
9. Jeff Komlo, 2–14, .125
6-T. Steve Stenstrom, 1–9, .100
6-T. Tony Adams, 1–9, .100
6-T. Chris Weinke, 2–18, .100
3-T. Tyler Thigpen, 1–10, .091 (active)
3-T. Dan Darragh, 1–10, .091
3-T. Rick Norton, 1–10, .091
1-T. Stan Gelbaugh, 1–11, .083
1-T. Tommy Hodson, 1–11, .083

Gary Hogeboom

QPR 4.0

Height: 6'4" **Weight:** 205 lbs. **Birthdate:** 8/21/1958
College: Central Michigan **Draft:** Dallas 1980-5th
1980–85 Dallas Cowboys; 1986–88 Indianapolis Colts; 1989 Arizona Cardinals
Regular Season Record: 18–19, 5 comebacks
Postseason Record: 0–0, no comebacks
Relative Rating: 96%

Passing

Year	G	Comp./Att.	%	Yards	Y/Att.	TD	INT	Rating
1980	2	0/0	0.0	0	0	0	0	0.0
1981	1	0/0	0.0	0	0	0	0	0.0
1982	4	3/8	37.5	45	5.6	0	1	17.2
1983	6	11/17	64.7	161	9.5	1	1	90.6
1984	16	195/367	53.1	2,366	6.4	7	14	63.7
1985	16	70/126	55.6	978	7.8	5	7	70.8
1986	5	85/144	59.0	1,154	8.0	6	6	81.2
1987	6	99/168	58.9	1,145	6.8	9	5	85.0
1988	9	76/131	58.0	996	7.6	7	7	77.7
1989	14	204/364	56.0	2,591	7.1	14	19	69.5
Total	79	743/1,325	56.1	9,436	7.1	49	60	71.9
PS:	1	14/29	48.3	162	5.6	2	2	59.8

Rushing

Year	Att.	Yards	Avg.	TD
1982	3	0	0.0	0
1983	6	-10	-1.7	0
1984	15	19	1.3	0
1985	8	48	6.0	1
1986	10	20	2.0	1
1987	3	3	1.0	0
1988	11	-8	-0.7	1
1989	27	89	3.3	1
Total	83	161	1.9	4
PS:	0	0	0.0	0

One of the things that angered his Cowboy teammates about Danny White was his seemingly pro-management stance during the protracted 1982 players strike. Gary Hogeboom's impressive performance in a playoff loss to Washington later that season helped propel a pro-Hogeboom faction on the team, and Gary finally got his chance to start in 1984. He threw just seven touchdowns to 14 interceptions that year and lost the starting job back to White in 1985. By 1986, he was traded to Indianapolis. During the 1987 players strike, Hogeboom played along with the replacement players, and the two wins he engineered as the starter helped ensure the Colts of making the playoffs. Gary started just a dozen games for Indianapolis in three seasons before leaving as a Plan B free agent in 1989. He signed a $3 million, four-year contract with Arizona and had the best season in his mediocre career with 14 touchdown passes as well as 19 interceptions. Suffering with elbow and shoulder problems, he was released, and his 10-year career was over. The tall, angular pocket passer gained greater fame 16 years later when he turned up as one of the contestants on the popular reality television show *Survivor*, although he didn't win the million-dollar prize.

Kelly Holcomb

QPR 2.5

Height: 6'2" **Weight:** 212 lbs. **Birthdate:** 7/9/1973
College: Middle Tennessee State **Draft:** Free agent
1996 NFL Europe; 1997 Indianapolis Colts; 2001–04 Cleveland Browns; 2005 Buffalo Bills; 2007 Minnesota Vikings
Regular Season Record: 8–16, 3 comebacks
Postseason Record: 0–1, no comebacks
Relative Rating: 100%

Passing

Year	G	Comp./Att.	%	Yards	Y/Att.	TD	INT	Rating
1997	5	45/73	61.6	454	6.2	1	8	44.3
2001	1	7/12	58.3	114	9.5	1	0	118.1
2002	4	64/106	60.4	790	7.5	8	4	92.9
2003	10	193/302	63.9	1,797	6.0	10	12	74.6
2004	4	59/87	67.8	737	8.5	7	5	96.8
2005	10	155/230	67.4	1,509	6.6	10	8	85.6
2007	3	42/83	50.6	515	6.2	2	1	73.1
Total	37	565/893	63.3	5,916	6.6	39	38	79.9
PS:	1	26/43	60.5	429	10.0	3	1	107.6

Rushing

Year	Att.	Yards	Avg.	TD
1997	5	5	1.0	0
2001	1	0	0.0	0
2002	8	9	1.1	0
2003	8	7	0.9	0
2004	3	-2	-0.7	0
2005	18	11	0.6	1
Total	43	30	0.7	1
PS:	2	3	1.5	0

Kelly Holcomb made a career of relieving disappointing top draft picks. After a year on the Tampa practice squad and a season in NFL Europe, Holcomb joined the Colts in 1997 and saw his first NFL action, throwing just one touchdown to eight interceptions. Holcomb was one of Peyton Manning's unseen backups over the next three years until landing in Cleveland where one-time overall No. 1 pick Tim Couch was struggling to live up to his potential. The sight of the undrafted Holcomb playing about as well as the ballyhooed Couch did not make things easier for Tim with Cleveland fans. When the Browns made the playoffs in 2002, Couch got hurt, and Holcomb played magnificently in a 36–33 postseason loss to Pittsburgh by throwing for 429 yards and three touchdowns.

Couch was gone by 2004, and Holcomb left for Buffalo in 2005 where he outplayed second-year high draft pick J.P. Losman. Losman beat out Holcomb in 2006, and Kelly was traded to Philadelphia in the Takeo Spikes deal the next year. Cut by the Eagles, Holcomb made his way to Minnesota where he briefly took over for the young Tarvaris Jackson before retiring. Holcomb was not mobile and did not have much of an arm, but he used his brains to stay in the league for 10 years on very modest gifts.

Don Horn

QPR 1.0

Height: 6'2" **Weight:** 195 lbs. **Birthdate:** 3/9/1945
College: San Diego State **Draft:** Green Bay 1967-1st
**1967–70 Green Bay Packers; 1971–72 Denver
Broncos; 1973 Cleveland Browns; 1974 San Diego
Chargers; 1975 WFL**
Regular Season Record: 6-8-1, 1 comeback
Postseason Record: NA
Relative Rating: 85%

Passing

Year	G	Comp./Att.	%	Yards	Y/Att.	TD	INT	Rating
1967	3	12/24	50.0	171	7.1	1	1	70.0
1968	1	10/16	62.5	187	11.7	2	0	142.4
1969	9	89/168	53.0	1,505	9.0	11	11	78.1
1970	7	28/76	36.8	428	5.6	2	10	25.4
1971	9	89/173	51.4	1,056	6.1	3	14	42.4
1972	2	0/0	0.0	0	0.0	0	0	0.0
1973	14	4/8	50.0	22	2.8	1	0	95.8
1974	12	0/0	0.0	0	0.0	0	0	0.0
Total	57	232/465	49.9	3,369	7.2	20	36	55.9

Rushing

Year	Att.	Yards	Avg.	TD
1967	1	-2	-2.0	0
1968	3	-7	-2.3	0
1969	3	-7	-2.3	1
1970	5	4	0.8	0
1971	6	15	2.5	0
Total	18	3	0.2	1

Don Horn had a good arm and a good record under coach Don Coryell at San Diego State and was groomed to be Bart Starr's successor in Green Bay. That never worked out for the unsteady bomber. Horn seemed to be developing in his first few seasons. In 1969, he won four of five starts and set a team record by throwing for 410 yards and five touchdowns in the season finale. The next year, though, he threw just two touchdowns and 10 interceptions in a part-time role and was traded to Denver. Given the chance to start for the Broncos, Horn was a disaster with three touchdown passes, 14 interceptions, and a 3–8–1 record. He finished his NFL career as a backup in Cleveland and San Diego before spending a season with the Portland Thunder of the WFL. Horn never learned to read defenses and became easily rattled under pressure,

causing his teammates to lose faith in him. He also threw a lot of interceptions.

Jeff Hostetler

QPR 8.0

Height: 6'3" **Weight:** 215 lbs. **Birthdate:** 4/22/1961
College: West Virginia **Draft:** New York Giants 1984-3rd
**1985–86, 1988–92 New York Giants; 1993–96 Los
Angeles/Oakland Raiders; 1997 Washington Redskins**
Regular Season Record: 51–32, 11 comebacks
Postseason Record: 4–1, 2 comebacks
Relative Rating: 105%

Passing

Year	G	Comp./Att.	%	Yards	Y/Att.	TD	INT	Rating
1985	5	0/0	0.0	0	0	0	0	0.0
1986	13	0/0	0.0	0	0	0	0	0.0
1988	16	16/29	55.2	244	8.4	1	2	65.9
1989	16	20/39	51.3	294	7.5	3	2	80.5
1990	16	47/87	54.0	614	7.1	3	1	83.2
1991	12	179/285	62.8	2,032	7.1	5	4	84.1
1992	13	103/192	53.6	1,225	6.4	8	3	80.8
1993	15	236/419	56.3	3,242	7.7	14	10	82.5
1994	16	263/455	57.8	3,334	7.3	20	16	80.8
1995	11	172/286	60.1	1,998	7.0	12	9	82.2
1996	13	242/402	60.2	2,548	6.3	23	14	83.2
1997	6	79/144	54.9	899	6.2	5	10	56.5
Total	152	1,357/2,338	58.0	16,430	7.0	94	71	80.5
PS:	5	72/115	62.6	1,034	9.0	7	0	112

Rushing

Year	Att.	Yards	Avg.	TD
1986	1	1	1.0	0
1988	5	-3	-0.6	0
1989	11	71	6.5	2
1990	39	190	4.9	2
1991	42	273	6.5	2
1992	35	172	4.9	3
1993	55	202	3.7	5
1994	46	159	3.5	2
1995	31	119	3.8	0
1996	37	179	4.8	1
1997	14	28	2.0	0
Total	316	1,391	4.4	17
PS:	24	98	4.1	0

Todd Blackledge beat Jeff Hostetler out for the starting job at Penn State, so Jeff transferred to West Virginia where he was an Academic All-

American, led the Mountaineers to an 18-6 record, and eventually married the daughter of coach Don Nehlen. The Giants drafted him in the third round of the 1984 draft, but he was buried behind both Phil Simms and Jeff Rutledge and would not throw his first pass until 1988. Jeff also served as emergency tight end and even blocked a punt during that time as the third quarterback. When Simms broke his foot at the end of the 1990 season, though, Hostetler was ready despite having thrown just 58 passes in six and a half years as the Giants' frustrated backup quarterback. Jeff led New York to wins in its last two games and then beat the Bears and 49ers in the playoffs to get to the Super Bowl against the ballyhooed Buffalo Bills. Hostetler's steady field generalship helped the Giants score one of the biggest upsets in Super Bowl history in beating the Bills 20–19 with a ball-control offense that held the ball for more than 40 minutes.

His postseason success led to an immediate quarterback controversy. New coach Ray Handley chose the younger and more mobile Hostetler, but Simms still got playing time during the next two unsuccessful seasons. Both quarterbacks found this to be intolerable, so when new coach Dan Reeves chose Simms as his starter, Hostetler was allowed to leave as a free agent. Jeff spent four seasons as the starter with the Raiders, throwing for more than 3,000 yards twice, but his time there is most remembered for his coach Art Shell sneeringly calling him just another "white quarterback." Hostetler moved on to the Redskins for a season and then retired to spend more time with his family.

Hostetler has admitted to having regrets about not getting a chance to play until his seventh NFL season. Lacking a big arm, he still proved himself to be an able NFL quarterback: very smart, an accurate passer, and an elusive runner. He is the only quarterback to never throw a postseason interception on at least 100 passes. When the Giants were making their 2007 playoff run, Hostetler remarked to ESPN, "The thing I'm most proud of was being prepared and taking advantage when the opportunity finally presented itself. Quarterbacks have come to realize that Super Bowls are a different type of pressure than they've ever experienced. To play well under those circumstances was very rewarding."

Bobby Hoying

QPR 2.5

Height: 6'3"   **Weight:** 221 lbs.   **Birthdate:** 9/20/1972
College: Ohio State   **Draft:** Philadelphia 1996-3rd
1996–98 Philadelphia Eagles; 1999–2000 Oakland Raiders
Regular Season Record: 3–9–1, 2 comebacks
Postseason Record: 0–0, no comebacks
Relative Rating: 83%

Passing

Year	G	Comp./Att.	%	Yards	Y/Att.	TD	INT	Rating
1996	1	0/0	0.0	0	0.0	0	0	0.0
1997	7	128/225	56.9	1,573	7.0	11	6	83.8
1998	8	114/224	50.9	961	4.3	0	9	45.6
1999	2	2/5	40.0	10	2.0	0	0	47.9
2000	4	0/2	0.0	0	0.0	0	0	39.6
Total	22	244/456	53.5	2,544	5.6	11	15	64.3
PS:	1	8/16	50.0	107	6.7	0	2	32

Rushing

Year	Att.	Yards	Avg.	TD
1997	16	78	4.9	0
1998	22	84	3.8	0
1999	2	-3	-1.5	0
2000	2	-3	-1.5	0
Total	42	156	3.7	0
PS:	3	13	4.3	0

One of Ray Rhodes' weaknesses in his four-year stint as Eagles coach was his inability to settle on a quarterback. He went from Randall Cunningham to Rodney Peete to Ty Detmer, back to Peete, to Bobby Hoying, back to Peete, back to Hoying, and then to Koy Detmer. Hoying inspired a lot of excitement in Eagle fans in his first three starts in 1997 when he threw for six touchdowns and just one interception while the team went 2–0–1. The demand for Hoying jerseys was so great that there were shortages in local stores. Unfortunately, in the last three games of the year, Hoying's touchdown-interception ratio was down to 4:5 and the Eagles lost all three. In an understatement after the season, Hoying admitted, "Let's say I wasn't ready for all [the defenses] threw at me."

Hoying opened the 1998 season as the starter but regressed even further, now definitely looking like a deer mesmerized by headlights whenever the defense blitzed. Hoying threw zero touchdowns and nine interceptions in seven starts. The team went 1–6 in those games and averaged just six points a game. Bobby was traded to Oakland after the year where he was reunited with former Eagles offensive coordinator Jon Gruden. Hoying spent two seasons as Rich Gannon's caddy but threw just seven passes and retired after injuring his elbow.

Damon Huard

QPR 5.0

Height: 6'3"   **Weight:** 215 lbs.   **Birthdate:** 7/9/1973
College: Washington   **Draft:** Free agent
1998–2000 Miami Dolphins; 2002–03 New England Patriots; 2006–08 Kansas City Chiefs
Regular Season Record: 15–12, 7 comebacks
Postseason Record: 0–0, no comebacks
Relative Rating: 102%

Passing

Year	G	Comp./Att.	%	Yards	Y/Att.	TD	INT	Rating
1998	2	6/9	66.7	85	9.4	0	1	57.4
1999	16	125/216	57.9	1,288	6.0	8	4	79.8
2000	16	39/63	61.9	318	5.0	1	3	60.2
2002	2	0/0	0.0	0	0.0	0	0	0.0
2003	2	0/1	0.0	0	0.0	0	0	39.6
2006	10	148/244	60.7	1,878	7.7	11	1	98.0
2007	11	206/332	62	2,257	6.8	11	13	76.8
2008	5	50/81	61.7	477	5.9	2	4	65.7
Total	64	574/946	60.7	6,303	6.7	33	26	80.6
PS:	1	5/16	31.3	46	2.9	0	0	40.6

Rushing

Year	Att.	Yards	Avg.	TD
1999	28	124	4.4	0
2002	1	4	4.0	0
2003	1	-1	-1.0	0
2006	9	9	1.0	0
2007	9	-1	-0.1	0
2008	4	13	3.3	0
Total	52	148	2.8	0
PS:	0	0	0.0	0

Damon Huard landed the job of Dan Marino's backup in 1998 and even got to start five games for the injured Hall of Famer in 1999. After Marino retired at the end of that season, though, the newly signed Jay Fiedler beat out Huard as Dan's successor. Damon moved on to New England to spend three seasons backing up Drew Bledsoe and then Tom Brady. Damon threw just one pass as a Patriot but did win two Super Bowl rings for carrying a clipboard so calmly. In 2004, Huard signed with the Chiefs as Trent Green's backup and did not get to play until Green suffered such a severe concussion in 2006 that he missed half the season. Huard played well in Green's absence, throwing 11 touchdowns to just one interception and winning five of eight starts. Although he cannot throw the bomb or the deep-out pattern, Damon compensates by being very accurate on the shorter throws. Since Green left in 2007, Huard has battled unproven prospects Brodie Croyle and Tyler Thigpen for the starting job. Huard is little more than a career backup who understands his place, stating, "I understand that my job is to get the ball to our playmakers." Damon, who was succeeded at quarterback for the University of Washington by his brother Brock, does not have the talent to be a starter, but he is one of the most reliable backups in the league.

Gary Huff

QPR 1.0

Height: 6'1"   **Weight:** 195 lbs.   **Birthdate:** 4/27/1951
Florida State   **Draft:** Chicago Bears 1973-2nd
1973–76 Chicago Bears; 1977–78 Tampa Bay Bucs; 1985 USFL
Regular Season Record: 7–21, 1 comeback
Postseason Record: NA
Relative Rating: 72%

Passing

Year	G	Comp./Att.	%	Yards	Y/Att.	TD	INT	Rating
1973	8	54/126	42.9	525	4.2	3	8	36.6
1974	13	142/283	50.2	1,663	5.9	6	17	50.4
1975	14	114/205	55.6	1,083	5.3	3	9	57.0
1976	8	0/0	0.0	0	0.0	0	0	0.0
1977	8	67/138	48.6	889	6.4	3	13	37.4
1978	6	15/36	41.7	169	4.7	1	3	30.9
Total	57	392/788	49.7	4,329	5.5	16	50	46.8

Rushing

Year	Att.	Yards	Avg.	TD
1973	11	22	2.0	0
1974	23	37	1.6	2
1975	5	7	1.4	0
1977	8	10	1.3	0
1978	3	10	3.3	0
Total	50	86	1.7	2

At Florida State, the fans called Gary Huff "The Magic Dragon" because his name rhymed with "Puff." For his unimpressive, weak-armed stint in the NFL, though, Puff would have been a more accurate description. Huff was still another failed Bear quarterback who threw three times as many interceptions as touchdowns and averaged a paltry 5.5 yards per throw. Chicago released him in 1977, and Huff returned to Florida to sign with the winless Bucs. Gary's claim to fame is that he quarterbacked Tampa to its very first victory after the team had dropped the first 26 games played. In Week 13, Tampa beat New Orleans 33–14 by returning three interceptions of Archie Manning's for touchdowns. Gary whipped out a victory cigar and said, "I've been carrying this so long, it's stale." Then they beat the Cardinals the next week in the season finale. Those were Huff's last two starts. In 1978, Doug Williams and Mike Rae joined the Bucs, and Gary threw just 36 passes in his last year. Huff did some coaching—even serving as a player/coach seven years later

---

TOP 10
Quarterbacks With the Most Passes Without an NFL Start

10. Brian Dowling, 55 passes
8-T. Jeff Brohm, 58 passes
8-T. Fred Benners, 58 passes
7. John Walton, 65 passes
5-T. Guy Benjamin, 68 passes
5-T. Rich Campbell, 68 passes
4. Bev Wallace, 69 passes
3. Paul Held, 77 passes
2. Casey Weldon, 120 passes
1. Jim Sorgi, 156 passes

---

with Memphis in the USFL—before becoming the chief financial officer of the Los Angeles Raiders in the late 1980s.

Stan Humphries

QPR **7.5**

Height: 6'2" **Weight:** 223 lbs. **Birthdate:** 4/14/1965
College: Northeast Louisiana **Draft:** Washington 1988-6th
1989–90 Washington Redskins; 1992–97 San Diego Chargers
Regular Season Record: 50–31, 13 comebacks
Postseason Record: 3–3, 2 comebacks
Relative Rating: 98%

Passing

Year	G	Comp./Att.	%	Yards	Y/Att.	TD	INT	Rating
1989	2	5/10	50.0	91	9.1	1	1	75.4
1990	7	91/156	58.3	1,015	6.5	3	10	57.5
1992	16	263/454	57.9	3,356	7.4	16	18	76.4
1993	12	173/324	53.4	1,981	6.1	12	10	71.5
1994	15	264/453	58.3	3,209	7.1	17	12	81.6
1995	15	282/478	59.0	3,381	7.1	17	14	80.4
1996	13	232/416	55.8	2,670	6.4	18	13	76.7
1997	8	121/225	53.8	1,488	6.6	5	6	70.8
Total	88	1,431/2,516	56.9	17,191	6.8	89	84	75.8
PS:	6	118/228	51.8	1,347	5.9	6	13	54.8

Rushing

Year	Att.	Yards	Avg.	TD
1989	5	10	2.0	0
1990	23	106	4.6	2
1992	28	79	2.8	4
1993	8	37	4.6	0
1994	19	19	1.0	0
1995	33	53	1.6	1
1996	21	28	1.3	0
1997	13	24	1.8	0
Total	150	356	2.4	7
PS:	13	43	3.3	0

Stan Humphries led Northeast Louisiana to the Division I-AA championship in 1987 and was drafted in the late rounds by the Redskins. The chunky Humphries spent four years as a backup in Washington, but his disinterest in Washington's off-season weight-training program caused Joe Gibbs to sour on him. Former Redskin GM Bobby

Beathard traded the forgettable Clarence Verdin to Washington to bring Stan to San Diego, and Humphries would go on to accumulate more yards and touchdown passes than any Charger quarterback other than John Hadl and Dan Fouts. Humphries did something else that neither Hadl nor Fouts could manage; he took San Diego to the Super Bowl.

The Chargers' 1994 Super Bowl run was highlighted by Humphries leading the league in fourth-quarter game-winning drives with six. Soon after, however, the team was driven apart by dissension among players, management, and coach Bobby Ross. Some players even questioned the toughness of the banged-up Humphries toward the end of his career. Stan liked to work off of play-action and made a number of big plays down the field. Humphries was immobile but had a quick release, so he kept sacks to a minimum. Still, he took some bad hits and eventually retired after suffering a series of concussions.

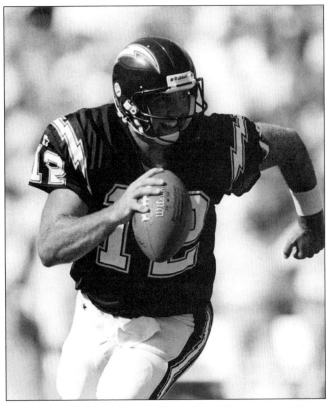

Stan Humphries threw a 99-yard touchdown pass to Tony Martin on September 18, 1994 against Seattle.

Scott Hunter

QPR **4.0**

Height: 6'2" **Weight:** 205 lbs. **Birthdate:** 11/11/1947
College: Alabama **Draft:** Green Bay 1971-6th
1971–73 Green Bay Packers; 1974 Buffalo Bills;
1976–77 Atlanta Falcons; 1979 Detroit Lions
Regular Season Record: 21–18–3, 8 comebacks
Postseason Record: 0–1, no comebacks
Relative Rating: 84%

Passing

Year	G	Comp./Att.	%	Yards	Y/Att.	TD	INT	Rating
1971	13	75/163	46.0	1,210	7.4	7	17	46.1
1972	14	86/199	43.2	1,252	6.3	6	9	55.5
1973	8	35/84	41.7	442	5.3	2	4	46.8
1974	1	0/0	0.0	0	0.0	0	0	0.0
1976	8	51/110	46.4	633	5.8	5	4	64.7
1977	7	70/151	46.4	898	5.9	2	3	61.6
1979	13	18/41	43.9	321	7.8	1	1	69.3
Total	64	335/748	44.8	4,756	6.4	23	38	55.0
PS:	1	12/24	50.0	150	6.3	0	1	52.4

Rushing

Year	Att.	Yards	Avg.	TD
1971	21	50	2.4	4
1972	22	37	1.7	5
1973	8	3	0.4	1
1976	14	41	2.9	1
1977	28	70	2.5	1
1979	2	3	1.5	1
Total	95	204	2.1	13
PS:	2	13	6.5	0

Like Bart Starr, Scott Hunter was late-round draft pick from Alabama who was a cool-headed leader on the field, and Packer fans were hoping that Crimson Tide lightning would strike twice in Wisconsin. Unfortunately, Hunter had suffered a severe shoulder separation in college that drained him of arm strength. Forced to start as a rookie when Starr got hurt, Hunter looked hopeless at times. In 1972 he told *Sports Illustrated*, "I didn't know what I was doing, but I learned. Working with Bart was like reading an encyclopedia."

In his second season, though, the Packers rode a punishing ground attack to the Central Division crown despite Hunter completing just 43 percent of his passes. In the playoffs, the Redskins came out in a five-man defensive front to shut down Green Bay's running, but the Packers didn't trust Hunter's arm enough to go to the pass and Washington won easily. The next year, Hunter had injury problems, and coach Dan Devine gave him up, trading for a washed up John Hadl. Scott moved on to Buffalo, Atlanta, and Detroit but never completed more than 46 percent of his passes anywhere. Hunter was a fine leader but was a spray passer who threw interceptions. Ultimately, he was no Bart Starr.

Chad Hutchinson

QPR 1.0

Height: 6'5" **Weight:** 237 lbs. **Birthdate:** 2/21/1977
College: Stanford **Draft:** Free agent
2002–03 Dallas Cowboys; 2004 Chicago Bears
Regular Season Record: 3–11, 1 comeback
Postseason Record: NA
Relative Rating: 86%

Passing

Year	G	Comp./Att.	%	Yards	Y/Att.	TD	INT	Rating
2002	9	127/250	50.8	1,555	6.2	7	8	66.3
2003	1	1/2	50.0	8	4.0	0	0	60.4
2004	5	92/161	57.1	903	5.6	4	3	73.6
Total	15	220/413	53.3	2,466	6.0	11	11	69.1

Rushing

Year	Att.	Yards	Avg.	TD
2002	18	74	4.1	0
2003	2	-3	-1.5	0
2004	6	14	2.3	0
Total	26	85	3.3	0

Chad Hutchinson was highly recruited for both baseball and football coming out of high school but chose to go to Stanford, where he pitched on the baseball team and played quarterback for the football team. After his junior year, Chad signed a $3.5 million contract with baseball's St. Louis Cardinals in 1997 to forego his senior year of eligibility. Four years later, Hutchinson spent two weeks in the big leagues and appeared in three games as a relief pitcher, giving up 11 runs in four innings.

At this point, Hutchinson realized he must be a football player after all and provoked a bidding war for his services as a free agent. The Cowboys gave Chad a $3.1 million bonus to sign with them

---

TOP 10
Dropoffs from Legendary Quarterbacks

10. From Bob Griese to David Woodley in Miami
9. From Terry Bradshaw to Cliff Stoudt in Pittsburgh
8. From Len Dawson to Mike Livingston in Kansas City
7. From Jim Kelly to Todd Collins in Buffalo
6. From Warren Moon to Billy Joe Tolliver in Houston
5. From Dan Fouts to Mark Malone in San Diego
4. From Troy Aikman to Quincy Carter in Dallas
3. From Bart Starr to Scott Hunter in Green Bay
2. From Johnny Unitas to Marty Domres in Baltimore
1. From Otto Graham to Tommy O'Connell in Cleveland

---

in 2002, but the green and rusty Hutchinson won just two of nine starts as a rookie and didn't look much better the next year. So he was released and landed with the Bears in 2004. After one season in Chicago, the hard-throwing, 6'5" 230-pound Hutchinson found himself behind Kyle Orton, Jeff Blake, and Kurt Kittner and was released. He made more than $3 million in two different sports but could not play either one at a big-league level.

Cecil Isbell

QPR 9.0

Height: 6'1" **Weight:** 190 lbs. **Birthdate:** 7/11/1915
College: Purdue **Draft:** Green Bay 1938-1st
1938–42 Green Bay Packers
Regular Season Record: 40–12–2 est., 5 comebacks
Postseason Record: 0–1, no comebacks
Relative Rating: 188%

Passing

Year	G	Comp./Att.	%	Yards	Y/Att.	TD	INT	Rating
1938	11	37/91	40.7	659	7.2	8	10	55.9
1939	11	43/103	41.7	749	7.3	6	5	66.4
1940	10	68/150	45.3	1,037	6.9	8	12	53.1
1941	11	117/206	56.8	1,479	7.2	15	11	81.4
1942	11	146/268	54.5	2,021	7.5	24	14	87.0
Total	24	411/818	50.2	5,945	7.3	61	52	72.6
PS:	3	13/26	50.0	235	9.0	2	1	91.0

Rushing

Year	Att.	Yards	Avg.	TD
1938	85	445	5.2	2
1939	132	407	3.1	2
1940	97	270	2.8	4
1941	72	317	4.4	1
1942	36	83	2.3	1
Total	422	1,522	3.6	10
PS:	25	48	1.9	0

During the five seasons that Cecil Isbell was the Packers' single-wing tailback, Hall of Famers Sammy Baugh and Sid Luckman were his contemporaries. Comparing their statistics for that time period, Isbell threw for the most yards and touchdown passes and had the lowest interception percentage. Baugh had the highest completion percentage and Luckman the highest average gain per pass. Overall, Isbell compares very well to both passers. That's why Packers coach Curly Lambeau said that Isbell was the best passer he ever saw. "Isbell was the master at any range. He could throw soft passes, bullet passes, or feathery lobs. He was the best with Sid Luckman of the Bears a close second and Sammy Baugh of the Redskins a long third. Luckman wasn't as versatile and Baugh couldn't compare on the long ones." Unlike the other two, however, Isbell never got to play quarterback in the T formation. Furthermore, because Cecil had dislocated his left shoulder several times in college, he wore a chain that went from his arm to his torso to keep him from raising his arm too high and damaging the shoulder. Isbell also had nine interceptions on defense and rushed for 1,522 yards on 422 attempts in his brief career.

The Packers already had an All-League tailback in Arnie Herber in 1938, but Isbell was so talented that the two generally would alternate for Cecil's first three years in the league. Sometimes both would play at the same time and occasionally even would throw passes to each other, but most of the time they would throw to Don Hutson. In 1942, Hutson caught 17 of Isbell's record 24 touchdown passes. From 1940 through 1942, Cecil threw a touchdown pass in 23 straight games, a record that Johnny Unitas would break in 1958 en route to an ultimate total of 47 straight.

Isbell twice was All-League and three times was second-team All-League in his five seasons in the NFL. Isbell said that he had seen Lambeau coldly cast aside loyal veterans such as Arnie Herber and was determined that would never happen to him. When his alma mater, Purdue, offered him a coaching job in 1943, Cecil took it so he did not get the chance to accumulate more impressive career totals like Baugh and Luckman. Isbell served as head coach for three years at Purdue before moving on to coach the Baltimore Colts of the All-America Football Conference for a few years, tutoring a rookie quarterback named Y.A. Tittle in 1948.

Packer passer Cecil Isbell, flanked by end Don Hutson and coach Curly Lambeau, studies the X's and O's in 1940.

Tarvaris Jackson

Height: 6'2" **Weight:** 226 lbs. **Birthdate:** 4/21/1983
College: Alabama State **Draft:** Minnesota 2006-2nd
2006–08 Minnesota Vikings
Regular Season Record: 10–9, 4 comebacks
Postseason Record: 0–1, no comebacks
Relative Rating: 95%

Passing

Year	G	Comp./Att.	%	Yards	Y/Att.	TD	INT	Rating
2006	4	47/81	58.0	475	5.9	2	4	62.5
2007	12	171/294	58.2	1,911	6.5	9	12	70.8
2008	9	88/149	59.1	1,056	7.1	9	2	95.4
Total	23	306/524	58.4	3,442	6.6	20	18	76.5
PS:	1	15/35	42.9	164	4.7	0	1	45.4

Rushing

Year	Att.	Yards	Avg.	TD
2006	15	77	5.1	1
2007	54	260	4.8	3
2008	26	145	5.6	0
Total	95	482	5.1	4
PS:	2	17	8.5	0

During the 2008 preseason, Vikings coaches raved about the progress third-year man Tarvaris Jackson had made in his development as a pro quarterback, but after two shaky performances at the start of the year, Jackson was benched for the mediocre graybeard Gus Frerotte for the balance of the season. Jackson possesses a powerful gun for an arm and runs like a rampaging bull when scrambling but still was making bad reads of coverage and throwing the ball too erratically to hold the starting job. The talented Jackson came out of tiny Alabama State with a great deal to learn about playing quarterback at the professional level. When Frerotte got hurt in December, Jackson returned and drove the Vikings to the playoffs. Tarvaris kept the job even after Frerotte was ready again because he seemed to have matured a bit. Jackson has the physical tools and is a fiery leader but needs to get more consistent at the mechanical fundamentals of passing and better at recognizing

defenses. His play in the postseason indicated that he has a long way to go to become a quality quarterback.

Jack Jacobs

Height: 6'1" **Weight:** 196 lbs. **Birthdate:** 8/7/1919
College: Oklahoma **Draft:** Cleveland Rams 1942-2nd
1942, 1945 Cleveland Rams; 1946 Washington Redskins; 1947–49 Green Bay Packers; 1950–54 CFL
Regular Season Record: 10–14–1 est., 1 comeback
Postseason Record: NA
Relative Rating: 81%

Passing

Year	G	Comp./Att.	%	Yards	Y/Att.	TD	INT	Rating
1942	8	43/93	46.2	640	6.9	6	6	63.9
1945	2	3/5	60.0	12	2.4	0	0	64.6
1946	9	5/12	41.7	98	8.2	0	2	31.2
1947	12	108/242	44.6	1,615	6.7	16	17	59.8
1948	12	82/184	44.6	848	4.6	5	21	27.9
1949	12	3/16	18.8	55	3.4	0	3	1.8
Total	55	244/552	44.2	3,268	5.9	27	49	42.9

Rushing

Year	Att.	Yards	Avg.	TD
1942	32	-31	-1.0	0
1945	2	0	0.0	0
1946	18	34	1.9	0
1947	18	64	3.6	1
1948	24	73	3.0	1
Total	94	140	1.5	2

"Indian" Jack Jacobs, who was once Sammy Baugh's backup in Washington, was the Slingin' Sam of Canadian Football in the early 1950s, introducing a wide-open passing attack to the Great White North. Jacobs, a Creek Indian, began his career as tailback Parker Hall's backup with the Rams in 1942 and then went into the war. After he returned to the NFL, he was traded to the Redskins for quarterback Jim Hardy and two other players in 1946. Jacobs threw only 12 passes that year behind Baugh and was traded to the Packers for Bob Nussbaumer the following year. With Green Bay finally switching to the T formation, Jacobs became the Packers' first real quarterback in 1947 and enjoyed his finest NFL season with 16 touchdown passes. During the next two seasons, though, the team fell apart, and Jacobs struggled with injuries, although he did lead the league in punting in 1948.

Released in 1950, he went north to Winnipeg in the Western Division of Canadian football. Over the next five years, Jacobs threw for 104 touchdowns, only 53 interceptions, and more than 11,000 yards. He became the first professional quarterback to throw for 30 touchdowns and more than 3,000 yards in a season in 1951 and exceeded 30 touchdown passes again in 1952. He led the Blue Bombers to the championship game in both 1951 and 1953 but lost each time. Nonetheless, Jacobs was immensely popular, and Winnipeg's new stadium in 1953 was commonly known as "The House that Jack Built." Jacobs was elected to the CFL Hall of Fame in 1963.

Rushing

Year	Att.	Yards	Avg.	TD
1974	7	34	4.9	1
1975	12	33	2.8	2
1976	2	15	7.5	1
1977	40	127	3.2	5
1978	30	79	2.6	0
1979	43	119	2.8	2
1980	27	95	3.5	1
1981	22	128	5.8	0
1982	10	9	0.9	0
1983	25	129	5.2	1
1984	5	18	3.6	1
1985	17	35	2.1	2
1986	13	33	2.5	0
1989	4	5	1.3	0
Total	257	859	3.3	16
PS:	23	49	2.1	1

Ron Jaworski

QPR 7.5

Height: 6'2" **Weight:** 196 lbs. **Birthdate:** 3/23/1951

College: Youngstown State **Draft:** Los Angeles Rams 1973-2nd

1974–76 Los Angeles Rams; 1977–86 Philadelphia Eagles; 1988 Miami Dolphins; 1989 Kansas City Chiefs

Regular Season Record: 73–69–1, 23 comebacks

Postseason Record: 4–5, 1 comeback

Relative Rating: 101%

Passing

Year	G	Comp./Att.	%	Yards	Y/Att.	TD	INT	Rating
1974	5	10/24	41.7	144	6.0	0	1	44.4
1975	14	24/48	50.0	302	6.3	0	2	52.6
1976	5	20/52	38.5	273	5.3	1	5	22.8
1977	14	166/346	48.0	2,183	6.3	18	21	60.4
1978	16	206/398	51.8	2,487	6.2	16	16	67.9
1979	16	190/374	50.8	2,669	7.1	18	12	76.8
1980	16	257/451	57.0	3,529	7.8	27	12	91.0
1981	16	250/461	54.2	3,095	6.7	23	20	73.8
1982	9	167/286	58.4	2,076	7.3	12	12	77.5
1983	16	235/446	52.7	3,315	7.4	20	18	75.1
1984	13	234/427	54.8	2,754	6.4	16	14	73.5
1985	16	255/484	52.7	3,450	7.1	17	20	70.2
1986	10	128/245	52.2	1,405	5.7	8	6	70.2
1988	16	9/14	64.3	123	8.8	1	0	116.1
1989	6	36/61	59.0	385	6.3	2	5	54.3
Total	188	2,187/4,117	53.1	28,190	6.8	179	164	72.8
PS:	9	126/270	46.5	1,669	6.2	10	10	63.4

Ron Jaworski is famous today for being perhaps the most analytical football broadcaster on television, but he was once a sturdy quarterback who endured 32 concussions and was sacked nearly 400 times during his 15-year NFL career. It was his record of 116 consecutive quarterback starts that Brett Favre broke in 1999. Ron was booed heavily at times in his 10 years in Philadelphia, but the upbeat, talkative "Jaws" transformed the boos into a positive force by using them as a motivation to improve and win the respect of the league's roughest fans with his toughness, his play, and his attitude.

After getting just three starts in four years in Los Angeles, Jaworski got lucky and was traded to Philadelphia for tight end Charlie Young. Coach Dick Vermeil was trying to rebuild a decimated Eagle franchise and needed a quarterback. Jaworski, the son of a steelworker, was installed as a starter in 1977 and showed potential but was very raw. In his first two years in Philadelphia, he completed just 50 percent of his passes and threw 34 touchdowns against 37 interceptions while being sacked 88 times. In 1979, Vermeil brought in retired offensive genius Sid Gillman to redesign the passing offense and to tutor Jaworski. Under Gillman's guidance, Jaws threw for 45 touchdowns and only 24 interceptions in 1979–80. In 1980, he threw for a personal high of 3,529 yards and 27 TDs and won the NFL MVP award as he led the Eagles to the Super Bowl.

Jaworski threw three interceptions in the Super Bowl as the Eagles were upset by the Raiders, and he never again had seasons as good as 1979 and 1980, although he was still a solid pro. Ron's biggest highlight was the 99-yard touchdown pass to Mike Quick to win in overtime against Atlanta in 1985. After Buddy Ryan arrived as the blustering coach in 1986, Jaworski's playing time was cut, and then he was cut from the team. He caught on for a couple of seasons as a backup in Miami and Kansas City and at 38 was part of the oldest center-quarterback combination in NFL history with 37-year-old Mike Webster of the Chiefs.

Brad Johnson

 QPR 8.5

Height: 6'5" **Weight:** 226 lbs. **Birthdate:** 9/13/1968
College: Florida State **Draft:** Minnesota 1992-9th
**1994-98, 2005-06 Minnesota Vikings; 1999-2000
Washington Redskins; 2001-04 Tampa Bay Bucs;
2007-08 Dallas Cowboys**
Regular Season Record: 72-53, 29 comebacks
Postseason Record: 4-3, no comebacks
Relative Rating: 104%

Passing

Year	G	Comp./Att.	%	Yards	Y/Att.	TD	INT	Rating
1994	4	22/37	59.5	150	4.1	0	0	68.5
1995	5	25/36	69.4	272	7.6	0	2	68.3
1996	12	195/311	62.7	2,258	7.3	17	10	89.4
1997	13	275/452	60.8	3,036	6.7	20	12	84.5
1998	4	65/101	64.4	747	7.4	7	5	89.0
1999	16	316/519	60.9	4,005	7.7	24	13	90.0
2000	12	228/365	62.5	2,505	6.9	11	15	75.7
2001	16	340/559	60.8	3,406	6.1	13	11	77.7
2002	13	281/451	62.3	3,049	6.8	22	6	92.9
2003	16	354/570	62.1	3,811	6.7	26	21	81.5
2004	4	65/103	63.1	674	6.5	3	3	79.5
2005	15	184/294	62.6	1,885	6.4	12	4	88.9
2006	15	270/439	61.5	2,750	6.3	9	15	72.0
2007	16	7/11	63.6	79	7.2	0	0	85.0
2008	16	41/78	52.6	427	5.5	2	5	50.5
Total	164	2,668/4,326	61.7	29,054	6.7	166	122	82.5
PS:	7	125/224	55.8	1,403	6.3	7	12	62.8

Rushing

Year	Att.	Yards	Avg.	TD
1994	2	-2	-1.0	0
1995	9	-9	-1.0	0
1996	34	90	2.6	1
1997	35	139	4.0	0
1998	12	15	1.3	0
1999	26	31	1.2	2
2000	22	58	2.6	1
2001	39	120	3.1	3
2002	13	30	2.3	0
2003	25	33	1.3	0
2004	5	23	4.6	0
2005	18	53	2.9	0
2006	29	82	2.8	1
2007	5	-5	-1.0	0
2008	2	-1	-0.5	0
Total	276	657	2.4	8
PS:	12	29	2.4	1

Brad Johnson was never the full-time starter at Florida State and was not rated highly by scouts for the NFL draft, establishing a pattern of underestimation that would haunt Johnson's 15-year professional career. Brad did not appear in a game for Minnesota until his third year and did not start one until his fifth. Finally in his sixth season, Johnson began 1997 as the Vikings' regular starter and then hurt his neck in the 13th game. He tried again in 1998 but broke his leg in the second game and watched Randall Cunningham lead Minnesota to a 15-1 record.

Traded to Washington in 1999, Johnson had his best year, throwing for more than 4,000 yards and 24 touchdowns. After two seasons with the Redskins, Johnson signed with Tampa as a free agent in 2001. One year later, Jon Gruden arrived as coach and the two uneasy partners led the Bucs to the world championship that season. Brad held the starting job for just one more year in Tampa before losing out to Brian Griese in 2004. He returned to Minnesota as a backup in 2005 and moved on to Dallas in 2007. Although he rarely has been considered among the top quarterbacks in the league, he's won more than 70 games as a starter and has gone to two Pro Bowls.

Despite being 6'5" and more than 225 pounds, Johnson has never been much of a long-ball passer. Instead, he relies on a short, accurate passing attack. The only year in which he averaged more than 12 yards per completion was his first year in Washington. Johnson has been the epitome of the smart game manager. He completes more than 60 percent of his passes each year, has twice led the league in lowest interception percentage, and is not prone to being sacked. Since turning 38 in 2006, though, his arm had clearly declined to the point where he couldn't make basic throws, and he was no longer even a quality backup.

Charley Johnson

QPR 8.0

Height: 6'0" **Weight:** 190 lbs. **Birthdate:** 11/22/1938
College: New Mexico State **Draft:** St. Louis Cardinals 1960-10th; San Diego Chargers 1961-8th
1961–69 St. Louis Cardinals; 1970–71 Houston Oilers; 1972–75 Denver Broncos
Regular Season Record: 59–57–8, 17 comebacks
Postseason Record: NA
Relative Rating: 103%

Passing

Year	G	Comp./Att.	%	Yards	Y/Att.	TD	INT	Rating
1961	4	5/13	38.5	51	3.9	0	2	10.9
1962	11	150/308	48.7	2,440	7.9	16	20	65.9
1963	14	222/423	52.5	3,280	7.8	28	21	79.5
1964	14	223/420	53.1	3,045	7.3	21	24	69.4
1965	11	155/322	48.1	2,439	7.6	18	15	73.0
1966	9	103/205	50.2	1,334	6.5	10	11	65.0
1967	5	12/29	41.4	162	5.6	1	3	31.8
1968	7	29/67	43.3	330	4.9	1	1	57.4
1969	12	131/260	50.4	1,847	7.1	13	13	69.5
1970	10	144/281	51.2	1,652	5.9	7	12	59.8
1971	14	46/94	48.9	592	6.3	3	7	48.7
1972	12	132/238	55.5	1,783	7.5	14	14	74.6
1973	14	184/346	53.2	2,465	7.1	20	17	74.9
1974	14	136/244	55.7	1,969	8.1	13	9	84.5
1975	14	65/142	45.8	1,021	7.2	5	12	46.7
Total	165	1,737/3,392	51.2	24,410	7.2	170	181	69.2

Rushing

Year	Att.	Yards	Avg.	TD
1961	1	-3	-3.0	0
1962	25	138	5.5	3
1963	41	143	3.5	1
1964	31	93	3.0	2
1965	25	60	2.4	1
1966	20	39	2.0	2
1968	5	-1	-0.2	0
1969	17	51	3.0	1
1970	5	3	0.6	0
1971	2	0	0.0	0
1972	3	0	0.0	0
1973	7	-2	-0.3	0
1974	4	-3	-0.8	0
1975	10	21	2.1	0
Total	196	539	2.8	10

Along with Frank Ryan, Charley Johnson was one of two 1960s quarterbacks to earn a doctorate. Charley's was in chemical engineering, and he eventually returned to his alma mater as a chemical engineering professor who is also involved with the athletic department.

Johnson spent 15 years in the NFL, the first nine with the St. Louis Cardinals, but his career was frequently interrupted by injuries and military obligations. In 1965 and 1966, he missed eight games due to knee and shoulder problems and then started just two games in 1967 and 1968 while he was fulfilling his Army Reserve duty. When he returned in 1969, he was battling Jim Hart for the starting job and was traded to the Oilers for Pete Beathard the next season. After two years in Houston where he worked with touted rookie Dan Pastorini, Johnson was sent to the Broncos for a draft pick. Charley proved he could still play in Denver by leading the Broncos to the first two winning seasons in their history before he retired in 1975.

As a quarterback, Johnson was streaky and threw interceptions. He had a quick release, was an accurate pocket passer, and was a smart play caller. On the Cardinals, Johnson was trained to use his brain to call audibles about one-quarter of the time. Although he didn't have the most powerful arm, he was good at throwing the ball down the field. Of quarterbacks who retired after 1975 and who threw at least 1,000 passes, only Joe Namath, John Hadl, and Steve Grogan threw for a higher yards per completion average than Charley's 14.1. Johnson's backup, Buddy Humphrey, summed him up in 1965, "Charley is a great quarterback. He makes the team move." If he had been able to stay in the lineup in the mid-1960s, Charley might have gotten the Cardinals to the postseason, but he never did appear in a playoff game.

Doug Johnson

Height: 6'2" **Weight:** 225 lbs. **Birthdate:** 10/27/1977
College: Florida **Draft:** Free agent
2000–03 Atlanta Falcons; 2004 Tennessee Titans
Regular Season Record: 2–9, 2 comebacks
Postseason Record: 0–0, no comebacks
Relative Rating: 87%

Passing

Year	G	Comp./Att.	%	Yards	Y/Att.	TD	INT	Rating
2000	4	36/67	53.7	406	6.1	2	3	63.4
2001	3	3/5	60.0	23	4.6	1	0	110.8
2002	6	37/57	64.9	448	7.9	2	3	78.7
2003	10	136/243	56.0	1,655	6.8	8	12	67.5
2004	2	6/12	50.0	68	5.7	0	0	67.4
Total	25	218/384	56.8	2,600	6.8	13	18	69.4
PS:	1	1/1	100.0	14	14.0	0	0	118.8

Rushing

Year	Att.	Yards	Avg.	TD
2000	3	11	3.7	0
2001	5	12	2.4	0
2002	8	16	2.0	1
2003	14	21	1.5	1
2004	2	-2	-1.0	0
Total	32	58	1.8	2
PS:	0	0	0.0	0

Doug Johnson was one of a flock of Florida Gator quarterbacks who excelled in Steve Spurrier's "Fun 'n' Gun" offense playing against overmatched opponents and who then were complete washouts in the pros. Johnson shared the quarterback job at Florida with Jesse "the Bachelor" Palmer and simultaneously played minor league baseball. Johnson went undrafted by the NFL and signed with Atlanta as a free agent in 2000. Coach Dan Reeves took a liking to Doug and handed him

the starting job when Michael Vick was hurt in the 2003 preseason. Johnson led the Falcons over the Cowboys in the opener; then the team dropped its next five games, and Kurt Kittner replaced him. Johnson got to start and lose two more games that year to push his record to 2–9 and earn inclusion in this book. He was later on the rosters of the Titans, Bengals, and Browns but threw just 12 passes in Tennessee in his final playing opportunities.

Randy Johnson

Height: 6'3" **Weight:** 205 lbs. **Birthdate:** 6/17/1944
College: Texas A&I **Draft:** Atlanta 1966-1st; Denver 1966-4th
1966–70 Atlanta Falcons; 1971–73 New York Giants; 1974 WFL; 1975 Washington Redskins; 1976 Green Bay Packers
Regular Season Record: 10–38–1, 2 comebacks
Postseason Record: NA
Relative Rating: 84%

Passing

Year	G	Comp./Att.	%	Yards	Y/Att.	TD	INT	Rating
1966	14	129/295	43.7	1,795	6.1	12	21	47.8
1967	14	142/288	49.3	1,620	5.6	10	21	47.8
1968	8	73/156	46.8	892	5.7	2	10	42.5
1969	6	51/93	54.8	788	8.5	8	5	89.4
1970	4	40/72	55.6	443	6.2	2	8	43.7
1971	5	41/74	55.4	477	6.4	3	3	71.7
1972	4	10/17	58.8	230	13.5	3	3	103.2
1973	9	99/177	55.9	1,279	7.2	7	8	73.2
1975	8	41/79	51.9	556	7.0	4	10	52.0
1976	3	21/35	60.0	249	7.1	0	1	69.8
Total	75	647/1,286	50.3	8,329	7.0	51	90	55.1

Rushing

Year	Att.	Yards	Avg.	TD
1966	35	142	4.1	4
1967	24	144	6.0	1
1968	11	97	8.8	1
1969	11	55	5.0	1
1970	7	21	3.0	0
1971	6	29	4.8	0
1972	9	26	2.9	1
1973	4	24	6.0	1
1975	2	10	5.0	0
1976	5	25	5.0	1
Total	114	573	5.0	10

Along with Tommy Nobis, Randy Johnson was one of two first-round picks of the Atlanta Falcons in their first season. Johnson had good size, a good arm, and good mobility. He had been a Little All-American at Texas A&I and won the MVP awards in the Blue-Gray game, the Senior Bowl, and the Coaches' All-America game. Johnson began 1966 behind Dennis Claridge but took over as the starter by the end of the preseason. Randy was overmatched in the NFL and threw 21 interceptions in each of his first two seasons while getting beaten up behind a horrible offensive line. By 1969, Johnson had lost his job to Bob Berry and was deemed expendable. When Giants backup Dick Shiner walked out of training camp in 1971 because he was upset at his lack of playing time, the two unhappy backups were swapped for each other.

In New York, Johnson backed up Fran Tarkenton in 1971 and Norm Snead in 1972. By 1973, Randy was fed up and on October 9, after the fourth game of the season, he announced his "retirement" in order to shake things up. Owner Wellington Mara wished Randy well and said the team would go on. Ten days later, Johnson was back and apologetic. Ten days after that, he started for the first time of the year and lost. Johnson went 1–6 as a starter that year and spent the next three seasons in three different cities for two different leagues. His career winning percentage is the lowest ever for quarterbacks who started at least 30 games. Randy had great physical tools but made poor decisions on the field, throwing nearly twice as many interceptions as touchdown passes for his career.

Rob Johnson

QPR 5.5

Height: 6'4" **Weight:** 204 lbs. **Birthdate:** 3/18/1973
College: USC **Draft:** Jacksonville 1995-4th
1995–97 Jacksonville Jaguars; 1998–2001 Buffalo Bills; 2002 Tampa Bay Bucs; 2003 Oakland Raiders; 2003 Washington Redskins
Regular Season Record: 12–17, 4 comebacks
Postseason Record: 0–1, no comebacks
Relative Rating: 107%

Passing

Year	G	Comp./Att.	%	Yards	Y/Att.	TD	INT	Rating
1995	1	3/7	42.9	24	3.4	0	1	12.5
1996	2	0/0	0.0	0	0.0	0	0	0.0
1997	5	22/28	78.6	344	12.3	2	2	111.9
1998	8	67/107	62.6	910	8.5	8	3	102.9
1999	2	25/34	73.5	298	8.8	2	0	119.5
2000	12	175/306	57.2	2,125	6.9	12	7	82.2
2001	8	134/216	62.0	1,465	6.8	5	7	76.3
2002	6	57/88	64.8	536	6.1	1	2	75.8
2003	4	11/20	55.0	93	4.7	0	1	46.5
Total	48	494/806	61.3	5,795	7.2	30	23	83.6
PS:	2	11/23	47.8	152	6.6	0	0	69.5

Rushing

Year	Att.	Yards	Avg.	TD
1995	3	17	5.7	0
1997	10	34	3.4	1
1998	24	123	5.1	1
1999	8	61	7.6	0
2000	42	307	7.3	1
2001	36	241	6.7	1
2002	14	73	5.2	0
2003	3	21	7.0	0
Total	140	877	6.3	4
PS:	4	16	4.0	0

Some scouts wrote off Rob Johnson as a prima donna for failing to show up for a pre-draft workout, but instead he was having a private quarterback tutoring session with offensive guru Bill Walsh at the time. Johnson dropped into the fourth round of the draft and was snagged by Jacksonville, where he found himself behind Mark Brunell for three years. In that time, Johnson appeared in a few regular-season games but made a big name for himself starring in preseason games each year.

With Johnson approaching free agency, Tom Coughlin traded him to the Bills in 1998 for a first-round draft pick. In Buffalo, the 25-year-old Johnson was beaten out by 36-year-old Doug Flutie, newly returned from Canada. Over the next three years the two would battle fiercely in a quarterback controversy that split the team in half. In 1999, Johnson hurt his ribs and was replaced by Flutie, who turned around a losing season. Flutie started the first 15 games in 1999 before coach Wade Phillips let Johnson start the season finale, and then, in a bizarre decision, kept him as starter in the next week's playoff game in Tennessee that was won by the Titans on the last-minute play known as the Music City Miracle. Johnson started for most of the 2000 season, but when he got hurt and was replaced, the team began to win again.

Flutie had had enough of being jerked around in 2001 and signed with San Diego. By midseason, the 1–7 Johnson had lost his starting job to backup Alex Van Pelt. Rob played for three teams in the next three years before drifting out of the game. Johnson's one claim to fame is that he has the highest sack percentage of any quarterback since sacks have been recorded. Despite being touted as a mobile roll-out quarterback, Johnson was sacked on almost 15 percent of all pass plays. Superficially his numbers look pretty good—he completed more than 60 percent of his passes, threw more touchdowns than interceptions, and averaged 7.2 yards per pass. However, he was a putrid, indecisive leader who went 12–17 as a starter for some pretty good teams and helped drive a wedge right through the Buffalo Bills.

QPR 8.5

Bert Jones

Height: 6'3" **Weight:** 210 lbs. **Birthdate:** 9/7/1951
College: LSU **Draft:** Baltimore Colts 1973-1st
1973–81 Baltimore Colts; 1982 Los Angeles Rams
Regular Season Record: 47–49, 10 comebacks
Postseason Record: 0–3, no comebacks
Relative Rating: 114%

Passing

Year	G	Comp./Att.	%	Yards	Y/Att.	TD	INT	Rating
1973	8	43/108	39.8	539	5.0	4	12	28.8
1974	11	143/270	53.0	1,610	6.0	8	12	62.4
1975	14	203/344	59.0	2,483	7.2	18	8	89.1
1976	14	207/343	60.3	3,104	9.0	24	9	102.5
1977	14	224/393	57.0	2,686	6.8	17	11	80.8
1978	3	27/42	64.3	370	8.8	4	1	114.2
1979	4	43/92	46.7	643	7.0	3	3	67.4
1980	15	248/446	55.6	3,134	7.0	23	21	75.3
1981	15	244/426	57.3	3,094	7.3	21	20	76.9
1982	4	48/87	55.2	527	6.1	2	4	61.8
Total	102	1,430/2,551	56.1	18,190	7.1	124	101	78.2
PS:	3	29/62	46.8	399	6.4	1	2	59.8

TOP 10

Regular-Season Overtime Game-Winning Touchdown Passes

10. Joe Namath to Emerson Boozer for 5 yards in a 26–20 Jets win over the Giants on November 10, 1974. It was the first overtime touchdown pass in NFL history and was the first overtime game to have a winner.

9. Ryan Fitzpatrick to Kevin Curtis for 56 yards in a 33–27 Rams win over the Texans on November 27, 2005. In his NFL debut, Fitzpatrick threw for 310 yards. St. Louis scored the last 16 points in the game.

8. Cleo Lemon to Greg Camarillo for 64 yards in a 22–16 Dolphins win over the Ravens on December 16, 2007. It was Miami's only win of the year.

7. Warren Moon to Cris Carter for 65 yards in a 33–27 Vikings win over the Bears on December 1, 1994.

6. Ben Roethlisberger to Santonio Holmes for 67 yards in a 23–17 Steelers win over the Bengals on December 31, 2006.

5. Danny Kanell to Chris Calloway for 68 yards in a 26–20 Giants win over the Lions on October 19, 1997.

4. Mark Brunell to Santana Moss for 68 yards in a 36–30 Redskins win over the Jaguars on October 1, 2006.

3. Troy Aikman to Rocket Ismail for 76 yards in a 41–35 Cowboys win over the Redskins on September 12, 1999. The Cowboys came back from a 21-point fourth-quarter deficit.

2. Brett Favre to Greg Jennings for 82 yards in a 19–13 Packers win over the Broncos on October 29, 2007. The touchdown came on the first play from scrimmage in overtime.

1. Ron Jaworski to Mike Quick for 99 yards in a 23–17 Eagles win over the Falcons on November 10, 1985. One minute and 49 seconds into the overtime period, Jaworski hit his receiver at the 30-yard line, and Quick raced 70 yards to score.

Rushing

Year	Att.	Yards	Avg.	TD
1973	18	58	3.2	0
1974	39	279	7.2	4
1975	47	321	6.8	3
1976	38	214	5.6	2
1977	28	146	5.2	2
1978	9	38	4.2	0
1979	10	40	4.0	1
1980	27	175	6.5	2
1981	20	85	4.3	0
1982	11	73	6.6	0
Total	247	1,429	5.8	14
PS:	10	39	3.9	0

Bert Jones grew up as the Browns' ball boy since his father Dub Jones was coaching for the team on which he formerly played, and Bert was a natural leader of football players. He was drafted No. 1 by the Colts in 1973 and just missed playing with Johnny Unitas, who was brusquely discarded after the 1972 season. Bert himself would experience the bombastic ignorance of Colts owner Robert Irsay on more than one occasion in his nine years in Baltimore.

Jones first shared the starting job with journeyman Marty Domres and found himself at the center of a controversy when coach Howard Schnellenberger was fired in 1974 for not playing Jones enough. Under new coach Ted Marchibroda in 1975, the Colts resurfaced at the top of the division, winning three division titles in a row and losing in the first round of the playoffs each time. Even this success was tempered by conflict with the front office that culminated in Marchibroda resigning in 1976, only to have Jones lead a team revolt backing their coach in his protest of management's abusive treatment.

Jones missed 25 of 32 games in 1978–79 with shoulder injuries, and the team crumpled. By the time Bert was again healthy, the Colts were a pathetic team. In 1981, Jones felt he was being used as a scapegoat for the team's failures and filed two grievances against management. Although he lost both grievances, Jones was traded to the Rams in 1982 for first- and second-round draft choices. Unfortunately, Bert's career ended after just four games with the Rams due to a serious neck injury.

Bill Belichick, who began his coaching career under Marchibroda on the Colts, remembered Jones at a press conference before Super Bowl XLII as the best "pure passer" he ever saw. Some have compared him to John Elway for his combined skill set of an exemplary passing arm and nimble feet. In 1976, his greatest season, Bert completed 60 percent of his passes for 3,104 yards and 24 touchdowns while averaging 9 yards per pass. In his injury-shortened career, Jones lost more games than he won, but for three exemplary years, he was arguably the finest quarterback in football.

QPR 9.5

Sonny Jurgensen

Height: 5'11" **Weight:** 202 lbs. **Birthdate:** 8/23/1934
College: Duke **Draft:** Philadelphia 1957-4th
1957–63 Philadelphia Eagles; 1964–74 Washington Redskins
Regular Season Record: 69–73–7, 15 comebacks
Postseason Record: 0–0, no comebacks
Relative Rating: 123%

Passing

Year	G	Comp./Att.	%	Yards	Y/Att.	TD	INT	Rating
1957	10	33/70	47.1	470	6.7	5	8	53.6
1958	12	12/22	54.5	259	11.8	0	1	77.7
1959	12	3/5	60.0	27	5.4	1	0	114.2
1960	12	24/44	54.5	486	11.0	5	1	122.0
1961	14	235/416	56.5	3,723	8.9	32	24	88.1
1962	14	196/366	53.6	3,261	8.9	22	26	74.3
1963	9	99/184	53.8	1,413	7.7	11	13	69.4
1964	14	207/385	53.8	2,934	7.6	24	13	85.4
1965	13	190/356	53.4	2,367	6.6	15	16	69.6
1966	14	254/436	58.3	3,209	7.4	28	19	84.5
1967	14	288/508	56.7	3,747	7.4	31	16	87.3
1968	12	167/292	57.2	1,980	6.8	17	11	81.7
1969	14	274/442	62.0	3,102	7.0	22	15	85.4
1970	14	202/337	59.9	2,354	7.0	23	10	91.5
1971	5	16/28	57.1	170	6.1	0	2	45.2
1972	7	39/59	66.1	633	10.7	2	4	84.9
1973	14	87/145	60.0	904	6.2	6	5	77.5
1974	14	107/167	64.1	1,185	7.1	11	5	94.5
Total	218	2,433/4,262	57.1	32,224	7.6	255	189	82.6
PS:	1	6/12	50.0	78	6.5	0	3	31.3

Rushing

Year	Att.	Yards	Avg.	TD
1957	10	-3	-0.3	2
1958	1	1	1.0	0
1960	4	5	1.3	0
1961	20	27	1.4	0
1962	17	44	2.6	2
1963	13	38	2.9	1
1964	27	57	2.1	3
1965	17	23	1.4	2
1966	12	14	1.2	0
1967	15	46	3.1	2
1968	8	21	2.6	1
1969	17	156	9.2	1
1970	6	39	6.5	1
1971	3	29	9.7	0
1972	4	-5	-1.3	0
1973	3	7	2.3	0
1974	4	-6	-1.5	0
Total	181	493	2.7	15
PS:	0	0	0.0	0

Christian Adolph "Sonny" Jurgensen had more 300-yard games during the 1960s than any other quarterback. He threw a 99-yard touchdown pass to Gerry Allen in 1968.

Sonny Jurgensen played football at Duke when the Blue Devils hardly ever threw the ball, so Sonny's skills were mostly wasted in college. Jurgensen threw the ball only 59 times as a senior and tossed just six touchdown passes as an undergraduate. Former Duke star Ace Parker recommended Sonny to the Eagles, though, and Philadelphia drafted Jurgensen in the fourth round in 1957.

Sonny got to start four games as a rookie, winning three of them, but the Eagles obtained Norm Van Brocklin the next year. Sonny was relegated to the bench for three years to learn from the gruff pass master. Although their personalities were markedly different, the two were both tough, pudgy pocket passers who could throw any sort of pass, long or short, as well as any other quarterback in the league. Philadelphia won the title behind Van Brocklin in 1960; Sonny did not appear in the championship game.

With Van Brocklin retired, Sonny was the starting quarterback at last. Starting with the 1961 College All-Star Game where Jurgensen showed a flair for the spectacular by completing a pass behind his back to Pete Retzlaff, 1961 was a great year for Sonny and the team. He threw for a league-record 3,723 yards and 32 touchdowns with his deadly sidearm delivery while leading the Eagles to 10–4 record, good for second place in the East.

Unfortunately, in the meaningless Playoff Bowl that pitted the second-place Eagles against the second-place Lions in January, Jurgensen suffered a severe shoulder separation that would linger in its effects over the next two years.

The combination of Sonny's declining production, reputation as a frivolous playboy, and a bad relationship with management led to new coach/GM Joe Kuharich trading Jurgensen to the Redskins for Norm Snead in one of the most lopsided quarterback trades of all time. Reportedly, Jurgensen had been offered first to Minnesota for Fran Tarkenton, but Vikings coach Van Brocklin nixed that deal.

Over the next 11 seasons in Washington, Jurgensen faced the Eagles 18 times. The Redskins won 12, lost three, and tied three as Sonny threw for 33 touchdowns and only 16 interceptions in those games. Jurgensen led the NFL in passing yards five times, attempts three times, touchdown passes twice, and interceptions twice. Among pre-1980 quarterbacks, only Johnny Unitas had more 300-yard games than Jurgy's 25. However, the Redskins did not begin to win until George Allen arrived in 1971 when Sonny turned 37. Hampered by knee, elbow, rib, shoulder, and Achilles problems, Jurgensen started just 13 games in his last four years under Allen. Besides, the conservative Allen preferred the less flashy Billy Kilmer as his quarterback. To their credit, not only did the two veteran signal-callers support each other, they became fast friends and drinking buddies united in keeping young Joe Theismann off the field. Sonny's last appearance as a pro quarterback was his first appearance in the postseason as he played part of the 1974 playoff game the Skins lost to the Rams. Jurgensen has served as a Redskins radio broadcaster for three decades.

Paul Justin

Height: 6'4"   **Weight:** 211 lbs.   **Birthdate:** 5/19/1968
College: Arizona State   **Draft:** Chicago Bears 1991-7th
1993 Arena Football; 1995 NFL Europe; 1995-97 Indianapolis Colts; 1998 Cincinnati Bengals; 1999 St. Louis Rams
Regular Season Record: 3-7, 1 comeback
Postseason Record: NA
Relative Rating: 96%

Passing

Year	G	Comp./Att.	%	Yards	Y/Att.	TD	INT	Rating
1995	3	20/36	55.6	212	5.9	0	2	49.8
1996	8	74/127	58.3	839	6.6	2	0	83.4
1997	8	83/140	59.3	1,046	7.5	5	5	79.6
1998	5	34/63	54.0	426	6.8	1	3	60.7
1999	10	9/14	64.3	91	6.5	0	0	82.7
Total	34	220/380	57.9	2,614	6.9	8	10	75.0

Rushing

Year	Att.	Yards	Avg.	TD
1995	3	1	0.3	0
1996	2	7	3.5	0
1997	6	2	0.3	0
1998	1	2	2.0	0
1999	5	-1	-0.2	0
Total	17	11	0.6	0

Paul Justin was a tall, skinny quarterback with moderate skills who received increasing playing time behind Jim Harbaugh for three years in Indianapolis. In 1997, he started for the 0–10 Colts against the 8–2 defending champion Packers and threw for 340 yards in a 41–38 victory. It was the

only time Justin exceeded 300 yards passing and it marked the final win of his career. The Colts traded Justin to the Bengals for a fifth-round pick the next year, and he finished his career as Kurt Warner's backup on the 1999 world champion Rams.

Danny Kanell

Height: 6'3"   **Weight:** 218 lbs.   **Birthdate:** 11/21/1973
College: Florida State   **Draft:** New York Giants 1996-4th
1996-98 New York Giants; 1999-2000 Atlanta Falcons; 2003 Denver Broncos
Regular Season Record: 10-13-1, 2 comebacks
Postseason Record: 0-1, no comebacks
Relative Rating: 80%

Passing

Year	G	Comp./Att.	%	Yards	Y/Att.	TD	INT	Rating
1996	4	23/60	38.3	227	3.8	1	1	48.4
1997	16	156/294	53.1	1,740	5.9	11	9	70.7
1998	10	160/299	53.5	1,603	5.4	11	10	67.3
1999	3	42/84	50.0	593	7.1	4	4	69.2
2000	5	57/116	49.1	524	4.5	2	5	49.6
2003	5	53/103	51.5	442	4.3	2	5	49.1
Total	43	491/956	51.4	5,129	5.4	31	34	63.2
PS:	1	16/32	50.0	199	6.2	1	0	80.1

Rushing

Year	Att.	Yards	Avg.	TD
1996	7	6	0.9	0
1997	15	2	0.1	0
1998	15	36	2.4	0
2000	1	0	0.0	0
2003	6	5	0.8	0
Total	44	49	1.1	0
PS:	0	0	0.0	0

Danny Kanell was the Danny Wuerffel of Florida State. Although Wuerffel won the Heisman, it was hard to distinguish between the two college stars. They were contemporaries, but Kanell graduated a year before Wuerffel and joined the Giants in 1996 as a fourth-round pick. When the struggling Dave Brown was injured in the sixth game of 1997, Kanell stepped in and went 7-2-1 in the last 10 games as the Giants made the playoffs. Kanell averaged only 164 yards per start passing and 5.9 yards per pass that year, but coach Jim Fassell directed his team to play a ball-control, field-position game that allowed the questionable Kanell to enjoy some success. As Danny himself put it, "The idea was to play mistake-free football. Don't screw it up. Let the defense win it."

The next year, reality sank in and Kanell lost seven of 10 starts before being relieved by the middling Kent Graham for the remainder of the season. After two seasons as a backup in Atlanta, Kanell tried a season of minor league baseball and then a year in the arena league before returning to the NFL in 2003 with the Broncos. In Denver, Danny started two more games despite the fact that his average yards per pass was down to 4.3. It wasn't too much of a surprise that yet another Florida State quarterback failed in the NFL. In addition, Kanell's quarterback coach in high school was the unforgettable Browns draft bust from the 1970s, Mike Phipps.

Joe Kapp

Height: 6'2" **Weight:** 215 lbs. **Birthdate:** 3/19/1938
College: California **Draft:** Washington 1959-18th
1959–66 CFL; 1967–69 Minnesota Vikings; 1970 New England Patriots
Regular Season Record: 24–21–3, 6 comebacks
Postseason Record: 2–2, 1 comeback
Relative Rating: 81%

Passing

Year	G	Comp./Att.	%	Yards	Y/Att.	TD	INT	Rating
1967	13	102/214	47.7	1,386	6.5	8	17	48.2
1968	14	129/248	52.0	1,695	6.8	10	17	58.8
1969	13	120/237	50.6	1,726	7.3	19	13	78.5
1970	11	98/219	44.7	1,104	5.0	3	17	32.6
Total	**51**	**449/918**	**48.9**	**5,911**	**6.4**	**40**	**64**	**55.1**
PS:	4	61/101	60.4	835	8.3	3	6	72.0

Rushing

Year	Att.	Yards	Avg.	TD
1967	27	167	6.2	2
1968	50	269	5.4	3
1969	22	104	4.7	0
1970	20	71	3.6	0
Total	**119**	**611**	**5.1**	**5**
PS:	27	160	5.9	1

If Billy Kilmer was the poor man's Bobby Layne, then Joe Kapp was the poor man's Billy Kilmer. All three signal-callers were winners known equally for their fiery temperaments and wobbly passes. Kapp told *Sports Illustrated* in 1970, "It's a fundamental fact about quarterbacks, almost every one of them, that they're not good enough to play any other position. Quarterback is the natural refuge for a guy with a big mouth and few natural abilities." Joe was a tough, charismatic leader who liked to throw on the run. His passes were not pretty because he grabbed the ball from the center and did not shift it in his hands before unloading it. If the receivers were covered, Kapp was happy to run with the ball and seemed to seek out contact with defenders, trying to run over people and avoid the sidelines.

Kapp was an option quarterback at California who led the Golden Bears to the 1959 Rose Bowl just a year after the team had finished 1–7. The school has not returned to Pasadena in the ensuing 50 years. The Redskins drafted the lightly regarded Kapp in the 18th round, but Joe signed with Calgary in the CFL instead. Two years later, he was traded to the British Columbia Lions where he had his greatest success in Canada, leading the Lions to the Grey Cup game in 1963 and the title in 1964. After the 1966 season, the celebrated Kapp signed with the Houston Oilers, foreshadowing the signing of CFL star Warren Moon by nearly 30 years. However, Pete Rozelle ruled that Houston had tampered with a player who had a valid contract and quashed the deal. Eventually, a complicated three-way trade was worked out between the BC Lions, Toronto Argonauts, and Minnesota to make Joe a proud Viking in 1967.

With the team around him improving, Kapp's play got better as well. Joe started off the 1969 season by throwing seven touchdown passes against the Colts in Week 2, and that began a 12-game winning streak that vaulted the Vikings to the Super Bowl where they were thumped by the Chiefs. It was during that year that Kapp originated the "40 for 60" slogan that captured his team-oriented approach, 40 players together for 60 minutes of football. Joe was voted NFL Player of the Year and the Vikings' MVP, but he refused the team MVP because, "there are 40 most valuable Vikings."

TOP 10
Sacked Quarterbacks
(100 sack minimum)

10. Steve Ramsey, sacked on 10.7 percent of pass plays

9. Joe Pisarcik, sacked on 11.1 percent of pass plays

8. Bart Starr, sacked on 11.3 percent of pass plays (based on incomplete data)

7. Dennis Shaw, sacked on 11.8 percent of pass plays

6. Greg Landry, sacked on 11.9 percent of pass plays

5. Hugh Millen, sacked on 12 percent of pass plays

4. Steve Fuller, sacked on 12.5 percent of pass plays

3. Bobby Douglass, sacked on 13.3 percent of pass plays

2. Bob Berry, sacked on 14 percent of pass plays

1. Rob Johnson, sacked on 14.8 percent of pass plays.

Passing

Year	G	Comp./Att.	%	Yards	Y/Att.	TD	INT	Rating
1986	16	285/480	59.4	3,593	7.5	22	17	83.3
1987	12	250/419	59.7	2,798	6.7	19	11	83.8
1988	16	269/452	59.5	3,380	7.5	15	17	78.2
1989	13	228/391	58.3	3,130	8.0	25	18	86.2
1990	14	219/346	63.3	2,829	8.2	24	9	101.2
1991	15	304/474	64.1	3,844	8.1	33	17	97.6
1992	16	269/462	58.2	3,457	7.5	23	19	81.2
1993	16	288/470	61.3	3,382	7.2	18	18	79.9
1994	14	285/448	63.6	3,114	7.0	22	17	84.6
1995	15	255/458	55.7	3,130	6.8	22	13	81.1
1996	13	222/379	58.6	2,810	7.4	14	19	73.2
Total	160	2,874/4,779	60.1	35,467	7.4	237	175	84.4
PS:	17	322/545	59.1	3,863	7.1	21	28	72.3

Rushing

Year	Att.	Yards	Avg.	TD
1986	41	199	4.9	0
1987	29	133	4.6	0
1988	35	154	4.4	0
1989	29	137	4.7	2
1990	22	63	2.9	0
1991	20	45	2.3	1
1992	31	53	1.7	1
1993	36	102	2.8	0
1994	25	77	3.1	1
1995	17	20	1.2	0
1996	19	66	3.5	2
Total	304	1,049	3.5	7
PS:	44	161	3.7	0

From that high point, Kapp played out his option and signed with the lowly Patriots in 1970 but threw just three touchdown passes to 17 interceptions in Boston. When New England wanted him to take a pay cut in 1971, Kapp quit and sued the league on antitrust grounds (he lost). In later years, this self-styled "toughest Chicano" returned to his roots and served as California's head coach and then British Columbia's GM but in neither case was he able to re-create the glory of his playing days.

QPR 9.5

Jim Kelly

Height: 6'3" **Weight:** 217 lbs. **Birthdate:** 2/14/1960
College: Miami **Draft:** Buffalo 1983-1st
1984–85 USFL; 1986–96 Buffalo Bills
Regular Season Record: 101–59, 29 comebacks
Postseason Record: 9–8, 1 comeback
Relative Rating: 110%

Jim Kelly is overshadowed by two other Hall of Fame quarterbacks from the same 1983 draft class, John Elway and Dan Marino, but he was very much their match despite having a relatively abbreviated career. In fact, Kelly's Bills scored 11 percent more points than the league average during his tenure as starter compared to the 12 percent figure achieved by Marino's Dolphins and Elway's Broncos in their careers. Jim started the long line of pro-style quarterbacks at the University of Miami in 1980 but played only two and a half games of his senior season before suffering a severe shoulder separation that ended his college career.

Despite the injury, Kelly was still a first-round draft pick of the Bills but spent the 1983 season recovering from his shoulder surgery before signing with the Houston Gamblers of the USFL. In two

TOP 10
Overrated Quarterbacks

10. Brett Favre
9. Joe Namath
8. Drew Bledsoe
7. Carson Palmer
6. Michael Vick
5. Jim McMahon
4. Randall Cunningham
3. Sonny Jurgensen
2. Y.A. Tittle
1. Warren Moon

Jack Kemp

QPR 9.0

Height: 6'1" **Weight:** 201 lbs. **Birthdate:** 7/13/1935
College: Occidental **Draft:** Detroit 1957-17th
1957 Pittsburgh Steelers; 1960–62 Los Angeles/San Diego Chargers; 1962–67, 1969 Buffalo Bills
Regular Season Record: 65–37–3, 10 comebacks
Postseason Record: 2–4, no comebacks
Relative Rating: 93%

Passing

Year	G	Comp./Att.	%	Yards	Y/Att.	TD	INT	Rating
1957	4	8/18	44.4	88	4.9	0	2	19.9
1960	14	211/406	52.0	3,018	7.4	20	25	67.1
1961	14	165/364	45.3	2,686	7.4	15	22	59.2
1962	6	64/139	46.0	928	6.7	5	6	62.3
1963	14	193/384	50.3	2,910	7.6	13	20	65.1
1964	14	119/269	44.2	2,285	8.5	13	26	50.9
1965	14	179/391	45.8	2,368	6.1	10	18	54.8
1966	14	166/389	42.7	2,451	6.3	11	16	56.2
1967	14	161/369	43.6	2,503	6.8	14	26	50.0
1969	14	170/344	49.4	1,981	5.8	13	22	53.2
Total	**122**	**1,436/3,073**	**46.7**	**21,218**	**6.9**	**118**	**183**	**57.3**
PS:	6	78/160	48.8	1,126	7.0	2	10	50.2

Rushing

Year	Att.	Yards	Avg.	TD
1957	3	-1	-0.3	0
1960	54	238	4.4	8
1961	43	105	2.4	6
1962	20	84	4.2	2
1963	50	239	4.8	8
1964	37	124	3.4	5
1965	36	49	1.4	4
1966	40	130	3.3	5
1967	36	58	1.6	2
1969	37	124	3.4	0
Total	**356**	**1,150**	**3.2**	**40**
PS:	18	11	0.6	1

seasons directing the Gamblers' explosive run-and-shoot offense, Jim threw for 83 touchdowns and nearly 10,000 yards. After the USFL folded, Kelly finally signed with the improving Bills under Marv Levy and was spectacular right from the start. After his debut, noted football writer Paul Zimmerman wrote that Kelly "is Joe Namath with knees" due to his toughness and attacking style of play. Kelly's college coach, Howard Schnellenberger, who was an offensive coach under Bear Bryant at Alabama, compared Kelly favorably not only to Namath but to other great Tide quarterbacks Ken Stabler and Steve Sloan.

Kelly was a rugged player that Joe Paterno had tried to recruit to Penn State as a linebacker, but Jim was also the essence of a field general. He was one of the the last NFL quarterbacks to regularly call his own plays in the Bills' no-huddle K-gun attack that was similar to the run-and-shoot except that the Bills used three wideouts and a tight end rather than four wideouts. It was the offense that took Buffalo to an unprecedented four straight Super Bowls in the early 1990s. If only Scott Norwood had not been wide right in his 47-yard field goal attempt at the end of the first Bills' Super Bowl appearance, Jim would have earned a championship ring and probably would be considered more of an equal to his 1983 classmates.

For as successful a quarterback as Jack Kemp was, he has terrible statistics. Kemp played in five AFL title games in seven years—and lost a divisional playoff game in a sixth season—but threw 114 touchdowns to 183 interceptions. He is the all-time AFL leader in attempts, completions, and passing yards but also in fumbles as well as being second in interceptions to George Blanda. Kemp was a scrambler who did not stay in the pocket. He had a very strong arm and liked to throw on the run, although he was often an erratic passer.

Buddy Parker drafted Kemp for Detroit in the 17th round in 1957 and then acquired Jack in Pittsburgh when Buddy was hired as the Steelers' coach later that year. Kemp backed up Earl Morrall that year but spent the following season on the practice squad of the Giants. In 1959, he tried out for Calgary in the CFL but was cut. Finally in 1960, Sid Gillman gave Jack the chance to run the wide-open passing attack of the brand-new Los Angeles Chargers of the American Football League, and Kemp took the Chargers to the title game in both 1960 and 1961, although they lost to the Oilers both years. In 1962, Jack broke his finger, and Gillman mistakenly put him on waivers, where he was claimed by Buffalo and Denver. AFL commissioner Joe Foss awarded Kemp to the Bills. In a quid pro quo move, Buffalo later relinquished their territorial claim to CFL quarterback Tobin Rote so he could sign with San Diego in 1963. Gillman told a booster club at the time that he could not win with Kemp.

Kemp instantly gave the defensive-minded Bills an inspirational leader with a cannon arm on offense, and he led them to three straight title games. Jack had the satisfaction of beating Gillman and the Chargers in 1964 and 1965 but lost to the Chiefs in 1966 and thus missed out on the first Super Bowl. The team quickly declined after that, and Kemp missed 1968 with a knee injury before returning for one last year in 1969.

The affable, intelligent, and conservative Kemp then went into politics. He had already campaigned for Nixon and Goldwater and worked for Governor Ronald Reagan when he was elected to Congress from Buffalo in 1970. He was reelected seven times and then joined the cabinet of President George H.W. Bush as Secretary of Housing and Urban Development in 1989. In 1996, Bob Dole picked Jack as his running mate in their ill-fated presidential campaign. Jack's sons both played professional football—Jeff in the NFL and Jimmy in the CFL. Kemp passed away in 2009 at the age of 73.

Jeff Kemp

QPR 5.5

Height: 6'0" **Weight:** 201 lbs. **Birthdate:** 7/11/1959
College: Dartmouth **Draft:** Free agent
1981, 1983–85 Los Angeles Rams; 1986 San Francisco 49ers; 1987–91 Seattle Seahawks; 1991 Philadelphia Eagles
Regular Season Record: 16–12–1, 5 comebacks
Postseason Record: 0–1, no comebacks
Relative Rating: 94%

Passing

Year	G	Comp./Att.	%	Yards	Y/Att.	TD	INT	Rating
1981	1	2/6	33.3	25	4.2	0	1	7.6
1983	4	12/25	48.0	135	5.4	1	0	77.9
1984	14	143/284	50.4	2,021	7.1	13	7	78.7
1985	5	16/38	42.1	214	5.6	0	1	49.7
1986	10	119/200	59.5	1,554	7.8	11	8	85.7
1987	13	23/33	69.7	396	12.0	5	1	137.1
1988	11	13/35	37.1	132	3.8	0	5	9.2
1989	9	0/0	0.0	0	0.0	0	0	0.0
1990	15	0/0	0.0	0	0.0	0	0	0.0
1991	14	151/295	51.2	1,753	5.9	9	17	55.7
Total	96	479/916	52.3	6,230	6.8	39	40	70.0
PS:	2	18/37	48.6	173	4.7	0	1	50.8

Rushing

Year	Att.	Yards	Avg.	TD
1981	2	9	4.5	0
1983	3	-2	-0.7	0
1984	34	153	4.5	1
1985	5	0	0.0	0
1986	15	49	3.3	0
1987	5	9	1.8	0
1988	6	51	8.5	0
1989	1	0	0.0	0
1991	38	179	4.7	0
Total	109	448	4.1	1
PS:	1	2	2.0	0

Not surprisingly, there was little clamor in 1981 among pro teams to sign the undrafted Dartmouth quarterback Jeff Kemp, whose favorite target was Don Shula's son David, but the Rams brought him in as a training camp arm and he managed to stick around. Jeff did not get to play much until 1984, when he worked his way up No. 2 on the depth chart behind Vince Ferragamo, who then broke his hand. Kemp went 9–4 as a starter that year but found himself back on the bench in 1985 behind newly acquired Dieter Brock. The following year, Kemp spent half the season filling in for an injured Joe Montana in San Francisco and then moved up the coast to Seattle for the next five seasons. Jeff finished his career in Philadelphia in 1991. Although he didn't have the arm or the professional success that his father did, Jeff was a reliable backup in the NFL for a decade.

Bill Kenney

 QPR 7.5

Height: 6'4" **Weight:** 211 lbs. **Birthdate:** 1/20/1955
College: Northern Colorado **Draft:** Miami 1978-12th
1980–88 Kansas City Chiefs
Regular Season Record: 34–43, 7 comebacks
Postseason Record: 0–0, no comebacks
Relative Rating: 103%

Passing

Year	G	Comp./Att.	%	Yards	Y/Att.	TD	INT	Rating
1980	3	37/69	53.6	542	7.9	5	2	91.6
1981	13	147/274	53.6	1,983	7.2	9	16	63.6
1982	7	95/169	56.2	1,192	7.1	7	6	77.3
1983	16	346/603	57.4	4,348	7.2	24	18	80.8
1984	9	151/282	53.5	2,098	7.4	15	10	80.7
1985	16	181/338	53.6	2,536	7.5	17	9	83.6
1986	15	161/308	52.3	1,922	6.2	13	11	70.8
1987	11	154/273	56.4	2,107	7.7	15	9	85.8
1988	16	58/114	50.9	549	4.8	0	5	46.3
Total	106	1,330/2,430	54.7	17,277	7.1	105	86	77.0
PS:	1	8/16	50.0	97	6.1	0	0	69.0

Rushing

Year	Att.	Yards	Avg.	TD
1980	8	8	1.0	0
1981	24	89	3.7	1
1982	13	40	3.1	0
1983	23	59	2.6	3
1984	9	-8	-0.9	0
1985	14	1	0.1	1
1986	18	0	0.0	0
1987	12	-2	-0.2	0
1988	2	4	2.0	0
Total	123	191	1.6	5
PS:	0	0	0.0	0

In 1976, former NFL receiver Paul Salata founded the Mr. Irrelevant Award to be given annually to the last player selected in the NFL draft. Although Bill Kenney was merely the penultimate pick by the Dolphins in 1978, he was awarded the "Irrelevant" mantle because the final draft pick, Lee Washburn, hurt his back and never reported to the Cowboys. Kenney is one of five quarterbacks to win this dubious honor and is the only one to actually start a game in the league.

Kenney was cut in his first training camp by Miami but two years later made the Chiefs' roster as Steve Fuller's backup. By his second year, Bill was the starter and held the job in Kansas City for most of the decade, even holding off the celebrated Todd Blackledge from the 1983 quarterback class. Kenney had good size but was generally average in every category. He was emblematic of the mediocrity of the Chiefs' franchise in the 1980s. When Marty Schottenheimer took over the team in 1989, Kenney was cut and spent a season as the Redskins' third quarterback but never appeared in a game. After football, Bill served in the Missouri State Senate for eight years, just one year shy of his tenure with the Chiefs.

Gary Kerkorian

QPR 1.0

Height: 5'11" **Weight:** 185 lbs. **Birthdate:** 1/14/1930
College: Stanford **Draft:** Pittsburgh 1952-19th
1952 Pittsburgh Steelers; 1954–56 Baltimore Colts
Regular Season Record: 3–7, 2 comebacks
Postseason Record: NA
Relative Rating: 109%

Passing

Year	G	Comp./Att.	%	Yards	Y/Att.	TD	INT	Rating
1952	12	5/11	45.5	79	7.2	1	3	60.6
1954	10	117/217	53.9	1,515	7.0	9	12	66.9
1955	7	15/29	51.7	209	7.2	1	3	47.1
1956	3	2/2	100.0	59	29.5	1	0	158.3
Total	32	139/259	53.7	1,862	7.2	12	18	63.2

Rushing

Year	Att.	Yards	Avg.	TD
1952	2	20	10.0	0
1954	22	36	1.6	1
1955	6	20	3.3	1
Total	30	76	2.5	2

Gary Kerkorian led Stanford to the 1952 Rose Bowl, handing off to Olympic decathalon champion Bob Mathias at fullback and throwing to future Bears end Bill McColl. Kerkorian, though, was drafted by the Steelers and backed up Jim Finks at quarterback while handling the team's place-kicking duties in 1952. After the season, Gary was part of a U.S. rugby team that toured Australia, and he did not play in the NFL in 1953. Returning to the league in 1954, Kerkorian was the Colts' starting quarterback throughout the season. Although he was an accurate passer, he did not have a big-league arm, and Baltimore drafted George Shaw in the first round of 1955. Kerkorian backed up Shaw in 1955, just as Shaw's brother Tom had once backed up Gary at Stanford. In 1956, the unheralded Johnny Unitas arrived in camp and both Shaw and Kerkorian dropped on the depth chart. Kerkorian went to law school at Georgetown and briefly returned to the Colts in 1958 when Unitas hurt his back, but he never played. Gary set up a law practice in his native Southern California and eventually became a State Superior Court judge.

Billy Kilmer

QPR 8.5

Height: 6'0" **Weight:** 204 lbs. **Birthdate:** 9/5/1939
College: UCLA **Draft:** San Francisco 1961-1st; San Diego 1961-5th
1961–62, 1964, 1966 San Francisco 49ers; 1967–70 New Orleans Saints; 1971–78 Washington Redskins
Regular Season Record: 61–52–1, 15 comebacks
Postseason: 2–5, no comebacks
Relative Rating: 108%

Passing

Year	G	Comp./Att.	%	Yards	Y/Att.	TD	INT	Rating
1961	11	19/34	55.9	286	8.4	0	4	44.1
1962	12	8/13	61.5	191	14.7	1	3	91.5
1964	10	8/14	57.1	92	6.6	1	1	71.1
1966	6	5/16	31.3	84	5.3	0	1	24.0
1967	10	97/204	47.5	1,341	6.6	6	11	56.4
1968	12	167/315	53.0	2,060	6.5	15	17	66.9
1969	14	193/360	53.6	2,532	7.0	20	17	74.9
1970	13	135/237	57.0	1,557	6.6	6	17	55.5
1971	14	166/306	54.2	2,221	7.3	13	13	74.0
1972	12	120/225	53.3	1,648	7.3	19	11	84.8
1973	10	122/227	53.7	1,656	7.3	14	9	81.3
1974	11	137/234	58.5	1,632	7.0	10	6	83.5
1975	12	178/346	51.4	2,440	7.1	23	16	77.2
1976	10	108/206	52.4	1,252	6.1	12	10	70.3
1977	8	99/201	49.3	1,187	5.9	8	7	66.5
1978	5	23/46	50.0	316	6.9	4	3	74.2
Total	170	1,585/2,984	53.1	20,495	6.9	152	146	71.6
PS:	7	92/178	51.7	1,060	6.0	8	7	68.6

Rushing

Year	Att.	Yards	Avg.	TD
1961	96	509	5.3	10
1962	93	478	5.1	5
1964	36	113	3.1	0
1966	3	23	7.7	0
1967	20	142	7.1	1
1968	21	97	4.6	2
1969	11	18	1.6	0
1970	12	42	3.5	0
1971	17	5	0.3	2
1972	3	-3	-1.0	0
1973	9	10	1.1	0
1974	6	27	4.5	0
1975	11	34	3.1	1
1976	13	-7	-0.5	0
1977	10	20	2.0	0
1978	1	1	1.0	0
Total	362	1,509	4.2	21
PS:9	41		4.6	0

With Billy Kilmer (17) and Sonny Jurgensen (9), the team always came first, no matter who started at quarterback.

As noted with Joe Kapp, Billy Kilmer was a lowercase version of Bobby Layne. Both were brash leaders who spent their evenings in taprooms but came to play when the game started. Neither threw many perfect spirals, but both drove their teams to championship games. Kilmer, though, could not overcome the unbeaten Dolphins in Super Bowl VII in 1973 and never won a title.

Kilmer began as a single-wing tailback at UCLA who also played on the basketball team under legendary coach John Wooden. Billy was San Francisco's top pick in 1961 and walked into what seemed to be an ideal situation with 49ers coach Red Hickey installing the shotgun formation as the team's offense that season. In this offense, Kilmer was the first-down quarterback who generally ran with the ball. Bob Waters came in on second down to run or pass, and John Brodie came in on third down to pass. By midseason, the rest of the league had caught up to the predictable approach, and the 49ers went back to the T. In those first six games though, Kilmer ran for more than 100 yards three times. In the T formation, Billy was switched to running back until he broke his leg in a car wreck in 1962 and nearly had to have it amputated. He missed the rest of that season and all of 1963 in recovery.

Kilmer returned to the 49ers as a courageous, somewhat gimpy-legged third-string quarterback in 1964. Three years later, the New Orleans Saints picked him up in the expansion draft, and Billy was the heavily booed starter of the ungodly awful Saints for four years until Archie Manning arrived in 1971. In New Orleans, though, Kilmer played against the Rams twice in 1970 and impressed coach George Allen with his bold leadership. When Allen took over the Redskins and fashioned them into the "Over the Hill Gang," he traded for Kilmer despite having All-Pro Sonny Jurgensen on hand. When Jurgensen got hurt, Billy made the most of his opportunity to play on a good team and drove them to the playoffs. Although Washington fans were divided with some sporting bumper stickers reading "I Like Billy" and others "I Like Sonny," the two quarterbacks got along well. Jurgensen helped Kilmer with his throwing mechanics, and the two met with teammates in the same saloons at night. After all, Billy was commonly known as "Whiskey."

Kilmer led the NFL in touchdown passes and passer rating in 1972, the Super Bowl season, and united with Jurgensen in two goals: to win games and to keep mouthy Joe Theismann on the bench.

Sonny retired after the 1974 season, but Kilmer continued with the Redskins through 1978 when he became, at last, Theismann's backup. After Jurgensen retired, Kilmer noted, "Everybody says that I'm throwing better, but that's because they don't have Sonny Jurgensen to compare me with anymore." Jurgensen and Kilmer remained friends long after football.

Shaun King

Height: 6'1" **Weight:** 215 lbs. **Birthdate:** 5/29/1977
College: Tulane **Draft:** Tampa 1999-2nd
1999–2003 Tampa Bay Bucs; 2004 Arizona Cardinals; 2007 Arena Football; 2007 CFL
Regular Season Record: 14–10, 4 comebacks
Postseason Record: 1–2, 1 comeback
Relative Rating: 93%

Passing

Year	G	Comp./Att.	%	Yards	Y/Att.	TD	INT	Rating
1999	6	89/146	61.0	875	6.0	7	4	82.4
2000	16	233/428	54.4	2,769	6.5	18	13	75.8
2001	3	21/31	67.7	210	6.8	0	1	73.3
2002	3	10/27	37.0	80	3.0	0	1	30.0
2003	3	15/22	68.2	130	5.9	1	1	79.7
2004	3	47/84	56.0	502	6.0	1	4	57.7
Total	34	415/738	56.2	4,566	6.2	27	24	73.4
PS:	3	45/92	48.9	491	5.3	1	3	55.1

Rushing

Year	Att.	Yards	Avg.	TD
1999	18	38	2.1	0
2000	73	353	4.8	5
2001	5	-12	-2.4	0
2002	4	25	6.3	0
2003	4	20	5.0	0
2004	9	30	3.3	0
Total	113	454	4.0	5
PS:	7	12	1.7	0

After throwing for more than 3,300 yards and 36 touchdowns as a senior at Tulane, Shaun King was drafted in the second round by Tampa in 1999.

Although he did not become a star, he did have a better career than Cade McNown and Akili Smith, two of the five quarterbacks drafted in the first round that year.

By the end of his rookie season, King took over from a flailing Trent Dilfer and guided the Bucs to the NFC Championship Game, where they nearly upset the heavily favored Rams. The next season, King started all 16 games, threw for 18 touchdowns, and led the Bucs back to the playoffs, but his unimpressive showing in the postseason inspired Tampa to sign Brad Johnson as a free agent. King was short and pudgy and lacked a big arm. He was a good runner but not a terribly accurate passer and did not react well under a pass rush. Shaun started just one game in the next three years before signing with the Cardinals as a free agent in 2004. King was beaten out by a younger Josh McCown in Arizona and spent the next few seasons unsuccessfully trying to catch on with another NFL club before drifting to arena football and the CFL.

Jon Kitna

QPR 7.0

Height: 6'2" **Weight:** 220 lbs. **Birthdate:** 9/21/1972
College: Central Washington **Draft:** Free agent
1997 WLAF; 1997–2000 Seattle Seahawks; 2001–05 Cincinnati Bengals; 2006–08 Detroit Lions
Regular Season Record: 46–69, 19 comebacks
Postseason Record: 0–1, no comebacks
Relative Rating: 97%

Passing

Year	G	Comp./Att.	%	Yards	Y/Att.	TD	INT	Rating
1997	3	31/45	68.9	371	8.2	1	2	82.7
1998	6	98/172	57.0	1,177	6.8	7	8	72.3
1999	15	270/495	54.5	3,346	6.8	23	16	77.7
2000	15	259/418	62.0	2,658	6.4	18	19	75.6
2001	16	313/581	53.9	3,216	5.5	12	22	61.1
2002	14	294/473	62.2	3,178	6.7	16	16	79.1
2003	16	324/520	62.3	3,591	6.9	26	15	87.4
2004	4	61/104	58.7	623	6.0	5	4	75.9
2005	3	17/29	58.6	99	3.4	0	2	36.4
2006	16	372/596	62.4	4,208	7.1	21	22	79.9
2007	16	355/561	63.3	4,068	7.3	18	20	80.9
2008	4	68/120	56.7	758	6.3	5	5	72.2
Total	**128**	**2,642/4,114**	**59.8**	**27,293**	**6.6**	**152**	**151**	**76.6**
PS:	2	38/70	54.3	359	5.1	2	4	54.4

Rushing

Year	Att.	Yards	Avg.	TD
1997	10	9	0.9	1
1998	20	67	3.4	1
1999	35	56	1.6	0
2000	48	127	2.6	1
2001	27	73	2.7	1
2002	24	57	2.4	4
2003	38	113	3.0	0
2004	10	42	4.2	0
2005	2	14	7.0	0
2006	34	156	4.6	2
2007	25	63	2.5	0
2008	6	34	5.7	0
Total	**279**	**811**	**2.9**	**10**
PS:	5	26	5.2	0

Undrafted free agent Jon Kitna went from being named the MVP of the European League, where he led the Barcelona Dragons to the World Bowl title, to earning a backup job with Seattle in 1997. Kitna was the Seahawks' primary starting quarterback in both 1999 and 2000 but was let go in 2001 when the team traded for Matt Hasselbeck. After Cincinnati lost out on Elvis Grbac that year, they signed Kitna instead. Jon flailed away on the lowly Bengals for two years before throwing for 26 touchdowns in 2003 and being named Comeback Player of the Year. Top draft pick Carson Palmer took over in 2004 and got Cincinnati to the playoffs in 2005. On the first play of a wild-card game against Pittsburgh, Palmer went down to a knee injury while completing a 66-yard pass. Kitna took over and struggled as the Steelers won the game handily.

Signing with Detroit as a free agent in 2006, Kitna threw for more than 4,000 yards twice under full-throttle offensive coordinator Mike Martz. Of course, he also threw 42 interceptions to just 39 touchdowns. Kitna made headlines in 2007 when he predicted 10 wins for the Lions. He did get the team off to a 6–2 start, but Detroit ended up 7–9 on the year. His strength is throwing short touch passes. He does not have a strong arm, cannot avoid a pass rush, throws interceptions, and has fumbled 103 times in 128 games. He is all right as a backup quarterback but is miscast as a starter.

David Klingler

QPR 0.5

Height: 6'3"   **Weight:** 210 lbs.   **Birthdate:** 2/17/1969
College: Houston   **Draft:** Cincinnati 1992-1st
1992-95 Cincinnati Bengals; 1996-97 Oakland Raiders
Regular Season Record: 4-20, 1 comeback
Postseason Record: NA
Relative Rating: 84%

Passing

Year	G	Comp./Att.	%	Yards	Y/Att.	TD	INT	Rating
1992	4	47/98	48.0	530	5.4	3	2	66.3
1993	14	190/343	55.4	1,935	5.6	6	9	66.6
1994	10	131/231	56.7	1,327	5.7	6	9	65.7
1995	3	7/15	46.7	88	5.9	1	1	59.9
1996	1	10/24	41.7	87	3.6	0	0	51.9
1997	1	4/7	57.1	27	3.9	0	1	26.2
Total	33	419/718	54.2	3,994	5.6	16	22	65.1

Rushing

Year	Att.	Yards	Avg.	TD
1992	11	53	4.8	0
1993	41	282	6.9	0
1994	17	85	5.0	0
1996	4	36	9.0	0
1997	1	0	0.0	0
Total	74	456	6.2	0

Despite starting as a running quarterback in the veer offense in high school, David Klingler produced some astronomical passing numbers in the run-and-shoot offense at the University of Houston, where he followed Heisman Trophy winner Andre Ware. As a junior, Klingler threw for more than 5,000 yards and 54 touchdowns. In one game, he threw for 11 touchdowns and in another passed for 716 yards. In David's senior year, his numbers dropped to 3,300 yards and 29 touchdowns, but the Bengals still selected him with their top pick to prematurely replace Boomer Esiason. Ultimately, though, neither Klingler nor Ware was prepared for the pro game.

Klingler was a very hard thrower before a shoulder problem in his third season robbed his arm of its strength. He won just four of 24 starts in Cincinnati before finishing his career as a backup in Oakland. In the NFL, Klingler was a dink passer even before the shoulder injury and averaged

just more than a measly 10 yards per completion. Furthermore, his indecisiveness resulted in a drive-killing average of being sacked on 10.8 percent of pass plays. David instead found his calling in the doctoral program at the Dallas Theological Seminary.

Jeff Komlo

QPR 0.5

Height: 6'2"   **Weight:** 200 lbs.   **Birthdate:** 7/30/1956
College: Delaware   **Draft:** Detroit 1979-9th
1979-81 Detroit Lions; 1983 Tampa Bay Bucs
Regular Season Record: 2-14, 1 comeback
Postseason Record: NA
Relative Rating: 69%

Passing

Year	G	Comp./Att.	%	Yards	Y/Att.	TD	INT	Rating
1979	16	183/368	49.7	2,238	6.1	11	23	52.8
1980	4	2/4	50.0	26	6.5	0	1	31.2
1981	3	29/57	50.9	290	5.1	1	3	49.6
1983	2	4/8	50.0	49	6.1	0	1	29.7
Total	25	218/437	49.9	2,603	6.0	12	28	50.9

Rushing

Year	Att.	Yards	Avg.	TD
1979	30	107	3.6	2
1981	6	3	0.5	0
1983	2	11	5.5	0
Total	38	121	3.2	2

Jeff Komlo was a running quarterback in coach Tubby Raymond's split-T offense at the University of Delaware. Drafted in the ninth round, Komlo was a surprise starter for Detroit in his rookie season. However, Gary Danielson was lost for the year in the final 1979 exhibition game, and backup Joe Reed was unimpressive in the opener, so coach Monte Clark turned to Jeff in Week 2. Komlo was painfully overmatched in the NFL, particularly as a rookie. He completed fewer than half his passes, threw just 11 touchdowns to 23 interceptions, and was sacked at will. Detroit went just 2–12 in his starts in 1979, and Jeff started only two more games in his last two years with the Lions. He finished his career as a third-stringer in Tampa. Twenty years later, Komlo was featured on the TV series *America's Most Wanted* for allegedly going on the lam to avoid being sentenced for DUI convictions. The life on the run of this running quarterback ended when Komlo was killed in an auto accident in Greece in 2009.

Bernie Kosar

QPR 7.5

Height: 6'5" **Weight:** 210 lbs. **Birthdate:** 11/25/1963
College: Miami **Draft:** Cleveland 1985-1ˢᵗ(S)
1985–93 Cleveland Browns; 1993 Dallas Cowboys;
1994–96 Miami Dolphins
Regular Season Record: 53–54–1, 16 comebacks
Postseason Record: 3–4, 1 comeback
Relative Rating: 107%

Passing

Year	G	Comp./Att.	%	Yards	Y/Att.	TD	INT	Rating
1985	12	124/248	50.0	1,578	6.4	8	7	69.3
1986	16	310/531	58.4	3,854	7.3	17	10	83.8
1987	12	241/389	62.0	3,033	7.8	22	9	95.4
1988	9	156/259	60.2	1,890	7.3	10	7	84.3
1989	16	303/513	59.1	3,533	6.9	18	14	80.3
1990	13	230/423	54.4	2,562	6.1	10	15	65.7
1991	16	307/494	62.1	3,487	7.1	18	9	87.8
1992	7	103/155	66.5	1,160	7.5	8	7	87.0
1993	11	115/201	57.2	1,217	6.1	8	3	82.0
1994	2	7/12	58.3	80	6.7	1	1	71.5
1995	9	74/108	68.5	699	6.5	3	5	76.1
1996	3	24/32	75.0	208	6.5	1	0	102.1
Total	126	1,994/3,365	59.3	23,301	6.9	124	87	81.8
PS:	9	152/270	56.3	1,953	7.2	16	10	83.5

Rushing

Year	Att.	Yards	Avg.	TD
1985	26	-12	-0.5	1
1986	24	19	0.8	0
1987	15	22	1.5	1
1988	12	-1	-0.1	1
1989	30	70	2.3	1
1990	10	13	1.3	0
1991	26	74	2.8	0
1992	5	12	2.4	0
1993	23	26	1.1	0
1994	1	17	17.0	0
1995	7	19	2.7	1
1996	1	6	6.0	0
Total	180	265	1.5	5
PS:	14	27	1.9	0

Bernie Kosar was a very smart guy who did things his own way. As a redshirted freshman at the University of Miami, Kosar led the Hurricanes to the 1983 national championship. Bernie had another big season as a sophomore in 1984, but that season was marred by losses to Maryland, when Frank Reich led the Terrapins back from a 31–0 halftime deficit, and to Boston College, when Doug Flutie won the game on a 48-yard Hail Mary pass at the end. Kosar completed his college work in three years, applied for the 1985 supplemental NFL draft and expressed a desire to play for the Browns in his native Ohio. Cleveland traded three picks to Buffalo for Kosar's rights, and Bernie became an instant fan favorite in the Dawg Pound.

When starter Gary Danielson got hurt in the fifth game of 1985, coach Marty Schottenheimer was forced to use Kosar sooner than he had planned, but Bernie led Cleveland to the playoffs in his first season. Kosar solidified his status with the fans by leading the Browns to the AFC Championship Game in three of the next four years, but each time they lost painfully to John Elway and the Broncos. Meanwhile, the immobile Kosar was taking a beating that would ultimately shorten his career. When Bill Belichick arrived as coach in 1991, Bernie threw for more than 3,400 yards and completed 62 percent of his passes. However, by the time Belichick brought in Vinny Testaverde two years later, Kosar was no longer very good as a starter at age 30. In midseason 1993, Belichick found the whole situation too distracting and shocked Cleveland by cutting Kosar even though Testaverde himself was hurt at the time. Belichick withstood the public outcry, and the Browns made the playoffs in 1994 behind Testaverde.

Kosar was signed by Dallas as a backup in 1993 and won a Super Bowl ring under former Miami coach Jimmy Johnson. Bernie finished his career as Dan Marino's backup with the Dolphins. Kosar was very tall and skinny with an unimpressive body unlikely to withstand the shocks that an NFL quarterback must undergo, and he suffered frequent injuries to his elbows, knees, and ankles. Most quarterbacks with his fragile build end up with unimpressive careers, such as Dick Wood or Steve Tensi. Moreover, Kosar threw from an

TOP 10
Quarterback Politicians

10. J.C. Watts, Oklahoma congressman (CFL quarterback)
9. Earl Morrall, mayor of Davie, Florida
8. Gary Kerkorian, California Superior Court judge
7. Ed Rutkowski, Erie County (Pennsylvania) executive
6. Al Dekdebrun, Erie County (Pennsylvania) executive
5. Bill Kenney, Missouri State Senate
4. George Ratterman, sheriff of Campbell County, Kentucky
3. Carlos Brown (Alan Autry), mayor of Fresno, California
2. Heath Shuler, North Carolina congressman
1. Jack Kemp, New York congressman, George H.W. Bush cabinet member, 1996 vice-presidential candidate

Passing

Year	G	Comp./Att.	%	Yards	Y/Att.	TD	INT	Rating
1987	3	45/92	48.9	559	6.1	4	5	60.0
1991	13	136/265	51.3	1,635	6.2	11	8	71.8
1992	7	58/106	54.7	771	7.3	4	8	59.1
1993	5	87/138	63.0	1,002	7.3	8	3	95.1
1994	6	99/158	62.7	1,129	7.1	8	8	79.9
1995	16	315/522	60.3	3,838	7.4	29	10	93.5
1996	4	73/150	48.7	781	5.2	3	6	54.3
1997	15	275/477	57.7	3,011	6.3	14	14	74.0
1998	8	151/250	60.4	1,823	7.3	9	7	83.1
1999	6	78/141	55.3	788	5.6	2	10	46.6
Total	83	1,317/2,229	57.3	15,337	6.7	92	79	76.6
PS:	4	91/130	70.0	999	7.7	6	3	98.2

Rushing

Year	Att.	Yards	Avg.	TD
1987	2	10	5.0	0
1991	35	26	0.7	1
1992	12	34	2.8	0
1993	10	5	0.5	0
1994	6	-2	-0.3	0
1995	35	39	1.1	1
1996	8	4	0.5	0
1997	27	83	3.1	2
1998	13	17	1.3	1
1999	5	1	0.2	0
Total	153	217	1.4	5
PS:	5	5	1.0	0

awkward sidearm motion unlike anyone else that is somewhat similar to Philip Rivers today. Although he didn't have a rocket arm, Bernie was an expert at reading defenses and taking what the defense gave. He had great field vision and was a particularly accurate passer who threw very few interceptions. Above all, he was a leader whose championship challenges were all thwarted by his nemesis, John Elway. Kosar remains popular with Browns fans and is involved with the ownership group that returned the Browns to town in 1999.

Erik Kramer

QPR 6.5

Height: 6'1" **Weight:** 200 lbs. **Birthdate:** 11/6/1964
College: North Carolina State **Draft:** Free agent
1987 Atlanta Falcons; 1988–90 CFL; 1991–93 Detroit Lions; 1994–99 Chicago Bears; 1999 San Diego Chargers
Regular Season Record: 31–36, 13 comebacks
Postseason Record: 1–2, no comebacks
Relative Rating: 99%

Erik Kramer struggled to get noticed as a football player. He took his junior college team to the 1983 Potato Bowl and landed at North Carolina State. When no one drafted Erik, he began his NFL career as a replacement player during the 1987 players' strike and then went to Canada. After three years in the CFL, Kramer earned a spot with the Lions in 1991 and stepped in for the injured Rodney Peete at midseason. With a 6–2 record, Kramer led Detroit to the playoffs where they throttled the Cowboys 38–6 with Kramer throwing for 341 yards and three touchdowns. In the NFC championship, though, two Kramer turnovers in the first three minutes led to a 10–0 Washington lead that the Redskins never relinquished.

Still, one would think Kramer had earned the starting job, but he started just seven more games in the next two years in the Wayne Fontes quarterback merry-go-round. Erik signed with the Bears in 1994 and threw for 29 touchdowns a year later. In five seasons in Chicago, Kramer twice threw for more than 3,000 yards, but he was a streaky player who was best at throwing touch passes. He finished his career as a backup in San Diego.

Tommy Kramer

QPR **7.5**

Height: 6'2" **Weight:** 200 lbs. **Birthdate:** 3/7/1955
College: Rice **Draft:** Minnesota 1977-1st
1977–89 Minnesota Vikings; 1990 New Orleans Saints
Regular Season Record: 54–56, 19 comebacks
Postseason Record: 1–2, 1 comeback
Relative Rating: 99%

Passing

Year	G	Comp./Att.	%	Yards	Y/Att.	TD	INT	Rating
1977	6	30/57	52.6	425	7.5	5	4	77.0
1978	4	5/16	31.3	50	3.1	0	1	15.1
1979	16	315/566	55.7	3,397	6.0	23	24	69.3
1980	15	299/522	57.3	3,582	6.9	19	23	72.2
1981	14	322/593	54.3	3,912	6.6	26	24	72.6
1982	9	176/308	57.1	2,037	6.6	15	12	77.3
1983	3	55/82	67.1	550	6.7	3	4	77.8
1984	9	124/236	52.5	1,678	7.1	9	10	70.6
1985	15	277/506	54.7	3,522	7.0	19	26	67.8
1986	13	208/372	55.9	3,000	8.1	24	10	92.6
1987	6	40/81	49.4	452	5.6	4	3	67.5
1988	10	83/173	48.0	1,264	7.3	5	9	60.5
1989	8	77/136	56.6	906	6.7	7	7	72.7
1990	1	1/3	33.3	2	0.7	0	1	2.8
Total	**129**	**2,012/3,651**	**55.1**	**24,777**	**6.8**	**159**	**158**	**72.8**
PS:	5	71/140	50.7	874	6.2	3	7	56.7

Rushing

Year	Att.	Yards	Avg.	TD
1977	10	3	0.3	0
1978	1	10	10.0	0
1979	32	138	4.3	1
1980	31	115	3.7	1
1981	10	13	1.3	0
1982	21	77	3.7	3
1983	8	3	0.4	0
1984	15	9	0.6	0
1985	27	54	2.0	0
1986	23	48	2.1	1
1987	10	44	4.4	2
1988	14	8	0.6	0
1989	12	9	0.8	0
Total	**214**	**531**	**2.5**	**8**
PS:	11	18	1.6	0

Erik Kramer's greatest season came in 1995 when he threw for a Bears record 29 touchdowns and 3,838 yards.

Tommy Kramer was a frantic gunner somewhat like Brett Favre without the rocket arm. Some called him "Two-Minute Tommy" for his propensity for pulling out games with improbable finishes. He threw a game-winning touchdown one time with 17 seconds left and another with 13 seconds remaining and won a game against the Browns in 1980 on a 46-yard Hail Mary pass that bounced into Ahmad Rashad's hands at the final gun. Others called Kramer "494 Tommy" for his frequenting of the bars along that route in Minneapolis. Although not great, he was a lively player with spark and personality.

Kramer was drafted to replace Fran Tarkenton in 1977 and did so when Fran retired after the 1978 season. Like Tarkenton, Tommy liked to keep everyone involved and threw often to his backs and tight end. Kramer could not scramble like Tarkenton but was fairly mobile and had a good arm. He liked to take chances, too, and ended up throwing just one touchdown pass more than interceptions in his career. His finest year was 1986 when he led the league in passer rating and threw 24 touchdowns to just 10 interceptions. Through the later part of his career, Kramer battled injuries and the challenge of Wade Wilson. He was released after the 1989 season and finished his playing days as a backup in New Orleans in 1990.

QPR 8.5

Dave Krieg

Height: 6'1" **Weight:** 193 lbs. **Birthdate:** 10/20/1958
College: Milton **Draft:** Free agent
1980–91 Seattle Seahawks; 1992–93 Kansas City Chiefs; 1994 Detroit Lions; 1995 Chicago Bears; 1996 Arizona Cardinals; 1997–98 Tennessee Titans
Regular Season Record: 98–77, 31 comebacks
Postseason Record: 3–6, 1 comeback
Relative Rating: 107%

Passing

Year	G	Comp./Att.	%	Yards	Y/Att.	TD	INT	Rating
1980	1	0/2	0.0	0	0.0	0	0	39.6
1981	7	64/112	57.1	843	7.5	7	5	83.3
1982	3	49/78	62.8	501	6.4	2	2	79.1
1983	9	147/243	60.5	2,139	8.8	18	11	95.0
1984	16	276/480	57.5	3,671	7.6	32	24	83.3
1985	16	285/532	53.6	3,602	6.8	27	20	76.2
1986	15	225/375	60.0	2,921	7.8	21	11	91.0
1987	12	178/294	60.5	2,131	7.2	23	15	87.6
1988	9	134/228	58.8	1,741	7.6	18	8	94.6
1989	15	286/499	57.3	3,309	6.6	21	20	74.8
1990	16	265/448	59.2	3,194	7.1	15	20	73.6
1991	10	187/285	65.6	2,080	7.3	11	12	82.5
1992	16	230/413	55.7	3,115	7.5	15	12	79.9
1993	12	105/189	55.6	1,238	6.6	7	3	81.4
1994	14	131/212	61.8	1,629	7.7	14	3	101.7
1995	16	304/521	58.3	3,554	6.8	16	21	72.6
1996	13	226/377	59.9	2,278	6.0	14	12	76.3
1997	8	1/2	50.0	2	1.0	0	0	56.2
1998	5	12/21	57.1	199	9.5	0	0	89.2
Total	213	3,105/5,311	58.5	38,147	7.2	261	199	81.5
PS:	12	144/282	51.1	1,895	6.7	11	9	72.3

Rushing

Year	Att.	Yards	Avg.	TD
1981	11	56	5.1	1
1982	6	-3	-0.5	0
1983	16	55	3.4	2
1984	46	186	4.0	3
1985	35	121	3.5	1
1986	35	122	3.5	1
1987	36	155	4.3	2
1988	24	64	2.7	0
1989	40	160	4.0	0
1990	32	115	3.6	0
1991	13	59	4.5	0
1992	37	74	2.0	2
1993	21	24	1.1	0
1994	23	35	1.5	0
1995	19	29	1.5	0
1996	16	12	0.8	1
1997	4	-2	-0.5	0
1998	3	-1	-0.3	0
Total	417	1,261	3.0	13
PS:	17	20	1.2	1

Along with Warren Moon and Jim Hart, Dave Krieg is one of three undrafted quarterbacks who played more than 200 games in the NFL. Coming from the obscure private college of Milton, Krieg's 19-year career is even more remarkable. In Seattle, Krieg began as the backup to another prominent undrafted free-agent quarterback, Jim Zorn. As Zorn started to fade in 1983, Krieg took over and led the Seahawks to the playoffs four times in the next decade.

Krieg tended to be streaky and had some inconsistent periods but was especially noted for his skill in getting hot late and bringing Seattle back in the closing minutes of a game. When he retired, Dave's 31 fourth-quarter game-winning drives were seventh of all time. Everyone remembers that the sack-prone Krieg was once brought down seven times by Derrick Thomas in a game against Kansas City, but it should also be recalled that Krieg won that game in 1990 by eluding Thomas on the game's final play and hitting Paul Skansi for the 25-yard winning touchdown. He was always cool under pressure.

After the 1991 season, Seattle released the 33-year-old quarterback to retain younger passers Kelly Stouffer and Dan McGwire, but Krieg was still playing long after Stouffer and McGwire had flopped and dropped out of the league. Over the

TOP 10
Quarterback Draft Busts

10. Stan Heath—completed 24 percent of passes and threw one TD to 14 interceptions in only one season in Green Bay
9. Rich Campbell—never started a game for Green Bay
8. Heath Shuler—record of 8–14 for Washington and New Orleans
7. David Klingler—record of 4–20 in Cincinnati
6. Terry Baker—started just one game for the Rams before shifting to halfback
5. Randy Duncan—went to Canada first and then played in the AFL as a backup
4. Akili Smith—first of the 1999 draft class' five first-round quarterbacks; cut by Cincinnati
3. Art Schlichter—spent more time in prison than on the field with the Colts
2. Ryan Leaf—second overall pick, a disaster off the field, and a 4–17 record on it
1. Bobby Garrett—overall top pick of the Browns but never started a game due to stuttering problem

Passing

Year	G	Comp./Att.	%	Yards	Y/Att.	TD	INT	Rating
1963	14	33/71	46.5	437	6.2	3	4	57.1
1964	14	55/128	43.0	1,137	8.9	6	8	64.5
1965	14	29/70	41.4	376	5.4	3	6	37.6
1966	14	33/84	39.3	549	6.5	4	5	53.1
1967	14	220/425	51.8	3,228	7.6	30	20	80.8
1968	13	206/416	49.5	3,245	7.8	25	15	80.9
1969	14	221/426	51.9	3,302	7.8	34	25	79.8
1970	14	179/356	50.3	2,516	7.1	22	15	76.5
1971	14	118/242	48.8	1,717	7.1	16	16	66.8
1972	14	149/281	53.0	1,998	7.1	18	12	79.5
1973	8	42/93	45.2	614	6.6	2	8	38.6
1974	4	3/9	33.3	35	3.9	1	4	43.5
Total	**151**	**1,288/2,601**	**49.5**	**19,154**	**7.4**	**164**	**138**	**72.9**
PS:	11	117/263	44.5	1,928	7.3	19	10	77.9

Rushing

Year	Att.	Yards	Avg.	TD
1963	9	8	0.9	0
1964	55	289	5.3	6
1965	10	30	3.0	1
1966	9	6	0.7	1
1967	22	110	5.0	4
1968	19	98	5.2	1
1969	13	36	2.8	1
1970	8	24	3.0	0
1971	4	16	4.0	0
1972	10	33	3.3	0
1973	5	-7	-1.4	0
1974	2	-3	-1.5	0
Total	**166**	**640**	**3.9**	**14**
PS:	8	23	2.9	1

next seven years, Krieg made stops in Kansas City, Detroit, Arizona, Chicago, and Tennessee and was his team's regular starter in three of those years, enabling him to accumulate 261 touchdowns and more than 38,000 passing yards. On the downside, Krieg threw at least 20 interceptions five times, twice led the league in that category, and finished second all-time to Warren Moon in fumbles. Krieg was not a great quarterback but was a very good one for a very long time.

Daryle Lamonica  **QPR 9.5**

Height: 6'3" **Weight:** 215 lbs. **Birthdate:** 7/17/1941
College: Notre Dame **Draft:** Buffalo Bills 1963-24th; Green Bay Packers 1963-12th
1963–66 Buffalo Bills; 1967–74 Oakland Raiders; 1975 WFL
Regular Season Record: 66–16–6, 18 comebacks
Postseason Record: 4–5, no comebacks
Relative Rating: 115%

In Daryle Lamonica's 12 seasons in the NFL, his team played in the postseason 11 times. Those teams won 10 division titles and three AFL titles and went to one Super Bowl. Those teams also outscored the league average by an imposing 32 percent. Daryle's gaudy lifetime winning percentage as a starter of .793 is second only to Otto Graham, and yet he is not remembered as one of the greats because his career was short and he never won a Super Bowl.

Lamonica was known as the "Mad Bomber" for his affection for the deep pass and may have been the finest long passer ever. Although he spent most of his career in Oakland's vertical passing offense that emphasized his long-ball skills, Daryle was a bomber even in Buffalo where he began as Jack Kemp's backup. Lamonica was so proficient at relieving Kemp when Jack was struggling that he was known by Buffalo fans as the "Fireman" for his ace relief pitching. In his second season with the Bills, Lamonica completed only 43 percent of his passes but averaged more than 20 yards per completion. That year, Daryle also led all AFL quarterbacks with 289 yards rushing.

Lamonica lobbied for the starting role in Buffalo and was surprised to be traded to Oakland in 1967 along with Glenn Bass for quarterback Tom Flores and end Art Powell in one of the most lopsided trades in NFL history. In his first three years with the Raiders, Daryle threw for 89 touchdown passes and passed for more than 3,000 yards each year. His battles with the Jets' bomber Joe Namath were especially memorable examples of the best of the wide-open AFL-style of football. Lamonica summed up his approach to *Sports Illustrated* in 1970, "I'm throwing to win. If I only complete three passes in an entire game but they all go for touchdowns and we win, then I'm happy. There are quarterbacks who throw safe passes to get the big percentage of completions. That's not me. I'd rather look lousy and win than great and lose."

The better defenses adjusted, however, and found that Lamonica sometimes would panic under pressure and force long passes into deep zone coverage. Lamonica thought the Oakland game plans were getting too conservative and belittled coach John Madden as Ken Stabler began to eat into Daryle's playing time in the early 1970s. Lamonica played out his option in 1974 to sign with the Southern California Sun of the World Football League. He suffered a hernia in the preseason, though, and by the time he returned, rookie Pat Haden was firmly ensconced as the starter. Daryle threw only 19 passes before the Sun and the WFL folded and his career was over. Although he was not quite great, no quarterback other than Joe Namath evokes the freewheeling nature of the AFL more than Daryle Lamonica.

Greg Landry

QPR **8.0**

Height: 6'4" **Weight:** 210 lbs. **Birthdate:** 12/18/1946
College: Massachusetts **Draft:** Detroit 1968-1st
1968-78 Detroit Lions; 1979-81 Baltimore Colts;
1983-84 USFL; 1984 Chicago Bears
Regular Season Record: 44-51-3, 8 comebacks
Postseason Record: 0-1, no comebacks
Relative Rating: 106%

Passing

Year	G	Comp./Att.	%	Yards	Y/Att.	TD	INT	Rating
1968	4	23/48	47.9	338	7.0	2	7	45.7
1969	10	80/160	50.0	853	5.3	4	10	48.3
1970	12	83/136	61.0	1,072	7.9	9	5	92.5
1971	14	136/261	52.1	2,237	8.6	16	13	80.9
1972	14	134/268	50.0	2,066	7.7	18	17	71.8
1973	7	70/128	54.7	908	7.1	3	10	52.5
1974	5	49/82	59.8	572	7.0	3	3	77.9
1975	6	31/56	55.4	403	7.2	1	0	84.2
1976	14	168/291	57.7	2,191	7.5	17	8	89.6
1977	11	135/240	56.3	1,359	5.7	6	7	68.7
1978	5	48/77	62.3	452	5.9	1	1	77.4
1979	16	270/457	59.1	2,932	6.4	15	15	75.3
1980	16	24/47	51.1	275	5.9	2	3	56.6
1981	11	14/29	48.3	195	6.7	0	1	56.0
1984	1	11/20	55.0	199	10.0	1	3	66.5
Total	**146**	**1,276/2,300**	**55.5**	**16,052**	**7.0**	**98**	**103**	**72.9**
PS:	1	5/12	41.7	48	4.0	0	0	53.5

Rushing

Year	Att.	Yards	Avg.	TD
1968	7	39	5.6	1
1969	33	243	7.4	1
1970	35	350	10.0	1
1971	76	530	7.0	3
1972	81	524	6.5	9
1973	42	267	6.4	2
1974	22	95	4.3	1
1975	20	92	4.6	0
1976	43	234	5.4	1
1977	25	99	4.0	0
1978	5	29	5.8	0
1979	31	115	3.7	0
1980	7	26	3.7	1
1981	1	11	11.0	0
1984	2	1	0.5	1
Total	**430**	**2,655**	**6.2**	**21**
PS:	3	15	5.0	0

Greg Landry was one of the earliest running quarterbacks in the NFL. When the lanky 6'4" quarterback retired, his total of 2,655 rushing yards was topped only by Fran Tarkenton and Tobin Rote. His 76-yard quarterback sneak in 1970 was the longest run by a quarterback up to that point. His 530 yards rushing in 1971 broke Rote's record of 523 and was in turn broken by Bobby Douglass with 968 yards in 1972. Unlike Douglass, though, Landry was also an accurate passer who could read defenses. Overall, he was similar to Jim Harbaugh.

Landry was the first quarterback drafted in 1968 and was the Lions' primary quarterback for the next 11 years, although he often battled with Bill Munson for playing time. Landry went to the Pro Bowl in 1971 with his record rushing total and with 2,237 yards passing; no Detroit quarterback has been to the Pro Bowl since then. The mediocre Lions made it to the postseason only once in his tenure, and Landry had a terrible day in an ugly 5–0 loss to Dallas in the 1970 playoffs. Greg later played with the Colts, Bears, and the Chicago Blitz of the USFL. In fact, Landry was the first big-name player to sign with the USFL in 1982. He was a smart, steady, solid starter for several seasons and then coached for the Bears and Lions for another decade.

Bobby Layne

QPR 9.5

Height: 6'1" **Weight:** 201 lbs. **Birthdate:** 12/19/1926
College: Texas **Draft:** Chicago Bears 1948-1st
1948 Chicago Bears; 1949 NY Bulldogs; 1950–58 Detroit Lions; 1958–62 Pittsburgh Steelers
Regular Season Record: 82–61–5, 22 comebacks
Postseason Record: 3–1, 1 comeback
Relative Rating: 103%

Passing

Year	G	Comp./Att.	%	Yards	Y/Att.	TD	INT	Rating
1948	11	16/52	30.8	232	4.5	3	2	49.5
1949	12	155/299	51.8	1,796	6.0	9	18	55.3
1950	12	152/336	45.2	2,323	6.9	16	18	62.1
1951	12	152/332	45.8	2,403	7.2	26	23	67.6
1952	12	139/287	48.4	1,999	7.0	19	20	64.5
1953	12	125/273	45.8	2,088	7.6	16	21	59.6
1954	12	135/246	54.9	1,818	7.4	14	12	77.3
1955	12	143/270	53.0	1,830	6.8	11	17	61.8
1956	12	129/244	52.9	1,909	7.8	9	17	62.0
1957	11	87/179	48.6	1,169	6.5	6	12	53.0
1958	12	145/294	49.3	2,510	8.5	14	12	77.6
1959	12	142/297	47.8	1,986	6.7	20	21	62.8
1960	12	103/209	49.3	1,814	8.7	13	17	66.2
1961	8	75/149	50.3	1,205	8.1	11	16	62.8
1962	13	116/233	49.8	1,686	7.2	9	17	56.2
Total	**175**	**1,814/3,700**	**49.0**	**26,768**	**7.2**	**196**	**243**	**63.4**
PS:	4	46/97	47.4	568	5.9	1	12	29.9

Rushing

Year	Att.	Yards	Avg.	TD
1948	13	80	6.2	1
1949	54	196	3.6	3
1950	56	250	4.5	4
1951	61	290	4.8	1
1952	94	411	4.4	1
1953	87	343	3.9	0
1954	30	119	4.0	2
1955	31	111	3.6	0
1956	46	169	3.7	5
1957	24	99	4.1	0
1958	40	154	3.9	3
1959	33	181	5.5	2
1960	19	12	0.6	2
1961	8	11	1.4	0
1962	15	25	1.7	1
Total	**611**	**2,451**	**4.0**	**25**
PS:	33	120	3.6	1

Fellow Texan Yale Lary said of his Lion teammate Bobby Layne, "When Bobby said block, you blocked. And when Bobby said drink, you drank." Layne was the "greatest leader" according to his coach, Buddy Parker, and led the Lions and Steelers both on and off the field. He commanded the huddle, exhorting his teammates to play harder and berating poor play, and was at his best when the game was on the line. Bobby is frequently cited as being the first quarterback to master the two-minute offense. Although his passes were not the prettiest, Layne was the best deep passer of his time. In addition, Bobby led all quarterbacks in rushing yards three times and was a credible place-kicker who led the NFL in scoring in 1956. Of course, there is a seamier side, too. Layne was a heavy drinker, and there have long been allegations of his involvement with gamblers during his playing days, although Bobby always denied those rumors.

The single-wing Steelers were all set to draft Layne with the first pick in 1948, but Bobby made it clear he wanted to play in a T formation. George Halas traded tailback Ray Evans to Pittsburgh and signed Layne to go with Sid Luckman and Johnny Lujack. After one year, Halas decided that Lujack was his future and traded Bobby to the New York Bulldogs, where he got to start—but for a terrible team with a porous line. Layne took a beating that season but then was traded again in 1950 to the Detroit Lions, where he ushered in the glory era of Lion football in the 1950s, winning three titles in eight years.

Bobby led the Lions over the Browns in two of three championship games, winning the 1953 game on a 33-yard strike to Jim Doran in the final minute. Layne had injury problems in 1955 but had the Lions poised to win another divisional crown in 1956 in the season finale against the Bears. However, Chicago defensive end Ed Meadows drilled Layne, who was the last quarterback to play without a facemask, well after a handoff and knocked him out of the game with a concussion. Without Bobby, the Lions lost the game and the division title to the Bears.

Layne returned in 1957 but now had to share the quarterbacking with newly acquired Tobin Rote. When Layne broke his leg in Week 11, Rote stepped in and guided the Lions to the championship. With friction developing between Layne and coach George Wilson, Bobby was traded to Pittsburgh in 1958 where he reunited with coach Buddy Parker. Layne could not quite get the Steelers over the hump in five years, though, and his skills began to fade as the bumps and bruises caught up with him. Parker urged Bobby to retire after the 1962 season, and he did. Layne's final game was a loss in the 1963 Playoff Bowl to the Lions, and his final pass was intercepted by safety Yale Lary. Layne's high school and Detroit teammate, Doak Walker, once

said of him, "Bobby never lost a game. Time just ran out on him." By 1962, time had. Layne retired as the all-time leader in passing yards, touchdown passes, and interceptions and as a Hall of Famer.

Ryan Leaf

QPR 0.5

Height: 6'5" **Weight:** 245 lbs. **Birthdate:** 5/15/1976
College: Washington State **Draft:** San Diego 1998-1st
1998, 2000 San Diego Chargers; 2001 Dallas Cowboys
Regular Season Record: 4–17, 3 comebacks
Postseason Record: NA
Relative Rating: 64%

Passing

Year	G	Comp./Att.	%	Yards	Y/Att.	TD	INT	Rating
1998	10	111/245	45.3	1,289	5.3	2	15	39.0
2000	11	161/322	50.0	1,883	5.8	11	18	56.2
2001	4	45/88	51.1	494	5.6	1	3	57.7
Total	25	317/655	48.4	3,666	5.6	14	36	50.0

Rushing

Year	Att.	Yards	Avg.	TD
1998	27	80	3.0	0
2000	28	54	1.9	0
2001	4	-7	-1.8	0
Total	59	127	2.2	0

One of the reasons that Ryan Leaf is arguably the greatest draft bust in NFL history is that there was such a serious debate before the draft as to whether Leaf or Peyton Manning would be the better top pick. Colts GM Bill Pollian selected Manning because Peyton had started nearly twice as many games in college, was more mature, and showed a much better work ethic. Both were big quarterbacks with strong arms, but one turned out to be a combination of the Scarecrow who lacked brains and the Tin Man who lacked heart.

Leaf managed to win his first two games— the first rookie to do that since John Elway—but then imploded. He earned a 0.0 passer rating by completing just one of 15 passes with two interceptions against the Chiefs and lost four games in a row, including a 17–12 loss to the Colts for Peyton Manning's first win. Leaf fared no better off the field, cursing cameramen and sleeping through team meetings, and eventually was benched.

Injuries; profanity-laced tirades against fans, teammates, and Charger GM Bobby Beathard, and a suspension caused Leaf to miss all of 1999, but he returned to win just one of nine starts in 2000. San Diego waived him at the end of the year and cut its losses. Ryan failed a tryout with the Bucs in 2001 but was signed by the Cowboys, who let him start three games, all losses, before releasing him. Leaf tried out for Seattle in 2002 and then retired from the NFL. This was the man for whom Beathard traded two first-round picks, a second-rounder, and two players in 1998. This was the man Chargers owner Alex Spanos introduced as "the player who's going to lead us to the Super Bowl." This was the man who won four of 21 starts, completed fewer than half of his passes, threw just 12 touchdowns to 36 interceptions, and fumbled 24 times in 25 games. This was the greatest bust of all time.

Eddie LeBaron

QPR 6.5

Height: 5'7"   **Weight:** 168 lbs.   **Birthdate:** 1/7/1930
College: Pacific   **Draft:** Washington 1950-10th
1952–53, 1955–59 Washington Redskins; 1954 CFL;
1960–63 Dallas Cowboys
Regular Season Record: 29–57–4, 14 comebacks
Postseason Record: NA
Relative Rating: 96%

Passing

Year	G	Comp./Att.	%	Yards	Y/Att.	TD	INT	Rating
1952	12	96/194	49.5	1,420	7.3	14	15	65.7
1953	12	62/149	41.6	874	5.9	3	17	28.3
1955	12	79/178	44.4	1,270	7.1	9	15	50.5
1956	10	47/98	48.0	554	5.7	3	10	36.2
1957	12	99/167	59.3	1,508	9.0	11	10	86.1
1958	12	79/145	54.5	1,365	9.4	11	10	83.3
1959	12	77/173	44.5	1,077	6.2	8	11	54.0
1960	11	111/225	49.3	1,736	7.7	12	25	53.5
1961	14	120/236	50.8	1,741	7.4	14	16	66.7
1962	14	95/166	57.2	1,436	8.7	16	9	95.4
1963	13	33/65	50.8	418	6.4	3	3	67.3
Total	134	898/1,796	50.0	13,399	7.5	104	141	61.4

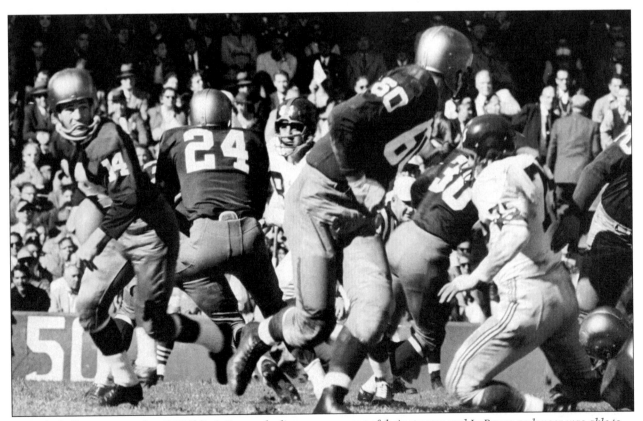

Once the ball was snapped to 5'7" Eddie LeBaron, the linemen came out of their stances and LaBaron no longer was able to see downfield.

Rushing

Year	Att.	Yards	Avg.	TD
1952	43	164	3.8	2
1953	21	95	4.5	2
1955	37	190	5.1	4
1956	11	6	0.5	0
1957	20	-12	-0.6	0
1958	12	30	2.5	0
1959	13	7	0.5	0
1960	17	94	5.5	1
1961	20	72	3.6	0
1962	6	-1	-0.2	0
1963	2	5	2.5	0
Total	202	650	3.2	9

At 16, Eddie LeBaron enrolled at the College of the Pacific, where the football coach was the legendary 84-year-old Amos Alonzo Stagg. Stagg retired after Eddie's freshman year, and the 5'7" LeBaron went on to achieve, appropriately, Little All-American honors for the next three years. Although the Redskins drafted Eddie in 1950, his pro career was put on hold by his U.S. Marine Corps service during the Korean War. LeBaron was the youngest commissioned officer in the marines at 20 and was decorated with the Purple Heart and the Bronze Star.

LeBaron joined the Redskins in 1952 for Sammy Baugh's final year and took over as the starter immediately. Eddie started in Washington for the rest of the decade, aside from 1954 when he went to play in Canada rather than endure a second season under bellicose coach Curly Lambeau. Washington posted only two winning seasons in those years, but LeBaron was named to four Pro Bowls. He was a magical ball handler and a fine passer when his passing lanes weren't blocked by the pass rush. His receivers had the odd sensation of not being able to see their quarterback when they looked back for the ball. Cowboys receiver Billy Howton described it as the ball seeming to come "out of a silo."

LeBaron was ready to retire in 1960 but was coaxed into playing for the expansion Dallas Cowboys. By 1962, the Cowboys had the most explosive offense in the league with alternating quarterbacks LeBaron and Don Meredith. Meredith took over in 1963, and LeBaron retired at the end of the season to practice law. Eddie returned to the game as the Falcons' GM in 1977 and served in Atlanta's front office for 10 years before returning to the law practice. LeBaron never played for very good teams but was an inspiring leader who twice led the league in fourth-quarter game-winning drives. In many ways, he was the Doug Flutie of his day. He had a big impact on everything he ever tried.

Bob Lee

Height: 6'2"   **Weight:** 195 lbs.   **Birthdate:** 8/7/1945
College: Pacific   **Draft:** Minnesota 1968-17th
1969–72, 1975–78 Minnesota Vikings; 1973–74 Atlanta Falcons; 1979–80 Los Angeles Rams
Regular Season Record: 19–11, 3 comebacks
Postseason Record: 1–1, no comebacks
Relative Rating: 95%

Passing

Year	G	Comp./Att.	%	Yards	Y/Att.	TD	INT	Rating
1969	14	7/11	63.6	79	7.2	1	0	115.3
1970	6	40/79	50.6	610	7.7	5	5	71.2
1971	14	45/90	50.0	598	6.6	2	4	60.3
1972	2	3/6	50.0	75	12.5	1	0	135.4
1973	12	120/230	52.2	1,786	7.8	10	8	77.9
1974	9	78/172	45.3	852	5.0	3	14	32.4
1975	4	5/14	35.7	103	7.4	2	1	72.3
1976	4	15/30	50.0	156	5.2	0	2	37.6
1977	5	42/72	58.3	522	7.3	4	4	76.3
1978	3	2/4	50.0	10	2.5	0	1	16.7
1979	3	11/22	50.0	243	11.0	2	1	101.1
1980	1	0/0	0.0	0	0.0	0	0	0.0
Total	77	368/730	50.4	5,034	6.9	30	40	63.7
PS:	5	33/67	49.3	382	5.7	1	3	53.2

Rushing

Year	Att.	Yards	Avg.	TD
1969	3	9	3.0	0
1970	10	20	2.0	1
1971	11	14	1.3	1
1973	29	67	2.3	0
1974	19	99	5.2	1
1975	1	0	0.0	0
1976	2	2	1.0	0
1977	12	-8	-0.7	0
1979	4	-5	-1.3	0
1980	1	-1	-1.0	0
Total	92	197	2.1	3
PS:	8	22	2.8	0

"General" Bob Lee was no relation to the Confederate leader, but he did have the best season of his career in Atlanta. Lee was the 441st player drafted in 1969. Only three quarterbacks were ever drafted any lower, and none of them ever played in the NFL. He was primarily a punter in his rookie season for the Super Bowl–bound Vikings but started to see some action as a backup quarterback in 1970. Itching to play more, Lee welcomed a trade to Atlanta in 1973 that returned Bob Berry to Minnesota.

Lee fell behind journeyman Dick Shiner due to a training camp injury but replaced the injured Shiner in Week 4 and led the Falcons to seven straight wins. Bob was an enthusiastic leader in the huddle and got the team on a roll. In his first start against the Bears in October, Lee achieved a perfect passer rating by completing 17 of 20 passes for 257 yards and two touchdowns. Later in the season, though, Bob scored a 0.0 rating in a dreary December game against St. Louis (in which rookie Cardinal quarterback Gary Keithley also rated 0.0 in winning his first-ever start). Atlanta finished at 9–5, just out of the playoffs, but fans were excited about next year. However, the team dropped to 3–11 in 1974, and Lee's numbers fell off to 45 percent completions and a ratio of three touchdown passes to 14 interceptions. Lee was released and returned to Minnesota as a backup replacing Bob Berry again.

Lee finished his career as a backup with the Vikings and Rams and played with two more Super Bowl teams. He even threw a touchdown pass in Super Bowl XI with the Vikings trailing Oakland by 25 points with 25 seconds to play. Lee was a slightly talented, inconsistent second-string quarterback who had two months of glory in Atlanta that got him written up in *Time* magazine in 1973. His daughter Jenna Lee is an anchor on the Fox Business Network.

Jacky Lee

Height: 6'1" **Weight:** 189 lbs. **Birthdate:** 7/11/1939
College: Cincinnati **Draft:** St. Louis Cardinals 1960-1st
1960–63, 1966–67 Houston Oilers 1964–65 Denver Broncos; 1967–69 Kansas City Chiefs
Regular Season Record: 7–15–1, 1 comeback
Postseason Record: NA
Relative Rating: 107%

Passing

Year	G	Comp./Att.	%	Yards	Y/Att.	TD	INT	Rating
1960	14	41/77	53.2	842	10.9	5	6	81.2
1961	14	66/127	52.0	1,205	9.5	12	6	96.7
1962	14	26/50	52.0	433	8.7	4	5	68.6
1963	14	37/75	49.3	475	6.3	2	8	38.9
1964	14	133/265	50.2	1,611	6.1	11	20	51.6
1965	4	44/80	55.0	692	8.7	5	3	89.2
1966	8	4/8	50.0	27	3.4	0	1	18.2
1967	9	42/91	46.2	414	4.5	3	6	43.0
1968	6	25/45	55.6	383	8.5	3	1	96.8
1969	3	12/20	60.0	109	5.5	1	1	70.6
Total	**100**	**430/838**	**51.3**	**6,191**	**7.4**	**46**	**57**	**65.6**

Rushing

Year	Att.	Yards	Avg.	TD
1960	6	11	1.8	0
1961	8	36	4.5	0
1962	4	1	0.3	0
1963	2	9	4.5	0
1964	42	163	3.9	3
1965	2	1	0.5	0
1966	1	-3	-3.0	0
1967	6	-3	-0.5	0
1969	1	3	3.0	0
Total	**72**	**218**	**3.0**	**3**

Facially, Jacky Lee bore an uncanny resemblance to Peyton Manning, but on the field, he was simply a dependable backup quarterback who played on the first two AFL champions and the last one. The pairing of Lee and George Blanda at quarterback for the Oilers gave Houston a big advantage that sent them to the AFL's first three title games. In both 1960 and 1961, Lee was called upon to start three games for Blanda and kept the Oilers on their winning ways. In one game against Boston in 1961, Lee threw for 457 yards. Jacky was more of a deep passer than Blanda was, and the two combined for 48 touchdowns passes in that year, with Lee contributing a dozen.

Lee and Blanda competed intensely both on and off the field and did not get along very well. Despite his penchant for throwing interceptions, Blanda had the confidence of the offense. Lee had a stronger arm and was better able to escape a pass rush. One anonymous player told *Sports Illustrated*, "[Lee] couldn't get us in a group and lead us across the street. He's cocky, like he wants us to think he's the man, but deep inside he knows he's really not."

With Don Trull on hand as the new backup in 1964, Houston struck a strange deal with quarterback-starved Denver, whose coach Jack Faulkner called Lee "the best quarterback in our league and the best backup quarterback in the game." The Oilers lent Lee to the Broncos for two years and in return got All-Pro defensive tackle Bud McFaddin and a No. 1 draft pick. Lee could do no better with the awful Broncos than previous Denver quarterbacks and lost the starting job back to John McCormick and Mickey Slaughter in 1965. Lee returned to Houston in 1966 but was traded to Kansas City for Pete Beathard in 1967. In 1969, Lee stepped in for an injured Len Dawson only to suffer a broken ankle the next week and miss out on the Chiefs' Super Bowl win over Minnesota. He was one of just 20 players who played all 10 years of the AFL's existence.

Rushing

Year	Att.	Yards	Avg.	TD
1947	18	143	7.9	0
1948	28	86	3.1	1
1949	13	58	4.5	1
Total	59	187	4.9	2

Clyde LeForce was a great college football player at Tulsa in the 1940s. As a sophomore in 1942, he backed up All-American senior tailback Glenn Dobbs and then took over as starter the next year. In 1943, LeForce was deferred from the military as a petroleum engineering major and led the Golden Hurricane in yards passing, rushing, scoring, punting, and punt returns. Clyde spent the next two years in the war before returning to Tulsa in 1946. The Hurricane switched to the T formation that year, and LeForce was the starting quarterback, backed up by future Steeler Jim Finks. In the 1947 East-West Shrine Game, Clyde enhanced his reputation by throwing for 230 yards in rallying the West team to victory.

Drafted by Detroit in 1945, LeForce signed with the Lions in 1947 and, along with Roy Zimmerman, became the first T-formation quarterbacks in team history. Clyde was very slightly built and not really up to the pounding of the pro game but stuck around for three years in Detroit, sharing the job with Fred Enke in 1948 and with Enke and Frank Tripucka in 1949. All three were swept aside in 1950 when Bobby Layne arrived in the Motor City and LeForce retired.

Clyde LeForce

QPR 4.0

Height: 5'11" **Weight:** 176 lbs. **Birthdate:** 6/4/1923
College: Tulsa **Draft:** Detroit 1945-19th
1947–49 Detroit Lions
Regular Season Record: 3–7 est., no comebacks
Postseason Record: NA
Relative Rating: 102%

Passing

Year	G	Comp./Att.	%	Yards	Y/Att.	TD	INT	Rating
1947	9	94/175	53.7	1,384	7.9	13	20	65.0
1948	12	50/101	49.5	912	9.0	9	8	77.7
1949	11	53/112	47.3	665	5.9	3	9	41.7
Total	32	197/388	50.8	2,961	7.6	25	37	58.1

TOP 10
Party Boys

10. Brett Favre and Kerry Collins (reformed)
9. Ryan Leaf
8. Cade McNown
7. Dan Pastorini
6. Ken Stabler
5. Don Meredith
4. Billy Kilmer
3. Sonny Jurgensen
2. Joe Namath
1. Bobby Layne

Byron Leftwich

QPR 5.0

Height: 6'5" **Weight:** 245 lbs. **Birthdate:** 1/14/1980
College: Marshall **Draft:** Jacksonville 2003-1st
**2003-06 Jacksonville Jaguars; 2007 Atlanta Falcons;
2008 Pittsburgh Steelers**
Regular Season Record: 24–22, 11 comebacks
Postseason Record: 0–1, no comebacks
Relative Rating: 100%

Passing

Year	G	Comp./Att.	%	Yards	Y/Att.	TD	INT	Rating
2003	15	239/418	57.2	2,819	6.7	14	16	73.0
2004	14	267/441	60.5	2,941	6.7	15	10	82.2
2005	11	175/302	57.9	2,123	7.0	15	5	89.3
2006	6	108/183	59.0	1,159	6.3	7	5	79.0
2007	3	32/58	55.2	279	4.8	1	2	59.5
2008	5	21/36	58.3	303	8.4	2	0	104.3
Total	54	842/1,438	58.6	9,624	6.7	54	38	80.3
PS:	2	18/32	56.3	179	5.6	0	1	59.2

Rushing

Year	Att.	Yards	Avg.	TD
2003	25	108	4.3	2
2004	39	148	3.8	2
2005	31	67	2.2	2
2006	25	41	1.6	2
2007	6	7	1.2	0
2008	4	7	1.8	1
Total	130	378	2.9	9
PS:	7	24	3.4	0

Byron Leftwich is a hefty log of a quarterback who took over for fan favorite Mark Brunell as a rookie in Jacksonville and was eventually beaten out by injuries and David Garrard. Leftwich can make all the throws accurately and is a great leader who will play through pain. The indelible image of Leftwich is when he broke his shin in a 2002 college game against Akron but refused to come out. Instead, two linemen would carry him down the field after every completion in his game-winning rally. Leftwich's work ethic inspires that kind of dedication from his teammates. However, Byron has also proven to be injury-prone and misses a lot of games. He is slow to set up and slow to deliver the ball and does not elude the rush well.

After missing 18 games due to injury in his four years with the Jaguars, Leftwich was replaced by Garrard and released by coach Jack Del Rio in 2007. Byron spent a disastrous year in Atlanta before landing with the Steelers as Ben Roethlisberger's able backup in 2008. At the start of the season in Pittsburgh, Leftwich outlined his admirable approach, "This is the situation I'm in. I'm the backup quarterback. If I'm called upon, I have to be ready, and, even if I'm not, I have to do the things they need me to do to help this team win. I've always looked at football like that. I love this game. I take it seriously."

Matt Leinart

QPR 2.5

Height: 6'5" **Weight:** 232 lbs. **Birthdate:** 5/11/1983
College: USC **Draft:** Arizona 2006-1st
2006-08 Arizona Cardinals
Regular Season Record: 7–9, 2 comebacks
Postseason Record: NA
Relative Rating: 89%

Passing

Year	G	Comp./Att.	%	Yards	Y/Att.	TD	INT	Rating
2006	12	214/377	56.8	2,547	6.8	11	12	74.0
2007	5	60/112	53.6	647	5.8	2	4	61.9
2008	4	15/29	51.7	264	9.1	1	1	80.2
Total	21	289/518	55.8	3,458	6.7	14	17	71.7

Rushing

Year	Att.	Yards	Avg.	TD
2006	22	49	2.2	2
2007	11	42	3.8	0
2008	4	5	1.3	0
Total	37	96	2.6	2

Being the life of the party doesn't preclude a quarterback from being a star as long as he keeps his focus. Ken Stabler famously pointed out that there's nothing wrong with reading your playbook by the light of the jukebox. In his first three seasons in the NFL, though, party animal Matt Leinart seemed to lack the focus to multitask on and off the field.

Leinart won a Heisman Trophy and two national championships at USC while winning 37 of 39 starts in three years. In the pros, he is just 7–9 as a starter and has been outplayed by his former backup Matt Cassell in New England. Leinart is a big left-hander with a strong and accurate arm who has battled injuries and immaturity in the desert. The self-proclaimed "King of Hollywood," who still had his mom paying his bills at the age of 25, was beaten out by 37-year-old Kurt Warner in 2008. Although Leinart is popular with teammates, he would become even more popular if he could harness his talent and help the team win.

Pete Liske

QPR 4.5

Height: 6'3" **Weight:** 200 lbs. **Birthdate:** 5/24/1942
College: Penn State **Draft:** NY Jets 1963-15th; Philadelphia 1963-10th
1964 New York Jets; 1965–68, 1973–75 CFL; 1969–70 Denver Broncos; 1971–72 Philadelphia Eagles
Regular Season Record: 13–15–1, 2 comebacks
Postseason Record: NA
Relative Rating: 95%

Passing

Year	G	Comp./Att.	%	Yards	Y/Att.	TD	INT	Rating
1964	2	9/18	50.0	55	3.1	0	2	16.9
1969	7	61/115	53.0	845	7.3	9	11	63.4
1970	11	112/238	47.1	1,340	5.6	7	11	55.3
1971	14	143/269	53.2	1,957	7.3	11	15	67.1
1972	14	71/138	51.4	973	7.1	3	7	60.4
Total	48	396/778	50.9	5,170	6.6	30	46	60.4

Rushing

Year	Att.	Yards	Avg.	TD
1964	1	0	0.0	0
1969	10	50	5.0	0
1970	7	42	6.0	1
1971	13	29	2.2	1
1972	7	20	2.9	0
Total	38	141	3.7	2

Penn State is known as "Linebacker U" for all the NFL linebackers it has produced. Several Nittany Lion quarterbacks have played in the pros as well but not with the same success. If you include Pete Liske's Canadian experience, he may have been the most successful of the lot between Milt Plum and Kerry Collins. Liske signed with the Jets in 1964 and got to start the season finale that year, but Weeb Ewbank was not impressed and traded Pete to Buffalo at season's end. Liske chose to sign with Toronto of the CFL instead and spent one year

with the Argonauts before being traded to Calgary in 1966. By 1967, Liske had mastered the Canadian game and threw for more than 4,000 yards in back-to-back seasons. Pete also tossed 40 touchdown passes, was named MVP in 1967, and then led the Stampeders to the Grey Cup game in 1968.

At this high-water mark of his career, Liske returned to the U.S. and signed with Denver as a free agent just as Joe Kapp had two years before. With the Broncos, Pete was unable to dislodge Steve Tensi in two seasons and was sent to the Eagles for a fifth-round pick in 1971. Former Calgary coach Jerry Williams led the Eagles, and Liske was the Birds' substandard primary starter for the next two losing seasons before he returned to Canada in 1973 for three more years in the CFL. Pete was a fine leader but had a rag arm, was suspect at reading defenses, and could not elude a pass rush. In a perfect world, he would have landed on a team with a good defense and a strong running game and may have achieved some success as a game manager. However, the Jet, Bronco, and Eagle teams that employed Liske were very far from that ideal.

Mike Livingston

QPR 6.5

Height: 6'4" **Weight:** 212 lbs. **Birthdate:** 11/14/1945
College: Southern Methodist **Draft:** Kansas City 1968-2nd
1968–79 Kansas City Chiefs
Regular Season Record: 31–43–1, 7 comebacks
Postseason Record: NA
Relative Rating: 97%

Passing

Year	G	Comp./Att.	%	Yards	Y/Att.	TD	INT	Rating
1968	1	0/0	0.0	0	0.0	0	0	0.0
1969	9	84/161	52.2	1,123	7.0	4	6	67.4
1970	4	11/22	50.0	122	5.5	0	1	47.9
1971	3	12/28	42.9	130	4.6	0	0	57.1
1972	5	41/78	52.6	480	6.2	7	8	61.9
1973	8	75/145	51.7	916	6.3	6	7	65.2
1974	8	66/141	46.8	732	5.2	4	10	42.6
1975	7	88/176	50.0	1,245	7.1	8	6	74.2
1976	14	189/338	55.9	2,682	7.9	12	13	77.6
1977	13	143/282	50.7	1,823	6.5	9	15	59.8
1978	14	159/290	54.8	1,573	5.4	5	13	57.4
1979	5	44/90	48.9	469	5.2	1	4	49.7
Total	91	912/1,751	52.1	11,295	6.5	56	83	63.3

Rushing

Year	Att.	Yards	Avg.	TD
1968	2	2	1.0	0
1969	15	102	6.8	0
1970	3	26	8.7	0
1971	5	11	2.2	0
1972	14	133	9.5	0
1973	19	94	4.9	2
1974	9	28	3.1	0
1975	13	68	5.2	1
1976	31	89	2.9	2
1977	19	78	4.1	1
1978	23	49	2.1	1
1979	3	2	0.7	0
Total	**156**	**682**	**4.4**	**7**

Mike Livingston did not throw a pass as a rookie, but in his second season, starter Len Dawson was lost to a knee injury in Week 2 and backup Jacky Lee broke his ankle the next week. Livingston was the next man up and led the Chiefs to five straight victories before Dawson returned in the second half of the year. In fact, Mike went 6–0 as a starter in that Super Bowl season for Kansas City and won his next four starts spread out over three more seasons before finally losing a start to Cincinnati in October 1972. After that 10–0 start, though, Livingston won just 21 of the remaining 65 starts in his 12-year career.

Looking closer at Livingston's undefeated 1969 season, we see that the five teams he faced finished 22–43–5 that year. Not one of the teams posted a winning season. Moreover, the Chiefs averaged 174 yards on the ground during those games, and Mike threw just four touchdown passes and five interceptions in support of that running game. Dawson faced the good teams in the league—the Raiders, Chargers, and Jets—otherwise the Chiefs may not have even reached the playoffs.

As Dawson started to fade in 1973, Livingston stepped in more often, starting half the games from 1973 through 1975. With Len's retirement, Livingston became the full-time starter for three losing seasons. Coach Paul Wiggin remarked that Mike was more of a "street fighter" than a "finesse player." Translated, that means he was not an accurate passer and was a born backup.

Lanky Neil Lomax was a streaky quarterback who went to two Pro Bowls and was elected to the College Football Hall of Fame.

Neil Lomax

QPR **8.0**

Height: 6'3" **Weight:** 215 lbs. **Birthdate:** 2/17/1959
College: Portland State **Draft:** St. Louis Cardinals 1981-2nd
1981–88 St. Louis/Arizona Cardinals
Regular Season Record: 47–52–2, 14 comebacks
Postseason Record: 0–1, no comebacks
Relative Rating: 111%

Passing

Year	G	Comp./Att.	%	Yards	Y/Att.	TD	INT	Rating
1981	14	119/236	50.4	1,575	6.7	4	10	59.9
1982	9	109/205	53.2	1,367	6.7	5	6	70.1
1983	13	209/354	59.0	2,636	7.4	24	11	92.0
1984	16	345/560	61.6	4,614	8.2	28	16	92.5
1985	16	265/471	56.3	3,214	6.8	18	12	79.5
1986	14	240/421	57.0	2,583	6.1	13	12	73.6
1987	12	275/463	59.4	3,387	7.3	24	12	88.5
1988	14	255/443	57.6	3,395	7.7	20	11	86.7
Total	108	1,817/3,153	57.6	22,771	7.2	136	90	82.7
PS:	1	32/51	62.7	385	7.5	2	2	82.6

Rushing

Year	Att.	Yards	Avg.	TD
1981	19	104	5.5	2
1982	28	119	4.3	1
1983	27	127	4.7	2
1984	35	184	5.3	3
1985	32	125	3.9	0
1986	35	148	4.2	1
1987	29	107	3.7	0
1988	17	55	3.2	1
Total	222	969	4.4	10
PS:	4	9	2.3	0

Neil Lomax went from fifth string to starter as a freshman at Portland State where he followed June Jones as the Vikings' quarterback in Mouse Davis' original run-and-shoot offense. Lomax threw 106 touchdowns in four years there, including a record seven in one quarter of one game. With that aerial record, Neil followed Jones into the pros when Lomax was drafted by the Cardinals.

By midseason of his rookie year, Lomax had replaced local legend Jim Hart as the team's starting quarterback, and Hart did not take that well, making for a tense relationship. Neil was a good-sized quarterback with an accurate arm, and Cardinals scout Harry Gilmer praised his field vision. He was very good at scrambling despite foot and hip problems but still took a lot of sacks—61 in 1985—and those hits took a toll. By 1984 when he threw for more than 4,600 yards and 28 touchdowns, he was being compared to Dan Marino as a passer. Lomax could not maintain that level, though. He had problems with consistency and with handling blitzes, but his biggest problem turned out to be degenerative arthritis in his hip

that forced him to sit out the 1989 season and to retire officially in 1990. When he was in college, he told *Sports Illustrated*, "You know, football is such a stupid game if you think about it, but it's all such a challenge—the miserable conditions, the defense knowing we're going to pass—I can't help it. I really enjoy playing it." His playing days were over at the age of 29. The next year, he underwent hip replacement surgery.

Chuck Long

Height: 6'4" **Weight:** 217 lbs. **Birthdate:** 2/18/1963
College: Iowa **Draft:** Detroit Lions 1986-1st
1986–89, 1991 Detroit Lions; 1990 Los Angeles Rams
Regular Season Record: 4–17, 1 comeback
Postseason Record: NA
Relative Rating: 86%

Passing

Year	G	Comp./Att.	%	Yards	Y/Att.	TD	INT	Rating
1986	3	21/40	52.5	247	6.2	2	2	67.4
1987	12	232/416	55.8	2,598	6.2	11	20	63.4
1988	7	75/141	53.2	856	6.1	6	6	68.2
1989	1	2/5	40.0	42	8.4	0	0	70.4
1990	4	1/5	20.0	4	0.8	0	0	39.6
1991	0	0/0	0.0	0	0.0	0	0	0.0
Total	27	331/607	54.5	3,747	6.2	19	28	64.5

Rushing

Year	Att.	Yards	Avg.	TD
1986	2	0	0.0	0
1987	22	64	2.9	0
1988	7	22	3.1	0
1989	3	2	0.7	0
Total	34	88	2.6	0

At Iowa, the 6'4" Chuck Long won the Davey O'Brien Award and the Maxwell Club Award and finished second to Bo Jackson for the Heisman Trophy. Drafted by Detroit, the dead-end street for pro quarterbacks, in the first round of the 1986 draft, Chuck started his NFL career with a 37-yard touchdown to Leonard Thompson on his first professional pass. It was all downhill from there.

Chuck won the starting job in 1987 but threw 20 interceptions to just 11 touchdowns and won just three of 12 starts. The following season, he injured his knee in the sixth game of the year and started only one more game as a pro. In fact, once Wayne Fontes took over as the permanent coach in 1989 and installed the run-and-shoot offense, Long would throw just 10 more passes in his career. A few years back, Long said of his pro years, "I went to a team that wasn't focused on winning. I learned a lot from it. I've taken a lot into my coaching from what I learned there. It was rough, physically rough. I started to get dinged up quite a bit." Long was immobile and never displayed the accuracy that made him the Big Ten's all-time completion percentage leader at 65 percent. The scary thing for Lions fans is that the second most accurate Big Ten passer is Drew Stanton, who can't get on the field in Detroit and who also completed his first NFL pass attempt for a touchdown. Long has been successful as an assistant coach in the college ranks but was fired from his first head coaching position at San Diego State in 2008.

J.P. Losman

QPR 4.5

Height: 6'2"   **Weight:** 217 lbs.   **Birthdate:** 3/12/1981
College: Tulane   **Draft:** Buffalo Bills 2004-1st
2004–08 Buffalo Bills
Regular Season Record: 10–23, 6 comebacks
Postseason Record: NA
Relative Rating: 94%

Passing

Year	G	Comp./Att.	%	Yards	Y/Att.	TD	INT	Rating
2004	4	3/5	60.0	32	6.4	0	1	39.2
2005	9	113/228	49.6	1,340	5.9	8	8	64.9
2006	16	268/429	62.5	3,051	7.1	19	14	84.9
2007	8	111/175	63.4	1,204	6.9	4	6	76.9
2008	5	63/104	60.6	584	5.6	2	5	62.3
Total	42	558/941	59.3	6,211	6.6	33	34	75.6

Rushing

Year	Att.	Yards	Avg.	TD
2004	2	15	7.5	0
2005	31	154	5.0	0
2006	38	140	3.7	1
2007	20	110	5.5	0
2008	12	70	5.8	2
Total	103	489	4.7	3

TOP 10
Quarterback Nicknames

10. Lenny "the Cool" Dawson
9. Dandy Don Meredith
8. Randall Cunningham, the Ultimate Weapon
7. Steve "Air" McNair
6. Billy "Whiskey" Kilmer
5. Slingin' Sammy Baugh
4. Roger "the Dodger" Staubach (also the original Captain Comeback)
3. Automatic Otto Graham
2. Daryle "the Mad Bomber" Lamonica
1. Broadway Joe Namath

J.P. Losman transferred from UCLA to Tulane as an undergraduate and backed up Patrick Ramsey for two years before taking charge of the Green Wave. Losman was the fourth quarterback selected in the first round of the 2004 draft and has been much less successful than Eli Manning, Philip Rivers, and Ben Roethlisberger.

In his first training camp, Losman broke a bone in his leg and appeared in only four games as a rookie. In his second year, he won just one of eight starts and was beaten out by journeyman Kelly Holcomb. J.P. started to show some progress in his third season but regressed in 2007 and was replaced by rookie Trent Edwards. Losman was unable to win back the starting job, so he complained about the team's lack of support and for two seasons asked to be traded. For Bills fans, Losman has been the second coming of the whiny Rob Johnson. Losman has a strong arm and throws a nice deep pass but is not reliably accurate. He is indecisive, too quick to opt for running from the pocket, takes a lot of sacks, and has fumbled 34 times in 42 games. He will try to resurrect his career elsewhere in 2009.

Ray Lucas

QPR **3.0**

Height: 6'3" **Weight:** 214 lbs. **Birthdate:** 8/6/1972
College: Rutgers **Draft:** Free agent
1996 New England Patriots; 1997–2000 New York Jets; 2001–02 Miami Dolphins
Regular Season Record: 8-7, 3
Postseason Record: NA
Relative Rating: 95%

Passing

Year	G	Comp./Att.	%	Yards	Y/Att.	TD	INT	Rating
1996	2	0/0	0.0	0	0.0	0	0	0.0
1997	5	3/4	75.0	28	7.0	0	1	54.2
1998	15	1/3	33.3	27	9.0	0	0	67.4
1999	9	161/272	59.2	1,678	6.2	14	6	85.1
2000	7	21/41	51.2	206	5.0	0	4	26.1
2001	10	2/3	66.7	45	15.0	0	0	109.7
2002	7	92/160	57.5	1,045	6.5	4	6	69.9
Total	55	280/483	58.0	3,029	6.3	18	17	74.3

Rushing

Year	Att.	Yards	Avg.	TD
1997	6	55	9.2	0
1998	5	23	4.6	0
1999	41	144	3.5	1
2000	6	42	7.0	0
2001	8	6	0.8	1
2002	36	126	3.5	2
Total	102	396	3.9	4

Rutgers' own Ray Lucas was one of Parcells' Guys, one of those players that coach Bill Parcells would bring with him from coaching stop to coaching stop. Lucas made the Patriots as a free agent in 1996 and then followed Parcells to the Jets the next season where he threw seven passes and ran with the ball 11 times in his first two seasons. When Vinny Testaverde tore his Achilles tendon in the 1999 season opener and Rick Mirer flopped as the new starter, Lucas got his chance at midseason and led the Jets to six wins in eight games to salvage an 8–8 record for the year. Lucas was nothing but a game manager with a weak arm and good running ability, though, and the Jets drafted Chad Pennington the next year while new coach Al Groh proclaimed that he still loved Ray's heart and moxie.

TOP 10
Lopsided Quarterback Trades

10. The Houston Oilers traded the rights to Joe Namath to the Jets for the rights to Jerry Rhome in 1965.
9. The Eagles traded Sonny Jurgensen to the Redskins for interception-prone Norm Snead in 1964.
8. The Packers gave up two first-round picks, two second-round picks, and a third-round pick to obtain the washed up John Hadl from the Rams in 1974.
7. The 49ers gave up three first-round picks, a second-round pick, and Tom Owen to obtain Jim Plunkett from the Patriots in 1976.
6. Pittsburgh traded the rights to Bobby Layne to the Bears for tailback Ray Evans in 1948.
5. Pittsburgh traded the rights to Sid Luckman to the Bears for end Ed Manske in 1939.
4. Buffalo traded Daryle Lamonica and Glenn Bass to Oakland for Tom Flores and Art Powell in 1967.
3. The 49ers sent Y.A. Tittle to the Giants for lineman Lou Cordileone in 1961.
2. The Bucs traded Steve Young to the 49ers for second- and fourth-round picks in 1987.
1. The Colts traded John Elway to Denver for Chris Hinton, Mark Herrmann, and a first-round pick in 1983.

In 2000, Lucas signed as a free agent with the Dolphins to back up Jay Fiedler. He got another chance to start when Fiedler was hurt in 2001, but his first start was a disaster. Ray completed just 13 of 33 passes, fumbled twice and threw four interceptions, including three to Buffalo's Nate Clements. It was so ugly that a Miami broadcaster wondered aloud whether Fiedler could come back in and throw left-handed. Lucas caught on briefly as a third quarterback for the Ravens but never appeared in another game. He now works as a sports analyst in New York.

Sid Luckman

Height: 6'0" **Weight:** 190 lbs. **Birthdate:** 11/21/1916
College: Columbia **Draft:** Chicago Bears 1939-1st
1939–50 Chicago Bears
Regular Season Record: 73–22–2 est., 10 comebacks
Postseason Record: 5–1, 1 comeback
Relative Rating: 158%

Sid Luckman's Signature Play: Midway through the fourth quarter of the 1946 NFL championship, the Bears and Giants were tied at 14. Luckman led the Bears on a 66-yard march that culminated in a surprise 19-yard bootleg touchdown run by the quarterback for the winning score.

Passing

Year	G	Comp./Att.	%	Yards	Y/Att.	TD	INT	Rating
1939	11	23/51	45.1	636	12.5	5	4	91.6
1940	11	48/105	45.7	941	9.0	4	9	54.5
1941	11	68/119	57.1	1,181	9.9	9	6	95.3
1942	11	57/105	54.3	1,024	9.8	10	13	80.1
1943	10	110/202	54.5	2,194	10.9	28	12	107.5
1944	7	71/143	49.7	1,018	7.1	11	12	63.8
1945	10	117/217	53.9	1,727	8.0	14	10	82.5
1946	11	110/229	48.0	1,826	8.0	17	16	71.0
1947	12	176/323	54.5	2,712	8.4	24	31	67.7
1948	12	89/163	54.6	1,047	6.4	13	14	65.1
1949	11	22/50	44.0	200	4.0	1	3	37.1
1950	11	13/37	35.1	180	4.9	1	2	38.1
Total	128	904/1,744	51.8	14,686	8.4	137	132	75.2
PS:	6	44/88	51.2	742	8.6	7	4	88.4

Rushing

Year	Att.	Yards	Avg.	TD
1939	24	42	1.8	0
1940	23	-65	-2.8	0
1941	18	18	1.0	1
1942	13	-6	-0.5	0
1943	22	-40	-1.8	1
1944	20	-96	-4.8	1
1945	36	-118	-3.3	0
1946	25	-76	-3.0	0
1947	10	86	8.6	1
1948	8	11	1.4	0
1949	3	4	1.3	0
1950	2	1	0.5	0
Total	204	-239	-1.2	4
PS:	14	61	4.4	2

The Bears had been running the T formation since their inception in 1919, but Sid Luckman was the first quarterback in the modernized version of the offense that Clark Shaughnessy polished up in 1939 and that is still the basis of the pro set 70 years later. George Halas handpicked the Columbia triple-threat single-wing tailback to unleash the full firepower of the modern T and traded end Eggs Manske to the Steelers to select Luckman with the second pick in the 1939 draft.

Luckman had no plans to play pro football at the time, but Halas signed Sid and turned him over to former Bear quarterback Carl Brumbaugh for intensive tutoring in quarterback footwork, ball handling, faking, and setting up. Even with the intensive study, Luckman was fumbling and stumbling so badly at the start that he began his rookie season as the Bears' left halfback. It was not till midseason that Sid began to take turns at quarterback, and he became the starter the next season when the Bears won their division. That 1940 championship game was the real coming-out

Sid Luckman in the Clutch: On December 26, 1943, before he left the Bears to join the Merchant Marines, Luckman threw five touchdown passes in leading Chicago over the Redskins for the NFL title. He ran eight times for 64 yards and completed 15 of 26 passes for 286 yards.

Sid Luckman was a two-way player who intercepted 17 passes on defense and returned punts and kickoffs on occasion.

Sid Luckman's Five Highest Honors

5. Member of the College Football Hall of Fame
4. Selected to three All-Star Games
3. Eight-time All-Pro and five-time consensus All-Pro
2. 1943 Player of the Year
1. Elected to the Pro Football Hall of Fame in 1965

The Five Quarterbacks Most Similar to Sid Luckman

5. Daryle Lamonica
4. Tom Brady
3. Bart Starr
2. Troy Aikman
1. Otto Graham

Sid Luckman's Five Top Touchdown Targets

5. Harry Clarke, 9 TDs
4. George Wilson, 13 TDs
3. Jim Keane, 14 TDs
2. Ray McLean, 14 TDs
1. Ken Kavanaugh, 29 TDs

Sid Luckman's Five Toughest Rivals

5. Luckman was 4–2 against the Giants in the regular season and 2–0 in the playoffs.
4. Luckman was 5–3 against the Redskins in the regular season and 2–1 in the playoffs.
3. Luckman was 14–4 against the Lions.
2. Luckman was 9–3 against the Cardinals.
1. Luckman was 14–4–1 against the Packers in the regular season and 1–0 in the playoffs.

Five Random Sid Luckman Statistics

5. Luckman played for three head coaches.
4. Luckman's Bears outscored the league average by 51 percent.
3. Luckman threw five touchdowns in the 1943 NFL championship against Washington and threw for seven against the Giants on November 14, 1943.
2. Luckman threw for more than 300 yards three times and over 400 the same day he tossed seven touchdowns.
1. Luckman led the league in yards three times, touchdown passes three times, yards per attempt three times, passer rating twice, and interceptions once.

party for the modern T and for Luckman as the Bears trampled the Redskins 73–0, although Sid threw just six passes all day with Chicago rushing for 381 yards. In fact, Luckman never had to throw the ball that much, but the Bears' running game set up a very effective passing attack. Luckman led the league in passing yards, yards per pass, and touchdown passes three times each.

Sid was known as a master technician, a brilliant play caller, and the undisputed leader of the team. He had a soft touch on his passes and could throw both long and short equally well. Behind Luckman, the Bears outscored their opponents by 22 points per game in 1941 and 26 points per game in 1942. During his playing days, the Bears' explosive offense outscored the league points-scored average by 51 percent. In 1943, Sid enlisted in the Merchant Marines but also found time to throw for 443 yards and seven touchdowns on Sid Luckman Day against the Giants on November 14. That year, he threw 28 touchdown passes in just 10 games, the equivalent of 45 touchdowns in today's 16-game season. Not bad for a year in which he threw just 20 passes per game.

Of most importance, Luckman was a winner who led the Bears to five championship games and won four of them. Although his career passing totals are not that impressive in contemporary terms, he still holds many team career marks because the Bears have never been able to adequately replace Luckman at quarterback. In fact, he set the standard for all T-formation quarterbacks to follow.

In the landmark 1940 championship game won by the Bears 73–0 over the Redskins, Sid Luckman completed three of four passes for 88 yards and one touchdown. He also contributed one yard to the Bears' rushing total of 381.

Johnny Lujack

QPR 6.0

Height: 6'0" **Weight:** 186 lbs. **Birthdate:** 1/4/1925
College: Notre Dame **Draft:** Chicago Bears 1947-1st
1948–51 Chicago Bears
Regular Season Record: 22–9, 1 comeback
Postseason Record: 0–1, no comebacks
Relative Rating: 118%

Passing

Year	G	Comp./Att.	%	Yards	Y/Att.	TD	INT	Rating
1948	9	36/66	54.5	611	9.3	6	3	97.5
1949	12	162/312	51.9	2,658	8.5	23	22	76.0
1950	12	121/254	47.6	1,731	6.8	4	21	41.0
1951	12	85/176	48.3	1,295	7.4	8	8	69.2
Total	45	404/808	50.0	6,295	7.8	41	54	65.3
PS:	1	15/29	51.7	193	6.7	0	3	33.3

Rushing

Year	Att.	Yards	Avg.	TD
1948	15	110	7.3	1
1949	8	64	8.0	2
1950	63	397	6.3	11
1951	47	171	3.6	7
Total	133	742	5.6	21
PS:	3	2	0.7	0

Nearly 60 years after his retirement in 1950, Sid Luckman is still the Bears' leader in passing yards, yards per attempt, and touchdowns despite playing in a time when passing was much less emphasized. Even though they employed the first modern T-formation quarterback in Luckman, the Bears have had a sorry history of signal-callers. Unfortunately, the best Bears quarterback since Luckman was his immediate successor, Johnny Lujack, but Lujack's career was cut short by injuries and he is little remembered today.

Lujack was the Heisman Trophy–winning quarterback of Frank Leahy's national champion Fighting Irish when he was drafted by the Bears. Both Lujack and Bobby Layne joined the team as rookies in 1948, but George Halas decided he could afford to pay only one of his expensive, talented understudies to Luckman. In 1949, Halas traded Layne to the New York Bulldogs, and Lujack earned the starting job. Johnny led the NFL that year in passes, completions, yards, and touchdown passes.

He also set a league record by passing for 468 yards in one game that year against the Cardinals, the same game in which he threw for six touchdowns. In addition, the mobile Lujack was an excellent runner, an able kicker who led the team in scoring four straight seasons, and a star defensive back who intercepted eight passes in his rookie year. His defensive play proved to be his downfall, though, when he hurt his shoulder making a tackle in 1950, and his touchdown passes fell from 23 to four. Johnny still ran for nearly 400 yards and scored 11 touchdowns on the ground and was named to the Pro Bowl. Lujack saw his playing time diminish in 1951 but was named to another Pro Bowl. He and George Halas, though, had an acrimonious relationship over salary issues. Johnny left the NFL at the end of the season with a weakened shoulder and bad knees. In his one healthy season, Lujack showed himself a worthy heir to Luckman, not only as a tremendous passer, but also as a better runner and defender than Sid. As with the Bengals' Greg Cook 20 years later, football fans were left wondering, "What if…?"

Tommy Maddox

QPR 5.5

Height: 6'4" **Weight:** 220 lbs. **Birthdate:** 9/2/1971
College: UCLA **Draft:** Denver 1992-1st
1992–93 Denver Broncos; 1994 Los Angeles Rams;
1995 New York Giants; 2000 Arena Football; 2001
XFL; 2001–2005 Pittsburgh Steelers
Regular Season Record: 15–20–1, 4 comebacks
Postseason Record: 1–1, 1 comeback
Relative Rating: 92%

Passing

Year	G	Comp./Att.	%	Yards	Y/Att.	TD	INT	Rating
1992	13	66/121	54.5	757	6.3	5	9	56.4
1993	16	1/1	100.0	1	1.0	1	0	118.7
1994	5	10/19	52.6	141	7.4	0	2	37.3
1995	16	6/23	26.1	49	2.1	0	3	0.0
2001	3	7/9	77.8	154	17.1	1	1	116.2
2002	15	234/377	62.1	2,836	7.5	20	16	85.2
2003	16	298/519	57.4	3,414	6.6	18	17	75.3
2004	4	30/60	50.0	329	5.5	1	2	58.3
2005	5	34/71	47.9	406	5.7	2	4	51.7
Total	93	686/1,200	57.2	8,087	6.7	48	54	72.4
PS:	3	54/96	56.3	667	6.9	5	3	82.2

Rushing

Year	Att.	Yards	Avg.	TD
1992	9	20	2.2	0
1993	2	-2	-1.0	0
1994	1	1	1.0	0
1995	1	4	4.0	0
2001	6	9	1.5	1
2002	19	43	2.3	0
2003	13	12	0.9	0
2004	9	15	1.7	0
2005	8	26	3.3	0
Total	68	128	1.9	1
PS:	3	8	2.7	0

Tommy Maddox was the ultimate Comeback Player of the Year in 2002, having gone 10 years between NFL starts while drifting into arena football and then the execrable XFL, which was sponsored by Vince McMahon's wrestling organization. Maddox was once a highly regarded UCLA quarterback who made the bad decision to enter the NFL draft after his sophomore season. Drafted in 1992 by Dan Reeves for the Broncos as insurance against his personal problems with John Elway, Maddox became just one more cause of friction between the two men.

Maddox started and lost four games as a rookie while sometimes alternating plays with fellow rookie Shawn Moore in Reeves' final year as coach. After Tommy's first start, Raiders defensive end Howie Long joked that the boyish Maddox resembled his paperboy. Tommy got to throw just one pass in his second year before being traded to the Rams in 1994 for a draft pick. Maddox appeared in just five games for Los Angeles before signing with the Giants, coached by Dan Reeves in 1995. Tommy looked completely overmatched in the few opportunities he got to play that year and was cut. When Reeves moved on to the Falcons in 1997, though, he brought Maddox to training camp again but cut him in the preseason. "Tommy Gun" became an insurance salesman until a stint in the Arena Football League a few years later led to the XFL, where Maddox was the league's MVP. That earned him a contract with the Steelers in 2001.

Maddox took over for a struggling Kordell Stewart in Week 3 of 2002, and Pittsburgh began to win. Tommy was left temporarily paralyzed after an awkward tackle in Tennessee in midseason but missed just two games and came back to lead the Steelers to the playoffs. In 2003, though, Maddox and the team came back to earth. Maddox was a pocket quarterback with a quick release but still made bad decisions trying to force passes and always had trouble with ball security. When he got hurt early in 2004, rookie Ben Roethlisberger took over and the fairy tale ended. Maddox was demoted to third string in 2005 and was out of football for good in 2006.

Don Majkowski

QPR **5.0**

Height: 6'2"   **Weight:** 197 lbs.   **Birthdate:** 2/25/1964
College: Virginia   **Draft:** Green Bay 1987-10th
1987-92 Green Bay Packers; 1993-94 Indianapolis Colts; 1995-96 Detroit Lions
Regular Season Record: 26-30-1, 13 comebacks
Postseason Record: 0-0, no comebacks
Relative Rating: 95%

Passing

Year	G	Comp./Att.	%	Yards	Y/Att.	TD	INT	Rating
1987	7	55/127	43.3	875	6.9	5	3	70.2
1988	13	178/336	53.0	2,119	6.3	9	11	67.8
1989	16	353/599	58.9	4,318	7.2	27	20	82.3
1990	9	150/264	56.8	1,925	7.3	10	12	73.5
1991	9	115/226	50.9	1,362	6.0	3	8	59.3
1992	14	38/55	69.1	271	4.9	2	2	77.2
1993	3	13/24	54.2	105	4.4	0	1	48.1
1994	9	84/152	55.3	1,010	6.6	6	7	69.8
1995	8	15/20	75.0	161	8.1	1	0	114.8
1996	5	55/102	53.9	554	5.4	3	3	67.2
Total	93	1,056/1,905	55.4	12,700	6.7	66	67	72.9
PS:	1	14/23	60.9	206	9.0	3	2	93.5

Rushing

Year	Att.	Yards	Avg.	TD
1987	15	127	8.5	0
1988	47	225	4.8	1
1989	75	358	4.8	5
1990	29	186	6.4	1
1991	25	108	4.3	2
1992	8	33	4.1	0
1993	2	4	2.0	0
1994	24	34	1.4	3
1995	9	1	0.1	0
1996	14	38	2.7	0
Total	248	1,114	4.5	12
PS:	3	16	5.3	0

Don Majkowski is football's Wally Pipp, a pretty good player who got hurt and watched his replacement not miss a game for the next decade and a half on the way to the Hall of Fame. Pipp's replacement was Lou Gehrig; Majkowski's was Brett Favre.

Majkowski separated his shoulder in his senior year at the University of Virginia and slipped off most teams' radar, but the Packers picked him in the 10th round of the 1987 draft. Don developed slowly in his first two seasons as he underwent more shoulder rehabilitation work, but in 1989, the Majik Man emerged for the one great season of his 10-year NFL career. He led the league in passing yards with 4,318 and led the team to a 10–6 record with 27 touchdown passes. Don achieved seven of those 10 victories by leading a furious fourth-quarter comeback, and the Packers just missed the playoffs that season. The most controversial comeback came against the Bears when Majkowski threw a fourth-down 14-yard touchdown pass to Sterling Sharpe with 32 seconds left to pull out a 14–13 win. Majkowski was flagged for being past the line of scrimmage when he unleashed the pass, but after a review the call was overturned and ruled a touchdown. The Bears were so disgusted that they listed the game with an asterisk in their media guide for years.

Majkowski made the Pro Bowl in 1989 and sat out the opening game of the next season in a contract holdout before coming back with quite a bit of rust. In the 10th game, Don was sacked hard on his shoulder and required rotator cuff surgery. He hadn't had a very strong arm to start with but returned in 1991 with diminished arm strength. Then he injured a hamstring and missed half the season. Majkowski still won the starting job under new coach Mike Holmgren in 1992, but Favre got his chance when Don went down with an ankle injury in the third game of the year. Majkowski moved on as a backup in Indianapolis in 1993 and then to Detroit in 1995. Although Don had very nimble feet and was a creative playmaker on the run, injuries short-circuited his career. After the 1996 season, the Majik Man was released and drifted out of football, although he still works as a football analyst in Wisconsin, where he maintains his popularity.

Ray Mallouf

QPR 5.5

Height: 5'11" **Weight:** 180 lbs. **Birthdate:** 7/11/1918
College: Southern Methodist **Draft:** Chicago Cardinals 1941-10th
1941, 1946–48 Chicago Cardinals;
1949 New York Giants
Regular Season Record: 7–4–1 est., no comebacks
Postseason Record: 0–1, no comebacks
Relative Rating: 143%

Passing

Year	G	Comp./Att.	%	Yards	Y/Att.	TD	INT	Rating
1941	9	48/96	50.0	725	7.6	2	4	64.8
1946	5	14/34	41.2	260	7.6	4	2	83.0
1947	11	21/36	58.3	340	9.4	1	2	76.2
1948	12	73/143	51.0	1,160	8.1	13	6	91.2
1949	11	3/16	18.8	19	1.2	0	2	0.0
Total	48	159/325	48.9	2,504	7.7	20	16	75.0
PS:	1	3/7	42.9	35	5.0	0	0	58.6

Rushing

Year	Att.	Yards	Avg.	TD
1941	43	104	2.4	0
1946	4	6	1.5	0
1947	5	13	2.6	0
1948	13	17	1.3	1
1949	1	-1	-1.0	0
Total	66	139	2.1	1
PS:	2	5	2.5	0

Ray Mallouf was an effective backup quarterback for the Cardinals in their glory days of the late 1940s when he was known as the Slingin' Syrian. After Pitchin' Paul Christman broke his wrist in October 1948, Mallouf took charge of the defending champions and helped lead them back to the title game. That month, he threw four touchdown passes in a 63–35 win over the Giants and three touchdowns the following week in a 49–27 victory over the Boston Yanks. Christman returned in November and shared the job with Mallouf the rest of the season. Ray still started at quarterback in the 1948 title game played in a blizzard in Philadelphia, but his fumbled handoff to Elmer Angsman at the Cardinal 17 led to the only score of the game as the Eagles won 7–0. Mallouf was traded to the Giants in the off-season and spent one year as Charlie Conerly's backup before retiring so he could return to his Dallas home.

Mark Malone

QPR 5.0

Height: 6'4" **Weight:** 223 lbs. **Birthdate:** 11/22/1958
College: Arizona State **Draft:** Pittsburgh 1980-1st
1980–81, 1983–87 Pittsburgh Steelers; 1988 San Diego Chargers; 1989 New York Jets
Regular Season Record: 23-30, 7 comebacks
Postseason Record: 1–1, 1 comeback
Relative Rating: 83%

Passing

Year	G	Comp./Att.	%	Yards	Y/Att.	TD	INT	Rating
1980	1	0/0	0.0	0	0.0	0	0	0.0
1981	8	45/88	51.1	553	6.3	3	5	58.6
1983	2	9/20	45.0	124	6.2	1	2	42.5
1984	13	147/272	54.0	2,137	7.9	16	17	73.4
1985	10	117/233	50.2	1,428	6.1	13	7	75.5
1986	14	216/425	50.8	2,444	5.8	15	18	62.5
1987	12	156/336	46.4	1,896	5.6	6	19	46.7
1988	12	147/272	54.0	1,580	5.8	6	13	58.8
1989	1	2/2	100.0	13	6.5	0	0	93.7
Total	73	839/1,648	50.9	10,175	6.2	60	81	61.9
PS:	3	40/71	56.3	558	7.9	4	3	83.0

Rushing

Year	Att.	Yards	Avg.	TD
1981	16	68	4.3	2
1984	25	42	1.7	3
1985	15	80	5.3	1
1986	31	107	3.5	5
1987	34	162	4.8	3
1988	37	169	4.6	4
1989	1	0	0.0	0
Total	159	628	3.9	18
PS:	5	-6	-1.2	0

Mark Malone once trained as a decathlete and was a better football player than quarterback. His biggest highlight in the NFL was catching a 90-yard touchdown pass from Terry Bradshaw in a 1981 game in which he started at wide receiver. It was the longest reception in Steeler history and foreshadowed the multiple skills of Kordell "Slash" Stewart in Pittsburgh. Also like Stewart, though, Malone was not so popular after he became the team's starting quarterback.

Malone injured his knee later that year and played the remainder of his career wearing a bulky knee brace that cut down on his effectiveness. With Bradshaw's injuries and his eventual retirement, Malone spent most of the decade competing for the starting quarterback position in Pittsburgh against Cliff Stoudt, David Woodley, and Bubby Brister. None of the four made anyone forget Bradshaw, and Terry didn't make it any easier for Malone when he told Sam Toperoff in *Lost Sundays*, "Mark's got good enough skills, but he can't carry a football team. Let's just say that he's not my kind of quarterback. And the fans here don't like his style."

Malone relied a lot on short passes but still was not very accurate and threw too many interceptions. In the 1987 strike season, Mark started all 12 non-strike games and threw just six touchdown passes, while replacement quarterbacks Steve Bono and Reggie Collier combined to throw for seven scores in just three games. Malone's high-water mark in Pittsburgh was leading a fourth-quarter comeback over John Elway's Broncos in the 1984 playoffs that took the Steelers to the AFC Championship Game against Dan Marino's Dolphins. In the title game, Malone threw for 300 yards for the first time in his career but also threw three interceptions, and Pittsburgh lost by 17 points. After retiring, the photogenic Malone went into sports broadcasting.

Archie Manning

QPR **6.5**

Height: 6'3" **Weight:** 212 lbs. **Birthdate:** 5/19/1949
College: Mississippi **Draft:** New Orleans 1971-1st
1971–75, 1977–82 New Orleans Saints; 1982–83
Houston Oilers; 1983–84 Minnesota Vikings
Regular Season Record: 35–101–3, 12 comebacks
Postseason Record: NA
Relative Rating: 97%

Passing

Year	G	Comp./Att.	%	Yards	Y/Att.	TD	INT	Rating
1971	12	86/177	48.6	1,164	6.6	6	9	60.1
1972	14	230/448	51.3	2,781	6.2	18	21	64.6
1973	13	140/267	52.4	1,642	6.1	10	12	65.2
1974	11	134/261	51.3	1,429	5.5	6	16	49.8
1975	13	159/338	47.0	1,683	5.0	7	20	44.3
1977	10	113/205	55.1	1,284	6.3	8	9	68.8
1978	16	291/471	61.8	3,416	7.3	17	16	81.7
1979	16	252/420	60.0	3,169	7.5	15	20	75.6
1980	16	309/509	60.7	3,716	7.3	23	20	81.8
1981	12	134/232	57.8	1,447	6.2	5	11	63.6
1982	7	67/132	50.8	880	6.7	6	8	62.1
1983	5	44/88	50.0	755	8.6	2	8	49.2
1984	6	52/94	55.3	545	5.8	2	3	66.1
Total	151	2,011/3,642	55.2	23,911	6.6	125	173	67.1

Rushing

Year	Att.	Yards	Avg.	TD
1971	33	172	5.2	4
1972	63	351	5.6	2
1973	63	293	4.7	2
1974	28	204	7.3	1
1975	33	186	5.6	1
1977	39	270	6.9	5
1978	38	202	5.3	1
1979	35	186	5.3	2
1980	23	166	7.2	0
1981	2	28	14.0	0
1982	13	85	6.5	0
1983	3	12	4.0	0
1984	11	42	3.8	0
Total	384	2,197	5.7	18

Archie Manning is still revered in Mississippi as the greatest of all Rebel players. Not only did the university retire his jersey, No. 18, but it also established 18 as the speed limit on campus in his honor. Despite boasting a strong arm and elusive

TOP 10

Worst Quarterback Winning Percentages (minimum 100 games)

10. Vinny Testaverde, 90–123–1, .423
9. Lynn Dickey, 45–63–3, .419
8. Jim Everett, 64–89, .418
7. Jim Zorn, 44–62, .415
6. Jon Kitna, 46–69, .400
5. Jeff Blake, 39–61, .390
4. Steve DeBerg, 53–86–1, .382
3. Jeff George, 46–78, .371
2. Norm Snead, 52–99–7, .351
1. Archie Manning, 35–101–3, .263

running skills, though, Manning never achieved similar success as a pro.

Archie had the misfortune of being the top draft pick of the New Orleans Saints in the days when the team was so bad that fans attended games with bags over their heads and referred to the squad as the "Ain'ts." In terms of winning percentage, Archie Manning is the losingest quarterback in NFL history, whether the minimum is 50, 75, or 100 starts. He never played for a winning team in 13 years spent in New Orleans, Houston, and Minnesota. In fact, Manning won the NFC Player of the Year Award in 1978 by leading the Saints to a 7–9 record. Archie's biggest highlight in all those years came in his very first game when he led a fourth-quarter comeback to beat the Rams on a touchdown run on the final play of the game in September 1971.

Manning's playing style was similar to that of Steve Young, but unlike Young, Archie never was traded to a championship club with a world-class quarterback coach to fine-tune his skills. Instead, Manning languished with losing teams under 10 different coaches, throwing way too many interceptions in the Big Easy. Off the field, though, he hit it big. Archie married the homecoming queen at Ole Miss and the two had three sons, two of whom became championship quarterbacks in the NFL. Archie's pro career was so dismal that it wasn't until 2008 and a combined 16 seasons for the two Manning sons, Peyton and Eli, that the first family of football achieved a cumulative winning record in games the three quarterbacks started.

Eli Manning

QPR 8.0

Height: 6'4" **Weight:** 218 lbs. **Birthdate:** 1/3/1981
College: Mississippi **Draft:** San Diego 2004-1st
2004–08 New York Giants
Regular Season Record: 42–29, 11 comebacks
Postseason Record: 4–3, 3 comebacks
Relative Rating: 95%

Passing

Year	G	Comp./Att.	%	Yards	Y/Att.	TD	INT	Rating
2004	9	95/197	48.2	1,043	5.3	6	9	55.4
2005	16	294/557	52.8	3,762	6.8	24	17	75.9
2006	16	301/522	57.7	3,244	6.2	24	18	77.0
2007	16	297/529	56.1	3,336	6.3	23	20	73.9
2008	16	289/479	60.3	3,238	6.8	21	10	86.4
Total	73	1,276/2,284	55.9	14,623	6.4	98	74	76.1
PS:	7	113/193	58.5	1,297	6.7	8	7	77.6

Rushing

Year	Att.	Yards	Avg.	TD
2004	6	35	5.8	0
2005	29	80	2.8	1
2006	25	21	0.8	0
2007	29	69	2.4	1
2008	20	10	0.5	1
Total	109	215	2.0	3
PS:	28	160	5.7	1

Steve Sabol of NFL Films called the scrambling Eli Manning pass that David Tyree pinned to the top of his helmet while being decked by aggressive Patriot safety Rodney Harrison the "greatest play in Super Bowl history." That play not only extended the Giants' game-winning drive in a gigantic Super Bowl upset, it also silenced all critics of Eli Manning. The maddeningly inconsistent and streaky Manning was now and forever a champion. Eli Manning followed his famous father Archie

(No. 2 overall draft pick, 1971) and brother Peyton (No. 1 overall draft pick, 1998) as the No. 1 overall draft choice of San Diego in 2004. Except, like John Elway in 1983, he announced before the draft that he would never play for the team holding the top pick and thus forced a trade from the Chargers to the Giants, who coveted him. New York gave up its 2004 No. 1 pick (quarterback Philip Rivers) as well as another No. 1 and a No. 3 and a No. 5 for Manning's rights. Just as Eli had played under a microscope by following his venerated father to the University of Mississippi, he put himself in the ultimate pressurized fishbowl by forcing the trade to New York. It wasn't until Super Bowl XLII that Giant fans saw that the mild-mannered, even-tempered, cool quarterback was worth the high price.

From season to season, there was incremental improvement in Manning's completion percentage and passer rating, but his skittish inaccuracy at times kept the team from succeeding. After Tiki Barber retired, he made some noise as a broadcaster by saying that Manning's attempts at leadership were "comical" at times. Although Eli's arm and ability were unquestioned, he was considered easy to intimidate into mistakes. Though there may be more games like the Minnesota meltdown in 2007 when Eli threw four interceptions, three of which were returned for touchdowns, he proved himself able in 2007. His proud brother Peyton said after the Super Bowl, "He throws the deep ball as good as anybody in the league. I find him, when I watch him on TV, getting out of a lot of tough situations. I just don't think this will be the last [championship] for him." Eli's decline at the end of the 2008 season coincided with the loss of his 6'6" security blanket, Plaxico Burress. Without the deep threat of Burress to keep the defense honest, Manning turned back into a pumpkin in the postseason.

Peyton Manning

Height: 6'5" **Weight:** 230 lbs. **Birthdate:** 3/24/1976
College: Tennessee **Draft:** Indianapolis Colts 1998-1st
1998–2008 Indianapolis Colts
Regular Season Record: 117–59, 38 comebacks
Postseason Record: 7–8, 1 comeback
Relative Rating: 119%

Passing

Year	G	Comp./Att.	%	Yards	Y/Att.	TD	INT	Rating
1998	16	326/575	56.7	3,739	6.5	26	28	71.2
1999	16	331/533	62.1	4,135	7.8	26	15	90.7
2000	16	357/571	62.5	4,413	7.7	33	15	94.7
2001	16	343/547	62.7	4,131	7.6	26	23	84.1
2002	16	392/591	66.3	4,200	7.1	27	19	88.8
2003	16	379/566	67.0	4,267	7.5	29	10	99.0
2004	16	336/497	67.6	4,557	9.2	49	10	121.1
2005	16	305/453	67.3	3,747	8.3	28	10	104.1
2006	16	362/557	65.0	4,397	7.9	31	9	101.0
2007	16	337/515	65.4	4,040	7.8	31	14	98.0
2008	16	371/555	66.8	4,002	7.2	27	12	95.0
Total	176	3,839/5,960	64.4	45,628	7.7	333	165	94.7
PS:	15	348/564	61.7	4,208	7.5	22	17	85.0

Rushing

Year	Att.	Yards	Avg.	TD
1998	15	62	4.1	0
1999	35	73	2.1	2
2000	37	116	3.1	1
2001	35	157	4.5	4
2002	38	148	3.9	2
2003	28	26	0.9	0
2004	25	38	1.5	0
2005	33	45	1.4	0
2006	23	36	1.6	4
2007	20	-5	-0.3	3
2008	20	21	1.1	1
Total	309	717	2.3	17
PS:	20	29	1.5	3

Through his first eight seasons, Peyton Manning was frequently compared to Dan Fouts and Dan Marino as three record-setting passers who could never win the big one. Peyton's Super Bowl ring for the 2006 season ended that talk for good. Despite being one of the two best quarterbacks of his time along with Tom Brady, Manning has been much ridiculed throughout his career. With his playoff frustrations, particularly against the Patriots, regularly occurring, columnists mocked the "Manning Face" of dejected frustration that Peyton displayed sitting on the sidelines of big games. The "chicken dance" of hand motions that Manning went through on each play while calling plays at the line of scrimmage in the Colts no-huddle attack was scorned, and Peyton was resented for the frequent commercial endorsements that made his long face ubiquitous on television screens.

What is lost in all of that is not only how good a quarterback Manning is but also how admirable his career has been. Aside from one misbegotten mooning incident in 1996 at the University of Tennessee, Manning's work ethic, study habits, citizenship, and leadership have been exemplary. There has been no finer role model in the NFL in the last decade. His play, of course, has been at a Hall of Fame level right from his rookie year. He has never missed a start in his pursuit of Brett

Peyton Manning in the Clutch: Down 21–3 late in the second quarter of the AFC championship to his personal nemesis, the New England Patriots, Manning led a furious second-half comeback to tie the game in the third quarter. He then bested Tom Brady in a back-and-forth finish that culminated with Manning leading an 80-yard drive in the final two minutes to give the Colts their first lead of the game with 1:02 left. From that 38–34 victory, the Colts went on to win the Super Bowl two weeks later.

Of quarterbacks who have thrown at least 2,000 passes, only Dan Marino and Doug Williams have a lower sack percentage than Peyton Manning's 3.3 percent.

Peyton Manning's Five Highest Honors

5. Won both the Walter Payton and Whizzer White Awards in 2005
4. Selected to eight Pro Bowls
3. Nine-time All-Pro and four-time consensus All-Pro
2. Super Bowl XLI MVP
1. 2003, 2004, and 2008 Player of the Year

The Five Quarterbacks Most Similar to Peyton Manning

5. Carson Palmer
4. Kurt Warner
3. Norm Van Brocklin
2. Dan Fouts
1. Dan Marino

Peyton Manning's Five Top Touchdown Targets

5. Brandon Stokley, 15 TDs
4. Dallas Clark, 31 TDs
3. Marcus Pollard, 34 TDs
2. Reggie Wayne, 52 TDs
1. Marvin Harrison, 112 TDs

Peyton Manning's Five Toughest Rivals

5. Manning is 5–2 against the Ravens in the regular season and 1–0 in the playoffs.
4. Manning is 11–4 against the Jaguars.
3. Manning is 9–5 against the Titans in the regular season and 0–1 in the playoffs.
2. Manning is 3–2 against the Chargers in the regular season and 0–2 in the playoffs.
1. Manning is 5–9 against the Patriots in the regular season and 1–2 in the playoffs.

Five Random Peyton Manning Statistics

5. Manning has played for three head coaches.
4. Manning's Colts have outscored the league average by 24 percent.
3. Manning has thrown for five touchdowns four times, and for six touchdowns against the Saints on September 28, 2003, and the Lions on November 25, 2004.
2. Manning has thrown for over 300 yards 44 times and more than 400 seven times.
1. Manning has led the league in completion percentage once, yards twice, touchdown passes three times, yards per attempt once, passer rating three times, and interceptions once.

Favre's record streak of consecutive starts, and his consistency from year to year and game to game is unbroken. He is big with a strong and accurate arm and the intelligence to call his own plays in the complicated modern game. He has more fourth-quarter game-winning drives than any other quarterback in the new century and is fast moving up the all-time list in every major passing category. Above all, each year his team outscores the league average by nearly 25 percent, wins at least 12 games, and makes the playoffs.

Manning's rivalry with Tom Brady has led to annual showdowns between the Colts and Patriots that rivet the attention of NFL fans, not only because the two are such great players, but also because they are the fiercest of competitors who play to win. He once told Peter King, "I play because I love the game, not because it's what I'm supposed to be doing. I think as soon as I'm not excited to be driving to training camp, then it will be over." Yes, he is such a perfectionist that he even loves practice.

Peyton Manning's Signature Play: Down by eight to the Chargers with one minute to play on December 26, 2004, Manning walked over to slot receiver Brandon Stokley and whispered, "Run a post." The Colts had not even practiced the play, but Manning coolly hit Stokley for six points, tied the game with a two-point conversion, and then led the winning drive in overtime. It was Manning's 49th touchdown pass of the season, breaking Dan Marino's record.

The Manning family of quarterbacks: brothers Eli and Peyton and their father Archie.

Ted Marchibroda

QPR 1.5

Height: 5'10" **Weight:** 178 lbs. **Birthdate:** 3/15/1931
College: St. Bonaventure **Draft:** Pittsburgh 1953-1st
1953, 1955–56 Pittsburgh Steelers; 1957 Chicago Cardinals
Regular Season Record: 4–7, no comebacks
Postseason Record: NA
Relative Rating: 78%

Passing

Year	G	Comp./Att.	%	Yards	Y/Att.	TD	INT	Rating
1953	4	9/22	40.9	66	3.0	1	2	25.9
1955	7	24/43	55.8	280	6.5	2	3	62.2
1956	12	124/275	45.1	1,585	5.8	12	19	49.4
1957	7	15/45	33.3	238	5.3	1	5	19.7
Total	30	172/385	44.7	2,169	5.6	16	29	45.3

Rushing

Year	Att.	Yards	Avg.	TD
1953	1	15	15.0	0
1955	6	-1	-0.2	1
1956	39	152	3.9	2
1957	4	10	2.5	0
Total	50	176	3.5	3

Steelers owner Art Rooney's brother Dan was a priest who was the athletic director at St. Bonaventure in New York. Thus, it was not a surprise when Pittsburgh drafted the Bonnies' star running quarterback, Ted Marchibroda, who hailed from nearby Franklin, with their first pick in 1953. However, the slightly built Marchibroda was only 5'10" with a weak and inaccurate arm and lasted just three years in Pittsburgh. In his one season as a starter, Ted completed just 45 percent of his passes for 12 touchdowns and 19 interceptions. He played one season for the Cardinals and then went into coaching. Over the decades, Marchibroda worked as the offensive coach for the Rams, Redskins, Bears, Lions, and Bills and worked with quarterbacks Roman Gabriel, Sonny Jurgensen, Billy Kilmer, Bert Jones, Jim Kelly, Jim Harbaugh, and Vinny Testaverde. There is a nice symmetry to his head coaching positions. From 1975 to 1979, Ted coached the Baltimore Colts. From 1992 to 1995, he coached the Indianapolis Colts, and then from 1996 to 1998 he returned to Baltimore as the first coach of the Ravens.

When Dan Marino broke three career passing records of Fran Tarkenton's in a 1995 Monday Night Football *game, his coach of 13 years, Don Shula, congratulated him.*

Dan Marino

QPR 9.5

Height: 6'4" **Weight:** 224 lbs. **Birthdate:** 9/15/1961
College: Pittsburgh **Draft:** Miami 1983-1st
1983–99 Miami Dolphins
Regular Season Record: 147–93, 42 comebacks
Postseason Record: 8–10, 4 comebacks
Relative Rating: 113%

Passing

Year	G	Comp./Att.	%	Yards	Y/Att.	TD	INT	Rating
1983	11	173/296	58.4	2,210	7.5	20	6	96.0
1984	16	362/564	64.2	5,084	9.0	48	17	108.9
1985	16	336/567	59.3	4,137	7.3	30	21	84.1
1986	16	378/623	60.7	4,746	7.6	44	23	92.5
1987	12	263/444	59.2	3,245	7.3	26	13	89.2
1988	16	354/606	58.4	4,434	7.3	28	23	80.8
1989	16	308/550	56.0	3,997	7.3	24	22	76.9
1990	16	306/531	57.6	3,563	6.7	21	11	82.6
1991	16	318/549	57.9	3,970	7.2	25	13	85.8
1992	16	330/554	59.6	4,116	7.4	24	16	85.1
1993	5	91/150	60.7	1,218	8.1	8	3	95.9
1994	16	385/615	62.6	4,453	7.2	30	17	89.2
1995	14	309/482	64.1	3,668	7.6	24	15	90.8
1996	13	221/373	59.2	2,795	7.5	17	9	87.8
1997	16	319/548	58.2	3,780	6.9	16	11	80.7
1998	16	310/537	57.7	3,497	6.5	23	15	80.0
1999	11	204/369	55.3	2,448	6.6	12	17	67.4
Total	242	4,967/8,358	59.4	61,361	7.3	420	252	86.4
PS:	18	385/687	56.0	4,510	6.6	32	24	77.1

Rushing

Year	Att.	Yards	Avg.	TD
1983	28	45	1.6	2
1984	28	-7	-0.3	0
1985	26	-24	-0.9	0
1986	12	-3	-0.3	0
1987	12	-5	-0.4	1
1988	20	-17	-0.9	0
1989	14	-7	-0.5	2
1990	16	29	1.8	0
1991	27	32	1.2	1
1992	20	66	3.3	0
1993	9	-4	-0.4	1
1994	22	-6	-0.3	1
1995	11	14	1.3	0
1996	11	-3	-0.3	0
1997	18	-14	-0.8	0
1998	21	-3	-0.1	1
1999	6	-6	-1.0	0
Total	301	87	0.3	9
PS:	13	-4	-0.3	1

By the end of the 1986 season, 25-year-old Dan Marino had played four years in the NFL and had led the league in passing yards and touchdown passes three times and in yards per pass and passer rating once each. He had thrown for more than 4,000 yards three times, thrown at least 30 touchdowns three times, and taken his team to the Super Bowl. In the next 13 seasons, Marino led the NFL in passing yards two more times and went more than 4,000 yards three times. He threw 30 touchdowns one more time but never again led the league in touchdown passes, yards per pass, or passer rating. And the Dolphins never made it back to the Super Bowl.

Marino, of course, continued to be a top quarterback through most of the rest of his career, but much like another Hall of Fame quarterback with the middle name Constantine who played for Don Shula (Johnny Unitas), his greatness was heavily frontloaded into the early years of his career. His rookie season is still the standard by which other hotshot rookie quarterbacks are judged. Dan had a cannon arm, great pocket awareness, and the quickest release since Joe Namath. Even though he was so stationary that he totaled just 87 rushing yards in 17 years, he was sacked at the lowest rate of any quarterback who threw at least 1,500 passes.

Dan played the first 13 seasons of his career for Don Shula and started more games for one coach than any other quarterback—184. In fact, if the three replacement player games are ignored, Marino achieved a streak of 145 consecutive starts during the 1980s. Shula could never supply Marino with a strong enough defense and running game to seriously compete for the Super Bowl after 1984. When Jimmy Johnson replaced Shula in 1996, he improved the team, but the aging Marino increasingly became a detriment to winning. The uneasy marriage of Johnson and Marino came to a sad conclusion when the Jaguars manhandled the Dolphins 62–7 in the 1999 playoffs. Both Marino and Johnson ended their great careers in frustration that day. The retirement of Marino marked the end of the line for the legendary quarterback class of 1983, and Dan joined John Elway and Jim Kelly from that group in the Hall of Fame five years later. Marino ended his career second only to Elway in both career wins and career fourth-quarter game-winning drives and as the all-time leader in 300-yard games with 63 and 400-yard games with 13—his uniform number. He retired with the most passes, completions, touchdown passes, and passing yards in history until Brett Favre topped Marino in all categories a decade later.

QPR 6.5

Bernie Masterson

Height: 6'3" **Weight:** 195 lbs. **Birthdate:** 8/10/11
College: Nebraska **Draft:** Free agent
1934–40 Chicago Bears
Regular Season Record: 35–16–3 est., 1 comeback
Postseason Record: 0–1, no comebacks
Relative Rating: 177%

Passing

Year	G	Comp./Att.	%	Yards	Y/Att.	TD	INT	Rating
1934	9	3/3	100.0	39	13.0	1	0	158.3
1935	12	18/44	40.9	446	10.1	6	4	80.1
1936	12	10/42	23.8	292	7.0	3	6	40.3
1937	10	26/72	36.1	615	8.5	9	7	67.8
1938	11	46/112	41.1	848	7.6	5	9	49.3
1939	11	44/113	38.9	914	8.1	8	9	58.6
1940	7	9/23	39.1	212	9.2	2	3	62.5
Total	72	156/409	38.1	3,366	8.2	34	38	57.2
PS:	1	4/17	23.5	131	7.7	2	2	58.8

Rushing

Year	Att.	Yards	Avg.	TD
1934	4	11	2.8	0
1935	21	2	0.1	0
1936	9	-7	-0.8	2
1937	30	-21	-0.7	1
1938	13	-16	-1.2	0
1939	21	-31	-1.5	2
1940	10	-7	-0.7	1
Total	108	-69	-0.6	6
PS:	1	-2	-2.0	0

The lanky Bernie Masterson was the tallest quarterback of his era and the Bears' signal-caller from 1935 through 1939, when Sid Luckman was drafted. Masterson starred at the University of Nebraska in the early 1930s and was set to go right into coaching for the Cornhuskers when the Bears offered him a contract in 1934. For the Bears, Masterson was known for his deep passes and averaged 21.6 yards per completion for his career. Bernie led the league in touchdown passes with nine in 1937, and in the title game against Washington that year completed just four of 17 passes, two going for scores in a 28–21 shootout loss to rookie Sammy Baugh. In 1938, Masterson became the first Bear passer to throw at least 100 passes in a season and repeated that in 1939. Luckman took over completely in 1940, and Masterson moved on to coaching, making several stops in both the pros and college ball.

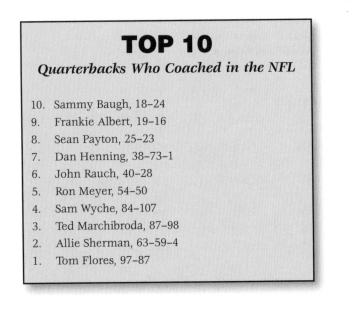

TOP 10
Quarterbacks Who Coached in the NFL

10. Sammy Baugh, 18–24
9. Frankie Albert, 19–16
8. Sean Payton, 25–23
7. Dan Henning, 38–73–1
6. John Rauch, 40–28
5. Ron Meyer, 54–50
4. Sam Wyche, 84–107
3. Ted Marchibroda, 87–98
2. Allie Sherman, 63–59–4
1. Tom Flores, 97–87

QPR **6.5**

Shane Matthews

Height: 6'3" **Weight:** 196 lbs. **Birthdate:** 6/1/1970
College: Florida **Draft:** Free agent
1996, 1999–2001 Chicago Bears; 2002 Washington Redskins; 2004 Buffalo Bills
Regular Season Record: 11–11, 2 comebacks
Postseason Record: 0–0, no comebacks
Relative Rating: 96%

Passing

Year	G	Comp./Att.	%	Yards	Y/Att.	TD	INT	Rating
1996	2	13/17	76.5	158	9.3	1	0	124.1
1999	8	167/275	60.7	1,645	6.0	10	6	80.6
2000	6	102/178	57.3	964	5.4	3	6	64.0
2001	5	84/129	65.1	694	5.4	5	6	72.3
2002	8	124/237	52.3	1,251	5.3	11	6	72.6
2004	3	2/3	66.7	44	14.7	1	0	149.3
Total	32	492/839	58.6	4,756	5.7	31	24	75.0
PS:	1	8/17	47.1	66	3.9	0	2	17.9

Rushing

Year	Att.	Yards	Avg.	TD
1996	1	2	2.0	1
1999	14	31	2.2	0
2000	10	35	3.5	0
2001	4	5	1.3	0
2002	12	31	2.6	0
2004	2	-3	-1.5	0
Total	43	101	2.3	1
PS:	1	-1	-1.0	0

Shane Matthews was another quarterback produced by Steve Spurrier at Florida, which made him ideally equipped to be a backup in the NFL. Although he was fairly accurate, he was a weak-armed dink passer who could not lead any team to the playoffs. He started 15 games in four years in Chicago and then was acquired by Washington when Spurrier was hired as the Redskins' coach. Matthews won the opening day starting job but was benched after three games for rookie Patrick Ramsey. Matthews returned as starter four games later. Four games after that, Shane was benched again, this time for fellow Spurrier alumnus Danny Wuerffel. Matthews stayed on the periphery of the league for four more years, drifting from practice squad to practice squad before retiring in 2006.

John McCormick

QPR 1.0

Height: 6'1" **Weight:** 208 lbs. **Birthdate:** 5/26/1937
College: Massachusetts **Draft:** Free agent
1962 Minnesota Vikings; 1963, 1965–66, 1968 Denver Broncos
Regular Season Record: 5–10, 3 comebacks
Postseason Record: NA
Relative Rating: 61%

Passing

Year	G	Comp./Att.	%	Yards	Y/Att.	TD	INT	Rating
1962	13	7/18	38.9	104	5.8	0	5	19.0
1963	9	28/72	38.9	417	5.8	4	3	59.8
1965	14	103/253	40.7	1,292	5.1	7	14	43.5
1966	14	68/193	35.2	993	5.1	6	15	30.9
1968	1	8/19	42.1	89	4.7	0	1	34.8
Total	51	214/555	38.6	2,895	5.2	17	38	37.6

Rushing

Year	Att.	Yards	Avg.	TD
1962	2	4	2	0
1963	3	-5	-1.7	0
1965	1	-2	-2	0
1966	4	2	0.5	0
Total	10	-1	-0.1	0

Big-armed John McCormick joined the 1962 Minnesota Vikings as the team's punter and backup to Fran Tarkenton. The following season, he was the last player cut in 1963 when rookie Ron Vander Kellen won the backup quarterback slot. McCormick signed with the desperate Denver Broncos that year and led the club to a fourth-quarter win over the Patriots in his first appearance on a 72-yard touchdown pass to Lionel Taylor. McCormick was an inaccurate bomber who was emblematic of the horrendous Bronco quarterbacking throughout that decade. He completed just 38 percent of his passes unless you factor in "completions" he threw to the opposing team. Then, his completion percentage rises to 45 percent. That he spent six seasons in the Mile High City helps explain why the team went 20–62–2 in that span even though Matt Millen was not the GM.

Josh McCown

QPR 4.0

Height: 6'4" **Weight:** 212 lbs. **Birthdate:** 7/4/1979
College: Sam Houston State **Draft:** Arizona Cardinals 2002-3rd
2002–05 Arizona Cardinals; 2006 Detroit Lions; 2007 Oakland Raiders; 2008 Carolina Panthers
Regular Season Record: 12–19, 4 comebacks
Postseason Record: NA
Relative Rating: 90%

Passing

Year	G	Comp./Att.	%	Yards	Y/Att.	TD	INT	Rating
2002	2	7/18	38.9	66	3.7	0	2	10.2
2003	10	95/166	57.2	1,018	6.1	5	6	70.3
2004	14	233/408	57.1	2,511	6.2	11	10	74.1
2005	9	163/270	60.4	1,836	6.8	9	11	74.9
2006	2	0/0	0.0	0	0.0	0	0	0.0
2007	9	111/190	58.4	1,151	6.1	10	11	69.4
2008	2	0/0	0.0	0	0.0	0	0	0.0
Total	48	609/1,052	57.9	6,582	6.3	35	40	71.6

Rushing

Year	Att.	Yards	Avg.	TD
2002	1	20	20.0	0
2003	28	158	5.6	1
2004	36	112	3.1	2
2005	29	139	4.8	0
2006	0	0	0.0	0
2007	29	143	4.9	0
2008	4	-3	-0.8	0
Total	127	569	4.5	3

Josh McCown is the better quarterback of the two mediocre NFL McCown brothers, because Luke has started just seven games in the league so far. A third brother, Randy, quarterbacked Texas A&M in the 1990s. Josh spent three years at SMU before transferring to Sam Houston State for his senior year to prove to scouts that he could operate an NFL-style offense. His 3,400 yards and 32 touchdowns at Sam Houston got Josh drafted in the third round by the Cardinals, whose coach, Denny Green, quickly predicted greatness for McCown. In the pros, though, McCown has shown himself to be a streaky, strong-armed gunslinger whose greatest moment came when he hit Nate Poole with a 28-yard touchdown pass on the final play of the 2003 season finale against Minnesota to knock the Vikings out of the playoffs. He's a fine athlete who sometimes lined up at wide receiver for the Lions but has trouble reading defenses and forces passes into coverage too often.

then cut a year later. As a quarterback, McDonald was immobile with questionable arm strength and not a very accurate passer. The Cowboys gave him a brief look before his career ended for good.

Paul McDonald

QPR **1.0**

Height: 6'2" **Weight:** 185 lbs. **Birthdate:** 2/23/1958
College: USC   **Draft:** Cleveland 1980-4th
1980–85 Cleveland Browns; 1986 Dallas Cowboys
Regular Season Record: 8–13, 4 comebacks
Postseason Record: 0–1, no comebacks
Relative Rating: 87%

Passing

Year	G	Comp./Att.	%	Yards	Y/Att.	TD	INT	Rating
1980	15	0/0	0.0	0	0.0	0	0	0.0
1981	12	35/57	61.4	463	8.1	4	2	95.9
1982	9	73/149	49.0	993	6.7	5	8	59.5
1983	16	32/68	47.1	341	5.0	1	4	42.6
1984	16	271/493	55.0	3,472	7.0	14	23	67.3
1985	16	0/0	0.0	0	0.0	0	0	0.0
1986	1	0/0	0.0	0	0.0	0	0	0.0
Total	85	411/767	53.6	5,269	6.9	24	37	65.7
PS:	1	18/37	48.6	281	7.6	1	0	83.3

Rushing

Year	Att.	Yards	Avg.	TD
1980	3	-2	-0.7	0
1981	2	0	0.0	0
1982	7	-13	-1.9	0
1983	3	17	5.7	0
1984	22	4	0.2	1
Total	37	6	0.2	1
PS:	1	7	7.0	0

Paul McDonald waited two years at USC for Vince Evans and then Rob Hertel to graduate before getting his shot. He then led the Trojans to a national championship one year and a two-year record of 22–1–1. Drafted by the Browns, the left-hander waited four years for Brian Sipe to "graduate," and finally Sipe jumped to the USFL in 1984. McDonald started all 16 games for the 5–11 Browns that year and threw just 14 touchdowns to 23 interceptions. The next year, Bernie Kosar and Gary Danielson arrived, and Paul was demoted to third string and

Lamar McHan

QPR **5.5**

Height: 6'1" **Weight:** 201 lbs. **Birthdate:** 12/16/1932
College: Arkansas   **Draft:** Chicago Cardinals 1954-1st
1954–58 Chicago Cardinals; 1959–60 Green Bay Packers; 1961–63 Baltimore Colts; 1963 San Francisco 49ers; 1965 CFL
Regular Season Record: 24–47–2, 7 comeback
Postseason Record: NA
Relative Rating: 76%

Passing

Year	G	Comp./Att.	%	Yards	Y/Att.	TD	INT	Rating
1954	12	105/255	41.2	1,475	5.8	6	22	32.4
1955	12	78/207	37.7	1,085	5.2	11	19	34.8
1956	12	72/152	47.4	1,159	7.6	10	8	73.3
1957	12	87/200	43.5	1,568	7.8	11	15	58.1
1958	12	91/198	46.0	1,291	6.5	12	13	60.4
1959	12	48/108	44.4	805	7.5	8	9	60.1
1960	12	33/91	36.3	517	5.7	3	5	44.1
1961	7	3/15	20.0	28	1.9	1	4	22.2
1962	10	10/20	50.0	278	13.9	3	2	95.8
1963	12	83/196	42.3	1,243	6.3	8	11	54.0
Total	113	610/1,442	42.3	9,449	6.6	73	108	50.3

Rushing

Year	Att.	Yards	Avg.	TD
1954	34	152	4.5	1
1955	56	194	3.5	2
1956	58	161	2.8	5
1957	25	82	3.3	2
1958	17	65	3.8	1
1959	16	64	4.0	0
1960	8	67	8.4	1
1961	4	1	0.3	0
1962	4	4	1.0	0
1963	17	59	3.5	0
Total	239	849	3.6	12

Lamar McHan spent a decade as the quarterbacks coach of the Saints, but as a player he was anything but a model citizen. The Cardinals drafted the running quarterback out of Arkansas in the first round in 1954 and put him right into the starting lineup as a rookie. McHan threw 22 interceptions to just six touchdowns in that first year and didn't improve a whole lot over the next decade. In his first few years, the Cardinals ran a split-T offense in which the mobile McHan often ran with the ball on the option play to try to take advantage of his skills. In 1956, the Cardinals got off to a 4–0 start before losing two of the next three when McHan began to unravel. Before a game in Pittsburgh, McHan told his teammates he didn't feel like playing, ignored plays that the coaches sent in, and refused to go back in the game after he was taken out. Two days later, McHan was suspended and fined $3,000, the largest fine in NFL history to that point. The suspension was lifted a week later, but Jim Root started the next two games before McHan got his job back at the end of the year.

Three years later, the Cardinals traded McHan to the Packers, and in Vince Lombardi's first year, fans were split into McHan and Starr camps regarding who should start. Lombardi originally gave the job to McHan, but when Lamar cursed Vince as a "Dago" after being yanked from a game, he fell out of favor in Green Bay. Lombardi would not tolerate bigotry or disrespect. The Packers traded him to the Colts to back up Johnny Unitas, and he finished his career as John Brodie's injury replacement in San Francisco in 1963.

McHan had a very strong but very inaccurate arm and completed just 42 percent of his passes over his career. On the plus side, his 15.5 yards per completion average is fifth of all time for quarterbacks who threw at least 1,000 passes. As a player, he was moody, opinionated, and unpredictable. He later summed up his career to a local newspaper reporter by saying, "Playing in the NFL required you to think. Playing tailback in college, all you had to do was fake to one side, run to the other, and prepare for shock. I was better at absorbing shocks than thinking." It's no wonder then that in the bottom six of quarterbacks with the worst winning percentages in a minimum of 50 starts are McHan and two of his pupils on the Saints, Archie Manning and Bobby Douglass.

Jim McMahon

QPR 8.5

Height: 6'1" **Weight:** 195 lbs. **Birthdate:** 8/21/1959
College: BYU **Draft:** Chicago Bears 1982-1st
1982–88 Chicago Bears; 1989 San Diego Chargers;
1990–92 Philadelphia Eagles; 1993 Minnesota Vikings;
1994 Arizona Cardinals; 1995–96 Green Bay Packers
Regular Season Record: 67–30, 15 comebacks
Postseason Record: 3–3, no comebacks
Relative Rating: 103%

Passing

Year	G	Comp./Att.	%	Yards	Y/Att.	TD	INT	Rating
1982	8	120/210	57.1	1,501	7.1	9	7	79.9
1983	14	175/295	59.3	2,184	7.4	12	13	77.6
1984	9	85/143	59.4	1,146	8.0	8	2	97.8
1985	13	178/313	56.9	2,392	7.6	15	11	82.6
1986	6	77/150	51.3	995	6.6	5	8	61.4
1987	7	125/210	59.5	1,639	7.8	12	8	87.4
1988	9	114/192	59.4	1,346	7.0	6	7	76.0
1989	12	176/318	55.3	2,132	6.7	10	10	73.5
1990	5	6/9	66.7	63	7.0	0	0	86.8
1991	12	187/311	60.1	2,239	7.2	12	11	80.3
1992	4	22/43	51.2	279	6.5	1	2	60.1
1993	12	200/331	60.4	1,968	5.9	9	8	76.2
1994	3	23/43	53.5	219	5.1	1	3	46.6
1995	1	1/1	100.0	6	6.0	0	0	91.7
1996	5	3/4	75.0	39	9.8	0	0	105.2
Total	120	1,492/2,573	58.0	18,148	7.1	100	90	78.2
PS:	8	82/155	52.9	1,112	7.2	5	4	76.1

Rushing

Year	Att.	Yards	Avg.	TD
1982	24	105	4.4	1
1983	55	307	5.6	2
1984	39	276	7.1	2
1985	47	252	5.4	3
1986	22	152	6.9	1
1987	22	88	4.0	2
1988	26	104	4.0	4
1989	29	141	4.9	0
1990	3	1	0.3	0
1991	22	55	2.5	1
1992	6	23	3.8	0
1993	33	96	2.9	0
1994	6	32	5.3	0
1996	4	-1	-0.3	0
Total	338	1,631	4.8	16
PS:	20	77	3.9	3

"I'm the punky QB known as McMahon/When I hit the turf, I've got no plan/I just throw my body all over the field." These were the opening lines for Jim McMahon in the 1985 Bears' Super Bowl Shuffle rap video, and they were two-thirds accurate. McMahon was a punk and he did throw his body all over the field, but he also was a very smart quarterback who knew exactly what he was doing. He didn't have the strongest arm but was a good rollout passer and a smart play caller who would do whatever it took to win. Bears Hall of Fame defensive lineman Dan Hampton said of McMahon in 1991, "He's not Marino or Montana and you don't build your team around him. But if he's focused, he'll find a way to win for a quality team."

McMahon was drafted out of BYU in the first round by the Bears in 1982 and played in Chicago for most of the decade while constantly feuding with volatile coach Mike Ditka. McMahon became as well known for wearing sunglasses at all times, sporting unapproved headbands counter to NFL Commissioner Pete Rozelle's orders, and mooning journalists at the Super Bowl as for his own gutsy play. "Outrageousness is nothing more than a way to wake people up," he would say. McMahon was a quarterback who thought and played like a lineman, and he was the respected leader of the offense whenever he was on the field. In his 15-year career, though, he never played a full season because of injuries. Jim's record as the Bears' starter was 46–15, but Chicago played 101 games over those seven seasons, and McMahon played in only 66. In Jim's last three years in Chicago, he was able to play in just 22 of 44 non-strike games and was a major irritant to Ditka, so the Bears traded him to San Diego for a third-round pick in 1989.

McMahon's season as a Charger was a disaster on and off the field, and so he signed with Philadelphia as Randall Cunningham's backup under Buddy Ryan. When Cunningham got hurt in 1991, Jim led the Eagles to a 10–6 record, but they still missed the playoffs. Two seasons later, he joined Minnesota and led the Vikings to the playoffs with a dink-and-dunk attack that relied entirely on guile, because McMahon's arm was completely shot. Ryan brought him back in Arizona, and he finished his career in

Green Bay as Brett Favre's backup for Super Bowl XXXI. After the Packers' victory, McMahon was released but was invited to come with the team to the White House to celebrate the win. In typical McMahon fashion, he did so in a Bears jersey to honor the 1985 Chicago team that was not invited to the White House because of the explosion of the *Challenger* space shuttle.

Mike McMahon

QPR **1.5**

Height: 6'2"   **Weight:** 215 lbs.   **Birthdate:** 2/8/1979
Rutgers   **Draft:** Detroit 2001-5th
2001–04 Detroit Lions; 2005 Philadelphia Eagles; 2007 CFL
Regular Season Record: 3–11, 3 comebacks
Postseason Record: NA
Relative Rating: 69%

Passing

Year	G	Comp./Att.	%	Yards	Y/Att.	TD	INT	Rating
2001	8	53/115	46.1	671	5.8	3	1	69.9
2002	8	62/147	42.2	874	5.9	7	9	52.4
2003	3	9/31	29.0	87	2.8	0	2	12.7
2004	1	11/15	73.3	77	5.1	0	1	56.8
2005	9	94/207	45.4	1,158	5.6	5	8	55.2
Total	29	229/515	44.5	2,867	5.6	15	21	55.1

Rushing

Year	Att.	Yards	Avg.	TD
2001	27	145	5.4	1
2002	14	96	6.9	3
2003	5	32	6.4	0
2004	2	18	9.0	0
2005	34	118	3.5	3
Total	82	409	5.0	7

In November 1869, Rutgers and Princeton met in New Brunswick, New Jersey, for what is often referred to as the first college football game. Football at the time was more like a combination of soccer and rugby, but that game eventually evolved into modern American football. The first Rutgers player to play in the pros was future singer and activist Paul Robeson in the 1920s, but the first Scarlet Knight quarterback to be drafted and play in the NFL had to wait until Mike McMahon in 2001.

McMahon was 8–25 as a starter for Rutgers squads that featured future Giants center Shaun O'Hara and future Eagles tight end L.J. Smith, but he finished 9–35 in his time there. Some of his teammates grew tired of McMahon bad-mouthing them while he was completing fewer than half of his passes and throwing 52 interceptions to 41 touchdowns. Mike, though, was chesty enough to tell the *New York Times,* "I think I'm the best quarterback in the draft personally." It is true that after you got past Drew Brees and Michael Vick, there wasn't much talent in the 2001 quarterback class, but aside from his elusive running skills, McMahon was a terribly inaccurate passer who made consistently bad decisions with the ball. As the Lions, Eagles, and Vikings found out, he wasn't even good enough to serve as a backup.

Donovan McNabb

QPR 9.0

Height: 6'2" **Weight:** 240 lbs. **Birthdate:** 11/25/1976
College: Syracuse **Draft:** Philadelphia 1999-1st
1999–2008 Philadelphia Eagles
Regular Season Record: 82–45–1, 17 comebacks
Postseason Record: 9–6, 1 comeback
Relative Rating: 108%

Passing

Year	G	Comp./Att.	%	Yards	Y/Att.	TD	INT	Rating
1999	12	106/216	49.1	948	4.4	8	7	60.1
2000	16	330/569	58.0	3,365	5.9	21	13	77.8
2001	16	285/493	57.8	3,233	6.6	25	12	84.3
2002	10	211/361	58.4	2,289	6.3	17	6	86.0
2003	16	275/478	57.5	3,216	6.7	16	11	79.6
2004	15	300/469	64.0	3,875	8.3	31	8	104.7
2005	9	211/357	59.1	2,507	7.0	16	9	85.0
2006	10	180/316	57.0	2,647	8.4	18	6	95.5
2007	14	291/473	61.5	3,324	7.0	19	7	89.9
2008	16	345/571	60.4	3,916	6.9	23	11	86.4
Total	134	2,534/4,303	58.9	29,230	6.8	194	90	85.9
PS:	15	322/540	59.6	3,522	6.5	23	16	80.2

Rushing

Year	Att.	Yards	Avg.	TD
1999	47	313	6.7	0
2000	86	629	7.3	6
2001	82	482	5.9	2
2002	63	460	7.3	6
2003	71	355	5.0	3
2004	41	220	5.4	3
2005	25	55	2.2	1
2006	32	212	6.6	3
2007	50	236	4.7	0
2008	39	147	3.8	2
Total	536	3,109	5.8	26
PS:	70	409	5.8	4

Donovan McNabb has had a great deal of success in Philadelphia but in many ways was poorly suited to play in the City of Brotherly Love. McNabb sensed that right from the moment he was drafted, when a group of 30 Eagles fans transported to the draft by a local sports talk radio announcer booed his selection because they wanted Texas running back Ricky Williams instead. Five quarterbacks were drafted in the first round in 1999, and Donovan, the second selected, turned out to be the best. He's led the Eagles to five NFC championship games and one Super Bowl while throwing twice as many touchdowns as interceptions and establishing new team career marks in most passing categories. In addition, he is a model citizen off the field, the reliable, practical good son in all ways. Yet his popularity in town has been as spotty as his accuracy.

One reason for the disparity is that Donovan is thin-skinned and doesn't take criticism very well. In Philadelphia, the fans literally have booed every quarterback since Tommy Thompson in the 1940s, even tough, winning ones they loved, such as Thompson, Norm Van Brocklin, and Ron Jaworski. An Eagle quarterback can't take the booing to heart, but McNabb seems to. Neither could fans understand how Donovan made a conscious effort to change his playing style after his first few years by de-emphasizing his extraordinary running ability to concentrate on being a pure pocket passer. McNabb implied that he resented being called a running quarterback because there were racial implications to that designation even though there have been several white running quarterbacks as well. Then there was the Terrell Owens disaster in 2005, the year after the Super Bowl trip, in which Donovan got sucked into the selfish receiver's vortex that tore the team apart. Finally, the Philly faithful have never liked coach Andy Reid's pass-happy West Coast offense and wish that McNabb would take more control on the field and audible out of questionable play calls from the bench. Donovan has never been the brash Unitas-style leader who would tell the coach to go to hell, but that's the commanding presence Eagle fans would like to see from their quarterback.

McNabb has been unable to win a championship in Philadelphia and appears to be slipping but still has enough talent to win a title in the right situation. He has been a very good quarterback for a decade but has fallen short of being a great one.

Steve McNair

QPR
9.0

Height: 6'2" **Weight:** 235 lbs. **Birthdate:** 2/14/1973
College: Alcorn State **Draft:** Houston Oilers 1995-1st
1995–2005 Houston Oilers/Tennessee Titans;
2006–07 Baltimore Ravens
Regular Season Record: 91–62, 21 comebacks
Postseason Record: 5–5, 2 comebacks
Relative Rating: 105%

Passing

Year	G	Comp./Att.	%	Yards	Y/Att.	TD	INT	Rating
1995	4	41/80	51.3	569	7.1	3	1	81.7
1996	9	88/143	61.5	1,197	8.4	6	4	90.6
1997	16	216/415	52.0	2,665	6.4	14	13	70.4
1998	16	289/492	58.7	3,228	6.6	15	10	80.1
1999	11	187/331	56.5	2,179	6.6	12	8	78.6
2000	16	248/396	62.6	2,847	7.2	15	13	83.2
2001	15	264/431	61.3	3,350	7.8	21	12	90.2
2002	16	301/492	61.2	3,387	6.9	22	15	84.0
2003	14	250/400	62.5	3,215	8.0	24	7	100.4
2004	8	129/215	60.0	1,343	6.2	8	9	73.1
2005	14	292/476	61.3	3,161	6.6	16	11	82.4
2006	16	295/468	63.0	3,050	6.5	16	12	82.5
2007	6	133/205	64.9	1,113	5.4	2	4	73.9
Total	161	2,733/4,544	60.1	31,304	6.9	174	119	82.8
PS:	10	184/311	59.2	1,764	5.7	6	11	66.7

Rushing

Year	Att.	Yards	Avg.	TD
1995	11	38	3.5	0
1996	31	169	5.5	2
1997	101	674	6.7	8
1998	77	559	7.3	4
1999	72	337	4.7	8
2000	72	403	5.6	0
2001	75	414	5.5	5
2002	82	440	5.4	3
2003	38	138	3.6	4
2004	23	128	5.6	1
2005	32	139	4.3	1
2006	45	119	2.6	1
2007	10	32	3.2	0
Total	669	3,590	5.4	37
PS:	55	355	6.5	6

The original "Air" McNair was not Steve but his older brother Fred, who preceded Steve to Alcorn State and to professional football. Fred was Steve's role model but did not have the success in the pros that his little brother did. Fred bounced from the CFL to arena football, where he threw 340 touchdowns in 10 seasons but never got much of a look in the NFL. Steve, however, for 13 years in Houston, Tennessee, and Baltimore, proved himself one of the finest field generals in the game, despite a series of injuries that would have truncated the careers of most quarterbacks.

Coach Jeff Fisher brought Steve along slowly with the Oilers and Titans as McNair eventually mastered all the facets of being an NFL quarterback. Coming from a small school, McNair had to work on reading defenses and also needed to improve his accuracy. From the start, he was a great runner and twice led all quarterbacks in yards rushing. In addition, he always was careful with the ball and threw few interceptions. Steve began to emerge in his third season as the team's starter when he led the Titans to the Super Bowl, where they memorably came within inches of tying the heavily favored Rams on the game's final play. From the following season on, McNair began connecting on at least 60 percent of his passes as he guided Tennessee to the playoffs in three of the next four seasons. The year 2003 was his greatest, when he threw 24 touchdown passes, just seven interceptions, and averaged eight yards per pass while being voted co-MVP of the league with Peyton Manning.

McNair had a powerful build and took a beating but played through one injury after another. In 2002, Steve was unable to practice for the last five weeks of the season due to several injuries, but played and won each Sunday to take the Titans to the playoffs. It was a good thing that his wife was a nurse. Over his career, McNair endured problems with his back, shoulder, knee, chest, groin, thumb, shin, and toe and kept on playing. The combination of those cumulative injuries and the realities of the salary cap led to a sad and strange spectacle in 2006. As McNair's contract was running out, the Titans banned him from their workout facility so they wouldn't be liable for a large salary cap hit should Steve suffer a serious injury on the team's grounds. The Titans traded McNair to the Ravens shortly after that, but Steve wasn't the same quarterback in Baltimore that he had been in Tennessee and retired two years later, saying, "My mind was there. Mentally, I could go out and play. But physically, I couldn't do it anymore. Not to the capacity that I needed to help my teammates win a football game." McNair was murdered in a tragic shooting in 2009 at the age of 36.

Cade McNown

QPR 1.0

Height: 6'1"　**Weight:** 208 lbs.　**Birthdate:** 1/12/1977
College: UCLA　**Draft:** Chicago 1999-1st
1999–2000 Chicago Bears
Regular Season Record: 3–12, 1 comeback
Postseason Record: NA
Relative Rating: 87%

Passing

Year	G	Comp./Att.	%	Yards	Y/Att.	TD	INT	Rating
1999	15	127/235	54.0	1,465	6.2	8	10	66.7
2000	10	154/280	55.0	1,646	5.9	8	9	68.5
Total	25	281/515	54.6	3,111	6.0	16	19	67.7

Rushing

Year	Att.	Yards	Avg.	TD
1999	32	160	5.0	0
2000	50	326	6.5	3
Total	82	486	5.9	3

TOP 10
Worst Quarterback Winning Percentages
(minimum 50 games)

10.　Rick Mirer, 24–44, .353
9.　Frank Tripucka, 19–34–1, .352
8.　Norm Snead, 52–99–7, .351
7.　Eddie LeBaron, 29–57–4, .344
6.　Joey Harrington, 26–50, .342
5.　Lamar McHan, 24–47–1, .342
4.　Mike Pagel, 17–36–1, .324
3.　Bobby Douglass, 16–36, .311
2.　David Carr, 23–56, .291
1.　Archie Manning, 35–101–3, .263

Cade McNown was the biggest flop of the celebrated but mostly unsuccessful 1999 quarterback class. McNown lasted just two seasons as an active player in Chicago and served on the practice squad for the Dolphins and 49ers for two more years before falling out of football entirely. He did make an impact off the field, though, stealing the Playboy Playmate girlfriend of his friend and fellow 1999 rookie quarterback Tim Couch and getting banned from the Playboy Mansion for whisking away Hugh Hefner's girlfriend as well. To think that UCLA alumnus Troy Aikman once said of the dating habits of his Bruin protégé, "He would rather sleep with his football."

On the field, McNown was short, had an inadequate arm, tended to overthrow receivers, and was too eager to break off a play and run. Teammates often found him to be untrustworthy and insincere. Reportedly before the 2000 season finale, a group of them went to Bears coach Dick Jauron and pleaded with him to sit McNown for the game. Jauron benched Cade, and Chicago traded the draft bust to Miami in the off-season.

Don Meredith

QPR 9.0

Height: 6'3" **Weight:** 210 lbs. **Birthdate:** 4/10/1938
College: Southern Methodist **Draft:** Chicago Bears 1960-3rd
1960–68 Dallas Cowboys
Regular Season Record: 50–36–4, 9 comebacks
Postseason Record: 1–3, no comebacks
Relative Rating: 107%

Passing

Year	G	Comp./Att.	%	Yards	Y/Att.	TD	INT	Rating
1960	6	29/68	42.6	281	4.1	2	5	34.0
1961	8	94/182	51.6	1,161	6.4	9	11	63.0
1962	13	105/212	49.5	1,679	7.9	15	8	84.2
1963	14	167/310	53.9	2,381	7.7	17	18	73.1
1964	12	158/323	48.9	2,143	6.6	9	16	59.1
1965	14	141/305	46.2	2,415	7.9	22	13	79.9
1966	13	177/344	51.5	2,805	8.2	24	12	87.7
1967	11	128/255	50.2	1,834	7.2	16	16	68.7
1968	13	171/309	55.3	2,500	8.1	21	12	88.4
Total	104	1,170/2,308	50.7	17,199	7.5	135	111	74.8
PS:	4	38/77	49.4	551	7.2	3	5	59.0

Rushing

Year	Att.	Yards	Avg.	TD
1960	3	4	1.3	0
1961	22	176	8.0	1
1962	21	74	3.5	0
1963	41	185	4.5	3
1964	32	81	2.5	4
1965	35	247	7.1	1
1966	38	242	6.4	5
1967	28	84	3.0	0
1968	22	123	5.6	1
Total	242	1,216	5.0	15
PS:	8	42	5.3	0

Cowboys coach Tom Landry sends Don Meredith in with the play but the two rarely saw eye to eye.

A quarterback's reputation can come down to the slightest movements of an offensive lineman. In the 1966 NFL championship, Don Meredith had the underdog Cowboys at the Green Bay 2 in the final minute, trailing by seven points. On second down, left tackle Jim Boeke moved, and Dallas was penalized five yards for offside and ultimately failed to score. One year later, the same two teams were in the opposite situation in the closing seconds of the 1967 NFL championship when Bart Starr slipped into the end zone on a quarterback sneak to win the game. However, when you closely examine the film, you can see Packers right guard Jerry Kramer anticipate the snap by a fraction of a millisecond, but no flag was thrown. The Packers won both games and the first two Super Bowls, and the Cowboys started to gain a reputation as the team that "couldn't win the big one." Don Meredith played just one more season and after that retired because the game wasn't much fun for him anymore.

A further irony is that Packers coach Vince Lombardi thought so highly of Meredith that he reportedly had offered Dallas any two Packers for Don back in 1960 but was turned down and so stuck with Starr instead. Meredith, meanwhile, took his lumps for the expansion Cowboys, having shoulder, knee, and elbow injuries nearly every year. Even though the Bears actually drafted Meredith from SMU, the Cowboys signed him for the NFL so that the Dallas Texans in the AFL couldn't and then gave the Bears draft picks in return. Meredith spent his entire football career—high school, college, and professional—in the city of Dallas.

However, Don may have been better off signing with Hank Stram's Texans because the team was more successful than the Cowboys at first. Tom Landry brought Meredith along slowly, even having him alternate plays with Eddie LeBaron in 1962 before taking over as starter in 1963. Dandy Don also took his lumps from the fans, who heavily booed the banged-up and inconsistent quarterback throughout much of his career. It wasn't until after Meredith retired that fans began to really admire his grit and wit. Meredith had good mobility in the pocket and threw a nice deep ball. In the huddle, he was much like Brett Favre—in command but one of the guys and aiming not only to win but to have fun doing so.

Meredith gained his greatest popularity as a broadcaster and foil of Howard Cosell on *Monday Night Football* for several years, famous for such irreverent touches as singing, "Turn out the lights, the party's over" when a game's outcome was decided. He also had a fairly successful run as an actor and TV pitchman before he chucked the public life entirely and retreated to the privacy of New Mexico. He was an excellent and underrated quarterback who always followed his own path at his own pace.

QPR
3.0

Hugh Millen

Height: 6'5"　**Weight:** 216 lbs.　**Birthdate:** 11/22/1963
College: Washington　**Draft:** Los Angeles Rams 1986-3rd
1987 Los Angeles Rams; 1988–90 Atlanta Falcons; 1991–92 New England Patriots; 1994–95 Denver Broncos
Regular Season Record: 7–18, 7 comebacks
Postseason Record: NA
Relative Rating: 96%

Passing

Year	G	Comp./Att.	%	Yards	Y/Att.	TD	INT	Rating
1987	1	1/1	100.0	0	0.0	0	0	79.2
1988	3	17/31	54.8	215	6.9	0	2	49.8
1989	5	31/50	62.0	432	8.6	1	2	79.7
1990	3	34/63	54.0	427	6.8	1	0	80.6
1991	13	246/409	60.1	3,073	7.5	9	18	72.5
1992	7	124/203	61.1	1,203	5.9	8	10	70.3
1994	5	81/131	61.8	893	6.8	2	3	77.6
1995	3	26/40	65.0	197	4.9	1	0	85.1
Total	40	560/928	60.3	6,440	6.9	22	35	73.5

Rushing

Year	Att.	Yards	Avg.	TD
1988	1	7	7.0	0
1989	1	0	0.0	0
1990	7	-12	-1.7	0
1991	31	92	3.0	1
1992	17	108	6.4	0
1994	5	57	11.4	0
1995	3	8	2.7	0
Total	65	260	4.0	1

As a walk-on to the University of Washington football team, Hugh Millen beat out the highly recruited Chris Chandler to start for the Huskies for two seasons

---

TOP 10
Losing Performances in a Title Game

10. Tommy Thompson in 1947 completed 27 of 44 for 297 yards, one touchdown, and three interceptions.

9. Tom Brady in Super Bowl XLII completed 29 of 48 for 266 yards, one touchdown, and no interceptions.

8. Steve McNair in Super Bowl XXXIV completed 22 of 36 for 214 yards, no touchdowns, and no interceptions.

7. Jim Kelly in Super Bowl XXV completed 18 of 30 for 212 yards, no touchdowns, and no interceptions.

6. Ken Anderson in Super Bowl XVI completed 25 of 34 for 300 yards, two touchdowns, and two interceptions.

5. Kurt Warner in Super Bowl XXXVI completed 28 of 44 for 365 yards, one touchdown, and two interceptions.

4. Charlie Conerly in 1958 completed 10 of 14 for 187 yards, one touchdown, and no interceptions.

3. Brett Favre in Super Bowl XXXII completed 25 of 42 for 256 yards, three touchdowns, and one interception.

2. Jake Delhomme in Super Bowl XXXVIII completed 16 of 34 for 323 yards, three touchdowns, and no interceptions.

1. Roger Staubach in Super Bowl XIII completed 17 of 30 for 228 yards, three touchdowns, and one interception.

and won the 1985 Orange Bowl over Oklahoma. Now a Huskies broadcaster, Millen made news in 2006 when his former Washington roommate Jim Mora Jr. told Hugh on air how much he coveted the UW job even though Mora was then the Atlanta Falcons' coach—although that changed soon after Mora's comments became widely dispersed.

Millen served as a backup in Los Angeles and Atlanta and started just three games in his first four years in the NFL. Hugh then signed with the 1–15 Patriots in 1991 as a Plan B free agent and helped lead the team to six victories that year. In fact, all the wins were the result of a league-high six fourth-quarter comebacks engineered by Hugh. The following season, Millen separated his shoulder, the team sank back to two wins, and Scott Zolak became the new fan favorite. Hugh moved on to Dallas as Troy Aikman's backup in 1993 but never played and then spent two seasons behind John Elway in Denver before signing with the Saints in 1996 to finish his career. Millen was very tall but was fairly mobile. He was a feisty leader but did not have a very good arm, threw a lot of interceptions, fumbled 28 times in 40 games, and was not a reliable starter.

Chris Miller

QPR

7.0

Height: 6'2" **Weight:** 212 lbs. **Birthdate:** 8/9/1965
College: Oregon **Draft:** Atlanta 1987-1st
1987–93 Atlanta Falcons; 1994–95 Los Angeles/St. Louis Rams; 1999 Denver Broncos
Regular Season Record: 34–58, 11 comebacks
Postseason Record: 1–1, 1 comeback
Relative Rating: 98%

Passing

Year	G	Comp./Att.	%	Yards	Y/Att.	TD	INT	Rating
1987	3	39/92	42.4	552	6.0	1	9	26.4
1988	13	184/351	52.4	2,133	6.1	11	12	67.3
1989	15	280/526	53.2	3,459	6.6	16	10	76.1
1990	12	222/388	57.2	2,735	7.0	17	14	78.7
1991	15	220/413	53.3	3,103	7.5	26	18	80.6
1992	8	152/253	60.1	1,739	6.9	15	6	90.7
1993	3	32/66	48.5	345	5.2	1	3	50.4
1994	13	173/317	54.6	2,104	6.6	16	14	73.6
1995	13	232/405	57.3	2,623	6.5	18	15	76.2
1999	3	46/81	56.8	527	6.5	2	1	79.6
Total	98	1,580/2,892	54.6	19,320	6.7	123	102	74.9
PS:	2	35/62	56.5	469	7.6	3	5	63.2

Rushing

Year	Att.	Yards	Avg.	TD
1987	4	21	5.3	0
1988	31	138	4.5	1
1989	10	20	2.0	0
1990	26	99	3.8	1
1991	32	229	7.2	0
1992	23	89	3.9	0
1993	2	11	5.5	0
1994	20	100	5.0	0
1995	22	67	3.0	0
1999	8	40	5.0	0
Total	178	814	4.6	2
PS:	4	18	4.5	0

Chris Miller's career illustrates both the danger and the allure of the game. Miller was a first-round pick out of Oregon where he displayed quick feet and a good arm. He came to a lousy Atlanta Falcons team in 1987 where he was knocked around quite a bit for four years and lost 31 of 42 starts. Chris had a breakout year in 1991, leading Atlanta to the playoffs with 26 touchdowns and 3,100 yards passing. On this basis, the Falcons saw Miller as their future and traded recalcitrant rookie quarterback Brett Favre to Green Bay. However, injuries sidelined Miller's career during the next two seasons, and then he left Atlanta to sign with the Rams in 1994.

Miller's first season with the Rams was interrupted twice by concussions that affected him so strongly that he got lost trying to drive himself home. Still, he came back in 1995 but suffered three more concussions during the season and was forced to retire. In retirement, a number of teams tried to entice him to return to the NFL as a backup, and Chris resisted for four years till he decided to give playing one more shot with Denver in 1999. Miller started three games in November for the Broncos. In the third one against Oakland, Chris suffered his sixth and final concussion that drove him from the league for good at the age of 34.

Jim Miller

QPR **5.0**

Height: 6'2" **Weight:** 226 lbs. **Birthdate:** 2/9/1971
College: Michigan State **Draft:** Pittsburgh 1994-6th
1995-96 Pittsburgh Steelers; 1999-2002 Chicago Bears
Regular Season Record: 15-12, 6 comebacks
Postseason Record: 0-1, no comebacks
Relative Rating: 96%

Passing

Year	G	Comp./Att.	%	Yards	Y/Att.	TD	INT	Rating
1995	3	32/56	57.1	397	7.1	2	5	53.9
1996	2	13/25	52.0	123	4.9	0	0	65.9
1999	5	110/174	63.2	1,242	7.1	7	6	83.5
2000	3	47/82	57.3	382	4.7	1	1	68.2
2001	14	228/395	57.7	2,299	5.8	13	10	74.9
2002	10	180/314	57.3	1,944	6.2	13	9	77.5
Total	37	610/1,046	58.3	6,387	6.1	36	31	75.2
PS:	1	3/5	60.0	23	4.6	0	1	31.7

Rushing

Year	Att.	Yards	Avg.	TD
1995	1	2	2.0	0
1996	2	-4	-2.0	0
1999	3	9	3.0	0
2000	7	5	0.7	0
2001	29	-19	-0.7	0
2002	13	11	0.8	0
Total	55	4	0.1	0
PS:	0	0	0.0	0

Jim Miller was a late-round pick of the Steelers in 1994 who worked hard to be named the team's starting quarterback for the 1996 season. However, that status lasted all of one-half game as coach Bill Cowher pulled the ineffective Miller for the legendary Mike Tomczak in the second half of the 1996 season opener against the Jaguars. Miller got into just one more game during that season before being released. Jim passed through the Jacksonville, Atlanta, and Detroit organizations over the next two years without playing a down and then landed with the Bears at the end of 1998.

By November 1999, Miller was the Bears' starter and threw for more than 300 yards two times in his first three starts before the league suspended him for four games for taking a dietary supplement that contained a steroid. Thus, Jim was the first quarterback to be suspended for taking steroids, however inadvertent it may have been. Miller missed most of the next season with an Achilles problem but returned in 2001 to lead the Bears to the playoffs, where they met the Eagles. In the first half of the division-round game, though, Jim was driven to the ground by Eagle defensive end Hugh Douglass after an interception and forced to leave the game. Miller missed half of 2002 with elbow tendinitis, and Chicago cut ties after the season. He caught on with the Bucs, Patriots, and Giants over the next three years but never played in another NFL game. The injury-prone Miller was essentially a game manager who was not able to stay healthy enough to hold a regular position in the league.

Chris Miller had good mobility, but his susceptibility to concussions prematurely ended his career...twice.

Rick Mirer

Height: 6'3" **Weight:** 210 lbs. **Birthdate:** 3/19/1970
College: Notre Dame **Draft:** Seattle 1993-1st
1993–96 Seattle Seahawks; 1997 Chicago Bears;
1999 New York Jets; 2000 San Francisco 49ers;
2003 Oakland Raiders
Regular Season Record: 24–44, 7 comebacks
Postseason Record: NA
Relative Rating: 81%

Passing

Year	G	Comp./Att.	%	Yards	Y/Att.	TD	INT	Rating
1993	16	274/486	56.4	2,833	5.8	12	17	67.0
1994	13	195/381	51.2	2,151	5.6	11	7	70.2
1995	15	209/391	53.5	2,564	6.6	13	20	63.7
1996	11	136/265	51.3	1,546	5.8	5	12	56.6
1997	7	53/103	51.5	420	4.1	0	6	37.7
1999	8	95/176	54.0	1,062	6.0	5	9	60.4
2000	1	10/20	50.0	126	6.3	1	0	86.7
2003	9	116/221	52.5	1,267	5.7	3	5	64.8
Total	80	1,088/2,043	53.3	11,969	5.9	50	76	63.5

Rushing

Year	Att.	Yards	Avg.	TD
1993	68	343	5.0	3
1994	34	153	4.5	0
1995	43	193	4.5	1
1996	33	191	5.8	2
1997	20	78	3.9	1
1999	21	89	4.2	1
2000	3	0	0.0	0
2003	20	83	4.2	1
Total	242	1,130	4.7	9

The 1998 pre-draft debate over whether Manning or Leaf would go first was predated by a similar debate in 1993 about Rick Mirer and Drew Bledsoe. Although neither Mirer nor Bledsoe proved to have either the upside or downside that Manning and Leaf had, the team with the top pick got the choice right in both instances. Bledsoe went to the Patriots as the first overall pick and had a good career, while Seattle took Mirer with the second pick and got less than it paid for. At the time, quarterback guru Bill Walsh had touted Mirer as the second coming of another Notre Dame alumnus, Joe Montana, which just goes to prove that even geniuses can be spectacularly wrong.

TOP 10
Odd Quarterback Draft Picks

10. Harry Agganis—Cleveland, 1952, round 1, played major league baseball instead
9. Don Klosterman—Cleveland, 1952, round 3, future NFL GM
8. Mike Shula—Tampa, 1987, round 12, Don Shula's son
7. Lee Corso—Chicago, 1957, round 29, future college coach
6. Jake Gibbs—Cleveland, 1961, round 9, played major league baseball instead
5. Ron Meyer—Chicago, 1966, round 7, future NFL coach
4. Jim Fassell—Chicago, 1972, round 7, future NFL coach
3. Mike Holmgren—St. Louis, 1970, round 8, future NFL coach
2. Brian Dowling—Minnesota, 1969, round 11, model for "BD" character in *Doonesbury* comic strip
1. Bill Buckner—Atlanta, 1967, round 17, played major league baseball instead

Mirer was a scrambler with a weak and inaccurate arm. Despite being a coach's son, he tended to lock in on one receiver, was indecisive, and took a lot of sacks. Rick threw for more yards and a better completion percentage than Bledsoe in their rookie seasons, but Bledsoe improved the next year. Mirer instead regressed as a dink passer over the next few years to the point where Seattle offered him to Atlanta in 1996 straight up for suspended malcontent Jeff George and were turned down. Instead, the Seahawks fleeced the Bears out of a first-round pick for Rick in 1997.

In Chicago, Mirer hit bottom, averaging just 4.1 yards per pass and throwing six interceptions and no touchdowns in seven games. Chicago cut Mirer after just one year and the Packers signed him to develop as a third-string quarterback in 1998. When the Jets lost Vinny Testaverde in the 1999 season opener, Bill Parcells' friend Ron Wolf essentially gave Mirer to New York for "past considerations." By midseason, though, Mirer was beaten out by the unheralded Ray Lucas. Mirer spent the next four years on the West Coast where the 49ers and Raiders also tried to unleash the potential that so many had once seen, but he lost six of eight starts and was finished in football.

QPR **7.0**
Scott Mitchell

Height: 6'6" **Weight:** 240 lbs. **Birthdate:** 1/2/1968
College: Utah **Draft:** Miami 1990-4th
1991–93 Miami Dolphins; 1994–98 Detroit Lions;
1999 Baltimore Ravens; 2000–01 Cincinnati Bengals
Regular Season Record: 32–39, 8 comebacks
Postseason Record: 0–2, no comebacks
Relative Rating: 97%

Passing

Year	G	Comp./Att.	%	Yards	Y/Att.	TD	INT	Rating
1991	2	0/0	0.0	0	0.0	0	0	0.0
1992	16	2/8	25.0	32	4.0	0	1	4.2
1993	13	133/233	57.1	1,773	7.6	12	8	84.2
1994	9	119/246	48.4	1,456	5.9	10	11	62.0
1995	16	346/583	59.3	4,338	7.4	32	12	92.3
1996	14	253/437	57.9	2,917	6.7	17	17	74.9
1997	16	293/509	57.6	3,484	6.8	19	14	79.6
1998	2	38/75	50.7	452	6.0	1	3	57.2
1999	2	24/56	42.9	236	4.2	1	4	31.5
2000	8	89/187	47.6	966	5.2	3	8	50.8
2001	1	4/12	33.3	38	3.2	0	3	3.5
Total	99	1,301/2,346	55.5	15,692	6.7	95	81	75.3
PS:	2	23/54	42.6	183	3.4	1	5	19.3

Rushing

Year	Att.	Yards	Avg.	TD
1992	8	10	1.3	0
1993	21	89	4.2	0
1994	15	24	1.6	1
1995	36	104	2.9	4
1996	37	83	2.2	4
1997	37	83	2.2	1
1998	7	30	4.3	0
1999	1	1	1.0	0
2000	10	61	6.1	1
Total	172	485	2.8	11
PS:	4	20	5.0	0

Scott Mitchell was a tall, immobile, left-handed quarterback who cashed in on seven starts in four years as Dan Marino's backup in Miami for a three-year, $11 million contract with the Lions in 1994.

Detroit won a bidding war for his services, but like most Lions' decisions, it didn't really work out. At crunch time, Mitchell was scatter-armed and threw game-changing interceptions.

Mitchell took a year of adjustment to starting at quarterback before putting up some big numbers from 1995 through 1997. In 1995 in particular, Mitchell threw for 4,338 yards and 32 touchdowns in leading the Lions to the playoffs. Unfortunately, Detroit lost that wild-card game to the Eagles 58–37, and Mitchell was lifted early in the second half after throwing three interceptions. Two years later, the Lions snuck into the postseason again, and again Mitchell came up very small, throwing a couple of interceptions in a 20–10 loss to the Bucs. Mitchell was benched for rookie Charlie Batch in 1998 and then traded to the Ravens, where coach Brian Billick benched him after two starts. Mitchell finished his dwindling career with two years as a backup in Cincinnati.

Surrounded by Barry Sanders, Herman Moore, Brett Perriman, and Johnny Morton, Scott Mitchell racked up some big numbers in Detroit, but not playoff wins.

Joe Montana

QPR 10.0

Height: 6'2"   **Weight:** 200 lbs.   **Birthdate:** 6/11/1956
College: Notre Dame   **Draft:** San Francisco 1979-3rd
1979–90, 1992 San Francisco 49ers; 1993–94 Kansas City Chiefs
Regular Season Record: 117–47, 29 comebacks
Postseason Record: 16–7, 5 comebacks
Relative Rating: 123%

Passing

Year	G	Comp./Att.	%	Yards	Y/Att.	TD	INT	Rating
1979	16	13/23	56.5	96	4.2	1	0	81.1
1980	15	176/273	64.5	1,795	6.6	15	9	87.8
1981	16	311/488	63.7	3,565	7.3	19	12	88.4
1982	9	213/346	61.6	2,613	7.6	17	11	88.0
1983	16	332/515	64.5	3,910	7.6	26	12	94.6
1984	16	279/432	64.6	3,630	8.4	28	10	102.9
1985	15	303/494	61.3	3,653	7.4	27	13	91.3
1986	8	191/307	62.2	2,236	7.3	8	9	80.7
1987	13	266/398	66.8	3,054	7.7	31	13	102.1
1988	14	238/397	59.9	2,981	7.5	18	10	87.9
1989	13	271/386	70.2	3,521	9.1	26	8	112.4
1990	15	321/520	61.7	3,944	7.6	26	16	89.0
1992	1	15/21	71.4	126	6.0	2	0	118.4
1993	11	181/298	60.7	2,144	7.2	13	7	87.4
1994	14	299/493	60.6	3,283	6.7	16	9	83.6
Total	192	3,409/5,391	63.2	40,551	7.5	273	139	92.3
PS:	23	460/734	62.7	5,772	7.9	45	21	95.6

Rushing

Year	Att.	Yards	Avg.	TD
1979	3	22	7.3	0
1980	32	77	2.4	2
1981	25	95	3.8	2
1982	30	118	3.9	1
1983	61	284	4.7	2
1984	39	118	3.0	2
1985	42	153	3.6	3
1986	17	38	2.2	0
1987	35	141	4.0	1
1988	38	132	3.5	3
1989	49	227	4.6	3
1990	40	162	4.1	1
1992	3	28	9.3	0
1993	25	64	2.6	0
1994	18	17	0.9	0
Total	457	1,676	3.7	20
PS:	64	300	4.7	2

The Joe Montana legend for coolness under pressure and for implausible comebacks was well established at Notre Dame, but NFL scouts still had their doubts. They saw Montana as slightly built, weak-armed, erratic, and unable to maintain his status as the Fighting Irish starting quarterback under Dan Devine. San Francisco selected Joe in the third round in 1979 after quarterbacks Jack Thompson, Phil Simms, and Steve Fuller had already been picked. Three years later, before Montana was to play in his first of four Super Bowls, former 49er great John Brodie said, "Joe Montana, I think, will become the best quarterback who ever played the game." Brodie's bold prediction has proven to be very arguably true.

Joe Montana's Signature Play: "The Catch." A retreating Montana, chased by Cowboys "Too Tall" Jones, Larry Bethea, and D.D. Lewis, unloads a high pass to the back of the end zone where only a leaping Dwight Clark can catch it for the winning touchdown in the final minute of the 1981 NFC championship.

Joe Montana in the Clutch: With the 49ers trailing 16–13 with 3:20 to play in Super Bowl XXIII, Montana calmed his teammates in the huddle by pointing out comedian John Candy in the stands. Montana then led the 49ers 92 yards in 2:46 by completing eight of nine passes for 87 yards, including the game-winning 10-yarder to John Taylor. Montana's only incompletion on the drive was because he was hyperventilating, but did not want to waste a timeout.

Montana's consistent excellence from year to year was reflected by his leading the league in completion percentage five times, exceeding 3,000 yards passing seven times, and leading the league in touchdown passes and passer rating twice each, while having a rating of more than 100 three times. Montana's signature was the fourth-quarter game-winning drives, and he led all quarterbacks in the 1980s with 24 such drives. His leadership was unquestioned, and he best displayed his toughness by coming back in two months from potentially career-ending back surgery in 1986. Most important was his postseason work, especially in Super Bowls where he was a three-time MVP and four-time champion. Joe is the all-time NFL postseason leader with 5,772 passing yards, 45 touchdown passes, and 16 wins. As college teammate Dave Waymer once put it, "He was a guy who wouldn't overheat."

Montana's first Super Bowl was a complete surprise. Joe led a 49er team that had finished 6–10 the year before over the dreaded Cowboys in the NFC championship by throwing the touchdown pass that Dwight Clark pulled in with "The Catch," and then the 49ers took apart the more experienced Bengals in the Super Bowl. Super Bowl number two cemented Montana's place as a great quarterback and not just a product of the West Coast offense when he thoroughly outdueled the celebrated Dan Marino in a game that was never close. After a lull of four years, Montana beat back the challenge of backup Steve Young to take San Francisco to a third Super Bowl that Montana won with a 92-yard drive in the final minutes, capped by his 10-yard touchdown pass to John Taylor with 34 seconds to play against the Bengals. The fourth Super Bowl the following year was a coronation for Montana ascending to the quarterback's Mount Rushmore as the 49ers destroyed the Broncos with Joe throwing five touchdown passes.

The year after the fourth championship, Joe was injured in the 1990 NFC championship loss to the Giants and missed nearly two seasons in recovery. He was traded to the Chiefs and never returned to the Super Bowl but did take Kansas City to the postseason twice before retiring. He was the most poised quarterback and fiercest competitor of his time and is on the short list of the greatest of all time.

Joe Montana and Coach Bill Walsh enjoy the end of another playoff victory during their third Super Bowl run.

Joe Montana's nimble feet allowed him to make plays when things broke down around him.

Joe Montana's Five Highest Honors

5. Selected to eight Pro Bowls
4. Eight-time All-Pro and two-time consensus All-Pro
3. Three-time Super Bowl MVP
2. 1989 and 1990 Player of the Year
1. Elected to the Pro Football Hall of Fame in 2000

The Five Quarterbacks Most Similar to Joe Montana

5. Ken Anderson
4. Rich Gannon
3. Ken Stabler
2. Joe Theismann
1. Len Dawson

Joe Montana's Five Top Touchdown Targets

5. John Taylor, 15 TDs
4. Roger Craig, 15 TDs
3. Freddie Solomon, 29 TDs
2. Dwight Clark 41 TDs
1. Jerry Rice, 55 TDs

Joe Montana's Five Toughest Rivals

5. Montana was 4–0 against the Cowboys in the regular season and 1–0 in the playoffs.
4. Montana was 3–1 against the Giants in the regular season and 2–3 in the playoffs.
3. Montana was 15–2 against the Saints.
2. Montana was 14–5 against the Falcons.
1. Montana was 12–8 against the Rams in the regular season and 1–0 in the playoffs.

Five Random Joe Montana Statistics

5. Montana played for three head coaches.
4. Montana's team outscored the league average by 18 percent.
3. Montana threw for five touchdowns against the Falcons on October 6, 1985, and the Eagles on September 24, 1989, while throwing six touchdown passes against the Falcons on October 14, 1990.
2. Montana threw for over 300 yards 38 times and more than 400 seven times.
1. Montana led the league in completion percentage five times, touchdown passes twice, yards per attempt once and passer rating twice.

Warren Moon

QPR **9.0**

Height: 6'3" **Weight:** 218 lbs. **Birthdate:** 11/18/1956
College: Washington **Draft:** Free agent
**1978–83 CFL; 1984-93 Houston Oilers; 1994–96
Minnesota Vikings; 1997–98 Seattle Seahawks;
1999–2000 Kansas City Chiefs**
Regular Season Record: 102–101, 35 comebacks
Postseason Record: 3-7, 2 comebacks
Relative Rating: 106%

Passing

Year	G	Comp./Att.	%	Yards	Y/Att.	TD	INT	Rating
1984	16	259/450	57.6	3,338	7.4	12	14	76.9
1985	14	200/377	53.1	2,709	7.2	15	19	68.5
1986	15	256/488	52.5	3,489	7.1	13	26	62.3
1987	12	184/368	50.0	2,806	7.6	21	18	74.2
1988	11	160/294	54.4	2,327	7.9	17	8	88.4
1989	16	280/464	60.3	3,631	7.8	23	14	88.9
1990	15	362/584	62.0	4,689	8.0	33	13	96.8
1991	16	404/655	61.7	4,690	7.2	23	21	81.7
1992	11	224/346	64.7	2,521	7.3	18	12	89.3
1993	15	303/520	58.3	3,485	6.7	21	21	75.2
1994	15	371/601	61.7	4,264	7.1	18	19	79.9
1995	16	377/606	62.2	4,228	7.0	33	14	91.5
1996	8	134/247	54.3	1,610	6.5	7	9	68.7
1997	15	313/528	59.3	3,678	7.0	25	16	83.7
1998	10	145/258	56.2	1,632	6.3	11	8	76.6
1999	1	1/3	33.3	20	6.7	0	0	57.6
2000	2	15/34	44.1	208	6.1	1	1	61.9
Total	208	3,988/6,823	58.4	49,325	7.2	291	233	80.9
PS:	10	259/403	64.3	2,870	7.1	17	14	84.9

Rushing

Year	Att.	Yards	Avg.	TD
1984	58	211	3.6	1
1985	39	130	3.3	0
1986	42	157	3.7	2
1987	34	112	3.3	3
1988	33	88	2.7	5
1989	70	268	3.8	4
1990	55	215	3.9	2
1991	33	68	2.1	2
1992	27	147	5.4	1
1993	48	145	3.0	1
1994	27	55	2.0	0
1995	33	82	2.5	0
1996	9	6	0.7	0
1997	17	40	2.4	1
1998	16	10	0.6	0
2000	2	2	1.0	0
Total	543	1,736	3.2	22
PS:	35	114	3.3	0

Although a handful of black quarterback pioneers had played in the NFL before Warren Moon, it was really the success of Moon, Randall Cunningham, and Doug Williams in the 1980s that forever broke down all barriers for black quarterbacks in the NFL. For the excellence of his long career, Moon became the first black quarterback elected to the Hall of Fame in 2006. He already was enshrined in the Canadian Football Hall of Fame, the only player elected to both.

Moon began his career at the University of Washington where he met with hostility from fans until he led the Huskies to the Rose Bowl as a senior. Despite his college success, NFL scouts talked to Moon about switching positions, and Warren decided to sign with Edmonton of the CFL instead. Moon was never drafted by the NFL and thus was an enticing free agent six years later when he returned to the United States in triumph after leading the Eskimos to five consecutive Grey Cup championships. Warren narrowed the choice to Seattle and Houston and then signed with the Oilers, who brought in Edmonton's coach, Hugh Campbell, as their new coach.

Moon struggled for his first few years and Campbell was fired before things got better when second-year coach Jerry Glanville instituted the run-and-shoot offense in 1987. Warren took to the new offense immediately. He had a strong arm, could throw very well on the run, and was tough enough to take the hits that came in an offense that was devoted to the pass but also featured weak pass protection schemes. Dyspeptic Oiler defensive coach Buddy Ryan famously derided the offense as the "chuck-and-duck." Moon, a calm and mature leader, led the Oilers to the playoffs seven straight seasons, but his failures in the postseason became an annual occurrence. Twice John Elway outdueled him, but the most memorable loss was the Bills' miracle comeback from a 35–3 second-half deficit in the 1992 playoffs despite Moon's four touchdown passes and 371 yards passing.

A year later, Moon was a gun for hire and spent three seasons in Minnesota, two in Seattle, and two in Kansas City before retiring at age 44, having thrown for more yards and touchdowns than any other professional football player. Although he lost as many games as he won in his long NFL career and never won a championship, Moon was elected to the Hall of Fame on the first ballot.

Earl Morrall

QPR 8.5

Height: 6'1" **Weight:** 205 lbs. **Birthdate:** 5/17/1934
College: Michigan State **Draft:** San Francisco 1956-1st
1956 San Francisco 49ers; 1957–58 Pittsburgh Steelers; 1958–64 Detroit Lions; 1965–67 New York Giants; 1968–71 Baltimore Colts; 1972–76 Miami Dolphins
Regular Season Record: 63–37–3, 10 comebacks
Postseason Record: 4-1, 2 comebacks
Relative Rating: 111%

Passing

Year	G	Comp./Att.	%	Yards	Y/Att.	TD	INT	Rating
1956	12	38/78	48.7	621	8.0	1	6	48.1
1957	12	139/289	48.1	1,900	6.6	11	12	64.9
1958	11	25/78	32.1	463	5.9	5	9	35.3
1959	12	65/137	47.4	1,102	8.0	5	6	69.1
1960	12	32/49	65.3	423	8.6	4	3	94.2
1961	13	69/150	46.0	909	6.1	7	9	56.2
1962	14	32/52	61.5	449	8.6	4	4	82.9
1963	14	174/328	53.0	2,621	8.0	24	14	86.2
1964	6	50/91	54.9	588	6.5	4	3	75.7
1965	14	155/302	51.3	2,446	8.1	22	12	86.3
1966	7	71/151	47.0	1,105	7.3	7	12	54.1
1967	8	13/24	54.2	181	7.5	3	1	100.9
1968	14	182/317	57.4	2,909	9.2	26	17	93.2
1969	9	46/99	46.5	755	7.6	5	7	60.0
1970	14	51/93	54.8	792	8.5	9	4	97.6
1971	14	84/167	50.3	1,210	7.2	7	12	58.2
1972	14	83/150	55.3	1,360	9.1	11	7	91.0
1973	14	17/38	44.7	253	6.7	0	4	27.5
1974	14	17/27	63.0	301	11.1	2	3	86.1
1975	13	26/43	60.5	273	6.3	3	2	82.8
1976	14	10/26	38.5	148	5.7	1	1	54.6
Total	255	1,379/2,689	51.3	20,809	7.7	161	148	74.1
PS:	6	50/103	48.5	806	7.8	3	7	56.5

Rushing

Year	Att.	Yards	Avg.	TD
1956	6	10	1.7	0
1957	41	81	2.0	2
1958	11	80	7.3	0
1959	26	112	4.3	0
1960	10	37	3.7	1
1961	20	86	4.3	0
1962	17	65	3.8	1
1963	26	105	4.0	1
1964	10	70	7.0	0
1965	17	52	3.1	0
1966	5	12	2.4	0
1967	4	11	2.8	1
1968	11	18	1.6	1
1970	2	6	3.0	0
1971	6	13	2.2	0
1972	17	67	3.9	1
1973	1	9	9.0	0
1974	1	11	11.0	0
1975	4	33	8.3	0
Total	235	878	3.7	8
PS:	8	2	0.3	0

The greatest backup quarterback in NFL history played as a starter and reserve with six teams over his 21-year career in the league and was on two Super Bowl championship teams. Earl Morrall competed with and backed up Hall of Fame quarterbacks at nearly every stop along the way. He was a respected leader who was skilled at reading defenses and threw a good deep ball. He even did a little punting, although his 37.7 punting average is the lowest of any quarterback who punted at least 100 times.

Morrall led his home state Michigan State Spartans to a Rose Bowl win in 1956 and then was the first pick of the 49ers that year. In San Francisco, Earl competed with Y.A. Tittle and was clearly overmatched as a rookie. He was traded the next year to Pittsburgh for linebacker Marv Matuszak. After a mediocre year as the Steelers' starter in 1957, Morrall was traded to Detroit at the beginning of the 1958 season for Bobby Layne. Earl spent the next seven years with the Lions but inexplicably was unable to beat out mediocrities Jim Ninowski and Milt Plum for any extended period of time as the starting quarterback. When the Lions decided to stick with Plum in 1965, they traded Earl to the Giants for a couple of players. Earl had a successful first year in New York leading the 2–10–2 Giants to a 7–7 season but got hurt in 1966 and found himself behind newly acquired Fran Tarkenton in 1967. The Colts traded for Morrall to back up Johnny Unitas in 1968. Then Unitas hurt his arm, and Earl led the Colts to a triumphant 13–1 record and a disastrous trip to Super Bowl III where he was denigrated by opposing quarterback Joe Namath as not as good as the six top quarterbacks in the AFL because he was an erratic passer who set up slow and could be pressured. When Morrall failed to spot Jimmy Orr alone in the end zone at the end of the first half on a flea flicker and instead threw one of his three interceptions on the day, the validity of Namath's view was borne out.

Earl continued as Unitas' backup in Baltimore and relieved an injured Unitas in Super Bowl V two years later to preside over a Colt win so ugly that it became known as the Blunder Bowl. Two years later, Don Shula acquired Morrall for the Dolphins because he remembered how well Earl had performed for him in Baltimore. In game five that year, starter Bob Griese broke his leg, and Morrall came in to win nine straight regular-season starts and one playoff game before Griese returned in the postseason to cap the Dolphins' undefeated 1972 season. Morrall lasted four more years as a backup in Miami before retiring in 1976 at 42. Earl later served as the mayor of Davie, Florida, and as the quarterback coach for Jim Kelly, Bernie Kosar, and Vinny Testaverde at the University of Miami.

John Elway wasn't the first Denver quarterback to wear No. 7 and take the Broncos to the Super Bowl. Craig Morton had one of his best years in the Mile High City in 1977.

Craig Morton

QPR  **9.0**

Height: 6'4" **Weight:** 214 lbs. **Birthdate:** 2/5/1943
College: California **Draft:** Dallas 1965-1st
1964–74 Dallas Cowboys; 1974–76 New York Giants; 1977–82 Denver Broncos
Regular Season Record: 81–62–1, 19 comebacks
Postseason Record: 5–5, no comebacks
Relative Rating: 108%

Passing

Year	G	Comp./Att.	%	Yards	Y/Att.	TD	INT	Rating
1965	4	17/34	50.0	173	5.1	2	4	45.0
1966	6	13/27	48.1	225	8.3	3	1	98.5
1967	9	69/137	50.4	978	7.1	10	10	67.7
1968	13	44/85	51.8	752	8.8	4	6	68.4
1969	13	162/302	53.6	2,619	8.7	21	15	85.4
1970	12	102/207	49.3	1,819	8.8	15	7	89.8
1971	10	78/143	54.5	1,131	7.9	7	8	73.5
1972	14	185/339	54.6	2,396	7.1	15	21	65.9
1973	14	13/32	40.6	174	5.4	3	1	76.8
1974	10	124/239	51.9	1,522	6.4	9	13	61.7
1975	14	186/363	51.2	2,359	6.5	11	16	63.6
1976	12	153/284	53.9	1,865	6.6	9	20	55.6
1977	14	131/254	51.6	1,929	7.6	14	8	82.0
1978	14	146/267	54.7	1,802	6.7	11	8	77.0
1979	14	204/370	55.1	2,626	7.1	16	19	70.6
1980	12	183/301	60.8	2,150	7.1	12	13	77.8
1981	15	225/376	59.8	3,195	8.5	21	14	90.5
1982	3	18/26	69.2	193	7.4	0	3	51.1
Total	**203**	**2,053/3,786**	**54.2**	**27,908**	**7.4**	**183**	**187**	**73.5**
PS:	12	91/227	40.1	1,235	5.4	9	16	42.0

Rushing

Year	Att.	Yards	Avg.	TD
1965	3	-8	-2.7	0
1966	7	50	7.1	0
1967	15	42	2.8	0
1968	4	28	7.0	2
1969	16	62	3.9	1
1970	16	37	2.3	0
1971	4	9	2.3	1
1972	8	26	3.3	2
1973	1	0	0.0	0
1974	4	5	1.3	0
1975	22	72	3.3	0
1976	15	48	3.2	0
1977	31	125	4.0	4
1978	17	71	4.2	0
1979	23	13	0.6	1
1980	21	29	1.4	1
1981	8	18	2.3	0
Total	215	627	2.9	12
PS:	20	28	1.4	1

Although Craig Morton was a fairly good quarterback on a good team, he will forever be remembered as having two of the worst Super Bowls a quarterback ever had. Morton was a tall pocket passer with a strong arm who was the No. 1 pick of the Cowboys in 1965. He spent four seasons behind Don Meredith before the 30-year-old Meredith surprised everyone by retiring in 1969.

The hard-throwing Morton assumed the starting role and took Dallas to the playoffs in his first year but had elbow and shoulder problems. Because Craig was so slow to set up and so immobile, he was a sitting duck in the pocket and was injury prone throughout his long career. As a player, he had major shoulder surgery and four knee operations. Of more importance, he folded under pressure. He was normally cool and calm and could read defenses, but in the postseason, Morton was awful. In 12 playoff games, he completed at least half his passes just three times and threw nearly twice as many interceptions as touchdowns. Morton rode the stellar Cowboy defense to the Super Bowl in 1971, but there he threw three picks, including one in the final minute that set up Jim O'Brien's winning field goal for the Colts. Although Craig predicted that he would settle the Dallas quarterback controversy quickly in 1971, Roger Staubach replaced Morton

as the starter that year and led Dallas to its first championship. Staubach got hurt the following year, though, so Morton returned and guided the Cowboys back to the playoffs in 1972. In the first game against the 49ers, Landry pulled Craig in the fourth quarter for the returning Staubach, who mounted a 17-point comeback to win the game and earn the start in the NFC championship against the Redskins. Although Staubach lost that game, he had won the starting job for good. Morton lasted another year and a half as a backup before he was traded to the Giants for a No. 1 pick in 1974.

With the abysmal Giants, Morton was an ineffective tackling dummy and was given to Denver for Steve Ramsey in 1977. Craig was reborn in Denver, though, and had one of the best years of his career in leading Denver to its first Super Bowl, where they met Roger Staubach and the Cowboys. Morton was painfully bad in this loss. He was relentlessly pummeled by the Dallas pass rush and threw four interceptions in the first half before being yanked in the second half.

Morton went on to have several fine seasons as the best Bronco quarterback before John Elway but never again made it to a Super Bowl. In Dallas, Craig was a playboy loner and not much of a leader but seemed to grow better with age in Denver. Although he was savagely booed in Dallas and New York, he is more fondly remembered in Denver despite that Super Bowl disaster.

TOP 10
Backup Quarterbacks

10. Don Heinrich, Giants
9. Steve DeBerg, 49ers, Broncos, Bucs, Falcons
8. Mike Livingston, Chiefs
7. George Ratterman, Browns
6. Pat Ryan, Jets
5. Zeke Bratkowski, Packers
4. Don Strock, Dolphins
3. Frank Reich, Bills
2. George Blanda, Raiders
1. Earl Morrall, Colts, Dolphins, Lions

Bill Munson

QPR 7.5

Height: 6'2"   **Weight:** 203 lbs.   **Birthdate:** 8/11/1941
College: Utah State   **Draft:** Los Angeles Rams 1964-1st; Houston Oilers 1964-16th
1964–67 Los Angeles Rams; 1968–75 Detroit Lions; 1976 Seattle Seahawks; 1977 San Diego Chargers; 1978–79 Buffalo Bills
Regular Season Record: 27–34–5, 7 comebacks
Postseason Record: 0–0, no comebacks
Relative Rating: 108%

Passing

Year	G	Comp./Att.	%	Yards	Y/Att.	TD	INT	Rating
1964	11	108/223	48.4	1,533	6.9	9	15	56.5
1965	10	144/267	53.9	1,701	6.4	10	14	64.2
1966	5	30/50	60.0	284	5.7	2	1	80.7
1967	5	5/10	50.0	38	3.8	1	2	53.3
1968	12	181/329	55.0	2,311	7.0	15	8	82.3
1969	8	84/166	50.6	1,062	6.4	7	8	64.9
1970	8	84/158	53.2	1,049	6.6	10	7	76.7
1971	4	21/38	55.3	216	5.7	1	1	69.6
1972	2	20/35	57.1	194	5.5	1	1	70.4
1973	10	95/187	50.8	1,129	6.0	9	8	67.8
1974	11	166/292	56.8	1,874	6.4	8	7	75.3
1975	5	65/109	59.6	626	5.7	5	2	83.4
1976	5	20/37	54.1	295	8.0	1	3	55.6
1977	4	20/31	64.5	225	7.3	1	1	83.4
1978	4	24/43	55.8	328	7.6	4	2	92.0
1979	3	3/7	42.9	31	4.4	0	0	56.2
Total	107	1,070/1,982	54.0	12,896	6.5	84	80	71.5
PS:	1	2/8	25.0	44	5.5	0	1	10.4

Rushing

Year	Att.	Yards	Avg.	TD
1964	19	150	7.9	0
1965	26	157	6.0	1
1966	4	3	0.8	0
1967	2	-22	-11.0	0
1968	25	109	4.4	1
1969	7	31	4.4	0
1970	9	33	3.7	0
1971	3	9	3.0	0
1972	1	0	0.0	0
1973	10	33	3.3	0
1974	18	40	2.2	1
1975	4	-3	-0.8	0
1976	1	6	6.0	0
1977	1	2	2.0	0
Total	130	548	4.2	3
PS:	0	0	0.0	0

When the Rams chose Bill Munson in the first round of the 1964 draft, it was the third year in a row they had used their first pick on a quarterback. While 1963's pick, Terry Baker, was being tried as halfback and flanker, Munson was busy beating out 1962's Roman Gabriel as the starter. Munson had a strong and accurate arm, but the Rams discovered over the next two seasons that the team played better behind Gabriel. When George Allen was hired as coach in 1966, Munson went to the bench, and Gabriel moved in as starter.

Two years later, Munson was traded to the Lions for three players and a No. 1 pick and spent the next eight years competing with Greg Landry to be the Lions' starter, with Landry starting about two-thirds of the time. Munson was a quiet, easygoing player who was not much of a leader and did not play particularly well under pressure. He was injury prone, had a tendency to hold on to the ball too long, and sometimes had trouble reading defenses. Ultimately, he was a fine backup who later had stints in Seattle, San Diego, and Buffalo.

Browning Nagle

QPR 0.5

Height: 6'3"   **Weight:** 225 lbs.   **Birthdate:** 4/29/1968
College: Louisville   **Draft:** NY Jets 1991-2nd
1991–93 New York Jets; 1994 Indianapolis Colts; 1996 Atlanta Falcons; 1999–2000 Arena Football
Regular Season Record: 4–10, no comebacks
Postseason Record: NA
Relative Rating: 70%

Passing

Year	G	Comp./Att.	%	Yards	Y/Att.	TD	INT	Rating
1991	1	1/2	50.0	10	5.0	0	0	64.6
1992	14	192/387	49.6	2,280	5.9	7	17	55.7
1993	3	6/14	42.9	71	5.1	0	0	58.9
1994	1	8/21	38.1	69	3.3	0	1	27.7
1996	5	6/13	46.2	59	4.5	1	2	45.5
Total	24	213/437	48.7	2,489	5.7	8	20	53.5

Rushing

Year	Att.	Yards	Avg.	TD
1991	1	-1	-1.0	0
1992	24	57	2.4	0
1994	1	12	12.0	0
Total	26	68	2.6	0

The long-forgotten Browning Nagle became a celebrity again in 2008 when the Jets finally acquired Brett Favre, 17 years after they had originally planned. Favre was the Jets' target in the 1991 draft, but they were aced out by Atlanta one pick before New York's turn. As consolation, the Jets turned to Nagle, who coincidentally would have been the Falcons' choice had Favre not been available.

Nagle starred at Louisville after having transferred out of West Virginia. He had a cannon for an arm but had no touch on his passes. As the Jets soon found out, he also had problems reading defenses. On the urging of the front office, Nagle replaced beleaguered starter Ken O'Brien in 1992, although coach Bruce Coslet later called that the biggest mistake of his career. The next year, Coslet brought in free agent Boomer Esiason, and Nagle's days as a Jet were numbered. Nagle was cut and spent brief periods with the Colts and Falcons over the next three years before falling out of the NFL. Nagle accused Coslet of blackballing him with other coaches, but Coslet denied it. As Browning tried to make himself marketable in the arena league in 1999, he told *Sports Illustrated*, "With my kind of talent I should be in the NFL. It's still not too late for me to change my career into a success story." After 2000 though, he retired because no one in the NFL agreed, despite his 74 arena football touchdowns.

TOP 10
Overall No. 1 Draft Picks

10. Carson Palmer, 2003
9. Bill Wade, 1952
8. Steve Bartkowski, 1975
7. Eli Manning, 2004
6. Jim Plunkett, 1971
5. Joe Namath, 1965
4. Terry Bradshaw, 1970
3. Troy Aikman, 1989
2. Peyton Manning, 1998
1. John Elway, 1983

QPR

Joe Namath

Height: 6'2" **Weight:** 200 lbs. **Birthdate:** 5/31/1943
College: Alabama **Draft:** New York Jets 1965-1st; St. Louis Cardinals 1965-1st
1965–76 New York Jets; 1977 Los Angeles Rams
Regular Season Record: 62–63–4, 15 comebacks
Postseason Record: 2–1, 1 comeback
Relative Rating: 103%

Passing

Year	G	Comp./Att.	%	Yards	Y/Att.	TD	INT	Rating
1965	13	164/340	48.2	2,220	6.5	18	15	68.7
1966	14	232/471	49.3	3,379	7.2	19	27	62.6
1967	14	258/491	52.5	4,007	8.2	26	28	73.8
1968	14	187/380	49.2	3,147	8.3	15	17	72.1
1969	14	185/361	51.2	2,734	7.6	19	17	74.3
1970	5	90/179	50.3	1,259	7.0	5	12	54.7
1971	4	28/59	47.5	537	9.1	5	6	68.2
1972	13	162/324	50.0	2,816	8.7	19	21	72.5
1973	6	68/133	51.1	966	7.3	5	6	68.7
1974	14	191/361	52.9	2,616	7.2	20	22	69.4
1975	14	157/326	48.2	2,286	7.0	15	28	51.0
1976	11	114/230	49.6	1,090	4.7	4	16	39.9
1977	4	50/107	46.7	606	5.7	3	5	54.5
Total	140	1,886/3,762	50.1	27,663	7.4	173	220	65.5
PS:	3	50/117	42.7	636	5.4	3	4	54.6

Rushing

Year	Att.	Yards	Avg.	TD
1965	8	19	2.4	0
1966	6	42	7.0	2
1967	6	14	2.3	0
1968	5	11	2.2	2
1969	11	33	3.0	2
1970	1	-1	-1.0	0
1971	3	-1	-0.3	0
1972	6	8	1.3	0
1973	1	-2	-2.0	0
1974	8	1	0.1	1
1975	10	6	0.6	0
1976	2	5	2.5	0
1977	4	5	1.3	0
Total	71	140	2.0	7
PS:	2	15	7.5	0

In *The Paolantonio Report*, ESPN reporter Sal Paolantonio discusses the most overrated and underrated NFL players at every position, and for most overrated quarterback, his pick is Joe Namath.

There is some merit to Paolantonio's argument. Namath is in the Hall of Fame primarily for two reasons: 1) his impact on the finances and style of the sport in the 1960s, and 2) leading the underdog Jets of the upstart AFL over the NFL's vaunted Colts in Super Bowl III after brashly guaranteeing a win the week before the game.

A cursory look at Namath's numbers is not very favorable to Joe. He threw 173 touchdowns but also 220 interceptions, barely completed 50 percent of his passes with a just-above-average 65.5 passer rating, and won fewer games than he lost. But with Namath, we have to take injuries into account. He came into the league on one leg, having blown out one knee in his senior year at Alabama, and showed tremendous courage in the pocket throughout his career despite his immobility. In his first five years, Joe did not miss a game due to injury, but over the next four seasons, he would go down to a season-ending injury three times. By 1973 he was finished as a useful quarterback but continued playing through 1977. Through those first five years, Namath threw for 97 touchdowns and 104 interceptions and went 37–23–4 as a starter. Despite the fact that his gambling, bomb-throwing playing style was not conducive to high passer ratings, his 70.1 for the period was 13 percent greater than the league average, and he led the league in passing yards twice and yards per attempt once. As a result, the Jets' offense scored 17 percent more than the league average in points during those five years. Expanding the view to Namath's first eight years, his passer rating was still 10 percent better than the league average, his record was 47–34–4, and the Jets were still scoring points at 16 percent better than the league. By the end of his career, though, Namath was just 3 percent better than the league in passer rating and the Jets were 7 percent better than the league in scoring over that time.

When Namath was healthy, he was an amazing quarterback. He had the quickest release in the game; was a master of reading defenses and calling plays, as he proved in Super Bowl III; and was an inspirational, charismatic leader that his teammates would follow anywhere. Yes, he forced too many passes and threw interceptions even at his healthiest, but he was the most exciting quarterback of his time. His 21 300-yard games are third behind

Johnny Unitas and Sonny Jurgensen among pre-1980 quarterbacks. The 1972 showdown between the hobbled Namath and aged Unitas when Namath threw for 496 yards and six touchdowns to overcome Unitas' 376 yards and three touchdowns is one of the most memorable games in NFL history. He was Unitas' heir—they shared the same first coach—but injuries robbed Joe of proving that statistically.

Bill Nelsen

Height: 6'0"   **Weight:** 195 lbs.   **Birthdate:** 1/29/1941
College: USC   **Draft:** Pittsburgh 1963-10th
1963–67 Pittsburgh Steelers; 1968–72 Cleveland Browns
Regular Season Record: 40–31–3, 7 comebacks
Postseason Record: 2–3, no comebacks
Relative Rating: 105%

Passing

Year	G	Comp./Att.	%	Yards	Y/Att.	TD	INT	Rating
1963	2	0/2	0.0	0	0.0	0	0	39.6
1964	5	16/42	38.1	276	6.6	2	3	47.3
1965	12	121/270	44.8	1,917	7.1	8	17	52.7
1966	5	63/112	56.3	1,122	10.0	7	1	107.8
1967	8	74/165	44.8	1,125	6.8	10	9	65.3
1968	14	152/293	51.9	2,366	8.1	19	10	86.4
1969	14	190/352	54.0	2,743	7.8	23	19	78.8
1970	12	159/313	50.8	2,156	6.9	16	16	68.9
1971	14	174/325	53.5	2,319	7.1	13	23	60.3
1972	4	14/31	45.2	141	4.5	0	3	19.1
Total	**90**	963/1,905	50.6	14,165	7.4	98	101	70.2
PS:	5	68/132	51.5	839	6.4	3	8	53.8

Rushing

Year	Att.	Yards	Avg.	TD
1963	1	-6	-6.0	0
1964	3	17	5.7	0
1965	26	84	3.2	1
1966	6	18	3.0	0
1967	9	-19	-2.1	0
1968	13	30	2.3	1
1969	5	-11	-2.2	0
1970	7	-4	-0.6	0
1971	13	-18	-1.4	0
1972	1	-2	-2.0	0
Total	**84**	**89**	**1.1**	**2**
PS:	4	-7	-1.8	0

Bill Nelsen's knees may have been even worse than Joe Namath's. One of Bill's knees was operated on four times and the other twice. Like Namath, Nelsen bravely played on in the teeth of the fiercest pass rush while sporting heavy aluminum braces to support his rickety knees. Unlike Namath, Nelsen managed to win more games than he lost and did not hang on playing way beyond the disappearance of his skills.

Nelsen battled Pete Beathard for the starting job at USC as the Trojans won the national championship in his senior year of 1962. Nelsen did not have the strongest arm and was not especially big, but he learned to read defenses and was very good at floating long passes in to his receivers. Although immobile, he had a confident attitude and was a respected leader on the field. After not playing much in his first two years in Pittsburgh, Nelsen became the team's primary starter from 1965 through 1967 but went down to knee injuries each year. Finally, the Steelers traded Bill to the Browns in 1968, and his career blossomed under coach Blanton Collier. Nelsen beat out Frank Ryan as starter that year and led the Browns to the playoffs in his first two years in Cleveland, although they lost the NFL championship both times, once to Baltimore and once to Minnesota, and missed going to the Super Bowl. In 1972, Nelsen's knees continued to deteriorate, so he lost his starting job to Mike Phipps. Bill retired and spent the next decade coaching for the Browns, Falcons, Bucs, and Lions.

Harry Newman

QPR 6.0

Height: 5'8" **Weight:** 179 lbs. **Birthdate:** 9/5/1909
College: Michigan **Draft:** Free Agent
1933–35 New York Giants; 1936–37 AFL II
Regular Season Record: 21–7 est., 3 comebacks
Postseason Record: 0–1, no comebacks
Relative Rating: 143%

Passing

Year	G	Comp./Att.	%	Yards	Y/Att.	TD	INT	Rating
1933	14	53/136	39.0	973	7.2	11	17	51.7
1934	10	35/93	37.6	391	4.2	1	12	15.0
1935	8	9/29	31.0	132	4.6	0	7	7.3
Total	32	97/258	37.6	1,496	5.8	12	36	33.5
PS:	2	13/25	52.0	209	8.4	2	2	73.6

Rushing

Year	Att.	Yards	Avg.	TD
1933	130	437	3.4	3
1934	141	483	3.4	3
1935	65	166	2.6	0
Total	336	1,086	3.2	6
PS:	0	0	0	0

Harry Newman was an exciting single-wing tailback in the early years of the NFL who was one of the best passers and ball handlers of his day. He grew up in Detroit and attended Benny Friedman's summer camp, where Friedman taught him how to pass and later recommended him to the University of Michigan. Newman enrolled there and was an All-American Wolverine just like Benny had been. In his tenure at Ann Arbor, Michigan lost just one game in three years, and Newman was the MVP of the Big Ten. The Giants signed the 5'8" passer upon graduation in 1933 to replace Friedman, who had left the team the year before.

Newman negotiated a smart deal with New York that included a percentage of the gate as a bonus to his salary. In Harry's rookie season, he led the NFL in passing yards with 973 and touchdowns with 12 as well as in attempts and completions. He also finished sixth in the league in rushing. In the thrilling 1933 championship game against the Bears that went down to the final play with Chicago prevailing, Newman threw for 201 yards, a total that was unheard of for the time. Harry fell off to just one touchdown pass in 1934, though, and averaged just four yards per completion that year. His second season ended badly late in the year when the crush of the Bears' pass rush injured his back. Ed Danowski took over as tailback, led the Giants to the title, and then kept the starting job the following season. Harry held out at the beginning of the 1935 season and played sporadically after that.

When the Giants weren't willing to meet Newman's contract demands in 1936, Harry helped form the second American Football League. However, after two lackluster seasons, the league went under and Newman retired. Harry's Brooklyn Tigers had to move to Rochester in the middle of the 1936 season and finished with 0–6–1 and 4–3 records for the two years of their existence.

Newman went on to have a successful career as a private businessman and lived vibrantly to the age of 90.

Gifford Nielsen

Height: 6'4" **Weight:** 205 lbs. **Birthdate:** 10/25/1954
College: BYU **Draft:** Houston Oilers 1978-3rd
1978–83 Houston Oilers
Regular Season Record: 3–11, 2 comebacks
Postseason Record: 1–0, no comebacks
Relative Rating: 96%

Passing

Year	G	Comp./Att.	%	Yards	Y/Att.	TD	INT	Rating
1978	2	2/4	50.0	0	0.0	0	0	56.2
1979	16	32/61	52.5	404	6.6	3	3	69.3
1980	16	2/4	50.0	12	3.0	1	0	95.8
1981	5	60/93	64.5	709	7.6	5	3	92.1
1982	9	87/161	54.0	1,005	6.2	6	8	64.8
1983	7	90/175	51.4	1,125	6.4	5	8	62.2
Total	55	273/498	54.8	3,255	6.5	20	22	70.0
PS:	3	13/24	54.2	129	5.4	1	2	48-8

Rushing

Year	Att.	Yards	Avg.	TD
1979	5	7	1.4	0
1980	1	0	0.0	0
1981	6	2	0.3	0
1982	9	37	4.1	0
1983	8	43	5.4	0
Total	29	89	3.1	0
PS:	2	12	6.0	0

After Gifford Nielsen replaced an injured Ken Stabler for the Oilers in 1981, Houston center Carl Mauck commented, "In the huddle, I can't get used to the smell of milkshakes on Gifford's breath." Nielsen, a clean-living Mormon, was a clear contrast to Snake Stabler both on and off the field. That may have been good news for the Houston community as a whole but not for the Oilers.

Nielsen was an earlier, taller version of another BYU quarterback, Ty Detmer. Both had a lot of success in college by throwing a ton of passes in the Cougars' aerial attack, but neither had the arm to succeed in the NFL. In fact, Gifford almost didn't make it to the NFL. As a senior, he tore up his knee so badly that he was told his playing days were over. Nielsen overcame that setback because he was smart and dedicated, the ideal backup quarterback. The biggest highlight of his career came in the 1979 playoffs when he took the place of injured Dan Pastorini and led the Oilers over the favored Chargers in San Diego. Although Nielsen's 111 yards passing didn't compare to Dan Fouts' 333 that day, Gifford threw just one interception while Dan tossed five in the 17–14 upset. Nielsen lost the last nine starts in his career.

Jim Ninowski

Height: 6'1" **Weight:** 206 lbs. **Birthdate:** 3/26/1936
College: Michigan State **Draft:** Cleveland 1958-4th
1958–59, 1962–66 Cleveland Browns; 1960–61
Detroit Lions; 1967–68 New Orleans Saints; 1969
Washington Redskins
Regular Season Record: 15–15–1, 2 comebacks
Postseason Record: 0–0, no comebacks
Relative Rating: 80%

Passing

Year	G	Comp./Att.	%	Yards	Y/Att.	TD	INT	Rating
1958	4	8/17	47.1	139	8.2	1	3	55.4
1959	2	3/10	30.0	41	4.1	0	1	4.6
1960	11	134/283	47.3	1,599	5.7	2	18	40.9
1961	13	117/247	47.4	1,921	7.8	7	18	53.0
1962	7	87/173	50.3	1,178	6.8	7	8	66.6
1963	4	29/61	47.5	423	6.9	2	6	41.9
1964	3	6/9	66.7	125	13.9	2	0	149.3
1965	6	40/83	48.2	549	6.6	4	3	70.8
1966	14	11/18	61.1	175	9.7	4	1	110.0
1967	14	12/18	66.7	123	6.8	0	1	63.0
1968	7	49/95	51.6	633	6.7	4	6	60.5
1969	4	17/34	50.0	227	6.7	1	2	56.9
Total	89	513/1,048	49.0	7,133	6.8	34	67	55.4
PS:	1	3/15	20.0	31	2.1	0	1	11.8

Rushing

Year	Att.	Yards	Avg.	TD
1958	2	1	0.5	0
1959	1	11	11.0	0
1960	32	81	2.5	5
1961	33	238	7.2	5
1962	9	15	1.7	0
1963	5	-19	-3.8	0
1964	1	-8	-8.0	0
1965	4	46	11.5	0
1966	3	-11	-3.7	0
1968	2	13	6.5	0
Total	**92**	**367**	**4.0**	**10**

| PS: | 0 | 0 | 0.0 | 0 |

Jim Ninowski followed his fellow Michigan native Earl Morrall to Michigan State and later competed with Earl in Detroit for the Lions' starting quarterback position. Cleveland drafted Ninowski as Milt Plum's backup, but he threw just 27 passes in his first two seasons. Jim was traded to Detroit in 1960 for a No. 1 draft pick but never lived up to that billing with the Lions. Although Jim got most of the playing time, Morrall was clearly the better player. Ninowski completed just 47 percent of his passes for nine touchdowns and 36 interceptions in 1960 and 1961. Morrall completed 50 percent of his passes for 11 touchdowns and 12 interceptions in that time. Furthermore, the Lions were 9–8–1 in Ninowski's starts and 6–2 in Morrall's starts.

Finally, Detroit pulled the plug on Ninowski in 1962 when they traded him back to Cleveland for Milt Plum. Ninowski threatened to quit rather than return to Paul Brown, who once dryly told a reporter, "Mr. Ninowski does not understand how I feel about interceptions." Jim played better in 1962 but was challenged strongly by Frank Ryan. Ninowski had a strong but very erratic arm and was a hard thrower. His best skill was running with the ball, and Jim led all quarterbacks in touchdowns scored in both years in Detroit. In fact, Brown even talked about having Ninowski run some option plays when he brought Jim back in 1962. Under new coach Blanton Collier, Ryan beat out Ninowski as starter in 1963, and Jim settled in as a backup for the last seven years of his career.

In the war with the AFL, Ninowski made out quite well, even as a backup. When the AFL went on its raid of NFL quarterbacks in 1966, Ninowski negotiated a four-year, $100,000 contract with Oakland that was sidelined by the merger of the leagues. When Ninowski threatened legal action, the NFL secretly paid him the difference between his real salary and the negotiated one for the four-year period.

Kent Nix

Height: 6'2" **Weight:** 195 lbs. **Birthdate:** 3/12/1944
College: Texas Christian **Draft:** Free agent
1967–69 Pittsburgh Steelers; 1970–71 Chicago Bears;
1972 Houston Oilers
Regular Season Record: 4–14, 3 comebacks
Postseason Record: NA
Relative Rating: 67%

Passing

Year	G	Comp./Att.	%	Yards	Y/Att.	TD	INT	Rating
1967	12	136/268	50.7	1,587	5.9	8	19	49.5
1968	8	56/130	43.1	720	5.5	4	8	45.7
1969	5	25/53	47.2	290	5.5	2	6	37.2
1970	1	0/1	0.0	0	0.0	0	0	39.6
1971	8	51/137	37.2	760	5.5	6	10	40.4
1972	12	33/63	52.4	287	4.6	3	6	41.0
Total	**46**	**301/652**	**46.2**	**3,644**	**5.6**	**23**	**49**	**44.3**

Rushing

Year	Att.	Yards	Avg.	TD
1967	15	45	3.0	2
1968	6	15	2.5	0
1969	10	70	7.0	0
1971	9	12	1.3	0
1972	3	3	1.0	0
Total	**43**	**145**	**3.4**	**2**

Kent Nix is the only Texas Christian passer aside from Sammy Baugh to throw at least 500 passes in the NFL and is the last Horned Frog quarterback to start a game in the league. The only other TCU quarterbacks who made it to the NFL were Hunter Enis and the 6'7" Sonny Gibbs in the 1960s. After Baugh, two other TCU single-wing tailbacks turned professional—Davey O'Brien in 1939 and Kent's dad, Emery, in 1943. In fact, Emery Nix's completion percentage of 47.2, passer rating of 78.8, and yards per pass average of 7.8 all exceed his son's numbers.

Kent signed with the Packers as an undrafted free agent and spent 1966 on Green Bay's practice squad. Steelers coach Bill Austin, a former Packer assistant, signed Nix in 1967 and gave him a shot when Bill Nelsen went down to another knee injury. Nix started nine games that year and threw 19 interceptions. He had a strong arm, but it was an inaccurate and erratic one as well. After three years in Pittsburgh, Nix spent two in Chicago and one in Houston and was found inadequate in all three cities. At least he lasted four years longer in the NFL than his dad did.

Rick Norton

Height: 6'2" **Weight:** 200 lbs. **Birthdate:** 11/16/1943
College: Kentucky **Draft:** Miami Dolphins 1966-1st; Cleveland Browns 1966-2nd
1966-69 Miami Dolphins; 1970 Green Bay Packers
Regular Season Record: 1–10, no comebacks
Postseason Record: NA
Relative Rating: 47%

Passing

Year	G	Comp./Att.	%	Yards	Y/Att.	TD	INT	Rating
1966	7	21/55	38.2	192	3.5	3	6	27.0
1967	14	53/133	39.8	596	4.5	1	9	28.3
1968	3	17/41	41.5	254	6.2	0	4	22.9
1969	7	65/148	43.9	709	4.8	2	11	32.2
1970	1	3/5	60.0	64	12.8	1	0	143.7
Total	32	159/382	41.6	1,815	4.8	7	30	30.0

Rushing

Year	Att.	Yards	Avg.	TD
1966	3	2	0.7	0
1967	7	14	2.0	0
1968	1	9	9.0	0
1969	8	16	2.0	0
Total	19	41	2.2	0

On his wedding day in 1966, Rick Norton was the second of two No. 1 draft picks of the expansion Miami Dolphins. The Dolphins' first pick that first year, Jim Grabowski, rebuffed Miami to sign with Green Bay. Norton signed with Miami but was a tremendous failure with a passer rating not even half that of the league average for his time. Dolphins' player personnel chief Joe Thomas said

at the time, "The young players are the ones who make us or break us in three years. They have to be good, and they have to glitter."

Norton fit neither category. Rick injured his knee as a senior in college and never fully recovered. He was not much of a scrambler to start with but was really immobile after that. Behind the leaky offensive line of an expansion team, Norton was pummeled. He suffered a fractured jaw as a rookie and broke his cheekbone and a couple of fingers in 1967.

Norton had a very strong arm but no real quarterbacking skills. Rick completed just 41 percent of his 382 passes for an average of fewer than 5 yards per pass. He threw just seven touchdown passes while tossing 30 interceptions and fumbling 15 times. Looking back years later, Norton told a reporter, "I wasn't near the athlete Bob [Griese] was. When you get into camp and see the other guy's ability—well you know you're in trouble. He was a great quarterback." Although Norton was cut after the 1970 season, he continued to receive deferred compensation checks to 1975 as the team's original bonus baby bust.

Davey O'Brien

Height: 5'7" **Weight:** 151 lbs. **Birthdate:** 6/22/1917
College: Texas Christian **Draft:** Philadelphia 1939-1st
1939–40 Philadelphia Eagles
Regular Season Record: 2–19–1 est., 2 comebacks
Postseason Record: NA
Relative Rating: 108%

Passing

Year	G	Comp./Att.	%	Yards	Y/Att.	TD	INT	Rating
1939	11	99/201	49.3	1,324	6.6	6	17	45.3
1940	11	124/277	44.8	1,290	4.7	5	17	39.2
Total	22	223/478	46.7	2,614	5.5	11	34	41.8

Rushing

Year	Att.	Yards	Avg.	TD
1939	108	-14	-0.1	1
1940	100	-180	-1.8	1
Total	208	-194	-0.9	2

The 5'7" 150-pound single-wing tailback Davey O'Brien succeeded the lanky Sammy Baugh at Texas

Christian in 1937 and was named All-Southwestern Conference quarterback. In his senior season of 1938, O'Brien completed 55 percent of his passes for 1,733 yards and 19 touchdowns while running for 10 more scores. And he played safety on defense. TCU won the Sugar Bowl and the national championship with an 11–0 record that year. Davey won the Walter Camp Memorial Trophy, the Heisman Trophy, and the Maxwell Club Award as the best player in college football.

Although Davey did not intend to play pro football, Bert Bell selected O'Brien with the Eagles' first pick in the 1939 draft and signed him for $10,000 plus a percentage of the gate. O'Brien was the first Heisman winner to play professional ball. Although Bell felt the need to take out an insurance policy with Lloyd's of London on the slightly built tailback, Davey never missed a game for Philadelphia. However, the team went 2–19–1 and was outscored 411 points to 216 over O'Brien's two-year NFL career. With Davey, the Philadelphia offense threw the ball more than any team in the league by far. Essentially, the Eagles were running their offense from the shotgun formation, but it was mostly short passes because O'Brien did not have the arm to throw the bomb. Philadelphia had a terrible offensive line and Davey regularly ran for his life to escape the relentless pass rush. Still, O'Brien broke Baugh's league record for passing yards in his rookie season and earned himself a $2,000 raise.

Davey ended his short career with his most memorable game in the 1940 season finale against Baugh's Redskins. O'Brien passed the ball on almost every down and completed a record 33 of 60 passes for 316 yards that day. Trailing 13–0 in the fourth quarter, Davey led a 98-yard scoring drive to get Philadelphia on the board. The Eagles' final drive took them from their own 31 to the Redskin 22 as time ran out. After the game, Bell presented Davey with a plaque inscribed, "To the greatest player of all time. Small in stature with the heart of a lion. A living inspiration to the youth of America." O'Brien quit the game in 1941 to join the FBI. Davey O'Brien was a fine person who claimed his most prized accomplishment was winning the Best All-Around Camper award when he was a schoolboy struggling to overcome a bad temper. He paved the way for

Eddie LeBaron in the 1950s and Doug Flutie in the 1990s to succeed in the NFL despite their lack of size.

Ken O'Brien

Height: 6'4" **Weight:** 210 lbs. **Birthdate:** 11/27/1960
College: California-Davis **Draft:** New York Jets 1983-1st
1984–92 New York Jets; 1993 Philadelphia Eagles
Regular Season Record: 50–59–1, 19 comebacks
Postseason Record: 0–2, no comebacks
Relative Rating: 107%

Passing
Year	G	Comp./Att.	%	Yards	Y/Att.	TD	INT	Rating
1984	10	116/203	57.1	1,402	6.9	6	7	74.0
1985	16	297/488	60.9	3,888	8.0	25	8	96.2
1986	15	300/482	62.2	3,690	7.7	25	20	85.8
1987	12	234/393	59.5	2,696	6.9	13	8	82.8
1988	14	236/424	55.7	2,567	6.1	15	7	78.6
1989	15	288/477	60.4	3,346	7.0	12	18	74.3
1990	16	226/411	55.0	2,855	6.9	13	10	77.3
1991	16	287/489	58.7	3,300	6.7	10	11	76.6
1992	10	55/98	56.1	642	6.6	5	6	67.6
1993	5	71/137	51.8	708	5.2	4	3	67.4
Total	129	2,110/3,602	58.6	25,094	7.0	128	98	80.4
PS:	3	45/67	67.2	504	7.5	2	4	74.5

Rushing
Year	Att.	Yards	Avg.	TD
1984	16	29	1.8	0
1985	25	58	2.3	0
1986	17	46	2.7	0
1987	30	61	2.0	0
1988	21	25	1.2	0
1989	9	18	2.0	0
1990	21	72	3.4	0
1991	23	60	2.6	0
1992	8	8	1.0	0
1993	4	17	4.3	0
Total	174	394	2.3	0
PS:	6	36	6.0	0

A Division II All-American at California-Davis, Ken O'Brien was the fifth of six quarterbacks taken in the celebrated 1983 NFL draft. Oddly, his college roommate, Bo Eason, was the brother of the fourth quarterback selected, Tony Eason. Tony later finished his career as O'Brien's backup on the 1990 Jets. The sixth quarterback taken, Dan Marino, reacted to being drafted behind the little-known O'Brien by saying, "Who?"

O'Brien had a very strange up-and-down career in New York. He did not play at all as a rookie. In 1984, his progress was delayed by his involvement in a trial concerning a brawl at the famous New York nightspot Studio 54. O'Brien finally became the Jets' starter for the last five games of that season and in 1985 made the Pro Bowl, throwing 25 touchdowns to just eight interceptions and leading the Jets to the playoffs. O'Brien and the Jets got off to a fast start in 1986, winning 10 of 11 games before they crash-landed. After the first 11 games, O'Brien had thrown 23 touchdowns and just eight interceptions. In the last five games, though, Ken threw just two touchdowns and 12 interceptions while the Jets lost all five. The team managed to get back into the playoffs, but coach Joe Walton then benched the ineffective, dead-armed O'Brien for backup Pat Ryan. New York beat Kansas City in the first round, but Ryan was hurt in the second-round game against Cleveland. O'Brien came in but was unimpressive as Bernie Kosar led the Browns to a comeback victory. Cumulatively over the course of Ken's career with the Jets, he was 42–37–1 in the first 12 games of the year and just 8–18 in the last quarter of the season.

O'Brien is most remembered for his duels with Marino and the Dolphins in the late 1980s. From 1986 through 1989, the two quarterbacks met six times, with each man winning three and with at least one team scoring more than 30 points in every game. The best game was a 51–45 overtime shootout in 1986 in which O'Brien tied the game with a 21-yard pass to Wesley Walker in the fourth quarter and won it in overtime with a 43-yard strike to Walker.

O'Brien was a very accurate passer who three times led the league with the lowest interception percentage, but he still managed to throw some untimely picks. Although he had a strong arm, he tended to rely more on the short passing game. His biggest problem was in not getting rid of the ball. Ken was sacked on nearly 9 percent of pass plays and twice was sacked the most times in the NFL, which shortened his career. After just seven years as the team's primary starter, O'Brien was pushed

aside by Browning Nagle in 1991 and traded to Green Bay in 1992. The Packers cut O'Brien in training camp, but he caught on briefly with the Eagles, coached by Rich Kotite, who had worked with Ken as the Jets' offensive coach in the 1980s. O'Brien lost all four starts in Philadelphia, and his career was over.

Tommy O'Connell

QPR 5.0

Height: 5'10"   **Weight:** 187 lbs.   **Birthdate:** 9/26/1930
College: Illinois   **Draft:** Chicago Bears 1952-18th
1953 Chicago Bears; 1956–57 Cleveland Browns; 1960–61 Buffalo Bills
Regular Season Record: 11-7-2, 2 comebacks
Postseason Record: 0-1, no comebacks
Relative Rating: 97%

Passing

Year	G	Comp./Att.	%	Yards	Y/Att.	TD	INT	Rating
1953	12	33/67	49.3	437	6.5	1	4	50.4
1956	7	42/96	43.8	551	5.7	4	8	41.6
1957	11	63/110	57.3	1,229	11.2	9	8	93.3
1960	14	65/145	44.8	1,033	7.1	7	13	47.9
1961	1	1/5	20.0	11	2.2	0	1	0.0
Total	45	204/423	48.2	3,261	7.7	21	34	57.5
PS:	1	4/8	50.0	61	7.6	0	2	35.9

Rushing

Year	Att.	Yards	Avg.	TD
1953	7	16	2.3	0
1956	24	40	1.7	2
1957	14	-5	-0.4	1
1960	16	21	1.3	1
Total	61	72	1.2	4
PS:	0	0	0.0	0

Little Tommy O'Connell had a sporadic professional career as a game manager quarterback for three teams. O'Connell led the University of Illinois to an undefeated season and Rose Bowl triumph in his junior year and was a late-round pick of the hometown Bears in 1952. Tommy saw his first NFL action in 1953, but that was solely as starter George Blanda's relief. After two years in the army, O'Connell was cut by the Bears in 1956 and picked up in midseason by the Browns when

TOP 10
Shortest Quarterbacks

10-T. Drew Brees, 6'
10-T. Fran Tarkenton, 6'
5-T. Marlin Briscoe, 5'10"
5-T. Frankie Filchock, 5'10"
5-T. Benny Friedman, 5'10" (tailback)
5-T. Frankie Albert, 5'10"
4.   Doug Flutie, 5'9"
3.   Harry Newman, 5'8" (tailback)
1-T. Davey O'Brien, 5'7" (tailback)
1-T. Eddie LeBaron, 5'7"

starter George Ratterman suffered a career-ending knee injury. Tommy started the last five games for Cleveland after backup Babe Parilli, too, got hurt but was scatter-armed with four touchdown passes and eight interceptions.

With rookie running back Jim Brown shouldering the load of the Cleveland offense in 1957, O'Connell had to throw just 10 passes a game to lead the Browns to the Eastern Conference crown. Because the league passing title was determined by average yards per pass in the 1950s, Tommy was the NFL's leading passer in 1957 with an average of 11 yards per attempt. His yards per completion figure was an amazing 19.5, he completed 57 percent of his passes, and was voted the team's MVP. Unfortunately, in the 10th game of the year, O'Connell broke his leg, although it was reported as just a sprained ankle. After three weeks of rest, Tommy started the NFL title game against the Lions and completed just four of eight passes with two interceptions in the first half before being lifted with Detroit ahead 31–7 on their way to the title.

The Browns cut O'Connell the next year—the first time an NFL passing leader, championship game starter, and team MVP was cut the following season. Tommy spent 1958 and 1959 as an assistant coach at Illinois before signing on as the first quarterback of the Buffalo Bills in 1960. O'Connell was unimpressive in Buffalo and lasted just one game into the 1961 season before being cut for good. Two of his sons, Mike and Tim, went on to

play professional hockey, and Mike advanced into the front office of the Boston Bruins and the Los Angeles Kings.

Neil O'Donnell
QPR 8.0

Height: 6'3" **Weight:** 228 lbs. **Birthdate:** 7/3/1966
College: Maryland **Draft:** Pittsburgh 1990-3rd
1990–95 Pittsburgh Steelers; 1996–97 New York Jets; 1998 Cincinnati Bengals; 1999–2003 Tennessee Titans
Regular Season Record: 55–45, 18 comebacks
Postseason Record: 3–4, 1 comeback
Relative Rating: 105%

Passing

Year	G	Comp./Att.	%	Yards	Y/Att.	TD	INT	Rating
1991	12	156/286	54.5	1,963	6.9	11	7	78.8
1992	12	185/313	59.1	2,283	7.3	13	9	83.6
1993	16	270/486	55.6	3,208	6.6	14	7	79.5
1994	14	212/370	57.3	2,443	6.6	13	9	78.9
1995	12	246/416	59.1	2,970	7.1	17	7	87.7
1996	6	110/188	58.5	1,147	6.1	4	7	67.8
1997	15	259/460	56.3	2,796	6.1	17	7	80.3
1998	13	212/343	61.8	2,216	6.5	15	4	90.2
1999	8	116/195	59.5	1,382	7.1	10	5	87.6
2000	6	36/64	56.3	530	8.3	2	3	74.3
2001	5	42/76	55.3	496	6.5	2	2	73.1
2002	4	3/5	60.0	24	4.8	0	0	72.1
2003	1	18/27	66.7	232	8.6	2	1	102.7
Total	**124**	**1,865/3,229**	**57.8**	**21,690**	**6.7**	**120**	**68**	**81.8**
PS:	9	159/275	57.8	1,705	6.2	9	8	74.9

Rushing

Year	Att.	Yards	Avg.	TD
1942	18	-17	-0.9	1
1946	47	50	1.1	1
1947	24	55	2.3	1
1948	7	15	2.1	1
Total	**215**	**446**	**2.1**	**4**
PS:	8	28	3.5	0

Neil O'Donnell's career was one of the most ironic in football history. The quarterback with the lowest interception percentage in league history will forever be remembered for throwing two of the lamest interceptions in Super Bowl history to cost the Steelers a possible championship. Those

While Neil O'Donnell had the intelligence and talent to be a starter, his personality was better matched to being a backup quarterback.

Rich Kotite. The team lost its first six games, and then O'Donnell had his shoulder separated during a sack. Six games later, Neil was ready to return but slipped on the Jets' logo on the field and tore a calf muscle that ended his season. The 1–15 Jets let Kotite go, and angry rookie receiver Keyshawn Johnson blasted everyone in his controversial book *Just Give Me the Damn Ball*. Johnson claimed that O'Donnell faked his injury, padded his stats, and was afraid to throw long. Bill Parcells was hired to straighten out this soap opera and a year later released O'Donnell to sign Vinny Testaverde because he felt Neil was overpriced. O'Donnell went to Cincinnati for a season before signing with Tennessee. Neil spent five years as Steve McNair's backup, a low-pressure job for which he was ideally suited.

two picks by Cowboy corner Larry Brown were so bad that Neil's teammates did not even make a pretense of protecting him after the game. Runner Erric Pegram grumbled, "We gave away the Super Bowl. We even gave away the MVP. It was like Christmas out there." One month later, O'Donnell left the Steelers as a free agent and signed a five-year, $25 million contract with the Jets.

O'Donnell had been a mid-round draft choice that Pittsburgh nurtured, and their conservative run-first offense brought out the best in such a cautious quarterback of moderate skills. Neil never threw more than 17 touchdowns or nine interceptions in any of his five seasons with the Steelers but led the team to four straight playoff berths. Pittsburgh made a strong effort to hold on to him even after the Super Bowl debacle, but ultimately the Jets had more green and O'Donnell jumped to New Jersey.

His first year with the Jets was a bizarre fiasco under the less-than-astute leadership of coach

Charlie O'Rourke

QPR 6.0

Height: 5'11" **Weight:** 175 lbs. **Birthdate:** 5/10/17
College: Boston College **Draft:** Chicago Bears 1941-5th
1942 Chicago Bears; 1946–47 Los Angeles Dons;
1948–49 Baltimore Colts
Regular Season Record: 14–12–2 est., 5 comebacks
Postseason Record: 0–0, no comebacks
Relative Rating: 113%

Passing

Year	G	Comp./Att.	%	Yards	Y/Att.	TD	INT	Rating
1942	11	37/88	42.0	951	10.8	11	16	82.1
1946	14	105/182	57.7	1,250	6.9	12	14	68.7
1947	14	89/178	50.0	1,449	8.1	13	16	64.6
1948	14	24/51	47.1	377	7.4	3	4	59.0
1949	5	1/7	14.3	12	1.7	0	1	0.0
Total	**58**	**256/506**	**50.6**	**4,039**	**8.0**	**39**	**51**	**63.6**
PS:	1	4/6	66.7	110	18.3	0	0	109.7

Rushing

Year	Att.	Yards	Avg.	TD
1942	18	-17	-0.9	1
1946	47	50	1.1	1
1947	24	55	2.3	1
1948	7	15	2.1	1
Total	**96**	**103**	**1.1**	**4**
PS:	0	0	0.0	0

Charlie O'Rourke was the original Doug Flutie at Boston College. Under coach Frank Leahy, the slightly built O'Rourke led the Eagles to a 20–2 record from 1939 to 1940 and a victory in the 1941 Sugar Bowl over Tennessee. O'Rourke was an All-American in his senior year and was drafted by the Bears. George Halas liked to rotate his backs to keep them fresh, so O'Rourke got to play enough as Sid Luckman's backup in 1942 to throw 11 touchdown passes as a rookie.

O'Rourke went into the navy for the duration of World War II and signed with the Los Angeles Dons of the All-America Football Conference in 1946. In Los Angeles, Charlie alternated at quarterback with Angelo Bertelli in 1946 and Glenn Dobbs in 1947, throwing 25 touchdown passes and 30 interceptions over two seasons. When the Dons decided to shift to the single-wing to accommodate the skills of Dobbs in 1948, O'Rourke was sold to the Baltimore Colts where he served as a player/coach under Cecil Isbell but played little behind the young Y.A. Tittle. With the demise of the AAFC in 1950, O'Rourke retired and went into coaching in his native New England.

Kyle Orton

QPR 4.5

Height: 6'4" **Weight:** 226 lbs. **Birthdate:** 11/14/1982
College: Purdue **Draft:** Chicago Bears 2005-4th
2005, 2007–08 Chicago Bears
Regular Season Record: 21–12, 2 comebacks
Postseason Record: NA
Relative Rating: 89%

Passing

Year	G	Comp./Att.	%	Yards	Y/Att.	TD	INT	Rating
2005	15	190/368	51.6	1,869	5.1	9	13	59.7
2007	3	43/80	53.8	478	6.0	3	2	73.9
2008	15	272/465	58.5	2,972	6.4	18	12	79.6
Total	33	505/913	55.3	5,319	5.8	30	27	71.1

Rushing

Year	Att.	Yards	Avg.	TD
2005	24	44	1.8	0
2007	5	-1	-0.2	0
2008	24	49	2.0	3
Total	53	92	1.7	3

TOP 10
Ugliest Interceptions

10. Jim Hardy threw eight picks in one game against the Eagles in 1950.
9. Raider Mike Davis intercepted Brian Sipe's end zone pass to Ozzie Newsome on a play called Red Right 88 with 41 seconds to play to preserve Oakland's divisional playoff win over Cleveland in January 1981.
8. Earl Morrall didn't see Jimmy Orr open in the end zone on a flea flicker and was picked by Jim Hudson in Super Bowl III.
7. Rex Grossman was picked off by Kelvin Hayden for the clinching touchdown in Super Bowl XLI.
6. Brett Favre threw a "pop-fly" interception that Brian Dawkins returned to set up the winning field goal in overtime during the 2003 playoffs.
5. Richard Todd was picked off by Dolphin A.J. Duhe three times in a muddy 1983 playoff loss.
4. Craig Morton's two fourth-quarter interceptions led to the Colts' final 10 points to win Super Bowl IV.
3. Joe Theismann's screen pass was intercepted by Raider linebacker Jack Squirek and returned for the clinching touchdown with 12 seconds left in the first half of Super Bowl XVIII.
2. Neil O'Donnell gift-wrapped two interceptions for mediocre Cowboy cornerback Larry Brown, who is named MVP of Super Bowl XXX.
1. Matt Hasselbeck announced during the overtime coin flip in a 2004 playoff game that the Seahawks wanted the ball and were going to score and then threw an out-pattern that Packer corner Al Harris jumped and returned for the winning score.

Like his immediate predecessor at Purdue, Drew Brees, Kyle Orton was a terrific college quarterback in a spread-passing offense that took the Boilermakers to three straight bowl games. Force-fed into a starting position as a rookie nearly destroyed Orton's NFL career, but he has made great strides in 2008 to prove that he belongs in the league.

As a rookie in 2005, Orton was made the starter when the highly touted Rex Grossman in his third year was hurt in the preseason and backup Chad Hutchinson demonstrated that he was a catastrophe behind center. Orton was badly overmatched at quarterback that year but was present for 10 wins in 15 starts as he averaged just 5.1 yards per pass and fewer than 10 yards per completion. The Bears relied on their defense and running attack to get them to the playoffs when Grossman came back to wreck the season. Still, Grossman returned as starter in 2006 when Chicago's defense took the team to the Super Bowl. Orton was demoted to third string that year behind free agent Brian Griese and began in the same spot in 2007. However, the cartoon adventures of Grossman and mediocrity of Griese led to Kyle getting some action in 2007 and showing enough to set up a quarterback competition in 2008.

Orton beat out Grossman in the 2008 preseason and showed much improvement in his fourth year. His completion percentage and yards per pass average both increased significantly, and he threw twice as many touchdowns as interceptions. Kyle will probably never be more than a game manager but has established himself as a viable quarterback in the NFL. In 2009, he was traded to Denver in exchange for Jay Cutler.

Mike Pagel

Height: 6'2" **Weight:** 206 lbs. **Birthdate:** 9/13/1960
College: Arizona State **Draft:** Baltimore Colts 1982-4th
1982–85 Baltimore/Indianapolis Colts; 1986–90 Cleveland Browns; 1991–93 Los Angeles Rams
Regular Season Record: 17–36–1, no comebacks
Postseason Record: 0–1, no comebacks
Relative Rating: 84%

Passing

Year	G	Comp./Att.	%	Yards	Y/Att.	TD	INT	Rating
1982	9	111/221	50.2	1,281	5.8	5	7	62.4
1983	15	163/328	49.7	2,353	7.2	12	17	64.0
1984	11	114/212	53.8	1,426	6.7	8	8	71.8
1985	16	199/393	50.6	2,414	6.1	14	15	65.8
1986	1	2/3	66.7	53	17.7	0	0	109.7
1987	4	0/0	0.0	0	0.0	0	0	0.0
1988	5	71/134	53.0	736	5.5	3	4	64.1
1989	16	5/14	35.7	60	4.3	1	1	43.8
1990	16	69/148	46.6	819	5.5	3	8	48.2
1991	16	11/27	40.7	150	5.6	2	0	83.9
1992	16	8/20	40.0	99	5.0	1	2	33.1
1993	7	3/9	33.3	23	2.6	0	1	2.8
Total	132	756/1,509	50.1	9,414	6.2	49	63	63.3
PS:	1	17/25	68.0	179	7.2	2	1	98.6

Rushing

Year	Att.	Yards	Avg.	TD
1982	19	82	4.3	1
1983	54	441	8.2	0
1984	26	149	5.7	1
1985	25	160	6.4	2
1986	2	0	0.0	0
1988	4	1	0.3	0
1989	2	-1	-0.5	0
1990	3	-1	-0.3	0
1992	1	0	0.0	0
Total	136	831	6.1	4
PS:	1	-1	-1.0	0

The same year that the Colts made Art Schlichter their top draft pick, they also selected Mike Pagel in the fourth round. As a rookie in 1982, Pagel made more starts than the troubled Schlichter would make in his career. Although Mike went 0–8–1 in those rookie starts, he went on to have a 12-year career in the NFL.

Wearing the No. 18 later made famous by Peyton Manning, Pagel was the Colts' primary quarterback for four years and was the first starter when the team moved to Indianapolis in 1984. After starting 47 games in four years, though, Mike was traded to Cleveland for a ninth-round draft pick to make way for Jack Trudeau and Gary Hogeboom. Pagel spent five years with the Browns and three with the Rams but started just seven more games in his career. Although Mike was a very good scrambler who led all quarterbacks with 441 yards rushing in 1984, he was a scatter-armed passer who barely completed half his passes, threw more interceptions than touchdowns, and lost two-thirds of his starts.

Carson Palmer

Height: 6'5" **Weight:** 230 lbs. **Birthdate:** 12/27/1979
College: USC **Draft:** Cincinnati 2003-1st
2004–08 Cincinnati Bengals
Regular Season Record: 32–33, 10 comebacks
Postseason Record: 0–1, no comebacks
Relative Rating: 111%

Passing

Year	G	Comp./Att.	%	Yards	Y/Att.	TD	INT	Rating
2004	13	263/432	60.9	2,897	6.7	18	18	77.3
2005	16	345/509	67.8	3,836	7.5	32	12	101.1
2006	16	324/520	62.3	4,035	7.8	28	13	93.9
2007	16	373/575	64.9	4,131	7.2	26	20	86.7
2008	4	75/129	58.1	731	5.7	3	4	69.0
Total	65	1,380/2,165	63.7	15,630	7.2	107	67	88.9
PS:	1	1/1	100.0	66	66.0	0	0	118.8

Rushing

Year	Att.	Yards	Avg.	TD
2004	18	47	2.6	1
2005	34	41	1.2	1
2006	26	37	1.4	0
2007	24	10	0.4	0
2008	6	38	6.3	0
Total	108	173	1.6	2
PS:	0	0	0.0	0

Carson Palmer is a picture-perfect quarterback who has one of the oddest postseason statistical lines ever recorded. Palmer, of course, lasted just two plays in the 2005 wild-card loss to the Steelers and got to throw just one pass that he completed for 66 yards before Pittsburgh's Kimo von Oelhoffen rolled into his knee. Von Oelhoffen's hit prompted the league to enact still tougher restrictions on pass rushers and forced Palmer to undergo strenuous rehabilitation of his injured knee to be able to return for opening day in 2006.

Palmer won the Heisman Trophy at USC and was the No. 1 overall draft pick in 2003. The Bengals kept him on the bench to learn the pro game from the sidelines that year, watching Jon Kitna at quarterback. Palmer took over the team in 2004 and started 51 straight regular-season games before elbow problems knocked him out in 2008. Even though he was unable to finish the year, Carson was part of an NFL first in 2008 when his younger brother Jordan signed with the Bengals as a backup quarterback and got to appear in a few games. It was the first time two brothers had played on the same team at the same time.

Palmer has accumulated some huge passing numbers in his four full seasons in the league, twice exceeding 4,000 yards passing and three times tossing at least 26 touchdowns while completing

63 percent of his passes. A pocket passer with a quick release who is good at reading defenses, he can make all the throws, short, long, with touch, or with extra mustard. Palmer has been the light version of Peyton Manning to this point in his career. The one question that remains is whether he can lead a team to a big season. Essentially, he has been a .500 quarterback so far—which is an accomplishment in itself in Cincinnati—but whether he can meld the talents and egos of his teammates into one highly functioning team remains unanswered.

QPR 0.5

Don Panciera

Height: 6'1" **Weight:** 192 lbs. **Birthdate:** 6/23/1927
College: San Francisco **Draft:** Philadelphia 1949-4th
1949 New York Yankees; 1950 Detroit Lions;
1952 Chicago Cardinals
Regular Season Record: 8–5, 3 comebacks
Postseason Record: 0–1, no comebacks
Relative Rating: 50%

Passing

Year	G	Comp./Att.	%	Yards	Y/Att.	TD	INT	Rating
1949	12	51/150	34.0	801	5.3	5	16	24.2
1950	4	0/0	0.0	0	0.0	0	0	0.0
1952	10	35/96	36.5	582	6.1	5	9	36.0
Total	26	86/246	35.0	1,383	5.6	10	25	28.6
PS:	1	7/25	28.0	116	4.6	0	3	6.8

Rushing

Year	Att.	Yards	Avg.	TD
1949	10	-4	-0.4	0
1950	0	0	0.0	0
1952	4	6	1.5	0
Total	14	2	0.1	0
PS:	0	0	0.0	0

The world champion Eagles selected three quarterbacks in the first four rounds of the 1949 draft, but none of them ever played in Philadelphia. First-rounder Frank Tripucka was waived to Detroit during the season, second-rounder Frank Burns of Rutgers was hired by the Scarlet Knights as an assistant coach, and fourth-rounder Don Panciera signed with the New York Yankees of the AAFC instead. In New York, Panciera beat out fellow rookie Gil Johnson for the starting quarterback position as the Yankees switched to the T formation in 1949. Don completed only one-third of his passes and threw more than three times as many interceptions as touchdowns, but the Yankees managed to win eight of 12 games with Panciera starting. When the AAFC was merged into the NFL, Panciera ended up with the Lions and played a season at defensive back. He surfaced again as a quarterback with the Cardinals in 1952 but had not improved since his rookie year. He finished his football career in Canada before doing some coaching.

Babe Parilli

QPR 7.0

Height: 6'1" **Weight:** 196 lbs. **Birthdate:** 5/7/1930
College: Kentucky **Draft:** Green Bay 1952-1st
1952–53, 1957–58 Green Bay Packers; 1956 Cleveland Browns; 1959 CFL; 1960 Oakland Raiders; 1961–67 Boston Patriots; 1968–69 New York Jets
Regular Season Record: 49–46–7, 8 comebacks
Postseason Record: 1–1, no comebacks
Relative Rating: 98%

Passing

Year	G	Comp./Att.	%	Yards	Y/Att.	TD	INT	Rating
1952	12	77/177	43.5	1,416	8.0	13	17	56.6
1953	12	74/166	44.6	830	5.0	4	19	28.5
1956	5	24/49	49.0	409	8.3	3	7	58.5
1957	12	39/102	38.2	669	6.6	4	12	34.8
1958	12	68/157	43.3	1,068	6.8	10	13	53.3
1960	14	87/187	46.5	1,003	5.4	5	11	47.6
1961	14	104/198	52.5	1,314	6.6	13	9	76.5
1962	10	140/253	55.3	1,988	7.9	18	8	91.5
1963	14	153/337	45.4	2,345	7.0	13	24	52.1
1964	14	228/473	48.2	3,465	7.3	31	27	70.8
1965	14	173/426	40.6	2,597	6.1	18	26	50.0
1966	14	181/382	47.4	2,721	7.1	20	20	66.9
1967	14	161/344	46.8	2,317	6.7	19	24	58.5
1968	14	29/55	52.7	401	7.3	5	2	91.6
1969	14	14/24	58.3	138	5.8	2	1	85.1
Total	189	1,552/3,330	46.6	2,2681	6.8	178	220	59.6

| PS: | 3 | 28/65 | 43.1 | 489 | 7.5 | 2 | 2 | 66.8 |

Rushing

Year	Att.	Yards	Avg.	TD
1952	32	106	3.3	1
1953	42	171	4.1	4
1956	18	65	3.6	0
1957	24	83	3.5	2
1958	8	15	1.9	0
1960	21	131	6.2	1
1961	38	183	4.8	4
1962	28	169	6.0	2
1963	36	126	3.5	5
1964	34	168	4.9	2
1965	50	200	4.0	0
1966	28	42	1.5	1
1967	14	61	4.4	0
1968	7	-2	-0.3	1
1969	3	4	1.3	0
Total	383	1,522	4.0	23

| PS: | 2 | 10 | 5.0 | 0 |

Babe Parilli played for Bear Bryant at Kentucky, where he followed George Blanda as the Wildcat quarterback. As an All-American, Parilli led Kentucky to victories in both the Sugar Bowl and Cotton Bowl before being drafted by the Packers in 1952. In Green Bay, Parilli split the quarterbacking with Tobin Rote, and the two combined for 26 touchdown passes and 25 interceptions while averaging eight yards per pass in 1952. However, the next year the two fell off to nine touchdown passes, 34 interceptions, and an average of just 5.25 yards per throw. The Packers then sent Parilli to Cleveland in a multiplayer deal that brought former overall No. 1 pick Bobby Garrett, a quarterback, to Green Bay.

Parilli went into the military for two years and came out in 1956 to back up George Ratterman in the Browns' first season without Otto Graham. When Ratterman went down to a career-ending knee injury midseason, Parilli took over but got hurt himself four games later. Tommy O'Connell finished the year as the Browns' quarterback. Parilli was very sensitive to the caustic criticism of Paul Brown in Cleveland and was glad to be traded in 1957—oddly enough back to Green Bay with a package of players for linebacker Roger Zatkoff and Bobby Garrett again. Babe spent two more years in Green Bay before being cut in Vince Lombardi's first training camp and drifting up to Canada.

When the American Football League began a year later, Parilli signed with the Oakland Raiders.

Babe spent one season in Oakland before being acquired by Boston in 1961. Over the next seven years Parilli kept the Patriots in continual contention in the Eastern Division and led them to the AFL title game in 1963. Although he could be up and down as a passer, Babe had a great arm, was a skilled play caller and a respected leader who threw for 132 touchdowns and 138 interceptions in Boston. In 1964, he led the AFL with 3,465 passing yards, 31 touchdowns, and 27 interceptions and in 1965 topped all AFL quarterbacks in rushing yards. When he was later elected to the Patriots' team Hall of Fame, teammate Gino Cappelletti said, "Babe had such great timing and anticipation that he knew exactly where the receiver and the ball should meet and that's where he would drop it, right between the defenders."

As a 10-year man in the AFL, Parilli was proud to take part in the epic Super Bowl III upset as Joe Namath's backup and holder for kicker Jim Turner. After retiring in 1970, Parilli was Terry Bradshaw's first quarterback coach in Pittsburgh. He also coached in the World Football League and then in arena ball for many years.

Ace Parker

QPR 8.0

Height: 6'0" **Weight:** 178 lbs. **Birthdate:** 5/17/1912
College: Duke **Draft:** Brooklyn Dodgers 1937-2nd
1937–41 Brooklyn Dodgers; 1945 Boston Yanks; 1946 New York Yankees
Regular Season Record: 33–21–7 est., 6 comebacks
Postseason Record: 0–1, no comebacks
Relative Rating: 131%

Passing

Year	G	Comp./Att.	%	Yards	Y/Att.	TD	INT	Rating
1937	4	28/61	45.9	514	8.4	1	7	41.3
1938	11	63/148	42.6	865	5.8	5	7	53.5
1939	11	72/157	45.9	977	6.2	4	13	40.2
1940	11	49/111	44.1	817	7.4	10	7	73.3
1941	11	51/102	50.0	639	6.3	2	8	43.7
1945	8	10/24	41.7	123	5.1	0	5	18.6
1946	12	62/115	53.9	763	6.6	8	3	87.0
Total	**68**	**335/718**	**46.7**	**4,698**	**6.5**	**30**	**50**	**53.2**
PS:	1	8/18	44.4	81	4.5	0	1	34.7

Rushing

Year	Att.	Yards	Avg.	TD
1937	34	26	0.8	1
1938	93	253	2.7	2
1939	104	271	2.6	5
1940	89	306	3.4	2
1941	85	301	3.5	0
1945	18	-49	-2.7	0
1946	75	184	2.5	3
Total	**498**	**1,292**	**2.6**	**13**
PS:	9	5	0.6	0

Clarence "Ace" Parker preferred baseball to football, but after having played both professionally, he found he was better on the gridiron. Parker went directly from Duke to Connie Mack's Philadelphia A's as a shortstop in 1937 but batted just .179 for two seasons in the major leagues. Concurrently, Ace began his NFL career in the fall of 1937 with the Brooklyn Dodgers and had much greater success as a smallish, triple-threat, single-wing tailback who passed, ran, punted, place-kicked, returned punts and kicks, and played safety on defense.

Brooklyn was a very weak team until Jock Sutherland was hired as coach in 1940. That year, Parker overcame having broken his ankle playing minor league baseball to be voted the MVP of the NFL. Even though he began the football season wearing a 10-pound brace from his knee to his ankle, he threw for 10 touchdowns, ran for more than 300 yards, led the league in extra points with 19 and in interceptions with six for the second-place Dodgers. Although his passing statistics don't look too impressive today, his passer rating was 30 percent better than the league average for his career and was nearly double the league average in 1940. After leading Brooklyn to another second-place finish in 1941, Ace entered the navy for three years. When he returned in 1945, the Brooklyn Dodgers were defunct, and Parker spent one season with the Boston Yanks before jumping to the New York Yankees of the AAFC in 1946.

The Yankees were owned by former Dodgers owner Dan Topping and coached by former Redskins coach Ray Flaherty. Ace shared the tailback position with Spec Sanders in New York. Sanders was more of a runner, while Parker did most of the team's passing. The Yankees met Cleveland for the

TOP 10

NFL Quarterbacks
Who Played Another Sport

10. Gary Kerkorian was on a national touring rugby team.

9. Dean Look was an outfielder who went hitless in six at-bats for the White Sox.

8. Tom Yewcic went 0-for-1 as a Detroit Tigers catcher.

7. Chad Hutchinson pitched in three games for the Cardinals with a 24.75 ERA.

6. Drew Henson batted .111 as a New York Yankee third baseman.

5. Josh Booty batted .269 as a third baseman for the Florida Marlins.

4. Ace Parker hit .179 in two years as a Philadelphia A's infielder.

3. Chris Chandler has won prize money as a golfer.

2. John Brodie played on the PGA Senior Tour.

1. Otto Graham played for the NBL–champion Rochester Royals in 1946.

Passing

Year	G	Comp./Att.	%	Yards	Y/Att.	TD	INT	Rating
1971	14	127/220	47.0	1,702	6.3	7	21	43.8
1972	14	144/299	48.2	1,711	5.7	7	12	57.1
1973	14	154/290	53.1	1,482	5.1	5	17	49.0
1974	11	140/247	56.7	1,571	6.4	10	10	72.4
1975	14	163/342	47.7	2,053	6.0	14	16	61.0
1976	13	167/309	54.0	1,795	5.8	10	10	68.6
1977	14	169/319	53.0	1,987	6.2	13	18	62.3
1978	16	199/368	54.1	2,473	6.7	16	17	70.4
1979	15	163/324	50.3	2,090	6.5	14	18	62.1
1980	5	66/130	50.8	932	7.2	5	8	61.4
1981	7	64/152	42.1	719	4.7	2	14	22.9
1983	3	0/5	0.0	0	0.0	0	0	39.6
Total	140	1,556/3,055	50.9	18,515	6.1	103	161	59.1
PS:	5	71/116	61.2	954	8.2	4	8	70.1

Rushing

Year	Att.	Yards	Avg.	TD
1971	26	140	5.4	3
1972	38	205	5.4	2
1973	31	102	3.3	0
1974	24	-6	-0.3	0
1975	23	97	4.2	1
1976	11	45	4.1	0
1977	18	39	2.2	2
1978	18	11	0.6	0
1979	15	23	1.5	0
1980	4	24	6.0	0
1981	7	5	0.7	0
1983	1	0	0.0	0
Total	216	685	3.2	8
PS:	3	-9	-3.0	0

first AAFC title that year and lost 14–9. Parker was driving the team at the end, but the final pass of his career was intercepted by Otto Graham to seal the game. Afterward, Ace was one of several players to criticize Flaherty's game strategy, and Parker returned to minor league baseball as a player and manager. Later, he returned to Duke as the head baseball coach and as a football assistant for many years before serving as an NFL scout. It was on his recommendation that the Eagles drafted Sonny Jurgensen in 1957. Parker was elected to the Hall of Fame in 1972.

Dan Pastorini

QPR 6.5

Height: 6'2" **Weight:** 208 lbs. **Birthdate:** 5/26/1949
College: Santa Clara **Draft:** Houston Oilers 1971-1st
1971–79 Houston Oilers; 1980 Oakland Raiders; 1981 Los Angeles Rams; 1983 Philadelphia Eagles
Regular Season Record: 56–61, 14 comebacks
Postseason Record: 2–3, 1 comeback
Relative Rating: 88%

Quarterbacks Jim Plunkett, Archie Manning, and Dan Pastorini went 1-2-3 in the 1971 draft, and all three had to endure some pretty tough times with some very bad football teams. Plunkett was the only one to win a championship, but Pastorini at least took the Oilers to the conference championship twice.

In Pastorini's first three years in Houston, the team finished 1–13 twice. In that time, Dan threw for 19 touchdowns to 50 interceptions, lost a record 21 starts in a row, and won just five of 30 starts. Over his next six years with the Oilers, though, Pastorini threw 77 touchdowns to 89 interceptions and went 48–29 as a starter. He had a great arm but often lacked accuracy and never threw more than 16 touchdowns in any season. Dan was also a fine ball handler and served as the Oilers' punter through 1976.

Pastorini had a bad temper and was known for his toughness. He missed just five games in Houston despite enduring broken ribs, a punctured lung, and elbow and knee problems. When the Oilers finally started winning under coach Bum Phillips in the late 1970s, only the Pittsburgh Steelers stood in their way to the Super Bowl, and the rivalry was fierce between the two rugged teams. It was in a December 1978 loss to Pittsburgh that Pastorini's ribs were broken, landing him in the hospital where he was visited by inventor Byron Donzis, who demonstrated his new flak jacket by having a friend hit him with a baseball bat. Pastorini ordered one right away and played the following week. However, both the 1978 and 1979 seasons ended with frustrating losses to the Steelers in the AFC Championship Games.

In 1980, Dan was traded to Oakland straight up for Kenny Stabler because the Raiders wanted a better deep passer and the Oilers wanted a change. Unfortunately, Pastorini broke his leg in the fifth game of the year. Dan's rival from his high school days in California, Jim Plunkett, stepped in to lead the Raiders to the Super Bowl and redeem his own stalled career. Pastorini moved on to the Rams the next year and finished his career with the Eagles two years after that.

Dan took life at top speed. He liked to race cars, married a pinup model nine years his senior, and posed nude for *Playgirl* magazine. All of this on and off the field led to Pastorini telling *Sports Illustrated* in 1978, "I feel weathered. The paint is starting to chip off. There is something about the pro game that taints one's perspective. As a kid, you really want it, but when you get there it's a whole different world. It's nothing but entertainment. Hollywood."

Passing

Year	G	Comp./Att.	%	Yards	Y/Att.	TD	INT	Rating
1993	7	4/8	50.0	41	5.1	0	0	65.1
1996	1	0/0	0.0	0	0.0	0	0	0.0
1997	1	0/0	0.0	0	0.0	0	0	0.0
1998	12	14/24	58.3	128	5.3	2	0	100.7
1999	16	119/227	52.4	1,276	5.6	7	9	62.9
2000	11	117/210	55.7	1,047	5.0	2	8	56.6
2001	16	0/0	0.0	0	0.0	0	0	0.0
2002	16	19/28	67.9	134	4.8	1	0	90.5
2003	16	2/2	100.0	16	8.0	0	0	100.0
2004	4	11/23	47.8	120	5.2	0	2	27.4
Total	100	286/522	54.8	2,762	5.3	12	19	62.3

Rushing

Year	Att.	Yards	Avg.	TD
1993	2	-1	-0.5	0
1997	3	-4	-1.3	0
1998	8	-4	-0.5	0
1999	20	33	1.7	0
2000	18	68	3.8	0
2001	1	-1	-1.0	0
2002	1	-1	-1.0	0
2003	6	-5	-0.8	0
2004	2	15	7.5	0
Total	61	100	1.6	0

Despite his modest skills, Doug Pederson spent 10 years in the NFL mostly because he had influential friends. As an undrafted free agent, Doug signed with the Dolphins in 1991, but the only game he got to throw the ball in was Don Shula's record-setting 325th win on November 14, 1993. Scott Mitchell was injured in the second half of that game, and Pederson came in to throw just eight passes in leading Miami to two second-half field goals to pull out the 19–14 victory.

Pederson had two stints backing up the indestructible Brett Favre in Green Bay. Those backup gigs were broken up by a season in Philadelphia mentoring rookie Donovan McNabb and one in Cleveland mentoring second-year man Tim Couch. Former Green Bay assistant Andy Reid signed Pederson to an unwarranted three-year, $4.5 million contract in Philadelphia because of his familiarity with the offense that Reid was installing for McNabb to run. Doug impressed no one with his play on the field, but his knowledgeable approach to the game led him into coaching after he retired.

QPR 0.5

Doug Pederson

Height: 6'3" **Weight:** 220 lbs. **Birthdate:** 1/31/1968
College: Louisiana-Monroe   **Draft:** Free agent
**1992, 1995 WLAF; 1993 Miami Dolphins; 1996–98,
2001–04 Green Bay Packers; 1999 Philadelphia
Eagles; 2000 Cleveland Browns**
Regular Season Record: 3–14, 1 comeback
Postseason Record: NA
Relative Rating: 80%

Rodney Peete

QPR 6.5

Height: 6'0" **Weight:** 230 lbs. **Birthdate:** 3/16/1966
College: USC **Draft:** Detroit 1989-6th
1989-93 Detroit Lions; 1994 Dallas Cowboys; 1995-98 Philadelphia Eagles; 1999 Washington Redskins; 2001 Oakland Raiders; 2002-04 Carolina Panthers
Regular Season Record: 45-42, 14 comebacks
Postseason Record: 1-1, no comebacks
Relative Rating: 94%

Passing

Year	G	Comp./Att.	%	Yards	Y/Att.	TD	INT	Rating
1989	8	103/195	52.8	1,479	7.6	5	9	67.0
1990	11	142/271	52.4	1,974	7.3	13	8	79.8
1991	8	116/194	59.8	1,339	6.9	5	9	69.9
1992	10	123/213	57.7	1,702	8.0	9	9	80.0
1993	10	157/252	62.3	1,670	6.6	6	14	66.4
1994	7	33/56	58.9	470	8.4	4	1	102.5
1995	15	215/375	57.3	2,326	6.2	8	14	67.3
1996	5	80/134	59.7	992	7.4	3	5	74.6
1997	5	68/118	57.6	869	7.4	4	4	78.0
1998	5	71/129	55.0	758	5.9	2	4	64.7
1999	3	8/17	47.1	107	6.3	2	1	82.2
2001	1	0/0	0.0	0	0.0	0	0	0.0
2002	14	223/381	58.5	2,630	6.9	15	14	77.4
2003	1	4/10	40.0	19	1.9	0	0	47.9
2004	1	1/1	100.0	3	3.0	0	0	79.2
Total	104	1,344/2,346	57.3	16,338	7.0	76	92	73.3
PS:	3	20/32	62.5	298	9.3	3	0	124.2

Rushing

Year	Att.	Yards	Avg.	TD
1989	33	148	4.5	4
1990	47	363	7.7	6
1991	25	125	5.0	2
1992	21	83	4.0	0
1993	45	165	3.7	1
1994	9	-2	-0.2	0
1995	32	147	4.6	1
1996	20	31	1.6	1
1997	8	37	4.6	0
1998	5	30	6.0	1
1999	2	-1	-0.5	0
2002	22	14	0.6	0
2004	1	-1	-1.0	0
Total	270	1,139	4.2	16
PS:	2	17	8.5	0

Rodney Peete was a journeyman quarterback who played for six teams over his 15-year NFL career.

Rodney Peete was never anybody's first choice at quarterback and never started a full season in his 15-year NFL career, but he did win more games than he lost and was a poised and smart leader. As befits the son and brother of coaches, Rodney was a coach on the field who found a way to win despite his shortcomings. Peete was short with a mediocre arm and threw passes that wobbled like those of Billy Kilmer or Jake Delhomme. Unlike those two fiery winners, though, Rodney had a very calm temperament on the field. All three were leaders.

Peete led USC to back-to-back wins over Troy Aikman's UCLA Bruins and two Rose Bowl appearances. He finished second to future Lion teammate Barry Sanders in the 1988 Heisman Trophy voting, but his size and arm relegated him to the sixth round of the NFL draft. In Detroit, Rodney was shuffled in and out of the lineup with Erik Kramer and Andre Ware by Wayne Fontes and left after five years to back up Aikman in Dallas for a year. Peete moved on to Philadelphia, where he found another coach who couldn't make up his mind about his quarterback in Ray Rhodes. In four years as an Eagle, Rodney went 15-9 while Randall Cunningham, Ty Detmer, Bobby Hoying, and Koy Detmer combined to go 14-25-1. Peete did lead the Eagles to a 58-37 thrashing of Wayne Fontes and the Lions in the 1995 playoffs but then got hurt the next week and the Eagles lost. In fact, Rodney tended to be injury prone, and that made it more difficult for him to hold down a starting job, too. Peete finished his career bouncing to Washington, Oakland, and Carolina. With the Panthers, he led John Fox's ball-control offense for one season before being beaten out by Delhomme in 2002. Peete is married to actress Holly Robinson Peete.

Pelluer was a tall, gangly rollout passer who was not very good at reading defenses and threw interceptions. He was the last quarterback to start for Landry and the last to record a win. When Jimmy Johnson arrived, Pelluer was cut and spent two years in Kansas City as a backup. He later played in Europe and Canada.

Steve Pelluer

QPR **5.0**

Height: 6'4" **Weight:** 209 lbs. **Birthdate:** 7/29/1962
College: Washington **Draft:** Dallas 1984-5th
1984–88 Dallas Cowboys; 1989–90 Kansas City Chiefs; 1992 WLAF; 1995 CFL
Regular Season Record: 9–20–1, 4 comebacks
Postseason Record: NA
Relative Rating: 95%

Passing

Year	G	Comp./Att.	%	Yards	Y/Att.	TD	INT	Rating
1984	1	0/0	0.0	0	0.0	0	0	0.0
1985	2	5/8	62.5	47	5.9	0	0	78.6
1986	16	215/378	56.9	2,727	7.2	8	17	67.9
1987	12	55/101	54.5	642	6.4	3	2	75.6
1988	16	245/435	56.3	3,139	7.2	17	19	73.9
1989	5	26/47	55.3	301	6.4	1	0	82.0
1990	13	2/5	40.0	14	2.8	0	1	8.3
Total	65	548/974	56.3	6,870	7.1	29	39	71.6

Rushing

Year	Att.	Yards	Avg.	TD
1985	3	-2	-0.7	0
1986	41	255	6.2	1
1987	25	142	5.7	1
1988	51	314	6.2	2
1989	17	143	8.4	2
1990	5	6	1.2	0
Total	142	858	6.0	6

When Steve Pelluer became the full-time starting quarterback for the Dallas Cowboys in 1988, it was a clear signal that it was time for the Cowboys' aging triumvirate of coach Tom Landry, GM Tex Schramm, and player personnel director Gil Brandt to step aside after 29 seasons. Dallas' unbroken string of fine quarterbacking from Eddie LeBaron, Don Meredith, Craig Morton, Roger Staubach, and Danny White was snapped by Steve Pelluer.

Chad Pennington

QPR **8.0**

Height: 6'3" **Weight:** 225 lbs. **Birthdate:** 6/26/1976
College: Marshall **Draft:** New York Jets 2000-1st
2000–07 New York Jets; 2008 Miami Dolphins
Regular Season Record: 43–34, 10 comebacks
Postseason Record: 2–4, 1 comeback
Relative Rating: 114%

Passing

Year	G	Comp./Att.	%	Yards	Y/Att.	TD	INT	Rating
2000	1	2/5	40.0	67	13.4	1	0	127.1
2001	2	10/20	50.0	92	4.6	1	0	79.6
2002	15	275/399	68.9	3,120	7.8	22	6	104.2
2003	10	189/297	63.6	2,139	7.2	13	12	82.9
2004	13	242/370	65.4	2,673	7.2	16	9	91.0
2005	3	49/83	59.0	530	6.4	2	3	70.9
2006	16	313/485	64.5	3,352	6.9	17	16	82.6
2007	9	179/260	68.8	1,765	6.8	10	9	86.1
2008	16	321/476	67.4	3,653	7.7	19	7	97.4
Total	85	1,580/2,395	66.0	17,391	7.3	101	62	90.6
PS:	6	132/216	61.1	1,418	6.6	8	8	77.3

Rushing

Year	Att.	Yards	Avg.	TD
2000	1	0	0.0	0
2001	1	11	11.0	0
2002	29	49	1.7	2
2003	21	42	2.0	2
2004	34	126	3.7	1
2005	6	27	4.5	0
2006	35	109	3.1	0
2007	20	32	1.6	1
2008	30	62	2.1	1
Total	177	458	2.6	7
PS:	11	20	1.8	0

As a young player, Chad Pennington was drawing comparisons to Joe Montana for his ability to carve up defenses efficiently. The man Chad replaced at

TOP 10
Worst Rookie Quarterback Seasons

10. John Elway—48 percent completions, seven touchdowns, and 14 interceptions in 1983
9. Jim Zorn—41 percent completions, 12 touchdowns, and 27 interceptions in 1976
8. Randy Johnson—41 percent completions, 12 touchdowns, and 21 interceptions in 1966
7. Dan Pastorini—47 percent completions, seven touchdowns, and 21 interceptions in 1971
6. Steve DeBerg—41 percent completions, eight touchdowns, and 22 interceptions in 1978
5. Dan Darragh—41 percent completions, three touchdowns, and 14 interceptions in 1968
4. Lamar McHan—41 percent completions, six touchdowns, and 22 interceptions in 1954
3. Tobin Rote—37 percent completions, seven touchdowns, and 24 interceptions in 1950
2. Ryan Leaf—45 percent completions, two touchdowns, and 15 interceptions in 1998
1. Terry Bradshaw—38 percent completions, six touchdowns, and 24 interceptions in 1970

quarterback in 2002, Vinny Testaverde, said, "Chad makes great decisions and his passing touch and leadership are surprising for a guy who is so early in his career." Pennington was very smart—he had been a Rhodes Scholar candidate at Marshall when he was throwing bombs to Randy Moss—and was a leader who commanded the huddle. He was so dedicated that he even took his playbook along on his honeymoon to study and was so accurate a thrower that he completed nearly 69 percent of his passes in his first full season.

The NFL is tough world, though, and Pennington's bright promise was greatly reduced by a series of severe injuries. Chad was not very mobile and got hit too much. In 2003, he broke his hand. In 2004, he tore his rotator cuff. Pennington returned in 2005 but then tore the rotator cuff again and ruined his arm for good. On guile, Chad was the NFL's Comeback Player of the Year in 2006 but struggled with his limitations and those of the team the following season. When the Jets acquired Brett Favre in 2008, Chad was released. Pennington signed with Miami, which was being

managed by the man who originally drafted him, Bill Parcells. The 1–15 Dolphins had a rebirth in 2008 when Pennington smartly moved the team to an 11–5 record and the division crown. Winning Comeback Player of the Year for the second time, Chad proved that working in the right offense he could still be a winner in the NFL.

Mike Phipps

QPR 5.5

Height: 6'3"　**Weight:** 208 lbs.　**Birthdate:** 11/19/1947
College: Purdue　**Draft:** Cleveland 1970-1st
1970–76 Cleveland Browns; 1977–81 Chicago Bears
Regular Season Record: 38–31–2, 12 comebacks
Postseason Record: 0–2, no comebacks
Relative Rating: 78%

Passing

Year	G	Comp./Att.	%	Yards	Y/Att.	TD	INT	Rating
1970	14	29/60	48.3	529	8.8	1	5	49.9
1971	14	13/47	27.7	179	3.8	1	4	14.6
1972	14	144/305	47.2	1,994	6.5	13	16	61.0
1973	14	148/299	49.5	1,719	5.7	9	20	49.4
1974	14	117/256	45.7	1,384	5.4	9	17	46.7
1975	14	162/313	51.8	1,749	5.6	4	19	47.5
1976	4	20/37	54.1	146	3.9	3	0	90.6
1977	3	3/5	60.0	5	1.0	0	0	64.6
1978	6	44/83	53.0	465	5.6	2	10	38.1
1979	12	134/255	52.5	1,535	6.0	9	8	69.6
1980	7	61/122	50.0	630	5.2	2	9	40.0
1981	3	11/17	64.7	171	10.1	2	0	137.1
Total	119	886/1,799	49.2	10,506	5.8	55	108	52.6
PS:	3	25/59	42.4	300	5.1	1	7	34.6

Rushing

Year	Att.	Yards	Avg.	TD
1970	11	94	8.5	0
1971	6	35	5.8	0
1972	60	256	4.3	5
1973	60	395	6.6	5
1974	39	279	7.2	1
1975	18	70	3.9	0
1976	4	26	6.5	0
1978	13	34	2.6	0
1979	27	51	1.9	0
1980	15	38	2.5	2
1981	1	0	0.0	0
Total	254	1,278	5.0	13
PS:	9	50	5.6	1

Over his career, Mike Phipps completed fewer than half of his passes, threw almost twice as many interceptions as touchdowns, averaged fewer than six yards per pass, and still posted a winning record as a starter. How is this possible? Primarily because he had two seasons in his career in which he was not completely terrible. In fact, they were the only two years in which he was within 10 percent of the league average in passer rating; in all the other full seasons of his career, his rating was at least 24 percent worse than the league's. With the 1972 Browns and 1978 Bears, Mike was supported by a good defense and strong running attack. In 1972 and 1978, Phipps went 19–4 as a starter; for the rest of his career he was 19–27–2. In 1972 and 1978, Mike threw 22 touchdowns and 24 interceptions; for the rest of his career, he threw 33 touchdowns and 84 interceptions.

Phipps had been a big star at Purdue, where he replaced Bob Griese. Mike was the first quarterback to beat Notre Dame three straight years, and the Browns traded Hall of Fame receiver Paul Warfield to the Dolphins to move up in the draft and grab Phipps with the third pick in 1970. Mike took over from the injury-ravaged Bill Nelsen in 1972 and led the Browns to the playoffs on the strength of a league-leading five fourth-quarter game-winning drives. He was an excellent runner and had a good arm but was sacked a lot and made terrible decisions throwing the ball. When Brian Sipe emerged as the starter in 1976, the Browns unloaded Phipps for a No. 1 pick to the Bears, where he finished his career competing with Vince Evans and Bob Avellini, although he did take the Bears to the playoffs in 1979. One glance at his statistics from the two playoff games he played in his two "best" years demonstrates how Phipps played against good teams—42 percent completions, just one touchdown pass, and seven interceptions.

Joe Pisarcik

Height: 6'4" **Weight:** 220 lbs. **Birthdate:** 7/2/1952
College: New Mexico State **Draft:** Free Agent
1974–76 CFL; 1977–79 New York Giants; 1980–84 Philadelphia Eagles
Regular Season Record: 9–21, 1 comeback
Postseason Record: NA
Relative Rating: 75%

Passing

Year	G	Comp./Att.	%	Yards	Y/Att.	TD	INT	Rating
1977	13	103/241	42.7	1,346	5.6	4	14	42.3
1978	15	143/301	47.5	2,096	7.0	12	23	52.1
1979	4	43/108	39.8	537	5.0	2	6	39.0
1980	9	15/22	68.2	187	8.5	0	0	94.3
1981	7	8/15	53.3	154	10.3	2	2	89.3
1982	1	1/1	100.0	24	24.0	0	0	118.7
1983	5	16/34	47.1	172	5.1	1	0	72.2
1984	7	96/176	54.5	1,036	5.9	3	3	70.6
Total	**61**	**425/898**	**47.3**	**5,552**	**6.2**	**24**	**48**	**53.9**

Rushing

Year	Att.	Yards	Avg.	TD
1977	27	57	2.1	2
1978	17	68	4.0	1
1979	1	6	6.0	0
1980	3	-3	-1.0	0
1981	7	1	0.1	0
1983	3	-1	-0.3	0
1984	7	19	2.7	2
Total	**65**	**147**	**2.3**	**5**

New York led Philadelphia 17–12 on November 19, 1978, with 31 seconds to play, and the Eagles were out of timeouts. In the huddle, Joe Pisarcik's teammates begged him to change the play sent in by Giants offensive coordinator Bob Gibson, but Joe had run into trouble doing that before. He stuck with the bizarre call, and it won him a dubious place in NFL history. One kneel-down would end the game, but Gibson sent in a running play. Pisarcik took the handoff gripping the back end of the ball and turned to the right before turning all the way around to find Csonka, who was headed to Joe's left. The aborted handoff bounced off Csonka's hip as he ploughed into the line. Pisarcik dove for the free ball, but cornerback Herman Edwards scooped it up and carried it 26 yards to the end zone for an impossible winning score. In New York, it's known as "The Fumble" but in Philadelphia as "The Miracle of the Meadowlands." Parkway Joe Pisarcik, who spent two and a half years as a bumbling starter in New York and then five years as Ron Jaworski's backup in Philadelphia, will never live it down.

Milt Plum

QPR 7.5

Height: 6'1" **Weight:** 205 lbs. **Birthdate:** 1/20/1935
College: Penn State **Draft:** Cleveland 1957-2nd
1957–61 Cleveland Browns; 1962–67 Detroit Lions;
1968 Los Angeles Rams; 1969 New York Giants
Regular Season Record: 56–40–6, 11 comebacks
Postseason Record: 0–1, no comebacks
Relative Rating: 105%

Passing

Year	G	Comp./Att.	%	Yards	Y/Att.	TD	INT	Rating
1957	9	41/76	53.9	590	7.8	2	5	60.7
1958	12	102/189	54.0	1,619	8.6	11	11	77.9
1959	12	156/266	58.6	1,992	7.5	14	8	87.2
1960	12	151/250	60.4	2,297	9.2	21	5	110.4
1961	14	177/302	58.6	2,416	8.0	18	10	90.3
1962	14	179/325	55.1	2,378	7.3	15	20	68.2
1963	10	27/77	35.1	339	4.4	2	12	18.7
1964	12	154/287	53.7	2,241	7.8	18	15	78.5
1965	14	143/308	46.4	1,710	5.6	12	19	51.2
1966	6	82/146	56.2	943	6.5	4	13	47.8
1967	9	86/172	50.0	925	5.4	4	8	54.5
1968	4	5/12	41.7	49	4.1	1	1	46.9
1969	1	3/9	33.3	37	4.1	0	0	47.0
Total	129	1,306/2,419	54.0	17,536	7.2	122	127	72.2
PS:	2	12/24	50.0	134	5.6	0	4	27.4

Rushing

Year	Att.	Yards	Avg.	TD
1957	26	118	4.5	0
1958	37	107	2.9	4
1959	21	20	1.0	1
1960	17	-24	-1.4	2
1961	24	-17	-0.7	1
1962	29	170	5.9	1
1963	9	26	2.9	0
1964	12	28	2.3	1
1965	21	37	1.8	3
1966	12	59	4.9	0
1967	6	5	0.8	0
1968	2	3	1.5	0
1969	1	-1	-1.0	0
Total	217	531	2.4	13
PS:	6	59	9.8	0

Milt Plum was living proof of the old admonition to be careful what you wish for because you just might get it. Plum was selected in the second round of the 1957 NFL draft by Cleveland as a sort of consolation prize. Browns coach Paul Brown had hoped to draft Purdue's Len Dawson with his first-round pick but was forced to "settle" for fullback Jim Brown when the Steelers nabbed Dawson. Brown then plucked Plum in the next round to help fill the void that Otto Graham's retirement had left a year before. In Milt's rookie year, he mostly watched as Jim Brown carried Cleveland to the championship game behind the weak-armed quarterback Tommy O'Connell. Cleveland was smashed in that title match, and Plum became the regular starter in 1958.

Over the next four seasons, Plum three times topped the NFL in passing percentage, led Cleveland to three second-place finishes, and went to two Pro Bowls. He was supported by perhaps the best offensive line in the league, a Hall of Fame runner in Jim Brown, and a shifty, speedy halfback, Bobby Mitchell, whose pass-catching abilities took him to Canton as a wide receiver. Although Cleveland's receiving corps was mediocre, Plum relied heavily on passes to his two-star backfield

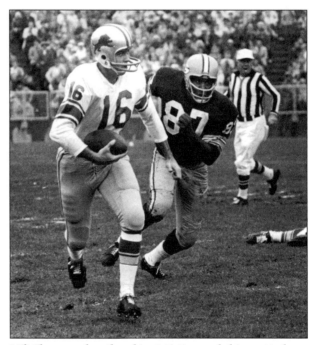

Milt Plum was less than his statistics made him out to be and was traded three times in his career.

mates and excelled. Despite all this success, Plum chafed under Paul Brown's autocratic attitude and yearned to call his own plays. After Milt voiced his discontent in the newspaper, Brown traded him to the Lions in 1962 for Milt's former backup in Cleveland, Jim Ninowski.

Plum had gotten what he wanted, but he quickly established that he was a product of his surroundings. Running Paul Brown's plays in Cleveland, he completed 58 percent of his passes, threw 66 touchdowns to 39 interceptions and had a passer rating of 89.9; calling his own plays in Detroit, those figures dropped to 51 percent, 55 touchdowns to 89 interceptions, and a passer rating of 58. Moreover, he lost the confidence of his teammates almost from the start. In a Week 4 showdown with archrival Green Bay, the Lions had the ball at midfield, leading 7–6 with less than 2:00 to play. Rather than call a safe running play on third and 8, Plum tried to hit flanker Terry Barr with a pass, but Barr slipped and Herb Adderley intercepted and returned the ball to the Lions' 18. A Paul Hornung field goal won the game for the Packers and led to a locker room insurrection by the furious and frustrated Lions defense. Alex Karras was said to have flung his helmet at Plum, and Joe Schmidt denied reports that he charged the quarterback.

Plum's inconsistent play in the following seasons took him in and out of the starting lineup and allowed team unity to deteriorate to the point where the Lions' management sent Plum to a leadership training program at the Dale Carnegie Institute in 1965, but it was too little too late. Plum was not a leader, and his tenure with the talented Lions was a disappointment.

Jake Plummer

QPR **7.0**

Height: 6'2" **Weight:** 212 lbs. **Birthdate:** 12/19/1974
College: Arizona State **Draft:** Arizona Cardinals 1997-1st
1997–02 Arizona Cardinals; 2003–06 Denver Broncos
Regular Season Record: 69–67, 29 comebacks
Postseason Record: 2–4, no comebacks
Relative Rating: 95%

Passing

Year	G	Comp./Att.	%	Yards	Y/Att.	TD	INT	Rating
1997	10	157/296	53.0	2,203	7.4	15	15	73.1
1998	16	324/547	59.2	3,737	6.8	17	20	75.0
1999	12	201/381	52.8	2,111	5.5	9	24	50.8
2000	14	270/475	56.8	2,946	6.2	13	21	66.0
2001	16	304/525	57.9	3,653	7.0	18	14	79.6
2002	16	284/530	53.6	2,972	5.6	18	20	65.7
2003	11	189/302	62.6	2,182	7.2	15	7	91.2
2004	16	303/521	58.2	4,089	7.8	27	20	84.5
2005	16	277/456	60.7	3,366	7.4	18	7	90.2
2006	16	175/317	55.2	1,994	6.3	11	13	68.8
Total	143	2,484/4,350	57.1	29,253	6.7	161	161	74.6
PS:	6	122/197	61.9	1,340	6.8	7	10	72.7

Rushing

Year	Att.	Yards	Avg.	TD
1997	39	216	5.5	2
1998	51	217	4.3	4
1999	39	121	3.1	2
2000	37	183	4.9	0
2001	35	163	4.7	0
2002	46	283	6.2	2
2003	37	205	5.5	3
2004	62	202	3.3	1
2005	46	151	3.3	2
2006	36	112	3.1	1
Total	428	1,853	4.3	17
PS:	25	66	2.6	0

The splits in Jake Plummer's numbers are pretty pronounced between his six years with the woebegone Cardinals and his four years with the talented Broncos. With the Cardinals, Jake completed 56 percent of his passes for 90 touchdowns and 114 interceptions and a passer rating of 69 while going 30–52 as a starter. With the Broncos, he completed 59 percent of his passes for 71 touchdowns and 47 interceptions for a rating of 84.3 and a record of 39–15. Even in Denver, though, Plummer wasn't what you would call reliable. In fact, the signature moment of his career occurred with Denver in a September 2004 game against the Chiefs. Plummer opened the second half with an interception that led to a Kansas City touchdown. The next time the Broncos had the ball, Jake was being sacked in the end zone but quickly switched the ball to his left hand and flung it across his body so that Chiefs linebacker Shawn Barber had an easy interception that led immediately to a game-tying touchdown.

The mercurial Plummer still managed to win that game in the fourth quarter, which was his specialty going back to his college days.

Jake the Snake was compared to Joe Montana by none other than Bill Walsh at the time of the 1997 draft, and Jake was selected by his hometown Arizona Cardinals. In his second season, Plummer led the Cardinals to their first playoff berth in 23 years on the strength of a league-leading seven fourth-quarter game-winning drives. However, that was the last winning season Jake would experience in the desert. He signed with the Broncos as a free agent in 2003 and three times took Denver to the playoffs. His problems in the postseason sealed his fate, though. In the 2005 AFC championship, Jake's two fumbles and two interceptions helped the Steelers upset the Broncos in Denver and sent Pittsburgh to the Super Bowl. The following season, coach Mike Shanahan benched Plummer while the Broncos were still in the playoff hunt and then traded him to Tampa in the off-season, although Jake chose to retire instead.

Plummer was an athletic scrambler and gambler. He was not big and his arm was nothing special, but he was a good ball handler and excelled at throwing on the run. He had good vision, quick feet, and nice touch on his passes but took too many risks that resulted in interceptions. In many ways, Eli Manning's career has been similar to Jake's, but Eli saved his greatest comeback for the biggest stage, while Jake always fell short.

Jim Plunkett

QPR 9.0

Height: 6'3" **Weight:** 220 lbs. **Birthdate:** 12/5/1947
College: Stanford **Draft:** New England 1971-1st
1971–75 New England Patriots; 1976–77 San Francisco 49ers; 1979–86 Oakland/Los Angeles Raiders
Regular Season Record: 72–72, 18 comebacks
Postseason Record: 8–2, 1 comeback
Relative Rating: 96%

Passing

Year	G	Comp./Att.	%	Yards	Y/Att.	TD	INT	Rating
1971	14	158/328	48.2	2,158	6.6	19	16	68.6
1972	14	169/355	47.6	2,196	6.2	8	25	45.7
1973	14	193/376	51.3	2,550	6.8	13	17	65.8
1974	14	173/352	49.1	2,457	7.0	19	22	64.1
1975	5	36/92	39.1	571	6.2	3	7	39.7
1976	12	126/243	51.9	1,592	6.6	13	16	63.0
1977	14	128/248	51.6	1,693	6.8	9	14	62.1
1979	4	7/15	46.7	89	5.9	1	1	60.1
1980	13	165/320	51.6	2,299	7.2	18	16	72.9
1981	9	94/179	52.5	1,045	5.8	4	9	56.7
1982	9	152/261	58.2	2,035	7.8	14	15	77.0
1983	14	230/379	60.7	2,935	7.7	20	18	82.7
1984	8	108/198	54.5	1,473	7.4	6	10	67.6
1985	3	71/103	68.9	803	7.8	3	3	89.6
1986	10	133/252	52.8	1,986	7.9	14	9	82.5
Total	**157**	**1,943/3,701**	**52.5**	**25,882**	**7.0**	**164**	**198**	**67.5**
PS:	10	162/272	59.6	2,293	8.4	11	12	81.9

Rushing

Year	Att.	Yards	Avg.	TD
1971	45	210	4.7	0
1972	36	230	6.4	1
1973	44	209	4.8	5
1974	30	161	5.4	2
1975	4	7	1.8	1
1976	19	95	5.0	0
1977	28	71	2.5	1
1979	3	18	6.0	0
1980	28	141	5.0	2
1981	12	38	3.2	1
1982	15	6	0.4	0
1983	26	78	3.0	0
1984	16	14	0.9	1
1985	5	12	2.4	0
1986	12	47	3.9	0
Total	**323**	**1,337**	**4.1**	**14**
PS:	28	97	3.5	0

In a year in which Archie Manning, Dan Pastorini, Ken Anderson, Joe Theismann, and Lynn Dickey were all drafted, Heisman Trophy winner Jim Plunkett was the first overall pick by the 2–12 New England Patriots in 1971. Plunkett was the Rookie of the Year, throwing 19 touchdowns to 16 interceptions and improving the Patriots to 6–8, but it was all downhill from there in New England. After being sacked and hit unmercifully behind the weak Patriot line for four years, Plunkett lost his starting job to rookie Steve Grogan in 1975 and was traded to San Francisco for three No. 1 draft picks and a No. 2 in 1976. Returning to his native Bay Area, Jim got the 49ers off to a 6–1 start in 1976, but the team went 2–5 in the second half of the year and then sank to 5–9 in 1977.

The 49ers released a despondent Plunkett in the 1978 preseason, and Al Davis signed him in Oakland across the bay. Plunkett did not get on the field at all in 1978 and threw just 15 passes in 1979. When the Raiders traded Kenny Stabler for Plunkett's old rival from high school and college, Dan Pastorini, in 1980, Jim wanted out, but Davis refused. Four weeks into the season, Pastorini broke his leg, and Plunkett stepped in to lead the Raiders to a Super Bowl championship. They were the first wild-card team to win it all. Plunkett won both the Comeback Player of the Year award and the Super Bowl MVP trophy. Oakland, with a deep passing attack, was the perfect spot for Plunkett's big arm to land. Three years later, Jim led the Raiders back to the Super Bowl for a second championship. It was the last time an AFC team would win the Super Bowl for 14 years until Denver beat Green Bay in Super Bowl XXXII.

Due to injuries and age, Plunkett was mostly a backup for the last three years of his resurrected career and retired after 1989. Jim's long career and late success were a tribute to hard work and persistence. Years later, he commented on his first Super Bowl, "I'm proud of that game. Many people felt I was washed up, and I wasn't sure they were wrong." To his credit, Plunkett never quit. He continues to serve the Raiders as a broadcaster.

Warren Rabb

Height: 6'3" **Weight:** 204 lbs. **Birthdate:** 12/12/1937
College: LSU **Draft:** Detroit Lions 1960-2nd
1960 Detroit Lions; 1961–62 Buffalo Bills
Regular Season Record: 6–3–1, 2 comebacks
Postseason Record: NA
Relative Rating: 100%

Passing
Year	G	Comp./Att.	%	Yards	Y/Att.	TD	INT	Rating
1960	7	0/0	0.0	0	00.	0	0	0.0
1961	9	34/74	45.9	586	7.9	5	2	84.6
1962	14	67/177	37.9	1,196	6.8	10	14	47.7
Total	30	101/251	40.2	1,782	7.1	15	16	58.6

Rushing
Year	Att.	Yards	Avg.	TD
1961	13	47	3.6	0
1962	37	77	2.1	3
Total	50	124	2.5	3

Warren Rabb was the quarterback on LSU's 1958 national championship team that featured future Heisman Trophy winner Billy Cannon. Rabb was pursued by both the Lions and the AFL's Dallas Texans but signed with Detroit on the advice of Packer fullback Jim Taylor, his former teammate both in high school and college. Warren spent one year in Detroit but never got to throw a pass and left to sign with Buffalo of the AFL in 1961. The Bills also signed quarterbacks M.C. Reynolds and Johnny Green to compete for the starting position. Reynolds was another former LSU teammate of Rabb's. By 1962, all the other quarterbacks were gone, but Al Dorow was brought in from New York, and Jack Kemp would arrive from San Diego in midseason. Still, Rabb went 5–1–1 as a starter during the year, although he was throwing only between 11 and 17 passes per game. Rabb was a good runner but a terrible passer and functioned solely as a game manager operating Buffalo's pounding rushing attack. When Kemp recovered from his thumb injury, though, Rabb went back to the bench. Warren was replaced as backup by rookie Daryle Lamonica in 1963 and headed to Canada for one last season of professional football.

Patrick Ramsey

QPR 3.5

Height: 6'2" **Weight:** 225 lbs. **Birthdate:** 2/14/1979
College: Tulane **Draft:** Washington 2002-1st
2002–05 Washington Redskins, 2006 New York Jets; 2007–08 Denver Broncos
Regular Season Record: 10–14, 2 comebacks
Postseason Record: 0–0, no comebacks
Relative Rating: 94%

Passing
Year	G	Comp./Att.	%	Yards	Y/Att.	TD	INT	Rating
2002	10	117/227	51.5	1,539	6.8	9	8	71.8
2003	11	179/337	53.1	2,166	6.4	14	9	75.8
2004	9	169/272	62.1	1,665	6.1	10	11	74.8
2005	4	15/25	60.0	279	11.2	1	1	95.2
2006	1	0/1	0.0	0	0.0	0	0	39.6
2007	2	29/48	60.4	262	5.5	1	1	73.4
2008	1	2/3	66.7	19	6.3	0	0	84.0
Total	38	511/913	56.0	59.3	6.5	35	30	74.9
PS:	1	1/1	100.0	-1	-1.0	0	0	79.2

Rushing
Year	Att.	Yards	Avg.	TD
2002	13	-1	-0.1	1
2003	15	62	4.1	1
2004	10	19	1.9	0
2005	7	3	0.4	0
2007	2	6	3	0
Total	47	89	1.9	2
PS:	0	0	0.0	0

Although he was the No. 1 pick of the Redskins in 2002, Patrick Ramsey just became part of the quarterback carousel that coach Steve Spurrier was running in unsuccessfully trying to implement his college offense in the NFL. New coach Joe Gibbs

gave Ramsey a trial late in 2004 but went back to veteran Mark Brunell the following year. Ramsey has good size and a decent arm but is not very mobile and tends to be a bit scatter-armed. He has spent the last three years as a backup with the Jets and Broncos, which is his niche in the league.

Steve Ramsey

QPR 5.5

Height: 6'2" **Weight:** 210 lbs. **Birthdate:** 4/22/1948
College: North Texas **Draft:** New Orleans 1970-5th
1970 New Orleans; 1971–76 Denver Broncos
Regular Season Record: 14–17, 6 comebacks
Postseason Record: NA
Relative Rating: 91%

Passing
Year	G	Comp./Att.	%	Yards	Y/Att.	TD	INT	Rating
1970	1	0/2	0.0	0	0.0	0	0	39.6
1971	9	84/178	47.2	1,120	6.3	5	13	46.6
1972	9	65/137	47.4	1,050	7.7	3	9	53.5
1973	5	10/27	37.0	194	7.2	2	2	56.7
1974	7	41/74	55.4	580	7.8	5	7	64.0
1975	11	128/233	54.9	1,562	6.7	9	14	63.6
1976	12	128/270	47.4	1,931	7.2	11	13	64.9
Total	54	456/921	49.5	6,437	7.0	35	58	58.9

Rushing
Year	Att.	Yards	Avg.	TD
1971	3	6	2.0	0
1972	6	15	2.5	2
1974	5	-2	-0.4	0
1975	6	38	6.3	0
1976	13	51	3.9	0
Total	33	108	3.3	2

After a season as the third quarterback for the 2–11–1 Saints in 1970, Steve Ramsey was traded to Denver for a fourth-round pick in 1971. At the same time, the Broncos also acquired quarterback Don Horn from the Packers for a higher price, but neither Ramsey nor Horn were very impressive as starters that year. Veteran Charlie Johnson was obtained in 1972 and Horn was traded away in 1973, with Ramsey left to serve as Johnson's backup for four years. Ramsey got his chance to be the main man in 1976 after Johnson retired but proved himself to be far from adequate. He had a quick release with his semi-sidearm delivery but was an insufficient passer with no leadership skills. Denver traded Ramsey to the Giants for Craig Morton in 1977, and Morton led the Broncos to the Super Bowl that year. Ramsey never played in the NFL again.

Tim Rattay

QPR 2.0

Height: 6'0" **Weight:** 200 lbs. **Birthdate:** 3/15/1977
College: Louisiana Tech **Draft:** San Francisco 2000-7th
2000–05 San Francisco 49ers; 2006 Tampa Bay Bucs; 2007 Arizona Cardinals
Regular Season Record: 5–13, 1 comeback
Postseason Record: NA
Relative Rating: 103%

Passing

Year	G	Comp./Att.	%	Yards	Y/Att.	TD	INT	Rating
2000	1	1/1	100.0	-4	-4.0	0	0	79.2
2001	3	2/2	100.0	21	10.5	0	0	110.4
2002	4	26/43	60.5	232	5.4	2	0	90.5
2003	11	73/118	61.9	856	7.3	7	2	96.6
2004	9	198/325	60.9	2,169	6.7	10	10	78.1
2005	4	56/97	57.7	667	6.9	5	6	70.3
2006	4	61/101	60.4	748	7.4	4	2	88.2
2007	4	15/27	55.6	164	6.1	3	3	71.1
Total	40	432/714	60.5	4,853	6.8	31	23	81.9

Rushing

Year	Att.	Yards	Avg.	TD
2000	2	-1	-0.5	0
2001	5	-3	-0.6	0
2002	5	0	0.0	0
2003	8	0	0.0	0
2004	12	55	4.6	0
2005	7	18	2.6	0
2006	4	3	0.8	0
2007	2	5	2.5	0
Total	45	77	1.7	0

Tim Rattay was no Tom Brady, but he was what you would expect out of a seventh-round draft pick. He was undersized but very smart. He had a decent arm but was not much of a runner and took a lot of sacks. He has proven to be an adequate backup, exceeding the production of the 49ers' third-round pick in 2000, Giovanni Carmazzi, who never appeared in an NFL game. Rattay is not the most famous quarterback to come out of Louisiana Tech; he is slightly overshadowed by Hall of Famer

Terry Bradshaw. Rattay was followed at Tech by Luke McCown, who replaced Tim as the backup for Tampa Bay in 2007.

George Ratterman

QPR 8.5

Height: 6'0" **Weight:** 192 lbs. **Birthdate:** 11/12/1926
College: Notre Dame **Draft:** Boston Yanks 1948-16th
1947–49 Buffalo Bills (AAFC); 1950–51 New York Yanks; 1952–56 Cleveland Browns
Regular Season Record: 29–23–5, 5 comebacks
Postseason Record: 1–2, 1 comeback
Relative Rating: 122%

Passing

Year	G	Comp./Att.	%	Yards	Y/Att.	TD	INT	Rating
1947	14	124/244	50.8	1,840	7.5	22	20	71.8
1948	14	168/335	50.1	2,577	7.7	16	22	64.5
1949	11	146/252	57.9	1,777	7.1	14	13	76.8
1950	12	140/294	47.6	2,251	7.7	22	24	64.6
1951	6	31/67	46.3	340	5.1	2	6	34.4
1952	6	2/6	33.3	20	3.3	1	2	43.7
1953	9	23/41	56.1	301	7.3	4	0	111.9
1954	6	32/53	60.4	465	8.8	3	3	84.2
1955	10	32/47	68.1	504	10.7	6	3	116.5
1956	4	39/57	68.4	398	7.0	1	3	72.1
Total	92	737/1,396	52.8	10,473	7.5	91	96	70.4
PS:	4	37/76	48.7	470	6.2	6	6	61.8

Rushing

Year	Att.	Yards	Avg.	TD
1947	17	-49	-2.9	1
1948	12	-18	-1.5	3
1949	36	85	2.4	4
1950	11	0	0.0	3
1951	3	9	3.0	0
1952	1	2	2.0	0
1953	2	6	3.0	0
1954	8	-13	-1.6	1
1955	6	8	1.3	1
1956	10	19	1.9	1
Total	106	49	0.5	14
PS:	0	0	0.0	0

George Ratterman was one of eight Notre Dame quarterbacks to enter professional football between 1945 and 1949, including Angelo Bertelli, Steve Nemeth, Boley Dancewicz, George Terlep, Joe Gasparella, Johnny Lujack, and Frank Tripucka.

Ratterman backed up Dancewicz and then Lujack for the Fighting Irish and lettered in four sports. After being suspended for missing curfew, he left school in 1947 to sign with the Buffalo Bills of the All-America Football Conference at age 20 and was the top rookie in the league that year with 22 touchdown passes. George also threw 20 interceptions that year and three times led the league in interceptions, operating by Brett Favre's credo of "No risk, no reward." Ratterman, though, was a skilled ball handler, an accurate passer, and a good deep thrower who played on just one losing team in 10 years.

When the Bills were dissolved in the AAFC's merger with the NFL, Ratterman ended up with the New York Yanks and led them to a 7–5 record in 1950. Negotiations with owner Ted Collins did not go well the next year, and George jumped to Montreal to play in the CFL. Midway through the year, he returned to the Yanks, but the deal he signed allowed him to become a free agent when the Yanks' franchise was transferred to Dallas. Ratterman signed with the Browns where he was the best backup in the league to the best quarterback in the league, Otto Graham, for the next four years.

On Graham's retirement, Ratterman became the starter just in time to experiment with Paul Brown's latest innovation, the radio helmet. Neither the helmet nor George lasted the season. The helmet was ineffective and banned, while Ratterman suffered a career-ending knee injury in the fourth game of the year. George, who was always a clever prankster, later wrote engagingly about his football life in *Confessions of a Gypsy Quarterback*. He went into broadcasting and then local politics. Ratterman was elected sheriff of Campbell County in Kentucky in 1961 despite being drugged and placed in a compromising position by mobsters seeking to sink his candidacy. Ratterman was elected anyway and cleaned up a very corrupt county in his term of office.

John Reaves

QPR 0.5

Height: 6'3" **Weight:** 210 lbs. **Birthdate:** 3/2/1950
College: Florida **Draft:** Philadelphia 1972-1st
1972–74 Philadelphia Eagles; 1975–78 Cincinnati Bengals; 1981 Houston Oilers; 1983–85 USFL; 1987 Tampa Bay Bucs
Regular Season Record: 4–13, 1 comeback
Postseason Record: NA
Relative Rating: 75%

Passing

Year	G	Comp./Att.	%	Yards	Y/Att.	TD	INT	Rating
1972	11	108/224	48.2	1,508	6.7	7	12	58.4
1973	1	5/19	26.3	17	0.9	0	1	17.7
1974	4	5/20	25.0	84	4.2	0	2	5.0
1975	7	25/51	49.0	297	5.8	2	3	55.8
1976	3	8/22	36.4	76	3.5	2	1	58.1
1977	9	24/59	40.7	383	6.5	0	5	27.7
1978	9	74/144	51.4	790	5.5	3	8	51.6
1981	5	31/61	50.8	379	6.2	2	2	67.6
1987	2	6/16	37.5	83	5.2	1	0	75.8
Total	**51**	**286/616**	**46.4**	**3,617**	**5.9**	**17**	**34**	**51.4**

Rushing

Year	Att.	Yards	Avg.	TD
1972	18	109	6.1	1
1973	2	2	1.0	0
1974	1	8	8.0	0
1975	6	13	2.2	2
1977	5	0	0.0	0
1978	6	50	8.3	0
1981	6	13	2.2	0
Total	**44**	**195**	**4.4**	**3**

As a candidate for the Heisman Trophy in 1971, Florida's John Reaves set an NCAA record for career passing yards with a little unethical help from his teammates. Leading the University of Miami 45–8, the Florida defenders literally dropped to the ground in what was called the Gator Flop and allowed Miami a cheap touchdown late in the game so Reaves could get the ball back and break the record. The Eagles selected the strong-armed Reaves in the first round of the 1972 draft and thrust him into the starting lineup by October, although he was far from ready to play. Press reports noted that Philly fans greeted Reaves with cheers at the start of the game against the Giants, but after he fumbled a snap that led to a New York score and

age of 37, John appeared in two games for the Bucs during the replacement player strike games in 1987. Reaves worked as an assistant coach at Florida, South Carolina, and Cornell after retiring. He was arrested on gun and drug charges in 2008 at the age of 58.

Chris Redman

Height: 6'3" **Weight:** 223 lbs. **Birthdate:** 7/7/1977
College: Louisville **Draft:** Baltimore Ravens 2000-3rd
2000–03 Baltimore Ravens; 2007–08 Atlanta Falcons
Regular Season Record: 4-6, 1 comeback
Postseason Record: NA
Relative Rating: 99%

Passing

Year	G	Comp./Att.	%	Yards	Y/Att.	TD	INT	Rating
2000	2	2/3	66.7	19	6.3	0	0	84.0
2001	0	0/0	0.0	0	0.0	0	0	0.0
2002	6	97/182	53.3	1,034	5.7	7	3	76.1
2003	2	7/13	53.8	58	4.5	0	2	26.0
2007	7	89/149	59.7	1,079	7.2	10	5	90.4
Total	**17**	**195/347**	**56.2**	**2,190**	**6.3**	**17**	**10**	**79.5**

Rushing

Year	Att.	Yards	Avg.	TD
2000	1	0	0.0	0
2002	10	8	0.8	0
2003	2	4	2.0	0
2007	8	16	2.0	0
Total	**21**	**28**	**1.3**	**0**

threw an end zone interception, John was booed as he left the field at halftime. Reaves had never called his own plays before, could not read defenses, and needed much more coaching than he received. To top it off, he tore ligaments in his ankle that year and could not move in the pocket very effectively.

New coach Mike McCormack traded for Roman Gabriel to replace Reaves in 1973. The year after that, McCormack acquired Mike Boryla and demoted Reaves to third string. John appeared in 11 games as a rookie, starting and losing seven but got into only five more games in his last two seasons with the Eagles before being traded to Cincinnati in 1975. In the ensuing years as he drifted unsuccessfully from the Bengals to the Vikings to the Oilers, he developed dependency problems with alcohol, marijuana, and cocaine and eventually bounced out of the league in 1982. He surfaced with the Tampa Bay Bandits of the USFL in 1983 and spent three successful seasons in Tampa under head coach Steve Spurrier, another former Gator QB who struggled in the pros. Reaves threw for more than 4,000 yards with the Bandits in 1985 which was more than he threw for in nine years in the NFL. As an NFL curtain call at the

Chris Redman was one of a long line of failed Baltimore Ravens quarterbacks in the Brian Billick era. Billick once said of Redman, "He has the attributes of a good quarterback, but this is the one position where you can never tell how good someone will be. You don't really know until you see him play." In Chris' rookie year in 2000, the third-round draft pick from Louisville won a Super Bowl ring as the Ravens' third-string quarterback. After throwing just three passes in his first two years, Redman went 3–3 as a starter in the first six games of 2002 before hurting his back and being replaced by Jeff Blake. The next season, Baltimore drafted Kyle Boller in the first round, and Chris fell behind both Boller and Anthony Wright on the depth chart. After having shoulder surgery in 2004, Redman was cut and struggled to catch on with another team. Finally in 2007, Redman's offensive coach from Louisville, Bobby Petrino, was hired by the Falcons and signed Chris to take the place of backup Matt Schaub, who had been traded. Although Redman has only an average arm, he is a nice touch passer and played well enough that Atlanta re-signed him in 2008, long after Petrino had scurried back to college ball.

Joe Reed

QPR 1.5

Height: 6'1" **Weight:** 195 lbs. **Birthdate:** 1/8/1948
College: Mississippi State **Draft:** San Francisco 1971-11th
1972–74 San Francisco 49ers; 1975–79 Detroit Lions
Regular Season Record: 9–10, 2 comebacks
Postseason Record: NA
Relative Rating: 73%

Passing

Year	G	Comp./Att.	%	Yards	Y/Att.	TD	INT	Rating
1972	9	0/0	0.0	0	0.0	0	0	0.0
1973	6	51/114	44.7	589	5.2	2	6	44.8
1974	6	29/74	39.2	316	4.3	2	7	22.1
1975	10	86/191	45.0	1,181	6.2	9	10	59.3
1976	13	32/62	51.6	425	6.9	3	3	69.6
1977	3	13/40	32.5	150	3.8	0	4	5.2
1978	1	0/0	0.0	0	0.0	0	0	0.0
1979	2	14/32	43.8	164	5.1	2	1	67.7
Total	50	225/513	43.9	2,825	5.5	18	31	48.1

Rushing

Year	Att.	Yards	Avg.	TD
1972	4	22	5.5	0
1973	15	85	5.7	0
1974	16	107	6.7	0
1975	34	193	5.7	1
1976	11	63	5.7	1
1977	1	3	3.0	0
1978	1	0	0.0	0
1979	2	11	5.5	0
Total	84	484	5.8	2

Joe Reed generally played only when a team was in desperate straits. A late-round pick of the 49ers, Reed stuck with the team as the third quarterback in 1972 and got his first start the following year when both John Brodie and Steve Spurrier were hurt. More injuries to the same two men meant more playing time for Joe in 1974, but he made a bigger name for himself by releasing a record called "Put Your Hand in the Hand" with the Niner Nuggets, a group of singing and dancing women dressed in red hot pants, white boots, and white cowboy hats who were used as a promotional tool by the team in the 1970s.

Traded to Detroit in 1975, Reed got to play extensively that year when both Greg Landry and Bill Munson were injured. Joe even quarterbacked the Lions over the 49ers that season with receiver Marlin Briscoe—the first black starting quarterback—serving as his emergency backup. He also continued his singing career in the next five seasons in Detroit by releasing a couple of gospel albums. Reed was a pretty good scrambler but was an awful passer who completed fewer than half his throws and threw more interceptions than touchdowns while averaging fewer than 6 yards per pass.

Frank Reich

QPR 3.0

Height: 6'4" **Weight:** 210 lbs. **Birthdate:** 12/4/1961
College: Maryland **Draft:** Buffalo 1985-3rd
1985-86, 1988-94 Buffalo Bills; 1995 Carolina Panthers; 1996 New York Jets; 1997-98 Detroit Lions
Regular Season Record: 5–15, 2 comebacks
Postseason Record: 2–0, 1 comeback
Relative Rating: 95%

Passing

Year	G	Comp./Att.	%	Yards	Y/Att.	TD	INT	Rating
1985	1	1/1	100.0	19	19.0	0	0	118.7
1986	3	9/19	47.4	104	5.5	0	2	24.8
1988	3	0/0	0.0	0	0.0	0	0	0.0
1989	7	53/87	60.9	701	8.1	7	2	103.7
1990	16	36/63	57.1	469	7.4	2	0	91.3
1991	16	27/41	65.9	305	7.4	6	2	107.2
1992	16	24/47	51.1	221	4.7	0	2	46.5
1993	15	16/26	61.5	153	5.9	2	0	103.5
1994	16	56/93	60.2	568	6.1	1	4	63.4
1995	3	37/84	44.0	441	5.3	2	2	58.7
1996	11	175/331	52.9	2,205	6.7	15	16	68.9
1997	6	11/30	36.7	121	4.0	0	2	21.7
1998	6	63/110	57.3	768	7.0	5	4	78.9
Total	119	508/932	54.5	6,075	6.5	40	36	72.9
PS:	5	67/104	64.4	783	7.5	7	3	97.6

Rushing

Year	Att.	Yards	Avg.	TD
1986	1	0	0.0	0
1988	3	-3	-1.0	0
1989	9	30	3.3	0
1990	15	24	1.6	0
1991	13	6	0.5	0
1992	9	-9	-1.0	0
1993	6	-6	-1.0	0
1994	6	3	0.5	0
1995	1	3	3.0	0
1996	18	31	1.7	0
1997	4	-4	-1.0	0
1998	6	3	0.5	0
Total	91	78	0.9	0
PS:	5	1	0.2	0

One of the most able backup quarterbacks in league history, Frank Reich is most famous for leading the Bills to the greatest comeback ever, in the 1992 postseason. At the time, Reich was also credited with the greatest comeback in college football history. When he was Stan Gelbaugh's backup at the University of Maryland, Reich led the Terrapins to a 42–40 win over the Miami Hurricanes in 1984 after Bernie Kosar had staked Miami to a 31–0 halftime lead. Although that comeback was exceeded by Michigan State in 2006, Reich's 32-point masterpiece against the Oilers has not been

Frank Reich takes over for an injured Jim Kelly. Reich was a born backup who played behind Kelly for nine years.

topped in the NFL. Trailing Houston 35–3 in the third quarter, Reich got hot and led Buffalo to four touchdowns in seven minutes. The Bills pulled ahead in the fourth quarter, were tied at the gun, and then won the game in overtime.

Reich started that day because Jim Kelly was hurt, and Frank started again the next week in a win over Pittsburgh. Kelly returned for the AFC championship and the Bills' annual Super Bowl loss. After 10 years in Buffalo and nine years backing up Kelly, Reich joined the expansion Carolina Panthers, who were directed by former Buffalo GM Bill Pollian. Reich's hold on the Panthers' starting quarterback post lasted just three games, all losses, before rookie Kerry Collins took over. Frank spent one season with the Jets and two with the Lions before retiring. The cerebral and spiritual Reich did not have the tools to be a starter in the NFL but was a dependable backup for 13 seasons.

QPR 8.0

Philip Rivers

Height: 6'5" **Weight:** 228 lbs. **Birthdate:** 12/8/1981
North Carolina State **Draft:** New York Giants 2004-1st
2004–08 San Diego Chargers
Regular Season Record: 33–15, 9 comebacks
Postseason Record: 3–3, 1 comeback
Relative Rating: 116%

Passing

Year	G	Comp./Att.	%	Yards	Y/Att.	TD	INT	Rating
2004	2	5/8	62.5	33	4.1	1	0	110.9
2005	2	12/22	54.5	115	5.2	0	1	50.4
2006	16	284/460	61.7	3,388	7.4	22	9	92.0
2007	16	277/460	60.2	3,152	6.9	21	15	82.4
2008	16	312/478	65.3	4,009	8.4	34	11	105.5
Total	52	890/1,428	62.3	10,697	7.5	78	36	92.9
PS:	6	107/189	56.6	1,522	8.1	7	7	79.7

Rushing

Year	Att.	Yards	Avg.	TD
2004	4	-5	-1.3	0
2005	1	-1	-1.0	0
2006	48	49	1.0	0
2007	29	33	1.1	1
2008	31	84	2.7	0
Total	113	160	1.4	1
PS:	9	14	1.6	0

TOP 10
One-Game Career Quarterbacks

10. Tulsa's Greg Barton threw one incomplete pass for the 1969 Lions and was traded to Philadelphia for three draft picks. He signed instead with Toronto of the CFL.
9. Texas Tech's Kliff Kingsbury completed one of two passes for 17 yards when he relieved an injured Vinny Testaverde in the final minute of a 27–0 Jets' loss to the Broncos in November 2005.
8. Chicago's Corey Sauter completed six of nine passes after relieving Henry Burris in the fourth quarter of the 2002 Bears' season finale. The 15–0 loss to Tampa was the Bucs' first win in sub-40-degree weather.
7. Iowa State's Dean Carlson completed seven of 15 passes for the 1974 Chiefs.
6. Tom Clements, former Notre Dame and CFL star, completed seven of 12 passes for the 1980 Chiefs.
5. Texas A&M's Will Cureton started in his only appearance and completed 10 of 32 passes for 95 yards for the 1975 Browns in a 21–10 loss to Detroit.
4. Lafayette's Ed Baker "completed" eight of 10 passes for the Oilers in their 1972 season finale after Dan Pastorini was hurt. Unfortunately, four of those "completions" were to Bengal defenders and three of those were returned for touchdowns in a 61–17 loss.
3. Ronnie Knox, the celebrated UCLA quarterback/aspiring actor who was suspended from the Bears for missing practice and for his stepfather's interference with the coaches, threw no passes in his only NFL appearance in the 1957 season opener against Green Bay.
2. Cincinnati's Tom O'Malley completed four of 15 passes with six interceptions as Tobin Rote's relief in the Packers' 45–7 opening day loss to Detroit.
1. Michigan State's Willie Thrower was the first black NFL quarterback; he completed three of eight passes in his only appearance for the 1953 Bears.

Philip Rivers' sidearm delivery is reminiscent of Bernie Kosar's, but Rivers does not look quite as awkward as Kosar did. Both sidearmers were 6'5", but Rivers is bit more solidly built. However, neither quarterback had any speed or running skills. Rivers was a four-year starter at North Carolina State who completed 72 percent of his passes as a senior. When the Chargers drafted Eli Manning with the overall No. 1 draft pick in 2004, they did so with the knowledge that Eli professed he would never play in San Diego and that the Giants coveted Manning. A last-minute draft day deal was worked out that called for the Giants to draft Rivers and trade him along with first-, third- and fifth-round picks to San Diego for Manning's rights.

Rivers held out while negotiating his contract and allowed third-year man Drew Brees to strengthen his hold on the starting position with a big year in 2004. Rivers continued to sit in 2005, but Brees made the quarterback decision easy for the Chargers in the season finale when he tore up his shoulder and was allowed to leave as a free agent. Rivers took over in 2006 and led San Diego to a 14–2 record, but the team stumbled against the Patriots in the playoffs. Under new coach Norv Turner, Rivers led the Chargers back to the postseason in 2007 and beat both the Titans and the defending champion Colts before falling to the Patriots in the AFC championship with Philip bravely playing despite a torn ACL in his knee.

Rivers delivers his passes with a smooth touch and great accuracy. He has a quick release and makes good decisions. Philip can be cocky and emotional at times—a memorable image from the 2007 playoffs is of Rivers jawing with Indianapolis fans in the stands—but is a tough leader who is cool at crunch time. During the playoffs, he told *Sports Illustrated*, "One thing I've learned is that all quarterbacks in this league can throw. It's the guys who can handle a little adversity, handle the *NFL Primetime* guys analyzing them or the fans saying things that last." Despite the Chargers falling to 4–8 during the 2008 season, Rivers kept his poise and drove the team into the playoffs by throwing a league-leading 34 touchdowns to just 11 interceptions.

John Roach

Height: 6'4" **Weight:** 197 lbs. **Birthdate:** 3/26/1933
College: Southern Methodist **Draft:** Chicago Cardinals 1956-3rd
1956, 1959–60 Chicago/St. Louis Cardinals; 1961–63
Green Bay Packers; 1964 Dallas Cowboys
Regular Season Record: 7–11–1, 3 comebacks
Postseason Record: NA
Relative Rating: 70%

Passing

Year	G	Comp./Att.	%	Yards	Y/Att.	TD	INT	Rating
1956	8	0/0	0.0	0	0.0	0	0	0.0
1959	12	22/57	38.6	340	6.0	2	4	41.6
1960	12	87/188	46.3	1,423	7.6	17	19	62.7
1961	7	0/4	0.0	0	0.0	0	0	39.6
1962	8	3/12	25.0	33	2.8	0	0	39.6
1963	8	38/84	45.2	620	7.4	4	8	46.8
1964	9	32/68	47.1	349	5.1	1	6	30.8
Total	64	182/413	44.1	2,765	6.7	24	37	48.7

Rushing

Year	Att.	Yards	Avg.	TD
1959	9	20	2.2	0
1960	19	39	2.1	1
1961	2	-5	-2.5	1
1962	1	5	5.0	0
1963	3	31	10.3	0
1964	8	9	1.1	0
Total	42	99	2.4	2

The only 6'4" professional quarterbacks to come before John Roach were Glenn Dobbs and Joe Gasparella in the 1940s. However, Dobbs was mostly a single-wing tailback and played solely in the All-America Football Conference, and Gasparella played for the single-wing Steelers mostly as a blocking back. Roach, a former defensive back, then was breaking new ground in the NFL when he first got to play some quarterback in 1959. John was joined on the Cardinals the following year by 6'4" George Izo from Notre Dame, but Roach was the team's starter.

After throwing 19 interceptions in 10 starts in 1960, Roach was traded to the Browns during training camp in 1961 and then traded to the Packers a few weeks later. John collected two championship rings in the next two years while throwing just 16 passes as Bart Starr's backup.

When Starr went down to injury in 1963, Roach stepped in and led the Packers' run-heavy offense to three straight wins but then stumbled against the Bears in late November in the game that cost Green Bay a chance at three straight titles. Dallas acquired Roach the next year, and he got to start four games for the 1964 Cowboys when Don Meredith was out with knee problems. But he lost all four games to close an unremarkable career as a gangly, inaccurate bomber prone to making mistakes.

Matt Robinson

Height: 6'2" **Weight:** 196 lbs. **Birthdate:** 6/28/1955
College: Georgia **Draft:** New York Jets 1977-9th
1977–79 New York Jets; 1980 Denver Broncos;
1981–82 Buffalo Bills; 1983–84 USFL
Regular Season Record: 10–10, 1 comeback
Postseason Record: NA
Relative Rating: 71%

Passing

Year	G	Comp./Att.	%	Yards	Y/Att.	TD	INT	Rating
1977	4	20/54	37.0	310	5.7	2	8	29.6
1978	16	124/266	46.6	2,002	7.5	13	16	63.5
1979	15	17/31	54.8	191	6.2	0	2	46.6
1980	14	78/162	48.1	942	5.8	2	12	39.7
1981	15	0/2	0.0	0	0.0	0	0	39.6
1982	5	5/8	62.5	74	9.3	1	0	132.3
Total	69	244/523	46.7	3,519	6.7	18	38	50.2

Rushing

Year	Att.	Yards	Avg.	TD
1977	5	45	9.0	0
1978	28	23	0.8	0
1979	3	4	1.3	1
1980	21	47	2.2	3
1981	1	-2	-2.0	0
Total	58	117	2.0	4

Matt Robinson was a ninth-round draft pick who spent three seasons competing with former No. 1 pick Richard Todd for the Jets' starting quarterback position, although that was more because of Todd's injury problems and inconsistencies than Robinson's great talent. Although the two young southern quarterbacks established a strong friendship, the New York quarterback controversy divided fans and teammates until Robinson was traded away to Denver in 1980.

In New York, Matt started 11 games in 1978 when Todd fractured his collarbone and the strong-armed scrambler led the Jets to six wins. Robinson won the quarterback competition outright in the 1979 preseason and started the first game of the season. However, Matt had mysteriously injured the thumb on his passing hand before the game and was benched for the second game. He never played another down for the Jets. The Broncos traded for Robinson the following February to replace the aging Craig Morton, but Matt threw just two touchdowns to 12 interceptions and was cut the following season. After two years as a backup in Buffalo, Robinson surfaced in the USFL as a starter in 1984 but threw 22 touchdowns to 32 interceptions in two seasons to close the unimpressive career of another overrated backup.

In his first year as a starter, Aaron Rodgers proved he could make all the throws and generate offense. Leading the Packers to a winning season is his next challenge.

Aaron Rodgers

QPR 6.0

Height: 6'0" **Weight:** 190 lbs. **Birthdate:** 12/2/1983
College: California **Draft:** Green Bay 2005-1ˢᵗ
2005–08 Green Bay Packers
Regular Season Record: 6–10, 2 comebacks
Postseason Record: NA
Relative Rating: 115%

Passing

Year	G	Comp./Att.	%	Yards	Y/Att.	TD	INT	Rating
2005	3	9/16	56.3	65	4.1	0	1	39.8
2006	2	6/15	40.0	46	3.1	0	0	48.2
2007	2	20/28	71.4	218	7.8	1	0	106.0
2008	16	341/536	63.6	4,038	7.5	28	13	93.8
Total	**23**	**376/595**	**63.2**	**4,367**	**6.8**	**29**	**14**	**91.8**

Rushing

Year	Att.	Yards	Avg.	TD
2005	2	7	3.5	0
2006	2	11	5.5	0
2007	7	29	4.1	0
2008	56	207	3.7	4
Total	**67**	**254**	**3.7**	**4**

Aaron Rodgers was one of a handful of projected top picks in the 2005 NFL draft who were invited to attend the proceedings. Over five hours of televised incredulous agony, Rodgers watched his star plummet from being considered for the overall No. 1 pick by San Francisco to falling into the laps of Green Bay at pick No. 24. Scouts worried about Rodgers' slight build and brief resume as well as the ominous history of the previous quarterbacks coached by Ted Tedford. Five of Tedford's former pupils became No. 1 draft picks but none of them (Trent Dilfer, Akili Smith, Joey Harrington, David Carr, and Kyle Boller) became a great quarterback in the NFL.

Rodgers backed up Brett Favre for three years, meaning he got to play very little but still managed to get hurt. He broke his foot in 2006 against the Patriots and pulled a hamstring in 2007 after an impressive relief appearance for Favre against the Cowboys. Then, Favre retired and unretired in 2008, leading to an ugly showdown between the aging gunslinger quarterback and Packers management with Rodgers hung in the middle in a state of disbelief that was similar to his draft day nightmare three years before. Favre was finally sent to the Jets in August to end the stalemate. Rodgers and the Packers began the 2008 season with two big wins, but the team struggled after that, particularly on defense. Rodgers played reliably well throughout the season, though, showing himself to be an accurate passer with good mobility and improvisational skills. Whether he will prove to be consistent and a winner is yet to be determined.

QPR **9.5**

Ben Roethlisberger

Height: 6'5" **Weight:** 240 lbs. **Birthdate:** 3/2/1982
College: Miami (OH) **Draft:** Pittsburgh 2004-1st
2004–08 Pittsburgh Steelers
Regular Season Record: 51–20, 16 comebacks
Postseason Record: 8–2, 2 comebacks
Relative Rating: 111%

Passing

Year	G	Comp./Att.	%	Yards	Y/Att.	TD	INT	Rating
2004	14	196/295	66.4	2,621	8.9	17	11	98.1
2005	12	168/268	62.7	2,385	8.9	17	9	98.6
2006	15	280/469	59.7	3,513	7.5	18	23	75.4
2007	15	264/404	65.3	3,154	7.8	32	11	104.1
2008	16	281/469	59.9	3,301	7.0	17	15	80.1
Total	72	1,189/1,905	62.4	14,974	7.9	101	69	89.4
PS:	10	172/278	61.9	2,239	8.1	15	12	87.2

Rushing

Year	Att.	Yards	Avg.	TD
2004	56	144	2.6	1
2005	31	69	2.2	3
2006	32	98	3.1	2
2007	35	204	5.8	2
2008	34	100	2.9	2
Total	188	616	3.3	10
PS:	38	125	3.3	2

Ben Roethlisberger follows the modern Daunte Culpepper model of enormous but surprisingly mobile quarterbacks who would have been middle linebackers in an earlier generation. After Culpepper hurt his knee and lost his mobility, though, he became a lead-footed liability. Roethlisberger tends to hold the ball too long, takes too many sacks and hits, and has been injury prone as a result. Whether the beating Big Ben takes will shorten the brilliant start to his career as a quarterback is the main question he has to answer.

Roethlisberger was the third quarterback taken in 2004 after Eli Manning and Philip Rivers but was the first to start, the first to the playoffs, and the first to win a Super Bowl. Ben replaced injured starter Tommy Maddox in the second game of the 2004 season and led the Steelers to 13 wins without a loss and the top seed in the AFC playoffs. Coach Bill Cowher kept the offense simple for the rookie and relied heavily on the running game so that Roethlisberger could pick his spots with the pass. Still, Ben found himself outclassed by Tom Brady and the defending champion Patriots in the AFC championship. The following season, Roethlisberger came back from knee problems to lead Pittsburgh all the way to the Super Bowl from their precarious final wild-card playoff berth. In the Super Bowl against the Seahawks, Ben completed just nine of 21 passes and threw two interceptions, but the Steelers prevailed anyway for their first championship since the days of Terry Bradshaw 26 years before.

On the verge of the next training camp, Roethlisberger was involved in a motorcycle accident that derailed his 2006 season, despite a move to open up the attack. Ben threw for 35 yards more per game but also led the league in interceptions during Cowher's final season as the quarterback came into increasing conflict with the intense coach. Roethlisberger welcomed the arrival of new coach Mike Tomlin in 2007 and responded with a Pro Bowl season of 32 touchdown passes and just 11 interceptions that took Pittsburgh back to the postseason where they lost to Jacksonville. In 2008, the Steeler offense struggled while the defense put up the best numbers in the league against the NFL's toughest schedule. Week after week, Roethlisberger brought the team back in the fourth quarter to score just enough points to eke out a win, and that continued right through the Super Bowl.

After five years, Roethlisberger has established himself as an elite quarterback, one of the best leaders in the game. He has a great arm and is particularly accurate on deep passes. His ability to improvise off a broken play has led to an abundance of big plays and the fifth-best career winning percentage among quarterbacks with at least 50 NFL starts. Big Ben is a winner and the best Steeler quarterback aside from Terry Bradshaw.

Steve Romanik

QPR **1.0**

Height: 6'1" **Weight:** 190 lbs. **Birthdate:** 5/27/1924
College: Villanova **Draft:** Chicago Bears 1950-3rd
1950-53 Chicago Bears; 1953-54 Arizona Cardinals
Regular Season Record: 6-7, 1 comeback
Postseason Record: NA
Relative Rating: 64%

Passing

Year	G	Comp./Att.	%	Yards	Y/Att.	TD	INT	Rating
1950	1	0/2	0.0	0	0.0	0	0	39.6
1951	12	43/101	42.6	791	7.8	3	9	43.0
1952	10	49/126	38.9	772	6.1	4	11	34.2
1953	7	51/125	40.8	650	5.2	4	11	31.7
1954	8	36/79	45.6	343	4.3	2	5	40.2
Total	38	179/433	41.3	2,556	5.9	13	36	36.5

Rushing

Year	Att.	Yards	Avg.	TD
1951	12	23	1.9	1
1952	6	9	1.5	0
1953	2	1	0.5	1
1954	7	2	0.3	1
Total	27	35	1.3	3

Steve Romanik was one of a group of failed Bear quarterbacks who competed with the three L's of 1954 (Luckman, Lujack, and Layne) and the three B's of 1948 (Blanda, Brown, and Bratkowski). Romanik was not very mobile, threw three times as many interceptions as touchdowns, and completed just 40 percent of his passes. He played safety on defense at times and was traded during the 1953 season to the crosstown Cardinals for a decent defensive back from Tulsa, S.J. Whitman. Both players finished their careers in 1954—Whitman intercepted five passes for the Bears, and Romanik threw five interceptions for the Cardinals, including one against his old Bear teammates. After retiring, Romanik returned to his hometown of Millville, New Jersey, where he served on the city council for 16 years.

Tony Romo

QPR **7.5**

Height: 6'2" **Weight:** 219 lbs. **Birthdate:** 4/21/1980
College: Eastern Illinois **Draft:** Free agent
2004-08 Dallas Cowboys
Regular Season Record: 27-12, 7 comebacks
Postseason Record: 0-2, no comebacks
Relative Rating: 118%

Passing

Year	G	Comp./Att.	%	Yards	Y/Att.	TD	INT	Rating
2004	6	0/0	0.0	0	0.0	0	0	0.0
2005	16	0/0	0.0	0	0.0	0	0	0.0
2006	16	220/337	65.3	2,903	8.6	19	13	95.1
2007	16	335/520	64.4	4,211	8.1	36	19	97.4
2008	13	276/450	61.3	3,448	7.7	26	14	91.4
Total	67	831/1,307	63.6	10,562	8.1	81	46	94.7
PS:	2	35/65	53.8	390		6	2	1	75.8

Rushing

Year	Att.	Yards	Avg.	TD
2005	2	-2	-1.0	0
2006	34	102	3.0	0
2007	31	129	4.2	2
2008	28	41	1.5	0
Total	95	270	2.8	2
PS:	4	17	4.3	0

Eastern Illinois Panther quarterback alums include Broncos coach Mike Shanahan, Saints coach Sean Payton, and Vikings coach Brad Childress, but Tony Romo has proven himself the best of all of them with the ball in his hands. Although Romo did not break Payton's school passing records, he did win the Walter Payton Award as the nation's best Division I-AA player in 2002. NFL scouts downgraded Romo for his poor passing mechanics, but Payton, then a Cowboys assistant under Bill Parcells, recommended Romo, and Dallas signed him as a free agent.

Tony did not get to take even one snap in 2003, 2004, or 2005, but he slowly developed as a series of more highly touted quarterbacks came and went in each Cowboy training camp. He outlasted and outplayed the competition of Quincy Carter, Chad Hutchinson, Drew Henson, Vinny Testaverde, and Drew Bledsoe and maintained his smile in the face of Bill Parcells' pointed barbs. By 2006, Romo was

TOP 10
Rookie Quarterback Seasons

10. Joe Flacco—60 percent completions, 14 touchdowns, and 12 interceptions in 2008
9. Jim Plunkett—48 percent completions, 19 touchdowns, and 16 interceptions in 1971
8. Matt Ryan—61 percent completions, 16 touchdowns, and 11 interceptions in 2008
7. Charlie Conerly—54 percent completions, 22 touchdowns, and 13 interceptions in 1948
6. Y.A. Tittle—56 percent completions, 16 touchdowns, and nine interceptions in 1948
5. Joe Namath—48 percent completions, 18 touchdowns, and 15 interceptions in 1965
4. Fran Tarkenton—56 percent completions, 18 touchdowns, and 17 interceptions in 1961
3. Jim Kelly—59 percent completions, 22 touchdowns, and 17 interceptions in 1986
2. Ben Roethlisberger—66 percent completions, 17 touchdowns, and 11 interceptions in 2004
1. Dan Marino—58 percent completions, 20 touchdowns, and six interceptions in 1983

Bledsoe's backup, and when the team struggled under Drew the Aging Dinosaur, Parcells went to Romo in the seventh game of the 2006 season. Romo was ready and provided an immediate spark that drove the team to the playoffs, where they lost a heartbreaker when Tony fumbled the snap to botch the game-winning field-goal attempt.

Romo built on his success in 2007 by throwing 36 touchdown passes and averaging more than 8 yards per pass in leading the Cowboys to a 13–3 season. Tony has a good arm and throws long and short with accuracy and touch. Much like Brett Favre, Romo, a Wisconsin native, is very creative in extending plays by slipping away from trouble and throwing on the run. He is adept at avoiding sacks but sometimes makes risky choices under pressure and forces passes into coverage. Thus far, his turnovers have increased in the biggest games.

Again like Favre, Romo cultivates a "one of the guys" persona and is a confident leader on the field. In the media circus that often encircles the Cowboys, Tony keeps an even disposition whether he's dealing with questions about which famous country singer he's dating or locker room tension involving selfish

receivers. Romo went from having egotistic receiver Terrell Owens' sniffling, "That's my quarterback," when Tony was criticized for his play in the 2007 playoffs to T.O. complaining that he wasn't getting the ball enough because of Romo's friendship with tight end Jason Witten in 2008. Through it all, Tony has proven himself a worthy heir to Don Meredith and Roger Staubach as the gambling, scrambling quarterback with the star on his helmet.

Timm Rosenbach
QPR 1.5

Height: 6'2" **Weight:** 210 lbs. **Birthdate:** 10/27/1966
College: Washington State **Draft:** Arizona 1989-1st(S)
1989–90, 1992 Arizona Cardinals; 1994 CFL
Regular Season Record: 5–15, 2 comebacks
Postseason Record: NA
Relative Rating: 87%

Passing
Year	G	Comp./Att.	%	Yards	Y/Att.	TD	INT	Rating
1989	2	9/22	40.9	95	4.3	0	1	35.2
1990	16	237/437	54.2	3,098	7.1	16	17	72.8
1992	8	49/92	53.3	483	5.3	0	6	41.2
Total	26	295/551	53.5	3,676	6.7	16	24	66.0

Rushing
Year	Att.	Yards	Avg.	TD
1989	6	26	4.3	0
1990	86	470	5.5	3
1992	9	11	1.2	0
Total	101	507	5.0	3

Timm Rosenbach gave up his final year of college eligibility and declared for the NFL draft in 1989. The Cardinals used the first pick in the supplemental draft that year to choose Timm, who then sat on the bench behind Gary Hogeboom as a rookie. In 1990, though, Rosenbach started all 16 games and showed that he was a tough, feisty gunslinger who loved to scramble. However, like many scramblers, Timm was sacked a lot. Although he threw for more than 3,000 yards and ran for 470, he also threw more interceptions than touchdowns, and the team went 5–11 in 1990. Rosenbach hurt his knee during training camp in 1991 and missed the whole season. In 1992, Timm suffered a concussion on opening day and then had his shoulder separated on a sack in game two. He played little for the rest of the year and then retired at the end of the year.

Rosenbach told the *New York Times* at the time that he found the game dehumanizing and began to despise the NFL. "I thought I was turning into some kind of animal. You go through a week getting yourself up for a game by hating the other team, the other players. You're so mean and hateful, you want to kill somebody. Football's so aggressive. Things get done by force." Upon further review, Rosenbach attempted a comeback a year later with Hamilton of the CFL. Then in 1995, he signed with the Saints as a free agent but ruptured a disk in his back and was forced to retire for good. He went into college coaching.

Sage Rosenfels

QPR 4.0

Height: 6'4" **Weight:** 222 lbs. **Birthdate:** 3/6/1978
College: Iowa State **Draft:** Washington 2001-4th
2002–05 Miami Dolphins; 2006–08 Houston Texans
Regular Season Record: 6–6, 2 comebacks
Postseason Record: NA
Relative Rating: 101%

Passing

Year	G	Comp./Att.	%	Yards	Y/Att.	TD	INT	Rating
2002	4	0/3	0.0	0	0.0	0	0	39.6
2003	2	4/6	66.7	50	8.3	1	0	131.9
2004	3	16/39	41.0	264	6.8	1	3	41.0
2005	4	34/61	55.7	462	7.6	4	3	81.5
2006	4	27/39	69.2	265	6.8	3	1	103.0
2007	9	154/240	64.2	1,684	7.0	15	12	84.8
2008	6	116/174	66.7	1,431	8.2	6	10	79.5
Total	32	357/562	62.5	4,156	7.4	30	29	81.2

Rushing

Year	Att.	Yards	Avg.	TD
2002	2	-9	-4.5	0
2003	1	-1	-1.0	0
2005	6	15	2.5	0
2006	4	5	1.3	0
2007	21	51	2.4	1
2008	11	37	3.4	0
Total	45	98	2.2	1

Sage Rosenfels is fearless on the field but is too often senseless as well. Rosenfels spent one year as the Redskins' third quarterback before being traded for a seventh-round pick to Miami in 2002. The highlight of Sage's four years in Florida was when he relieved Gus Frerotte against Buffalo in December 2005 and led the Dolphins to three fourth-quarter touchdowns to overcome a 20-point deficit and beat the Bills. The Texans signed Rosenfels as a free agent in 2006, and he has pushed starters David Carr and Matt Schaub hard in the past three years, with some fans calling for Sage when the starters struggled. Rosenfels can move the team, but he's not reliable enough to be the starter, as the heartbreaking game with Indianapolis October 5, 2008, demonstrated. Rosenfels completed 21 of 33 passes to drive the Texans to a 27–10 lead with 4:00 to play but then fumbled twice and threw an interception in the next 2:10 to let the Colts pull out an implausible victory. Rosenfels does not have a strong arm but is accurate and fairly mobile. It's his bizarre decision making that will continue to frustrate his teammates and employer.

Tobin Rote

QPR 9.0

Height: 6'3" **Weight:** 211 lbs. **Birthdate:** 1/18/1928
College: Rice **Draft:** Green Bay 1950-2nd
1950–56 Green Bay Packers; 1957–59 Detroit Lions; 1960–62 CFL; 1963–64 San Diego Chargers; 1966 Denver Broncos
Regular Season Record: 48–63–4, 7 comebacks
Postseason Record: 3–1, 1 comeback
Relative Rating: 95%

Passing

Year	G	Comp./Att.	%	Yards	Y/Att.	TD	INT	Rating
1950	12	83/224	37.1	1,231	5.5	7	24	26.7
1951	12	106/256	41.4	1,540	6.0	15	20	48.6
1952	12	82/157	52.2	1,268	8.1	13	8	85.6
1953	12	72/185	38.9	1,005	5.4	5	15	32.4
1954	12	180/382	47.1	2,311	6.0	14	18	59.1
1955	12	157/342	45.9	1,977	5.8	17	19	57.8
1956	12	146/308	47.4	2,203	7.2	18	15	70.6
1957	12	76/177	42.9	1,070	6.0	11	10	60.2
1958	12	118/257	45.9	1,678	6.5	14	10	69.5
1959	10	62/162	38.3	861	5.3	5	19	26.8
1963	14	170/286	59.4	2,510	8.8	20	17	86.7
1964	14	74/163	45.4	1,156	7.1	9	15	49.5
1966	3	3/8	37.5	40	5.0	0	1	14.6
Total	149	1,329/2,907	45.7	18,850	6.5	148	191	56.8
PS:	4	48/90	53.3	785	8.7	8	3	98.6

Rushing

Year	Att.	Yards	Avg.	TD
1950	27	158	5.9	0
1951	76	523	6.9	3
1952	58	313	5.4	2
1953	33	180	5.5	0
1954	67	301	4.5	8
1955	74	332	4.5	5
1956	84	398	4.7	11
1957	70	366	5.2	1
1958	77	351	4.6	3
1959	35	156	4.5	2
1963	24	62	2.6	2
1964	10	-12	-1.2	0
Total	635	3,128	4.9	37
PS:	16	53	3.3	0

Tobin Rote might have been better suited as a single-wing tailback. Although the tall, tough Texan twice led the NFL in attempts, completions, and touchdown passes and once in passing yardage, he was also the first quarterback to lead his team in rushing yards. In fact, Rote led his team in rushing four times and finished second three other times. He led all NFL quarterbacks in rushing yards six times and is one of just five quarterbacks to score at least 10 rushing touchdowns in one season. In 1951, Packer coach Gene Ronzani even installed an early version of the shotgun formation to take advantage of Tobin's strong arm and his bruising running skills.

Perhaps due to the battering he took as a ball carrier, Rote was maddeningly inconsistent as a passer. Another Packer coach complained, "When Tobin Rote is hot he is positively the greatest of them all, and when he is cold, well..." Well, Tobin had one of the most up-and-down careers of all quarterbacks. For Green Bay in 1952, he completed 52 percent of his passes and threw 13 touchdown passes to just eight interceptions for a passer rating of 85.6. The next year he completed only 39 percent of his passes, threw five touchdowns and 15 interceptions, and compiled a rating of 32.4. Traded to Detroit to share the quarterbacking with Bobby Layne in 1957, Rote took over when Layne broke his leg late in the year and led the Lions to the championship game against the Browns. There, Tobin ran for one score and passed for four others

as the Lions destroyed Cleveland 59–14. Yet, just two years later, Rote completed only 38 percent of his passes and threw 19 interceptions to five touchdowns for a passer rating of only 26.8.

When the Lions wouldn't give Tobin a no-cut contract in 1959, he played out his option and signed with the Toronto Argonauts of the Canadian Football League in 1960, topping the CFL with 38 touchdown passes and leading his team to a divisional title. Two years later, Rote was down to 12 touchdown passes and 17 interceptions and signed with San Diego in the AFL, his third professional league. In 1963, Tobin led the AFL in passing percentage at 59 percent and threw for two touchdowns in the Chargers' 51–10 clubbing of the Patriots in the title game. He became just the second quarterback after Otto Graham to win titles in two major leagues. In 1964, though, he dropped to 45 percent completions, nine touchdowns, and 15 interceptions and lost the title game to Buffalo 20–7. He finished his career with a brief appearance for Denver in 1966.

For his career, Rote passed for 148 touchdowns and ran for 37 more. However, he also threw 191 interceptions and completed half his passes only twice. Tobin did set the standard for the running quarterback that continues to evolve today. His 3,128 rushing yards was the record for quarterbacks until it was broken by Fran Tarkenton in 1972, and Rote remains in the top 10 even today.

JaMarcus Russell   QPR 1.5

Height: 6'6"   **Weight:** 265 lbs.   **Birthdate:** 8/9/1985
College: LSU   **Draft:** Oakland 2007-1st
2007–08 Oakland Raiders
Regular Season Record: 5–11, 2 comebacks
Postseason Record: NA
Relative Rating: 91%

Passing

Year	G	Comp./Att.	%	Yards	Y/Att.	TD	INT	Rating
2007	4	36/66	54.5	373	5.7	2	4	55.9
2008	15	198/368	53.8	2,423	6.6	13	8	77.1
Total	19	234/434	53.9	2,796	6.4	15	12	73.9

Rushing

Year	Att.	Yards	Avg.	TD
2007	5	4	0.8	0
2008	17	127	7.5	1
Total	22	131	6.0	1

JaMarcus Russell came out of LSU as the overall No. 1 pick in 2007 looking like the second coming of Daunte Culpepper, a huge quarterback who was both a powerful runner and skilled deep passer. Thus far, Russell has been overmatched in the NFL. After an abnormally long holdout that lasted into the start of the 2007 season, Russell did not see any action until December and didn't start his first game till the season finale. Russell won the starting job in 2008, but his progress was retarded by the ridiculous coaching drama played out by the Raider front office. Russell has shown that he is a very good runner and has a quick release and a big arm. However, his mechanics are not solid, his passing is inaccurate, and he has such trouble reading defenses that he makes poor decisions with the ball. He is also sacked a lot and is prone to fumble. Russell showed marked improvement by the end of 2008, but it's too bad he's stuck in Oakland for these crucial years at the beginning of his career.

TOP 10
American Quarterbacks Who Also Played in Canada

10. Sam Etcheverry
9. Frank Tripucka
8. Glenn Dobbs
7. Jack Jacobs
6. Joe Theismann
5. Tobin Rote
4. Joe Kapp
3. Jeff Garcia
2. Doug Flutie
1. Warren Moon

Jeff Rutledge

QPR 2.0

Height: 6'1" **Weight:** 195 lbs. **Birthdate:** 1/22/1957
College: Alabama **Draft:** Los Angeles Rams 1979-9th
1979–81 Los Angeles Rams; 1983–89 New York Giants; 1990–92 Washington Redskins
Regular Season Record: 2–7–1, 4 comebacks
Postseason Record: 0–0, no comebacks
Relative Rating: 82%

Passing

Year	G	Comp./Att.	%	Yards	Y/Att.	TD	INT	Rating
1979	3	13/32	40.6	125	3.9	1	4	23.0
1980	1	1/4	25.0	26	6.5	0	0	54.2
1981	4	30/50	60.0	442	8.8	3	4	75.6
1983	4	87/174	50.0	1,208	6.9	3	8	59.3
1984	16	1/1	100.0	9	9.0	0	0	104.2
1985	16	0/0	0.0	0	0.0	0	0	0.0
1986	16	1/3	33.3	13	4.3	1	0	87.5
1987	13	79/155	51.0	1,048	6.8	5	11	53.9
1988	1	11/17	64.7	113	6.6	0	1	59.2
1989	1	0/0	0.0	0	0.0	0	0	0.0
1990	10	40/68	58.8	455	6.7	2	1	82.7
1991	16	11/22	50.0	189	8.6	1	0	94.7
1992	16	0/0	0.0	0	0.0	0	0	0.0
Total	117	274/526	52.1	3,628	6.9	16	29	61.4
PS:	3	1/1	100	23	23.0	0	0	118.8

Rushing

Year	Att.	Yards	Avg.	TD
1979	5	27	5.4	0
1981	5	-3	-0.6	0
1983	7	27	3.9	0
1985	2	-6	-3.0	0
1986	3	19	6.3	0
1987	15	31	2.1	0
1988	3	-1	-0.3	0
1990	4	12	3.0	1
1991	8	-13	-1.6	0
Total	52	93	1.8	1
PS:	4	0	0.0	0

Jeff Rutledge went to three Super Bowls with three different teams in his 13-year career as a backup but never got to throw a pass in one. Nevertheless, he did win rings with the Giants in 1986 and Redskins in 1991. The Rams lost the Super Bowl to the Steelers in Jeff's rookie year. Although Rutledge was the MVP of the 1979 Sugar Bowl with Alabama, he wasn't drafted till the ninth round because he did not have the arm to start in the NFL. He got to start just once in three years in Los Angeles but twice started four games with the Giants as Phil Simms' backup before being demoted to third string behind Jeff Hostetler. With Washington in 1990, Rutledge replaced an ineffective Stan Humphries to rally the Redskins back from a 35–14 deficit and beat Detroit in overtime one week. His former coach, Bill Parcells, commented at the time, "Jeff was always at his best in helter-skelter games. The crazier things got, when everything was going wrong, the better he was." The next week against the Eagles, Rutledge started for the final time in the NFL in what became known as the "Body Bag Game." Philadelphia's defense knocked 11 Redskins out of the game, including both Rutledge and Humphries, leaving kick returner Brian Mitchell to finish the game under center for Washington. Starting isn't always what it's cracked up to be.

Frank Ryan

QPR 9.5

Height: 6'3" **Weight:** 199 lbs. **Birthdate:** 7/12/1936
College: Rice **Draft:** Los Angeles Rams 1958-5th
1958–61 Los Angeles Rams; 1962–68 Cleveland Browns; 1969–70 Washington Redskins
Regular Season Record: 57–27–3, 8 comebacks
Postseason Record: 1–2, no comebacks
Relative Rating: 113%

Passing
Year	G	Comp./Att.	%	Yards	Y/Att.	TD	INT	Rating
1958	5	5/14	35.7	34	2.4	1	3	28.6
1959	10	42/89	47.2	709	8.0	2	4	63.4
1960	11	62/128	48.4	816	6.4	7	9	57.9
1961	14	72/142	50.7	1,115	7.9	5	7	68.3
1962	11	112/194	57.7	1,541	7.9	10	7	85.4
1963	13	135/256	52.7	2,026	7.9	25	13	90.4
1964	14	174/334	52.1	2,404	7.2	25	19	76.7
1965	12	119/243	49.0	1,751	7.2	18	13	75.3
1966	14	200/382	52.4	2,974	7.8	29	14	88.2
1967	13	136/280	48.6	2,026	7.2	20	16	72.7
1968	7	31/66	47.0	639	9.7	7	6	79.0
1969	1	1/1	100.0	4	4.0	0	0	83.3
1970	1	1/4	25.0	3	0.8	0	0	39.6
Total	126	1,090/2,133	51.1	16,042	7.5	149	111	77.6
PS:	4	35/72	48.6	534	7.4	6	4	78.1

Rushing
Year	Att.	Yards	Avg.	TD
1958	5	45	9.0	0
1959	19	57	3.0	1
1960	19	85	4.5	1
1961	38	139	3.7	0
1962	42	242	5.8	1
1963	62	224	3.6	2
1964	37	217	5.9	1
1965	19	72	3.8	0
1966	36	156	4.3	0
1967	22	57	2.6	0
1968	11	64	5.8	0
Total	310	1,358	4.4	6
PS:	8	25	3.1	0

Along with Charlie Johnson, Frank Ryan was one of at least two NFL quarterbacks from the 1960s who earned a doctorate. Frank's was in mathematics, and much was made of Ryan's intelligence during his career, although the quarterback tried to downplay it. The brainy Ryan was drafted by the Rams in 1958 despite having been King Hill's backup at Rice University and went on to have a far superior career to Hill, who was the first overall pick in 1958 by the Cardinals.

Ryan struggled with the Rams and chafed under the reactionary coaching of legendary Ram quarterback Bob Waterfield. Frank's confidence wavered as he played in fear of being yanked after any mistake while he shared the Rams quarterbacking with Billy Wade and Zeke Bratkowski for four years. After the 1961 season, Ryan demanded a trade and was sent to Cleveland where he split the quarterbacking with Jim Ninowski in Paul Brown's last season. Under new coach Blanton Collier in 1963, Ryan took over as starter and blossomed by improving his mechanics, accuracy, and ability to read defenses. Over the next five seasons as the Browns' starter, Frank went to three Pro Bowls, averaged 22 touchdowns and 15 interceptions per year, topped the NFL twice in touchdown passes, and led Cleveland to an NFL championship over a heavily favored Colt team with Johnny Unitas.

Ryan took advantage of having Jim Brown and then Leroy Kelly in the backfield to set up a long-ball passing attack that allowed Cleveland to finish second in the league in points twice and third once. The tall and spindly Ryan was a shifty runner, able to keep plays alive, and a clever play caller with a clear preference for the bomb with receivers Paul Warfield and Gary Collins. Shoulder and knee problems caused Frank to slow down and be replaced by Bill Nelsen in 1968. Ryan finished his career as a backup to Sonny Jurgensen in Washington in 1969 and 1970. He later worked as the director of information systems for the House of Representatives and as the athletic director at Yale University.

Matt Ryan

Height: 6'4"   **Weight:** 228 lbs.   **Birthdate:** 5/17/1985
College: Boston College   **Draft:** Atlanta 2008-1st
2008 Atlanta Falcons
Regular Season Record: 11–5, 4 comebacks
Postseason Record: 0–1, no comebacks
Relative Rating: 108%

Passing

Year	G	Comp./Att.	%	Yards	Y/Att.	TD	INT	Rating
2008	16	265/434	61.1	3,440	7.9	16	11	87.7
PS:	1	26/40	65	199	5.0	2	2	72.8

Rushing

Year	Att.	Yards	Avg.	TD
2008	55	104	1.9	1
PS:	4	6	1.5	0

Matt Ryan's remarkable rookie season of 2008 has few parallels in NFL history. Of rookies who threw at least 250 passes, only Ben Roethlisberger had a higher completion percentage, only Big Ben and Y.A. Tittle averaged more yards per pass, and only Ben, Tittle, and Dan Marino had a higher passer rating. Furthermore, the amazing seven-game turnaround of Ryan's Falcons is topped only by the nine-game jump of Roethlisberger's Steelers in 2004.

After throwing a touchdown on his very first NFL pass, Ryan displayed the ability to make good reads and good decisions throughout his first season. He has great size, an accurate arm, and the toughness to withstand punishment. His accuracy with deep passes has been questioned, but Matt made all the throws in 2008 and took a team to the

playoffs that in the previous season had floundered through coaching and quarterbacking disasters.

Pat Ryan

Height: 6'3"   **Weight:** 210 lbs.   **Birthdate:** 9/16/1955
College: Tennessee   **Draft:** New York Jets 1978-11th
1978–89 New York Jets; 1991 Philadelphia Eagles
Regular Season Record: 11–8, 1 comeback
Postseason Record: 1–1, no comebacks
Relative Rating: 93%

Passing

Year	G	Comp./Att.	%	Yards	Y/Att.	TD	INT	Rating
1978	2	9/14	64.3	106	7.6	0	2	47.6
1979	1	2/4	50.0	13	3.3	0	1	17.7
1980	14	0/0	0.0	0	0.0	0	0	0.0
1981	15	4/10	40.0	48	4.8	1	1	49.2
1982	9	12/18	66.7	146	8.1	2	1	105.3
1983	16	21/40	52.5	259	6.5	2	2	68.6
1984	16	156/285	54.7	1,939	6.8	14	14	72.0
1985	16	6/9	66.7	95	10.6	0	0	101.6
1986	16	34/55	61.8	342	6.2	2	1	84.1
1987	13	32/53	60.4	314	5.9	4	2	86.5
1988	16	63/113	55.8	807	7.1	5	4	78.3
1989	7	15/30	50.0	153	5.1	1	3	36.5
1991	4	10/26	38.5	98	3.8	0	4	10.3
Total	145	364/657	55.4	4,320	6.6	31	35	69.2
PS:	3	32/51	62.7	340	6.7	5	1	106.7

Rushing

Year	Att.	Yards	Avg.	TD
1981	3	-5	-1.7	0
1982	1	-1	-1.0	0
1983	4	23	5.8	0
1984	23	92	4.0	0
1985	3	-5	-1.7	0
1986	8	28	3.5	0
1987	4	5	1.3	1
1988	5	22	4.4	0
1989	1	-1	-1.0	0
1991	1	-2	-2.0	0
Total	53	156	2.9	1
PS:	2	30	15.0	0

Pat Ryan was something of a forerunner to Matt Cassell. He didn't play football till his senior year of high school and then was no more than a sporadic starter at the University of Tennessee. The Jets drafted him in the 11th round, and Pat spent his first six seasons as a backup, throwing fewer than 100 passes and starting zero games. Finally, in 1984, with former starter Richard Todd traded to New Orleans and quarterback of the future Ken O'Brien tied up with legal problems, Ryan started the first 11 games of the year and led New York to a 6–5 record before O'Brien took over in Week 12.

Unlike the current situation where a player like Cassell can leave as a free agent and enrich himself, Ryan was tied to the Jets and continued as O'Brien's dependable backup for the next five years. In that time, he won five of eight starts and threw fewer passes than he had in 1984. His most memorable experience came when he replaced a slumping O'Brien for the 1986 playoffs and led the Jets to a win over the Chiefs before getting hurt in a loss to the Browns.

"Mr. Guts," as Ryan was called by teammates, had a good arm but the personality of a backup. In 1981, he told the *New York Times*, "Everybody has the conception that if you're not starting at quarterback, you're teed off, and that's not true. I don't want to sound like I want to be a backup quarterback the rest of my life. I wouldn't say I'm content. I have just resolved myself to not getting upset about it." Three years later, after his 11-game stint in 1984, he added, "There's worse things than being a backup quarterback in the NFL. Some people say if you're a competitor you should want to play. I'd rather play a long time than shoot off my mouth and only play eight years." Ryan had a 13-year career in the NFL.

TOP 10
Least Mobile Quarterbacks

10. Dick Wood
9. Byron Leftwich
8. Mark Rypien
7. Bernie Kosar
6. Bill Nelsen
5. Dan Fouts
4. Dan Marino
3. Drew Bledsoe
2. Norm Van Brocklin
1. Joe Namath

QPR 8.5

Mark Rypien

Height: 6'4" **Weight:** 231 lbs. **Birthdate:** 10/2/1962
College: Washington State **Draft:** Washington 1986-6th
1988–93 Washington Redskins; 1994 Cleveland Browns; 1995, 1997 St. Louis Rams; 1996 Philadelphia Eagles; 2001 Indianapolis Colts
Regular Season Record: 47–31, 12 comebacks
Postseason Record: 5–2, no comebacks
Relative Rating: 103%

Passing

Year	G	Comp./Att.	%	Yards	Y/Att.	TD	INT	Rating
1988	9	114/208	54.8	1,730	8.3	18	13	85.2
1989	14	280/476	58.8	3,768	7.9	22	13	88.1
1990	10	166/304	54.6	2,070	6.8	16	11	78.4
1991	16	249/421	59.1	3,564	8.5	28	11	97.9
1992	16	269/479	56.2	3,282	6.9	13	17	71.7
1993	12	166/319	52.0	1,514	4.7	4	10	56.3
1994	6	59/128	46.1	694	5.4	4	3	63.7
1995	11	129/217	59.4	1,448	6.7	9	8	77.9
1996	1	10/13	76.9	76	5.8	1	0	116.2
1997	5	19/39	48.7	270	6.9	0	2	50.2
2001	4	5/9	55.6	57	6.3	0	0	74.8
Total	104	1,466/2,613	56.1	18,473	7.1	115	88	78.9
PS:	8	126/234	53.8	1,776	7.6	8	10	72.2

Rushing

Year	Att.	Yards	Avg.	TD
1988	9	31	3.4	1
1989	26	56	2.2	1
1990	15	4	0.3	0
1991	15	6	0.4	1
1992	36	50	1.4	2
1993	9	4	0.4	3
1994	7	4	0.6	0
1995	9	10	1.1	0
1997	1	1	1.0	0
Total	127	166	1.3	8
PS:	20	-11	-0.6	1

Mark Rypien left Washington State early and was drafted in the sixth round of the 1986 draft by the Redskins. Rypien then spent the next two years stashed on injured reserve for some trumped-up injuries while Doug Williams and Jay Schroeder battled for the starting quarterback position. Williams led Washington to a Super Bowl championship for the 1987 season, so Shroeder was traded in 1988 and Rypien came off IR at last.

Rypien won the starting job in 1989 and went to the Pro Bowl after throwing for 22 touchdowns and more than 3,700 yards. Mark was bothered by a knee injury in 1990 and missed six games but came back strong in 1991 when he took the Redskins to a championship on the strength of 28 touchdown passes, 8.5 yards per pass, and a league-leading 14.3 yards per completion. Rypien was as immobile as any quarterback in football but also threw the best deep ball in the game at the time. Both Mark and the team declined drastically in 1992, and Rypien went from being the Super Bowl MVP to being booed during player introductions at RFK within one year.

After a series of acrimonious contract negotiations, the quiet, self-effacing Rypien left as a free agent in 1994 and ended up playing as a backup for four teams in five years. He signed with a fifth, the Atlanta Falcons, in 1998 but quit football when his son Andrew died from a brain tumor. Rypien

Mark Rypien led the Redskins to a Super Bowl win over the Bills by throwing for 292 yards and two touchdowns.

returned to the NFL to spend one more year as a backup in Indianapolis in 2001 before retiring to devote his time to the Rypien Foundation, set up to support families fighting cancer.

Sean Salisbury

QPR **3.0**

Height: 6'5" **Weight:** 225 lbs. **Birthdate:** 3/9/1963
College: USC **Draft:** Free agent
1987 Indianapolis Colts; 1988–89 CFL; 1992–94 Minnesota Vikings; 1996 San Diego Chargers
Regular Season Record: 6–6, 2 comebacks
Postseason Record: 0–1, no comebacks
Relative Rating: 94%

Passing

Year	G	Comp./Att.	%	Yards	Y/Att.	TD	INT	Rating
1987	2	8/12	66.7	68	5.7	0	2	41.7
1992	10	97/175	55.4	1,203	6.9	5	2	81.7
1993	11	115/195	59.0	1,413	7.2	9	6	84.0
1994	1	16/34	47.1	156	4.6	0	1	48.2
1996	16	82/161	50.9	984	6.1	5	8	59.6
Total	40	318/577	55.1	3,824	6.6	19	19	72.9
PS:	4	14/44	31.8	234	5.3	0	3	22.3

Rushing

Year	Att.	Yards	Avg.	TD
1992	11	0	0.0	0
1993	10	-1	-0.1	0
1994	3	2	0.7	0
1996	6	14	2.3	0
Total	30	15	0.5	0
PS:	1	0	0.0	0

Sean Salisbury is probably more famous for sending X-rated photographs of his anatomy around to fellow ESPN staffers in 2006 than for his flaccid career as a professional quarterback. Salisbury handed off to Marcus Allen at USC but went undrafted by the NFL. After failing to catch on with Seattle or Indianapolis, Sean headed north and to Winnipeg in the CFL where he threw 37 touchdown passes in two seasons and led the Blue Bombers to the 1989 Grey Cup. That success brought him to Minnesota, and Salisbury spent five years with the Viking organization competing with Rich Gannon, Jim McMahon, and Warren Moon but started just nine games in his three years on the active roster. Sean was tall, with an average arm and no mobility. After another season as an ordinary backup for the Chargers, Salisbury went into broadcasting, eventually landing with ESPN for a decade. After being let go by the network in 2008, Salisbury complained that he wasn't given as much respect at the network as other analysts who had been better NFL players but weren't as good on television.

Jack Scarbath

Height: 6'2" **Weight:** 206 lbs. **Birthdate:** 8/12/1930
College: Maryland **Draft:** Washington 1953-1st
1953–54 Washington Redskins; 1955 CFL;
1956 Pittsburgh Steelers
Regular Season Record: 6–9, no comebacks
Postseason Record: NA
Relative Rating: 72%

Passing

Year	G	Comp./Att.	%	Yards	Y/Att.	TD	INT	Rating
1953	12	45/129	34.9	862	6.7	9	12	43.5
1954	10	44/109	40.4	798	7.3	7	13	48.1
1956	7	12/41	29.3	208	5.1	2	5	24.9
Total	29	101/279	36.2	1,868	6.7	18	30	42.1

Rushing

Year	Att.	Yards	Avg.	TD
1953	22	98	4.5	0
1954	17	36	2.1	0
1956	4	19	4.8	0
Total	43	153	3.6	0

As a Maryland freshman in 1949, Jack Scarbath poured concrete for the university's new football stadium. One year later, Scarbath christened the place by scoring the first touchdown in Byrd Stadium as a sophomore starter in the season's first game. Scarbath was an option quarterback in the split-T formation for three years and attracted more notice when some gamblers approached him in 1952 about shaving points in an upcoming game against LSU. Jack reported the bribe attempt to his coach and went out and pummeled LSU 34–6. Scarbath was the third overall pick in the 1953 NFL draft by Washington, but the College Hall of Famer achieved no success at all as a professional.

The Redskins traded the wildly inaccurate passer to the Colts in 1955, but Baltimore cut him, and Scarbath spent the year in Ottawa playing for the Rough Riders. Jack wasn't much better in Canada, completing 47 percent of his passes and throwing just six touchdowns to 16 interceptions, but he signed with the Steelers in 1956 where he backed up the weak-armed Ted Marchibroda for one year. Scarbath spent some time in coaching before giving up football for business.

Matt Schaub

Height: 6'5" **Weight:** 235 lbs. **Birthdate:** 6/25/1981
College: Virginia **Draft:** Atlanta 2004-3rd
2004–06 Atlanta Falcons; 2007–08 Houston Texans
Regular Season Record: 10–14, 5 comebacks
Postseason Record: NA
Relative Rating: 107%

Passing

Year	G	Comp./Att.	%	Yards	Y/Att.	TD	INT	Rating
2004	6	33/70	47.1	330	4.7	1	4	42.0
2005	16	33/64	51.6	495	7.7	4	0	98.1
2006	16	18/27	66.7	208	7.7	1	2	71.2
2007	11	192/289	66.4	2,241	7.8	9	9	87.2
2008	11	251/380	66.1	3,043	8.0	15	10	92.7
Total	60	527/830	63.5	6,317	7.6	30	25	86.2

Rushing

Year	Att.	Yards	Avg.	TD
2004	8	26	3.3	0
2005	9	76	8.4	0
2006	7	21	3.0	0
2007	17	52	3.1	0
2008	31	68	2.2	2
Total	72	243	3.4	2

There has been a long line of overrated understudies in the NFL. On scant evidence, one team's young untested backup quarterback gets a reputation as a terrific prospect, and teams with quarterback problems come sniffing around with draft picks in hand to trade. Jim Hardy, Gary Cuozzo, Steve Tensi, Pete Beathard, Marty Domres, Clint Longley, Jack Thompson, Matt Robinson, Steve Walsh, Craig Erickson, Brett Favre, and Rob Johnson are some of the most prominent backups who delivered a

---

TOP 10
Emergency Quarterbacks

10. Punter Dave Lewis for the 1971 Bengals
9. Returner Brian Mitchell for the 1990 Redskins
8. Linebacker Bob Laraba for the 1960 Chargers
7. Defensive back Ed Mioduszewski for the 1953 Colts
6. Tailback George Taliaferro for the 1953 Colts
5. Defensive back Tony Dungy for the 1977 Steelers
4. Wide receiver Guido Merkens for the 1982 Saints
3. Defensive back Tom Landry for the 1952 Giants
2. Wide receiver Ed Rutkowski for the 1968 Bills
1. Halfback Tom Matte for the 1965 Colts

---

payload of high draft picks. Matt Schaub is the latest. Although these quarterbacks usually prove to be busts, Schaub has shown promise in Houston.

Schaub backed up Michael Vick in Atlanta for three years and then was traded to the Texans for two second-round picks and a draft slot switch in 2007 right before Vick was caught up in his dogfighting troubles. With Houston, Matt has displayed an accurate arm, good timing, and fair mobility. At times he seems to get rattled by a pass rush, though, and has had trouble holding off the challenge of veteran backup Sage Rosenfels, particularly since Schaub has been injury prone thus far in his career. Schaub has proven himself superior to former Texan quarterback David Carr but still has to establish whether he is the team's long-term solution at quarterback.

Turk Schonert
QPR 4.0

Height: 6'1" **Weight:** 191 lbs. **Birthdate:** 1/15/1957
College: Stanford **Draft:** Chicago Bears 1980-9th
1981-85, 1987-89 Cincinnati Bengals; 1986 Atlanta Falcons
Regular Season Record: 7-5, 1 comeback
Postseason Record: 0-0, no comebacks
Relative Rating: 101%

Passing

Year	G	Comp./Att.	%	Yards	Y/Att.	TD	INT	Rating
1981	4	10/19	52.6	166	8.7	0	0	82.3
1982	2	1/1	100.0	6	6.0	0	0	91.7
1983	9	92/156	59.0	1,159	7.4	2	5	73.1
1984	8	78/117	66.7	945	8.1	4	7	77.8
1985	7	33/51	64.7	460	9.0	1	0	100.1
1986	8	95/154	61.7	1,032	6.7	4	8	68.4
1987	11	0/0	0.0	0	0.0	0	0	0.0
1988	16	2/4	50.0	20	5.0	0	0	64.6
1989	7	0/2	0.0	0	0.0	0	0	39.6
Total	72	311/504	61.7	3,788	7.5	11	20	75.6
PS:	1	0/1	0.0	0	0	0	0	39.6

Rushing

Year	Att.	Yards	Avg.	TD
1981	7	41	5.9	0
1982	3	-8	-2.7	0
1983	29	117	4.0	2
1984	13	77	5.9	1
1985	8	39	4.9	0
1986	11	12	1.1	1
1988	2	10	5.0	0
Total	73	288	3.9	4
PS:	0	0	0.0	0

Turk Schonert bookended his forgettable nine-year career as a backup with the two Cincinnati Bengals' Super Bowl appearances. Schonert, who spent his senior year at Stanford leading the nation in passer rating while fighting off the challenge of freshman John Elway, landed with the Bengals as their third-string quarterback behind Ken Anderson and Jack Thompson in 1981. Nine years later, he finished up as Cincinnati's third quarterback behind Boomer Esiason and Erik Wilhelm when they returned to the Super Bowl in 1989. In between, he managed a couple of years as the rag-armed No. 2 quarterback in Cincinnati and Atlanta before going into coaching in the 1990s. In 15 years of coaching, he has worked with several young quarterbacks who have yet to develop into stars, including Craig Erickson, Trent Dilfer, Rob Johnson, Chris Weinke, Aaron Brooks, J.P. Losman, and Trent Edwards.

Jay Schroeder

Height: 6'4" **Weight:** 215 lbs. **Birthdate:** 6/28/1961
College: UCLA **Draft:** Washington 1984-3rd
1985–87 Washington Redskins; 1988–92 Los Angeles Raiders; 1993 Cincinnati Bengals; 1994 Arizona Cardinals
Regular Season Record: 61–38, 14 comebacks
Postseason Record: 3–2, 2 comebacks
Relative Rating: 95%

Passing

Year	G	Comp./Att.	%	Yards	Y/Att.	TD	INT	Rating
1985	9	112/209	53.6	1,458	7.0	5	5	73.8
1986	16	276/541	51.0	4,109	7.6	22	22	72.9
1987	11	129/267	48.3	1,878	7.0	12	10	71.0
1988	9	113/256	44.1	1,839	7.2	13	13	64.6
1989	11	91/194	46.9	1,550	8.0	8	13	60.3
1990	16	182/334	54.5	2,849	8.5	19	9	90.8
1991	15	189/357	52.9	2,562	7.2	15	16	71.4
1992	13	123/253	48.6	1,476	5.8	11	11	63.3
1993	9	78/159	49.1	832	5.2	5	2	70.0
1994	9	133/238	55.9	1,510	6.3	4	7	68.4
Total	118	1,426/2,808	50.8	20,063	7.1	114	108	71.7
PS:	7	72/158	45.6	791	5.0	5	8	50.4

Rushing

Year	Att.	Yards	Avg.	TD
1985	17	30	1.8	0
1986	36	47	1.3	1
1987	26	120	4.6	3
1988	29	109	3.8	1
1989	15	38	2.5	0
1990	37	81	2.2	0
1991	28	76	2.7	0
1992	28	160	5.7	0
1993	10	41	4.1	0
1994	16	59	3.7	0
Total	242	761	3.1	5
PS:	12	39	3.3	0

By his own admission, Jay Schroeder wanted to be Johnny Bench and spent three years in the Toronto Blue Jays' farm system proving he could not hit a slider before giving up baseball. Jay had played one year of football for UCLA, backing up Tom Ramsey in 1980, so the Redskins drafted him in the third round in 1984. A year later, Schroeder was thrust into the starting role when Joe Theismann's leg was snapped in a Monday night game against the division-rival Giants. Schroeder came in to lead Washington to a comeback victory that night, and the Redskins won four of their last five games but missed the playoffs.

Schroeder took over as starter full time in 1986 and guided Washington to the NFC Championship Game where they were shut out by the Giants in the windy Meadowlands with Jay completing just 20 of 50 passes. The following season, Schroeder separated his shoulder and was in and out of the starting lineup before Doug Williams was named as the starting quarterback for the playoffs and won the Super Bowl. Washington traded its forgotten younger quarterback to Los Angeles for All-Pro tackle Jim Lachey, and Jay became "Schroeder the Raider." Schroeder's playing style seemed ideal for the Raiders' vertical passing game. Jay had a rocket arm that allowed him to lead the league in yards per completion three times. However, his unpredictable inaccuracy kept him from being successful for any extended period. In addition, he tended to get rattled against the pass rush of the better defenses. Schroeder had his best year in 1992 with 19 touchdown passes and just nine interceptions and led the Raiders to the AFC Championship Game. Once again at crunch time, though, Schroeder came up small, throwing five interceptions and completing just 13 of 31 passes in a 51–3 loss to Buffalo.

Schroeder was a bit of a loner and not much of a team leader. Although his winning percentage as a starter is excellent, that is more reflective of the good teammates that surrounded him than of Jay's performance. Schroeder's inadequate 50.8 completion percentage was 10 percent below the league average of 56.2 during his career. He could play spectacularly in spurts but was mistake prone and could never establish the consistency of a top quarterback.

Bud Schwenk

QPR 1.5

Height: 6'2" **Weight:** 201 lbs. **Birthdate:** 8/26/1918
College: Washington (MO) **Draft:** Chicago Cardinals 1942-3rd
1942 Chicago Cardinals; 1946 Cleveland Browns;
1947 Baltimore Colts; 1948 New York Yankees
Regular Season Record: 5–19–1 est., 1 comeback
Postseason Record: NA
Relative Rating: 82%

Passing

Year	G	Comp./Att.	%	Yards	Y/Att.	TD	INT	Rating
1942	11	126/295	42.7	1,360	4.6	6	27	25.5
1946	4	15/23	65.2	276	12.0	4	0	146.0
1947	14	168/327	51.4	2,236	6.8	13	20	61.2
1948	8	6/17	35.3	52	3.1	0	3	4.7
Total	37	315/662	47.6	3,924	5.9	23	50	46.5

Rushing

Year	Att.	Yards	Avg.	TD
1942	111	313	2.8	2
1946	6	-1	-0.2	1
1947	25	58	2.3	1
1948	3	6	2.0	0
Total	145	376	2.6	4

After tying Davey O'Brien's season record of 234 passes in college, Bud Schwenk led two professional leagues in pass attempts and interceptions in his brief four-year career. The pass-happy Schwenk began as a single-wing tailback with the Chicago Cardinals in 1942 before going into the service for the duration of the war. As a rookie in Chicago, Bud showed some running talent but threw 27 interceptions to just six touchdowns. When he left the military in 1946, Schwenk signed on with Cleveland in the All-America Football Conference as Otto Graham's backup at quarterback. One year later, Bud was starting for the new Baltimore Colts' franchise and leading the league with 20 interceptions. When the Colts signed rookie Y.A. Tittle, Schwenk moved on to the New York Yankees, his fourth team in four years, and was back in a single-wing offense for his last year as a professional.

Bobby Scott

QPR 1.5

Height: 6'1" **Weight:** 201 lbs. **Birthdate:** 4/2/1949
College: Tennessee **Draft:** New Orleans 1971-14th
1973–81 New Orleans Saints; 1983 USFL
Regular Season Record: 4–10, 2 comebacks
Postseason Record: NA
Relative Rating: 75%

Passing

Year	G	Comp./Att.	%	Yards	Y/Att.	TD	INT	Rating
1973	6	18/54	33.3	245	4.5	1	3	31.8
1974	5	31/71	43.7	366	5.2	4	4	55.3
1975	1	8/17	47.1	96	5.6	0	1	40.3
1976	11	103/190	54.2	1,065	5.6	4	6	64.5
1977	5	36/82	43.9	516	6.3	3	8	37.5
1978	1	3/5	60.0	36	7.2	0	0	82.1
1979	3	2/2	100.0	12	6.0	0	0	91.7
1980	5	16/33	48.5	200	6.1	2	1	75.3
1981	4	20/46	43.5	245	5.3	1	5	28.2
Total	41	237/500	47.4	2,781	5.6	15	28	51.4

Rushing

Year	Att.	Yards	Avg.	TD
1973	9	18	2.0	0
1974	1	1	1.0	0
1976	12	48	4.0	1
1977	4	11	2.8	0
1978	1	0	0.0	0
1981	3	-4	-1.3	0
Total	30	74	2.5	1

Tennessee's Bobby Scott and Mississippi's Archie Manning met twice in college with the Volunteers ripping the Rebels 31–0 in 1968 and the Rebels returning the favor 38–0 in 1969. In the 1971 draft, Manning was the second overall pick by the Saints; 14 rounds later, New Orleans chose Scott with the 340th pick. For the next dozen years, the two southern quarterbacks would be teammates on a franchise that would win just 53 of 178 games with three ties. Most of Scott's starts came in 1976 when Manning was out for the season with a shoulder injury, and Scott split the quarterbacking with Bobby Douglass. Scott won just two of six starts that year and got to start only four more games in New Orleans. Even in 1982 with Manning traded away and both Ken Stabler and Dave Wilson hurt, coach Bum Phillips chose to go with wide receiver/handyman Guido Merkens instead of Scott at quarterback. Bobby was short and not very mobile with a weak arm, but he still dreamed of proving himself. The next season, Scott signed with the New Jersey Generals and split the first USFL season playing both with the Generals and the Chicago Blitz but threw just 11 touchdowns to 19 interceptions in his last shot as a professional quarterback.

Dennis Shaw

QPR 3.5

Height: 6'3" **Weight:** 217 lbs. **Birthdate:** 3/3/1947
College: San Diego State **Draft:** Buffalo 1970-2nd
1970–73 Buffalo Bills; 1974–75 St. Louis Cardinals; 1984 USFL
Regular Season Record: 8–27–2, 6 comebacks
Postseason Record: NA
Relative Rating: 88%

Passing

Year	G	Comp./Att.	%	Yards	Y/Att.	TD	INT	Rating
1970	14	178/321	55.5	2,507	7.8	10	20	65.3
1971	13	149/291	51.2	1,813	6.2	11	26	46.1
1972	14	136/258	52.7	1,666	6.5	14	17	63.5
1973	4	22/46	47.8	300	6.5	0	4	32.9
1974	2	0/0	0.0	0	0.0	0	0	0.0
1975	3	4/8	50.0	61	7.6	0	1	35.9
Total	**50**	**489/924**	**52.9**	**6,347**	**6.9**	**35**	**68**	**56.8**

Rushing

Year	Att.	Yards	Avg.	TD
1970	39	210	5.4	0
1971	14	82	5.9	0
1972	35	138	3.9	0
1973	4	2	0.5	0
1975	3	-12	-4.0	0
Total	**95**	**420**	**4.4**	**0**

Dennis Shaw followed Don Horn as the quarterback at San Diego State under Don Coryell in 1968 and led the Aztecs to a 20–0–1 record in two years. In 1969, with Brian Sipe as his backup, Shaw threw 39 touchdown passes, including nine in one game. After Terry Bradshaw and Mike Phipps were taken in the first round of the 1970 NFL draft, Shaw was the next quarterback taken in round two by Buffalo. By Week 3, Dennis beat out starter Dan Darragh and threw for more than 2,500 yards in 1970. Even though he led the league in fumbles and threw 20 interceptions, Shaw showed such promise that he

---

TOP 12

Worst Quarterback Winning Percentages (minimum 20 games)

9-T. King Hill, 7–22–1, .250
9-T. Timm Rosenbach, 5–15, .250
9-T. Frank Reich, 5–15, .250
9-T.. Gary Huff, 7–21, .250
8. Dennis Shaw, 8–27, .243
7. Fred Enke, 6–20, .231
6. Randy Wright, 7–25, .219
5. Randy Johnson, 10–38–1, .214
3-T. Chuck Long, 4–17, .190
3-T. Ryan Leaf, 4–17, .190
2. David Klingler, 4–20, .167
1. Chris Weinke, 2–18, .100

was the first quarterback named Rookie of the Year. He had toughness, good size, and a strong arm but took a lot of sacks, forced passes into coverage, and had trouble reading defenses and picking up secondary receivers. The next year, the team dropped to 1–13 and Dennis led the NFL with 26 interceptions. He rebounded a bit in 1972 but then hurt his knee and lost his job to rookie Joe Ferguson in 1973.

Shaw was aquired in 1974 by the St. Louis Cardinals, who were coached by Don Coryell. Shaw's college coach could not resuscitate his career, though, and Dennis was cut. Over the next few years, he had tryouts with the Giants and Chiefs but never played in the NFL again. Shaw did surface at the age of 36 as a player/coach under Marv Levy for the USFL's Chicago Blitz in 1984 but never got to throw a pass.

George Shaw

QPR 5.0

Height: 6'1" **Weight:** 183 lbs. **Birthdate:** 7/25/1933
College: Oregon **Draft:** Baltimore Colts 1955-1st
1955–58 Baltimore Colts; 1959–60 New York Giants; 1961 Minnesota Vikings; 1962 Denver Broncos
Regular Season Record: 11–16–2, no comebacks
Postseason Record: NA
Relative Rating: 93%

Passing

Year	G	Comp./Att.	%	Yards	Y/Att.	TD	INT	Rating
1955	12	119/237	50.2	1,586	6.7	10	19	52.5
1956	5	45/75	60.0	645	8.6	3	7	62.4
1957	7	5/9	55.6	58	6.4	1	1	72.7
1958	12	41/89	46.1	531	6.0	7	4	72.8
1959	5	24/36	66.7	433	12.0	1	1	105.4
1960	9	76/155	49.0	1,263	8.1	11	13	65.6
1961	8	46/91	50.5	530	5.8	4	4	64.8
1962	13	49/110	44.5	783	7.1	4	14	41.4
Total	71	405/802	50.5	5,829	7.3	41	63	58.8

Rushing

Year	Att.	Yards	Avg.	TD
1955	68	301	4.4	3
1956	20	63	3.2	0
1957	5	30	6.0	1
1958	5	-3	-0.6	1
1959	3	3	1.0	0
1960	15	-12	-0.8	0
1961	10	39	3.9	0
1962	4	10	2.5	1
Total	130	431	3.3	6

George Shaw was the overall No. 1 pick of the 1955 draft by Baltimore and helped improve the Colts to a 5–6–1 record in a promising rookie season as a scrambling quarterback who ran for 301 yards and passed for more than 1,500. Ultimately though, Shaw lacked the confidence to be a starter. In the fourth game of 1956, Shaw broke his kneecap, was replaced by unknown rookie Johnny Unitas, and never again was a regular starter. George did get to start two key games in 1958 when Unitas hurt his ribs but expressed misgivings to *Sports Illustrated*: "Maybe I shouldn't say it, but you know when you're out there that the guys up in the line aren't making as much money as the quarterback. When they are great players on a team which is about to win a championship, they demand a lot from a quarterback. They expect you to be as good as they are, or better. It's a big load."

After three years backing up Unitas, Shaw claimed he had developed "second string-itis" and began to doubt himself. He pushed for a trade, and the champion Colts sent George to the runner-up Giants in 1959 for a No. 1 pick. Shaw was hampered by a sore thumb that year but still had trouble trying to unseat 39-year-old veteran Charlie Conerly in 1960. Giants coach Jim Lee Howell felt that Shaw was too "bashful" a leader for a veteran team, and others commented that

George had the bland personality of a banker (which he was in the off-season) rather than that of a feisty field general. The Giants traded Shaw to the expansion Vikings for a fifth-round pick in 1961, but George was beaten out by fiery rookie Fran Tarkenton. Shaw left for Denver of the AFL in 1962 but merely supplied occasional relief there for the mediocre 35-year-old Frank Tripucka before retiring.

Dick Shiner

Height: 6'0" **Weight:** 201 lbs. **Birthdate:** 7/18/1942
College: Maryland **Draft:** Washington 1964-7th; New York Jets 1964-20th
1964–66 Washington Redskins; 1967 Cleveland Browns; 1968–69 Pittsburgh Steelers; 1970 New York Giants; 1971, 1973 Atlanta Falcons; 1973–74 New England Patriots
Regular Season Record: 7–21–1, 2 comebacks
Postseason Record: NA
Relative Rating: 92%

Passing

Year	G	Comp./Att.	%	Yards	Y/Att.	TD	INT	Rating
1964	1	0/1	0.0	0	0.0	0	0	39.6
1965	14	28/65	43.1	470	7.2	3	4	57.9
1966	14	0/5	0.0	0	0.0	0	1	0.0
1967	13	3/9	33.3	34	3.8	0	1	6.0
1968	13	148/304	48.7	1,856	6.1	18	17	64.5
1969	12	97/209	46.4	1,422	6.8	7	10	60.3
1970	14	9/12	75.0	87	7.3	0	0	94.8
1971	10	30/57	52.6	463	8.1	5	5	72.5
1973	7	36/68	52.9	432	6.4	3	4	62.9
1974	1	3/6	50.0	37	6.2	0	1	29.9
Total	99	354/736	48.1	4,801	6.5	36	43	61.3

Rushing

Year	Att.	Yards	Avg.	TD
1964	2	8	4.0	0
1965	12	35	2.9	0
1966	1	10	10.0	0
1967	2	-7	-3.5	0
1968	14	53	3.8	0
1969	14	55	3.9	1
1971	10	9	0.9	1
1973	3	-2	-0.7	0
Total	58	161	2.8	2

Dick Shiner's claim to fame was that he quarterbacked the only Maryland victory over

Penn State since 1960. As a professional, Shiner was the essence of a well-traveled, erratic, journeyman backup. Dick spent three seasons behind Sonny Jurgensen in Washington and would sometimes get booed by fans watching practice because they would rather watch the more exciting Jurgensen. The Redskins traded Shiner to Cleveland for backup Jim Ninowski in 1967, but Dick played very little before being traded to Pittsburgh for Bill Nelsen. Despite his bad knees, Nelsen developed into a star for the Browns, while Shiner's two-year record for the Steelers was 3–16–1 in the most extended starting stint of his career.

Pittsburgh traded Shiner to the Giants for runner Frenchy Fuqua and middle linebacker Henry Davis in 1970. Both became Steeler starters, but Dick backed up Fran Tarkenton in New York. Shiner made a bold move in 1971 by walking out of training camp and forcing the Giants to trade him for his fourth time, which they did, to Atlanta for failed No. 1 draft choice Randy Johnson. Shiner was beaten out by Bob Berry on the Falcons, but when Berry was traded for Bob Lee in 1973, Dick emerged as the starter on opening day. The Falcons beat New Orleans that day 62–7, and Shiner earned a perfect passer rating of 158.3 by completing 13 of 15 passes for 227 yards and three touchdowns. However, one week later, Dick earned a 0.0 passer rating by completing just two of nine passes for 17 yards and an interception against the Rams. After putting up 62 points in the first game, Atlanta scored just 15 points in the next three weeks. In short order, Shiner was replaced by Bob Lee and waived to New England where he finished his career a year later.

Passing

Year	G	Comp./Att.	%	Yards	Y/Att.	TD	INT	Rating
1994	11	120/265	45.3	1,658	6.3	10	12	59.6
1995	7	66/125	52.8	745	6.0	3	7	55.6
1996	1	0/0	0.0	0	0.0	0	0	0.0
1997	10	106/203	52.2	1,288	6.3	2	14	46.6
Total	29	292/593	49.2	3,691	6.2	15	33	54.2

Rushing

Year	Att.	Yards	Avg.	TD
1994	26	103	4.0	0
1995	18	57	3.2	0
1996	1	0	0.0	0
1997	22	38	1.7	1
Total	67	198	3.0	1

In January 2007, Heath Shuler returned to Washington in triumph as a freshman congressman from North Carolina, but in his first stay in D.C. he was practically impeached by Redskins fans. Shuler was the third overall pick in the 1994 draft but ended up being outshone by Washington's seventh-round pick, Gus Frerotte, who lasted in the league for 15 years. Although Shuler won just one of eight starts as a rookie and completed just 45 percent of his passes, the strong-armed quarterback did show some potential by leading the league in yards per completion. While throwing three touchdowns to seven interceptions in 1995, though, Shuler hurt his shoulder, and Frerotte stepped in. By 1996, Frerotte had beaten out a recovered Shuler as starter and went to the Pro Bowl that year. Washington dealt Heath to the Saints for a fifth-round pick, but he managed to throw just two touchdowns and 14 interceptions before breaking his foot in 1997. After two surgeries, Shuler tried to come back with the Raiders in 1999 but was forced to quit and get on with his life. He was re-elected to the House in 2008.

Heath Shuler

QPR 1.0

Height: 6'2"   **Weight:** 216 lbs.   **Birthdate:** 12/31/1971
College: Tennessee   **Draft:** Washington 1994-1st
1994–96 Washington Redskins; 1997 New Orleans Saints
Regular Season Record: 8–14, 2 comebacks
Postseason Record: NA
Relative Rating: 69%

Chris Simms

QPR 2.0

Height: 6'4"   **Weight:** 220 lbs.   **Birthdate:** 8/29/1980
College: Texas   **Draft:** Tampa 2003-3rd
2004–06 Tampa Bay Bucs; 2008 Tennessee Titans
Regular Season Record: 7–8, 3 comebacks
Postseason Record: 0–1, no comebacks
Relative Rating: 89%

Passing

Year	G	Comp./Att.	%	Yards	Y/Att.	TD	INT	Rating
2004	5	42/73	57.5	467	6.4	1	3	64.1
2005	11	191/313	61.0	2,035	6.5	10	7	81.4
2006	3	58/106	54.7	585	5.5	1	7	46.3
2008	1	1/2	50.0	7	3.5	0	0	58.3
Total	20	292/494	59.1	3,094	6.3	12	17	71.2
PS:	1	25/38	65.8	198	5.2	0	2	56.7

Rushing

Year	Att.	Yards	Avg.	TD
2004	7	14	2.0	0
2005	19	31	1.6	0
2006	4	7	1.8	1
Total	30	52	1.7	1
PS:	3	11	3.7	1

Early in a September 24, 2006, loss to Carolina, Tampa quarterback Chris Simms was awkwardly sandwiched by charging linebacker Thomas Davis and massive defensive tackle Kris Jenkins and went down hard. Simms played the rest of the game in pain, leaving the Bucs 0–3 and Simms with just one touchdown pass and seven interceptions on the season. He would never play for Tampa again. After the game, team doctors discovered that Simms' spleen had ruptured from the early hit, and he had lost five pints of blood in internal bleeding. After an emergency splenectomy, Simms spent the next year and a half on injured reserve before drawing his release from Tampa in 2008.

Chris is the son of former Giants star quarterback Phil Simms. Phil was a proud father who told Steve Young to back off when the broadcaster questioned the mental toughness of Chris during the 2005 season. As Chris advanced from third string to starter to leading the Bucs to the play-offs in 2005, coach Jon Gruden spoke of how good Simms was in the locker room and of his accurate left arm. By 2008, though, Simms reported the relationship between the quarterback and coach was broken, and Simms welcomed his release that summer. Although there were rumors of Chris landing in New England after Tom Brady injured his knee on opening day, Simms actually ended up with the Titans as the third quarterback behind Kerry Collins and Vince Young, two other quarterbacks who have gone through some hard times.

Simms was always a bit erratic and not very mobile but is a legitimate backup.

Phil Simms

Height: 6'3" **Weight:** 216 lbs. **Birthdate:** 11/3/1954
College: Morehead State **Draft:** New York Giants 1979-1st
1979–81, 1983–93 New York Giants
Regular Season Record: 95–64, 17 comebacks
Postseason Record: 6–4, no comebacks
Relative Rating: 105%

Passing

Year	G	Comp./Att.	%	Yards	Y/Att.	TD	INT	Rating
1979	12	134/265	50.6	1,743	6.6	13	14	66.0
1980	13	193/402	48.0	2,321	5.8	15	19	58.9
1981	10	172/316	54.4	2,031	6.4	11	9	74.0
1983	2	7/13	53.8	130	10.0	0	1	56.6
1984	16	286/533	53.7	4,044	7.6	22	18	78.1
1985	16	275/495	55.6	3,829	7.7	22	20	78.6
1986	16	259/468	55.3	3,487	7.5	21	22	74.6
1987	9	163/282	57.8	2,230	7.9	17	9	90.0
1988	15	263/479	54.9	3,359	7.0	21	11	82.1
1989	15	228/405	56.3	3,061	7.6	14	14	77.6
1990	14	184/311	59.2	2,284	7.3	15	4	92.7
1991	6	82/141	58.2	993	7.0	8	4	87.0
1992	4	83/137	60.6	912	6.7	5	3	83.3
1993	16	247/400	61.8	3,038	7.6	15	9	88.3
Total	164	2,576/4,647	55.4	33,462	7.2	199	157	78.5
PS:	10	157/279	56.3	1,679	6.0	10	6	77.0

Rushing

Year	Att.	Yards	Avg.	TD
1979	29	166	5.7	1
1980	36	190	5.3	1
1981	19	42	2.2	0
1984	42	162	3.9	0
1985	37	132	3.6	0
1986	43	72	1.7	1
1987	14	44	3.1	0
1988	33	152	4.6	0
1989	32	141	4.4	1
1990	21	61	2.9	1
1991	9	42	4.7	1
1992	6	17	2.8	0
1993	28	31	1.1	0
Total	349	1,252	3.6	6
PS:	30	68	2.3	0

In 1979, Bill Walsh and Sam Wyche worked out Phil Simms from tiny Morehead State, and Walsh pegged him as the perfect quarterback for the West Coast offense he was installing in San Francisco. The Giants, meanwhile, ranked Simms even with Washington State's Jack Thompson as the top quarterbacks in the draft. After Paul Brown selected Thompson, New York went with Simms, and Walsh had to settle for Joe Montana in the third round.

Simms and Montana would engage in a spirited rivalry that would elevate both teams over the next decade, but at the time the reaction of Giants fans attending the draft was to boo. In fact, because the television cameras missed the Simms draft announcement, NBC asked Pete Rozelle to make the announcement again, and Simms was booed a second time as Rozelle snickered. Unlike Philadelphia's Donovan McNabb, who also was booed on draft day, Simms did not spend his career whining about that day, even as the booing continued on the field with Phil beset by shoulder separations, a knee injury, and a fractured thumb in his first five years. With Simms' early tendency to throw interceptions, Parcells gave the starting job to the more conservative Scott Brunner in 1983. Simms demanded a trade, but the competition may have sharpened his skills. In 1984, he won the starting job back and threw for more than 4,000 yards, earning the respect and confidence of Parcells.

Simms was a hard thrower and a tough field general who wouldn't quit but never got the public notice that other quarterbacks of the time did because the Giants favored a more ball-control, smash-mouth attack suited to the harsh weather of the northeast. Parcells once said of Phil's critics, "Anybody who doesn't think Phil Simms is a great quarterback should be covering another sport." Simms rewarded that assurance by leading the team to its first Super Bowl championship in 1986 by completing 22 of 25 passes for 268 yards and three touchdowns in Super Bowl XXI against Denver and the more celebrated John Elway.

Four years later, Simms had the Giants on track for another Super Bowl run when Phil broke his foot in a late-season game against Buffalo. Simms watched from the sidelines as backup Jeff Hostetler stepped up to lead the Giants to a second title in Super Bowl XXV. When Parcells stepped down after that game, new coach Ray Handley gave the starting nod to the younger Hostetler in 1991. Simms didn't get his starting job back till 1993 when at age 37 he had one of the finest seasons of his 14-year career in leading New York to the playoffs one last time. In a sad move, the Giants cut Simms in the off-season as a casualty of the new salary cap. He still dominates the Giants' passing record book, and New York retired his No. 11 as their greatest quarterback.

Brian Sipe

QPR 8.0

Height: 6'1" **Weight:** 195 lbs. **Birthdate:** 8/8/1949
College: San Diego State **Draft:** Cleveland 1972-13th
1974–83 Cleveland Browns; 1984–85 USFL
Regular Season Record: 57–55, 23 comebacks
Postseason Record: 0–1, no comebacks
Relative Rating: 107%

Passing

Year	G	Comp./Att.	%	Yards	Y/Att.	TD	INT	Rating
1974	10	59/108	54.6	603	5.6	1	7	47.0
1975	7	45/88	51.1	427	4.9	1	3	54.5
1976	14	178/312	57.1	2,113	6.8	17	14	77.3
1977	9	112/195	57.4	1,233	6.3	9	14	61.8
1978	16	222/399	55.6	2,906	7.3	21	15	80.7
1979	16	286/535	53.5	3,793	7.1	28	26	73.4
1980	16	337/554	60.8	4,132	7.5	30	14	91.4
1981	16	313/567	55.2	3,876	6.8	17	25	68.2
1982	6	101/185	54.6	1,064	5.8	4	8	60.7
1983	15	291/496	58.7	3,566	7.2	26	23	79.1
Total	**125**	**1,944/3,439**	**56.5**	**23,713**	**6.9**	**154**	**149**	**74.8**
PS:	1	13/40	32.5	183	4.6	0	3	17.0

Rushing

Year	Att.	Yards	Avg.	TD
1974	16	44	2.8	4
1975	9	60	6.7	0
1976	18	71	3.9	0
1977	10	14	1.4	0
1978	28	87	3.1	3
1979	45	178	4.0	2
1980	20	55	2.8	1
1981	38	153	4.0	1
1982	13	44	3.4	0
1983	26	56	2.2	0
Total	**223**	**762**	**3.4**	**11**
PS:	6	13	2.2	0

Red Right 88 was Brian Sipe's Bill Buckner moment, a disastrous play of such consequence that it redefines a whole career. Trailing 14–12 to the Raiders, Sipe drove the Browns the length of the field in the closing minutes. The Browns had already failed on one extra-point try and missed two field goals on this bitterly cold day with a minus-37-degree windchill. On second down from the Oakland 13 with 46 seconds to play, Sipe called the play Red Right 88 and tried to force the ball to tight end Ozzie Newsome in the end zone, but it was picked off by Raider Mike Davis to end the season and poison the legacy of Cleveland's Kardiac Kids.

In college, Sipe was an outstanding quarterback under Don Coryell at San Diego State where he followed Dennis Shaw and preceded Jesse Freitas Jr. NFL scouts were not impressed by Brian's smallish size or so-so arm, but Cleveland picked him in the 13th round in 1972. Brian spent two years on the practice squad and then two more as the Browns' backup before he finally beat out one-time top draft pick Mike Phipps in 1976. Sipe benefited from low expectations and quickly became a fan favorite as he developed into a winning quarterback over the next few years. Brian was a gutsy, confident gambler who was at his best when the game was on the line. He led the Browns to so many late, improbable comebacks that they began to be called the Kardiac Kids. In 1979, Sipe became the first quarterback to lead seven fourth-quarter winning drives in one season, even though the team won only nine games that year. That year, too, Brian led the NFL in both touchdown passes and interceptions with 28 and 26 respectively and threw for 3,793 yards.

1980 was even better. The team went 11–5, and Sipe threw for 4,132 yards and 30 touchdowns while leading the league in passer rating. In the postseason, Red Right 88 undid all that. Sipe had off years in 1981 and 1982 but, pressured by backup Paul McDonald, played well again in 1983. Brian signed with Donald Trump's New Jersey Generals in the USFL in 1984 and led the team to a 14–4 mark. Trump rewarded him by bringing in Doug Flutie and dispatching Sipe to the Jacksonville Bulls where Brian finished his career as a backup in 1985. Although Sipe's career left an up-and-down track from year to year, he was a good runner and a

smart quarterback who could read defenses except for the agonizing end of one January 1981 day in Cleveland.

QPR 3.0

Mickey Slaughter

Height: 6'2" **Weight:** 204 lbs. **Birthdate:** 8/22/1941
College: Louisiana Tech **Draft:** Denver 1963-7th
1963–66 Denver Broncos
Regular Season Record: 2–15–2, no comebacks
Postseason Record: NA
Relative Rating: 90%

Passing

Year	G	Comp./Att.	%	Yards	Y/Att.	TD	INT	Rating
1963	13	112/223	50.2	1,689	7.6	12	15	65.4
1964	14	97/189	51.3	930	4.9	3	11	46.4
1965	10	75/147	51.0	864	5.9	6	12	48.7
1966	3	7/25	28.0	124	5.0	1	0	61.1
Total	40	291/584	49.8	3,607	6.2	22	38	55.4

Rushing

Year	Att.	Yards	Avg.	TD
1963	29	127	4.4	1
1964	20	54	2.7	0
1965	20	75	3.8	0
1966	1	10	10.0	0
Total	70	266	3.8	1

Along with Craig Morton, Mickey Slaughter is one of two Broncos to wear No. 7 before John Elway retired the number in Denver. He was an accurate short passer on some terrible Bronco teams in the 1960s but was injury prone and threw too many interceptions. After three forgettable years sharing the quarterbacking with the mediocre Jacky Lee and the terrible John McCormick, Slaughter hurt his thumb and missed most of 1966. In the off-season, he and cornerback Willie Brown were then traded to Oakland for a No. 1 pick and tackle Rex Mirich.

Instead of playing for the Raiders, Slaughter returned to his alma mater of Louisiana Tech as the offensive coach under Maxie Lambright and had his greatest impact on professional football over the next few years tutoring Terry Bradshaw at quarterback. Bradshaw later called Slaughter the "greatest influence on my life" because Mickey taught Terry how to read defenses and call plays while instilling confidence in the insecure blond bomber. Slaughter coached at Tech for several seasons before going into business and always remained a big booster of the school.

Akili Smith

QPR 0.5

Height: 6'3" **Weight:** 220 lbs. **Birthdate:** 8/21/1975
College: Oregon **Draft:** Cincinnati 1999-1st
1999–2002 Cincinnati Bengals; 2005 NFL Europe; 2007 CFL
Regular Season Record: 3–14, 1 comeback
Postseason Record: NA
Relative Rating: 67%

Passing

Year	G	Comp./Att.	%	Yards	Y/Att.	TD	INT	Rating
1999	7	80/153	52.3	805	5.3	2	6	55.6
2000	12	118/267	44.2	1,253	4.7	3	6	52.8
2001	2	5/8	62.5	37	4.6	0	0	73.4
2002	1	12/33	36.4	117	3.5	0	1	34.5
Total	22	215/461	46.6	2,212	4.8	5	13	52.8

Rushing

Year	Att.	Yards	Avg.	TD
1999	19	114	6.0	1
2000	41	232	5.7	0
2001	6	20	3.3	0
2002	4	5	1.3	0
Total	70	371	5.3	1

In 2002, Akili Smith became the second bust from the 1999 quarterback class to fall out of the NFL. Smith summarized his four-year experience in Cincinnati succinctly, "It's been hell for everybody. I'm kind of baffled they drafted me. Ten games into my second season, they benched me, and it was all over after that."

Seven years after the David Klingler flop, the Bengals revisited the crapshoot of picking a quarterback at the top of the draft and selected Smith even though the former professional baseball player was a junior-college transfer who started at quarterback for Oregon only in his senior year. Mike Ditka had offered Cincinnati his entire 1999 slate of draft picks plus two picks in 2000 to be able to draft runner Ricky Williams the Bengals'

TOP 10
Left-Handed NFL Quarterbacks

10. Allie Sherman (the NFL's first in 1943)
9. Matt Leinart
8. Bobby Douglass
7. Jim Zorn
6. Michael Vick
5. Boomer Esiason
4. Frankie Albert
3. Mark Brunell
2. Ken Stabler
1. Steve Young

slot, but they turned down Ditka, who found the Redskins willing to make a similar deal. Although Smith put on a big show at the NFL Combine with his strong arm, it quickly became apparent with the Bengals that he held the ball too long, couldn't read defenses, and threw inaccurately. It didn't help that Smith held out of training camp and fell behind right from the start. In his brief tenure, Smith threw just five touchdowns but tossed 13 interceptions and fumbled 19 times. Two months after Cincinnati drafted Carson Palmer with the overall No. 1 pick in 2003, Akili was cut. Smith tried to catch on with the Packers and Bucs and then NFL Europe and Canada but could not revive his career.

Alex Smith

QPR 2.0

Height: 6'4" **Weight:** 212 lbs. **Birthdate:** 5/7/1984
College: Utah **Draft:** San Francisco 2005-1st
2005–08 San Francisco 49ers
Regular Season Record: 11–19, 6 comebacks
Postseason Record: NA
Relative Rating: 80%

Passing

Year	G	Comp./Att.	%	Yards	Y/Att.	TD	INT	Rating
2005	9	84/165	50.9	875	5.3	1	11	40.8
2006	16	257/442	58.1	2,890	6.5	16	16	74.8
2007	7	94/193	48.7	914	4.7	2	4	57.2
Total	32	435/800	54.4	4,679	5.8	19	31	63.5

Rushing

Year	Att.	Yards	Avg.	TD
2005	30	103	3.4	0
2006	44	147	3.3	2
2007	13	89	6.8	0
Total	87	339	3.9	2

If not for the flicker of potential that Alex Smith exhibited in his second season, the first overall pick of the 2005 draft could safely be labeled as a bust. Coming out of the shotgun spread offense used at Utah, Smith was looked at as a risk by many scouts. Although he is intelligent and a good runner with good size, Alex has yet to display much confidence or leadership in the NFL. He has been a scatter-armed turnover machine, with 31 interceptions and 27 fumbles in 32 games. One theory is that Smith's problems stem from too much coaching change. In his dreadful rookie season when he threw just one touchdown pass and 11 interceptions, the offensive coordinator was Mike McCarthy, who left for Green Bay in 2006. Under new coordinator Norv Turner in 2006, Smith seemed to blossom. He threw 16 touchdowns to 16 interceptions and completed 58 percent of his passes, but then Turner moved on to San Diego, and Jim Hosler was hired to coach the offense in 2007. Smith regressed to 48 percent completions and 4.7 yards per pass while trying to overcome a serious shoulder separation that head coach Mike Nolan downplayed. Finally, Smith went on injured reserve in December. Mike Martz replaced Hosler in 2008, and Smith was demoted to second string behind J.T. O'Sullivan, a backup whom Martz brought with him from Detroit. Then, Alex broke a bone in his shoulder and went back on IR for the entire season. Smith restructured his contract to stay in San Francisco, and will compete for the starting position again under a new offensive coordinator.

QPR 7.5

Norm Snead

Height: 6'4" **Weight:** 215 lbs. **Birthdate:** 7/31/1939
College: Wake Forest **Draft:** Washington 1961-1st; Buffalo 1961-5th
1961–63 Washington Redskins; 1964–70 Philadelphia Eagles; 1971 Minnesota Vikings; 1972–74, 1976 New York Giants; 1974–75 San Francisco 49ers
Regular Season Record: 52–99–7, 19 comebacks
Postseason Record: NA
Relative Rating: 98%

Passing

Year	G	Comp./Att.	%	Yards	Y/Att.	TD	INT	Rating
1961	14	172/375	45.9	2,337	6.2	11	22	51.6
1962	14	184/354	52.0	2,926	8.3	22	22	74.7
1963	14	175/363	48.2	3,043	8.4	13	27	58.1
1964	12	138/283	48.8	1,906	6.7	14	12	69.6
1965	11	150/288	52.1	2,346	8.1	15	13	78.0
1966	10	103/226	45.6	1,275	5.6	8	11	55.1
1967	14	240/434	55.3	3,399	7.8	29	24	80.0
1968	11	152/291	52.2	1,655	5.7	11	21	51.8
1969	13	190/379	50.1	2,768	7.3	19	23	65.7
1970	14	181/335	54.0	2,323	6.9	15	20	66.1
1971	7	37/75	49.3	470	6.3	1	6	40.4
1972	14	196/325	60.3	2,307	7.1	17	12	84.0
1973	10	131/235	55.7	1,483	6.3	7	22	45.8
1974	8	97/159	61.0	983	6.2	5	8	68.2
1975	9	108/189	57.1	1,337	7.1	9	10	73.0
1976	3	22/42	52.4	239	5.7	0	4	29.9
Total	178	2,276/4,353	52.3	30,797	7.1	196	257	65.5

Rushing

Year	Att.	Yards	Avg.	TD
1961	34	47	1.4	3
1962	20	10	0.5	3
1963	23	100	4.3	2
1964	16	59	3.7	2
1965	24	81	3.4	3
1966	15	32	2.1	1
1967	9	30	3.3	2
1968	9	27	3.0	0
1969	8	2	0.3	2
1970	18	35	1.9	3
1971	6	6	1.0	1
1972	10	21	2.1	0
1973	4	13	3.3	0
1974	4	29	7.3	0
1975	9	30	3.3	1
1976	3	-1	-0.3	0
Total	212	521	2.5	23

Norm Snead was a tall, big-armed Virginian who threw for more than 4,000 yards at Wake Forest and was the second overall pick of the 1961 draft. It was the third year in a row that the Redskins selected a quarterback with their top pick. Neither Don Allard in 1959 nor Richie Lucas in 1960 worked out, so Washington chose Snead, even though Wake Forest had finished just 11–19 under his leadership. He would have the same indifferent relationship to winning in the pros, winning just 33 percent of his starts.

Snead was thrown into the starting lineup immediately as a rookie and showed a facility for throwing the long ball but took a pounding behind a permeable offensive line. In three years with the Redskins, he threw 46 touchdowns and 71 interceptions and went 9–30–3. Yet, twice he was named to the Pro Bowl, including in 1963 when he led the league in interceptions for the first of four times. On the questionable basis of Snead being four years younger, new Eagles coach Joe Kuharich traded future Hall of Famer Sonny Jurgensen to Washington for Norm in a blockbuster quarterback-for-quarterback exchange almost never seen in the NFL. As Malaprop Joe put it, "It's quite rare but not unusual." In the next seven seasons, Jurgensen's Redskins would go 9–3–2 against Snead's Eagles, and in one 1966 Eagle victory, the slumping Snead didn't even play. Norm made the Pro Bowl a third time in 1965 but played very poorly the next year, throwing just eight touchdown passes to 25 interceptions. He was benched for King Hill and Jack Concannon at the end of 1966, but that was the only winning season Norm would have in Philadelphia.

Snead threw a career-high 29 TD passes in 1967 for a losing Eagles team but continued his up-and-down pattern in 1968 by throwing almost twice as many picks as touchdowns. Just as in Washington, Norm was heavily booed in Philadelphia for his erratic, mistake-prone play. He was sturdy with a strong arm but did not move well in the pocket, folded under pressure, and lacked fire as a leader. One of his Eagle teammates once said of him, "He plays like what he is during the off-season: an insurance salesman. Snead dulls you to defeat."

Snead was traded to the Vikings in 1971 and was part of another three-man crowd at quarterback with Gary Cuozzo and Bob Lee. After playing little for the division-winning Vikings, Norm was sent on to the Giants the next year. In New York, he had his finest year by leading the NFL in passing in 1972 and leading the Giants to an 8–6 record. Both Snead and the Giants returned to losing form in 1973, and in midseason 1974, Norm was traded to the 49ers. After a Bay Area detour, Snead finished his career with New York as a backup in 1976.

Butch Songin

Height: 6'2" **Weight:** 190 lbs. **Birthdate:** 5/11/1924
College: Boston College **Draft:** Cleveland 1950-19th
1953–54 CFL; 1960–61 Boston Patriots; 1962 New York Titans
Regular Season Record: 8–11–1, 2 comebacks
Postseason Record: NA
Relative Rating: 112%

Passing

Year	G	Comp./Att.	%	Yards	Y/Att.	TD	INT	Rating
1960	14	187/392	47.7	2,476	6.3	22	15	70.9
1961	14	98/212	46.2	1,429	6.7	14	9	73.0
1962	7	42/90	46.7	442	4.9	2	7	36.4
Total	35	327/694	47.1	4,347	6.3	38	31	67.1

Rushing

Year	Att.	Yards	Avg.	TD
1960	11	40	3.6	2
1961	8	39	4.9	0
1962	4	11	2.8	0
Total	23	90	3.9	2

Edward "Butch" Songin was an All-American hockey defenseman for Boston College in the 1940s as well as the starting quarterback on the Eagle football team. Although drafted by the Browns in 1950, he never played for them. Songin went to Canada to play football a few years later but stayed only two seasons before returning to his native Massachusetts. Six years later, when the American Football League was formed, Songin signed with the hometown Patriots and was Boston's first starting quarterback. In fact, he played in the league's first game against Denver, threw the AFL's first pass, and registered the AFL's first completed pass to Jim Colclough. The 36-year-old Songin was a touch-passing game manager who was joined in Boston by the big-armed Babe Parilli in 1961. The two complementary quarterbacks alternated plays at one point for coach Lou Saban. After Parilli fully demonstrated his arm, though, Songin was sent to the New York Titans for his final year of 1962. After retiring, Butch coached semipro football in the 1960s.

Steve Spurrier

QPR 4.5

Height: 6'2" **Weight:** 204 lbs. **Birthdate:** 4/20/1945
College: Florida **Draft:** San Francisco 1967-1st
1967–75 San Francisco 49ers; 1976 Tampa Bay Bucs
Regular Season Record: 13–24–1, 2 comebacks
Postseason Record: NA
Relative Rating: 91%

Passing

Year	G	Comp./Att.	%	Yards	Y/Att.	TD	INT	Rating
1967	14	23/50	46.0	211	4.2	0	7	18.4
1968	14	0/0	0.0	0	0.0	0	0	0.0
1969	6	81/146	55.5	926	6.3	5	11	54.8
1970	14	3/4	75.0	49	12.3	1	0	155.2
1971	6	1/4	25.0	46	11.5	0	0	75.0
1972	13	147/269	54.6	1,983	7.4	18	16	75.9
1973	11	83/157	52.9	882	5.6	4	7	59.5
1974	3	1/3	33.3	2	0.7	0	0	42.4
1975	11	102/207	49.3	1,151	5.6	5	7	60.3
1976	14	156/311	50.2	1,628	5.2	7	12	57.1
Total	106	597/1,151	51.9	6,878	6.0	40	60	60.1

Rushing

Year	Att.	Yards	Avg.	TD
1967	5	18	3.6	0
1968	1	-15	-15.0	0
1969	5	49	9.8	0
1970	2	-18	-9.0	0
1971	1	2	2.0	0
1972	11	51	4.6	0
1973	9	32	3.6	2
1975	15	91	6.1	0
1976	12	48	4.0	0
Total	61	258	4.2	2

Steve Spurrier's long, successful college coaching career overshadows his time in the NFL as both a player and coach because Steve never found much success in the pros. Spurrier won the Heisman Trophy at Florida in 1966, and Miami fans expected the Dolphins to draft Steve that year. After interviewing him, though, the Dolphins went with Bob Griese, who they found to be more mature and dedicated. Spurrier was selected by the 49ers, where he served mostly as John Brodie's backup for the next nine years, accumulating nearly twice as many yards punting as passing. Spurrier was so cool that many saw him as a lackadaisical diva, and that perception followed Steve into his coaching career. Spurrier was slow in setting up and slow in releasing the ball. Although he was fairly good at the deep ball, he was not very effective on shorter throws, and his passes lacked zip.

Spurrier got to start nine games in 1972 and five in 1973 when Brodie was hurt and fading. When Brodie finally retired in 1974, Steve separated his shoulder. He fell behind veteran Norm Snead in 1975 and then was traded to the expansion Bucs in 1976. Spurrier started 12 games for the Bucs that first year and lost all of them. Steve retired after Tampa's winless season and began his coaching career as the quarterback coach at his alma mater in 1978. Through 2008, Spurrier's record as a college coach was 170–61–2, but he was just 12–20 in two years coaching the Redskins in the NFL.

Ken Stabler

QPR 9.5

Height: 6'3" **Weight:** 215 lbs. **Birthdate:** 12/25/1945
College: Alabama **Draft:** Oakland 1968-2nd
1970–79 Oakland Raiders; 1980–81 Houston Oilers;
1982–84 New Orleans Saints
Regular Season Record: 96–49–1, 25 comebacks
Postseason Record: 7–5, 2 comebacks
Relative Rating: 109%

Passing

Year	G	Comp./Att.	%	Yards	Y/Att.	TD	INT	Rating
1970	3	2/7	28.6	52	7.4	0	1	18.5
1971	14	24/48	50.0	268	5.6	1	4	39.2
1972	14	44/74	59.5	524	7.1	4	3	82.3
1973	14	163/260	62.7	1,997	7.7	14	10	88.3
1974	14	178/310	57.4	2,469	8.0	26	12	94.9
1975	14	171/293	58.4	2,296	7.8	16	24	67.4
1976	12	194/291	66.7	2,737	9.4	27	17	103.4
1977	13	169/294	57.5	2,176	7.4	20	20	75.2
1978	16	237/406	58.4	2,944	7.3	16	30	63.3
1979	16	304/498	61.0	3,615	7.3	26	22	82.2
1980	16	293/457	64.1	3,202	7.0	13	28	68.7
1981	13	165/285	57.9	1,988	7.0	14	18	69.5
1982	8	117/189	61.9	1,343	7.1	6	10	71.8
1983	14	176/311	56.6	1,988	6.4	9	18	61.4
1984	3	33/70	47.1	339	4.8	2	5	41.3
Total	184	2,270/3,793	59.8	27,938	7.4	194	222	75.3
PS:	13	203/351	57.8	2,641	7.5	19	13	84.2

Rushing

Year	Att.	Yards	Avg.	TD
1970	1	-4	-4.0	0
1971	4	29	7.3	2
1972	6	27	4.5	0
1973	21	101	4.8	0
1974	12	-2	-0.2	1
1975	6	-5	-0.8	0
1976	7	-2	-0.3	1
1977	3	-3	-1.0	0
1978	4	0	0.0	0
1979	16	-4	-0.3	0
1980	15	-22	-1.5	0
1981	10	-3	-0.3	0
1982	3	-4	-1.3	0
1983	9	-14	-1.6	0
1984	1	-1	-1.0	0
Total	118	93	0.8	4
PS:	8	34	4.3	2

Kenny "Snake" Stabler was the left-handed heir to Bobby Layne and Joe Namath as an NFL quarterback. He was an inspirational leader, cool under pressure, in command of the huddle, and not concerned about interceptions because he always figured he could pull out a win at the end. Off the field, he led the way to the nearest bar and made famous the concept of reading the playbook by the light of the jukebox.

Stabler was a three-sport star in high school and followed Joe Namath to Alabama under Bear Bryant. Sharing the quarterbacking with Steve Sloan in 1965, the two led the Crimson Tide to a national title. Stabler took over as the full-time starter in 1966, and Alabama was undefeated that year and 8–2–1 in 1967. Stabler was taken by the Raiders in the second round in 1968 behind black quarterback Eldridge Dickey, who was Oakland's top pick. Stabler ended up playing minor-league football in the Pacific Northwest for a year before joining Oakland as the third quarterback behind Daryle Lamonica and George Blanda in 1970.

Ken was a running quarterback in college. It was his 30-yard touchdown run on a scramble that led to the Immaculate Reception by Franco Harris of Pittsburgh in the 1972 playoffs. However, knee operations transformed Stabler into a pocket passer who could still throw on the run, and he was extremely accurate on the short and intermediate routes. Finally in 1973, Stabler pushed past the bomb-throwing Lamonica as the Raiders' starter. Al Davis commented that going from Lamonica to Stabler was like going from the fast break to finding the open man in basketball. Coach John Madden said that Stabler "moves the ball. Our offense all begins with Stabler." In distributing the ball, Kenny led the league in completion percentage and touchdown passes twice each.

The Snake was also a gambler who once threw seven interceptions in one game against Denver. More memorable, though, were such nicknamed games as the "Holy Roller" against San Diego when Stabler fumbled the ball forward for a touchdown with time running out, the "Sea of Hands" game when Clarence Davis caught Kenny's shot put pass into a triple coverage to beat Miami in the 1974 postseason, and the "Ghost to the Post" pass to Dave Caspar that keyed an overtime win over the Colts in the 1977 playoffs.

Stabler quarterbacked Oakland to their first Super Bowl title in 1976 but four years later was traded straight up for Houston's strong-armed Dan Pastorini. The Oilers wanted Stabler to get them over the hump to beat the rival Steelers. In reality, neither quarterback had much left in the tank, although Stabler stuck around for two years in Houston and three in New Orleans before retiring.

TOP 10

Most Disappointing Quarterbacks from Florida Schools

10. George Mira, Miami
9. Danny Kanell, Florida State
8. Ken Dorsey, Miami
7. Gary Huff, Florida State
6. Chris Weinke, Florida State
5. Gino Torretta, Miami
4. Danny Wuerffel, Florida
3. Steve Spurrier, Florida
2. John Reaves, Florida
1. Rex Grossman, Florida

Bart Starr

QPR **10.0**

Height: 6'1" **Weight:** 197 lbs. **Birthdate:** 1/9/1934
College: Alabama **Draft:** Green Bay 1956-17th
1956–71 Green Bay Packers
Regular Season Record: 94–57–6, 19 comebacks
Postseason Record: 9-1, 1 comeback
Relative Rating: 120%

Passing

Year	G	Comp./Att.	%	Yards	Y/Att.	TD	INT	Rating
1956	9	24/44	54.5	325	7.4	2	3	65.1
1957	12	117/215	54.4	1,489	6.9	8	10	69.3
1958	12	78/157	49.7	875	5.6	3	12	41.2
1959	12	70/134	52.2	972	7.3	6	7	69.0
1960	12	98/172	57.0	1,358	7.9	4	8	70.8
1961	14	172/295	58.3	2,418	8.2	16	16	80.3
1962	14	178/285	62.5	2,438	8.6	12	9	90.7
1963	13	132/244	54.1	1,855	7.6	15	10	82.3
1964	14	163/272	59.9	2,144	7.9	15	4	97.1
1965	14	140/251	55.8	2,055	8.2	16	9	89.0
1966	14	156/251	62.2	2,257	9.0	14	3	105.0
1967	14	115/210	54.8	1,823	8.7	9	17	64.4
1968	12	109/171	63.7	1,617	9.5	15	8	104.3
1969	12	92/148	62.2	1,161	7.8	9	6	89.9
1970	14	140/255	54.9	1,645	6.5	8	13	63.9
1971	4	24/45	53.3	286	6.4	0	3	45.2
Total	196	1,808/3,149	57.4	24,718	7.8	152	138	80.5
PS:	10	130/213	61.0	1,753	8.2	15	3	104.8

Rushing

Year	Att.	Yards	Avg.	TD
1956	5	35	7.0	0
1957	31	98	3.2	3
1958	25	113	4.5	1
1959	16	83	5.2	0
1960	7	12	1.7	0
1961	12	56	4.7	1
1962	21	72	3.4	1
1963	13	116	8.9	0
1964	24	165	6.9	3
1965	18	169	9.4	1
1966	21	104	5.0	2
1967	21	90	4.3	0
1968	11	62	5.6	1
1969	7	60	8.6	0
1970	12	62	5.2	1
1971	3	11	3.7	1
Total	247	1,308	5.3	15
PS:	8	26	3.3	1

Bart Starr in the Clutch: Down 17-14 to Dallas in the Ice Bowl, the Packers got the ball at their own 32 with 4:50 to play. The temperature was minus 13 and the windchill minus 46. In the finest hour of the Green Bay dynasty of the 1960s, Starr led the team on a 68-yard march in 12 plays by completing five of five passes for 57 yards, mixing in a brilliant trap call that took the ball to the Dallas 3, and then scoring the game-winning touchdown on a quarterback sneak with 16 seconds to play.

Bart Starr is rarely mentioned in the upper echelon of quarterbacks today, but articles in national magazines and books in his time often favorably compared him to Johnny Unitas. The showdowns between Starr's Packers and Unitas' Colts were of comparable interest to today's Tom Brady–Peyton Manning rivalry. In the 1960s, Green Bay was 86–30–5 while Baltimore was 85–32–4, aside from the times the two teams met. (The Packers held a 10–7 edge there.) The two best teams of the decade had virtually identical records, yet Starr's Packers won five titles and Unitas' Colts won none. In Vince Lombardi's opinion, "Bart Starr is the greatest quarterback who ever played football. Starr is the greatest because he won the most championships. It's as simple as that. Isn't winning the job of the quarterback?"

Starr was a lowly 17th-round draft choice out of Alabama in 1956, but Bart made the team as Tobin

Bart Starr and Vince Lombardi were an unbeatable team who combined to win five championships for Green Bay in the 1960s.

Bart Starr's Five Highest Honors

5. Selected to four Pro Bowls
4. Five-time All-Pro and consensus All-Pro once
3. Two-time Super Bowl MVP
2. 1966 Player of the Year
1. Elected to the Pro Football Hall of Fame in 1977

The Five Quarterbacks Most Similar to Bart Starr

5. Frank Ryan
4. Troy Aikman
3. Otto Graham
2. Bob Griese
1. Len Dawson

Bart Starr's Five Top Touchdown Targets

5. Paul Hornung, 11 TDs
4. Ron Kramer, 12 TDs
3. Carroll Dale, 19 TDs
2. Max McGee, 25 TDs
1. Boyd Dowler, 28 TDs

Bart Starr's Five Toughest Rivals

5. Starr was 4–1 against the Cowboys in the regular season and 2–0 in the playoffs.
4. Starr was 11–7 against the Vikings.
3. Starr was 11–10–3 against the Lions.
2. Starr was 15–8 against the Bears.
1. Starr was 9–9 against the Colts in the regular season and 1–0 in the playoffs.

Five Random Bart Starr Statistics

5. Starr played for five head coaches.
4. Starr's Packers outscored the league average by 5 percent.
3. Starr threw four touchdown passes against the Vikings on November 1, 1964, and the Cowboys on October 28, 1968, as well as against Dallas in the 1966 NFL championship.
2. Starr threw for more than 300 yards five times.
1. Starr led the league in completion percentage three times, yards per attempt twice, and passer rating three times.

Rote's backup. Starr showed potential with his accuracy, but his arm and leadership were weak. Although Lombardi arrived in 1959, he did not decide on Bart as his permanent starting quarterback until late in 1960, when Starr led Green Bay to its first Western Conference crown in 16 years. Although the Packers lost the championship game to the Eagles that year 17–13, 1960 would be the last time Bart would lose a playoff game. The Packers won each of the next nine postseason games in the decade, and Starr played well in nearly all of them. In fact, the disciplined, precise Packer passer outplayed rival star quarterbacks Y.A. Tittle, Don Meredith, Frank Ryan, Roman Gabriel, Len Dawson, and Daryle Lamonica in the playoffs to win five championships with the highest postseason quarterback rating in NFL history at 104.8 and the lowest interception percentage of any postseason quarterback who threw at least 200 passes.

Bart was a master at calling plays, reading defenses, and switching off to audibles at the line of scrimmage. Cool under pressure, his signature play was the deep pass on third or fourth and short yardage, where Bart would fake to the halfback or fullback and pass to an open receiver downfield. He did it consistently for long gains and touchdowns both in the regular season and the playoffs. Starr was a surprisingly good runner but also took a lot of sacks rather than risk an interception, and that pounding made him injury prone. Although Starr did not have a very strong arm, he could and did throw the deep ball when it was open. His yards per pass average of 7.85 is excellent and virtually identical to that of Unitas. In Lombardi's ball-control offense, though, Starr did not throw enough to accumulate the big passing numbers of Unitas and others.

Bart Starr's Signature Play: Up 7–0 in the second quarter of the Ice Bowl, the 1967 NFL championship, the Packers faced third and one on the Cowboys' 46. As he did so many times in his career when faced with a short yardage play on third or fourth down, Starr went to a play-action deep pass with the defense drawn up to stop the expected run. Starr faked to the fullback Ben Wilson, dropped back and launched an easy touchdown pass to Boyd Dowler running a post pattern.

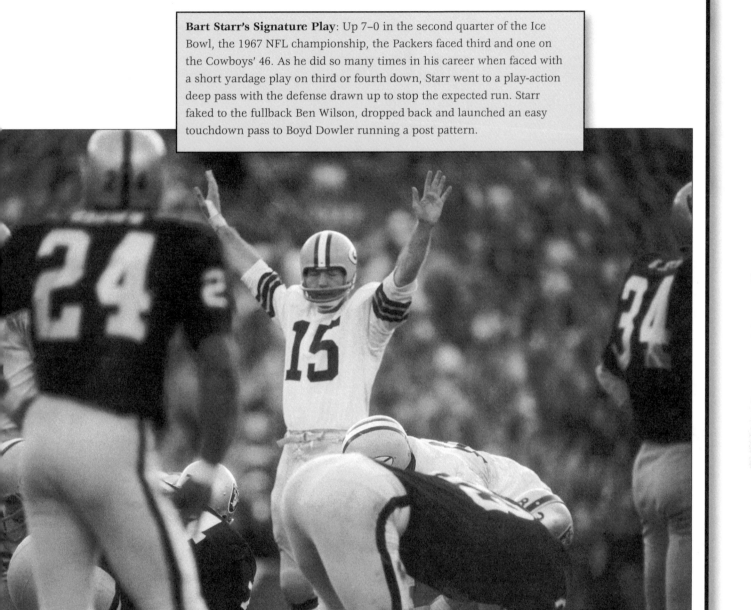

Starr was at his best in the postseason when his passer rating jumped 24 points from 80.5 to 104.8.

After his playing career ended, Bart was summoned back to Green Bay as coach. It was a mistake for the team to offer the job to the inexperienced Starr, and he recorded only two winning seasons in nine years. As a man, though, Starr was so respected that Athletes in Action instituted the Bart Starr Award in 1988 to honor an NFL player of strong character and leadership on and off the field each year. It is a fitting tribute to the greatest money quarterback of all.

Roger Staubach

Height: 6'3" **Weight:** 197 lbs. **Birthdate:** 2/5/1942
College: Navy **Draft:** Dallas 1964-10th; Kansas City 1964-16th
1969–79 Dallas Cowboys
Regular Season Record: 85–29, 21 comebacks
Postseason Record: 11-6, 2 comebacks
Relative Rating: 127%

Passing

Year	G	Comp./Att.	%	Yards	Y/Att.	TD	INT	Rating
1969	6	23/47	48.9	421	9.0	1	2	69.5
1970	8	44/82	53.7	542	6.6	2	8	42.9
1971	13	126/211	59.7	1,882	8.9	15	4	104.8
1972	4	9/20	45.0	98	4.9	0	2	20.4
1973	14	179/286	62.6	2,428	8.5	23	15	94.6
1974	14	190/360	52.8	2,552	7.1	11	15	68.4
1975	13	198/348	56.9	2,666	7.7	17	16	78.5
1976	14	208/369	56.4	2,715	7.4	14	11	79.9
1977	14	210/361	58.2	2,620	7.3	18	9	87.0
1978	15	231/413	55.9	3,190	7.7	25	16	84.9
1979	16	267/461	57.9	3,586	7.8	27	11	92.3
Total	131	1,685/2,958	57.0	22,700	7.7	153	109	83.4
PS:	19	224/410	54.4	2,817	6.9	24	19	76.4

Rushing

Year	Att.	Yards	Avg.	TD
1969	15	60	4.0	1
1970	27	221	8.2	0
1971	41	343	8.4	2
1972	6	45	7.5	0
1973	46	250	5.4	3
1974	47	320	6.8	3
1975	55	316	5.7	4
1976	43	184	4.3	3
1977	51	171	3.4	3
1978	42	182	4.3	1
1979	37	172	4.6	0
Total	410	2,264	5.5	20
PS:	76	432	5.7	0

Roger Staubach went to six Pro Bowls but never was named All-Pro. He led the league in passer rating four times in his NFL career but was never named MVP. He was a quarterback who did everything well but did it so efficiently that flashier quarterbacks with bigger numbers could steal the spotlight. Staubach has the fourth-highest winning percentage among all quarterbacks and was on the Cowboys for all five of Tom Landry's Super Bowls, winning two championships in four Super Bowl starts. Although Roger seldom got to call his own plays, the tall and wiry quarterback was an accurate passer and a shifty runner.

Unfortunately, Staubach's career was shortened on both ends. He got a late start because the 1963 Heisman Trophy winner from Annapolis first had to fulfill a four-year commitment to the navy during which he served in Vietnam. Then he retired at the top of his game when he began to feel the cumulative impact of 20 concussions suffered on the field. In between, Staubach was the most consistent quarterback of the 1970s. Known as Roger the Dodger, he was second only to Fran Tarkenton as a scrambler in his time. Roger led all quarterbacks in rushing yards in 1974 with 320, and he finished his career as sixth in 1980, although he has since fallen nearly out of the top 20 with the current proliferation of mobile quarterbacks. Redskins coach George Allen called Staubach "the best passer-runner I ever coached against."

Roger Staubach in the Clutch: Against the arch-rival Redskins on December 16, 1979, Captain Comeback led the Cowboys back from a 34–21 deficit in the last two minutes of the game by completing seven of 10 passes for two touchdowns to pull out the game 35–34 with just 39 seconds to play. Staubach had also led two touchdown drives in the final five minutes of the first half.

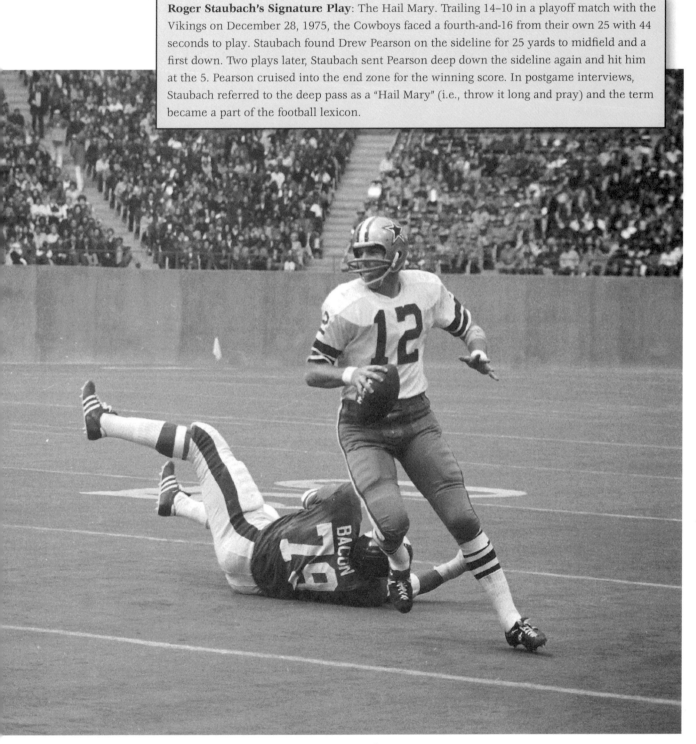

Roger Staubach's Signature Play: The Hail Mary. Trailing 14–10 in a playoff match with the Vikings on December 28, 1975, the Cowboys faced a fourth-and-16 from their own 25 with 44 seconds to play. Staubach found Drew Pearson on the sideline for 25 yards to midfield and a first down. Two plays later, Staubach sent Pearson deep down the sideline again and hit him at the 5. Pearson cruised into the end zone for the winning score. In postgame interviews, Staubach referred to the deep pass as a "Hail Mary" (i.e., throw it long and pray) and the term became a part of the football lexicon.

Rodger the Dodger eludes Coy Bacon on the Rams in November 1971.

Roger Staubach's Five Highest Honors

5. Won both the Whizzer White and the NFL Man of the Year Awards in 1978
4. Selected to six Pro Bowls
3. Five-time All-Pro and four-time consensus All-Pro
2. 1971 Player of the Year
1. Elected to the Pro Football Hall of Fame in 1985.

The Five Quarterbacks Most Similar to Roger Staubach

5. Jeff Hostetler
4. Danny White
3. Doug Flutie
2. Fran Tarkenton
1. Steve Young

Roger Staubach's Five Top Touchdown Targets

5. Bob Hayes, 11 TDs
4. Golden Richards, 13 TDs
3. Tony Hill, 15 TDs
2. Billy Joe Dupree, 27 TDs
1. Drew Pearson, 27 TDs

Roger Staubach's Five Toughest Rivals

5. Staubach was 13–5 against the Cardinals.
4. Staubach was 0–2 against the Steelers in the regular season and 0–2 in the Super Bowl.
3. Staubach was 3–2 against the Rams in the regular season and 3–2 in the playoffs.
2. Staubach was 1–2 against the Vikings in the regular season and 3–1 in the playoffs.
1. Staubach was 9–6 against the Redskins in the regular season and 0–1 in the playoffs.

Five Random Roger Staubach Statistics

5. Staubach played for only one head coach.
4. Staubach's Cowboys outscored the league average by 8 percent.
3. Staubach threw four touchdown passes against the Colts on September 4, 1978.
2. Staubach threw for more than 300 yards five times.
1. Staubach led the league in touchdown passes once, yards per attempt twice, and passer rating four times.

Staubach was also called Captain Comeback for his regular heroics in the last few minutes of games. Although he led the league in fourth-quarter game-winning drives only once, he led more comebacks than any other quarterback in the 1970s with 23, one more than Ken Stabler. Borrowing from his Catholic background, he coined a familiar football term when his 50-yard last-minute pass to Drew Pearson beat the Vikings in the 1975 playoffs, and after the game, Roger said, "I just closed my eyes and said a Hail Mary." Even in his two Super Bowl losses to the Steelers, Staubach had the Cowboys driving at the end, trying to beat the clock and the opponent. Tom Landry once said, "We always felt Roger would pull it out, no matter what was happening."

As the quarterback on the self-proclaimed America's Team, Staubach derisively was referred to as Captain America at times for his image of purity, but he was a thoroughly decent man and the finest leader in the NFL in his day.

The Cowboys never felt out of any game in which Roger Staubach was playing.

Steve Stenstrom

QPR 2.0

Height: 6'2"   **Weight:** 206 lbs.   **Birthdate:** 12/23/1971
College: Stanford   **Draft:** Kansas City 1995-4th
1996–98 Chicago Bears; 1999 San Francisco 49ers
Regular Season Record: 1–9, no comebacks
Postseason Record: NA
Relative Rating: 80%

Passing

Year	G	Comp./Att.	%	Yards	Y/Att.	TD	INT	Rating
1996	1	3/4	75.0	37	9.3	0	0	103.1
1997	3	8/14	57.1	70	5.0	0	2	31.0
1998	7	112/196	57.1	1,252	6.4	4	6	70.4
1999	6	54/100	54.0	536	5.4	0	4	52.7
Total	17	177/314	56.4	1,895	6.0	4	12	62.5

Rushing

Year	Att.	Yards	Avg.	TD
1997	1	6	6.0	0
1998	18	79	4.4	2
1999	3	15	5.0	0
Total	22	100	4.5	2

Steve Stenstrom was a four-year starter at Stanford and was Bill Walsh's last starting quarterback in the coach's second stint at Stanford from 1992 to 1994.

Stenstrom still holds most of the passing records for the Cardinal but was not much of a success in the pros. Steve didn't have a very strong arm and wasn't very mobile, but the Chiefs drafted him in the fourth round. Stenstrom never played in Kansas City but was picked up by the Bears, for whom he went 1–6 as a starter in 1998. By 1999, Walsh was back in the 49er front office and signed him as Steve Young's backup. Stenstrom lost all three of his starts after Young had his final concussion and lost out to Jeff Garcia as the new 49er quarterback. He was out of football the next year.

Kordell Stewart

QPR 6.5

Height: 6'1"   **Weight:** 218 lbs.   **Birthdate:** 10/16/1972
College: Colorado   **Draft:** Pittsburgh 1995-2nd
1995–2002 Pittsburgh Steelers; 2003 Chicago Bears;
2004–05 Baltimore Ravens
Regular Season Record: 48–34, 12 comebacks
Postseason Record: 1–3, no comebacks
Relative Rating: 90%

TOP 10

Game-Winning Drives

10. Roger Staubach's 50-yard Hail Mary pass to Drew Pearson to beat the Vikings in 1975.
9. Bobby Layne's 33-yard touchdown pass to Jim Doran to win the 1953 title in the last 2:00 over the Browns
8. Otto Graham leading the upstart Browns on a 60-yard drive for the winning field goal in the last 2:00 of the 1950 title game against the Rams.
7. Tom Brady leading the Patriots back from a 10-point fourth-quarter deficit in the snow to beat Oakland in January 2002.
6. Joe Montana's 89-yard drive in the closing minutes against the Cowboys in the NFC Championship Game in January 1982. Montana culminated the drive with a high pass to the back of the end zone that Dwight Clark made famous as "The Catch."
5. "The Drive" by John Elway—98 yards to tie Cleveland in the closing minutes. Denver won in overtime in the 1986 playoffs.
4. Eli Manning's 83-yard drive highlighted by the impossible catch by David Tyree to win Super Bowl XLII.
3. Joe Montana's 92-yard drive capped by a 10-yard touchdown pass to John Taylor in Super Bowl XXIII.
2. Bart Starr's quarterback sneak with 13 seconds left to finish a 68-yard game-winning drive in the Ice Bowl in 1967.
1. Johnny Unitas' two drives to tie and win the first sudden-death championship game in 1958.

Passing

Year	G	Comp./Att.	%	Yards	Y/Att.	TD	INT	Rating
1995	10	5/7	71.4	60	8.6	1	0	136.9
1996	16	11/30	36.7	100	3.3	0	2	18.8
1997	16	236/440	53.6	3,020	6.9	21	17	75.2
1998	16	252/458	55.0	2,560	5.6	11	18	62.9
1999	16	160/275	58.2	1,464	5.3	6	10	64.9
2000	16	151/289	52.2	1,860	6.4	11	8	73.6
2001	16	266/442	60.2	3,109	7.0	14	11	81.7
2002	8	109/166	65.7	1,155	7.0	6	6	82.8
2003	9	126/251	50.2	1,418	5.6	7	12	56.8
2004	2	0/0	0.0	0	0.0	0	0	0.0
2005	1	0/0	0.0	0	0.0	0	0	0.0
Total	126	1,316/2,358	55.8	14,746	6.3	77	84	70.8
PS:	6	69/142	48.6	744	5.2	2	8	45.6

Rushing

Year	Att.	Yards	Avg.	TD
1995	15	86	5.7	1
1996	39	171	4.4	5
1997	88	476	5.4	11
1998	81	406	5.0	2
1999	56	258	4.6	2
2000	78	436	5.6	7
2001	96	537	5.6	5
2002	43	191	4.4	2
2003	59	290	4.9	3
2004	1	-1	-1.0	0
2005	4	24	6.0	0
Total	560	2,874	5.1	38
PS:	45	250	5.6	2

When things were going well as a runner, receiver, and passer for Kordell "Slash" Stewart during his rookie season of 1995, coach Bill Cowher said, "He's bubbly, he's enthusiastic, he's bright-eyed. I think anyone who spends any time with Kordell will walk away thinking, 'Isn't it refreshing to see a player like that in the National Football League?'" Six years later, Cowher struck a different tone in praising his quarterback, "I'm sure he'll never forget some of the things he's had to go through, and I wouldn't wish them upon anyone, but he's buried the hatchet and handled himself like the consummate pro. It wasn't easy, but he has won back this city and this team."

Stewart's inconsistent career bounced from spectacular plays to infuriating, bumbling incompetence. As a starting quarterback he had some good years and some bad years, some winning seasons and some losing ones but was never very good in the biggest games, as his postseason statistics show. Stewart was a very erratic, streaky passer who often lost his composure in the pocket and tried to rely on his athletic talents too much to rescue a bad situation.

Kordell got his first chance to start in 1997 when he passed for 21 touchdowns and ran for 11 more in leading the Steelers to the playoffs. In the AFC championship against the Broncos, though, Stewart threw two end zone interceptions and was taunted and mocked by intense linebacker Bill Romanowski. The next year, Stewart was terrible and after being yanked from one game by Cowher was seen crying on the sidelines. Around that time, unsubstantiated rumors circulated that Kordell was gay. The year 1999 brought more of the same with Stewart getting beer dumped on him after one benching.

Offensive coordinators came and went until Mike Mullarkey arrived and simplified the offense in 2001. Stewart had his best season, throwing for 3,107 yards and leading all quarterbacks with 537 rushing yards. He even beat the Ravens in the playoffs when the Steeler defense picked off Elvis Grbac three times. The next week, though, it was Stewart's turn to be intercepted three times in a loss to New England in the AFC championship. The next year, Stewart lost his job to Tommy Maddox and then signed with Chicago as free agent in 2003. He flopped with the Bears and moved on to Baltimore. With the Ravens for the last two years of his career, Slash ran the ball five times, punted five times, and threw no passes.

QPR

Cliff Stoudt

Height: 6'4" **Weight:** 215 lbs. **Birthdate:** 3/27/1955
College: Youngstown State **Draft:** Pittsburgh 1977-5th
1980–83 Pittsburgh Steelers; 1984–85 USFL; 1986–88 St. Louis/Arizona Cardinals; 1989 Miami Dolphins
Regular Season Record: 9–11, 4 comebacks
Postseason Record: 0–1, no comebacks
Relative Rating: 78%

Passing

Year	G	Comp./Att.	%	Yards	Y/Att.	TD	INT	Rating
1980	6	32/60	53.3	493	8.2	2	2	78.0
1981	2	1/3	33.3	17	5.7	0	0	53.5
1982	6	14/35	40.0	154	4.4	0	5	14.2
1983	16	197/381	51.7	2,553	6.7	12	21	60.6
1986	5	52/91	57.1	542	6.0	3	7	53.5
1987	12	0/1	0.0	0	0.0	0	0	39.6
1988	16	63/113	55.8	747	6.6	6	8	64.3
1989	3	0/0	0.0	0	0.0	0	0	0.0
Total	66	359/684	52.5	4,506	6.6	23	43	58.3
PS:	1	10/20	50.0	187	9.4	1	1	78.5

Rushing

Year	Att.	Yards	Avg.	TD
1980	9	35	3.9	0
1981	3	11	3.7	0
1982	11	28	2.5	0
1983	77	479	6.2	4
1986	7	53	7.6	0
1987	1	-2	-2.0	0
1988	14	57	4.1	0
Total	122	651	5.4	4
PS:	9	50	5.6	0

Cliff Stoudt qualified for an NFL pension before he ever got on the field with the Steelers. He joked to the press, "I reach my threshold of pain when my toes get cold in the fourth quarter." As Pittsburgh's third quarterback for three and a half years, Cliff earned two Super Bowl rings for carrying a clipboard. When backup Mike Kruczek left as a free agent in 1980, Stoudt exclaimed, "I've graduated from clipboard to headset." At least Cliff had a self-deprecating sense of humor; he needed it in the Steel City.

Stoudt followed Ron Jaworski at Youngstown State and was a fifth-round pick by the Steelers in 1977, mostly for his size and arm strength. He didn't get to play at all until 1980 and finally replaced injured legend Terry Bradshaw in 1983. Although Pittsburgh won nine of Stoudt's 15 starts that year, he played terribly, throwing 21 interceptions to just 12 touchdowns and getting sacked 51 times, although he did run for 479 yards. Cliff was nervous in the pocket and an inaccurate passer with no touch who usually would lock onto his primary receiver.

Bradshaw returned for the beginning of the next-to-last game to spur the Steelers into the playoffs. Three weeks later, Stoudt was unimpressive in a 38–10 first-round loss to the Raiders.

Stoudt jumped to the Birmingham Stallions of the USFL in 1984 and helped the league get its first sellout crowd when he brought the Stallions to Pittsburgh to play the Maulers. Steeler fans filled the stadium to boo Stoudt and pelt him with food and beer. After the USFL folded, Stoudt spent four years as a backup with the Cardinals and Dolphins and then retired. In 2007, Stoudt's son Zack committed to attend Pitt, and Cliff remarked that he was happy with his son's choice because his years in Pittsburgh were the best of his career.

Kelly Stouffer

Height: 6'3" **Weight:** 210 lbs. **Birthdate:** 7/6/1964
College: Colorado State **Draft:** St. Louis Cardinals 1987-1st
1988–89, 1991–92 Seattle Seahawks
Regular Season Record: 5–11, no comebacks
Postseason Record: NA
Relative Rating: 73%

Passing

Year	G	Comp./Att.	%	Yards	Y/Att.	TD	INT	Rating
1988	8	98/173	56.6	1,106	6.4	4	6	69.2
1989	3	29/59	49.2	270	4.6	0	3	40.9
1991	2	6/15	40.0	57	3.8	0	1	23.5
1992	9	92/190	48.4	900	4.7	3	9	47.7
Total	22	226/437	51.5	2,333	5.3	7	19	54.5

Rushing

Year	Att.	Yards	Avg.	TD
1988	19	27	1.4	0
1989	2	11	5.5	0
1992	9	37	4.1	0
Total	30	75	2.5	0

Kelly Stouffer was the top pick of the Cardinals in 1987, but the team made a lowball offer and was slow to come off it. Stouffer hardened in his response, and the two sides could not reach agreement. Stouffer sat out the season and forced a trade to Seattle in 1988. The Seahawks gave up first-, second-, and fifth-round picks for Stouffer, but he was booed in his first exhibition game and never amounted to much in five years in the Pacific Northwest. He had good size and was a good runner, but he was injury prone and an inaccurate passer and fumbled 20 times in 22 games. He managed to complete 56 percent of his passes for four touchdowns and six interceptions in his six starts as a rookie but completed fewer than half his passes for just three touchdowns and 13 interceptions for the remainder of his disappointing career.

Don Strock

Height: 6'5" **Weight:** 220 lbs. **Birthdate:** 11/27/1950
College: Virginia Tech **Draft:** Miami 1973-5th
1974–87 Miami Dolphins; 1988 Cleveland Browns
Regular Season Record: 16–6, 7 comebacks
Postseason Record: 0–0, no comebacks
Relative Rating: 104%

Passing

Year	G	Comp./Att.	%	Yards	Y/Att.	TD	INT	Rating
1974	1	0/0	0.0	0	0.0	0	0	0.0
1975	6	26/45	57.8	230	5.1	2	2	67.8
1976	4	21/47	44.7	359	7.6	3	2	74.7
1977	4	2/4	50.0	12	3.0	0	1	16.7
1978	16	72/135	53.3	825	6.1	12	6	83.1
1979	16	56/100	56.0	830	8.3	6	6	78.3
1980	16	30/62	48.4	313	5.0	1	5	35.2
1981	16	79/130	60.8	901	6.9	6	8	71.3
1982	9	30/55	54.5	306	5.6	2	5	45.0
1983	15	34/52	65.4	403	7.8	4	1	106.5
1984	16	4/6	66.7	27	4.5	0	0	76.4
1985	16	7/9	77.8	141	15.7	1	0	155.8
1986	16	14/20	70.0	152	7.6	2	0	125.4
1987	12	13/23	56.5	114	5.0	0	1	51.7
1988	4	55/91	60.4	736	8.1	6	5	85.2
Total	**167**	**443/779**	**56.9**	**5,349**	**6.9**	**45**	**42**	**74.9**

| PS: | 5 | 40/65 | 61.5 | 564 | 8.7 | 4 | 3 | 90.8 |

Rushing

Year	Att.	Yards	Avg.	TD
1974	1	-7	-7.0	0
1975	6	38	6.3	1
1976	2	13	6.5	1
1978	10	23	2.3	0
1979	3	18	6.0	0
1980	1	-3	-3.0	0
1981	14	-26	-1.9	0
1982	3	-9	-3.0	0
1983	6	-16	-2.7	0
1984	2	-5	-2.5	0
1985	2	-6	-3.0	0
1986	1	0	0.0	0
1988	6	-2	-0.3	0
Total	**57**	**18**	**0.3**	**2**

| PS: | 1 | 0 | 0.0 | 0 |

Don Strock spent his entire 15-year career as a backup quarterback, 14 of it under Don Shula in Miami. Actually, Strock was with Shula for 15 years, because he joined the Dolphins in 1973 even though he never played in that first year as a fifth-round draft pick. In Miami, Strock backed up Bob Greise, Earl Morrall, David Woodley, and Dan Marino. The most games he ever started in one season was seven in 1978 when Greise was hurt; Don won five and lost two that year. Strock did see extensive relief action in the late 1970s and the early 1980s. With the inexperienced David Woodley starting, Strock was called on in relief so often that the two quarterbacks were seen as a package and known as "Woodstrock."

"Woodstrock" took Miami to the Super Bowl in 1982, but Don's most famous game came the year before in a playoff contest against the Chargers. That day, Woodley was pulled in the second quarter with Miami down 24–0. Strock, a fine pocket passer, came in and started firing. Don led the Dolphins to two scores and then, with 36 seconds left in the half, pulled the old hook-and-lateral play on the unsuspecting Chargers and went into the half down just 24–17. The second half was a back-and-forth battle that led to overtime and an eventual Charger victory even after Strock had put his field-goal kicker in position to win twice. Both Strock and Dan Fouts threw for more than 400 yards in that 41–38 classic.

The easygoing Strock was a success coming off the bench because his teammates had confidence in him. Although he barely got to throw more than one season's worth of passes in 15 years—earning "more money per bruise than anyone in the game" as Griese needled him—Strock was one of the greatest backup quarterbacks in history. He finished up his career as Bernie Kosar's backup in Cleveland and went into coaching, most notably at Florida International University where he resigned in 2006 after his team was involved in an ugly sideline-clearing brawl with the University of Miami.

Karl Sweetan

QPR 1.0

Height: 6'1" **Weight:** 203 lbs. **Birthdate:** 10/2/1942
College: Wake Forest **Draft:** Detroit 1965-18th
1964 CFL; 1966–67 Detroit Lions; 1968 New Orleans Saints; 1969–70 Los Angeles Rams
Regular Season Record: 6–10–3, 1 comeback
Postseason Record: NA
Relative Rating: 71%

Passing

Year	G	Comp./Att.	%	Yards	Y/Att.	TD	INT	Rating
1966	10	157/309	50.8	1,809	5.9	4	14	54.3
1967	10	74/177	41.8	901	5.1	10	11	51.1
1968	5	27/78	34.6	318	4.1	1	9	12.6
1969	5	5/13	38.5	101	7.8	1	0	92.1
1970	6	6/13	46.2	81	6.2	1	0	92.1
Total	36	269/590	45.6	3,210	5.4	17	34	48.3

Rushing

Year	Att.	Yards	Avg.	TD
1966	34	219	6.4	1
1967	17	93	5.5	1
1968	4	-5	-1.3	0
1969	1	-1	-1.0	0
Total	56	306	5.5	2

Karl Sweetan was the quarterback and kicker for Wake Forest when Brian Piccolo of *Brian's Song* fame was on campus. Sweetan did not finish school but signed with Toronto in the CFL instead. He joined the Lions after they drafted him in the 18th round in 1965 but was not very successful on the field. Karl threw twice as many interceptions as touchdowns and did not have much of an arm,

although he did tie an NFL record by connecting with Pat Studstill in 1966 for a 99-yard touchdown pass. He was a better runner than passer. Off the field, Sweetan was a little wild. George Plimpton later noted that while he was in the Lions' training camp for the *Paper Lion* project, he delivered food to a girl that Sweetan had stashed in the boiler room. After bouncing around the league a bit, Karl was arrested by the FBI in 1972 when he allegedly offered to sell a photocopy of the Rams' playbook to Saints coach J.D. Roberts. Because the playbook was not deemed of much monetary value, the case was dropped. Karl said at his arraignment, "Once this is cleared up, I'd like to play again." It's not surprising that there was no longer a market for his services. Sweetan went on to work as a blackjack dealer in Las Vegas for 27 years.

Jerry Tagge

QPR 1.5

Height: 6'2" **Weight:** 220 lbs. **Birthdate:** 4/12/1950
College: Nebraska **Draft:** Green Bay 1972-1st
1972–74 Green Bay Packers; 1975 WFL; 1977–79 CFL
Regular Season Record: 6–6, 1 comeback
Postseason Record: NA
Relative Rating: 68%

Passing

Year	G	Comp./Att.	%	Yards	Y/Att.	TD	INT	Rating
1972	4	10/29	34.5	154	5.3	0	0	52.9
1973	7	56/106	52.8	720	6.8	2	7	53.2
1974	7	70/146	47.9	709	4.9	1	10	36.0
Total	18	136/281	48.4	1,583	5.6	3	17	44.2

Rushing

Year	Att.	Yards	Avg.	TD
1972	8	-3	-0.4	1
1973	15	62	4.1	2
1974	18	58	3.2	0
Total	41	117	2.9	3

Jerry Tagge was a hometown boy. He was born in Nebraska and went to high school in Green Bay; as a football player, Tagge played for the Nebraska Cornhuskers and the Green Bay Packers. Jerry won consecutive national championships as the Nebraska quarterback and led the Huskers over the No. 2 ranked Oklahoma Sooners 35–31 in what was called the "Game of the Century" in 1971. Drafted by the Packers in 1972, Tagge was weak-armed and found the pro game too fast. He threw just three touchdowns to 17 interceptions in three disappointing years with the Packers. Jerry tried the World Football League in 1975 and then signed with British Columbia in the CFL in 1977 and threw 32 touchdowns and 38 interceptions in three years in Canada. In 1977, he finished second in the MVP voting for the league. A knee injury ended his career.

Mike Taliaferro

 QPR 2.5

Height: 6'2" **Weight:** 202 lbs. **Birthdate:** 7/26/1941
College: Illinois **Draft:** New York Jets 1963-28th; New York Giants1963-10th
1964–67 New York Jets; 1968–70 Boston Patriots; 1972 Buffalo Bills
Regular Season Record: 11–20, 2 comebacks
Postseason Record: NA
Relative Rating: 73%

Passing

Year	G	Comp./Att.	%	Yards	Y/Att.	TD	INT	Rating
1964	14	23/73	31.5	341	4.7	2	5	28.4
1965	14	45/119	37.8	531	4.5	3	7	36.1
1966	14	19/41	46.3	177	4.3	2	2	54.6
1967	3	11/20	55.0	96	4.8	1	1	63.7
1968	7	67/176	38.1	889	5.1	4	15	26.9
1969	14	160/331	48.3	2,160	6.5	19	18	66.0
1970	11	78/173	45.1	871	5.0	4	11	41.8
1972	5	16/33	48.5	176	5.3	1	4	35.2
Total	82	419/966	42.4	5,241	5.4	36	63	46.1

Rushing

Year	Att.	Yards	Avg.	TD
1964	9	45	5.0	0
1965	7	4	0.6	0
1967	2	20	10.0	0
1968	8	51	6.4	0
1969	12	-16	-1.3	0
1970	3	11	3.7	0
1972	5	19	3.8	0
Total	46	134	2.9	0

Mike Taliaferro's name was Italian but the pronunciation was anglicized to "Tolliver." Mike was the quarterback on the powerful 1964 Illinois Rose Bowl team that featured Dick Butkus at center

and Jim Grabowski at fullback. Drafted by both New York teams, Taliaferro signed with the Jets because they offered him a better chance to play. Mike backed up Dick Wood for one season, and then owner Sonny Werblin signed college stars Joe Namath for $427,000 and Heisman Trophy winner John Huarte for $200,000 in 1965.

Taliaferro admitted that he found it discouraging to read about Namath and Huarte constantly in the papers, but the $15,000 plugger beat out the high-priced rookies on opening day of 1965 and got to start several games that year as the inconsistent Namath was in and out of the lineup. But Taliaferro lacked confidence and assertiveness as a leader and was an inaccurate passer with a windup motion. After four years as a 39-percent passer with the Jets, he was traded to the Patriots for veteran Babe Parilli. Mike got a chance to start in Boston and even went to the AFL All-Star Game in 1969 on the strength of 19 touchdown passes but won just eight of 25 starts and threw 27 touchdowns to 44 interceptions. When Joe Kapp was acquired in 1970, Patriot fans immediately started calling for the former Viking, and Taliaferro moved on to Buffalo as a backup in 1972. Taliaferro surfaced briefly with the Houston Texans of the World Football League in 1974. There, Mike replaced Eldridge Dickey, who failed to report to training camp, but when the team moved to Shreveport, Louisiana, late in the year, Taliaferro quit instead.

TOP 10
Shady Quarterbacks

10. Frankie Filchock—suspended for not reporting a bribe
9. Jim McMahon—cultivated an image of antisocial punk
8. Karl Sweetan—tried to sell his former team's playbook
7. Quincy Carter—drug problems
6. Todd Marinovich—drug problems
5. Kerry Collins—alcohol-induced problems
4. Clint Longley—sucker punched Roger Staubach
3. Art Schlichter—gambling
2. Ryan Leaf—dysfunctional and immature
1. Michael Vick—implicated in dogfighting ring

Fran Tarkenton

Height: 6'0" **Weight:** 190 lbs. **Birthdate:** 2/3/1940
College: Georgia **Draft:** Minnesota 1961-3rd; Boston Patriots 1961-5th
1961–66, 1972–78 Minnesota Vikings; 1967–71 New York Giants
Regular Season Record: 124–109–6, 36 comebacks
Postseason Record: 6–5, 1 comeback
Relative Rating: 121%

Passing

Year	G	Comp./Att.	%	Yards	Y/Att.	TD	INT	Rating
1961	14	157/280	56.1	1,997	7.1	18	17	74.7
1962	14	163/329	49.5	2,595	7.9	22	25	66.9
1963	14	170/297	57.2	2,311	7.8	15	15	78.0
1964	14	171/306	55.9	2,506	8.2	22	11	91.8
1965	14	171/329	52.0	2,609	7.9	19	11	83.8
1966	14	192/358	53.6	2,561	7.2	17	16	73.8
1967	14	204/377	54.1	3,088	8.2	29	19	85.9
1968	14	182/337	54.0	2,555	7.6	21	12	84.6
1969	14	220/409	53.8	2,918	7.1	23	8	87.2
1970	14	219/389	56.3	2,777	7.1	19	12	82.2
1971	13	226/386	58.5	2,567	6.7	11	21	65.4
1972	14	215/378	56.9	2,651	7.0	18	13	80.2
1973	14	169/274	61.7	2,113	7.7	15	7	93.2
1974	13	199/351	56.7	2,598	7.4	17	12	82.1
1975	14	273/425	64.2	2,994	7.0	25	13	91.8
1976	13	255/412	61.9	2,961	7.2	17	8	89.3
1977	9	155/258	60.1	1,734	6.7	9	14	69.2
1978	16	345/572	60.3	3,468	6.1	25	32	68.9
Total	246	3,686/6,467	57.0	47,003	7.3	342	266	80.4
PS:	11	149/292	51.0	1,803	6.2	11	17	58.6

Rushing

Year	Att.	Yards	Avg.	TD
1961	56	308	5.5	5
1962	41	361	8.8	2
1963	28	162	5.8	1
1964	50	330	6.6	2
1965	56	356	6.4	1
1966	62	376	6.1	4
1967	44	306	7.0	2
1968	57	301	5.3	3
1969	37	172	4.6	0
1970	43	236	5.5	2
1971	30	111	3.7	3
1972	27	180	6.7	0
1973	41	202	4.9	1
1974	21	120	5.7	2
1975	16	108	6.8	2
1976	27	45	1.7	1
1977	15	6	0.4	0
1978	24	-6	-0.3	1
Total	675	3,674	5.4	32
PS:	25	70	2.8	1

The original scrambling quarterback, Fran Tarkenton left the game as the all-time leader in attempts, completions, touchdown passes, passing yards, rushing yards by a quarterback, and victories. He was second only to Johnny Unitas in fourth-quarter game-winning drives. Four times he led the league in fourth-quarter

Fran Tarkenton's Signature Play: On October 4, 1964, the Vikings trailed the Packers 23–21 in the closing minute and faced a fourth-and-22 at their own 35. Tarkenton rolled to the right but found no one open. Pursued by Willie Davis, he scrambled back to the middle of the field and then back again to the right before spotting a receiver free at last. Tight end Gordon Smith made a leaping catch at the Packers 30 and then ran another 10 yards before jumping out of bounds. With 18 seconds to play, Fred Cox booted the winning field goal and Minnesota beat Green Bay for the first time ever.

Fran Tarkenton in the Clutch: Behind 33–14 to the Redskins with under 10 minutes to play, Tarkenton drove the Giants to three late touchdowns for a 35–33 victory on November 15, 1970. The lengthy touchdown drives covered 71, 65, and 73 yards and propelled the Giants to their sixth straight win.

Fran Tarkenton was the most elusive scrambler of his time.

comebacks and seven times—five in a row—led the league in rushing yards by a quarterback. He was a great quarterback, but when *Sports Illustrated* asked him about his legacy in 1975, Tarkenton said, "I'd like to be thought of as a good one. I hate to think I won't be unless I win a Super Bowl." He never did win that championship.

The smallish, weak-armed Tarkenton was drafted in the third round in 1961 by the expansion Vikings. Fran relieved starter George Shaw in Minnesota's first game against the Bears and threw four touchdown passes to upset Chicago 37–13. Right from the outset, he was a dynamic leader who made an outmanned team competitive. Ultimately,

Fran Tarkenton's Five Highest Honors

5. Member of the College Football Hall of Fame.
4. Selected to nine Pro Bowls.
3. 11-time All–Pro and consensus All–Pro once.
2. 1975 Player of the Year.
1. Elected to the Pro Football Hall of Fame in 1986.

The Five Quarterbacks Most Similar to Fran Tarkenton

5. Tommy Kramer
4. David Woodley
3. Pat Haden
2. Roger Staubach
1. Doug Flutie

Fran Tarkenton's Five Top Touchdown Targets

5. Joe Morrison and Bill Brown, 18 TDs
4. Homer Jones, 20 TDs
3. Chuck Foreman, 23 TDs
2. Sammy White, 24 TDs
1. John Gilliam, 25 TDs

Fran Tarkenton's Five Toughest Rivals

5. Tarkenton was 9–7–3 against the Rams in the regular season and 2–1 in the playoffs.
4. Tarkenton was 4–9 against the Cowboys in the regular season and 1–1 in the playoffs.
3. Tarkenton was 14–12–1 against the Bears.
2. Tarkenton was 13–13–1 against the Lions.
1. Tarkenton was 13–14–1 against the Packers.

Five Random Fran Tarkenton Statistics

5. Tarkenton played for four head coaches.
4. Tarkenton's teams outscored the league average by 5 percent.
3. Tarkenton threw five touchdown passes against the Cardinals on October 25, 1970.
2. Tarkenton threw for more than 300 yards 13 times and over 400 on October 24, 1965, against the 49ers.
1. Tarkenton led the league in completion percentage twice, touchdown passes once, passer rating once, and interceptions once.

Tarkenton had a falling out with the Vikings' abrasive coach, Norm Van Brocklin, who did not trust running quarterbacks. In 1967, the Giants gave up two first-round picks and a No. 2 to acquire Fran. In his first year in New York, Tarkenton threw for 29 touchdowns and 3,000 yards. He was a clever play caller who compensated for his arm limitations with an effective, short-passing offense that emphasized dump passes to check down receivers. Brains and guile took him to four Pro Bowls for the Giants and nine in his career.

In 1971, Tarkenton got into a contract dispute with the Giants because he wanted a business loan from the team, and things turned so sour that for spite he was held out of the season finale—the first game he had missed in his 11 years as a professional. New York traded him back to Minnesota for first- and second-round draft picks and three nondescript players. Fran led the Vikings to three Super Bowls in his second tour in Minnesota but did not play well in any of them, throwing just one touchdown and six interceptions in those title games.

Tarkenton was smart and resourceful but could also come across as egotistic and self-serving. He showed how a scrambling quarterback could be effective in the NFL and introduced the quarterback slide as a way to protect himself on the field. Fran didn't miss a game due to injury until he broke his leg in his 17th year at the age of 37. He returned for one last year and led the league in passes, completions, passing yards, and a career-high 32 interceptions. In retirement, Tarkenton remained visible as a broadcaster on *Monday Night Football* and *That's Incredible* as well as an infomercial pitchman in his second career as an entrepreneur.

Tarkenton was a very clever play caller who commanded the huddle.

Steve Tensi

QPR 4.5

Height: 6'5" **Weight:** 215 lbs. **Birthdate:** 12/8/1942
College: Florida State **Draft:** San Diego 1965-4th; Baltimore
Colts 1965-16th
**1965–66 San Diego Chargers; 1967–70 Denver
Broncos**
Regular Season Record: 10–23–1, 1 comeback
Postseason Record: NA
Relative Rating: 93%

Passing

Year	G	Comp./Att.	%	Yards	Y/Att.	TD	INT	Rating
1965	1	0/0	0.0	0	0.0	0	0	0.0
1966	14	21/52	40.4	405	7.8	5	1	92.2
1967	14	131/325	40.3	1,915	5.9	16	17	54.8
1968	7	48/119	40.3	709	6.0	5	8	46.5
1969	13	131/286	45.8	1,990	7.0	14	12	68.1
1970	7	38/80	47.5	539	6.7	3	8	42.7
Total	56	369/862	42.8	5,558	6.4	43	46	59.0

Rushing

Year	Att.	Yards	Avg.	TD
1966	1	-1	-1.0	0
1967	24	4	0.2	0
1968	6	2	0.3	0
1969	12	63	5.3	0
1970	4	14	3.5	0
Total	47	82	1.7	0

Steve Tensi was tall, stiff, slow, and brittle. He moved in the pocket as easily as the rusty Tin Man in *The Wizard of Oz* and was sacked frequently, causing him to miss time each year due to injuries. As a passer, he could throw the bomb but was so inaccurate that he completed only 43 percent of his passes. At Florida State, he had teamed with Fred Biletnikoff to form a top passing combination in coach Bill Peterson's pro set offense. Sid Gillman helped Peterson install his offense at FSU and then drafted Tensi in 1965. At the time, Gillman claimed that Tensi was the equal of Joe Namath. Sid clearly either was trying to boost Steve's confidence or boost Tensi's perceived trade value because Steve Tensi was no Joe Namath. The desperate Broncos thought he was close enough, though, and sent San Diego two first-round picks for him in 1967. They remained desperate on offense after Tensi arrived.

Steve Tensi never completed half his passes in any season in the league.

Vinny Testaverde

QPR 7.5

Height: 6'5" **Weight:** 235 lbs. **Birthdate:** 11/13/1963
College: Miami **Draft:** Tampa 1987-1st
**1987–92 Tampa Bay Bucs; 1993–95 Cleveland
Browns; 1996–97 Baltimore Ravens; 1998–2003,
2005 New York Jets; 2004 Dallas Cowboys; 2006 New
England Patriots; 2007 Carolina Panthers**
Regular Season Record: 90–123–1, 34 comebacks
Postseason Record: 3–3, no comebacks
Relative Rating: 96%

Passing

Year	G	Comp./Att.	%	Yards	Y/Att.	TD	INT	Rating
1987	6	71/165	43.0	1,081	6.6	5	6	60.2
1988	15	222/466	47.6	3,240	7.0	13	35	48.8
1989	14	258/480	53.8	3,133	6.5	20	22	68.9
1990	14	203/365	55.6	2,818	7.7	17	18	75.6
1991	13	166/326	50.9	1,994	6.1	8	15	59.0
1992	14	206/358	57.5	2,554	7.1	14	16	74.2
1993	10	130/230	56.5	1,797	7.8	14	9	85.7
1994	14	207/376	55.1	2,575	6.8	16	18	70.7
1995	13	241/392	61.5	2,883	7.4	17	10	87.8
1996	16	325/549	59.2	4,177	7.6	33	19	88.7
1997	13	271/470	57.7	2,971	6.3	18	15	75.9
1998	14	259/421	61.5	3,256	7.7	29	7	101.6
1999	1	10/15	66.7	96	6.4	1	1	78.7
2000	16	328/590	55.6	3,732	6.3	21	25	69.0
2001	16	260/441	59.0	2,752	6.2	15	14	75.3
2002	5	54/83	65.1	499	6.0	3	3	78.3
2003	7	123/198	62.1	1,385	7.0	7	2	90.6
2004	16	297/495	60.0	3,532	7.1	17	20	76.4
2005	6	60/106	56.6	777	7.3	1	6	59.4
2006	3	2/3	66.7	29	9.7	1	0	137.5
2007	7	94/172	54.7	952	5.5	5	6	65.8
Total	233	3,787/6,701	56.5	46,233	6.9	275	267	75.0
PS:	7	115/190	60.5	1,329	7.0	6	5	81.2

Rushing

Year	Att.	Yards	Avg.	TD
1987	13	50	3.8	1
1988	28	138	4.9	1
1989	25	139	5.6	0
1990	38	280	7.4	1
1991	32	101	3.2	0
1992	36	197	5.5	2
1993	18	74	4.1	0
1994	21	37	1.8	2
1995	18	62	3.4	2
1996	34	188	5.5	2
1997	34	138	4.1	0
1998	24	104	4.3	1
2000	25	32	1.3	0
2001	31	25	0.8	0
2002	2	23	11.5	0
2003	6	17	2.8	0
2004	21	38	1.8	1
2005	7	4	0.6	2
2006	8	-8	-1.0	0
2007	9	22	2.4	0
Total	430	1,661	3.9	15
PS:	10	16	1.6	0

It's tempting to look at Vinny Testaverde as the Dave Kingman of quarterbacks, that is, someone who racked up huge numbers during his career but will never be considered for the Hall of Fame. However, Testaverde was not a one-dimensional performer like the "home run or strikeout" Kingman was. After a rough start, Vinny developed into a very solid pro field general.

Heisman Trophy winner Testaverde was the first overall pick in the 1987 NFL draft, relegated to the lowly Tampa Bay Bucs, coached by Ray Perkins. In just his second season, Vinny tossed 35 interceptions, the second highest total in NFL history; no one has thrown more than 29 in the 20 seasons since then. The struggling Testaverde was hampered by weak coaching at the outset of his career and seemed to be a bust when Bill Belichick picked him up in Cleveland in 1992, but he immediately blossomed under more favorable coaching. There, he succeeded despite the fact that he was replacing his old Miami Hurricane teammate, a fading Bernie Kosar who was still the hometown favorite of Browns fans. If you take away Vinny's first six seasons under three coaches in Tampa, his touchdown to interception ratio improves to 198–155 and his record as a starter perks up to 66–75. In fact, if you remove his last few seasons in his 40s as the wandering ancient mariner of quarterbacks, his record evens out to 58–58.

The 6'5" Testaverde always had a big arm and could throw the deep pass well. He is less remembered for being fairly mobile in the pocket until rupturing his Achilles tendon in 1999. He ran for more than 1,600 yards in his career, including 280 in 1990, and averaged almost 4 yards per carry. Vinny was at his best in Cleveland, Baltimore, and New York under Belichick, Ted Marchibroda, and Bill Parcells and retired in the top 10 in passes, completions, yards, touchdowns, and interceptions. He was not a great quarterback, but the two-time Pro Bowler was often a very good one.

Rushing

Year	Att.	Yards	Avg.	TD
1974	3	12	4.0	1
1975	3	34	11.3	0
1976	17	97	5.7	1
1977	29	149	5.1	1
1978	37	177	4.8	1
1979	46	181	3.9	4
1980	29	175	6.0	3
1981	36	177	4.9	2
1982	31	150	4.8	0
1983	37	234	6.3	1
1984	62	314	5.1	1
1985	25	115	4.6	2
Total	355	1,815	5.1	17
PS:	19	95	5.0	0

Joe Theismann

QPR 9.5

Height: 6'0" **Weight:** 192 lbs. **Birthdate:** 9/9/1949
College: Notre Dame **Draft:** Miami 1971-4th
1971–73 CFL; 1974–85 Washington Redskins
Regular Season Record: 77–47, 23 comebacks
Postseason Record: 3–3, 2 comebacks
Relative Rating: 109%

Passing

Year	G	Comp./Att.	%	Yards	Y/Att.	TD	INT	Rating
1974	9	9/11	81.8	145	13.2	1	0	149.1
1975	14	10/22	45.5	96	4.4	1	3	33.7
1976	14	79/163	48.5	1,036	6.4	8	10	59.8
1977	14	84/182	46.2	1,097	6.0	7	9	57.9
1978	16	187/390	47.9	2,593	6.6	13	18	61.6
1979	16	233/395	59.0	2,797	7.1	20	13	83.9
1980	16	262/454	57.7	2,962	6.5	17	16	75.2
1981	16	293/496	59.1	3,568	7.2	19	20	77.3
1982	9	161/252	63.9	2,033	8.1	13	9	91.3
1983	16	276/459	60.1	3,714	8.1	29	11	97.0
1984	16	283/477	59.3	3,391	7.1	24	13	86.6
1985	11	167/301	55.5	1,774	5.9	8	16	59.6
Total	167	2,044/3,602	56.7	25,206	7.0	160	138	77.4
PS:	7	128/211	60.7	1,782	8.4	11	7	91.4

Joe Theismann was a skilled quarterback who relied on his legs as a scrambler. His career ended abruptly with a violent leg fracture on Monday Night Football.

Joe Theismann was as full of himself as any two wide receivers and always had an eye for the camera and the spotlight. Joe was hyperactive, cocky, abrasive, and mouthy. He was also a very good quarterback, just not a real popular one.

Theismann came to Notre Dame as a 150-pound freshman who pronounced his name "Theezman"; he left four years later at 170 pounds pronouncing his name "Theismann as in Heisman" although he was the runner-up to Jim Plunkett for that esteemed award. NFL scouts deemed him too small, and Miami drafted him in the fourth round in 1971 after quarterbacks Plunkett, Manning, Pastorini, Lynn Dickey, Leo Hart, Ken Anderson, and Karl Douglass were selected but before Scott Hunter, Joe Reed, and Bobby Scott. Theismann didn't like the Dolphins' lowball offer and signed with Toronto of the CFL instead. Joe was a two-time All-Star in Canada who led his team to the Grey Cup game in his first year and came back from a broken leg in his second year.

After three seasons, Theismann returned to the United States in 1974 when the Redskins traded a No. 1 pick for his rights. Joe was disliked and ostracized by Washington's veteran quarterbacks Sonny Jurgensen and Billy Kilmer and volunteered to return punts just to get on the field as a rookie. Jurgensen retired, but Kilmer persisted in keeping Theismann on the sidelines for four more years till Joe got his chance to start in 1978. He would miss just three starts in the next eight years until his career ended with a hideous leg fracture against the Giants on *Monday Night Football* in 1985.

Joe was small but tough and played through several injuries in his career. He was a scrambler with quick feet, a sharp mind, and a good arm. Hollywood Joe may not have been the most popular Redskin, but he was a fiery, flamboyant leader in whom the team believed. He led Washington to back-to-back Super Bowl appearances, winning the first over Miami and losing the second to his old college rival Jim Plunkett and the Raiders. That second year was his greatest season, as he threw 29 touchdowns and just 11 interceptions in being named All-Pro for the only time in his career. The next year, Joe threw for 24 touchdowns and just 13

interceptions but declined badly in 1985, throwing just eight touchdowns and 16 interceptions before the broken leg ended his career. Theismann immediately went into broadcasting and spent the next 22 years with ESPN before being dumped for Ron Jaworski in 2007.

Tyler Thigpen

Height: 6'1" **Weight:** 235 lbs. **Birthdate:** 4/14/1984
College: Coastal Carolina **Draft:** Minnesota 2007-7th
2007-08 Kansas City Chiefs
Regular Season Record: 1–10, no comebacks
Postseason Record: NA
Relative Rating: 92%

Passing

Year	G	Comp./Att.	%	Yards	Y/Att.	TD	INT	Rating
2007	1	2/6	33.3	41	6.8	0	1	18.7
2008	14	230/420	54.8	2,608	6.2	18	12	76.0
Total	15	232/426	54.5	2,649	6.2	18	13	74.7

Rushing

Year	Att.	Yards	Avg.	TD
2008	62	386	6.2	3

Tyler Thigpen impressed the Vikings as a late-round draft pick out of tiny Coastal Carolina in 2007, but they weren't the only ones. When Minnesota waived Tyler to move him to their practice squad, Kansas City claimed him. With the woeful Chiefs, Thigpen quickly moved up from third quarterback to starter when both Brodie Croyle and Damon Huard were lost for the season to injuries early in 2008. Tyler showed good touch on his passes and elusive movement with his feet, but his lack of experience, particularly against high-level competition, led to bad decisions at crucial times. He led all quarterbacks in yards rushing and rushing average and remains a promising player.

Bobby Thomason

QPR 6.0

Height: 6'1" **Weight:** 196 lbs. **Birthdate:** 3/26/1928
College: VMI **Draft:** Los Angeles Rams 1949-1st
1949-50 Los Angeles Rams; 1951 Green Bay Packers;
1952-57 Philadelphia Eagles
Regular Season Record: 19-22-1, 5 comebacks
Postseason Record: NA
Relative Rating: 108%

Passing

Year	G	Comp./Att.	%	Yards	Y/Att.	TD	INT	Rating
1949	6	6/12	50.0	50	4.2	0	1	26.4
1951	11	125/221	56.6	1,306	5.9	11	9	73.5
1952	12	95/212	44.8	1,334	6.3	8	9	60.5
1953	12	162/304	53.3	2,462	8.1	21	20	75.8
1954	10	83/170	48.8	1,242	7.3	10	13	61.0
1955	10	88/171	51.5	1,337	7.8	10	7	80.0
1956	12	82/164	50.0	1,119	6.8	4	21	40.7
1957	12	46/92	50.0	630	6.8	4	10	47.2
Total	85	687/1,346	51.0	9,480	7.0	68	90	62.9

Rushing

Year	Att.	Yards	Avg.	TD
1951	5	-5	-1.0	0
1952	17	88	5.2	0
1953	9	23	2.6	1
1954	10	45	4.5	0
1955	17	29	1.7	0
1956	21	48	2.3	2
1957	15	62	4.1	3
Total	94	290	3.1	6

The Los Angeles Rams drafted Bobby Thomason in the first round in 1949, but Bobby was beaten out as Bob Waterfield's backup by fourth-round pick Norm Van Brocklin. Thomason was the best third quarterback in football, so the Rams traded him to the Packers in 1951 for two draft picks that were conditional on the Packers keeping him. Sharing the quarterbacking with Tobin Rote, Bobby led the league in completion percentage and interception percentage, but Green Bay figured they could finish next-to-last without Thomason and returned him to Los Angeles rather than give up first- and second-round draft picks. The Rams immediately repackaged Thomason and Jack Zilly for Jack Myers and a No. 1 pick from Philadelphia, and Bobby was an Eagle.

In Philadelphia, Thomason shared the quarterbacking for the next five years with Adrian Burk and had good years and bad years. In one 1953 game against the Giants, Bobby threw for 437 yards, and that remained a team record for 36 years. Thomason went to the Pro Bowl three times, inexplicably including 1956 when he threw four touchdown passes to a league-leading 21 interceptions and a passer rating of 40. When the Eagles acquired Van Brocklin in 1958, Bobby retired at age 30 and went into broadcasting.

Jack Thompson

QPR 1.0

Height: 6'3" **Weight:** 217 lbs. **Birthdate:** 5/19/1956
College: Washington State **Draft:** Cincinnati 1979-1st
1979-82 Cincinnati Bengals; 1983-84 Tampa Bay Bucs
Regular Season Record: 4-17, 4 comebacks
Postseason Record: NA
Relative Rating: 85%

Passing

Year	G	Comp./Att.	%	Yards	Y/Att.	TD	INT	Rating
1979	9	39/87	44.8	481	5.5	1	5	42.4
1980	14	115/234	49.1	1,324	5.7	11	12	60.9
1981	8	21/49	42.9	267	5.4	1	2	50.3
1982	1	0/0	0.0	0	0.0	0	0	0.0
1983	14	249/423	58.9	2,906	6.9	18	21	73.3
1984	5	25/52	48.1	337	6.5	2	5	42.4
Total	51	449/845	53.1	5,315	6.3	33	45	63.4

Rushing

Year	Att.	Yards	Avg.	TD
1979	21	116	5.5	5
1980	18	84	4.7	1
1983	26	27	1.0	0
1984	5	35	7.0	0
Total	70	262	3.7	6

When Jack Thompson finished his college career at Washington State in 1978, the "Throwin' Samoan" had thrown for more yards than anyone to that point. The Bengals were afraid that Ken Anderson was slipping and drafted Jack with the third overall pick in 1979, passing on both Phil Simms and Joe Montana. Anderson revived his career, while Thompson started a mere five games in four years and completed just 47 percent of his passes. Jack had an average arm and slow release, and he could not read defenses. He had trouble avoiding the rush and was jittery in the pocket, leading to interceptions. For once, Cincinnati didn't totally lose out, though. They were able to unload Thompson to Tampa in 1983 for a No. 1 draft pick because the Bucs were frantic to replace Doug Williams, who had bolted to the USFL. In 16 starts over two seasons in Tampa, Thompson was 3–13 and threw 20 touchdowns to 26 interceptions before the Bucs brought in Steve DeBerg to replace him.

Tommy Thompson

QPR 9.5

Height: 6'1" **Weight:** 192 lbs. **Birthdate:** 8/15/1916
College: Tulsa **Draft:** Free Agent
1940 Pittsburgh Steelers; 1941–42, 1945–50 Philadelphia Eagles
Regular Season Record: 39–32–2 est., 5 comebacks
Postseason Record: 3–1, 1 comeback
Relative Rating: 134%

Passing

Year	G	Comp./Att.	%	Yards	Y/Att.	TD	INT	Rating
1940	11	9/28	32.1	145	5.2	1	3	22.8
1941	11	86/162	53.1	959	5.9	8	14	51.4
1942	11	95/203	46.8	1,410	6.9	8	16	50.3
1945	8	15/28	53.6	146	5.2	0	2	38.7
1946	10	57/103	55.3	745	7.2	6	9	61.3
1947	12	106/201	52.7	1,680	8.4	16	15	76.3
1948	12	141/246	57.3	1,965	8.0	25	11	98.4
1949	12	116/214	54.2	1,727	8.1	16	11	84.4
1950	12	107/239	44.8	1,608	6.7	11	22	44.4
Total	99	732/1,424	51.4	10,385	7.3	91	103	66.5
PS:	4	45/82	54.9	503	6.1	4	7	54.1

Rushing

Year	Att.	Yards	Avg.	TD
1940	40	39	1.0	0
1941	54	-2	0.0	0
1942	92	-32	-0.3	1
1945	8	-13	-1.6	0
1946	34	-116	-3.4	0
1947	23	52	2.3	2
1948	12	46	3.8	1
1949	15	17	1.1	2
1950	15	34	2.3	0
Total	293	25	0.1	6
PS:	22	64	2.9	0

As a boy, Tossin' Tommy Thompson, the Tulsa Typhoon was left legally blind when he was struck in one eye with a stone. However, his strong arm took him to the University of Tulsa where he passed the team to two straight Missouri Valley Conference titles. Tommy was an All-MVC selection in 1938 but left school in 1939 because Tulsa declared him ineligible for football for having gotten married. Thompson could not play in the NFL for another year either, because his class had not graduated, so he joined the minor-league St. Louis Gunners for the 1939 season. In 1940, the Steelers signed Tommy as a tailback in Pittsburgh's run-oriented single-wing. Luckily for Thompson, the Pittsburgh and Philadelphia franchises were swapped, and Greasy Neale was hired to coach the new Eagles in 1941.

Neale installed the T formation that Thompson was born to run. After two losing seasons of learning the quarterback position, the one-eyed Thompson joined the army in 1943 and won a Purple Heart at Normandy. He rejoined the Eagles in October 1945 and shared the quarterbacking with Roy Zimmerman in 1945 and 1946, with the Eagles finishing second in the division both years. Thompson not only had better touch on his passes than Zimmerman, he was a more fiery leader as well. Tommy was popular with both his teammates and his coach. Prior to the 1947 season, Neale traded Zimmerman to the Lions for two linemen.

In 1947, the Eagles faced a playoff with the Steelers for the Eastern crown. In that game, Thompson completed 11 of 18 passes for 255 yards. Neale pointed out afterward, "That Tommy Thompson played a great game. His signal calling was just about perfect." The next week the Eagles lost the championship to the Cardinals on an icy field despite Tommy's 297 yards passing. Thompson was unruffled in any situation and was an excellent bad-weather quarterback.

Thompson had his greatest season in 1948, throwing 25 touchdown passes to just 11 interceptions. He was just the third NFL quarterback to throw 25 touchdowns in a season—and that would be a 12-game season. Thompson had the highest passer rating in the NFL in 1948 and 1949, and Philadelphia won the NFL title both years. Decline set in for both Thompson and the Eagles in 1950, and the remarkable one-eyed marksman retired to go into coaching.

Y.A. Tittle

QPR 9.5

Height: 6'0" **Weight:** 192 lbs. **Birthdate:** 10/24/1926
College: LSU **Draft:** Detroit 1948-1st
1948–50 Baltimore Colts; 1951–60 San Francisco 49ers; 1961–64 New York Giants
Regular Season Record: 86–70–5, 24 comebacks
Postseason Record: 0–5, no comebacks
Relative Rating: 117%

Passing

Year	G	Comp./Att.	%	Yards	Y/Att.	TD	INT	Rating
1948	14	161/289	55.7	2,522	8.7	16	9	90.3
1949	11	148/289	51.2	2,209	7.6	14	18	66.8
1950	12	161/315	51.1	1,884	6.0	8	19	52.9
1951	12	63/114	55.3	808	7.1	8	9	68.2
1952	12	106/208	51.0	1,407	6.8	11	12	66.3
1953	11	149/259	57.5	2,121	8.2	20	16	84.1
1954	12	170/295	57.6	2,205	7.5	9	9	78.7
1955	12	147/287	51.2	2,185	7.6	17	28	56.6
1956	10	124/218	56.9	1,641	7.5	7	12	68.6
1957	12	176/279	63.1	2,157	7.7	13	15	80.0
1958	11	120/208	57.7	1,467	7.1	9	15	63.9
1959	11	102/199	51.3	1,331	6.7	10	15	58.0
1960	9	69/127	54.3	694	5.5	4	3	70.8
1961	13	163/285	57.2	2,272	8.0	17	12	85.3
1962	14	200/375	53.3	3,224	8.6	33	20	89.5
1963	13	221/367	60.2	3,145	8.6	36	14	104.8
1964	14	147/281	52.3	1,798	6.4	10	22	51.6
Total	203	2,427/4,395	55.2	33,070	7.5	242	248	74.3
PS:	5	70/157	44.6	874	5.6	4	14	33.8

Rushing

Year	Att.	Yards	Avg.	TD
1948	52	157	3.0	4
1949	29	89	3.1	2
1950	20	77	3.9	2
1951	13	18	1.4	1
1952	11	-11	-1.0	0
1953	14	41	2.9	6
1954	28	68	2.4	4
1955	23	114	5.0	0
1956	24	67	2.8	4
1957	40	220	5.5	6
1958	22	35	1.6	2
1959	11	24	2.2	0
1960	10	61	6.1	0
1961	25	85	3.4	3
1962	17	108	6.4	2
1963	18	99	5.5	2
1964	15	-7	-0.5	1
Total	372	1,245	3.3	39
PS:	5	-14	-2.8	0

If Y.A. Tittle hadn't been traded from the 49ers to the Giants in 1961, he would never have been elected to the Hall of Fame. In his first 13 seasons, Tittle was just 54–57–2 as a starter and had never been to a championship game. To that point, Y.A. had thrown 146 touchdowns and 180 interceptions and had led the league in touchdown passes once, completion percentage once, and interceptions twice. In his four years in New York, Tittle was 32–13–3, went to three straight title games, threw 96 touchdowns to just 68 interceptions, and led

TOP 10

Worst Postseason Quarterbacks

10. Richard Todd, 2–2 record, four touchdowns, and 12 interceptions
9. Pat Haden, 2–3 record, four touchdowns, and 12 interceptions
8. Steve Grogan, 0–3 record, three touchdowns, and seven interceptions
7. Steve McNair, 5–5 record, 5 touchdowns, and 11 interceptions
6. Dan Fouts, 3–4 record, 12 touchdowns, and 16 interceptions
5. Warren Moon, 3–7 record, 17 touchdowns, and 14 interceptions
4. John Hadl, 0–2 record, one touchdown, and four interceptions
3. Kordell Stewart, 1–3 record, two touchdowns, and eight interceptions
2. Craig Morton, 6–6 record, 0–2 in Super Bowls, nine touchdowns, and 16 interceptions
1. Y.A. Tittle, 0–5 record, 0–3 in title games, four touchdowns, and 14 interceptions

the league in touchdowns two times, completion percentage once, and passer rating once. As a Giant, he was just the third quarterback to throw for seven touchdowns in one game and was the first to throw for more than 30 touchdown passes in consecutive seasons; his 36 TDs in 1963 would not be exceeded until Dan Marino threw for 48 in 1984. Tittle always maintained, "The game is about putting the ball in the air."

Tittle began his career in the All-America Football Conference with the original Baltimore Colts and then spent a decade in San Francisco as part of the 49ers' Million Dollar Backfield with Joe Perry, Hugh McElhenny, and John Henry Johnson. Y.A. was a deceptive ball handler, a master of the screen pass, and a very precise passer with a three-quarters throwing motion similar to Sammy Baugh. He remained one of the better quarterbacks in the league while fending off challenges from Frankie Albert, Earl Morrall, and John Brodie throughout the 1950s. During that decade, Tittle had the most fourth-quarter game-winning drives in the league with 19. Tittle was actually a pretty good runner as well, particularly on bootlegs, and ran for 39 touchdowns. The *Los Angeles Times* even referred to Tittle as a "scrambler" in 1960, a year before Fran Tarkenton fully defined that term. In 1961, the 49ers shifted to the shotgun offense and felt they had no need for a 35-year-old quarterback. So they traded Tittle to New York for the forgettable lineman Lou Cordileone, whose reaction was, "They traded me for Tittle? Just me?"

Tittle came into a difficult situation in New York where he was replacing the 40-year-old legendary veteran Charlie Conerly, but ultimately Y.A.'s feisty, emotional leadership blended the whole team together into one unit. Tittle led the aging Giants to three straight NFL Championship Games from 1961 to 1963, and he won Player of the Year recognition each year. However, the Giants lost all three title games, and Y.A. did not play well in any of them. Time ran out on Tittle and the team in 1964, but the Giants retired his No. 14 for his unequalled passing excellence.

QPR 6.5

Richard Todd

Height: 6'2" **Weight:** 207 lbs. **Birthdate:** 11/19/1953
College: Alabama **Draft:** New York Jets 1976-1st
1976–83 New York Jets; 1984–85 New Orleans Saints
Regular Season Record: 48–59–1, 13 comebacks
Postseason Record: 2–2, 1 comeback
Relative Rating: 94%

Passing

Year	G	Comp./Att.	%	Yards	Y/Att.	TD	INT	Rating
1976	13	65/162	40.1	870	5.4	3	12	33.2
1977	12	133/265	50.2	1,863	7.0	11	17	60.3
1978	5	60/107	56.1	849	7.9	6	10	61.6
1979	15	171/334	51.2	2,660	8.0	16	22	66.5
1980	16	264/479	55.1	3,329	6.9	17	30	62.7
1981	16	279/497	56.1	3,231	6.5	25	13	81.8
1982	9	153/261	58.6	1,961	7.5	14	8	87.3
1983	16	308/518	59.5	3,478	6.7	18	26	70.3
1984	15	161/312	51.6	2,178	7.0	11	19	60.6
1985	2	16/32	50.0	191	6.0	3	4	60.3
Total	119	1,610/2,967	54.3	20,610	6.9	124	161	67.6
PS:	4	78/140	55.7	1,026	7.3	4	12	52.9

Rushing

Year	Att.	Yards	Avg.	TD
1976	28	107	3.8	1
1977	24	46	1.9	2
1978	14	18	1.3	0
1979	36	93	2.6	5
1980	49	330	6.7	5
1981	32	131	4.1	0
1982	13	-5	-0.4	1
1983	35	101	2.9	0
1984	28	111	4.0	0
Total	259	932	3.6	14
PS:	14	32	2.3	0

Eleven years after the Jets chose Joe Namath with their No. 1 draft pick in 1965, the team drafted Richard Todd with its top pick in 1976. Both were single, handsome, strong-armed quarterbacks coached by Bear Bryant at Alabama. In fact, Todd grew up idolizing Namath and then spent his rookie season splitting the team's starts in Joe's last season in New York. Neither quarterback was very good that year. Both played in the season finale against the Bengals, and each scored a 0.0 passer rating that day on a combined seven completions in 28 attempts for 43 yards and six interceptions.

There are other similarities. Both had lifetime losing records. Both took the Jets to the playoffs twice. Both forced passes into coverage and threw a lot of interceptions. Namath's ratio of 173 touchdown passes to 220 interceptions isn't a whole lot better than Todd's 124 touchdowns to 161 interceptions, and Todd's 67.6 passer rating is slightly better than Namath's 65.5. Yet, Namath is in the Hall of Fame while Todd is in most Jet fans' Hall of Shame. What is missing from this picture?

First of all, Todd had two healthy legs and Namath didn't. Second, although Namath would refuse to speak to reporters he felt were unfair, he never stuffed one in a locker like Todd did to Steve Serby of the *New York Post*. Third, Namath loved New York, his life, and Jet fans. Todd was moody and came off as downright miserable, even flipping off the fans at one point. Fourth, Namath was always the unquestioned leader of his team, while Todd had trouble competing with the likes of Matt Robinson and Pat Ryan. Fifth, Namath is remembered for winning Super Bowl III and legitimizing a league; Todd is remembered for throwing three interceptions to Miami's linebacker A.J. Duhe and single-handedly short-circuiting a Super Bowl run.

Furthermore, if you examine the best five-year period for each quarterback, the differences in their peak value are striking. In Namath's first five seasons before he was completely decimated by injuries, Broadway Joe threw 97 touchdowns and 104 interceptions, averaged 7.6 yards per pass and 15.1 yards per completion, and went 37–23–4 with a Super Bowl win from 1965 to 1969. In Todd's best stretch from 1979 to 1983, Wall Street Richard threw 90 touchdowns and 99 interceptions, averaged 7.0 yards per pass and 12.5 yards per catch and went 35–36–1 with no championships.

Finally, because the style of the game has changed so radically over time, Broadway Joe's passer rating of 65.5 was actually 3 percent better than the league average; Just Plain Richard's 67.6 was 6 percent below the league average.

Billy Joe Tolliver

QPR 3.5

Height: 6'1" **Weight:** 217 lbs. **Birthdate:** 2/7/1966
College: Texas Tech **Draft:** San Diego 1989-2nd
1989–90 San Diego Chargers; 1991–93, 1997 Atlanta Falcons; 1994 Houston Oilers; 1995–96 CFL; 1997 Kansas City Chiefs; 1998–99 New Orleans Saints
Regular Season Record: 15-32, 4 comebacks
Postseason Record: NA
Relative Rating: 88%

Passing

Year	G	Comp./Att.	%	Yards	Y/Att.	TD	INT	Rating
1989	5	89/185	48.1	1,097	5.9	5	8	57.9
1990	15	216/410	52.7	2,574	6.3	16	16	68.9
1991	7	40/82	48.8	531	6.5	4	2	75.8
1992	9	73/131	55.7	787	6.0	5	5	70.4
1993	7	39/76	51.3	464	6.1	3	5	56.0
1994	10	121/240	50.4	1,287	5.4	6	7	62.6
1997	9	64/116	55.2	677	5.8	5	1	83.2
1998	7	110/199	55.3	1,427	7.2	8	4	83.1
1999	10	139/268	51.9	1,916	7.1	7	16	58.9
Total	**79**	**891/1,707**	**52.2**	**10,760**	**6.3**	**59**	**64**	**67.8**

Rushing

Year	Att.	Yards	Avg.	TD
1989	7	0	0.0	0
1990	14	22	1.6	0
1991	9	6	0.7	0
1992	4	15	3.8	0
1993	7	48	6.9	0
1994	12	37	3.1	2
1997	9	7	0.8	0
1998	11	43	3.9	0
1999	26	142	5.5	3
Total	**99**	**320**	**3.2**	**0**

The hard-throwing Billy Joe Tolliver is the very definition of a journeyman quarterback, playing with seven teams in two leagues over a forgettable 12-year career. To make Tolliver even harder to remember, there have been two NFL quarterbacks named Billy Joe in NFL history, and not only did both play in the 1990s, but both also ended their careers with the New Orleans Saints in 1999. One would assume that coach Mike Ditka called them by their last names. Although Tolliver threw three times as many passes as Hobert in their careers, both completed 52.2 percent of their passes, both had passer ratings of 67, both threw more interceptions than touchdowns, and both won fewer than one-third of their starts. Hobert averaged 6.4 yards per pass, while Tolliver averaged 6.3. Tolliver was more dedicated to his craft and a better team guy, but neither was an effective quarterback in the NFL.

Mike Tomczak

QPR **6.5**

Height: 6'1"   **Weight:** 202 lbs.   **Birthdate:** 10/23/1962
College: Ohio State   **Draft:** Free agent
1985–90 Chicago Bears; 1991 Green Bay Packers;
1992 Cleveland Browns; 1993–99 Pittsburgh Steelers
Regular Season Record: 42–31, 10 comebacks
Postseason Record: 3–2, no comebacks
Relative Rating: 90%

Passing

Year	G	Comp./Att.	%	Yards	Y/Att.	TD	INT	Rating
1985	6	2/6	33.3	33	5.5	0	0	52.8
1986	13	74/151	49.0	1,105	7.3	2	10	50.2
1987	12	97/178	54.5	1,220	6.9	5	10	62.0
1988	14	86/170	50.6	1,310	7.7	7	6	75.4
1989	16	156/306	51.0	2,058	6.7	16	16	68.2
1990	16	39/104	37.5	521	5.0	3	5	43.8
1991	12	128/238	53.8	1,490	6.3	11	9	72.6
1992	12	120/211	56.9	1,693	8.0	7	7	80.1
1993	7	29/54	53.7	398	7.4	2	5	51.3
1994	6	54/93	58.1	804	8.6	4	0	100.8
1995	7	65/113	57.5	666	5.9	1	9	44.3
1996	16	222/401	55.4	2,767	6.9	15	17	71.8
1997	16	16/24	66.7	185	7.7	1	2	68.9
1998	16	21/30	70.0	204	6.8	2	2	83.2
1999	16	139/258	53.9	1,625	6.3	12	8	75.8
Total	185	1,248/2,337	53.4	16,079	6.9	88	106	68.9
PS:	6	74/143	51.7	884	6.2	2	9	49.4

Rushing

Year	Att.	Yards	Avg.	TD
1985	2	3	1.5	0
1986	23	117	5.1	3
1987	18	54	3.0	1
1988	13	40	3.1	1
1989	24	71	3.0	1
1990	12	41	3.4	2
1991	17	93	5.5	1
1992	24	39	1.6	0
1993	5	-4	-0.8	0
1994	4	22	5.5	0
1995	11	25	2.3	0
1996	22	-7	-0.3	0
1997	7	13	1.9	0
1999	16	19	1.2	0
Total	198	526	2.7	9
PS:	5	27	5.4	0

What's remarkable about Mike Tomczak is that he lasted 15 years in the NFL and even maintained a winning record as a starter despite being a full 10 percent worse than the league average in passer rating. Tomczak was a coach's son who led Ohio State, featuring Jim Lachey and Keith Byars, to two Big Ten titles but went undrafted by the NFL. The Bears signed him as a free agent and he battled with Jim McMahon, Doug Flutie, and Jim Harbaugh for playing time for six years in Chicago. The combination of Tomczak's frustrating playing style and Ditka's temper was a volatile mix that led to a rough ride for Tomczak. Tomczak spent a year in Green Bay and a year in Cleveland before landing in Pittsburgh for the last seven years of his very ordinary career as a mistake-prone game manager.

Charley Trippi

QPR **1.0**

Height: 6'0"   **Weight:** 186 lbs.   **Birthdate:** 12/14/1922
College: Georgia   **Draft:** Chicago Cardinals 1947-1st
1947–55 Chicago Cardinals
Regular Season Record: 5–11, 3 comebacks
Postseason Record: 0–0, no comebacks
Relative Rating: 86%

Passing

Year	G	Comp./Att.	%	Yards	Y/Att.	TD	INT	Rating
1947	11	1/2	50.0	49	24.5	0	1	56.2
1948	12	4/8	50.0	118	14.8	1	0	135.4
1949	12	0/2	0.0	0	0.0	0	0	39.6
1950	12	1/3	33.3	19	6.3	0	0	56.2
1951	12	88/191	46.1	1,191	6.2	8	13	52.1
1952	11	84/181	46.4	890	4.9	5	13	40.5
1953	12	20/34	58.8	195	5.7	2	1	82.4
1954	12	7/13	53.8	85	6.5	0	3	34.6
Total	99	205/434	47.2	2,547	5.9	16	31	48.4
PS:	2	0/0	0.0	0	0.0	0	0	0.0

Rushing

Year	Att.	Yards	Avg.	TD
1947	83	401	4.8	2
1948	128	690	5.4	6
1949	112	553	4.9	3
1950	99	426	4.3	3
1951	78	501	6.4	4
1952	72	350	4.9	4
1953	97	433	4.5	0
1954	18	152	8.4	1
1955	0	0	0.0	0
Total	687	3,506	5.1	23
PS:	11	84	7.6	1

Charley Trippi is in the Hall of Fame as a halfback and the leading member of the Cardinals' "Dream Backfield" of the late 1940s when the team won its only championship. Trippi signed with the Cardinals in 1947 after a bidding war with the Yankees of the All-America Football Conference. At Georgia, Charley was a triple-threat tailback who played in four College All-Star Games in 1943, 1944, 1945, and 1947 on the side of the All-Stars and once in 1948 for the champion Cardinals. He also played some minor league baseball.

After four years starring at halfback, Trippi switched to quarterback in 1951 despite never having played the position before. Regular starting quarterback Jim Hardy had retired, so Curly Lambeau in desperation imposed on the talented Trippi to step in. Charley later told Bob Barnett and Bob Carroll in *The Coffin Corner*, "It didn't make any difference to me as long as I helped the team. Of course, I liked running the ball the best. I really wasn't a good quarterback. I didn't have the background in the techniques it takes to be a good quarterback." Trippi was right; he was no

quarterback. Hardy returned midway through the season, and Trippi played both quarterback and halfback after that.

In 1952, Lambeau was fired, and Hardy was traded. New coach Joe Kuharich brought in journeyman Don Panciera to join Trippi and Frank Tripucka as the team's quarterbacks. Charley took most of the snaps during the season, including some from a shotgun spread formation that allowed Trippi to run or pass. Joe Stydahar replaced Kuharich in 1954 and brought in three new quarterbacks—Jim Root, Steve Romanik, and Ray Nagel. Charley returned to halfback full time for one year and then moved to defense for the last two years of his versatile career.

Frank Tripucka

Height: 6'2" **Weight:** 192 lbs. **Birthdate:** 12/8/1927
College: Notre Dame **Draft:** Philadelphia 1949-1st
1949 Detroit Lions; 1950–52 Chicago Cardinals; 1952 Dallas Texans; 1953–59, 1963 CFL; 1960–63 Denver Broncos
Regular Season Record: 19–34–1, 9 comebacks
Postseason Record: NA
Relative Rating: 91%

Passing

Year	G	Comp./Att.	%	Yards	Y/Att.	TD	INT	Rating
1949	6	62/145	42.8	833	5.7	9	14	42.8
1950	10	47/108	43.5	720	6.7	4	7	51.5
1951	3	17/29	58.6	244	8.4	2	1	94.6
1952	12	91/186	48.9	809	4.3	3	17	28.3
1960	14	248/478	51.9	3,038	6.4	24	34	58.9
1961	14	167/344	48.5	1,690	4.9	10	21	47.3
1962	14	240/440	54.5	2,917	6.6	17	25	64.4
1963	2	7/15	46.7	31	2.1	0	5	13.9
Total	75	879/1,745	50.4	10,282	7.1	69	124	52.2

Rushing

Year	Att.	Yards	Avg.	TD
1949	12	36	3.0	1
1950	4	35	8.8	1
1951	1	14	14.0	0
1952	10	25	2.5	3
1960	10	0	0.0	0
1961	4	-8	-2.0	0
1962	2	-1	-0.5	1
Total	43	101	2.3	6

Frank Tripucka, seen here as a rookie in Philadelphia, played professionally for 15 years in three leagues.

Frank Tripucka is the only quarterback drafted in the first round who was then waived by that team in his rookie year. The world champion Eagles drafted the Notre Dame star quarterback in 1949, but Tripucka never appeared in a game for Philadelphia before they dumped him off to Detroit in the middle of the 1949 season. A year later, Detroit dealt Frank to the Chicago Cardinals where he spent two and a half seasons before being sent to the homeless Dallas Texans in the middle of 1952.

The next year, Frank signed with Saskatchewan in Canada where he played under coach Frankie Filchock for the next several seasons. In 1957, Tripucka told *Sports Illustrated* that his only regret was that he didn't come to Canada earlier, because they were paying him $4,000 a year more than he got in the States. When the American Football League started up in 1960, the Denver Broncos hired Filchock to be their first head coach, and Frankie hired the 33-year-old Tripucka as an assistant coach. When the two Franks saw the caliber of Bronco quarterbacks Tom Dublinski and George Herring, though, Tripucka slipped back into uniform. Denver was a very loosely run organization, and Tripucka used to draw up plays in the dirt as if he were playing on the sandlot. He was not much of a runner and relied solely on short

and medium-range passes. Frank threw the first touchdown pass in AFL history when he connected on a swing pass to halfback Al Carmichael, who ran 59 yards for the score in the first game against Boston. That year, Frank also became the first AFL or NFL quarterback to pass for more than 3,000, a feat he had already accomplished in Canada.

Frank threw 24 touchdown passes that first year but also led the league with 34 interceptions, and that was his biggest flaw as a quarterback. In four NFL seasons, Tripucka threw 18 touchdowns and 39 interceptions; in four AFL seasons, he threw 51 touchdowns and 85 interceptions; in seven seasons in Canada, he threw 82 touchdowns and 136 interceptions. Thus for his 15-year professional career, Frank threw 151 touchdowns and a whopping 260 interceptions. With these numbers and his 13–25–1 record as a Bronco starter, the shocking thing is that Denver retired Frank's No. 18 in the 1960s. One of Frank's sons, Kelly, played basketball for Notre Dame and in the NBA.

QPR

Bill Troup

Height: 6'5" **Weight:** 220 lbs. **Birthdate:** 4/2/1951
College: South Carolina **Draft:** Free Agent
1974, 1976–78 Baltimore Colts; 1980 Green Bay Packers
Regular Season Record: 3–8, no comebacks
Postseason Record: NA
Relative Rating: 69%

Passing

Year	G	Comp./Att.	%	Yards	Y/Att.	TD	INT	Rating
1974	1	0/0	0.0	0	0.0	0	0	0.0
1976	14	8/18	44.4	117	6.5	0	1	43.1
1977	14	0/2	0.0	0	0.0	0	1	0.0
1978	12	154/296	52.0	1,882	6.4	10	21	53.6
1980	2	4/12	33.3	48	4.0	0	3	6.9
Total	**43**	**166/328**	**50.6**	**2,047**	**6.2**	**10**	**26**	**47.4**

Rushing

Year	Att.	Yards	Avg.	TD
1976	5	-1	-0.2	1
1977	7	-8	-1.1	0
1978	18	25	1.4	1
Total	**30**	**16**	**0.5**	**2**

Bill Troup was the typical tall, geeky, immobile, incompetent pocket passer some uneasy teams employ as backups while praying that the starter stays upright. In 1978, the Colts lost the bet they'd been placing since 1974 and were left with Troup as the starting quarterback after Bert Jones separated his shoulder. With his long moustache, Troup resembled actor Donald Sutherland, and he entertained the fans on the field with sacks and interceptions in his moment in the spotlight. He later played in Green Bay.

Jack Trudeau

Height: 6'3" **Weight:** 227 lbs. **Birthdate:** 9/9/1962
College: Illinois **Draft:** Indianapolis 1986-1st
1986–93 Indianapolis Colts; 1994 New York Jets; 1995 Carolina Panthers
Regular Season Record: 19–30, 7 comebacks
Postseason Record: 0–1, no comebacks
Relative Rating: 83%

Passing

Year	G	Comp./Att.	%	Yards	Y/Att.	TD	INT	Rating
1986	12	204/417	48.9	2,225	5.3	8	18	53.5
1987	10	128/229	55.9	1,587	6.9	6	6	75.4
1988	2	14/34	41.2	158	4.6	0	3	19.0
1989	13	190/362	52.5	2,317	6.4	15	13	71.3
1990	6	84/144	58.3	1,078	7.5	6	6	78.4
1991	2	2/7	28.6	19	2.7	0	1	0.0
1992	11	105/181	58.0	1,271	7.0	4	8	68.6
1993	5	85/162	52.5	992	6.1	2	7	57.4
1994	5	50/91	54.9	496	5.5	1	4	55.9
1995	1	11/17	64.7	100	5.9	0	3	40.9
Total	67	873/1,644	53.1	10,243	6.2	43	69	63.3

PS:	1	21/33	63.6	251	7.6	2	1	94.4

Rushing

Year	Att.	Yards	Avg.	TD
1986	13	21	1.6	1
1987	15	7	0.5	0
1989	35	91	2.6	2
1990	10	28	2.8	0
1992	13	6	0.5	0
1993	5	3	0.6	0
1994	6	30	5.0	0
Total	97	186	1.9	3

PS:	2	4	2.0	0

Jack Trudeau led Illinois to the 1984 Rose Bowl as a sophomore where they lost to UCLA 45–9. Two years later the Colts drafted Jack in the second round. Trudeau was pushed into the starting lineup in Week 3 and was overmatched. He lost all 11 starts that year. Jack improved in his second year and shared the job with Gary Hogeboom. Indianapolis slipped into the playoffs that year but lost to the Browns even though Trudeau played respectably as the Colts' starter. For most of his 10-year NFL career, Jack was a backup, and that fit his skills better. He had a weak, inaccurate arm; floated nothing but dinky passes; and threw interceptions freely.

Don Trull

Height: 6'1" **Weight:** 195 lbs. **Birthdate:** 10/20/1941
College: Baylor **Draft:** Houston 1963-14th; Baltimore Colts 1963-9th
1964–69 Houston Oilers; 1967 Boston Patriots
Regular Season Record: 4–12–2, 1 comeback
Postseason Record: NA
Relative Rating: 99%

Passing

Year	G	Comp./Att.	%	Yards	Y/Att.	TD	INT	Rating
1964	14	36/86	41.9	439	5.1	1	2	52.4
1965	14	38/107	35.5	528	4.9	5	5	48.3
1966	14	84/172	48.8	1,200	7.0	10	5	79.1
1967	10	31/92	33.7	480	5.2	1	7	23.8
1968	11	53/105	50.5	864	8.2	10	3	98.3
1969	14	34/75	45.3	469	6.3	3	6	45.9
Total	77	276/637	43.3	3,980	6.2	30	28	61.6

Rushing

Year	Att.	Yards	Avg.	TD
1964	12	42	3.5	0
1965	29	145	5.0	2
1966	38	139	3.7	7
1967	22	30	1.4	3
1968	14	47	3.4	0
1969	8	25	3.1	2
Total	123	428	3.5	14

At Baylor, Don Trull threw what has been called the most famous interception in Southwest Conference history in 1963 when his pass to Larry Elkins in the Texas end zone was picked off by Duke Carlisle to preserve a 7–0 Longhorn win. Trull and Elkins were an All-American combination in college and both played for the Oilers, but neither achieved any success as a pro. Elkins had injury troubles; Trull just didn't have the arm.

Don signed with Houston rather than the Colts, who also drafted him, because Oiler starter George Blanda was older than Johnny Unitas on the Colts. Blanda, of course, was still playing after both Unitas and Trull retired. Don played for three head coaches in his first two years in Houston, moving up from third string to backup, but in three and a half years, he started just eight games. In 1967, the short-passing scrambler was traded to Boston for a ninth-round pick but failed to impress the Patriots and returned to Houston in 1968. In his second tour, Don backed up Pete Beathard for two seasons before heading for Canada for his last two seasons as a player. Trull did some college coaching after retiring.

Tom Tupa

 QPR 0.5

Height: 6'4" **Weight:** 225 lbs. **Birthdate:** 2/6/1966
College: Ohio State **Draft:** Arizona 1988-3rd
1988–91 Arizona Cardinals; 1992 Indianapolis Colts; 1994–95 Cleveland Browns; 1996–98 New England Patriots; 1999–01 New York Jets; 2002–03 Tampa Bay Bucs; 2004 Washington Redskins
Regular Season Record: 4–9, 1 comeback
Postseason Record: NA
Relative Rating: 80%

Passing

Year	G	Comp./Att.	%	Yards	Y/Att.	TD	INT	Rating
1988	2	4/6	66.7	49	8.2	0	0	91.7
1989	14	65/134	48.5	973	7.3	3	9	52.2
1991	11	165/315	52.4	2,053	6.5	6	13	62.0
1992	3	17/33	51.5	156	4.7	1	2	49.6
1995	16	1/1	100.0	25	25.0	0	0	118.7
1996	16	0/2	0.0	0	0.0	0	0	39.6
1999	16	6/11	54.5	165	15.0	2	0	139.2
2001	15	1/1	100.0	9	9.0	0	0	104.2
2002	16	0/1	0.0	0	0.0	0	1	0.0
Total	220	259/504	51.4	3,430	6.8	12	25	60.5

Rushing

Year	Att.	Yards	Avg.	TD
1989	15	75	5.0	0
1990	1	0	0.0	0
1991	28	97	3.5	1
1992	3	9	3.0	0
1995	1	9	9.0	0
1998	2	-2	-1.0	0
1999	2	8	4.0	0
2002	1	-9	-9.0	0
Total	53	187	3.5	1

Tom Tupa was a punter for his first three years at Ohio State, where his roommate was linebacker Chris Spielman. As a senior, Tupa was elevated to starting quarterback in Earle Bruce's final disappointing year as coach. The Cardinals drafted the punting quarterback in the third round and used him almost exclusively as a backup quarterback for four years. Tom got all 13 of his career starts in Arizona. With it then clearly established that the weak-armed Tupa had no business under center, he moved on to Indianapolis as a strong-legged punter.

In 1993, Tupa fell into the Belichick/Parcells orbit when Belichick signed him in Cleveland as a punter. Tupa did not actually play for the Browns in 1993, but from 1994 through 2001, Tom was punting for one of those coaches (or hand-picked replacement Al Groh) in Cleveland, New England, and New York. Tupa even got to play a little emergency quarterback for the Jets when Vinny Testaverde was hurt in 1999. Tom finished his career punting for the Bucs and Redskins.

TOP 10
Numbers Retired for Just One Quarterback

10. 4, Brett Favre (retirement forthcoming)
9. 18, Frank Tripucka
8. 8, Archie Manning
7. 11, Phil Simms
6. 1, Warren Moon
5. 15, Bart Starr
4. 13, Dan Marino
3. 22, Bobby Layne
2. 33, Sammy Baugh
1. 19, Johnny Unitas

Johnny Unitas

Height: 6'1" **Weight:** 194 lbs. **Birthdate:** 5/7/1933
College: Louisville **Draft:** Pittsburgh 1955-9th
1956–72 Baltimore Colts; 1973 San Diego Chargers
Regular Season Record: 118–64–4, 37 comebacks
Postseason Record: 6–2
Relative Rating: 117%

Passing

Year	G	Comp./Att.	%	Yards	Y/Att.	TD	INT	Rating
1956	12	110/198	55.6	1,498	7.6	9	10	74.0
1957	12	172/301	57.1	2,550	8.5	24	17	88.0
1958	10	136/263	51.7	2,007	7.6	19	7	90.0
1959	12	193/367	52.6	2,899	7.9	32	14	92.0
1960	12	190/378	50.3	3,099	8.2	25	24	73.7
1961	14	229/420	54.5	2,990	7.1	16	24	66.1
1962	14	222/389	57.1	2,967	7.6	23	23	76.5
1963	14	237/410	57.8	3,481	8.5	20	12	89.7
1964	14	158/305	51.8	2,824	9.3	19	6	96.4
1965	11	164/282	58.2	2,530	9.0	23	12	97.4
1966	14	195/348	56.0	2,748	7.9	22	24	74.0
1967	14	255/436	58.5	3,428	7.9	20	16	83.6
1968	5	11/32	34.4	139	4.3	2	4	30.1
1969	13	178/327	54.4	2,342	7.2	12	20	64.0
1970	14	166/321	51.7	2,213	6.9	14	18	65.1
1971	13	92/176	52.3	942	5.4	3	9	52.3
1972	8	88/157	56.1	1,111	7.1	4	6	70.8
1973	5	34/76	44.7	471	6.2	3	7	40.0
Total	211	2,830/5,186	54.6	40,239	7.8	290	253	78.2
PS:	9	120/226	53.1	1,676	7.4	7	10	69.1

Rushing

Year	Att.	Yards	Avg.	TD
1956	28	155	5.5	1
1957	42	171	4.1	1
1958	33	139	4.2	3
1959	29	145	5.0	2
1960	36	195	5.4	0
1961	54	190	3.5	2
1962	50	137	2.7	0
1963	47	224	4.8	0
1964	37	162	4.4	2
1965	17	68	4.0	1
1966	20	44	2.2	1
1967	22	89	4.0	0
1968	3	-1	-0.3	0
1969	11	23	2.1	0
1970	9	16	1.8	0
1971	9	5	0.6	0
1972	3	15	5.0	0
Total	450	1,777	3.9	13
PS:	19	98	5.2	1

Johnny Unitas established the image of the quarterback gunslinger more than any other signal-caller. Although great quarterbacks who came before, such as Luckman, Baugh, Graham, and Layne, certainly captured the public's imagination, it was Unitas who really defined the quarterback as the most important position in sports. From his crew cut to his high-top cleats, Unitas was fearless and deadly—a laconic Gary Cooper in a gridiron *High Noon* each week. The expressionless Johnny U looked like a man simply doing his job as he'd turn and walk slump-shouldered off the field after the most thrilling clutch touchdown pass. Even after Alan Ameche scored the winning touchdown in overtime in the 1958 championship game, Unitas just turned and left the field.

His backstory was right out of Hollywood. Cut by the hometown Pittsburgh Steelers so they

> **Johnny Unitas' Signature Play**: On November 13, 1960, the Bears led the Colts 20–17 in the final minute. On third down, Unitas was whipsawed by linebacker Bill George and defensive end Doug Atkins and gushed blood from a huge gash in his face. To stop the bleeding, Unitas reached down, grabbed a handful of mud and covered the wound. On fourth down from the Bears' 39, Unitas hit a streaking Lenny Moore for the winning score with 42 seconds to play.

Johnny Unitas in the Clutch: December 28, 1958. The very first sudden-death NFL championship. Unitas leads the Colts 73 yards in the last 1:53 to tie the game and then drives Baltimore 80 yards in 13 plays for the winning touchdown in overtime.

The perfect passing form of Johnny Unitas on display against the Cardinals.

could keep the more versatile Vic Eaton, Unitas had to labor for a year with the low-level semipro Bloomfield Rams before receiving an auspicious phone call from the Colts, who were looking for a backup quarterback in 1956. When Colts starter George Shaw broke his kneecap in the fourth game, he lost his job for good because Unitas took over the position with authority based on his total command on the field. Two years after that, Unitas led Baltimore to the championship in the

Johnny U was the face of the NFL when pro football became America's Game in the 1960s.

first sudden-death game in league history and helped hook the burgeoning American television audience on our most compelling sport. After another decade and a half of excellence behind center, Johnny U retired, having thrown and completed the most passes for the most yards and touchdowns in NFL history. He won more starts (119), led more fourth-quarter game-winning drives (39), and threw for 300 yards more times (26) than any quarterback who came before him and almost everyone who came after him.

What if the Steelers had held on to Unitas and cut Eaton instead? History would likely have been very different. The Steelers were a tough but lousy team and were unimaginatively coached by Walt Kiesling. Buddy Parker replaced Kiesling in 1957 and traded for Bobby Layne a year later because he preferred veterans. Unitas' career may have foundered had he not landed with the superior team that Weeb Ewbank was building in Baltimore. It was a perfect fit for the man born to be quarterback and a fortunate bit of fate for the NFL.

Unitas was a great, unpredictable, gambling play caller, which is a lost art among contemporary quarterbacks. He had flawless passing mechanics with a fast setup and quick release and could make every throw, long or short. He was so tough that he ignored punishment and stood his ground in the face of the fiercest pass rush without it affecting his throws. At one point, he held the NFL record for consecutive starts at quarterback with 92. Other quarterbacks have passed most of his records, and a very few quarterbacks arguably have been slightly better, but no one has personified the position like Johnny Unitas.

Johnny Unitas' Five Highest Honors

5. Selected to 10 Pro Bowls.
4. 11-time All-Pro and five-time consensus All-Pro.
3. Two-time NFL Championship Game MVP.
2. 1959, 1964, and 1967 Player of the Year.
1. Elected to the Pro Football Hall of Fame in 1979.

The Five Quarterbacks Most Similar to Johnny Unitas

5. Gary Cuozzo
4. Dan Marino
3. Joe Namath
2. Dan Fouts
1. Kurt Warner

Johnny Unitas' Five Top Touchdown Targets

5. Jim Mutscheller, 31 TDs
4. John Mackey, 32 TDs
3. Jimmy Orr, 41 TDs
2. Lenny Moore, 43 TDs
1. Raymond Berry, 63 TDs

Johnny Unitas' Five Toughest Rivals

5. Unitas was 11–2 against the Redskins.
4. Unitas was 15–8–1 against the Rams.
3. Unitas was 12–9–1 against the Lions.
2. Unitas was 13–9 against the Bears.
1. Unitas was 13–10 against the Packers.

Five Random Johnny Unitas Statistics

5. Unitas played for four head coaches.
4. Unitas' Colts outscored the league average by 8 percent.
3. Unitas threw for four touchdowns 17 times.
2. Unitas threw for over 300 yards 26 times and more than 400 on September 17, 1967, against the Falcons.
1. Unitas led the league in completion percentage once, yards four times, touchdown passes four times, yards per attempt three times, passer rating three times, and interceptions twice.

Sam Vacanti

QPR 1.5

Height: 5'11"   **Weight:** 203 lbs.   **Birthdate:** 3/20/1922
College: Nebraska   **Draft:** New York Giants 1945-21st
1947–48 Chicago Rockets (AAFC); 1948–49 Baltimore Colts (AAFC)
Regular Season Record: 1–10 est., 1 comeback
Postseason Record: NA
Relative Rating: 70%

Passing

Year	G	Comp./Att.	%	Yards	Y/Att.	TD	INT	Rating
1947	13	96/225	42.7	1,571	7.0	16	16	60.8
1948	14	47/116	40.5	633	5.5	2	15	24.7
1949	12	11/27	40.7	134	5.0	0	1	41.3
Total	39	154/368	41.8	2,338	6.4	18	32	43.5

Rushing

Year	Att.	Yards	Avg.	TD
1947	11	-9	-0.8	1
1948	7	7	1.0	2
1949	7	10	1.4	0
Total	25	8	0.3	3

Short, pudgy Sam Vacanti played football for three major universities during the war years: Iowa in 1942, Purdue in 1943, and Nebraska in 1946. He is even in the Nebraska Hall of Fame despite the Cornhuskers having finished just 3–6 in his one year in Lincoln. Vacanti signed with the lowly Chicago Rockets of the All-America Football Conference in 1947 and was the team's primary quarterback after Angelo Bertelli was hurt. Sam was not a very good passer, and the Rockets recorded back-to-back 1–13 seasons in his tenure. Near the end of 1948, though, the Colts acquired Vacanti as Y.A. Tittle's backup, and Baltimore finished out the year 7–7. Sam got a good taste of the familiar in 1949 when the Colts reverted to last place and won just one of 12 games. In three years as a professional, Vacanti had played for three one-win teams. In 1950, he went back in the marines and starred in service ball over the next few years.

TOP 10
Quarterback Controversies

10. Super Bowl champion Trent Dilfer released by Ravens coach Brian Billick to make way for Elvis Grbac in 2001
9. John Hadl, James Harris, and Ron Jaworski for the Rams in 1973–76
8. Roman Gabriel and Bill Munson for the Rams in 1964–67
7. Sonny Jurgenson and Billy Kilmer for the Redskins in 1971–74
6. Craig Morton and Roger Staubach for the Cowboys in 1969–74
5. Browns' fan favorite Bernie Kosar being cut by Bill Belichick mid-season for Vinny Testaverde
4. Doug Flutie and Rob Johnson for the Bills in 1998–2000
3. Whether the injured Drew Bledsoe would get his job back from Tom Brady for the Patriots in 2001 after he was healthy
2. Joe Montana and Steve Young for the 49ers in 1988–91
1. Norm Van Brocklin and Bob Waterfield for the Rams in 1949–52

TOP 10
NFL Quarterbacks Who Played Semipro Football

10. King Corcoran—Patriots and Pottstown Firebirds
9. Tom Kennedy—Giants and Brooklyn Dodgers
8. Karl Sweetan—Lions and Pontiac Arrows
7. Sam Wyche—Bengals and Wheeling Ironmen
6. John Walton—Eagles and Columbus Barons
5. Butch Songin—Patriots and Erie Vets
4. Tom Flores—Raiders and Bakersfield Spoilers
3. Tommy Thompson—Eagles and St. Louis Gunners
2. Ken Stabler—Raiders and Spokane Shockers
1. Johnny Unitas—Colts and Bloomfield Rams

TOP 10
Devastating Quarterback Injuries

10. Joe Namath suffered a series of knee injuries during his senior year at Alabama that altered his pro football future.
9. The Bears' Ed Meadows drilled Bobby Layne after a handoff and knocked Layne out of the 1956 season finale with a concussion. Without Layne, the Lions lost the game and the Bears won the conference title.
8. Packer defensive end Charles Martin grabbed Bear quarterback Jim McMahon and bodyslammed him to the turf after an interception in a 1986 game. McMahon suffered a season-ending shoulder injury, and Chicago made an early exit from the playoffs.
7. Steve Young was sacked by a blitzing Aeneas Williams in 1999 and suffered a severe concussion that ended his career.
6. In the first quarter of the first game of the 2008 season, the Chiefs' safety Bernard Pollard rolled into Tom Brady's knee and ended his season. The hit had playoff implications throughout the league.
5. Bert Jones missed 25 of 32 games in 1978 and 1979 due to repeated shoulder injuries. A Colt team that won three straight divisional titles in 1975–77 would not have another winning season until 1987.
4. Packer Lynn Dickey broke his leg so badly in the ninth game in 1977 against the Rams that he did not return to action until the 12th game in 1979.
3. Joe Montana was sacked by Leonard Marshall of the Giants in the 1990 playoffs, injured his elbow, and did not return until season finale of the 1992 season. He was then traded to Kansas City in the off-season.
2. Greg Cook was tackled hard in his third NFL game against the Chiefs in 1969 and injured his shoulder. The torn rotator cuff was misdiagnosed, so Cook aggravated the injury all year and effectively destroyed his promising career.
1. Lawrence Taylor and Harry Carson sandwiched Joe Theismann on a *Monday Night Football* game in 1985, and Joe's leg gruesomely was snapped in the pileup on national TV. Theismann's career ended that night.

TOP 10
African American Quarterback Firsts

10. 1947—The Los Angeles Dons of the AAFC give Morgan State's Oscar Givens a tryout. Givens is cut but does play in the Pacific Coast Football League.
9. 1951—Bernie Custis becomes the first African American professional quarterback with the Hamilton Tiger-Cats in Canada.
8. 1953—Willie Thrower becomes the first African American NFL quarterback with the Bears.
7. 1955—The Green Bay Packers draft Charlie Brackins from Prairie View, the first quarterback drafted from an African American college.
6. 1960—Pete Hall becomes the first African American quarterback in the College All-Star Game and the North-South Game.
5. 1966—Hank Washington becomes the first African American quarterback on the South team in the North-South Game and the first in the Senior Bowl as well. Dave Lewis becomes the first African American quarterback in the East-West Game.
4. 1968—Eldridge Dickey becomes the first African American quarterback drafted in the first round by the Oakland Raiders.
3. 1968—Marlin Briscoe becomes the first African American quarterback to start an NFL game for Denver and leads the league with an average of 17.5 yards per completion.
2. 1974—The Rams' James Harris becomes the first regular stating quarterback to lead his team to the playoffs and to play in the Pro Bowl.
1. 1988—The Redskins' Doug Williams is the first African American quarterback both to play in and win the Super Bowl.

Norm Van Brocklin

QPR **10.0**

Height: 6'1" **Weight:** 190 lbs. **Birthdate:** 3/15/1926
College: Oregon **Draft:** Pittsburgh 1949-4th
1949–57 Los Angeles Rams; 1958–60 Philadelphia Eagles
Regular Season Record: 75–44–4, 17 comebacks
Postseason Record: 2–3, 2 comebacks
Relative Rating: 127%

Norm Van Brocklin's Signature Play: In the 1951 NFL championship, Norm Van Brocklin was in Coach Joe Stydahar's doghouse, but was sent into a tie game with eight minutes to play. The bomb-throwing Dutchman quickly unloaded a 73-yard shot to Tom Fears for the title-winning touchdown.

Passing

Year	G	Comp./Att.	%	Yards	Y/Att.	TD	INT	Rating
1949	8	32/58	55.2	601	10.4	6	2	111.4
1950	12	127/233	54.5	2,061	8.8	18	14	85.1
1951	12	100/194	51.5	1,725	8.9	13	11	80.8
1952	12	113/205	55.1	1,736	8.5	14	17	71.5
1953	12	156/286	54.5	2,393	8.4	19	14	84.1
1954	12	139/260	53.5	2,637	10.1	13	21	71.9
1955	12	144/272	52.9	1,890	6.9	8	15	62.0
1956	12	68/124	54.8	966	7.8	7	12	59.5
1957	12	132/265	49.8	2,105	7.9	20	21	68.8
1958	12	198/374	52.9	2,409	6.4	15	20	64.1
1959	12	191/340	56.2	2,617	7.7	16	14	79.5
1960	12	153/284	53.9	2,471	8.7	24	17	86.5
Total	140	1,553/2,895	53.6	23,611	8.2	173	178	75.1
PS:	7	46/95	48.4	736	7.7	4	8	53.7

Rushing

Year	Att.	Yards	Avg.	TD
1949	4	-1	-0.3	0
1950	15	22	1.5	1
1951	7	2	0.3	2
1952	7	-10	-1.4	0
1953	8	11	1.4	0
1954	6	-10	-1.7	0
1955	11	24	2.2	0
1956	4	1	0.3	1
1957	10	-4	-0.4	4
1958	8	5	0.6	1
1959	11	13	1.2	2
1960	11	-13	-1.2	0
Total	102	40	0.4	11
PS:	5	-10	-2.0	0

With two Hall of Fame quarterbacks, Norm Van Brocklin and Bob Waterfield, the 1950s Los Angeles Rams were the original Greatest Show on Turf, real turf that is. From 1950 to 1952, the Rams averaged 33.5 points per game and led the NFL in scoring each year. The two star quarterbacks alternated quarters and competed in trying to outdo each other. In a game against Detroit in 1950, Norm put up 41 points in the third quarter alone. On opening day in 1951 with Waterfield sidelined with an injury, Van Brocklin played the whole game and accumulated a record 554 yards passing against the New York Yanks. The Dutchman was no backup.

The Rams were able to grab him in the fourth round of the 1949 NFL draft because they were the only team that realized Norm had completed his class work early at Oregon. It was clear from the start that Van Brocklin was as pure a passer as the game had ever seen. His arm was strong and accurate, and he had the quickest release in football. Norm could throw with touch or fire bullet passes, and his timing on both long and short passes was second to none. Van Brocklin was especially deadly on the long pass and led the NFL four times in yards per pass. In fact, Norm won the 1951 title game over the Browns with a fourth-quarter 73-yard touchdown bomb to Tom Fears. Still, he had his critics. George Halas scoffed, "All he has is an arm. He runs like a girl with her girdle slipping. Van Brocklin can throw. Period. In the full sense

Norm Van Brocklin lets one fly in the 1961 Pro Bowl (hence the odd uniforms). Van Brocklin had the best passing arm of his time.

Norm Van Brocklin in the Clutch:
Van Brocklin led fourth-quarter game-winning drives in five of the Eagles' 10 regular-season victories in the 1960 season. Against the Browns on October 24, Philadelphia trailed at one point 22–7 and in the final minute still trailed 29–28 with the ball on their own 10. Van Brocklin led a furious final drive to the Cleveland 31 where Bobby Walston kicked the winning field goal with 10 seconds to play.

Norm Van Brocklin has held the NFL record for passing yards in a game for nearly 60 years when he threw 554 against the Yanks in 1951.

of the word, he is not a professional player." Furthermore, one of Norm's own coaches questioned the efficacy of his fiery nature. Hampton Pool said of his quarterback, "Soon he'll break every existing record—if some lineman doesn't break his neck first."

The Waterfield/Van Brocklin Show broke up when Bob retired in 1953, and Norm fended off youngster Billy Wade for the next few years before the Rams returned to the title game in 1955. In that game, though, Cleveland intercepted six of the Dutchman's passes and pummeled Los Angeles. The Rams' coach by this time was Sid Gillman, who did not get along with Van Brocklin. After three years of being jerked around by Gillman, Norm demanded a trade and was sent to Philadelphia. Driven by Van Brocklin, the lowly Eagles advanced from two to seven to 10 wins in three years and won the championship in 1960 on the back of Norm's six fourth-quarter comebacks that year. Van Brocklin retired after the game and expected to be named the Eagles' next coach. However, when Philadelphia hired Nick Skorich instead, Van Brocklin became the first coach of the expansion Minnesota Vikings. Van Brocklin went on to coach seven years in Minnesota and another seven in Atlanta without much success. Both situations ended badly for the mouthy Dutchman, and he was out of football after 1974.

Norm Van Brocklin's Five Highest Honors

5. Member of the College Football Hall of Fame.
4. Selected to nine Pro Bowls.
3. Eight-time All-Pro and consensus All-Pro once.
2. 1960 Player of the Year.
1. Elected to the Pro Football Hall of Fame in 1971.

The Five Quarterbacks Most Similar to Norm Van Brocklin

5. Bobby Layne
4. Kurt Warner
3. Sonny Jurgensen
2. Dan Fouts
1. Dan Marino

Norm Van Brocklin's Five Top Touchdown Targets

5. Bobby Walston, 9 TDs
4. Tom Fears, 20 TDs
3. Bob Boyd, 21 TDs
2. Tommy McDonald, 29 TDs
1. Elroy Hirsch, 32 TDs

Norm Van Brocklin's Five Toughest Rivals

5. Van Brocklin was 6–2 against the Giants.
4. Van Brocklin was 1–8 against the Browns in the regular season and 1–1 in the playoffs.
3. Van Brocklin was 9–6–1 against the 49ers.
2. Van Brocklin was 5–8 against the Bears in the regular season and 1–0 in the playoffs.
1. Van Brocklin was 9–8 against the Lions in the regular season and 0–1 in the playoffs.

Five Random Norm Van Brocklin Statistics

5. Van Brocklin played for five head coaches.
4. Van Brocklin's teams outscored the league average by 25 percent.
3. Van Brocklin threw for five touchdowns against the Lions on October 29, 1950, and the Yankees on September 28, 1951.
2. Van Brocklin threw for more than 300 yards six times and more than 500 once (554 yards against the Yankees on September 28, 1951).
1. Van Brocklin led the league in completion percentage once, yards once, yards per attempt four times, and passer rating twice.

Alex Van Pelt

QPR 1.5

Height: 6'1" **Weight:** 220 lbs. **Birthdate:** 5/1/1970
College: Pittsburgh **Draft:** Buffalo 1993-8th
1995–2003 Buffalo Bills
Regular Season Record: 3-8, 3 comebacks
Postseason Record: 0-0, no comebacks
Relative Rating: 82%

Passing

Year	G	Comp./Att.	%	Yards	Y/Att.	TD	INT	Rating
1995	1	10/18	55.6	106	5.9	2	0	110.0
1996	1	2/5	40.0	9	1.8	0	0	47.9
1997	6	60/124	48.4	684	5.5	2	10	37.2
1998	1	0/0	0.0	0	0.0	0	0	0.0
1999	1	1/1	100	9	9.0	0	0	104.2
2000	1	4/8	50.0	67	8.4	0	0	78.6
2001	12	178/307	58.0	2,056	6.7	12	11	76.4
2002	2	2/2	100	5	2.5	0	0	79.2
2003	6	5/12	41.7	49	4.1	0	3	14.2
Total	31	262/477	54.9	2,985	6.3	16	24	64.1
PS:	1	4/10	40.0	27	2.7	1	0	81.3

Rushing

Year	Att.	Yards	Avg.	TD
1996	3	-5	-1.7	0
1997	11	33	3.0	1
1998	1	-1	-1.0	0
1999	1	-1	-1.0	0
2001	12	33	2.8	0
2003	4	-6	-1.5	0
Total	32	53	1.7	1
PS:	0	0	0.0	0

That Alex Van Pelt broke most of Dan Marino's passing records at Pitt is proof that there is a wide gulf between college and pro football. Van Pelt was drafted by his hometown Steelers in 1993 but was cut and spent his entire career as a backup quarterback in Buffalo. Van Pelt's first start came in 1997 against Marino's Dolphins, and Buffalo won 9–6 with Alex throwing for all of 89 yards in an ugly game. The smart but talent-challenged Van Pelt lasted in the NFL for nine years. After retiring, he spent two seasons as a Bills broadcaster before joining the coaching staff in 2006.

Michael Vick

QPR 6.5

Height: 6'0" **Weight:** 215 lbs. **Birthdate:** 6/26/1980
College: Virginia Tech **Draft:** Atlanta 2001-1st
2001–06 Atlanta Falcons
Regular Season Record: 38-28-1, 8 comebacks
Postseason Record: 2-2, no comebacks
Relative Rating: 95%

Passing

Year	G	Comp./Att.	%	Yards	Y/Att.	TD	INT	Rating
2001	8	50/113	44.2	785	6.9	2	3	62.7
2002	15	231/421	54.9	2,936	7.0	16	8	81.6
2003	5	50/100	50.0	585	5.9	4	3	69.0
2004	15	181/321	56.4	2,313	7.2	14	12	78.1
2005	15	214/387	55.3	2,412	6.2	15	13	73.1
2006	16	204/388	52.6	2,474	6.4	20	13	75.7
Total	74	930/1,730	53.8	11,505	6.7	71	52	75.7
PS:	4	58/103	56.3	609	5.9	3	3	71.2

Rushing

Year	Att.	Yards	Avg.	TD
2001	31	289	9.3	1
2002	113	777	6.9	8
2003	40	255	6.4	1
2004	120	902	7.5	3
2005	102	597	5.9	6
2006	123	1039	8.4	2
Total	529	3,859	7.3	21
PS:	28	239	8.5	0

Michael Vick has had eight 100-yard rushing games, has led all quarterbacks in rushing four times, and is the only quarterback to rush for more than 1,000 yards in a season. With four 500-yard rushing seasons, he is second only to Randall Cunningham and is third behind Cunningham and Steve Young in career quarterback rushing yards. In many ways, Vick is similar to Cunningham and could be said to be a shorter and quicker version of the Eagles' Ultimate Weapon from the 1980s. Both were elusive, speedy runners and wild-armed passers who stressed spectacular highlight plays over teamwork. Both were undisciplined streetball scramblers who were sacked on roughly 10 percent of all pass plays and league-leading fumblers who tended to make mistakes at crucial points in key games. Neither quarterback was much of a team leader, neither responded well to coaching, and both were instrumental in getting coaches fired.

Randall was a much better quarterback, though. He was the more consistent and accurate passer of the two, while Vick was the faster and slinkier runner. Cunningham was about 5 percent better than the league average in passer rating, compared to Vick, who has been 5 percent below the league average. Although Vick led the NFL in rushing average four times, he has never led the league in any passing category. Although a bit flighty, Randall was also a much more reliable citizen off the field.

As for the dogfighting felonies that sent Vick to prison for two years in 2007, Vick's involvement illustrates the folly of ghetto loyalty and the dangers of allowing parasitic friends to suck you dry and destroy the success you have earned for yourself. Even if all goes well and Vick gets out on parole and is reinstated from his NFL suspension, he still will miss at least three prime years of his career and return as a rusty 30-year-old ballplayer. How much spark he will be able to regain is an open question. Of course, some team is going to have to sign him first and take on the inevitable sideshow that would accompany his return. We have most likely seen the best, if not the last, of Michael Vick.

Rushing

Year	Att.	Yards	Avg.	TD
2003	11	4	0.4	1
2004	11	50	4.5	1
2005	1	3	3.0	0
2006	3	-3	-1.0	0
2007	11	-7	-0.6	0
Total	37	47	1.3	2
PS:	3	-1	-0.3	0

A Ted Tedford–coached quarterback at Fresno State, Billy Volek went undrafted and signed with the Titans as a free agent in 2000. Although Volek did not play in each season, he was with the team for six years. His biggest opportunity came in 2004 when Steve McNair battled several injuries and missed half the season. Stepping in, Billy joined the exclusive club of Dan Fouts, Dan Marino, and Phil Simms by throwing for more than 400 yards in consecutive weeks. Unfortunately, the Titans lost both of those games with Volek and finished 2–6 in his eight starts.

Still, when McNair was traded in 2006, Volek was named the starter. After coach Jeff Fisher signed Kerry Collins to compete with Volek, though, Billy reacted petulantly. A displeased Fisher indicated that Volek was not being honest with him and traded Billy to San Diego. One year later, Volek replaced an injured Philip Rivers in the fourth quarter of a playoff game against the Colts and led the Chargers to the go-ahead touchdown in the final minutes. Volek re-signed with San Diego as a backup in 2008, but did not play.

Billy Volek

QPR 4.5

Height: 6'2"   **Weight:** 214 lbs.   **Birthdate:** 4/28/1976
College: Fresno State   **Draft:** Free agent
2001, 2003–05 Tennessee Titans; 2006–07 San Diego Chargers
Regular Season Record: 3–7, 1 comeback
Postseason Record: 0–0, 1 comeback
Relative Rating: 107%

Passing

Year	G	Comp./Att.	%	Yards	Y/Att.	TD	INT	Rating
2001	1	0/3	0.0	0	0.0	0	0	39.6
2003	7	44/69	63.8	545	7.9	4	1	101.4
2004	10	218/357	61.1	2,486	7.0	18	10	87.1
2005	6	50/88	56.8	474	5.4	4	2	77.6
2006	1	1/2	50.0	4	2.0	0	0	56.2
2007	5	3/10	30.0	6	0.6	0	1	0.0
Total	30	316/529	59.7	3,515	6.6	26	14	84.9
PS:	1	3/4	75.0	48	12.0	0	0	114.6

Billy Wade

QPR 9.0

Height: 6'2"   **Weight:** 202 lbs.   **Birthdate:** 10/4/1932
Collge: Vanderbilt   **Draft:** Los Angeles Rams 1952-1st
1954–60 Los Angeles Rams; 1961–66 Chicago Bears
Regular Season Record: 40–43-2, 10 comebacks
Postseason Record: 1–0, no comebacks
Relative Rating: 107%

Passing

Year	G	Comp./Att.	%	Yards	Y/Att.	TD	INT	Rating
1954	10	31/59	52.5	509	8.6	2	1	86.1
1955	7	31/71	43.7	316	4.5	1	3	44.1
1956	12	91/178	51.1	1,461	8.2	10	13	67.2
1957	5	10/24	41.7	116	4.8	1	1	53.5
1958	12	181/341	53.1	2,875	8.4	18	22	72.2
1959	12	153/261	58.6	2,001	7.7	12	17	71.1
1960	11	106/182	58.2	1,294	7.1	12	11	77.0
1961	13	139/250	55.6	2,258	9.0	22	13	93.7
1962	14	225/412	54.6	3,172	7.7	18	24	70.0
1963	14	192/356	53.9	2,301	6.5	15	12	74.0
1964	11	182/327	55.7	1,944	5.9	13	14	68.6
1965	5	20/41	48.8	204	5.0	0	2	43.1
1966	2	9/21	42.9	79	3.8	0	1	33.6
Total	128	1,370/2,523	54.3	18,530	7.3	124	134	72.2
PS:	2	10/31	32.3	138	4.5	0	1	34.1

Rushing

Year	Att.	Yards	Avg.	TD
1954	28	190	6.8	1
1955	11	43	3.9	0
1956	26	93	3.6	3
1957	1	5	5.0	0
1958	42	90	2.1	2
1959	25	95	3.8	2
1960	26	171	6.6	2
1961	45	255	5.7	2
1962	40	146	3.7	5
1963	45	132	2.9	6
1964	24	96	4.0	1
1965	5	18	3.6	0
Total	318	1,334	4.2	24
PS:	9	40	4.4	2

When the Bears' Billy Wade won the 1963 NFL championship over Y.A. Tittle and the Giants, it represented the ultimate triumph of the game-manager quarterback. Wade's job during the 1963 season had been to manage a short passing attack, to not make mistakes, and to let the Bears' opportunistic defense win the game. In Chicago's 14–10 victory over New York for the title, he did just that. Wade scored both Bear touchdowns on quarterback sneaks after leading drives of 14 and 5 yards that were both set up by intercepted screen passes. One bitter Giant said after the game, "Wade can't score on you if he gets the ball far enough away from the goal line so that he has to make a

first down before he goes in. If the defense doesn't give him the ball on the 5, he's dead."

By that point, Wade's reputation had fallen pretty far from his being the overall No. 1 pick of the 1952 draft by the Rams. After two years in the military, Wade backed up Norm Van Brocklin for a couple of seasons before coach Sid Gillman named Billy the starter in 1956. By the end of the year, though, Wade had played himself back to the bench. Two years later, the Rams traded Van Brocklin to the Eagles, and Wade got a second chance in 1958. Over the next three years, Billy once again played himself out of a job. On the recommendation of former Rams assistant George Allen, the Bears acquired Wade for Zeke Bratkowski in 1961.

Wade had his best season that year with 22 touchdowns and just 13 interceptions but was back up to 24 interceptions the following year, so the Bears constricted the offense in 1963 and won a championship. Previously in Los Angeles, Wade had showed a strong arm that was too erratic to be trusted. He was a fine ball handler and a fairly nifty scrambler but an awkward passer. There was more inconsistency and disappointment in 1964, and the 34-year-old Wade was eventually replaced in a "youth" movement by 32-year-old Bears backup Rudy Bukich. For one glorious season, though, Wade designed the blueprint that Trent Dilfer followed on the Baltimore Ravens nearly 40 years later.

Seneca Wallace

QPR 3.0

Height: 5'11" **Weight:** 196 lbs. **Birthdate:** 8/6/1980
College: Iowa State **Draft:** Seattle 2003-4th
2005–08 Seattle Seahawks
Regular Season Record: 5–7, 2 comebacks
Postseason Record: NA
Relative Rating: 105%

Passing

Year	G	Comp./Att.	%	Yards	Y/Att.	TD	INT	Rating
2005	7	13/25	52.0	173	6.9	1	1	70.9
2006	8	82/141	58.2	927	6.6	8	7	76.2
2007	10	19/28	67.9	215	7.7	2	1	99.6
2008	10	141/242	58.3	1,532	6.3	11	3	87.0
Total	35	255/436	58.5	2,847	6.5	22	12	81.3

Rushing

Year	Att.	Yards	Avg.	TD
2005	6	-5	-0.8	0
2006	12	122	10.2	0
2007	4	17	4.3	0
2008	16	78	4.9	0
Total	38	212	5.6	0

Seneca Wallace has to have two helmets on the Seahawks, a radio helmet for when he plays quarterback and a regular one for the occasions when he lines up at wide receiver. Although Seattle drafted him in 2003, he didn't appear in a game until 2005, after backup Trent Dilfer had moved on. Wallace got to start four games in 2006 and eight more in 2008 when Matt Hasselbeck was hurt but proved that he is solely a backup quarterback. He is the shortest quarterback in the league and is a good scrambler, but he is not a pocket passer. He has a weak arm, which makes him a careful little dink passer who doesn't make many mistakes but doesn't generate much offense either.

Steve Walsh

QPR 4.5

Height: 6'3" **Weight:** 207 lbs. **Birthdate:** 12/1/1966
College: Miami **Draft:** Dallas 1989-1st(S)
1989–90 Dallas Cowboys; 1990–91, 1993 New Orleans Saints; 1994–95 Chicago Bears; 1996 St. Louis Rams; 1997–98 Tampa Bay Bucs; 1999 Indianapolis Colts
Regular Season Record: 20–18, 8 comebacks
Postseason Record: 1–2, no comebacks
Relative Rating: 86%

Passing

Year	G	Comp./Att.	%	Yards	Y/Att.	TD	INT	Rating
1989	8	110/219	50.2	1,371	6.3	5	9	60.5
1990	13	179/336	53.3	2,010	6.0	12	13	67.2
1991	8	141/255	55.3	1,638	6.4	11	6	79.5
1993	2	20/38	52.6	271	7.1	2	3	60.3
1994	12	208/343	60.6	2,078	6.1	10	8	77.9
1995	1	0/0	0.0	0	0.0	0	0	0.0
1996	3	33/77	42.9	344	4.5	0	5	29.4
1997	12	6/17	35.3	58	3.4	0	1	21.2
1998	5	9/19	47.4	58	3.1	0	3	14.7
1999	16	7/13	53.8	47	3.6	0	2	22.4
Total	80	713/1,317	54.1	7,875	6.0	40	50	66.4
PS:	4	32/59	54.2	373	6.3	2	4	56.7

Rushing

Year	Att.	Yards	Avg.	TD
1989	6	16	2.7	0
1990	20	25	1.3	0
1991	8	0	0.0	0
1993	4	-4	-1.0	0
1994	30	4	0.1	1
1996	6	10	1.7	0
1997	6	-4	-0.7	0
Total	80	47	0.6	1
PS:	7	5	0.7	0

At Miami under coach Jimmy Johnson, Steve Walsh went 23–1 and led the Hurricanes to a national championship. Still, when Johnson selected Walsh in the 1989 supplemental draft after having taken Troy Aikman with the overall No. 1 pick in the regular draft, Steve's response was, "Why?" As it turned out, there were a number of good reasons.

First, it was hedge against the Cowboys' bet on Aikman being a franchise quarterback. Second, Walsh provided an extra push for Aikman to succeed. Third, after Aikman proved he was the real deal, Walsh was then traded to New Orleans for first-, second-, and third-round draft picks, so Dallas came out ahead. Walsh was a smart game manager who lasted a decade in the NFL as an occasional starter and backup with six teams because he understood his role and his limitations. "I always get beaten up in the media over the lack of arm strength. When I do something, everybody acts surprised. My strength is making good decisions. I protect the football, and I get it into the receiver's hands," he told *Sports Illustrated* in 1994. That year he led Chicago into the playoffs just as he had guided the Saints to the postseason four years before. Once there, Walsh was not good enough to go very far, but he was a capable backup.

Kurt Warner

Height: 6'2" **Weight:** 220 lbs. **Birthdate:** 6/22/1971
College: Northern Iowa **Draft:** Free Agent
**1995–97 Arena Football; 1998 NFL Europe; 1998–03
St. Louis Rams; 2004 New York Giants; 2005–08
Arizona Cardinals**
Regular Season Record: 57–44, 8 comebacks
Postseason Record: 8–3, 3 comebacks
Relative Rating: 118%

Passing

Year	G	Comp./Att.	%	Yards	Y/Att.	TD	INT	Rating
1998	1	4/11	36.4	39	3.5	0	0	47.2
1999	16	325/499	65.1	4,353	8.7	41	13	109.2
2000	11	235/347	67.7	3,429	9.9	21	18	98.3
2001	16	375/546	68.7	4,830	8.8	36	22	101.4
2002	7	144/220	65.5	1,431	6.5	3	11	67.4
2003	2	38/65	58.5	365	5.6	1	1	72.9
2004	10	174/277	62.8	2,054	7.4	6	4	86.5
2005	10	242/375	64.5	2,713	7.2	11	9	85.8
2006	7	108/168	64.3	1,377	8.2	6	5	89.3
2007	14	281/451	62.3	3,417	7.6	27	17	89.8
2008	16	401/598	67.1	4,583	7.7	30	14	96.9
Total	110	2,327/3,557	65.4	28,591	8.0	182	114	93.8
PS:	11	261/403	64.8	3,368	8.4	26	13	98.9

Rushing

Year	Att.	Yards	Avg.	TD
1999	23	92	4.0	1
2000	18	17	0.9	0
2001	28	60	2.1	0
2002	8	33	4.1	0
2003	1	0	0.0	0
2004	13	30	2.3	1
2005	13	28	2.2	0
2006	13	3	0.2	0
2007	17	15	0.9	1
2008	18	-2	-0.1	0
Total	152	276	1.8	3
PS:	24	17	0.7	1

In a story that echoed that of Johnny Unitas, Kurt Warner came out of nowhere in 1999 to lead the lowly Rams to a Super Bowl championship. Just a year before, Warner had worked in a grocery store and played minor-league football to keep his dream alive. In the wide-open Arena Football League, Kurt threw 183 touchdowns in three years. Signed by the Rams and sent to NFL Europe for seasoning, Warner got his chance when new starter Trent Green hurt his knee in a preseason game. Kurt threw for 4,353 yards while leading the league with 41 touchdown passes. Unlike Johnny U though, Warner's crash was just as meteoric as his initial rise had been.

In his first three full seasons, Warner led the league in yards per pass three times, in touchdown passes and passer rating twice, and in passing yards once. The two-time league MVP also led the Rams to Super Bowls following the 1999 and 2001 seasons, and Kurt threw for the two highest Super Bowl passing yardage totals in those games, 414 in Super Bowl XXXIV and 365 in the last-second loss to New England in Super Bowl XXXVI. In between, Warner broke his hand in 2000 and missed five games. Warner had the quickest release of any

Kurt Warner in the Clutch: In the 2008 NFC championship, the Eagles rallied from a 24–6 deficit to take a fourth quarter 25–24 lead with 10:45 to play. Warner drove the Cardinals on a brilliant 14-play, 72-yard drive that mixed passes and runs and culminated with an 8-yard screen pass to Tim Hightower for the winning touchdown. The drive used up 7 minutes and 52 seconds and put the Cardinals in their first Super Bowl.

Kurt Warner's Signature Play: After the Titans tied the score in Super Bowl XXXIV with two minutes to play, Warner launched a 73-yard touchdown pass to Isaac Bruce on the next play to win the championship for the Rams.

Kurt Warner threw for 400 yards in leading the Rams to their first championship in 48 years in Super Bowl XXXIV.

Kurt Warner's Five Highest Honors

5. Walter Payton Man of the Year in 2008
4. Selected for four Pro Bowls
3. Two-time consensus All-Pro
2. Super Bowl XXXIV MVP
1. 1999 and 2001 Player of the Year

The Five Quarterbacks Most Similar to Kurt Warner

5. Peyton Manning
4. Joe Namath
3. Norm Van Brocklin
2. Dan Fouts
1. Johnny Unitas

Kurt Warner's Five Top Touchdown Targets

5. Marshall Faulk, 18 TDs
4. Torry Holt, 18 TDs
3. Isaac Bruce, 22 TDs
2. Anquan Boldin, 23 TDs
1. Larry Fitzgerald, 27 TDs

Kurt Warner's Five Toughest Rivals

5. Warner is 8–1 against the 49ers.
4. Warner is 3–4 against the Seahawks.
3. Warner is 4–2 against the Saints in the regular season and 0–1 in the playoffs.
2. Warner is 0–4 against the Bucs in the regular season and 1–0 in the playoffs.
1. Warner is 1–3 against the Eagles in the regular season and 2–0 in the playoffs.

Five Random Kurt Warner Statistics

5. Warner has played for five head coaches.
4. Warner's teams scored 22 percent more points than the league average.
3. Warner threw for five touchdowns against the 49ers on October 10, 1999.
2. Warner threw for more than 300 yards 48 times and over 400 yards four times.
1. Warner led the league in completion percentage three times, passing yards once, touchdown passes twice, yards per attempts three times, and passer rating once.

quarterback and was deadly accurate in hitting receivers in stride downfield. Defenses found that the best way to counter Warner was to blitz him and hit him hard and often. Warner's performance began to deteriorate as the beatings piled up.

Warner began 2002 by throwing just one touchdown pass and seven interceptions in the first three games of the season and then broke his finger. The next season, Kurt fumbled six times in the opening game loss to the Giants and was replaced for good by backup Marc Bulger. Kurt appeared in only one more game that season and left the Rams for the Giants as a free agent the next season. After one season as rookie Eli Manning's mentor, Warner moved on to Arizona to battle with pedestrian Josh McCown for playing time in 2005. The year 2006 brought a new rookie to mentor in Matt Leinart, but Warner never gave up and regained the starting job in 2008. Once again directing a high-powered aerial attack, Kurt led the Cardinals to a playoff slot—from the weak NFC West— with another 4,000-yard passing season at age 37 and guided the team to the Super Bowl for the first time in franchise history. In the process, he moved into fifth place with 48 300-yard games. For his stop-and-start career, Warner's teams have outscored the league average by an impressive 22 percent, and at times he has been as spectacular a passer as any in history.

In 2008, Kurt "Lazarus" Warner led the Cardinals to their first NFL championship game appearance in 60 years.

Bob Waterfield

QPR **9.5**

Height: 6'1" **Weight:** 200 lbs. **Birthdate:** 7/26/1920
College: UCLA **Draft:** Cleveland Rams 1944-5th
1945–52 Cleveland/Los Angeles Rams
Regular Season Record: 59–26–4, 11 comebacks
Postseason Record: 3–3, no comebacks
Relative Rating: 113%

Passing

Year	G	Comp./Att.	%	Yards	Y/Att.	TD	INT	Rating
1945	10	89/171	52.0	1,609	9.4	14	17	72.4
1946	11	127/251	50.6	1,747	7.0	17	17	67.6
1947	12	96/221	43.4	1,210	5.5	8	18	39.2
1948	11	87/180	48.3	1,354	7.5	14	18	60.0
1949	12	154/296	52.0	2,168	7.3	17	24	61.3
1950	12	122/213	57.3	1,540	7.2	11	13	71.7
1951	11	88/176	50.0	1,566	8.9	13	10	81.8
1952	12	51/109	46.8	655	6.0	3	11	35.7
Total	**91**	814/1,617	50.3	11,849	7.3	97	128	61.6
PS:	6	63/125	50.4	965	7.7	6	11	55.6

Rushing

Year	Att.	Yards	Avg.	TD
1945	18	18	1.0	5
1946	16	-60	-3.8	1
1947	3	6	2.0	1
1948	7	12	1.7	0
1949	5	-4	-0.8	1
1950	8	14	1.8	1
1951	9	49	5.4	3
1952	9	-14	-1.6	1
Total	**75**	**21**	**0.3**	**13**
PS:	10	14	1.4	0

In a glib and shallow attack on Bob Waterfield in a 2001 issue of *Sports Illustrated*, writer Peter King dismissed the Hall of Famer as the most overrated NFL quarterback because his cumulative stats were relatively light from an eight-year career and he was beaten out by Norm Van Brocklin. King is missing a number of points.

First, Waterfield played in four championship games in eight years and won two titles. His first title came in his rookie season of 1945 when he was voted the NFL's Most Valuable Player. In that championship game, Waterfield outdueled Sammy Baugh by throwing two touchdown passes on a freezing 6-degree day with 18 inches of snow on the ground and the wind whipping off Lake Erie. Second, Waterfield led the NFL twice each in touchdown passes and yards per attempt, as well as interceptions, and once in completion percentage. Although he completed just 50 percent of his passes, his passer rating is a full 13 percent better than the league average for his time. Third, Waterfield was not "beaten out" by fellow Hall of Famer Van Brocklin. He and Van Brocklin shared the quarterbacking, alternating quarters from 1950 through Waterfield's final season of 1952. It was an arrangement that neither quarterback was happy about, but the Rams in that era led the league in scoring each year by a wide margin. Behind either quarterback, Los Angeles was the greatest scoring machine of its time. Fourth, Waterfield was more than a quarterback; he was a football player who played both ways. From 1945 to 1948, Bob intercepted 20 passes on defense. He was the Rams' punter and place-kicker, and his 573 points scored is second only to George Blanda's 2,002 among quarterbacks.

The team captain, Waterfield was a cool, quiet leader known as "Waterbuckets" among his teammates. He was an expert ball handler and a top passer even if he did throw too many interceptions. Off the field, Waterfield married his high school sweetheart in his senior year at UCLA. She soon became famous as the actress and sex symbol Jane Russell. Russell once told Marilyn Monroe, who was about to marry Joe DiMaggio, "They're birds of a feather, and you'll get to know lots of other athletes. Otherwise, it's great." Waterfield later tried coaching with the Rams but went just 9–24–1 in less than three seasons.

Chris Weinke

QPR **1.0**

Height: 6'4" **Weight:** 232 lbs. **Birthdate:** 7/31/1972
College: Florida State **Draft:** Carolina 2001-4th
2001–02, 2005–06 Carolina Panthers; 2007 San Francisco 49ers
Regular Season Record: 2–18, 1 comeback
Postseason Record: NA
Relative Rating: 78%

Passing

Year	G	Comp./Att.	%	Yards	Y/Att.	TD	INT	Rating
2001	15	293/540	54.3	2,931	5.4	11	19	62.0
2002	6	17/38	44.7	180	4.7	0	3	26.2
2005	3	7/13	53.8	64	4.9	1	0	93.1
2006	3	56/96	58.3	625	6.5	2	4	67.4
2007	2	13/22	59.1	104	4.7	1	0	86.2
Total	29	386/709	54.4	3,904	5.5	15	26	62.2

Rushing

Year	Att.	Yards	Avg.	TD
2001	37	128	3.5	6
2002	5	9	1.8	0
2005	8	-5	-0.6	0
2006	4	16	4.0	0
Total	54	148	2.7	6

What a bizarre career Chris Weinke had. After choosing baseball as a teenager, Weinke spent six years in the Toronto Blue Jay organization as a weak-hitting first baseman before deciding to play football for Florida State, where he had originally committed to play. Chris started at quarterback for the Seminoles for three years, led them to a national championship as a junior, and became the oldest player ever to win the Heisman Trophy as a 28-year-old senior. Drafted by the Panthers in 2001, Weinke was named the starting quarterback and won the season opener. He lost his next 14 starts that year for the 1–15 Panthers and then lost his only start in 2002. From 2003 through 2005, Weinke was the Panthers' third quarterback and never appeared in a game. He was very slow with no agility and was unable to throw short passes accurately. Some compared him to a less-athletic Kent Graham, as if Kent Graham could be any less athletic. When Carolina lost two quarterbacks to injury in 2006, Weinke was back. Playing down to the challenge, Chris lost his first two starts, which brought him to a record-low lifetime winning percentage of .056. In the season's penultimate game, though, coach John Fox got tricky. He started Weinke but let him throw just seven passes. Weinke would leave the field on third down, and running back DeShaun Foster would take a direct snap rather than have Chris screw it up. Carolina won 10–3 over Atlanta, and starter Jake Delhomme returned for the season finale. Weinke's final act came the following year when the 49ers lost three quarterbacks and

brought in Chris to lose the final game of the year to Cleveland, bringing his winning percentage back down to .100—the worst ever among quarterbacks who started 20 or more games.

Craig Whelihan

QPR 1.5

Height: 6'5" **Weight:** 220 lbs. **Birthdate:** 4/15/1971
College: Pacific **Draft:** San Diego 1995-6th
1997–98 San Diego Chargers; 2001 XFL; 2001–07 Arena Football
Regular Season Record: 2–12, 2 comebacks
Postseason Record: NA
Relative Rating: 67%

Passing

Year	G	Comp./Att.	%	Yards	Y/Att.	TD	INT	Rating
1997	9	118/237	49.8	1,357	5.7	6	10	58.3
1998	10	149/320	46.6	1,803	5.6	8	19	48.0
Total	19	267/557	47.9	3,160	5.7	14	29	52.4

Rushing

Year	Att.	Yards	Avg.	TD
1997	13	29	2.2	0
1998	18	38	2.1	0
Total	31	67	2.2	0

In 1998, the San Diego Chargers had the NFL's top-ranked defense in yards allowed but won just five games because its quarterbacks were second-year man Craig Whelihan and rookie Ryan Leaf. Those two 6'5" superstars combined for 10 touchdown passes and 34 interceptions. Whelihan had lost all seven of his starts as a rookie in 1997 and went 2–5 in his second and last year in the NFL. He spent 2001 as a reserve with the Memphis Maniax and the Chicago Enforcers in the XFL and then spent seven years as a backup in arena football, where he threw 110 touchdowns to just 28 interceptions, finally finding his niche.

Danny White

QPR 9.0

Height: 6'2" **Weight:** 193 lbs. **Birthdate:** 2/9/1952
College: Arizona State **Draft:** Dallas 1974-3rd
1976–88 Dallas Cowboys
Regular Season Record: 62–30, 14 comebacks
Postseason Record: 5–5, 2 comebacks
Relative Rating: 113%

Passing

Year	G	Comp./Att.	%	Yards	Y/Att.	TD	INT	Rating
1976	14	13/20	65.0	213	10.7	2	2	94.4
1977	14	4/10	40.0	35	3.5	0	1	10.4
1978	16	20/34	58.8	215	6.3	0	1	65.2
1979	16	19/39	48.7	267	6.8	1	2	58.4
1980	16	260/436	59.6	3,287	7.5	28	25	80.7
1981	16	223/391	57.0	3,098	7.9	22	13	87.5
1982	9	156/247	63.2	2,079	8.4	16	12	91.1
1983	16	334/533	62.7	3,980	7.5	29	23	85.6
1984	14	126/233	54.1	1,580	6.8	11	11	71.5
1985	14	267/450	59.3	3,157	7.0	21	17	80.6
1986	7	95/153	62.1	1,157	7.6	12	5	97.9
1987	11	215/362	59.4	2,617	7.2	12	17	73.2
1988	3	29/42	69.0	274	6.5	1	3	65.0
Total	166	1,761/2,950	59.7	21,959	7.4	155	132	81.7
PS:	12	206/360	57.2	2,284	6.3	15	16	71.6

Rushing

Year	Att.	Yards	Avg.	TD
1976	6	17	2.8	0
1977	1	-2	-2.0	0
1978	5	7	1.4	0
1979	1	25	25	0
1980	27	114	4.2	1
1981	38	104	2.7	0
1982	17	91	5.4	0
1983	18	31	1.7	4
1984	6	21	3.5	0
1985	22	44	2.0	1
1986	8	16	2.0	1
1987	10	14	1.4	1
Total	159	482	3.0	8
PS:	18	1	0.1	0

People often described Danny White's relationship with Roger Staubach—while White was the backup in Dallas—as that of a little brother. The two competed in nearly everything, but Roger usually got the best of it. Staubach used to tease Danny by calling him "America's Punter" in reference to the Cowboys' designation as "America's Team." Coach Tom Landry later said, "I don't think anybody could have followed Roger and done as well as Danny. Danny was a solid winner."

The most similar situations to White following Hall of Famer Staubach after a four-year apprenticeship were Billy Wade following Norm Van Brocklin in Los Angeles, Sonny Jurgensen following Norm Van Brocklin in Philadelphia, and Steve Young following Joe Montana in San Francisco. In his first four years as the Cowboys' starter, White went 42–15 and threw 95 touchdowns to 73 interceptions while taking Dallas to three straight NFC Championship Games. Wade went 15–21 as a starter, threw 64 touchdowns to 63 interceptions, and was traded to Chicago. Jurgensen went 21–27–2 as a starter with 89 touchdowns and 76 interceptions and was traded to Washington. Young was two years older than White at 30 when he replaced Montana and went 42–16 as a starter with 106 touchdowns and 41 interceptions while taking the 49ers to three straight NFC championships and winning a Super Bowl. Although White was not quite Steve Young, he was an excellent quarterback who provided Dallas with a nice transition from a legend.

White was the son of Wilford White, a Bear running back in the 1950s who was the second NFL back known as Whizzer White. Danny followed his father to Arizona State and went 32–4 in three years as the Sun Devil starter. He signed with Memphis of the World Football League rather than Dallas out of college and got to start right away. After the WFL folded, White joined the Cowboys and spent the next four years as the team's backup quarterback and punter. He continued as the Cowboy punter into 1984 and was the last double-duty quarterback/punter in the NFL.

In many ways White was similar in style to Staubach as a quarterback; he just wasn't as good. But few were. Danny had the Cowboys right in the thick of the playoff mix for his first six seasons but started to slip as the team declined in general. White found himself pushed by first Gary Hogeboom and then Steve Pelluer, and that did not reflect well on the team's fortunes. Landry was right in that White was a solid winner, and Danny took Landry as a model and went into coaching himself. White spent 15 years coaching arena football and posted a 163–95 record with one championship.

David Whitehurst

Height: 6'2"   **Weight:** 204 lbs.   **Birthdate:** 4/27/1955
College: Furman   **Draft:** Green Bay 1977-8th
1977–83 Green Bay Packers
Regular Season Record: 16–20–1, 1 comeback
Postseason Record: NA
Relative Rating: 83%

Passing

Year	G	Comp./Att.	%	Yards	Y/Att.	TD	INT	Rating
1977	7	50/105	47.6	634	6.0	1	7	42.3
1978	16	168/328	51.2	2,093	6.4	10	17	59.9
1979	13	179/322	55.6	2,247	7.0	10	18	64.5
1980	2	5/15	33.3	55	3.7	0	1	17.4
1981	9	66/128	51.6	792	6.2	7	5	72.8
1982	3	18/47	38.3	235	5.0	0	1	46.0
1983	4	18/35	51.4	149	4.3	0	2	38.9
Total	54	980/504	51.4	6,205	6.3	28	51	59.2

Rushing

Year	Att.	Yards	Avg.	TD
1977	14	55	3.9	1
1978	28	67	2.4	1
1979	18	73	4.1	4
1981	15	51	3.4	1
1983	2	-4	-2.0	0
Total	77	242	3.1	7

David Whitehurst was a late-round draft pick of Green Bay who became the starter as a rookie when Lynn Dickey was severely injured in 1977. Dickey did not return till late in 1979, and Whitehurst piloted the Packers in the interim. After Dickey returned to the starting lineup, David fell into place as the team's backup for the next four years. When coach Bart Starr was fired and replaced by Forrest Gregg in 1984, Whitehurst was cut. David had limited quarterback skills but was a hard worker. He was just barely a 50 percent passer, took a lot of sacks and threw 51 interceptions to just 28 touchdowns. His son Charlie was a third-round draft pick of San Diego in 2006 and has served as the Chargers' third quarterback ever since.

Doug Williams

Height: 6'4"   **Weight:** 220 lbs.   **Birthdate:** 8/9/1955
College: Grambling   **Draft:** Tampa 1978-1st
1978–82 Tampa Bay Bucs; 1983–85 USFL; 1986–89 Washington Redskins
Regular Season Record: 38–42–1, 19 comebacks
Postseason Record: 4–3, 1 comeback
Relative Rating: 95%

Passing

Year	G	Comp./Att.	%	Yards	Y/Att.	TD	INT	Rating
1978	10	73/194	37.6	1,170	6.0	7	8	53.4
1979	16	166/397	41.8	2,448	6.2	18	24	52.5
1980	16	254/521	48.8	3,396	6.5	20	16	69.9
1981	16	238/471	50.5	3,563	7.6	19	14	76.8
1982	9	164/307	53.4	2,071	6.7	9	11	69.6
1986	1	0/1	0.0	0	0.0	0	0	39.6
1987	5	81/143	56.6	1,156	8.1	11	5	94.0
1988	11	213/380	56.1	2,609	6.9	15	12	77.4
1989	4	51/93	54.8	585	6.3	1	3	64.1
Total	88	1,240/2,507	49.5	16,998	6.8	100	93	69.4
PS:	7	68/169	40.2	1,110	6.6	9	11	53.6

Rushing

Year	Att.	Yards	Avg.	TD
1978	27	23	0.9	1
1979	35	119	3.4	2
1980	58	370	6.4	4
1981	48	209	4.4	4
1982	35	158	4.5	2
1987	7	9	1.3	1
1988	9	0	0.0	1
1989	1	-4	-4.0	0
Total	220	884	4.0	15
PS:	16	32	2.0	0

When critics would attack John McKay's quarterback Doug Williams, McKay would say, "You say his percentage isn't high enough? Well, that's tough. I wouldn't trade him for anyone." As a rookie, Williams took over a Bucs team that had gone 2–26 in its first two years, and he went 33–33–1 over the next five seasons as a starter. Doug led the Bucs to three playoff berths in four years as he steadily improved his game.

In 1978, Williams was Tampa's No. 1 pick out of Grambling, where he had led the Tigers to three straight national black college championships. Still, the competition level at Grambling was far from that of a major college program, and Doug had a lot to learn in the pros. In his first year, his completion percentage was just 37.6, but he raised that each year in Tampa as he became less scatter-armed and learned to put more touch and less zip on his passes. Williams was big and tough with a strong arm and release so quick that he ranks just behind Dan Marino and just ahead of Peyton Manning for the lowest sacked percentage among quarterbacks. He was also a good runner and protected the ball well.

After five seasons, though, Williams found out there were more than 40 NFL quarterbacks who were paid more money than he was, so he jumped to the USFL. When that league folded, Doug returned to the NFL in 1986 with the Redskins who were coached by Williams' former offensive coach at Tampa, Joe Gibbs. With starter Jay Schroeder struggling in 1987, Gibbs named Williams the starter for the playoffs, and Doug took Washington to the Super Bowl. As the first black Super Bowl quarterback, Williams spent the two weeks of pre–Big Game media hype under more scrutiny than any player ever. Although the story that a reporter asked Doug how long he had been a black quarterback never actually happened, there was nowhere that Williams could go to get away from the historical significance of his upcoming performance.

In the Super Bowl, the Redskins fell behind Denver 10–0 in the first quarter, and then Williams hyperextended his knee while dropping back to pass and had to leave the game for two plays. With the start of the second quarter, though, everything slowed down, and Doug had the best quarter any quarterback ever had at the Super Bowl. In five drives, Williams led the Redskins to 35 points. As a passer, he completed nine of 11 for 228 yards and four scores. Washington called off the dogs in the second half, and Williams cruised to 340 yards passing in the 42–10 rout that made the Redskins champions. Under enormous pressure, Williams had buried forever the demeaning stereotype of black quarterbacks not being winners.

Williams battled knee and back problems over the next couple of years and lost his starting job to Mark Rypien. Doug adjusted to that but was bitter

when the Redskins cut him after the 1989 season. He went into coaching and rose through the ranks to succeed his legendary college coach Eddie Robinson at Grambling in 1998. Over six seasons at Grambling, Williams achieved a 52–18 record. He left in 2004 to join the front office of Tampa Bay.

Dave Wilson

Height: 6'3" **Weight:** 206 lbs. **Birthdate:** 4/27/1959
College: Illinois **Draft:** New Orleans 1981-1st (S)
1981, 1983–88 New Orleans Saints
Regular Season Record: 12–19, 7 comebacks
Postseason Record: 0–0, no comebacks
Relative Rating: 86%

Passing

Year	G	Comp./Att.	%	Yards	Y/Att.	TD	INT	Rating
1981	11	82/159	51.6	1,058	6.7	1	11	46.1
1983	8	66/112	58.9	770	6.9	5	7	68.7
1984	5	51/93	54.8	647	7.0	7	4	83.9
1985	10	145/293	49.5	1,843	6.3	11	15	60.7
1986	14	189/342	55.3	2,353	6.9	10	17	65.8
1987	4	13/24	54.2	243	10.1	2	0	117.2
1988	1	5/16	31.3	73	4.6	0	1	21.1
Total	53	1,039/551	53.0	6,987	6.7	36	55	63.8
PS:	1	2/12	16.7	20	1.7	0	2	0

Rushing

Year	Att.	Yards	Avg.	TD
1981	5	1	0.2	0
1983	5	3	0.6	1
1984	3	-7	-2.3	0
1985	18	7	0.4	0
1986	14	19	1.4	1
Total	45	23	0.5	2
PS:	0	0	0.0	0

At Illinois, Dave Wilson once passed for 621 yards and six touchdowns in a loss to Ohio State in 1980, and he paved the way for future Illini quarterbacks Tony Eason and Jack Trudeau. Wilson sued the Big Ten because the conference ruled that he used up a year of eligibility when he broke his arm in his first game in junior college in 1977. Wilson contended that with another year at Illinois, he would have commanded a greater salary from the pros. The suit was eventually settled for $100,000. As it was,

Wilson was a No. 1 pick in the supplemental draft in 1980 but was not a very successful professional quarterback. He was a stationary pocket passer who grew flustered by pressure and threw a lot of interceptions. In one game against Kansas City in 1985, Wilson completed two of his first three passes and then threw 19 straight incompletions before he was replaced by Richard Todd in the second half. Wilson was the Saints' primary starter in 1985 and 1986 but was replaced by Bobby Hebert in 1987.

Marc Wilson

QPR 6.0

Height: 6'6" **Weight:** 205 lbs. **Birthdate:** 2/15/1957
College: BYU **Draft:** Oakland 1980-1st
1980–87 Oakland/Los Angeles Raiders; 1989–90 New England Patriots
Regular Season Record: 32–28, 14 comebacks
Postseason Record: 0–1, no comebacks
Relative Rating: 90%

Passing

Year	G	Comp./Att.	%	Yards	Y/Att.	TD	INT	Rating
1980	2	3/5	60.0	31	6.2	0	0	77.9
1981	13	173/366	47.3	2,311	6.3	14	19	58.9
1982	8	1/2	50.0	4	2.0	0	0	56.2
1983	10	67/117	57.3	864	7.4	8	6	82.0
1984	16	153/282	54.3	2,151	7.6	15	17	71.7
1985	16	193/388	49.7	2,608	6.7	16	21	62.7
1986	16	129/240	53.8	1,721	7.2	12	15	67.4
1987	15	152/266	57.1	2,070	7.8	12	8	84.6
1989	14	75/150	50.0	1,006	6.7	3	5	64.5
1990	16	139/265	52.5	1,625	6.1	6	11	61.6
Total	126	1,085/2,081	52.1	14,391	6.9	86	102	67.7
PS:	1	11/27	40.7	135	5.0	1	3	29.6

Rushing

Year	Att.	Yards	Avg.	TD
1980	1	3	3.0	0
1981	30	147	4.9	2
1983	13	122	9.4	0
1984	30	56	1.9	1
1985	24	98	4.1	2
1986	14	45	3.2	0
1987	17	91	5.4	0
1989	7	42	6.0	0
1990	5	7	1.4	0
Total	141	611	4.3	5
PS:	1	9	9.0	0

TOP 10
Quarterback Coach Killers

10. Benny Friedman
9. Lamar McHan
8. Randall Cunningham
7. Jake Plummer
6. Daunte Culpepper
5. Aaron Brooks
4. Richard Todd
3. Jeff George
2. Ryan Leaf
1. Michael Vick

Marc Wilson replaced Gifford Nielsen at BYU when Nielsen tore up his knee in 1977 and went 22–4 over the next two and a half years in Utah. Like Nielsen, Wilson was tall and skinny and put up record passing numbers in the BYU pass-happy offense. Oakland made Wilson their top pick in 1980, but Marc flopped in the NFL. He had a decent arm and lasted a decade but tended to guide the ball and either overthrow or underthrow receivers, resulting in interceptions. He was not much of a leader, and some players and coaches questioned his heart, although he did play his last season for a 1–15 team in New England with a broken hand and separated shoulder. The Raiders kept trying to have the youthful Wilson replace the aging Jim Plunkett but then would have to recall Plunkett to try to rescue the season. As it turned out, Wilson lasted only one year more in the Silver and Black than the 39-year-old Plunkett, who ended his career in 1986.

Wade Wilson

QPR 7.5

Height: 6'3" **Weight:** 210 lbs. **Birthdate:** 2/1/1959
College: Texas A&M-Commerce **Draft:** Minnesota 1981-8th
1981, 1983–91 Minnesota Vikings; 1992 Atlanta Falcons; 1993–94 New Orleans Saints; 1995–97 Dallas Cowboys; 1998 Oakland Raiders
Regular Season Record: 36–33, 7 comebacks
Postseason Record: 3–3, no comebacks
Relative Rating: 99%

Passing

Year	G	Comp./Att.	%	Yards	Y/Att.	TD	INT	Rating
1981	3	6/13	46.2	48	3.7	0	2	16.3
1983	1	16/28	57.1	124	4.4	1	2	50.3
1984	8	102/195	52.3	1,019	5.2	5	11	52.5
1985	4	33/60	55.0	404	6.7	3	3	71.8
1986	9	80/143	55.9	1,165	8.1	7	5	84.4
1987	12	140/264	53.0	2,106	8.0	14	13	76.7
1988	14	204/332	61.4	2,746	8.3	15	9	91.5
1989	14	194/362	53.6	2,543	7.0	9	12	70.5
1990	6	82/146	56.2	1,155	7.9	9	8	79.6
1991	5	72/122	59.0	825	6.8	3	10	53.5
1992	9	111/163	68.1	1,366	8.4	13	4	110.1
1993	14	221/388	57.0	2,457	6.3	12	15	70.1
1994	4	20/28	71.4	172	6.1	0	0	87.2
1995	7	38/57	66.7	391	6.9	1	3	70.1
1996	3	8/18	44.4	79	4.4	0	1	34.3
1997	7	12/21	57.1	115	5.5	0	0	72.5
1998	5	52/88	59.1	568	6.5	7	4	85.8
Total	125	1,391/2,428	57.3	17,283	7.1	99	102	75.6
PS:	6	99/185	53.5	1,322	7.1	7	6	75.6

Rushing

Year	Att.	Yards	Avg.	TD
1983	3	-3	-1.0	0
1984	9	30	3.3	0
1986	13	9	0.7	1
1987	41	263	6.4	5
1988	36	136	3.8	2
1989	32	132	4.1	1
1990	12	79	6.6	0
1991	13	33	2.5	0
1992	15	62	4.1	0
1993	31	230	7.4	0
1994	7	15	2.1	0
1995	10	12	1.2	0
1996	4	5	1.3	0
1997	6	-2	-0.3	0
1998	7	24	3.4	0
Total	239	1,025	4.3	9
PS:	23	105	4.6	0

Wade Wilson threw just 99 touchdown passes across a 17-year career in the NFL in which he never played a full year as a starter. Although he was the primary starter in a handful of seasons, Wilson was generally a backup. Wade spent his first six years behind Tommy Kramer before finally edging past Kramer in 1987. Wilson was a smart player who had his own ideas, as indicated from his very visible screaming arguments on

the Minnesota sidelines with offensive coach Bob Schnelker in the late 1980s. From 1987 through 1989, Wade was the Vikings' primary starter and led the team to three straight playoff berths and even the 1987 NFC Championship Game, but he was ordinary in every way. He was gutsy and a hard worker who played despite being diabetic, but he never threw more than 15 touchdown passes in any season, his passer rating mirrored the league average, and his winning percentage was just a bit better than .500.

Wilson fell behind Rich Gannon in 1990 and was cut in 1992 by new coach Denny Green. He hit the road as an itinerant quarterback and drifted from Atlanta to New Orleans to Dallas to Oakland over the next seven years. Wilson went directly into coaching after he retired, and in 2007, as the Cowboys' quarterbacks coach, was suspended by the NFL for five games for buying HGH, a banned substance, to help with his diabetes.

Dick Wood

 QPR 3.5

Height: 6'5" **Weight:** 205 lbs. **Birthdate:** 2/29/1936
College: Auburn **Draft:** Baltimore Colts 1959-12th
1962 San Diego Chargers; 1962 Denver Broncos;
1963–64 New York Jets; 1965 Oakland Raiders; 1966 Miami Dolphins
Regular Season Record: 13–19–2, 1 comeback
Postseason Record: NA
Relative Rating: 87%

Passing

Year	G	Comp./Att.	%	Yards	Y/Att.	TD	INT	Rating
1962	7	41/97	42.3	655	6.8	4	7	49.1
1963	12	160/352	45.5	2,204	6.3	18	19	60.6
1964	13	169/358	47.2	2,298	6.4	17	25	54.9
1965	14	69/157	43.9	1,003	6.4	8	6	66.4
1966	14	83/230	36.1	993	4.3	4	14	30.6
Total	60	522/1,194	43.7	7,153	6.0	51	71	52.9

Rushing

Year	Att.	Yards	Avg.	TD
1962	1	0	0.0	0
1963	7	17	2.4	1
1964	9	6	0.7	1
1965	4	16	4.0	1
1966	5	6	1.2	1
Total	26	45	1.7	4

Dick Wood was the poster child for tall, skinny, clumsy, inept, bomb-throwing quarterbacks. Wood was Joe Namath's predecessor as the Jets' passer with bad knees. Dick had had five knee operations when he came to New York and was even less mobile than Namath. Wood was originally drafted by Weeb Ewbank in Baltimore but never made the Colts. Dick had brief trials with both the Chargers and Broncos in 1962 before Ewbank brought him to New York in 1963. In two years as the Jets' starter, Wood helped the team rise to mediocrity by completing 46 percent of his passes for 35 touchdowns and 44 interceptions. With the arrival of Namath in 1965, Ewbank sent Dick to Oakland to add to Al Davis' collection of inaccurate, big-armed throwers. Wood went to the Dolphins in the expansion draft and became Miami's first quarterback while his daughter served as the mascot of the Dolphin Doll cheerleaders. After a miserable year in which he completed just 36 percent of his passes for four touchdowns and 14 interceptions, Wood retired and spent the next 30 years coaching at both the college and pro level.

Al Woodall was the 1970s version of Dick Wood for the Jets: tall, thin, and strong-armed, with bad knees and without any agility. Woodall left Duke early and played a year of semipro football before the Jets drafted him right after they won the Super Bowl. Woodall replaced Namath in 1970, 1971, and 1973 when Joe went down to season-ending injuries, but Al had knee problems himself in 1973 and 1975. Woodall wanted to start and kept threatening to play out his option. Wide receiver Eddie Bell summarized the difference between Namath and Woodall as, "Joe gives the team confidence, but the team gave Al confidence." In 1976, the Jets drafted Richard Todd and tried to trade Woodall, but there was no interest so he was cut.

David Woodley

Height: 6'2" **Weight:** 210 lbs. **Birthdate:** 10/25/1958
College: LSU **Draft:** Miami 1980-8th
1980–83 Miami Dolphins; 1984–85 Pittsburgh Steelers
Regular Season Record: 34–18–1, 6 comebacks
Postseason Record: 3–2, no comebacks
Relative Rating: 87%

Passing

Year	G	Comp./Att.	%	Yards	Y/Att.	TD	INT	Rating
1980	13	176/327	53.8	1,850	5.7	14	17	63.1
1981	15	191/366	52.2	2,470	6.7	12	13	69.8
1982	9	98/179	54.7	1,080	6.0	5	8	63.5
1983	5	43/89	48.3	528	5.9	3	4	59.6
1984	7	85/156	54.5	1,273	8.2	8	7	79.9
1985	9	94/183	51.4	1,357	7.4	6	14	54.8
Total	58	687/1,300	52.8	8,558	6.6	48	63	65.7
PS:	5	48/81	59.3	645	8.0	5	6	74.4

Rushing

Year	Att.	Yards	Avg.	TD
1980	55	214	3.9	3
1981	63	272	4.3	4
1982	36	207	5.8	2
1983	19	78	4.1	0
1984	11	14	1.3	0
1985	17	71	4.2	2
Total	201	856	4.3	11
PS:	17	101	5.9	1

Al Woodall

Height: 6'5" **Weight:** 205 lbs. **Birthdate:** 12/7/1945
College: Duke **Draft:** New York Jets 1969-2nd
1969–71, 1973–74 New York Jets
Regular Season Record: 5–14, 1 comeback
Postseason Record: NA
Relative Rating: 94%

Passing

Year	G	Comp./Att.	%	Yards	Y/Att.	TD	INT	Rating
1969	4	4/9	44.4	67	7.4	0	2	30.6
1970	10	96/188	51.1	1,265	6.7	9	9	68.7
1971	5	42/97	43.3	395	4.1	0	2	46.5
1973	9	101/201	50.2	1,228	6.1	9	8	67.8
1974	3	3/8	37.5	15	1.9	0	2	6.2
Total	31	246/503	48.9	2,970	5.9	18	23	60.3

Rushing

Year	Att.	Yards	Avg.	TD
1969	4	13	3.3	0
1970	28	110	3.9	0
1971	13	26	2.0	0
1973	13	68	5.2	0
1974	2	-3	-1.5	0
Total	60	214	3.6	0

David Woodley was a running quarterback. When he was a senior at LSU, he threw for eight touchdowns and ran for 14. As a late-round Miami draft pick, Woodley surprised everyone in his rookie season by taking over as starting quarterback for the aging Bob Griese. Coach Don Shula tailored his offense to Woodley's sprint-out passing style and brought in fireman Don Strock to save the day whenever Woodley struggled. The "Woodstrock" combination drove the Dolphins to the playoffs in Woodley's second season and to the Super Bowl in his third. At 24 years old, David was the youngest quarterback to start a Super Bowl to that point.

That Super Bowl was a metaphor for Woodley's career. David's first pass was a 76-yard touchdown to Jimmy Cefalo, but after that fast start, Woodley was just three of 13 for 21 yards and went 0-for-8 in the second half in the loss to Washington. Woodley was the polar opposite of Redskins quarterback Joe Theismann, who loved to talk and loved the spotlight. Woodley was a quiet, unflappable loner who retreated from public life. After the apex of reaching the Super Bowl, though, David's career would only decline.

The Dolphins drafted Dan Marino in 1983, and Woodley quickly fell from starter to third string. A year later, Shula traded him to Pittsburgh, where David shared the job with Mark Malone for two years but was very unhappy. About to play the Chargers in 1985, Woodley called his wife from the locker room to say he was quitting football right there. She had to talk him into playing that day. At the end of the season, he did quit. Although he missed the game and had a tryout with Green Bay in 1987, he did not miss life in the limelight.

Woodley's father had been an alcoholic, and David turned to the bottle to escape his life, too. In 2003 at the age of 44, Woodley died of liver and kidney failure. Of Super Bowl quarterbacks, he died the youngest.

Anthony Wright

QPR 2.5

Height: 6'1" **Weight:** 211 lbs. **Birthdate:** 2/14/1976
College: South Carolina **Draft:** Free agent
2000–01 Dallas Cowboys; 2003, 2005 Baltimore Ravens; 2006 Cincinnati Bengals; 2007 New York Giants
Regular Season Record: 8–11, 3 comebacks
Postseason Record: 0–1, no comebacks
Relative Rating: 84%

Passing

Year	G	Comp./Att.	%	Yards	Y/Att.	TD	INT	Rating
2000	4	22/53	41.5	237	4.5	0	3	31.7
2001	4	48/98	49.0	529	5.4	5	5	61.1
2003	7	94/178	52.8	1,199	6.7	9	8	72.3
2005	9	164/266	61.7	1,582	5.9	6	9	71.7
2006	4	3/3	100.0	31	10.3	0	0	109.7
2007	4	1/7	14.3	12	1.7	0	0	39.6
Total	32	332/605	54.9	3,590	5.9	20	25	66.3
PS:	1	20/37	54.1	214	5.8	1	2	57.7

Rushing

Year	Att.	Yards	Avg.	TD
2000	12	36	3.0	0
2001	17	57	3.4	0
2003	28	73	2.6	0
2005	18	68	3.8	0
2006	4	-12	-3.0	0
2007	1	-1	-1.0	0
Total	80	221	2.8	0
PS:	2	19	9.5	0

Every year, Anthony Wright finds himself in a scramble for a spot as a backup or third quarterback somewhere in the league. Both mistake and injury prone, Wright is an unremarkable backup quarterback. His greatest success came in 2003 when he took over for injured starter Kyle Boller to lead the Ravens to the playoffs by winning five of the last seven games. Wright threw two interceptions in the first-round game, and Baltimore made a quick exit from the postseason. He missed the next season with an injury but returned to Baltimore in 2005 and lost five of seven starts to even out his Ravens record. After a year in Cincinnati, Wright won a Super Bowl ring watching Eli Manning direct the Giants past the Patriots in the 2007 postseason.

Randy Wright

Height: 6'2" **Weight:** 200 lbs. **Birthdate:** 1/12/1961
Wisconsin **Draft:** Green Bay 1984-6th
1984–88 Green Bay Packers
Regular Season Record: 7-25, 2 comebacks
Postseason Record: NA
Relative Rating: 83%

Passing

Year	G	Comp./Att.	%	Yards	Y/Att.	TD	INT	Rating
1984	8	27/62	43.5	310	5.0	2	6	30.4
1985	5	39/74	52.7	552	7.5	2	4	63.6
1986	16	263/492	53.5	3,247	6.6	17	23	66.2
1987	9	132/247	53.4	1,507	6.1	6	11	61.6
1988	8	141/244	57.8	1,490	6.1	4	13	58.9
Total	46	602/1,119	53.8	7,106	6.4	31	57	61.4

Rushing

Year	Att.	Yards	Avg.	TD
1984	8	11	1.4	0
1985	8	8	1.0	0
1986	18	41	2.3	1
1987	13	70	5.4	0
1988	8	43	5.4	2
Total	55	173	3.1	3

Randy Wright threw nearly twice as many interceptions as touchdowns. His .219 winning percentage is second only to Randy Johnson's .214 as the lowest among quarterbacks who started at least 30 games. Wright had losing streaks of six, six, and seven games in his career. He was completely over his head in the NFL and once fainted in the huddle of a game against the Vikings. The only question about his career is why did coaches Forrest Gregg and Lindy Infante give this man 32 starts?

Danny Wuerffel

Height: 6'1" **Weight:** 212 lbs. **Birthdate:** 5/27/1974
College: Florida **Draft:** New Orleans 1997-4th
1997–99 New Orleans Saints; 2000 NFL Europe;
2000 Green Bay Packers; 2001 Chicago Bears; 2002
Washington Redskins
Regular Season Record: 4-6, 2 comebacks
Postseason Record: NA
Relative Rating: 72%

Passing

Year	G	Comp./Att.	%	Yards	Y/Att.	TD	INT	Rating
1997	7	42/91	46.2	518	5.7	4	8	42.3
1998	5	62/119	52.1	695	5.8	5	5	66.3
1999	4	22/48	45.8	191	4.0	0	3	30.8
2000	1	0/0	0.0	0	0.0	0	0	0.0
2001	1	0/0	0.0	0	0.0	0	0	0.0
2002	7	58/92	63.0	719	7.8	3	6	70.9
Total	25	184/350	52.6	2,123	6.1	12	22	56.4

Rushing

Year	Att.	Yards	Avg.	TD
1997	6	26	4.3	0
1998	11	60	5.5	0
1999	2	29	14.5	1
2000	2	-2	-1.0	0
2002	10	76	7.6	0
Total	31	189	6.1	1

Danny Wuerffel was a four-year starter at Florida. In Gainesville, he won a national championship and a Heisman Trophy while throwing 114 touchdown passes. After each touchdown, the religious Wuerffel would clasp his hands together in prayer to celebrate. In the pros, Danny got to clasp his hands only 12 times in six years.

Former Florida coach Steve Spurrier said of Wuerffel, "We learned a lot more from him than he did from us." When the Redskins hired Spurrier in 2002, he brought in Wuerffel—who had already washed out with three teams—to run his fun 'n' gun offense. Danny showed that he knew the offense as well as Spurrier but also proved that he did not have the talent to run it in the NFL. Wuerffel was small and had an inadequate arm. He reached his highest level when he won the World Bowl MVP in 2000 after throwing 25 touchdown passes in NFL Europe.

Because of his intelligence, though, Danny was offered a number of coaching jobs as his playing career was ending. Instead, Wuerffel chose to accept a position with Desire Street Ministries, a faith-based charity in New Orleans, and has worked hard to rebuild the ministry in the wake of the devastation of Hurricane Katrina.

Steve Young

QPR 10.0

Height: 6'2" **Weight:** 215 lbs. **Birthdate:** 10/11/1961

College: BYU **Draft:** Tampa 1984-1st(S)

1984-85 USFL; 1985-86 Tampa Bay Bucs; 1987-99 San Francisco 49ers

Regular Season Record: 94–49, 17 comebacks

Postseason Record: 8–6, 1 comeback

Relative Rating: 127%

Passing

Year	G	Comp./Att.	%	Yards	Y/Att.	TD	INT	Rating
1985	5	72/138	52.2	935	6.8	3	8	56.9
1986	14	195/363	53.7	2,282	6.3	8	13	65.5
1987	8	37/69	53.6	570	8.3	10	0	120.8
1988	11	54/101	53.5	680	6.7	3	3	72.2
1989	10	64/92	69.6	1,001	10.9	8	3	120.8
1990	6	38/62	61.3	427	6.9	2	0	92.6
1991	11	180/279	64.5	2,517	9.0	17	8	101.8
1992	16	268/402	66.7	3,465	8.6	25	7	107.0
1993	16	314/462	68.0	4,023	8.7	29	16	101.5
1994	16	324/461	70.3	3,969	8.6	35	10	112.8
1995	11	299/447	66.9	3,200	7.2	20	11	92.3
1996	12	214/316	67.7	2,410	7.6	14	6	97.2
1997	15	241/356	67.7	3,029	8.5	19	6	104.7
1998	15	322/517	62.3	4,170	8.1	36	12	101.1
1999	3	45/84	53.6	446	5.3	3	4	60.9
Total	169	2,667/4,149	64.3	33,124	8.0	232	107	96.8
PS:	20	292/471	62.0	3,326	7.1	20	13	85.8

Steve Young in the Clutch: In a back-and-forth playoff game with the Packers on January 3, 1999, Steve Young started the 49ers' final possession at his own 24 with 1:58 to play. Young drove the 49ers to the Packers' 25 and then with three seconds to play hit Terrell Owens between three defenders for the game-winning score with three seconds left. It was the only time Young ever beat Brett Favre.

Rushing

Year	Att.	Yards	Avg.	TD
1985	40	233	5.8	1
1986	74	425	5.7	5
1987	26	190	7.3	1
1988	27	184	6.8	1
1989	38	126	3.3	2
1990	15	159	10.6	0
1991	66	415	6.3	4
1992	76	537	7.1	4
1993	69	407	5.9	2
1994	58	293	5.1	7
1995	50	250	5.0	3
1996	52	310	6.0	4
1997	50	199	4.0	3
1998	70	454	6.5	6
1999	11	57	5.2	0
Total	722	4,239	5.9	43
PS:	96	535	5.6	7

Steve Young's football career was an exercise in delayed gratification that would have tried the patience of a Buddhist monk. Leaving BYU in 1984, the left-handed descendant of Brigham Young signed an annuitized $40 million contract with the Los Angeles Express but soon found that no one in L.A. actually cared about having a third professional football team in town. The raw Young threw just 16 touchdowns to 22 interceptions in two seasons in front of sparse crowds before the USFL folded.

Unfortunately for Young, Tampa held his draft rights, and Steve spent two frustrating 2–14 seasons with the Bucs. New coach Ray Perkins drafted Vinny Testaverde in 1987 and traded Young to the 49ers for second- and fourth-round picks. Steve would never play on another losing team, but for a while had to wonder if he would ever play. Behind Joe Montana, Young got to start just 10 games in four years but threw 23 touchdowns to just six

The greatest left-handed quarterback in NFL history, Steve Young, near the end of his career in 1998.

interceptions while earning two Super Bowl rings as the best backup in football. After Montana was seriously injured in the 1990 playoffs, Young finally got a chance to start in 1991 at the age of 30.

Although some 49er fans seemed to resent Young and prefer backup Steve Bono, Young quickly established that he was the greatest running quarterback in history. Steve was even better than Roger Staubach at combining his great running talents with superb passing efficiency. Young was unerringly accurate as a passer. He retired as the all-time leader in passer rating and was 27 percent better than the league average in that for his career. Young's six passing titles are equaled

Steve Young's Signature Play: On October 30, 1988, in relief of an injured Joe Montana, Steve Young dropped back to pass from midfield trailing Minnesota 21–17 with 1:58 to play. Finding no one open, Young started to run and both eluded and bounced off tacklers down to the five where he stumbled the last few yards for the 49-yard winning touchdown run.

Steve Young led all quarterbacks in rushing touchdowns three times and scored just one touchdown fewer than all-time leader Otto Graham.

only by Sammy Baugh. He led the NFL in completion percentage five times, yards per pass five times, and touchdown passes four times. As a runner, Steve topped all quarterbacks in rushing yards four times and in rushing average four times. He is second only to Randall Cunningham with 4,239 yards rushing and to just Otto Graham with 43 touchdowns in the regular season; in the postseason, Young ran for more yards, 535, and more touchdowns, seven, than anyone.

Those statistics also translated into winning. The 49ers went to three straight NFC championships before Steve finally reached the Super Bowl, where his victorious six-touchdown performance removed all doubt as to how great a quarterback he was. In the next three seasons, Young and the 49ers were topped in the playoffs each year by Brett Favre's Packers but finally got the best of Green Bay in 1998 when Young's last-second touchdown pass to Terrell Owens won the first-round game. It would be his last postseason victory. Young was tackled hard by Aeneas Williams in the third game of the 1999 season and suffered his third concussion in four years. At age 38, Young decided to retire, although his former offensive coordinators, Mike Shanahan and Mike Holmgren, were courting him to come to Denver or Seattle respectively.

Looking back, Young's 49ers scored 31 percent more points than league average, while Montana's 49ers outscored the league by 20 percent, although Joe won four titles to Steve's one. In retirement, Young has gotten married, had children, earned a law degree, and worked for ESPN. He and his old rival, Joe Montana, also seem to have reached the warm relationship between formerly intense competitors that can occur only after the struggle is over.

Steve Young's Five Highest Honors
5. Selected to seven Pro Bowls.
4. Seven-time All-Pro and three-time consensus All-Pro.
3. Super Bowl XXIX MVP.
2. 1992 and 1994 Player of the Year.
1. Elected to the Pro Football Hall of Fame in 2005.

The Five Quarterbacks Most Similar to Steve Young
5. Randall Cunningham
4. Archie Manning
3. Johnny Lujack
2. Tobin Rote
1. Mark Brunell

Steve Young's Five Top Touchdown Targets
5. J.J. Stokes, 13 TDs
4. Brent Jones, 22 TDs
3. John Taylor, 23 TDs
2. Terrell Owens, 24 TDs
1. Jerry Rice, 86 TDs

Steve Young's Five Toughest Rivals
5. Young was 11–6 against the Falcons in the regular season and 0–1 in the playoffs.
4. Young was 13–1 against the Rams.
3. Young was 12–4 against the Saints.
2. Young was 3–2 against the Cowboys in the regular season and 1–2 in the playoffs.
1. Young was 0–5 against the Packers in the regular season and 1–3 in the playoffs.

Five Random Steve Young Statistics
5. Young played for four head coaches.
4. Young's teams outscored the league average by 31 percent.
3. Young threw for four touchdowns nine times.
2. Young threw for over 300 yards 28 times and more than 400 three times.
1. Young led the league in completion percentage five times, touchdown passes four times, yards per attempt five times and passer rating six times.

Vince Young

QPR 4.5

Height: 6'5" **Weight:** 230 lbs. **Birthdate:** 5/18/1983
College: Texas **Draft:** Tennessee 2006-1st
2006–08 Tennessee Titans
Regular Season Record: 18–11, 5 comebacks
Postseason Record: 0–1, no comebacks
Relative Rating: 86%

Passing

Year	G	Comp./Att.	%	Yards	Y/Att.	TD	INT	Rating
2006	15	184/357	51.5	2,199	6.2	12	13	66.7
2007	15	238/382	62.3	2,546	6.7	9	17	71.1
2008	3	22/36	61.1	219	6.1	1	2	64.5
Total	33	444/775	57.3	4,964	6.4	22	32	68.8
PS:	1	16/29	55.2	138	4.8	0	1	53.5

Rushing

Year	Att.	Yards	Avg.	TD
2006	83	552	6.7	7
2007	93	395	4.2	3
2008	8	27	3.4	0
Total	184	974	5.3	10
PS:	2	12	6.0	0

Vince Young peaked in college. How could anyone ever top his amazing performance in his second Rose Bowl when he threw for 257 yards and ran for 200 in willing Texas over USC for the 2005 national championship?

The next year, the fast and powerful quarterback was playing in Tennessee, where he took over as the starter in October of his rookie season. Young drove the Titans to the playoffs on the strength of a league-leading five fourth-quarter game-winning drives, but he was far from a flawless field general. His sidearm passing delivery is unorthodox, and Vince is not always very accurate. He is still learning to read defenses and throws interceptions. What's more troubling about Young's future is his mind-set.

After his rookie season Young was quoted as saying he had considered quitting the game because, "It was crazy being an NFL quarterback. It wasn't fun anymore. All of the fun was out of it. All of the excitement was gone. All I was doing was worrying about things." Whether he has the mental toughness to succeed as an NFL quarterback is an open question. Young took a step backward in his second year and then reacted badly when the fans started to boo him after interceptions. At the outset of 2008, there were reports that he didn't want to return to the field after throwing a second interception in the opener against Jacksonville. When he did return, he hurt his leg almost immediately and was replaced by Kerry Collins. Coach Jeff Fisher stuck with Collins even after Young was healthy again, as the Longhorn hero from three years ago became the forgotten man in Tennessee during the Titans' playoff run in 2008.

Vince Young led all quarterbacks in rushing touchdowns with six in 2006 and in rushing yards with 395 in 2007.

Eric Zeier

QPR 3.0

Height: 6'1"   **Weight:** 214 lbs.   **Birthdate:** 9/6/1972
College: Georgia   **Draft:** Cleveland 1995-3rd
1995 Cleveland Browns; 1996–98 Baltimore Ravens;
1999-00 Tampa Bay Bucs
Regular Season Record: 4–8, 1 comeback
Postseason Record: NA
Relative Rating: 95%

Passing

Year	G	Comp./Att.	%	Yards	Y/Att.	TD	INT	Rating
1995	7	82/161	50.9	864	5.4	4	9	51.9
1996	1	10/21	47.6	97	4.6	1	1	57.0
1997	5	67/116	57.8	958	8.3	7	1	101.1
1998	10	107/181	59.1	1,312	7.2	4	3	82.0
1999	2	32/55	58.2	270	4.9	0	1	63.4
2000	3	3/3	100.0	19	6.3	0	0	93.1
Total	28	301/537	56.1	3,520	6.6	16	15	74.4

Rushing

Year	Att.	Yards	Avg.	TD
1995	15	80	5.3	0
1996	2	8	4.0	0
1997	10	17	1.7	0
1998	11	17	1.5	0
1999	3	7	2.3	0
2000	2	-2	-1.0	0
Total	43	127	3.0	0

Eric Zeier was a rookie in the Browns' final season before moving to Baltimore to become the Ravens. With the Browns, Zeier replaced starter Vinny Testaverde to beat the Bengals in his first start. Eric then went nine quarters over the next three games without leading the offense to a touchdown and was benched for Testaverde. Zeier watched the final game in Cleveland's Municipal Stadium from the sidelines that year, but two years later he again replaced Vinny as the starter at the end of 1997 and threw three touchdown passes in the final game in Baltimore's Memorial Stadium. That won him a congratulatory handshake from Johnny Unitas, a genuine brush with greatness for a generally inept game manager. Zeier finished his career as a backup to Trent Dilfer and Shaun King in Tampa.

TOP 10
Quarterbacks Who Followed Legends

10. Dan Fouts followed Johnny Unitas in San Diego.
9. Brad Johnson followed Warren Moon in Minnesota.
8. Tommy Kramer followed Fran Tarkenton in Minnesota.
7. John Brodie followed Y.A. Tittle in San Francisco.
6. Johnny Lujack followed Sid Luckman in Chicago.
5. Jeff Garcia followed Steve Young in San Francisco.
4. Danny White followed Roger Staubach in Dallas.
3. Billy Kilmer followed Sonny Jurgensen in Washington.
2. Norm Van Brocklin followed Bob Waterfield in Los Angeles.
1. Steve Young followed Joe Montana in San Francisco.

Roy Zimmerman

QPR 6.0

Height: 6'0"   **Weight:** 190 lbs.   **Birthdate:** 2/20/1918
College: San Jose State   **Draft:** Washington 1940-7th
1940–42 Washington Redskins; 1943–46 Philadelphia Eagles; 1947 Detroit Lions; 1948 Boston Yanks
Regular Season Record: 26–23–3 est., 2 comebacks
Postseason Record: 0–0, no comebacks
Relative Rating: 101%

Passing

Year	G	Comp./Att.	%	Yards	Y/Att.	TD	INT	Rating
1940	6	4/12	33.3	53	4.4	0	3	8.7
1941	9	0/1	0.0	0	0.0	0	0	39.6
1942	7	2/10	20.0	13	1.3	0	2	0.0
1943	10	43/124	34.7	846	6.8	9	17	44.0
1944	10	39/105	37.1	785	7.5	8	10	50.0
1945	10	67/127	52.8	991	7.8	9	8	75.9
1946	11	41/79	51.9	597	7.6	4	8	54.1
1947	12	57/138	41.3	867	6.3	7	9	52.4
1948	9	46/107	43.0	649	6.1	7	13	45.4
Total	84	299/703	42.5	4,801	6.8	44	70	46.7
PS:	1	3/12	25.0	34	2.8	0	2	0.0

Rushing

Year	Att.	Yards	Avg.	TD
1940	31	127	4.1	0
1941	20	54	2.7	0
1942	12	56	4.7	0
1943	33	-41	-1.2	1
1944	26	-84	-3.2	2
1945	29	-11	-0.4	1
1946	23	43	1.9	1
1947	13	28	2.2	1
1948	13	72	5.5	0
Total	200	244	1.2	6
PS:	1	2	2.0	0

Roy Zimmerman was a complete football player in the days of two-way football. He was a good place-kicker and a decent punter, and as a defensive back he intercepted 19 passes, including a league-leading seven in 1945. Roy was a fine ball handler, not much of a runner, and just about average as a passer for his time. He spent his first three years as the third-string tailback behind Sammy Baugh and Frankie Filchock and got to throw 12 passes in the 73–0 championship game loss to Chicago in his rookie season. Zimmerman got into a salary dispute with Washington owner George Preston Marshall that turned nasty in 1943. Greasy Neale swooped in and acquired Zimmerman to play T-formation quarterback in Philadelphia while Tommy Thompson was in the service. Zimmerman led the Eagles to their first three winning seasons ever from 1943 through 1945. With Thompson back in 1946, though, Zimmerman lost his job because Tommy was a better passer and more inspiring leader. Zimmerman was best at the deep pass, and his 16.1 yards per completion average is eighth best of all time. The Eagles traded Roy to Detroit for two linemen in 1947, and he and Clyde LeForce became the first T-formation quarterbacks for the Lions. The next year, Detroit sent Zimmerman to the Boston Yanks for John Grigas. Roy retired after one year in Boston to take up with a fast-pitch softball outfit as a pitcher and was very successful in his second career.

Jim Zorn

QPR 7.0

Height: 6'2" **Weight:** 200 lbs. **Birthdate:** 5/10/1953
College: Cal. Poly-Pomona **Draft:** Free agent
1976–84 Seattle Seahawks; 1985 Green Bay Packers;
1986 CFL; 1987 Tampa Bay Bucs
Regular Season Record: 44–62, 13 comebacks
Postseason Record: 0–0, no comebacks
Relative Rating: 93%

Passing

Year	G	Comp./Att.	%	Yards	Y/Att.	TD	INT	Rating
1976	14	208/439	47.4	2,571	5.9	12	27	49.5
1977	10	104/251	41.4	1,687	6.7	16	19	54.3
1978	16	248/443	56.0	3,283	7.4	15	20	72.1
1979	16	285/505	56.4	3,661	7.2	20	18	77.7
1980	16	276/488	56.6	3,346	6.9	17	20	72.3
1981	13	236/397	59.4	2,788	7.0	13	9	82.4
1982	9	126/245	51.4	1,540	6.3	7	11	61.9
1983	16	103/205	50.2	1,166	5.7	7	7	64.8
1984	16	7/17	41.2	80	4.7	0	2	16.4
1985	13	56/123	45.5	794	6.5	4	6	57.4
1987	1	20/36	55.6	199	5.5	0	2	48.3
Total	140	1,669/3,149	53.0	21,115	6.7	111	141	67.3
PS:	2	14/28	50.0	134	4.8	2	2	57.7

Rushing

Year	Att.	Yards	Avg.	TD
1976	52	246	4.7	4
1977	25	141	5.6	1
1978	59	290	4.9	6
1979	46	279	6.1	2
1980	44	214	4.9	1
1981	30	140	4.7	1
1982	15	113	7.5	1
1983	30	71	2.4	1
1984	7	-3	-0.4	0
1985	10	9	0.9	0
1987	4	4	1.0	0
Total	322	1,504	4.7	17
PS:	0	0	0.0	0

The left-handed Jim Zorn is a football lifer who has been out of the game for only one year since he left college in 1975. That year, Zorn was an undrafted free agent in the Cowboys' training camp but was the last player cut when Dallas acquired versatile back Preston Pearson. Before the expansion draft in 1976, though, the new Seattle Seahawks signed the former small-college star, and Jim became the first Seahawk quarterback that fall. In Seattle, Zorn teamed up with another unheralded rookie, Steve Largent, to form one of the most potent passing combinations in the league. Zorn would connect with Largent for 43 touchdowns over the next nine years.

Zorn set a rookie record with 2,571 yards passing in 1976 and became just the third quarterback after Norm Snead and Joe Namath to throw for more than 10,000 yards in his first four seasons. Jim was a slippery scrambler who threw best on the run. He had a very quick release but was also inconsistent and threw a lot more interceptions than touchdowns. He was beaten out by Dave Krieg in 1983 and lasted just one more year in Seattle as a backup. Zorn started five games for the Packers in 1985 and then went to Canada and threw 25 passes for the Winnipeg Blue Bombers in 1986. Zorn returned to the NFL as a replacement player for Tampa during the 1987 strike to finish his playing career. He then went into college coaching for the next nine years. Jim resurfaced in the NFL as a coach with Seattle in 1997 and finally got his chance to be a head coach with the Redskins in 2008.

TOP 10
Regular-Season Last-Play Game-Winning Touchdown Passes

10. Byron Leftwich to Ernest Wilford for seven yards in a 13–10 Jacksonville win over Buffalo on September 12, 2004

9. Jake Delhomme to Dante Rosario for 14 yards in a 26–24 Carolina win over San Diego on September 6, 2008

8. Joe Montana to Jerry Rice for 25 yards in a 27–26 San Francisco win over Cincinnati on September 20, 1987

7. Dave Krieg to Paul Skansi for 25 yards in a 17–16 Seattle win over Kansas City on November 11, 1990. Krieg was sacked by Derrick Thomas seven times that day.

6. Josh McCown to Nathan Poole for 28 yards in an 18–17 Arizona win over Minnesota on December 28, 2003. The fourth-down pass kept the Vikings out of the playoffs.

5. John Elway to Rod Smith for 43 yards in a 38–31 Denver win over Washington on September 17, 1995. It was Smith's first NFL catch.

4. Tommy Kramer to Ahmad Rashad for 46 yards in a 28–23 Minnesota win over Cleveland on December 14, 1980.

3. Steve Bartkowski to Billy "White Shoes" Johnson for 47 yards on a play called "Big Ben Right" in a 28–24 Atlanta win over San Francisco on November 20, 1983. Johnson caught the ball at the 7-yard line and had to slither and dive into the end zone. On November 12, 1978, Bartkowski connected with Alfred Jackson for a 57-yard Hail Mary also, but there were 19 seconds left in that game.

2. Tim Couch to Kevin Johnson for 56 yards in a 21–16 Cleveland win over New Orleans on October 31, 1999. It was the first win for the newly re-created Browns franchise. Couch had a second Hail Mary of 50 yards to Quincy Morgan to beat Jacksonville on December 8, 2002.

1. Earl Morrall to Jim Gibbons for 65 yards in a 20–15 Detroit win over Baltimore on December 4, 1960. With the Colts focusing solely on the Lion wide receivers, Morrall hit his tight end across the middle, and Gibbons raced into the end zone.

Appendix
More Starting Quarterbacks

Quarterbacks who have started fewer than 10 games since 1950 are listed by most wins and then by fewest losses. Quarterbacks from 1987 replacement-player strike games are indicated with an (r). The second list is of T-formation quarterbacks from the 1940s. Also included there are the Bears' two primary quarterbacks from the early 1930s, Carl Brumbaugh and Keith Molesworth.

Quarterback	Wins	Losses	Ties	%
Mike Kruczek	6	1	0	.857
Jason Garrett	6	3	0	.667
Norris Weese	5	2	0	.714
George Mira	5	3	0	.625
Tom Dublinski	4	1	0	.800
Joe Gilliam	4	2	1	.643
Don Hollas	4	4	0	.500
Jamie Martin	4	4	0	.500
Mike Rae	4	4	0	.500
Tom Owen	4	5	0	.444
John Stofa	4	5	0	.444
Ed Rubbert (r)	3	0	0	1.000
Travis Tidwell	3	0	1	.875
Bill Mackrides	3	1	0	.750
Craig Penrose	3	1	0	.750
Craig Krenzel	3	2	0	.600
Gary Kubiak	3	2	0	.600
Tom Yewcic	3	2	0	.600
M.C. Reynolds	3	3	0	.500
Stoney Case	3	3	0	.500
George Izo	3	3	0	.500
Andre Ware	3	3	0	.500
Bob Williams	3	4	0	.429
Scott Bull	3	4	0	.429
Max Choboian	3	4	0	.429
Scott Zolak	3	4	0	.429
Kellen Clemens	3	5	0	.375
Koy Detmer	3	5	0	.375
Todd Marinovich	3	5	0	.375
Oliver Luck	3	6	0	.333
Mike Moroski	3	6	0	.333
Larry Lawrence	2	0	0	1.000
Clint Longley	2	0	0	1.000
Mike Hohensee (r)	2	0	0	1.000
Rick Neuheisel (r)	2	0	0	1.000
Matt Moore	2	1	0	.667
Ken Karcher (r)	2	1	0	.667
Brent Pease (r)	2	1	0	.667
Alan Risher (r)	2	1	0	.667
Bobby Clatterbuck	2	2	0	.500
Quinn Gray	2	2	0	.500
Steve Pisarkiewicz	2	2	0	.500
Mark Vlasic	2	2	0	.500
Kevin Sweeney (r)	2	2	0	.500
Marlin Briscoe	2	3	0	.400
Tony Graziani	2	3	0	.400
Dan McGwire	2	3	0	.400
Todd Philcox	2	3	0	.400
Tom Ramsey	2	3	0	.400
Anthony Dilweg	2	5	0	.286
Jesse Freitas Jr.	2	5	0	.286
Babe Laufenberg	2	5	0	.286
Kim McQuilken	2	5	0	.286
T.J. Rubley	2	5	0	.286
Ron Smith	2	5	0	.286
George Wilson	2	5	0	.286
J.T. O'Sullivan	2	6	0	.250
Andrew Walter	2	7	0	.222
Glenn Foley	2	7	0	.222
Jerry Golsteyn	2	7	0	.222
Ed Luther	2	7	0	.222
Bruce Mathison	2	7	0	.222
Sam Wyche	2	7	0	.222
Bob Brodhead	1	0	0	1.000
Glenn Carano	1	0	0	1.000
Scott Covington	1	0	0	1.000
Jim Druckenmiller	1	0	0	1.000
Drew Henson	1	0	0	1.000
Dick Jamieson	1	0	0	1.000
Cliff Lewis	1	0	0	1.000
Tom Matte	1	0	0	1.000
Steve Matthews	1	0	0	1.000
Cliff Olander	1	0	0	1.000

Player	W	L	T	Pct
Mike Kelley (r)	1	0	0	1.000
Brian McClure (r)	1	0	0	1.000
Don Gault	1	0	0	1.000
Jim Cason	1	0	0	1.000
Dave Walter (r)	1	1	0	.500
Randy Duncan	1	1	0	.500
Hunter Enis	1	1	0	.500
Tom Greene	1	1	0	.500
Gary Keithley	1	1	0	.500
Jim Powers	1	1	0	.500
Troy Smith	1	1	0	.500
Clint Stoerner	1	1	0	.500
Bob Bleier (r)	1	1	0	.500
Jeff Christensen (r)	1	1	0	.500
Shawn Halloran (r)	1	1	0	.500
Larry Cipa	1	2	0	.333
Randy Dean	1	2	0	.333
Bill Demory	1	2	0	.333
Tom Flick	1	2	0	.333
Brady Quinn	1	2	0	.333
Todd Hons (r)	1	2	0	.333
Rick Arrington	1	3	1	.300
Tim Van Galder	1	3	1	.300
Lee Grosscup	1	3	0	.250
Richie Lucas	1	3	0	.250
Dave Mays	1	3	0	.250
Steve Myer	1	3	0	.250
Bucky Richardson	1	3	0	.250
Kyle Mackey (r)	1	3	0	.250
Kurt Kittner	1	3	0	.250
Edd Hargett	1	5	1	.214
Jerry Rhome	1	5	1	.214
Wayne Clark	1	4	0	.200
Joe Dufek	1	4	0	.200
Tim Hasselbeck	1	4	0	.200
June Jones	1	4	0	.200
Ron Vanderkelen	1	4	0	.200
Jim Root	1	6	1	.188
Todd Bouman	1	5	0	.167
Jim DelGaizo	1	5	0	.167
Terry Nofsinger	1	5	0	.167
Jonathan Quinn	1	5	0	.167
Luke McCown	1	6	0	.143
Tom Sherman	1	6	0	.143
Cleo Lemon	1	7	0	.125
Gary Wood	1	8	0	.111
Eddie Wilson	0	0	2	.500
Al Pastrana	0	2	1	.167
Terry Baker	0	1	0	0.00
Brock Berlin	0	1	0	0.00
Mike Buck	0	1	0	0.00
Henry Burris	0	1	0	0.00
Reggie Collier	0	1	0	0.00
Ogden Compton	0	1	0	0.00
Will Cureton	0	1	0	0.00
Eagle Day	0	1	0	0.00
Parnell Dickinson	0	1	0	0.00
Randy Fasani	0	1	0	0.00
Joe Francis	0	1	0	0.00
Arnold Galiffa	0	1	0	0.00
Scotty Glacken	0	1	0	0.00
Leo Hart	0	1	0	0.00
Stan Heath	0	1	0	0.00
John Huarte	0	1	0	0.00
John Hufnagel	0	1	0	0.00
David Humm	0	1	0	0.00
Jarious Jackson	0	1	0	0.00
John Jones	0	1	0	0.00
Tom Kennedy	0	1	0	0.00
Matt Kofler	0	1	0	0.00
Tom Landry	0	1	0	0.00
Gary Lane	0	1	0	0.00
Rusty Lisch	0	1	0	0.00
Mike Loyd	0	1	0	0.00
Terry Luck	0	1	0	0.00
Matt Lytle	0	1	0	0.00
Matt Mauck	0	1	0	0.00
Don Milan	0	1	0	0.00
Ron Miller	0	1	0	0.00
Ed Miodszewski	0	1	0	0.00
Bill Musgrave	0	1	0	0.00
John Navarre	0	1	0	0.00
Steve Sloan	0	1	0	0.00
Jim Still	0	1	0	0.00
Erik Wilhelm	0	1	0	0.00
John Witkowski	0	1	0	0.00
Steve Bradley (r)	0	1	0	0.00
Adrian Breen (r)	0	1	0	0.00
Mike Busch (r)	0	1	0	0.00
Jim Crocicchia (r)	0	1	0	0.00
Sammy Garza (r)	0	1	0	0.00
Doug Hudson (r)	0	1	0	0.00
Dan Manucci (r)	0	1	0	0.00
Willie Totten (r)	0	1	0	0.00
Jeff Van Raaphorst (r)	0	1	0	0.00
Tom Keane	0	1	0	0.00
Perry Moss	0	1	0	0.00
Don Breaux	0	2	0	0.00
Cary Conklin	0	2	0	0.00
Will Furrer	0	2	0	0.00
Brad Goebel	0	2	0	0.00
Neil Graff	0	2	0	0.00
Galen Hall	0	2	0	0.00
Mike Kirkland	0	2	0	0.00
Bruce Lemmerman	0	2	0	0.00
Dennis Morrison	0	2	0	0.00
Ray Nagel	0	2	0	0.00
Doug Nussmeier	0	2	0	0.00
Cody Pickett	0	2	0	0.00
Dave Ragone	0	2	0	0.00
Frank Seurer	0	2	0	0.00
Marques Tuiasosopo	0	2	0	0.00
Tommy Wade	0	2	0	0.00
Bob Waters	0	2	0	0.00
Guido Merkens (r)	0	2	0	0.00
David Norrie (r)	0	2	0	0.00

Matt Stevens (r)	0	2	0	0.00
Scott Tinsley (r)	0	2	0	0.00
Chuck Ortman	0	2	0	0.00
Tommy Mont	0	2	0	0.00
George Taliaferro	0	3	0	0.00
John Rauch	0	3	0	0.00
Carlos Brown	0	3	0	0.00
Jeff Carlson	0	3	0	0.00
Dennis Claridge	0	3	0	0.00
Blair Kiel	0	3	0	0.00
Moses Moreno	0	3	0	0.00
Jesse Palmer	0	3	0	0.00
Ed Rutkowski	0	3	0	0.00
Kay Stephenson	0	3	0	0.00
Peter Tom Willis	0	3	0	0.00
Spergon Wynn	0	3	0	0.00
John Beck	0	4	0	0.00
Jeb Blount	0	4	0	0.00
Gale Gilbert	0	4	0	0.00
Randy Hedberg	0	4	0	0.00
George Herring	0	4	0	0.00
Brock Huard	0	4	0	0.00
Jim LeClair	0	4	0	0.00
Larry Rakestraw	0	4	0	0.00
Scott Secules	0	4	0	0.00
Dewey Warren	0	4	0	0.00
Buddy Humphrey	0	5	0	0.00
Pat Sullivan	0	4	0	0.00
Art Schlichter	0	6	0	0.00
Gary Marangi	0	7	0	0.00
Dan Orlovsky	0	7	0	0.00
Brodie Croyle	0	8	0	0.00

More 1940s T-formation Quarterbacks:

Ermal Allen
Len Barnum
Carl Brumbaugh
Young Bussey
George Cafego
Ernie Case
Paul Collins
Boley Dancewicz
Bob DeMoss
Charley Eikenberg
Tom Farris
John Galvin
Bill Glenn
Scott Gudmundson
Stan Heath
Gil Johnson
John Ksionzyk
Cliff Lewis
Jonny Long
Howie Maley
Gene Malinowski
Joe Margucci

Keith Molesworth
Tommy Mont
Perry Moss
Steve Nemeth
Vince Oliver
Albie Reisz
Paul Rickards
Gene Ronzani
Frank Sachse
Nick Sacrinty
Allie Sherman
Bob Snyder
Leo Stasica
Jim Still
Ken Stofer
George Terlep
Bev Wallace
Foster Watkins
Larry Weldon
Jim Youel

Comments on these quarterbacks can be found at my website: www.rci.rutgers.edu/~maxymuk/home/home.html.

Bibliography

Books

Allen, George, with Ben Olan. *Pro Football's 100 Greatest Players: Rating the Stars of Past and Present.* Indianapolis: Bobbs-Merrill, 1982.

Ashe, Arthur. *A Hard Road to Glory: A History of the African-American Athlete.* 3 vols. New York: Warner Books, 1988.

Carroll, Bob. *When the Grass Was Real: Unitas, Brown, Lombardi, Sayers, Butkus, Namath and All the Rest: The Ten Best Years of Pro Football.* New York: Simon and Schuster, 1993.

Carroll, Bob, Michael Gershman, David Neft, and John Thorn. *Total Quarterbacks.* New York: Total Sports, 1998.

——. *Total Football: The Official Encyclopedia of the National Football League.* New York: Harper Collins, 1999.

Carroll, Bob, Pete Palmer, and John Thorn. *The Hidden Game of Football: The Next Edition.* New York: Total Sports, 1998.

Cavanaugh, Jack. *Giants Among Men: How Robustelli, Huff, Gifford and the Giants Made New York a Football Town and Changed the NFL.* New York: Random House, 2008

Cohen, Richard M., Jordan A. Deutsch, Roland T. Johnson, and David S. Neft. *The Scrapbook History of Pro Football.* Indianapolis, IN: Bobbs-Merrill, 1976.

Cope, Myron. *The Game That Was: An Illustrated Account of the Tumultuous Early Days of Pro Football.* New York: Crowell, 1974.

Curran, Bob. *Pro Football's Rag Days.* Englewood Cliffs, NJ: Prentice-Hall, 1969.

Daly, Dan, and Bob O'Donnell. *The Pro Football Chronicle: The Complete (Well Almost) Record of the Best Players, the Greatest Photos, the Hardest Hits, the Biggest Scandals, and the Funniest Stories in Pro Football.* New York: Collier Books, 1990.

Fleder, Rob, ed. *Sports Illustrated: The Football Book.* New York: Time Inc. Home Entertainment, 2005.

Garraty, John A., and Mark C. Carnes, general editors. *American National Biography.* New York: Oxford University Press, 1999.

Gillette, Gary, Matt Silverman, Pete Palmer, Ken Pullis, and Sean Lahman. *The ESPN Pro Football Encyclopedia.* New York: Sterling, 2007.

Herskowitz, Mickey. *The Golden Age of Pro Football: NFL Football in the 1950s.* Dallas, TX: Taylor Publishing, 1990.

——. *The Quarterbacks: The Uncensored Truth About the Men in the Pocket.* New York: Morrow, 1990.

King, Peter. *Football: A History of the Professional Game.* New York: Bishop Books [Time. Inc. Home Entertainment], 1997.

——. *Greatest Quarterbacks.* New York: Bishop Books [Time. Inc. Home Entertainment], 1999.

Leuthner, Stuart. *Iron Men: Bucko, Crazy Legs, and the Boys Recall the Golden Days of Professional Football.* New York: Doubleday, 1988.

Maule, Tex. *The Game: The Official Picture History of the NFL and AFL.* New York: Random House, 1967.

Maxymuk, John. *Strong Arm Tactics: A History and Statistical Analysis of the Professional Quarterback.* Jefferson, NC: McFarland, 2008.

Miller, Jeff. *Going Long: The Wild 10-Year Saga of the Renegade American Football League in the Words of Those Who Lived It.* New York: Contemporary Books, 2003.

Neft, David S., Richard M. Cohen, and Richard Korch. *The Football Encyclopedia: The Complete History of Professional Football from 1892 to the Present.* New York: St. Martin's, 1994.

Olderman, Murray. *The Pro Quarterback.* Englewood Cliffs, NJ: Prentice-Hall, 1966.

Peterson, Robert. *Pigskin: The Early Years of Pro Football*. New York: Oxford University Press, 1997.

Porter, David L., ed. *Biographical Dictionary of American Sports: Football*. New York: Greenwood Press, 1987.

——. *Biographical Dictionary of American Sports: 1989-1992 Supplement for Baseball, Football, Basketball, and Other Sports*. New York: Greenwood Press, 1992.

——. *Biographical Dictionary of American Sports: 1992-1995 Supplement for Baseball, Football, Basketball, and Other Sports*. New York: Greenwood Press, 1995.

Rand, Jonathan. *The Gridiron's Greatest Quarterbacks*. Champaign, IL: Sports Pub, 2004.

Rhoden, William C. *Third and a Mile: The Trials and Triumph of the Black Quarterback*. New York: ESPN Books, 2007.

Riffenburgh, Beau. *Great Ones: NFL Quarterbacks from Baugh to Montana*. New York: Viking, 1989.

Ross, Charles K. *Outside the Lines: African Americans and the Integration of the National Football League*. New York: New York University Press, 1999.

Schaap, Dick. *Quarterbacks Have All the Fun: The Good Life and Hard Times of Bart, Johnny, Joe, Francis, and Other Great Quarterbacks*. Chicago: Playboy Press, 1974.

75 Seasons: The Complete Story of the National Football League 1920-1995. Atlanta, GA: Turner Publishing Inc., 1994.

Smith, Myron J. *Pro Football: The Official Pro Football Hall of Fame Bibliography*. Westport, CT: Greenwood Press, 1993.

Smith, Ron. *The Sporting News Selects Football's 100 Greatest Players: A Celebration of the 20th Century's Best*. St. Louis, MO: Sporting News, 1999.

——. *Sporting News Books Presents Pro Football's Heroes of the Hall*. St. Louis, MO: Sporting News, 2003.

——. *The Sporting News Selects Pro Football's Greatest Quarterbacks*. St. Louis, MO: Sporting News, 2005.

Whittingham, Richard. *What a Game They Played*. New York: Harper and Row, 1974.

Zimmerman, Paul. *The New Thinking Man's Guide to Pro Football*. New York: Simon and Schuster, 1984.

Newspapers and Magazines

The following were checked extensively:

Chicago Tribune

Los Angeles Times

New York Times

Sport

Sports Illustrated

Washington Post

Websites

College Football Hall of Fame
http://collegefootball.org/

Current Team Histories http://www.jt-sw.com/football/pro/teams.nsf

DatabaseFootball.com
http://www.databasefootball.com/

Draft History http://www.drafthistory.com/index.php

NFL.com http://www.nfl.com/

Pro Football Hall of Fame
http://www.profootballhof.com/

Pro-Football-Reference.com
http://www.pro-football-reference.com/

Professional Football Researchers Association
http://www.profootballresearchers.org/